## Trademarks, Etc.

This book mentions many attractions, fictional characters, product names, entities, and works that are trademarks, registered trademarks, or service marks of their various creators and owners. They are used in this book solely for editorial purposes. Neither the author nor the publisher makes any commercial claim to their use.

## Cover Photo Credits

Other Books by Kelly Monaghan

*Air Courier Bargains:*
*How To Travel World-Wide For Next To Nothing*

*Home-Based Travel Agent:*
*How To Cash In On The Exciting*
*NEW World Of Travel Marketing*

*The Intrepid Traveler's Complete Desk Reference*
(co–author)

*A Shopper's Guide To Independent Agent Opportunities*

*Consolidators: Air Travel's Bargain Basement*

# Table of Contents

# List of Maps

# CHAPTER ONE:

# Introduction & Orientation

Don't get me wrong. I love Disney World and the wonderful creatures who live therein. I visit every chance I get.

As a travel writer, however, I must cast a canny eye on the marketplace. In doing so, I determined two things. First, the definitive book on Disney World has already been written. I refer, of course, to the estimable *The Unofficial Guide To Walt Disney World* by Bob Sehlinger (Macmillan, $15.95), available at fine bookstores everywhere. Anyone planning a visit to the Magic Kingdom and environs should have a copy in their kit bag. I wish I had written it, but I didn't and that's that.

Second, because Disney World is the 900-pound gorilla of Central Florida tourism, any guidebook to Central Florida must, of necessity, devote so much space to Disney's multitude of attractions that the area's other attractions receive short shrift, if they are covered at all.

This book, then, turns away from Disney World, not out of disdain, but to lavish on Orlando's *other* attractions the in-depth treatment that Disney has long enjoyed. I strongly suspect that readers of this book have already visited Disney World, perhaps many times, and are ready to explore the myriad other possibilities of a Central Florida vacation.

## When to Come

There are three major questions you must ask yourself when planning a trip to Orlando: How crowded will it be? What will the weather be like? When will my schedule allow me go? For most people, the third question will determine when they go, regardless of the answers to the other two. The dictates of business or the carved-in-stone school calendar will tend to dictate when you come to Orlando. For those who can be flexible, however, carefully picking the time of your visit will offer a number of benefits. And parents should bear in mind that school officials will often allow kids out of classes for a week, especially if there's something "educational" (like a visit to SeaWorld) in the offing.

During slow periods, the crowds at Orlando's major theme parks are noticeably thinner than they are at the height of the summer or during the madness of Christmas week. On top of that, hotel rates are substantially lower and airfare deals abound. Likewise, Orlando in winter can seem positively balmy to those from the North, although it's unlikely you will find the temperature conducive to swimming (except in heated pools). Spring and fall temperatures are close to ideal.

Let's take a look at these two variables: the tourist traffic and the weather. Then you can make a determination as to which dates will offer *your* ideal Orlando vacation.

## Orlando's Tourist Traffic

Most major tourist destinations seem to have two seasons — high and low. For most of Florida, the high season stretches from late fall to early spring, the cooler months up North. Low season is the blisteringly hot summer, when Floridians who can afford it head North. Orlando, thanks to its multitude of family-oriented attractions has five or six distinct "seasons," alternating between high and low, reflecting the vacation patterns of its prime customers — kids and their parents.

The heaviest tourist "season" is Christmas vacation, roughly from Christmas eve through January first. Next comes Easter week and Thanksgiving weekend. The entire summer, from Memorial Day in late May to Labor Day in early September, is on a par with Easter and Thanksgiving. There are two other "spikes" in attendance: President's Week in February and College Spring Break. Various colleges have different dates for their Spring Break, which may or may not coincide with Easter; the result is that the period from mid-March through mid-April shows a larger than usual volume of tourist traffic. The slowest period is the lull between Thanksgiving and Christmas. Next slowest (excluding the holidays mentioned earlier) are the months of September, October, November, January, and February. Tourism starts to build again in March, spiking sharply upward for Easter/Spring Break, then dropping off somewhat until Memorial Day.

Hotel occupancy figures (Orlando has more hotel rooms than any city in the United States except Las Vegas) seem to bear out the patterns cited above. In 1997, the last year for which figures are available, hotel occupancy in the tri-county Orlando metropolitan area looked like this:

| | |
|---|---|
| January | 78.3% |
| February | 84.9% |
| March | 88.7% |
| April | 85.6% |
| May | 80.1% |
| June | 83.1% |
| July | 85.6% |
| August | 81.4% |
| September | 65.8% |
| October | 78.6% |
| November | 71.5% |
| December | 65.3% |

*(Source: Smith Travel Research, cited by Orlando Convention & Visitors Bureau)*

Orlando has approximately 88,000 hotel rooms (more by the time you read this). Let's assume that the average occupied room holds three people (probably a low estimate given the high percentage of families that visit). That means that in December, the least popular month, there are about 172,000 tourists in Orlando on any given day; in March, the most popular month, there are close to 234,000. Of course, average monthly occupancy rates do not reflect the sharp spikes that occur during holiday periods like Thanksgiving, Christmas, and Easter. Another thing to bear in mind is that, when we speak of crowds, we are speaking of the major theme parks: Disney World, Universal Studios Florida, SeaWorld, and Busch Gardens. Here are annual attendance figures for Orlando area parks for 1997 as estimated by the trade paper *Amusement Business*:

| Rank* | Park | Attendance |
|---|---|---|
| 1 | The Magic Kingdom | 17,000,000 |
| 3 | EPCOT | 11,796,000 |
| 4 | Disney–MGM Studios | 10,473,000 |
| 5 | Universal Studios Florida | 8,900,000 |
| 7 | SeaWorld Orlando | 4,900,000 |
| 8 | Busch Gardens Tampa | 4,200,000 |

*\*Numbers represent the parks' **national** rankings. Disneyland, California, was number two.*

Cypress Gardens doesn't even make the top 50.

In other words, on any given day, the largest crowds will tend to be at the Disney parks. If you've been a Disney regular, SeaWorld and Universal will seem quite manageable by comparison. And regardless of when you visit, any attraction other than the big ones will seem almost deserted compared to Disney. While there is a definite advantage to timing your visit for one of Orlando's slack periods, you will probably still be amazed at how many other people are lining up to see the same things you are. What counts as a small crowd to an Orlando theme park may seem like a horde to you. Unless you come on a blustery January day, the crowds will still seem formidable. Orlando has become such a global tourist mecca that the tourist business is remarkably robust throughout the year.

The best advice is to avoid the absolutely busiest times of the year if possible. I find the slow months of fall and spring to be ideal. I even enjoy January, but I'm not the sunbathing type. If you come during the summer, as many families must, plan to deal with crowds at the major parks when you arrive and console yourself with the thought that, if you're bypassing Disney, you've automatically avoided the worst crowds.

## Orlando's Weather

Orlando's average annual temperature is a lovely 72.4 degrees. But as we've already noted, averages are deceptive. Here are the generally cited "average" figures for temperature and rainfall throughout the year:

|  | High (°F) | Low (°F) | Rain (in.) |
|---|---|---|---|
| January | 72 | 49 | 2.1 |
| February | 73 | 50 | 2.8 |
| March | 78 | 55 | 3.2 |
| April | 84 | 60 | 2.2 |
| May | 88 | 66 | 4.0 |
| June | 91 | 71 | 7.4 |
| July | 92 | 73 | 7.8 |
| August | 92 | 73 | 6.3 |
| September | 90 | 73 | 5.6 |
| October | 84 | 65 | 2.8 |
| November | 78 | 57 | 1.8 |
| December | 73 | 51 | 1.8 |

Use these figures as general guidelines rather than guarantees. While the average monthly rainfall in January might be 2.1 over the course of many years, in 1994 there were 4.9 inches of rain that month and in 1996 almost 4 inches fell in the first two days alone. January of '96 also saw lows dip into the twenties.

I find Orlando's weather most predictable in the summer when "hot, humid, in the low nineties, with a chance of afternoon thunderstorms" becomes something of a mantra for the TV weather report. Winter weather tends to be more unpredictable with "killer" freezes a possibility. As to those summer thunderstorms, they tend to be localized and mercifully brief (although occasionally quite intense) and needn't disrupt your touring schedule. I was once in Orlando for a summer week when it rained somewhere every day but never on me. Another thing to bear in mind is that June through September is hurricane season, with July and August the most likely months for severe weather.

## Getting Oriented in Orlando

Orlando can be confusing.

The Orlando metropolitan area comprises three counties and, since you will often hear location indicated by naming the county, it is worth knowing their names and relation to one another. From north to south they are Seminole, Orange, and Osceola. Orlando is in Orange County, Kissimmee is in Osceola. Most of the attractions covered in this book are in Orange and Osceola; only a few are in Seminole.

The area is dotted with lakes, both large and small; so streets stop, start, and take circuitous detours. In European fashion, streets change names as they cross municipal boundaries. On top of that, the area's major highway, Interstate 4, which runs east-west across the state, runs roughly from northeast to southwest through the Orlando metropolitan area and almost directly north-south in the heart of Orlando's tourist district. As a result, streets that are "east" or "south" of I-4 at one point are "west" or "north" of it at another. (See map, page 20.) All of this complicates the process of giving, receiving, and following directions.

Fortunately, most of the Orlando area's attractions are located in two fairly compact tourist districts: International Drive in Orlando and US 192 in Kissimmee, with I-4 forming a direct and easy-to-follow link between them. Attractions that are not located in these two areas are seldom more than a short drive away from an I-4 exit.

International Drive (sometimes abbreviated I Drive and pronounced "Eye Drive," just as I-4 is pronounced "Eye Four") is in Orlando. It is a meandering boulevard that roughly parallels I-4 from Exit 30 on the north to Exit 26 on the south. Many of the major attractions profiled in this book are on it or near it. At the northern end, you will find Universal Studios Florida (just across I-4) and Wet 'n Wild. At the southern end lies SeaWorld. In between, there are several dinner attractions and a number of smaller attractions, along with dozens of hotels, scores of eateries, several discount outlet malls, and the mammoth Orlando Convention Center. International Drive is glitzy, garish, hyperactive, and a traffic nightmare in the evening and at rush hours.

The second major tourist axis is US 192 (also called Highway 192, and Irlo Bronson Highway), which runs east to west through Kissimmee crossing I-4 at Exit 25. West of I-4 you will find Splendid China and the entrance to the Disney properties; to the east of I-4 is a gaudy strip of hotels, restaurants, dinner attractions, smaller attractions, miniature golf courses, and discount shopping outlets. This strip is thoughtfully marked with numbered "Mile Markers," which I have used in the text to give directions.

*Tip:* Chances are you will be staying in or very close to one of the two major tourist areas. When you are traveling from Point A to Point B in the Orlando area, my advice is to travel via US 192 and I-4. This may not always be the most direct or shortest route but it will be the surest route and very often the quickest. When I give directions in this book I try, wherever possible, to route you via these major arteries.

# Keeping Posted

For the very latest in information about what's going on in Orlando, your indispensable source of information is the *Orlando Sentinel*, the local daily newspaper. It costs 50 cents daily, except Sunday when it is $1.50. If you purchase the paper from a vending machine (as opposed to a store), you avoid paying the sales tax. Cheapskates take note.

Every Friday, the *Sentinel's* "Calendar" section offers an entire week's worth of information about films, plays, concerts, nightclubs, art exhibits, and the like, along with capsule reviews of many of the area's restaurants and a guide to area radio stations. Music buffs will appreciate the exhaustive listings of who's playing what where and film fans will find show times for every multiplex from Orlando to the Atlantic coast. There is even a listing of area attractions and a section of personal ads just in case you start feeling lonely.

Orlando has a number of free weekly newspapers. Among the more interesting are *Orlando Weekly*, which is especially strong on the pop music scene, and *artsLink,* which covers the visual arts as well as theater and writers groups. These and other free papers can be found in racks near the entrance to book stores, coffee shops, supermarkets, and drugstores.

The Intrepid Traveler, the publisher of this book, maintains a web site containing updated information about all of Orlando's non-Disney attractions along with other valuable information. Log on at

**http://www.intrepidtraveler.com**

# The Orlando FlexTicket

For readers of this book, there is some very good news. Borrowing a page from the Disney marketing manual, several of Mickey's competitors have banded together to offer what has long been a Disney staple — multi-day, multi-park passes at an attractive price. The participating parks are Universal Studios Florida, SeaWorld, Wet 'n Wild, and Busch Gardens Tampa.

It's called the Orlando FlexTicket and it works like this:

***Three-Park, Seven-Day Pass*** — Universal, SeaWorld, Wet 'n Wild

| | |
|---|---|
| Adults | $105.95 |
| Children (3 to 9) | $87.93 |

***Four-Park, Ten-Day Pass*** — adds Busch Gardens Tampa

| | |
|---|---|
| Adults | $137.75 |
| Children (3 to 9) | $114.43 |

Prices include tax. These passes offer unlimited visits to all three or four parks for their period of validity and represent an excellent value. On top of that, they offer the come and go as you please convenience of annual passes, albeit for a much shorter time.

Passes may be purchased at any of the participating parks' ticket booths or through your travel agent before coming. They are valid for seven or ten consecutive days beginning on the day you first use them. As for parking, you pay at the first park you visit on any given day. Then show your parking ticket and Orlando FlexTicket at the other parks on the same day for complimentary parking.

There are a number of attractive vacation packages now being offered that include the Orlando FlexTicket, as well as hotel accommodations in the International Drive area and a range of additional freebies (like lunch at the Hard Rock Café) along with discounts. For more information, call the Universal City Travel Company at (800) 711-0080, or contact your nearest travel agent.

## All About Discounts

Throughout this book, I have listed the standard admission price for every attraction. However, thanks to the cutthroat competition for the attention of tourists in tourist-saturated Orlando, an entire industry of dollars-off coupons and discount ticket outlets has grown up. With a little effort, you will seldom have to pay the posted price.

### Coupons

The most ubiquitous money-saving vehicle is the coupon. Coupons are distributed through a variety of free visitors' guides — magazine-sized publications filled with ads for area attractions and restaurants. The coupons you want are either in the ads or in a separate section of the magazine. There are some booklets distributed in the area that are nothing but coupons.

There's a good chance you will find several of these throwaway publications in your hotel room or be handed them with your room key or when you pick up your rental car. If not, look around for displays at the airport, car rental agencies, hotel lobbies, and restaurants in the tourist areas. You won't have to look far. Another source of dollars-off coupons is the brochures for individual attractions. Many of them contain a coupon. You will find them in the same places you find the larger, magazine-format coupon books. Many lobby and restaurant display racks contain dozens of these brochures.

The discounts available from dollars-off coupons are relatively modest, usually a few dollars. Some attractions make their coupons valid for up to four or six people, hence the headlines that shout "up to $16 off!" While you will find coupons for major parks like Universal Studios and SeaWorld (typically offering about $3 off), most of the dollars-off coupons are for smaller attractions, go kart tracks, miniature golf courses, airboat rides, and the like. You are unlikely to find coupons for museums, botanical gardens (except Cypress Gardens), and state parks (although anything is possible in this overheated competitive environment).

My suggestion is that you collect as many free visitors' guides as you can get your hands on. Browse the brochure racks and pull out those that appeal. Then, in the comfort of your hotel room, select and cut out offers that appeal to you and keep them in your rental car for ready use.

Yet another option for getting a wide range of modest discounts is the *Orlando Magicard*. Sponsored by the Orlando Convention and Visitors Bureau, the *Magicard* looks like a credit card. Flashing it will get you discounts at most area attractions and dinner shows, as well as at some restaurants and area hotels. You can obtain a card prior to your arrival by writing to the Orlando Visitors Center, 8723 International Drive, Orlando, FL 32819. Or call (407) 363-5872. They will send you the card free of charge. You can also pick up the card at the Center once you are in Orlando. Along with the card, you will receive a brochure with the current list of discount offers. The card is good forever; the list of attractions, restaurants, and hotels offering discounts changes periodically.

*Tip:* If you find yourself near an attraction you'd like to visit but don't have a coupon, stop into nearby restaurants, or even the entrance to a nearby attraction, and look for brochure racks. Chances are you'll find a brochure and coupon for the attraction that caught your eye.

## Ticket Brokers

The second major source of discounts is ticket brokers. There are dozens of them scattered around the tourist areas, many of them located in hotel lobbies. Ticket brokers concentrate on the major attractions and the dinner shows that are an Orlando staple. Discounts can be substantial — except for Disney. A 4% discount on Disney tickets is pretty standard. On the other hand, some brokers offer Universal at nearly 15% off and some dinner attractions at 34% off.

Using ticket brokers requires careful comparison shopping since discounts can vary widely from outlet to outlet. As a general rule, the discount ticket booths you find in your hotel lobby or in local restaurants seldom have the best prices. You'll do better at the free-standing ticket outlets. Nonetheless, it's still a good idea to shop around. Sometimes even the lowest of the low-price dealers will be undercut by someone else for a particular attraction. Virtually every reputable ticket broker will have a printed price list; collect a goodly supply of these and examine them later in your hotel room to smoke out the best deals.

## Protecting Yourself

While fraud is rare, it does occur. You can take some simple precautions when dealing with ticket brokers.

- Ticket brokers are regulated by both the state of Florida and local authorities. They are required to prominently post the appropriate licenses. If you don't see these certificates displayed, ask to see them.
- Ask about "restocking fees." If you find a lower price elsewhere, you may be able to return your tickets, but many outlets charge a 15% fee when you do so.
- Does the printed price list contain the name, address, and phone number of the broker? The absence of these elements does not, in and of itself, signal fraud, but there is no reason for a reputable broker to omit them.
- Don't accept Universal Studios tickets that are all white or that bear a "K" designation. These are not for resale and will not be honored for admission.
- Look for brokers that advertise that they will meet or beat any advertised price. That way, if you find a better deal, you will be protected.

## "Free" Tickets

It is actually possible to get "free" tickets to some major attractions. The catch is that, in return, you must agree to sit through a presentation for a local timeshare resort. You will be assured that there is no obligation, that these are not high pressure sales pitches. If you insist that you will never, ever buy a timeshare, they will tell you that's no problem, that you'll be able to tell your friends back home about their resort and that's good enough for them. All this may be true. But for me, sitting through a timeshare presentation is about as appealing as a visit to the dentist for root canal work. If you feel differently, you can find this kind of offer through ticket brokers or little booths along the tourist strips emblazoned with the words "FREE TICKETS."

## Some Orlando Ticket Brokers

Here are some stand-alone ticket brokers that ply their trade in the Orlando-Kissimmee area. A listing here does not constitute an endorsement, let alone a guarantee. Shop carefully.

**Central Florida Amusements**
4786 West US 192, Kissimmee, (407) 390-0466
**Orlando Visitors Center**
8723 International Drive, Orlando, (407) 363-5872
This private, nonprofit organization, sponsored by Orange County, also offers discounted tickets.
**Vacation Works**
4834 West US 192, Kissimmee, (407) 396-1883
7802 West US 192, Kissimmee, (407) 396-6363
6181 Westwood Boulevard, Orlando, (407) 363-5307
These folks advertise "We will not be beaten on price."

# How This Book Is Organized

Chapters 2 through 8 cover the major Orlando area attractions, ones which will occupy anywhere from a half a day to several days of your time. I have attempted to cover them in some depth, offering guidance on dining and shopping. Chapters 9 and 10 cover Kennedy Space Center to the east and Busch Gardens Tampa to the west. These, too, are major attractions.

The remaining chapters are omnibus chapters; that is, they cover three or more attractions that all have a common theme. The attractions described in these chapters are scattered throughout the Orlando area.

There is an index of rides and attractions, which will be most useful in locating the smaller attractions covered in chapters 12 through 20. It can also be used to locate descriptions of rides and attractions at the major theme parks.

As a general rule, I have tried to restrict the geographic scope of this book to Orlando and its immediate environs. That means that the farther you drive from Orlando, the more likely you will be to encounter attractions not covered in this book. For example, with the exception of

Kennedy Space Center and the nearby Astronaut Hall of Fame, I have not included any attractions on the Atlantic coast. Nor have I mentioned the many things to see and do in the Tampa Bay area aside from Busch Gardens and Adventure Island, its next-door water park.

Price ranges for restaurants (cost of an average meal) and hotels (cost of one night's stay in a double room) are indicated as follows:

|  | Restaurants | Hotels |
|---|---|---|
| $ | Under $5 | Under $50 |
| $$ | $5 – $10 | $50 – $100 |
| $$$ | Over $10 | Over $100 |
| $$$$ | Over $20 | Over $150 |

Finally, a note on highway and route abbreviations. I stands for Interstate; US for United States (i.e. federal) Highway; SR for State Route; CR for County Road.

## Accuracy and Other Impossible Dreams

While I have tried to be as accurate, comprehensive, and up-to-date as possible, these are all unattainable goals. What's most likely to change, alas, are prices. When available, I have quoted 1999 prices. However, many attractions do not make decisions about whether or not to increase their prices until after the deadline for this book. If you do run into price increases they will typically be modest.

Once again I refer you to The Intrepid Traveler's web site for the latest updated information. Check in here for the latest on prices and new rides and attractions:

http://www.intrepidtraveler.com

Perhaps more disconcerting will be the disappearance of entire attractions, usually smaller and/or newer ones. There always seem to be rumors that one attraction or another is "in trouble." I sincerely hope, for everyone's sake, that none of the wonderful attractions listed here close down before you get to experience them. Before driving any great distance, however, you may want to call to make sure the attraction that caught your eye is still open and get current hours and pricing information.

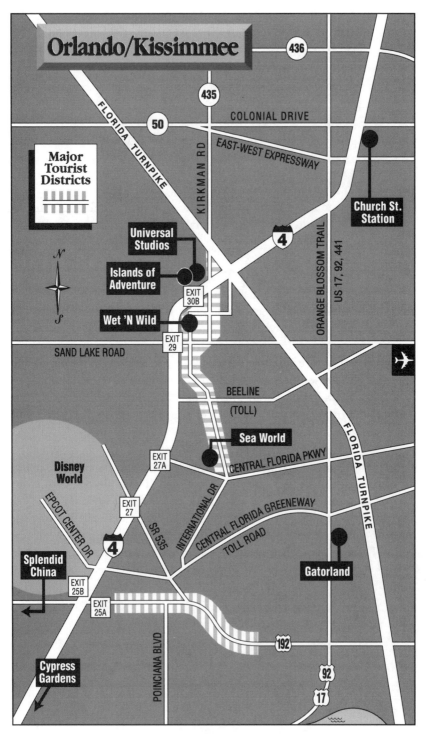

Orlando/Kissimmee

Major Tourist Districts

436

435

50

COLONIAL DRIVE

FLORIDA TURNPIKE

KIRKMAN RD

EAST-WEST EXPRESSWAY

Church St. Station

Universal Studios

4

Islands of Adventure

EXIT 30B

ORANGE BLOSSOM TRAIL

US 17, 92, 441

Wet 'N Wild

EXIT 29

SAND LAKE ROAD

BEELINE

(TOLL)

Sea World

EXIT 27A

CENTRAL FLORIDA PKWY

FLORIDA TURNPIKE

Disney World

EXIT 27

SR 535

INTERNATIONAL DR

CENTRAL FLORIDA GREENEWAY

EPCOT CENTER DR

4

TOLL ROAD

Splendid China

EXIT 25B

Gatorland

EXIT 25A

Cypress Gardens

POINCIANA BLVD

192

92

17

# CHAPTER TWO:

# Universal Studios Florida

R ide The Movies!" Universal Studios Florida's brilliant ad slogan (attributed to Steven Spielberg), says it all. Here is a movie-based theme park containing some of the greatest thrill rides in the world — along with a short course in the filmmaker's art (cleverly disguised as entertainment) — all sprinkled through a huge, meticulously detailed, working movie set that can make the simple act of sitting down to eat a hot dog seem like an adventure.

When Universal Studios Florida opened in 1990, it instantaneously became the number two draw in Orlando, right after Mickey's realm down the Interstate. With a just over 100 acres and a price tag of just $650 million, Universal couldn't match Disney in size and scope. But that doesn't mean Universal was willing to accept perennial also-ran status. There are a number of elements that set Universal Studios Florida apart from Disney and, say some, make it superior to Disney.

The word that visitors and locals most frequently use to differentiate Universal from Disney is "adult." Whereas Disney World is perceived by many as a kiddie park that adults will enjoy, they see Universal as a park conceived with grown-ups in mind. There are a number of reasons for this:

*Adult Themes.* Many Universal attractions are based on films and shows that appeal primarily to adults — *Jaws, Earthquake,* and *Psycho* are a far cry from *Honey, I Shrunk the Kids.*

*Intensity.* Whereas Disney (at least in its early days) would tend to tone down rides in the development stage lest they frighten young children, Universal Studios seems to delight in seeing just how intense they can be. *Jaws* and *Back To The Future* are prime examples.

*Beer and Wine.* One of the differences adults will notice very quickly at Universal is that they can drink. In fact, they are *encouraged* to drink. And not just in the restaurants. Don't be surprised to see a beer vendor plying those long lines on hot summer days. Some of the sit-down restaurants serve pretty decent wines by the bottle and at a few places you can get a mixed drink.

In spite of the ready availability of alcohol, there is remarkably little evidence of drunkenness. Evening crowds may tend to be a bit more boisterous, but I have never seen any real unpleasantness.

There are two other elements that, while not necessarily contributing to the "adult" nature of the park, tend to set Universal apart:

*Film Production.* Universal Studios Florida is (as they never tire of telling you) a working studio. Virtually every corner of the park was designed in such a way that it could serve the needs of Universal's own film makers as well as those of other producers who use the facility to shoot films, TV shows, and television commercials. The New York set can be "dressed" to stand in for virtually any urban setting in the world, they claim.

Don't be surprised if you see a film crew at work during your visit. You are welcome to watch if you are discreet. And something is almost always going on at Nickelodeon.

Yes, there is film production at Disney-MGM Studios, but nothing approaching the volume at Universal and Nickelodeon.

*Pyrotechnics.* If Universal Studios Florida has a stylistic signature, something that tells you that this is a Universal attraction and not someone else's, it has to be their lavish use of fire, fireworks, and loud explosions. You can almost feel your eyebrows singe on *Earthquake, Twister,* and *Jaws,* and when those grenade launchers go off during the *Dynamite Nights Stuntacular* you'll feel the concussion in your gut.

# Before You Come

## Gathering Information

Universal Studios Florida maintains a recorded message at (407) 363-8000, with the latest on prices, opening hours, and special events. By pressing "zero," you can speak with an "attraction representative" if you have specific questions or requests. Universal's web site at http://www.usf.com is another good source of general information.

If you are interested in booking a package vacation that includes a hotel room and other add-ons, in addition to your Universal Studios admission, call the Universal City Travel Company at (800) 711-0080.

## Doing Your Homework

It's perfectly possible to arrive at Universal Studios knowing nothing about any of the films or TV shows on which its attractions are based (although it's hard to imagine that being possible), and have a perfectly good time. Indeed, you don't need to understand a word of English to be entertained here, as the happy hordes of foreign tourists prove.

Nonetheless, there are a few attractions which, in my humble opinion, will benefit from a bit of research prior to your visit. Fortunately, this is the kind of homework that's easy and fun to do. Any well-stocked video rental store will have all the research material you need.

*E. T. Adventure* will make a lot more sense to those who have seen the film. This is especially true for younger kids who might find E.T.'s odd appearance a bit off-putting if they haven't seen the film.

The Hitchcock show is one of the best at Universal, and it will teach you a lot about the art of movie making. If you are unfamiliar with Hitch's work, the show should whet your appetite. However, knowing some of Hitchcock's films will make the show even more enjoyable. I recommend at least checking out *Psycho*. If you have time, you might want to screen the films that figure prominently in the show: *Dial M for Murder, The Birds, Strangers on a Train, Saboteur* (an overlooked masterpiece, in my opinion), and *Vertigo*. Of course, virtually any Hitchcock film is worth watching.

As for *Jaws, Back To The Future*, and *Twister*, while they're all based on popular films, knowing the films adds little to the fun of the rides. *Kongfrontation* is based on an updated remake of the old 1930s classic. If you want to show your kids what King Kong is all about, stick with the original.

## Getting There

Universal Studios is located just off I-4 at Exit 30, Kirkman Road. It is bounded by Kirkman on the east, Vineland Road on the north and Turkey Lake Road on the west. To the south lies its sister park, **Islands of Adventure**, described in *Chapter Three*.

There are four entrances to the park, one via the Universal Boulevard overpass from International Drive, one on Kirkman, one on Vineland, and one on Turkey Lake. All entrances feed cars down broad, palm-lined boulevards to toll-plaza-like entrances at the two huge, multi-level parking garages along Kirkman Road. The Kirkman Road entrance is clearly the "main" entrance to the park. It is flanked by beautifully manicured hedges, towering palm trees, and the words "UNIVERSAL STUDIOS" in huge bronze-gold letters. However, the overpass that crosses I-4 from the International Drive district is the obvious choice for those staying in that hotbed of hostelries; it also provides a nice view of **CityWalk** and **Islands of Adventure** as you cross the bridge over the Interstate. The other entrances seem almost anonymous by comparison. Perhaps because of that, they seem to be the lesser used and, therefore, the quickest ways into the park. However, the entrance you wind up using will probably depend on the direction from which you approach.

Coming from the south (that is, traveling "east" on I-4), the most direct route into the park is to take Exit 30A, International Drive, and turn left at the top of the ramp. This takes you over I-4 and onto Universal property. There are two other alternatives, however. On especially busy days, when the overpass at Exit 30A is backed up, you might save a little time by getting off at Exit 29, Sand Lake Road. Turn left off the ramp, under the Interstate and then right almost immediately onto Turkey Lake Road. You can't miss it; just follow the "Universal Studios" signs. Just opposite Dr. Phillips High School, you will see the Universal sign on your right. Your third choice is to drive past Exit 30A and take the lefthand Exit 30B, which feeds you onto Kirkman Road; the entrance to the park will be on your left at the first light.

For visitors approaching from the north (that is, traveling "west" on I-4) your best bet is Exit 30B, but you won't be able to take the immediate left turn into the park. That's because there's not enough room to get across four or five lanes of traffic to the far left lanes to turn into the park. In fact, a wisely-placed road divider prevents you from even trying. The signs direct you to proceed north to Vineland, turn left, and use the entrance on Vineland. Another alternative is to turn right onto Major Boulevard almost immediately upon exiting I-4. Major is a divided road, so it's easy to make a U-turn. Once you do so, you will be pointed straight at the Universal Studios' Kirkman Road entrance when you return to the intersection.

## Parking at Universal Studios Florida

Whichever entrance you use, you will arrive at the toll-booth entrances to the parking garages. Here, the attendants will collect your daily parking fee of $6 ($7 for RVs and trailers), and you will be directed to your parking spot. You will also be handed a "Studio Guide," a fold-out brochure with a map of the park and a show schedule on one side and a listing of restaurants, shops, and helpful information on the other. On the front will be listed the park's official opening and closing times and the dates for which the information in the brochure is valid, which could be for just the one day on which you receive it or for a range of several days. Additional copies of the guide are available just inside the gates and at various shops throughout the park.

If you have been to Disney World, the parking lot drill will be familiar, except that your car will be in a multi-level building rather than baking in the merciless Florida sun. Your options are virtually nonexistent. You will be directed in such a way that the lot is filled in the most efficient way possible. The parking structures are ingeniously designed so that as one level fills up cars are routed directly to the next level, without having to corkscrew upwards as you do in most multi-story parking lots.

The various sections in the two lots are named after movies (*Jaws, Jurassic Park,* and so forth); rows are indicated by numbers, with the first digit indicating the level. Thus "Jaws 305" would be on the third level. As always in these situations, it's a good idea to make a note of your parking lot location.

*Handicapped Parking.* Handicapped parking spaces are provided close to the main entrance. Follow the signs for handicapped parking and you will be directed accordingly.

*Valet Parking.* Get in the Hollywood spirit by having an attractive young attendant park your car for you. The fee is $12 ($6 for annual pass holders).

## Arriving at Universal Studios Florida

From your parking space, you will walk to the nearest of a series of escalators and moving sidewalks that will funnel you to "the hub," a large circular space on the third level with access from both parking structures. Universal claims that no parking space in either structure is more than a nine-minute walk from the hub. From the hub, it's a straight shot along more moving sidewalks to **CityWalk**, Universal's dining, shopping, and entertainment venue. You can continue straight ahead to **Islands of Adventure** or hang a sharp right and head for **Universal Studios**. These three major destinations — Universal Studios, Islands of Adventure, and CityWalk — together with several themed resort hotels being built nearby, comprise **Universal Studios Escape**, a new and evolving vacation extravaganza designed to go head to head with Disney World, the old vacation extravaganza down the Interstate.

Crossing the bridge from CityWalk, you arrive at the arched entrance to Universal Studios Florida. Just through the stately arch is an attractive plaza where you will find a row of ticket windows and, to your right, a Guest Services window, of which more later.

# Opening and Closing Times

Universal Studios is open 365 days a year. In the slow seasons, the park may open at nine and close at six. During the high season, the park may open at eight and close at eleven. These will be the "official" hours listed on the Studio Guide brochure and provided by Universal's telephone information line, but they are not the "actual" opening and closing times. The gates typically open anywhere from 15 minutes to one hour prior to the "official" time. Likewise, the park closes about an hour or more after the official closing time. In the amusement park business, it's known as "soft opening," that is the park's actual hours of operation ebb and flow with the demand.

Bear in mind that most people flood to the exits immediately after the *Dynamite Nights Stuntacular* which officially caps the park's day but it takes time to empty a large park of tens of thousands of people, so you needn't feel any rush to reach your car. The parking lot will be in gridlock anyway. So relax, take your time, do some shopping, have a dessert and coffee.

## The Price of Admission

Universal Studios has a limited number of ticket options. Most visitors will be looking at either a one- or two-day studio pass. At press time, prices (including tax) were as follows:

*One-Day Pass:*
| | |
|---|---|
| Adults: | $44.52 |
| Children (3 to 9): | $36.04 |

*Two-Day Pass:*
| | |
|---|---|
| Adults: | $65.72 |
| Children (3 to 9): | $55.12 |

*Celebrity Annual Pass:*
| | |
|---|---|
| Adults: | $79.50 |
| Children (3 to 9): | $63.60 |

Universal Studios Florida participates in the Orlando FlexTicket program described in *Chapter One: Introduction & Orientation*. Prices are as follows:

*Three-Park, Seven-Day Pass* — Universal, SeaWorld, Wet 'n Wild
| | |
|---|---|
| Adults: | $105.95 |
| Children (3 to 9): | $87.93 |

*Four-Park, Ten-Day Pass* — adds Busch Gardens Tampa
| | |
|---|---|
| Adults: | $137.75 |
| Children (3 to 9): | $114.43 |

Children under three are admitted **free**.

## Which Price Is Right?

If your schedule only allows one day at Universal, the choice is simple. If, however, you think you might want to give Universal two days out of your busy schedule, you have some options to weigh. My advice is to hedge your bets. Buy a one-day pass. If you decide during the day that the place definitely rates another visit you can upgrade to a two-day pass or the Orlando FlexTicket *while you are still at the park.* The price you pay will be exactly what you would have paid if you'd purchased a two-day pass when you first arrived. And if you are visiting during one of the park's slow seasons, be alert to "Second Day Free" promotions; they'll be prominently posted near the entrance.

There are some additional considerations for the two-day pass. The second day can be used *at any time* — even twenty years later. So if you know that you will be returning to Orlando at some point in the future, a two-day pass might be worth considering. The same applies to second day upgrades purchased while in the park: They're valid forever. However, "Second Day Free" passes, when available, must be used within the next seven days.

The Orlando FlexTicket is also an excellent buy for people whose main interest is Universal. You can spend one day at SeaWorld, one day at Wet 'n Wild, and the remaining five days of a seven-day pass at Universal.

## Annual Pass

The Celebrity Annual Pass confers unlimited admission and free parking for a year. What's more, it's less than $15 more than a two-day pass. Does it make sense for you? That depends. If you are planning to take another vacation in Florida next year, you might want to consider the annual pass. As long as you schedule next year's vacation a week or two earlier than this year's, your pass will still be good. However, if you will only spend one day at Universal on each visit, then a two-day pass is cheaper.

Still, there's more than price to consider. With an annual pass, you don't need to fret about cramming everything into one day. You might consider the extra cost worth the convenience of coming and going as you please. Annual pass holders get free parking, remember, and can bring in as many as six others at a 10% discount. Annual pass holders also receive an across-the-board 10% discount on most meals and purchases at Universal shops. The savings can mount up quickly.

There are still other advantages to the annual pass. I have had the 10% discount on souvenirs mushroom to 25% or 40% on occasion. You get a discount on valet parking ($6 as opposed to $12). Your pass also qualifies you for 10% discounts at some hotels and shops and reduced admission to some local dinner shows. Most of all, as an annual pass holder, I appreciate the freedom of strolling in whenever the spirit moves me, knowing that if a line is too long I can come back tomorrow.

All things considered, if you will spend three or more days in Orlando in a one-year period, the annual pass is worth it. Bear in mind that annual passes take the form of a photo ID card, so there's no chance of lending, passing on, or selling your annual pass to someone else. Every time I visit, the cheerful gate attendant checks my annual pass to see if that's my smiling face on my card.

## The Star Treatment

If an annual pass doesn't offer enough ego gratification, consider a VIP Tour. For $110 (plus $6.60 tax) you can join a group of other VIPs for a five-hour escorted behind-the-scenes tour of the studio. Not only will you see things that ordinary visitors don't, you will be whisked to the head of the line for "up to seven" rides and be guaranteed the best seats.

If you'd like to corral up to fourteen close friends, you can all take a private eight-hour "Exclusive VIP Tour" for $1,200 (plus $72 tax). That gives you 60 percent more time and three people go along for "free." What's more, this tour starts when you want it to and can be customized to your group's special interests and proclivities (so it doesn't have to last eight hours if you don't want it to). The group must be pre-formed, that is you can't join another group.

You can get more information about both kinds of VIP tours by calling (407) 363-8295. Reservations must be made at least 72 hours in advance (two weeks during summer and holiday periods) and prepayment is required.

## Discounts

There's no reason to pay full price for your one- or two-day pass. With a little planning you can get up to 20% off. Here's how:

*Coupons.* The Orlando area is awash in throwaway publications aimed at the tourist trade. They all contain discount coupons for many attractions in the area. A typical discount is $2.50 off for up to six people. See *Chapter One: Introduction & Orientation* for more information.

*AAA & AARP.* Members of these organizations receive a walk-up discount of $2.50 off for up to six people. AAA members can buy their tickets through a local AAA office, in which case the discount might be greater. Once inside, your AAA card is good for a 10% discount at many shops and restaurants.

*Military.* Active duty, reserve, and retired members of the U.S. military receive a 10% discount.

*Medical Discounts.* If you have a medical condition that prevents you from enjoying Universal's more intense or active rides, and if you have a note from your doctor to that effect, you can qualify for a 20% discount. Without the doctor's note, you can still get 10% off. This is a good strategy for grandparents who know they'll be sitting out *Back To The Future* and some others. Your doctor should be happy to provide the note.

Discount coupons do not apply to annual passes or VIP tours.

# Buying Tickets

You can purchase tickets at the park when you arrive, but I recommend purchasing your tickets before then, especially if you have only one day to spend in the park during high season. This will save precious time.

Your best bet is to buy tickets at the park a day or so before your visit. That way you can also get a free preview of the park. (See *The Shooting Script: Your Day at Universal Studios*, below.) A good time to purchase tickets at the park is in the late afternoon. Lines will be short then and you can avoid paying for parking by parking in the Hard Rock Cafe lot and walking the short distance to the ticket booths.

Tickets can also be purchased at the Universal Studios store in the Orlando International Airport, or through your travel agent (allow several weeks to receive your tickets).

# Staying Near the Park

If Universal Studios Florida is your primary Orlando destination, you may want to consider staying just outside the main gate. The following hotels are located along Major Boulevard, just opposite the main gate. It is possible to walk into the park from these hotels (although it can be an uncomfortably warm walk on hot days). They are listed in order of their distance to the front gate.

## Portofino Bay Resort

Kirkman and Vineland Roads
Orlando, FL 32819
(800) 235-6397
**Opens Spring of 1999**

The first of the on-property Universal Studios Escape resort hotels, this luxury waterside property is styled to evoke the atmosphere of the fabled Italian seaside village from which it takes its name.

*Price Range:* $$$ - $$$$
*Amenities:* Everything you'd expect of a major resort
*Shuttle:* Regular boat service to CityWalk, close to Universal Studios' entrance.
*Walk to Park:* 5 minutes

## Radisson Twin Towers

5780 Major Boulevard
Orlando, FL 32819
(800) 333-3333; (407) 351-1000; fax (407) 363-0106

A sleek corporate-style hotel (there's a convention center attached) that is a favorite with upscale overseas visitors.

*Price Range:* $$ - $$$$
*Amenities:* Large pool, five restaurants, playground, exercise room, business center, shops
*Shuttle:* Three departures in the morning and three returns in the afternoon; free to guests
*Walk to Park:* 5 to 10 minutes

## Holiday Inn

5905 South Kirkman Road
Orlando, FL 32819
(800) 327-1364; (407) 351-3333; fax (407) 351-3577

Standard mid-range hotel with ten-story all-suite tower.

*Price Range:* $$ - $$$$
*Amenities:* Pool, volleyball, TGI Friday's restaurant, fitness center, business center
*Shuttle:* Schedule varies with demand; free to guests
*Walk to Park:* 10 minutes

## Days Inn

5827 Caravan Court
Orlando, FL 32819
(800) 329-7466; (407) 351-3800; fax (407) 363-0907

Typical budget-class motel.

*Price Range:* $ - $$
*Amenities:* Pools, in-room movies, game rooms
*Shuttle:* $6
*Walk to Park:* 10 to 15 minutes

## Delta Orlando Resort

5715 Major Boulevard

Orlando, FL 32819

(800) 877-1133; (407) 351-3340; fax (407) 345-2872

Moderately priced resort, perhaps the best value in this group.

*Price Range:* $$ - $$$

*Amenities:* Three pools, sauna, tennis, 9-hole mini golf, volleyball, basketball, supervised kids' program, three restaurants, two lounges

*Shuttle:* Free to guests

*Walk to Park:* 10 to 15 minutes

# Special Events

The year is sprinkled with special events tied to the holiday calendar. Typically that means two admissions to the park, one for a regular daytime visit and another for the evening's special event. Daytime visitors can get a discounted admission for the evening's festivities, but this will still boost the cost of a full day by $16 or so.

Among the holiday themed events Universal Studios puts on are:

*Mardi Gras.* New Orleans' pre-Lenten bacchanalia comes to Florida in the form of a nighttime parade, complete with garish and gaudy floats, lots of Dixieland jazz, and plenty of baubles and beads that are flung into the outstretched hands of the crowd.

*Fourth of July.* Universal Studios celebrates America's birthday with a small town celebration on steroids. It's Universal's biggest fireworks display of the year, one you will feel in the core of your being as well as see and hear.

*Halloween.* If you come from a part of the country where "Haunted Houses" are a well-established Halloween tradition, Universal's version may not strike you as all that special. But the spooky-funny atmosphere in the park is infectious, with goblins and ghouls leaping out at visitors. Special walk-through attractions are created just for this event, featuring dark narrow passages with "scary" surprises around every corner and tableaux vivants based on horror movie themes.

*Christmas.* Ho, ho, ho! It's a Hollywood version of a heartwarming family holiday, complete with Franken-Santas and Christmas lights on the Bates Motel.

*New Year's Eve.* Expect a wild street party, often with a live pop concert being taped for later television broadcast. There is an awesome fireworks display at midnight and the park stays open until 1 a.m. The Hard Rock Café stays open an hour later for hard-core revelers.

These special events evenings can be fun if you're in the right mood. However, some people may find them an awkward and distracting overlay to the park's main business. In my opinion, the Fourth of July and New Year's Eve are the best.

# Character Breakfasts

Monday through Friday (Tuesdays and Thursdays during slower periods), Universal has its own version of the "character breakfast" — an early-morning, pre-opening event that lets kids meet and mingle with some of their favorite cartoon characters. On any given day, you might chow down with Woody Woodpecker, Rocky and Bullwinkle, or Scooby-Doo. It's great fun for younger kids and a terrific time to snap some very special photos.

There's an all-you-can-eat buffet breakfast. Danish, orange juice, scrambled eggs and sausage, cereal, and milk. Nothing fancy but plentiful. There's also coffee and tea for the grown-ups. And you'll probably need it because these affairs kick off at 8:00 a.m. The usual venue is the International Food Bazaar, although another location may be used.

The cost is $13.50 for adults and $8.75 for children 3 to 9. Prices include tax. This is in addition to the regular day's admission, of course. You can't come just for the breakfast.

Besides being fun for the kids, the character breakfasts get the family to the park bright and early, before other guests are admitted, and guarantee priority admission to *E. T. Adventure.*

You must reserve your seats at least 24 hours in advance but earlier reservations are highly recommended, especially if you will be visiting during a busy time. To make a reservation call (407) 224-6339 between 9 a.m. and 5 p.m. You can also book through the concierge or front desk of many area hotels.

# Dining at Universal Studios Florida

Dining at Universal is unlikely to win any kudos from gourmets. Like Disney, Universal sometimes is criticized for offering lackluster fare at inflated prices. Still, if you want to have a nice meal while visiting the park, you can do pretty well. Each of the full-service restaurants — Finnegan's, Lombard's Landing, and Monster Cafe — has at least a dish or two that's better than average. Try fish at Lombard's or one of the Irish specialties at Finnegan's, for example, and you will feel well fed indeed.

The major difference at Universal for those used to dining a la Disney is the beer and wine. Now you no longer have to go outside the park to satisfy that deeper thirst. Beer is available just about everywhere, including from outdoor vendors. Lombard's and Studio Stars also feature short, but serviceable, wine lists.

For most families, however, the fare will be of the standard fast-food variety — most of it pretty good and not too outrageously priced considering you are a captive audience. The most conspicuous bit of price gouging is to be found in the soft drinks. You can purchase your large soft drink in a "souvenir container" and get it refilled throughout the day at a reduced price, but even that option prices soft drinks at about what you'd expect to pay for a beer back home. Cost-conscious parents might want to steer thirsty little ones to the water fountains which are, mercifully, dotted throughout the park.

In addition to the standard eateries, which are described in detail later, there are innumerable street-side kiosks that appear and disappear as the crowds and weather dictate. From these vendors you can get everything from a frosty beer, to candy-coated peanuts, to fresh fruit, to barbecued turkey legs.

## Shopping at Universal Studios Florida

Without thinking too much about it, it's easy to spend more on gifts and souvenirs at Universal than you spent on admission. The standard, all-American souvenirs (t-shirts and the like) are priced only slightly higher than their off-park equivalents, and some of them are very nicely designed. Universal also offers a line of upscale clothing, with the Universal logo displayed very discreetly. You can find these items at Studio Styles and the Universal Studios Store, as well as at a few other locations in the park. They are expensive, but worth it.

Among the best buys I found were the stuffed animals at Safari Outfitters. They are nicely designed and very reasonably priced for the evident quality.

If you prefer, as I do, to spend your day on the rides, you can save all your shopping for the end of your visit. Plan to stop into the Universal Studios Store while the rest of the crowd is rushing to the gate after the *Dynamite Nights Stuntacular* — the grand finale to every day at the park. This shop has a good, although not complete, selection of merchandise from virtually every other shop in the park. All of Universal Studios Florida's shops will be described in some detail later.

## Good Things to Know About . . .

### Access for the Disabled

Universal Studios Florida makes a special effort for its disabled guests. (In fact, you are likely to see disabled people among the staff at the park.) Special viewing areas are set aside at most rides; there are even kennels for guide dogs who cannot accompany their masters on some rides.

Wheelchairs can be rented on the Front Lot for $6 per day. Electric carts are $30 per day, with a $25 deposit or your driver's license.

An extremely helpful and thorough booklet, *Studio Guide for Guests with Disabilities*, contains detailed information about access to specific rides. It is available from Guest Services. You can also request that a copy be sent to you prior to your visit. Call (407) 363-8000, then press "zero" to speak to a human being; allow four to six weeks for delivery.

## Babies

Little ones under three are admitted free and strollers are available for rent if you don't have your own. There are also diaper changing stations in all the major restrooms (men's and women's). But that's as far as it goes. Make sure you have an adequate supply of diapers, formula, and baby food before you head for the park.

Strollers can be rented on the Front Lot. Single strollers are $6 per day and doubles are $12.

## Baby "Swaps"

All rides can accommodate parents whose little ones are too small to ride. One parent rides, while the other waits in a holding area with the child. Then the parents switch off and the second parent rides without a second wait in line. It's a great system.

## Breakdowns

Rides break down. They are highly complex mechanical wonders and are subjected to a great deal of stress. Some mechanical failure is inevitable. According to some reports, Universal's rides break down with greater frequency than those at Disney. If you are in line for a ride when it breaks down, you are entitled to a pass that will give you priority access to the ride once it's working again. Since most rides are repaired fairly quickly, a breakdown can be a blessing in disguise. Simply return at your convenience once the ride is back up and be escorted to the head of the line.

## Car Trouble

If you return to your car and find the battery's dead, Universal will give you a free jump start. If the problem is more serious, they will help you get help.

## Drinking

As noted elsewhere, Universal Studios provides beer in all restaurants and many fast-food outlets as well as at outdoor stands. Wine is available indoors only. Hard liquor is served at the Hard Rock Cafe and the Cantina in Cafe La Bamba.

The legal drinking age in Florida is 21 and photo IDs will be requested if there is the slightest doubt. Try to feel flattered rather than annoyed. Taking alcoholic beverages through the turnstiles as you leave the park (even to the Hard Rock) is not allowed.

## Emergencies

As a general rule, the moment something goes amiss speak with the nearest Universal employee (and one won't be far away). They will contact security or medical assistance and get the ball rolling toward a solution.

*First Aid.* There is a first aid station on Canal Street, across from *Beetlejuice's Rock-n-Roll Graveyard Revue* and just beside Louie's Italian Restaurant (see map, page 43). There is also assistance to be found at Family & Health Services on the Front Lot.

*Lost Children.* It happens all the time and there's a good chance an alert employee will have spotted your wandering child before you notice he or she is gone. Rather than frantically search on your own, contact an employee. Found kids are escorted to Guest Services and entertained until parents can be located.

*Lost Property.* Go to Lost & Found on the Front Lot and report any loss as soon as you notice it. Be prepared to provide as accurate a description as possible. Universal has an excellent track record for recovering the seemingly unrecoverable.

## Height Restrictions and Other Warnings

Due to a variety of considerations, usually revolving around sudden movements and the configuration of lap restraints, a few rides will be off-limits to shorter (typically younger) guests. The following rides have a minimum height requirement of 40 inches:

*The FUNtastic World of Hanna Barbera* (stationery seating is provided)
*Back To The Future . . . The Ride*
*E. T. Adventure* (special seating for those under 40 inches)

## Leaving the Park

You can leave the park at any time and be readmitted free the same day. Just have your hand stamped with a fluorescent symbol on the way out; when you come back, look for the "same day reentry" line and pass your hand under the ultraviolet lamp. Most people use this system when they visit the Hard Rock Café, but it's a good idea for Mom and Dad to have their hands stamped when leaving the park for the day. Why? Just in case you get to the car and discover that Junior has left his E.T. doll somewhere on the grounds. The hand stamp will speed up your visit to Lost & Found.

## Lockers

Lockers are $2 a day. You rent a key to a locker at Lost and Found for $5 and get $3 back when you return it. You can open and relock your locker as many times as you like during the day.

## Pets

If you have pets of whatever description, the attendant will direct you to the Universal Studios kennels. Pet boarding is $5 a day for each animal and the accommodations are comfortable if not precisely luxurious. You supply the food, they supply the bowl and water.

## PG Ratings

Universal urges "parental discretion" for kids under 13 on the following rides and attractions:

*The Gory, Gruesome & Grotesque Horror Make-Up Show*
*Alfred Hitchcock, The Art of Making Movies*
*Jaws* (for very young children)

Most parents seem to ignore the warnings. In this day and age (sadly, perhaps), it's hard to imagine a child being shocked by anything. They've seen it all on *Oprah*!

## Reservations

Lombard's Landing is the only one of Universal Studios' full-service restaurants to accept dining reservations. They are highly recommended at any time and especially if you are visiting during the busy season, although a reservation is not an absolute guarantee of avoiding a short wait. You can make your reservations first thing in the morning when you arrive or by phone up to 24 hours in advance. The direct line to Lombard's Landing is (407) 224-6400.

## Smoking

There are smoking sections in all restaurants and smoking is, of course, permitted outside. However, smoking is not permitted in lines to the rides and attractions. Many smokers ignore this rule, probably out of ignorance. Bear in mind that many foreigners visit Universal Studios Florida and most of them come from countries where America's fetish with secondhand smoke seems quaint if not absurd. So before you learn how to say "Put that #@*!!% cigarette out," in French, German, Spanish, and Portuguese, signal a passing attendant and let them take the heat.

### Special Diets

Lombard's Landing and Classic Monsters Café can provide **kosher** meals with 45 minutes advance notice. Drop by Guest Services for a listing of **vegetarian** choices at the park's various eateries. If you're trying to stick to a **low-fat** regimen, lotsa luck. Your best bet will be the salads and fruit plates.

## The Shooting Script: Your Day at Universal

It is perfectly possible to spend a full day at Universal Studios Florida and see everything. This is especially true if you've heeded the advice in *Chapter One* and arrived during one of the less hectic times of year.

If circumstances or perversity have led you to ignore this sage advice, you will have to plan carefully to assure seeing as much of the park as possible in a one-day time span. At the very least, you will be able to see enough to feel satisfied. Not everyone, after all, will be equally interested in all of the attractions, and missing a few won't break anyone's heart. Even at less busy times, you might want to consider following some of the strategies set forth in this section. Lines for more popular rides can grow long enough to make the wait seem tedious even in slack periods.

A little later, I will give you a blow-by-blow description of every attraction, eatery, and shop in the park. Here, I will provide an overview, some general guidance, and a step-by-step plan for seeing the park during busier periods.

## When's the Best Time to Come?

Saturdays and Sundays seem to be the park's slowest days. During the slow seasons, Universal offers special prices for Florida residents. That tends to boost weekend attendance but not enough to make the park particularly crowded.

For optimum touring conditions, plan on arriving at the park early, very early. The gates open anywhere from 15 minutes to an hour prior to the official opening time. The parking lot opens even earlier.

Arriving crowds peak at about 11:00 a.m. and then level off. Many families and the faint of heart start leaving about 4:00 p.m. Thus, your best shot at the more popular rides is before 11 and after 4. During the heat of the day you can catch the shows with larger theaters, posted starting times, and shorter lines.

# What to Expect

It will help to have a basic understanding of the different types of rides, shows, and attractions Universal Studios Florida has to offer. Each type of attraction has its own peculiarities and dictates a different viewing pattern.

**Rides.** As the term indicates, these attractions involve getting into a vehicle and going somewhere. Some, like *E. T. Adventure*, are the descendants of the so-called "dark rides" of old-fashioned amusement parks; you ride through a darkened tunnel environment lined with things to look at. Others, like *Back To The Future*, use up-to-the-minute simulator technology to provide the illusion of hurtling across vast distances while your vehicle actually moves only a few feet in any direction.

Rides are the first major attractions to open in the morning and should be your first priority.

Rides have a limited seating capacity, at least compared to the theater shows. They don't last long either; most at Universal are no longer than five minutes. They tend to be the most popular attractions because of the thrills they promise (and deliver). The result: Lines form early and grow longer as the day wears on and more people pack the park.

**Theater Shows.** Whereas the rides offer thrills, theater shows offer entertainment and, more often than not, education as well. They occur indoors, out of the heat and sun, in comfortable theaters. They last about 25 minutes on average. Most theater shows start running about an hour after opening time.

Theater shows run continuously, that is, as soon as one group exits another is ushered in. While there is no schedule listed in the Studio Guide brochure, the starting time of the next show will be posted outside the theater.

Because they seat 250 to 500 people at a time, a long line outside a theater show may be deceptive. Many times you can get on line as the next group is entering and still make the show. This is not always true during the busier times, however. Ask an attendant if getting on line now will guarantee a seat at the next show.

**Amphitheater Shows.** These shows differ from theater shows in two major respects: They seat up to 2,000 and take place in covered arenas that are open to the elements on the sides. Thus they can be hot during the summer and bitterly cold during the winter. Unlike theater shows, amphitheater shows perform on a set schedule which is listed in the Studio

Guide brochure. Because of their large seating capacity, even on the busiest days you can usually arrive for an amphitheater show 15 minutes before show time and still get a decent seat. On slower days you can stroll in exactly on time or even a little late. Amphitheater shows generally don't have their first performance until at least two hours after opening.

**Outdoor Shows.** These are small-scale shows, typically involving a few entertainers. They occur on the streets at set times announced in the Studio Guide brochure.

**Displays and Interactive Areas.** These two different types of attractions are similar in that you can simply walk into them at will and stay as long as you wish. That's not to say you won't find a line, but, with the exception of *Fievel's Playland*, lines are rare at these attractions.

**All the Rest.** There's a great deal of enjoyment to be derived from simply walking around in Universal Studios Florida. The imaginative and beautifully executed sets make wonderful photo backdrops and you can even find a grassy knoll on which to stretch out, rest, and survey the passing scene.

## Academy Awards

If you have a limited time at Universal Studios Florida, you probably won't be able to see everything. However, it would be a shame if you missed the very best the park has to offer. Here, then, is my list of Academy Awards:

**Back To The Future . . . The Ride.** Still the most exciting and imaginative simulator ride ever created.

**T2: 3-D Battle Across Time.** With this attraction, the award for "best 3-D attraction in Orlando" moves from Disney to Universal.

**Jaws.** A wet and wild updating of those old haunted house rides on the boardwalk. Ride it at night.

**Earthquake — The Big One.** Special effects explained and demonstrated.

**Twister.** A perfect opportunity to get blown away.

**Alfred Hitchcock, The Art of Making Movies.** A salute to the master and an eye-opener for kids who haven't figured out yet that films are art.

**Animal Actors Stage.** Hilarious and heart-warming antics of your favorite stars.

**The FUNtastic World of Hanna-Barbera.** *Back To The Future* on training wheels still packs a wallop.

## Runners-Up

These aren't on my list of the best of the best but they make many other people's lists and they are very, very good.

***E. T. Adventure.*** A bicycle ride to E.T.'s home planet is like *It's a Small World* on acid.

***Kongfrontation.*** Face to face with a beautifully crafted Kong, but too slow and stately to be truly scary.

***The Gory, Gruesome & Grotesque Horror Make-Up Show.*** Fun and games with dead bodies and strange critters.

# Sneak Preview

Seeing the park in one day during the high season requires careful planning, and what better way to get a jump on the crowds than by scouting the landscape before your official visit to the park. Here's how to do it:

1. Arrive at the park the day before your visit. About 4 p.m. is a good time but at least two hours before closing. Use the Kirkman Road entrance and hug the right as you enter. Look for the signs for the Hard Rock Cafe parking lot and turn right. Park your car in the Hard Rock lot. It's free and just a short walk to the ticket booths.

2. Purchase your one-day pass at the ticket booth and collect your Preview and Official Studio Guide brochures. Put your tickets in a safe place.

3. Walk over to the Guest Services window (to your right as you face the ticket booth). Tell them you'd like a "shopper's pass" for your family. They will ask for your credit card and take an impression on a charge slip, just as if you were making a purchase. But this is just a deposit. (You may leave cash if you prefer.) Everyone in your party will have their hand stamped and will be given one hour's access to the park. If you return to Guest Services within the hour, your credit card slip is returned. If not . . . too bad, you just bought a one-day pass *for that day!*

The idea of the shopper's pass is to let you do just that — shop. But you don't have to. (If it soothes your conscience, pick up a t-shirt.) Use your hour to quickly reconnoiter the park. I recommend turning right and walking down Hollywood Boulevard and then walking around the lagoon counterclockwise, past Expo Center (note the plaza on your right that leads to E.T.), Amity, and San Francisco. Turn right onto Fifth Avenue and walk through the New York set past *Kongfrontation.* Turn left at the end and walk past the Boneyard through Production Central. The park exit is dead ahead. Note the road to your right that leads to Nickelodeon.

This quickie tour will take you past all the major rides; it will also give you the lay of the land and a sense of the distance between attractions. It should serve to whet your appetite for your visit.

4. Return to the Guest Services window outside the gates and retrieve your deposit before your hour is up. Thank them profusely and be

on your way. If it fits your schedule, eat at the Hard Rock Cafe. Since it has a separate entrance and free parking, I don't recommend taking time out of your day at the park to eat there.

5. Back at your hotel, look over the brochures you received. Note the shows you want to see most and their scheduled times. Review the notes below for The One-Day Stay.

## The One-Day Stay

1. Get up early. Real early. You want to arrive at the gate about one and a half hours prior to the official opening time. This allows half an hour to park your car and get to the main entrance in hopes that they will open the gates a full hour before the official opening. If they don't, don't worry, there will already be people there waiting and Universal Studios will do its best to keep you all amused, usually by having costumed characters come out to mix and mingle and pose for photos.

2. Since you were smart enough to buy your tickets the day before, you don't have to wait in line again, at least not for tickets. Position yourself for the opening of the gates and go over your plan one more time.

3. As soon as the gates open, have your pass validated and move briskly to *Back To The Future*. Many people will break into a run. Many people will stop first at *T2: 3-D Battle Across Time*, but resist the temptation. *Back To The Future* has a much more limited capacity and the wait gets lengthy very soon after opening.

As soon as you exit *Back To The Future*, move quickly to *Jaws* and ride. (Option: If *E. T. Adventure* is high on your list, go there first and then head for *Jaws*; if not, save E.T. for late in the day when many of the kiddies and their exhausted parents have left.)

4. After *Jaws*, head past *Earthquake* to ride *Kongfrontation*. Due to its popularity and more limited seating capacity, the line for Kong gets longer faster, so it's wise to see it first. After Kong, see *Twister*, then backtrack and ride *Earthquake*.

5. If *The FUNtastic World of Hanna-Barbera* is on your list, head there now. If the line is short, ride it. If the line looks too long, head on to *T2*. Now the time has come to start checking out the theater and amphitheater shows. Hitchcock is just across the street from Hanna-Barbera and well worth seeing.

6. By now you will have been on the most popular rides and seen a show or maybe even two. The crowds are beginning to get noticeably larger and the sun is high in the sky. Take a break, maybe eat lunch. If the park is particularly crowded and you feel you are "running late" you may want to limit your lunch to quick snacks you can carry with you as you

move from line to line. There are plenty of outdoor kiosks dispensing this kind of "finger food."

7. Continue your rounds of the shows you want to see. Check in periodically at any rides you missed (or would like to try again). You may be pleasantly surprised.

8. As the crowd thins towards closing time, circle back to the rides you missed. A great time to find shorter lines to even the most popular rides is about half an hour before the scheduled start of the *Dynamite Nights Stuntacular*, which "closes" the day's activities. If you can bear to miss this show, you can have some rides all to yourself.

9. While the stunt show ends the day, the park doesn't close immediately. The shows will be over but some rides may still be squeezing a few more people through. (Ride operators like to show an efficient "through-put" for the day.) Many shops will still be open, so this is a good time to buy your souvenirs; you'll have saved some prime touring time and won't have to lug them around for so long. Many of the smaller eateries will be open as well. And you'll have plenty of time to visit *Lucy: A Tribute* before heading for your car.

## The One-Day Stay for Kids

For selfless parents who are willing to place their child's agenda ahead of their own, I submit an alternative one-day plan that will serve the needs of younger children — age eleven and below, maybe seven or eight and below. In my experience, many young children are preternaturally sophisticated and often better equipped to handle the more intense rides than their elders. Presumably, you know your own child and will be able to adapt the following outline as needed.

1. Get to the park bright and early. As soon as you are in, visit *E. T. Adventure*.

2. If you have very young kids, it'll be too early for Barney so head to Hanna-Barbera.

3. Depending on your kid's tolerance, check out *Jaws*, *Kongfrontation* and *Earthquake*, in that order. (I am assuming your child is too short for *Back To The Future*.)

4. Next, check starting times for Barney and the *Animal Actors Stage*. See them in the appropriate order. Try to steer your little ones away from *Barney's Backyard* and *Fievel's Playland*, explaining that you'll return later.

5. Take the Nickelodeon tour and break for lunch.

6. After lunch, let the kids burn off steam at *Fievel's Playland* and/or *Barney's Backyard* while you get some much-needed rest and plot out the remainder of the day.

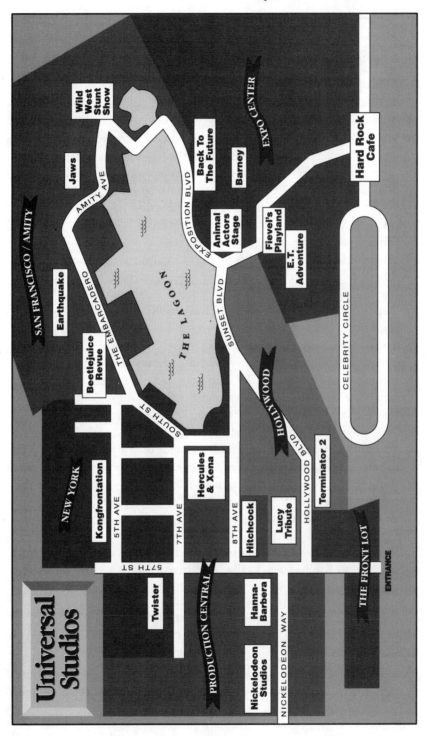

# THE FRONT LOT

In movie studio parlance, the front lot is where all the soundstages, as well as the administrative and creative offices are located — as opposed to the back lot which contains the outdoor sets.

Here at Universal Studios Florida, the Front Lot is a small antechamber of sorts to the theme park proper, which can be looked on as one huge back lot. Here you can take care of minor pieces of business on your way into the park — like picking up more money from the ATM or renting a stroller — and here you can also return when things go wrong — to register a complaint at Guest Services, or seek nursing aid for an injured child, or check Lost & Found for that priceless pearl earring that flew off in Back To The Future. Here are the services you will find on the Front Lot:

To your left as you enter the park are . . .

*Stamp Machine and Mail Box.* Read the instructions on the stamp vending machine carefully; in some cases you will not receive the change that is "due" you. Near the vending machine is a mail box. All mail posted here will bear a special Universal Studios cancellation.

*Lockers.* Lockers cost $2 for the day. Despite what the sign here says, you must go to the Lost and Found desk at the other end of the Front Lot to rent a locker key for $5 (you will receive $3 back when you return it).

*Second-Day Pass Sales.* Like what you see at Universal? If so you can upgrade your one-day pass to a second day for no more than you would have paid for a two-day pass to begin with. There are some simple rules: Second-day passes must be purchased before you leave the park. Everyone in your party who wants one must show up with their one-day pass stub in hand. Free or complimentary passes are not eligible for upgrades.

Second-day passes are non-transferable and Universal enforces this feature by requiring your signature on the pass and requesting photo ID when you return, which can be the next day or five years hence. The pass stays valid until you use it.

*Stroller and Wheelchair Rentals.* Wheelchairs and strollers are just $6 a day. Double strollers are $12. A motorized "convenience vehicle" is yours for $30 for the day.

To your right as you enter the park are . . .

*Guest Services.* This office performs a wide variety of functions. You can pick up information and brochures about services for the disabled and vegetarians. If you have a complaint (and, just as important, a compliment) about anything in the park, make your feelings known here. Guest Services personnel will often make good on an unfortunate experience by issuing a free pass for another day.

*First Union Bank.* This is a full-service branch of a local bank. This is where to head if you need to cash (or buy) traveler's checks, exchange foreign currency, or get a cash advance on your credit card.

*ATM.* Next to the bank is an outdoor ATM, where you can get a cash advance on your Visa or MasterCard at any time. The machine is also hooked into the Cirrus, Honor, Plus, and Exchange (the Armed Forces Financial Network) systems for those who would like to withdraw money from their bank account back home.

*Family & Health Services.* Nursing aid is available here should you need it. There is also a "family bathroom" if, for example, you need to assist a disabled spouse. If you just need to change a diaper, you will find diaper-changing facilities in all restrooms throughout the park.

*Lost & Found.* Items that if lost elsewhere would probably be gone forever have a surprising way of turning up at theme parks. The good feelings the park experience generates must make people ever so slightly less larcenous. Universal personnel always check the rides for forgotten belongings.

*Lockers.* Here are more lockers, with still more lockers just around the corner in a narrow passageway that leads to Hollywood Boulevard and the *T2* theater. Rent your key at the nearby Lost and Found counter.

# Shopping on the Front Lot

The Front Lot may be a prelude to the park proper, but Universal has shrewdly located a number of shops here that cater to the needs of both the arriving and departing guest.

## On Location

This should be your first stop if you've left the camera at the hotel or find yourself short of film. And if you forgot sunscreen or sunglasses, On Location can help you out there as well. You will find glossy photos of stars of the past and present here ($4 for black and whites, $5 for color) as well as tote bags to carry your day's purchases and autograph books in case you meet any stars. If you feel lucky, you can buy a Florida lottery ticket. At the back of the shop and dominating the decor is what looks like a huge blow-up aerial photo of the park. Closer examination reveals it to be a remarkably life-like computer-generated "portrait" of Universal Studios. It was created shortly after the park opened. After your visit, stop back and see if you can spot which newer attractions are missing.

## The Fudge Shoppe

You can't miss this small and rather spartanly decorated shop on your left as you enter the park. I'm sure there will be people who will stop here for lunch, dinner, and mid afternoon snack and feel well-fed indeed. But I will restrain myself and treat it as a shopping, rather than a dining, experience.

Fudge, pure and simple, is the name of the game here, despite the recent addition of made-from-scratch soft pretzels. Best of all, you can watch it being made. First, the delectable brown glop is brewed up in an enormous copper kettle. Then the fudgemeister pours the whole gooey mass onto one of two 1,700 pound marble tables. Working quickly as the fudge cools, he rhythmically massages and folds a large, thin rectangle of chocolate goodness into a long loaf-shaped mass. The process takes about ten minutes or so. Those who watch and comment admiringly on the fudgemeister's obvious skill may be rewarded with a sample of the scraps of fudge that don't make it into the loaf.

The fudge, which comes in a variety of flavors, often with added nuts, is sold for about $11 a pound, in irregular slices that weigh in at about $4.50 to $5 each. Buy three and get a fourth free. In case you need an excuse, Universal uses a low-fat recipe ("It's mostly sugar," they confide) that averages just five grams of fat per slice. Enjoy!

## Universal Studios Store

By far the largest store in the park, the Universal Studios Store is located just next to (in fact, it surrounds) The Fudge Shoppe. Here you will find a representative sampling of the wears to be found in the various smaller shops scattered about the park. If you want to save all your souvenir shopping until the end of your visit, you should be able to get something appropriate here. Just be aware that the selection is not exhaustive and that the plush toy animal you admired in Safari Outfitters might not be for sale here.

If you enter through the door that opens directly on the main plaza of the Front Lot (to the left of The Fudge Shoppe), you will find yourself in the store's children's section, with a selection of t-shirts and other kiddie gear priced from about $11 to $40. Further along, on your left, is adult clothing. You'll find a wide variety of options, starting with simple t-shirts at about $15 and going all the way to jackets for over $100. In between, you are sure to find something you'll like. Even with the inevitable Universal Studios logos, much of the clothing displayed here is very stylish and in impeccable taste. At the other end of the store is another children's section, clothing to one side, toys and dolls to the other.

And, of course, the Universal Studios Store has a generous selection of other souvenir merchandise, everything from refrigerator magnets to mugs, emblazoned with various film and TV series names, faces, and logos.

### It's A Wrap

It's A Wrap is a nifty name for this vest-pocket souvenir stand that thoughtfully straddles the exit to the park. That means, if you're on your way to the car and suddenly remember that you forgot a present for Auntie Em, you can run back and get something without reentering the park. The something you get will be small, however. The selection is minimal and limited to mostly small gewgaws like key chains, pens, postcards, and the like.

# HOLLYWOOD

Although I haven't taken out a tape measure to check, Hollywood is probably the smallest "set" at Universal Studios Florida. It is about two city blocks long, stretching from *Lucy: A Tribute* near the park entrance to The Garden of Allah motel near the lagoon. Along the way is an imaginative and loving recreation of the Hollywood of our collective subconscious. The Hollywood set was primarily a shopping and dining venue until the opening of *Terminator 2: 3-D Battle Across Time* made it a major stop on everybody's tour of Universal's Greatest Hits.

## Terminator 2: 3-D Battle Across Time

*Rating:* ★ ★ ★ ★ ★
*Type:* A "3-D Virtual Adventure"
*Time:* About 20 minutes
*Kelly says:* The best 3-D attraction in Orlando

Most attractions based on movies are created and developed by specialists at the parks. This time, *Terminator 2* director, James Cameron, and Arnold (The Austrian Oak) Schwarzenegger figured they could do it better themselves. And, boy, did they ever! Reports are that $60 million was spent to create this show. You'll get their money's worth.

Given its location at the top of Hollywood Boulevard, near the Studio gates, T2 has become *everyone's* first stop when entering the park, so be prepared for long lines. Even if you don't see lines outside, the huge interior queue can hold over 1,100 people, about a show and a half's worth. On the other hand, the theater holds 700 people and the line moves fairly quickly.

Once you step off the street, you are in the newly rebuilt headquarters of Cyberdyne, the not so nice corporate giant of the T2 flick, which is out to refurbish its image and show off its latest technology. The pre-show warm up, which takes place in a large anteroom to the theater itself, features a delicious parody of the sort of "Vision of the Future" corporate videos and television commercials that are becoming increasingly common these days. The pre-show also gets the plot rolling: Sarah Connor and her son John have invaded Cyberdyne and commandeered the video screen to warn us against the new SkyNet project (which sounds remarkably like an updated version of President Reagan's beloved Strategic Defense Initiative). According to these "terrorists" (as the Cyberdyne people describe them), SkyNet will enslave us all. The Cyberdyne flack who is our host glosses over this "unfortunate interruption" and ushers us into the large auditorium. There we settle into deceptively normal looking theater seats, don our "protective glasses," and the show begins.

And what a show it is. I don't want to give too much away, but suffice it to say that it involves a spectacular three-screen 3-D movie starring Ahnold himself, along with Linda Hamilton and Eddie Furlong (the kid from *Terminator 2*). In one of the more inspired touches, the on-screen actors move from screen to stage and back again, Arnold aboard a roaring motorcycle. The film's special effects are spectacular and the slam-bang, smoke-filled finale has people screaming and shrieking in their seats.

If you think you saw the state of the art in *Honey, I Shrunk The Audience* and the Muppet show over at the Disney parks, *T2: 3-D Battle Across Time* will quickly change your mind.

# The Gory, Gruesome & Grotesque Horror Make-Up Show

*Rating:*        ★ ★ ★ +
*Type:*          Theater show
*Time:*          25 minutes
*Kelly says:*    For younger teens and horror movie buffs

How to take something gory, gruesome, and downright disgusting and turn it into wholesome, funny family fare? Universal has solved the problem with this enjoyable (not to mention educational) foray into the ghastly art of make-up and special effects for the horror genre. The key is a horror make-up "expert" with a bizarre and goofy sense of humor who is interviewed in his make-up lab by an on-stage host and straight-man. During a laugh-filled 25 minutes, he leads us through a grisly show-and-tell of basic horror movie tricks and gimmicks.

Using the inevitable volunteer from the audience (to very amusing effect), we learn how harmlessly dull knifes can be made to leave bloody trails on bare human flesh and how real human skeletons are used as the basis for constructing decomposing zombies and ghouls. "We have to use real bones," the expert explains blithely, "so they don't melt when we bake them."

The on-stage demonstrations are supplemented with clips from actual films that illustrate the latest techniques in computer altered special effects. Also on hand are the actual mechanical werewolf heads that were used for the still stunning transformation scene in *An American Werewolf in London*. The show ends with a delicious send-up of the teleportation experiment gone wrong from the remake of *The Fly*.

As always, the show instructs while it entertains. Everyone will have a keener understanding of basic horror effects, and young children will be sternly warned about the importance of safety at all times. ("Don't do this at home . . . Do it at a friend's house!")

The waiting area for this show is the lobby of the Pantages Theater, where you will see a short, entertaining pre-show warm-up on video.

**The best seats in the house.** If all you want to do is enjoy the show, the oft repeated Universal refrain is absolutely true — every seat's a good seat. Key parts of the show are videoed and projected on large screens flanking the stage. Exhibitionists hoping to be selected as a volunteer should be aware that the performers have a predilection for young women seated in the center sections about three rows back.

# Lucy: A Tribute

*Rating:* ★ ★
*Type:* Museum-style display, with video
*Time:* Continuous viewing
*Kelly says:* Best for adults with a sense of history

*Lucy: A Tribute* is a walk-in display honoring the immortal Lucille Darlene Ball. It's hard to miss, since you bump into it almost as soon as you enter the park. There's hardly ever a crowd, so feel free to breeze on by and take it in later. If you run out of time . . . well, truth to tell, you haven't missed much. Still, fans of the great redhead (and who isn't?) will find at least something of interest here, even if it's just a reminder to pull down those Lucy videos at home and take a four hundredth look.

The "tribute" is simply a large open room ringed with glassed-in display cases, like shop windows, crammed with Lucy memorabilia — photos, letters, scripts, costumes, and Lucy's six Emmys — including the posthumous Governor's Award presented on September 17, 1989. One of the more interesting windows contains a model of the studio in which the ground-breaking *I Love Lucy* show was shot. It was the first show shot with the three-camera method still used today. A fascinating footnote: The sets in those days of black-and-white TV were actually painted in shades of gray (furniture, too) to provide optimum contrast on the home screen.

Continuously running videos feature Bob Hope and Gale Gordon reminiscing about Lucy, while brief clips remind us of just how much we really did love Lucy. You'll hear the people next to you saying, "Oh, I remember that one," or "I lo-o-o-ved that one." There's some interesting material here about Lucy's career before she became a television icon. In one corner, an interactive video system offers an *I Love Lucy* trivia quiz. The idea is to get the Ricardos and Mertzes cross-country to Hollywood by answering five multiple-choice questions. But, careful! You lose gas by guessing wrong. Real Lucy and Ricky fanatics should have no problem, but for most people the quiz will prove to be no pushover.

The "worst" part of *Lucy: A Tribute* is that it reminds you that almost nothing Universal Studios Florida has to offer is as entertaining as yet another viewing of the Vitameatavegemin episode (or the grape stomping episode, or the Bill Holden episode, for that matter). At least you can wander into the inevitable shop at the end of the display and buy some videos to take home. And that, perhaps, is the whole point. The shop is easily twice as large as the display!

# AT&T at the Movies

*Rating:* ★ +
*Type:* Advertising display with interactive games
*Time:* Continuous viewing
*Kelly says:* Some fun bits

Located at the end of the Hollywood section in a replica of the Garden of Allah Villas, but facing into the Expo Center plaza, lies this oddity. It's essentially one long advertisement for AT&T and, while it's genial enough, there is so much razzle dazzle going on just a few paces away that a visit here will rank way down on most people's priority list.

All that being said, some of the displays inside are actually quite interesting if you're in the mood. And if you'd care to make a phone call using a phone that's bigger than you are, then this is definitely the place to be.

*Tip:* If you enter the Garden of Allah Villas from the lagoon side, you can take a shortcut to Expo Center Plaza and the *E. T. Adventure*.

# Selected Short Subjects

### Legends of the Silver Screen

Wouldn't it have been great to meet W.C. Fields? Or Mae West? Or Lucy and Desi? Well, at Universal Studios it's never too late. Startling look-alikes of these and other stars — like Marilyn Monroe, Chaplin, and the Marx Brothers — regularly stroll along Hollywood Boulevard.

And they'd be absolutely delighted to pose for a photo. Not all stars appear every day and stars have been known to pop up elsewhere on the lot. (I once saw Lucy and Desi sprawled on the grass in the park by the lagoon and Bill Fields driving a Model-A down Park Avenue.)

### Universal Studios Radio Broadcast Center

Right next to the Brown Derby (see below) is a fairly inconspicuous radio studio. From here popular disk jockeys from around the U.S. and Canada, and from as far away as London and Belo Horizonte, Brazil, broadcast live shows to the folks back home.

If something's going on during your visit, you'll be able to watch through the picture windows. The audio feed will be piped to the outside. Even if there's no show on the air, peek in and check out the clever ceiling treatment inside.

### Kodak Trick Photography Photo Spot

This is one of several spots in the park where you can take your own souvenir photo using the "hanging miniature" technique pioneered in the early days of filmmaking. You get a stand on which to position your camera and step-by-step instructions to make double sure you get it right. There are even footprints telling you where to place your subjects. The results are a delight and guaranteed to be among your favorite (not to mention cheapest) souvenirs of your visit. Here, you can photograph your family in front of the Pantages Theater, with the Hollywood hills and the rest of the Los Angeles skyline stretching into the distance.

## Eating in Hollywood

### Beverly Hills Boulangerie

*What:*         Sandwiches, sweets, and coffee
*Where:*        At the corner of Hollywood Boulevard and
                Plaza of the Stars
*Price Range:*  $ - $$

According to the official Universal Studios map, the Beverly Hills Boulangerie is on the Front Lot but, given its theme and its location across Hollywood Boulevard from *Lucy: A Tribute*, it seems to make more sense to discuss it here.

This charming little bistro blends the current craze for coffee bars with a tasty array of breakfast and dessert baked goods. It's an unbeatable combination. If you're visiting during one of the less crowded times of year (so you don't have to dash right off to *Back To The Future*), you might want to pause here for a fortifying, if calorie-laden breakfast. Sit outside on sunny days to entertain yourself with the passing parade.

There are gigantic blueberry, banana-nut, and bran muffins and roly-poly chocolate croissants. If you subscribe to the when-on-vacation-start-with-dessert philosophy, why not start the day off right with an eclair, or a slice of raspberry cheesecake? Most pastries and muffins are in the $2 to $3 range. Coffees range from the plain (for about a dollar) to fancy cappuccinos for a little over $2.

Later in the day, you can stop in for a smoked turkey or ham and Swiss sandwich on your choice of baguette or croissant. Or soothe your conscience with a Health Sandwich of Swiss cheese, sprouts, cucumbers, and avocados. Sandwiches are in the $6 to $7 range. You can also get salads here if you purchase them with soup ($5) or a sandwich ($7). French wines are available for a bit over $3, or splurge on a glass of the bubbly for about $8.

## Mel's Drive-In

| | |
|---|---|
| *What:* | Fast-food burger joint |
| *Where:* | At the end of Hollywood Boulevard, across from the lagoon |
| *Price Range:* | $$ |

Remember the nostalgia drenched drive-in restaurant from *American Graffiti?* Well here it is in some of its splendor. No curvy car hops, alas, but you will see a mouth-watering array of customized vintage cars parked outside.

Inside, you will find a fairly typical 1990s fast-food emporium with fifties decor. Place and pay for your burger or hot dog and fries order at the cashier, then step forward to pick it up, wrapped in paper. If the food and non-service won't bring back memories of those great cheeseburgers and real-milk shakes you had way back when, at least there are jukeboxes to flip through at the tables. There is also an outdoor seating area that looks out to the park's central lagoon.

The menu is limited and prices low to moderate. The typical burger and fries meal will set you back about $8. Soft drinks are your only beverage choice here. Mel's is a good spot for a quick bite with kids who like no surprises with their meals, but I can't help but think that Universal is missing a bet here. I for one would be willing to pay a higher price for a dining experience that would more closely evoke the ambiance of the diner in the movie, complete with gum-chewing waitresses on rollerskates.

## Schwab's Pharmacy

| | |
|---|---|
| *What:* | Ice-cream parlor |
| *Where:* | In the middle of Hollywood Boulevard |
| *Price Range:* | $ - $$ |

Schwab's has a place in Hollywood lore as the place where a sharp-eyed talent scout discovered a sweater-clad, teenaged Lana Turner sipping soda at the counter. At Universal Studios, Schwab's lends its name to a small, black-and-white tiled, vaguely forties-ish ice-cream parlor featuring Häagen-Dazs products. Milk shakes and ice cream floats run about $3; sundaes are $4, and apple pie a la mode just a bit less. Or you can order a turkey breast, chicken salad, or tuna salad sandwich ($6 to $7). Although there are a few tables, Schwab's is primarily aimed at those looking for a quick — and portable — snack.

In keeping with its namesake's primary business, Schwab's also stocks a small supply of over-the-counter headache and heartburn remedies. For those intent on spending the whole day riding *Back To The Future*, Schwab's very thoughtfully provides Dramamine.

## Cafe La Bamba

| | |
|---|---|
| *What:* | Cafeteria-style barbecue restaurant |
| *Where:* | Across from Mel's and the lagoon in the Hollywood Hotel |
| *Price Range:* | $ - $$ |

Cafe La Bamba serves up ample portions of rotisserie chicken and barbecued ribs at moderate prices. On top of that, the ambiance is a cut above your average fast-food restaurant. Evoking a Spanish mission courtyard with adobe walls and tiled floors, it offers some charming corners just a few steps away from the cafeteria lines plus a delightful outdoor seating area that looks across to Mel's and the lagoon.

Most chicken entrees are in the $5 to $8 range. The barbecued baby back ribs are $10 and various burger platters are available for $6 to $7. Desserts are in the $2 to $3 range. At the Cantina, you can get a frozen alcoholic drink or have a cocktail mixed.

# Shopping in Hollywood

Hollywood Boulevard funnels visitors from the studio entrance to the central lagoon and serves as a primary route for visitors on their way out. Much of it has been given over to a variety of shopping experiences. The Boulevard itself is an imaginative recreation of major Hollywood facades, some of which still exist and others of which have vanished into the realm of cherished memories. It makes for a pleasant stroll and a fitting introduction to the movie-themed fun that awaits you in the rest of the park. Don't be surprised to see Mae West, W.C. Fields, or the Marx Brothers on your stroll, and don't hesitate to ask them to pose for a picture with you.

The following description begins at the end of the Boulevard closest to the entrance and proceeds towards the lagoon.

## Silver Screen Collectibles

Silver Screen Collectibles opens onto the Plaza of the Stars, just across the street from the Universal Studios Store. At the other end, it merges with *Lucy: A Tribute.*

Expect to find t-shirts and other merchandise featuring cartoon characters. Farther along is a hodgepodge of blown up publicity photos of stars past and present and large movie posters. There is also a selection of Universal Studios shirts and sweats in a variety of styles and prices.

The too-small book selection revolves around a few major stars like W.C. Fields and Elvis Presley.

The real star of Silver Screen Collectibles is the special Lucy section, strategically located at the entrance/exit to *Lucy: A Tribute.* Here you will find the Lucy Collection, a series of videos with two shows per cassette ($15 each). In addition, you'll find a generous selection of books, which the true Lucy fan will find to be invaluable references, and a series of t-shirts in homage to the great redhead. (My favorite is the Vitameata-vegemin shirt at $17).

## The Brown Derby

The original Brown Derby was a hat-shaped eatery that opened in Hollywood in 1929 and has long since been demolished. Universal Studio has copied the shape (in smaller scale) and devoted the tiny space to — what else? — hats! Inside you will find a cozy circular space, topped with a photographic frieze of famous stars of the past in a variety of headgear and filled to the brim with hats of all descriptions. Casual, stylish, or downright wacky — they're all here.

If your idea of sartorial splendor is a hat that makes you look like Bullwinkle Moose (complete with droopy antlers) or Woody Woodpecker, you'll find them here for about $20. For little girls, there are adorable pink and lavender pointed princess hats, complete with wispy veil, for the same price.

There are plenty of more practical toppers, too. Baseball caps in all colors, memorializing a wide assortment of characters, range from $15 to $20. Very stylish men's hats in leather and suede go for $35 to $50, while women's straw hats can be had for $13 to $23.

*Photo Op:* The central table carries a selection of wonderfully way-out creations. Although they have price tags, my guess is that they are seldom purchased but tried on hundreds of times a day. It's a great chance for some fun family portraits.

## Studio Styles

Clothes snobs who still want to wear something that says "Universal" should head straight for Studio Styles, located in the Hollywood Chamber of Commerce building. Here you'll find Universal's nicest, most fashionable logo-ed t-shirts, sweats, sweaters, and jackets at prices that keep the riffraff out. In addition to the $100 jackets, $70 sweaters, and $55 denim shirts with leather Universal logos, you will find high-style, high-tech sunglasses and watches at prices from $50 to $125.

## The Darkroom

If you didn't pick up film at On Location, it's not too late: The Dark-room has it, too. It also offers one-hour film developing if you just can't wait till you get back home. The typical tourist-sized roll of 36 exposures is processed for about $13 in the standard 4x6 size. But consider popping for 5x7 prints ($16) and then picking up (at On Location or the Universal Studios Store) picture frames in the shape of scene slates to enshrine them.

If you had your photo taken by a roving photographer in the park, here's where you claim your prints. Don't forget to check the number of your claim check against the "lucky numbers" posted here. Your photo just may be free!

## Cyber Image

If you see *T2 3-D: Battle Across Time* (and you should), you can't miss this T2 memorabilia shop; you walk right through it when you leave the theater. Here's your chance to dress just like Arnold in black leather jacket ($150), muscles not included. For the less well-heeled there are T2 and "No Fate" t-shirts for about $18 and Cyberdyne polo shirts for $13. The T800 exoskeleton model is $25.

## Movietime Portrait and Celebrity News

Back across Hollywood Boulevard, you'll find Universal's somewhat wan version of what has become a fairly familiar tourist town come-on. Here you can take advantage of a small costume and prop collection to dress up and have a solo or group photo taken in your choice of themes

— wild West or prohibition gangster ($25 to $45 depending on the number of people in the shot). Or, in another section, you can have the video image of your face superimposed on the body of a bathing beauty or bodybuilder, or inserted into some incongruous location. There are more elaborate (and cheaper) versions of this concession to be found elsewhere in Orlando.

# EXPO CENTER

The theme of Expo Center is, I suppose, the future, or at least the cutting edge of modernism. The result is a display of contemporary architecture and design that manages to be at once very attractive and rather characterless. Fortunately, people don't come here to muse on aesthetics.

As home to two of the park's most popular rides (*E. T. Adventure* and *Back To The Future . . . The Ride* ), Expo Center's broad open spaces are filled with happy people, making a visit here a highly enjoyable experience. The presence of *A Day in the Park With Barney* and *Fievel's Playland*, in addition to *E. T.*, make it a favorite with kids.

## Back To The Future . . . The Ride

| | |
|---|---|
| *Rating:* | ★ ★ ★ ★ ★ |
| *Type:* | Slam-bang simulator thrill ride |
| *Time:* | 4.5 minutes |
| *Kelly says:* | The best theme park ride in Orlando |

For many people, this is the ride that made Universal Studios Florida famous. And with good reason. *Back To The Future . . . The Ride* is a bone-jarring, stomach-churning (the official disclaimer posted outside describes it as "dynamically aggressive") thrill-a-second rocket ride through time and space. For once the warnings directed towards expectant mothers and those with heart problems, bad backs, and a tendency to motion sickness don't seem like lawyers' overkill. It's easy to see how this ride could trigger a premature birth or otherwise encourage what's inside to come outside in dramatic fashion.

*Tip:* Those in wheelchairs can still take this ride if they are able to transfer themselves from their wheelchair to the ride vehicle. Ask the attendant if you're not sure.

That mammoth building at the back of Expo Center is the Institute of Future Technology where that wild and wacky Doc Brown (played on video monitors with gleeful aplomb by Christopher Lloyd) is conducting yet another series of time travel experiments. Those of us who willingly get on the invariably long lines to this attraction are "volunteers" who have agreed to test out Doc's new eight-seater convertible DeLorean — all in the interests of science.

Trouble is, that not-too-bright but very resourceful Biff Tannen has stowed away in 1955 and is loose on the premises — a key bit of intelligence which we discover (via those video monitors) before Doc does. Biff has tied up some attendants and stolen the keys to one of the experimental DeLoreans. When he learns the truth, Doc goes, well, ballistic. "This could end the universe as we know it," he screams with characteristic understatement.

Suddenly, our mission has changed. Far from being mere passengers, we are now charged with giving chase to the evil Biff and engineering a time/space collision that will send Biff and his vehicle reeling back to the present.

That's the set-up. What follows is harder to describe. Suffice it to say that you're off on a four and a half minute, high-speed odyssey that will seem like eternity to some and all too brief to others. Along the way, you will zoom through the streets of Hill Valley's future, into the ice caves of its distant past, and smack into the slavering maw of a Tyrannosaurus Rex, always just a few tantalizing feet behind the errant Biff.

This ride raised the bar on thrill rides when it first opened. It has yet to be matched. It is, quite simply, the best simulator-based ride in Orlando — at least until Islands of Adventure opens (see *Chapter Three*).

*Back To The Future . . . The Ride* is actually two identical rides, located side by side in the same building. Each ride contains twelve identical eight-seater DeLoreans, each in its own "garage." The cars are arranged on three levels: four on the bottom, five in the middle, and three on the top. As you proceed into the maze of ramps that lead into the Institute, you will be guided to one of these levels. Once inside, you will wait first in a staging area and then in a cramped anteroom to your vehicle's garage. All along, the imaginative video introduction keeps you posted on Biff's caper while preparing you for the rigors of time travel. When you are in the final anteroom, an amusing safety warning featuring a family of hapless crash dummies explains the dangers of the DeLorean you're about to squeeze into.

At last the door opens and you see your DeLorean (and the wobbly group who just rode in it groping for the exit). If you look up you can see a gray void looming overhead. Once everyone is seated, the padded lap bars lock into place and the sides of the car fold down. It's a tight fit.

*Tip:* Try for the front seats. The view is better and rear seat passengers can expect to get their heads banged against the (padded) rear wall of the car. And heed the warnings about securing your personal belongings. Cameras, wallets, glasses, and the like have been known to disappear into the time-space continuum.

Suddenly you're airborne in a cloud of liquid nitrogen smoke and a flash of strobe lights that mask the DeLorean's rise up and out of the garage below. Your vehicle is actually an open-air cousin to the high-tech simulators used to train airline pilots. Like a box on stilts it hovers a few feet off the ground, but for all you know or care you might as well be in the depths of interstellar space.

You are now facing a mammoth, curved movie screen that completely fills your line of vision and represents the true genius of this ride. Other simulator-based rides (like the Hanna-Barbera ride here at Universal) use a movie screen that serves as a window to the outside of your spaceship or other vehicle. With *Back To The Future, you* are outside and the environment wraps around you. The illusion is startling, not to mention sometimes terrifying.

The movement of the simulator's stilts is surprisingly modest. You never actually move more than two feet in any direction. But try telling that to your brain. The kinetic signals sent by your body combine with the visual signals received from the screen to convince you that you are zooming along at supersonic speeds, making white-knuckle turns at dizzying angles.

Matching the technological wonder of the concept is the care that went into making the multi-million dollar 70-mm Omnimax film in which you become a key participant. Its budget reportedly rivaled that of most major feature-length films. It was directed by that living legend of special effects, Douglas Trumbull, and as they say in the movie biz, every penny they spent is on the screen.

*The best seats in the house.* The best way to experience this mind-boggling attraction is from the front row of the middle car of the middle row of DeLoreans. Regardless of which of the two "theaters" you enter, this car is designated as "Car Six." This position points you directly at the center of the domed screen. You'll experience less distortion of the image (and, not incidentally reduce any tendency towards motion sickness) and you'll be less likely to be distracted by glimpsing other cars out of your peripheral vision. (By the way, in the unlikely event you find yourself bored during your umpty-umpth ride, especially if you're off to the side of the bottom row, looking around at the other cars will give you a deeper appreciation of just how clever this ride is.)

Unfortunately, there's no easy way to position yourself to get the optimum seat. It's pretty much luck of the draw. If the lines are short or nonexistent, you might ask an attendant to point you to car number six (they'll know what you're talking about). That might at least get you to the right level. Otherwise, you'll just have to keep trying until your lucky number comes up. For die-hard fans that'll be something they can live with.

*Tip:* If you're prone to motion sickness but still want to savor the special thrills of this ride, take a Dramamine, or a similar over-the-counter anti-motion sickness pill, before you leave for the park. Popping one just before entering will probably not protect you. During the ride, keep your eyes focused on Biff's car dead ahead to avoid too much conflict with your inner ear's balancing mechanism. If you find yourself getting uncomfortably nauseated, shut your eyes and tell yourself to relax. Remember, the ride lasts less than five minutes. Some queasy riders report getting relief by turning their gaze away from the screen and focusing on an adjacent car.

## E.T. Adventure

| | |
|---|---|
| *Rating:* | ★ ★ ★ |
| *Type:* | Gondola ride |
| *Time:* | 5 minutes |
| *Kelly says:* | Kids love this one (some adults do, too) |

E.T. is one of Universal's most popular rides for people of all ages, with the result that the lines can become dauntingly long. While signs announcing wait times can generally be trusted, the sign here is misleading. It only tells you how long it will take to get inside. On busy days, there can be another wait of 15 to 20 minutes inside the building before you reach the ride itself. Plan accordingly.

Based on the blockbuster movie that crossed sci-fi with cuddly toys, the *E.T. Adventure* takes us where the movie didn't — back to E.T.'s home planet. In a filmed introduction to the ride, Steven Spielberg, who directed the film, sets up the premise: E.T.'s home, the Green Planet, is in some unspecified trouble, although it looks like an advanced case of ozone hole which is turning the place a none-too-healthy looking orange. You have to return with E.T. to help save the old folks at home. How to get there? Aboard the flying bicycles from the film's final sequence, of course. The fact that Spielberg doesn't bother to explain how we'll survive the rigors of interstellar travel aboard mountain bikes, tells us that this ride is aimed at the very young. How to save the planet? That's not explained either although it seems that E.T.'s "healing touch" and our mere presence will be enough to revive the place.

*Tip:* Moving to the far right (as you face the screen), will put you closer to the doors to the next chamber, thus first in line for the next phase of the adventure.

After this brief setup, the doors to the right open and we line up to get the "passports" we will need for the journey. Here, the ride reverts to the movie-making metaphor of so many of the attractions at Universal. Once again we are "actors" and a call-board on the front wall reminds us that we must give our first names to get our identification cards. The passports are thin pieces of plastic with bar-codes and a subtle message from the folks at AT&T reminding us which service to use next time *we* have to phone home.

Our plastic cards firmly in hand, we walk through a cave-like tunnel into the misty, night-time redwood forests of the Northwest. This set is a minor masterpiece of scenic design and some people think it's the best part of the adventure. As we wend our way along a winding "nature trail" amidst the towering trees, we make out the animated figure of Botanicus, a wise elder from E.T.'s planet, urging us to hurry back. Here, too, we glimpse the jury-rigged contraption E.T. used to communicate in the film.

As we get ready to collect our "bikes" (look for E.T. to pop his head out of the basket on the front), we turn in our plastic "passports" to another attendant and are directed to the staging area. The bikes are actually nine-passenger, open-sided gondolas with bicycle-like seats, each with its own set of handlebars. The gondolas hang from a ceiling track and soon "take off" on our adventure.

This ride might be likened to a bike with training wheels. It has many of the aspects of more thrilling rides — sudden acceleration, swoops, and turns — but toned down so as not to be truly frightening.

In the first phase of the ride, we are zipping through the redwoods, dodging the unenlightened grown-ups who want to capture E.T. for study and analysis. Police cars and jeeps roar out of the darkness on seeming collision course with our frail vehicle. This section might be a little scary for small kids and a little loud for older adults. Soon, however, we are soaring high above the city in one of the ride's most enchanting interludes. We rise higher until we are in the stars themselves and are then shot down a hyperspace tunnel before we decelerate abruptly and find ourselves in the steamy world of E.T.'s home planet.

It's an odd cave-like place but soon, apparently buoyed by our arrival, the place perks up and we are flying through a psychedelic world of huge multi-colored flowers in wondrous shapes, past talking mushrooms and plants (or are they creatures?) with dozens of eyes. All around are little E.T.s, peeping from under plants, climbing over them, and playing them like percussion instruments. It's all rather like Disney's *It's a*

*Small World* on acid. Those who were in San Francisco during the sixties have seen this all before, but youngsters will doubtless find it enchanting.

All too soon, E.T. is sending us back to *our* home but not before a final farewell. Here is where we get the payoff for giving the attendant our name at the beginning of the ride. E.T. thanks each of us personally in his croaking computer-generated voice. The computer system seems to handle some names better than others and on your subsequent trips you might find it amusing (as I did) to try to stump the system with off-beat names.

I will confess that I am not as captivated by this ride as some. Apparently, Spielberg created a whole new cast of characters for this ride, but, other than Botanicus, they are hard to identify, much less get to know or understand their place in E.T.'s world. And the humans in the woods look too much like department store mannequins for my taste. Still, these are minor carps. Much of the ride is fun, indeed, and will appeal to younger children and their timid elders, who can get a taste of a "thrill" ride without actually putting the contents of their stomachs at risk.

This is also one of the few rides at Universal where seeing the film on which it is based will definitely add to the appreciation of the experience. Without this background, much of the ride may seem merely odd. This will be especially true for younger children who will be better able to empathize with E.T. and his plight if they've seen the movie.

**The best seats in the house.** On the whole, the left side of the gondola provides better views than the right, especially of the city. Best of all is the far left seat in the first of the three rows.

**Tip:** When the *Animal Actors* show lets out (about 25 minutes after the posted show time), the crowds stream over to get on line for E.T. Time your visit accordingly.

## Animal Actors Stage

*Rating:* ★ ★ ★ ★ +
*Type:* Amphitheater show
*Time:* About 25 minutes
*Kelly says:* Fun for just about everybody

This show opens with one of the most amazing sights you will ever see: a trained cat that does not merely one trick but a whole series of them, and then unfurls a banner announcing the show. What follows is pretty amazing, too, but cat owners will be especially impressed with the opening act.

This vastly entertaining spectacle shows off the handiwork of Universal's animal trainers and their furry and feathery charges. It's all done with the droll good humor and audience participation that characterize all of Universal's shows. One lucky (or hapless) kid is pulled from the audience to serve as a foil for several amusing routines.

Just which animals you see will depend to some extent on what's hot and recent in Universal's film line up. A Saint Bernard and a piglet were added to the show after the successes of *Beethoven* and *Babe*. You're also almost guaranteed to see appearances by Benji and Lassie (striking a stirring pose high on a cliff) and Mr. Ed hams it up, although his lip syncing can be a bit off now and then.

Most entertaining on a recent visit was an orangutan whose comic timing would be the envy of most human professionals. Intellectually, you know that the animal is merely running through a series of learned responses. You can even spot the trainer giving the signals. But the interplay between them is so sharp and the ape's broad takes to the audience so casually hilarious that you'll really believe this is comic acting at its best.

In between the fun and games, the host makes enlightening points about the serious business of producing "behaviors" that can be put to use in films. Most interestingly, when an animal balks at performing a trick, the trainer doesn't merely gloss over the rough spot and get on with the show. Instead, he works patiently with the animal until the behavior is performed correctly. We learn that what for us is light entertainment is serious business for the folks (both two- and four-legged) on the stage.

No matter how extraordinary the performances of the other animals in the show, I keep thinking back to that darned cat. I'm half convinced it's actually a dog disguised as a cat.

*The best seats in the house.* There really are no bad seats for this one. However, if you'd like a shot at serving as a landing strip for a very mercenary bird, try sitting in the middle section about eight rows back.

# Fievel's Playland

| | |
|---|---|
| *Rating:* | ★ ★ ★ |
| *Type:* | Hands-on activity |
| *Time:* | As long as you want |
| *Kelly says:* | For young and very active kids |

Based on Steven Spielberg's charming animated film, *An American Tail*, about a shtetl mouse making his way in the New World, *Fievel's Playland* is a convoluted maze of climb-up, run-through, slide-down activities that will keep kids amused while their exhausted parents take a well-deserved break.

Don't forget to bring your camera for great photo ops of the kids amidst the larger-than-life cowboy hats, victrolas, water barrels, playing cards, and cattle skeletons that make up this maze of exploration. And half way to the top of the giant victrola is a great place to snap another picture of the Bates Motel mansion from *Psycho*.

The highlight is a Mouse Climb — a rope tunnel that spirals upwards. At the top, kids can climb into two-man (well, two-kid) rubber rafts to slide down through yet another tunnel to arrive at ground level with enormous grins and wet bottoms. Don't worry, there's also a set of stairs to the top of the slide.

This is a place you can safely let the kids explore on their own. The ground is padded. However, kids less than 40 inches high will have to drag a grown-up (or maybe a bigger sibling) along to ride the water slide. There's seldom a wait to get in but long lines do form for the water slide. If time is a factor and if you will be visiting one of the water-themed parks on another day, you can tell the kids that there are bigger, better water slides awaiting them tomorrow.

Even though this attraction is aimed squarely at the younger set, don't be surprised if your young teens get in the spirit and momentarily forget that romping through a kid's playground is not the 'cool' thing to do.

## A Day in the Park with Barney

| | |
|---|---|
| *Rating:* | ★ ★ ★ |
| *Type:* | Theater show with singing |
| *Time:* | About 20 minutes |
| *Kelly says:* | For toddlers and their long-suffering parents |

According to the publicity, Universal's Barney attraction is the only place in the United States where you can see Barney "live." For some people, that may be one place too many. But for his legions of adoring wee fans and the parents who love them, this show will prove an irresistible draw. Even old curmudgeons will grudgingly have to admit that the show's pretty sweet.

The first tip off that this is a kiddie show is the fact that it's the only attraction at Universal with its own stroller parking lot. And it's usually full. After the young guests have availed themselves of Mom and Dad's valet parking service, they enter through a gate into Barney's park, complete with a bronze Barney cavorting in an Italianate fountain.

When the show begins, we are all ushered into a stand-up pre-show area where Mr. Peekaboo and his gaudy bird friend Bartholomew put on a singing, dancing warm-up act that wouldn't be complete unless the audience got splashed. Then, using our imaginations, we pass through a misty cave entrance sprinkled with star dust to enter the main theater.

Inside is a completely circular space cheerfully decorated as a forest park at dusk. Low benches surround the raised central stage, but old fogies may want to make for the more comfortable park benches against the walls. The sightlines are excellent no matter where you sit, although Mr. Peekaboo reminds us that once we've chosen a seat we must stay there for the entire show.

The show is brief and cheery and almost entirely given over to sing-alongs that are already familiar to Barney's little fans. Barney is soon joined by Baby Bop and B.J. and the merriment proceeds apace, complete with falling autumn leaves, a brief snowfall, and shooting streamers. By the end, the air is filled with love — literally.

True star that he is, Barney stays behind after the show to greet his young admirers, a few of whom seem overawed to be so close to this giant vision in purple. One point I found particularly amusing was that the stage crew has very little to clean up after the show. The kids are remarkably efficient in policing up the fallen leaves and streamers. Now if only we could get them to do that back home!

The theater audience empties out into **Barney's Backyard**, which is the day-care center of your dreams. Here, beautifully executed by Universal scenic artists, is a collection of imaginative and involving activities for the very young, from making music to splashing in water, to drawing on the walls. For parents who are a bit on the slow side, there are signs to explain the significance of what their kids are up to. A sample: "Young children have a natural inclination towards music [which] encourages the release of stress through listening and dancing." Duh!

Barney's Backyard is where little kids get their revenge. Whereas many rides in the park bar younger children on the basis of height, here there are activities that are off limits to those *over* 48 inches or even 36 inches. Kids will love it. Grown-ups will only wish there were more of it.

*Tip:* This wonderful space has a separate entrance and you don't have to sit through the show to get in here. Keep this in mind if the family's youngest member needs some special attention or a chance to unwind from the frustrations of being a little person in a big persons' amusement park.

# Previews of Coming Attractions

*E. T. Adventure*, *A Day in the Park with Barney*, and *Fievel's Playland*, not to mention the fun-for-all-ages *Animal Actors Stage*, already make Expo Center a happenin' place for younger children but, come the summer of

1999, your younger kids may never leave the place. At press time, Universal announced the creation of two new children's attractions, aimed at the five-to-twelve set, under the omnibus name of **Woody Woodpecker's KidZone**.

**Woody Woodpecker's Nuthouse Coaster** is described as a "gentle" children's roller coaster, knocked together by Woody from bits of this and that, running through a nut factory. The cars are modeled after nut crates and are labled "salted," "unsalted," and "certifiable." **Curious George Goes To Town** is an elaborate play area themed after the illustrated books about the playful monkey. Various sections of the attraction include a zoo where Curious George has freed all the animals, a cityscape full of climb up, crawl through, slide down possibilities and a toy factory filled with foam balls that kids can "shoot, dump, blast, and haul." Water plays a big part in the design of the Curious George attraction and kids can expect to get plenty wet.

In addition to the new attractions, the KidZone area will have a water-play fountain, a "themed" restaurant, and a shop. Woody's KidZone will be located behind the existing Barney and Fievel attractions. Presumably this will mean that the *Psycho* House (see below) will be moved or eliminated. The Hard Rock Café, which is also back here, will move to much larger quarters in CityWalk (See *Chapter Three*).

# Selected Short Subjects

## Cartoon Casting Call

Here's your chance to meet and mingle with some of Hollywood's heavyweights. That's right, Fred Flintstone, Woody Woodpecker, Yogi Bear, and the rest of the gang. They show up periodically in front of Universal's Cartoon Store to meet their adoring public and, yes, sign autographs. Don't expect much in the way of scintillating conversation, however; they're the strong silent type. Appearances of cartoon characters are announced in the Studio Guide brochure.

## The "Psycho" House

Curious about that brooding old mansion up on the hill behind Barney's park? It's the "*Psycho*" house, and the one you see was actually used as a set in *Psycho IV*, filmed here at Universal Studios Florida. This is another Kodak photo spot, although this one doesn't involve any tricks. Simply stand where you're told and have your subjects walk to the end of the little path. Now turn your camera sideways and you've got another perfectly composed shot with a spooky backdrop.

**Note:** The *Psycho* House may go the way of Mom Bates as Universal begins construction on *Woody Woodpecker's KidZone*, described above.

# Eating in Expo Center

## International Food Bazaar

| | |
|---|---|
| *What:* | A multicultural cafeteria |
| *Where:* | On Exposition Boulevard, next to *Back To The Future* |
| *Price Range:* | $$ |

This is as fancy as it gets in Expo Center. This large, loud cafeteria-style food emporium is divided into sections by cuisine. From left to right, you can choose among Italian, American, German, Mexican, Chinese, or Ice Cream (my nationality). Entrees range from $3 to about $7.50, and the food is typical fast-food quality. In addition to the usual American beers, you can pick up Tsingtao (from China) for $4 and Italian wine for a little less. Be aware that some sections may be closed when you visit. The American, Italian, and Chinese sections seem to be open on the most regular basis.

More entertaining than the food is the ambiance, which follows both the food and international themes. Video monitors scattered around the large seating area play clips from old TV shows like *Leave It to Beaver* and movies like *Animal House* (remember the food fight sequence?). If a particular clip catches your fancy, you're in luck; at the end of each cycle of clips you are told where you can buy your own copy of the original.

On the walls are posters from foreign language versions of hit movies. *Great Balls of Fire* comes out as *Zampate di Fuoco* in Italian and *Back To The Future* is *Retours Vers Le Futur* in French. There is also a large outdoor seating area, if you feel like watching the crowds stream by.

*Tip:* The rear wall is all glass and looks out on the *Animal Actors Stage* — a great opportunity to take a second (if somewhat obstructed) look at one of Universal's most enjoyable attractions.

## Animal Crackers

| | |
|---|---|
| *What:* | Hot dog stand with outdoor seating |
| *Where:* | On Exposition Plaza, next to Universal's Cartoon Store |
| *Price Range:* | $ - $$ |

This walk-up fast-food counter serves up a restricted menu of quick snacks. Hot dogs and fries are about $4.50. Add chili and the price rises to about $5. A grilled chicken sandwich (about $7) is the most expensive item on the menu. Chocolate dipped cones can be had for about $2.50.

### Hard Rock Café

*What:*         World's busiest branch of wildly popular rock and roll beanery

*Where:*        At the edge of the park, past Barney and Fievel (see Note, below)

*Price Range:*  $$ - $$$

The Hard Rock Café is not really *in* Expo Center — or in Universal Studios, for that matter — but it does straddle the border of the park and a surprising number of people choose to exit into the Hard Rock, getting their hand stamped for re-entry, to have lunch or dinner.

*Tip:* Don't do it! Not because the Hard Rock Café isn't good. It is. Better than good. But you can eat at the Hard Rock without buying a ticket to the theme park, so use your precious time inside Universal Studios to concentrate on the rides, shows, and other attractions. Come back to the Hard Rock later — much later! It's open until 2 a.m.

That being said, the Hard Rock Café will appeal mostly to its die-hard fans who find the combination of ear-splitting rock and roll and above average American diner fare irresistible. For those who have never visited one of the other branches, this offers an excellent introduction. Not only is this branch the world's largest, but it sits on a guitar-shaped base, best appreciated from the air.

Inside is an amazing collection of rock and roll memorabilia, casually distributed on the walls of the restaurant. Most people are too reticent to wander about and take it all in, but feel free to do so if the spirit moves you.

*Note:* As I write, a new and much enlarged Hard Rock is being constructed just outside the front gate. When it opens in late 1998, this one will be closed.

# Shopping in Expo Center

### Back To The Future — The Store

There's a DeLorean smashing through the walls of this compact circular shop, and the walls themselves are plastered with newspaper headlines of the past and future. There are the expected *Back To The Future* souvenirs to be found here, including OUTATIME vanity license plates ($5). A DeLorean toy car goes for $25 and a boxed set of the film trilogy, complete with a bonus cassette about the "secrets" of making the films, will set you back $60. For little ones, there's an Einstein doll (Doc Brown's dog, not the wild-haired scientist) for $25.

Picking up on the time theme, the store features an intriguing variety of clocks, some of which celebrate the 1950s of the first film and others of which evoke a high-tech future yet unseen. Prices range from around $50 to several hundred dollars. There are also some fun "science" toys, including an "ooze tube" ($13) and a 10-minute timer in which the hopelessly old-fashioned sand has been replaced with slow moving goo.

## Expo Art

On Exposition Boulevard, outside the International Food Bazaar, you will find several tent-like structures housing some of Universal Studios' most attractive souvenirs. Under one tent, as many as four caricaturists hold forth, turning out devastatingly accurate portraits for remarkably reasonable prices. Black and white sketches are just $12, or $18 for a couple. With color added, the prices go to $18 and $30 respectively. For an extra $12, you get a frame with glass.

Next door is the Rainbow Art painting tent. Here a team of artists will paint your name in letters about six inches high formed by fanciful palm trees, fish, bamboo shoots, sea waves, and colorfully plumed birds. No letter seems to be painted the same way twice. The cost: just $2 per letter. You can have your finished masterpieces held for later pick-up or mailed to your home.

## E.T.'s Toy Closet

This vest-pocket shop is devoted to everybody's favorite alien, surely the homeliest homunculus ever to worm his way into a child's heart. E.T.s with rather unattractive hard plastic faces are $25. A video of the film is $25 here; children's t-shirts are around $10 to $13. Perhaps your best bet is a souvenir photo of your child on a bike with E.T. in the basket and a huge silver moon as backdrop ($5).

## Universal's Cartoon Store

Despite the name, a lot of live animals are represented in this store that's aimed squarely at your child's heart. You'll find Beethoven, Babe, and Lassie along with Rocky, Bullwinkle, Fievel, and Woody Woodpecker. All are available as plush dolls at prices ranging from $13 to about $40. There is also the usual assortment of kid-oriented t-shirts ($13) and videos. Rounding out the kid appeal of this cheerfully decorated circular space is a Nickelodeon section.

### The Barney Shop

Here's where your little one will plead with you for a Barney doll. Reflecting the powers of persuasion wee ones have over parents and grandparents, they range in price from $25 for smallish Barneys to $40 for the larger varieties. For children who balk at taking naps, there is a Barney pillow for $20. Videos are about $15 and t-shirts $13. There are Barney books and a series of Barney toys ($13 to $20).

# SAN FRANCISCO / AMITY

Juxtaposing California's San Francisco and New England's Amity might seem jarring at first, but in the movies anything is possible. In fact, the two areas are quite separate; the double-barreled name for this "set" is more a matter of convenience than anything else.

San Francisco/Amity is distinguished by the presence of *Jaws*, the wonderfully scary boat ride. The San Francisco part is also packed with eating places, some of them quite nice indeed.

## Jaws

| | |
|---|---|
| *Rating:* | ★ ★ ★ ★ + |
| *Type:* | Water ride |
| *Time:* | 5 minutes |
| *Kelly says:* | A scare-fest for kids of all ages |

Welcome aboard, as Captain Jake takes you on a sight-seeing tour of peaceful Amity harbor. As the waiting line snakes toward the dock, you get your first inkling that something might be amiss. Television monitors broadcast an appropriately hokey local news broadcast of strange doings in Amity, complete with interviews with the real Sheriff Brody (who complains that Arnold Schwarzenegger would have been a much better choice than Roy Scheider to play him in the movie).

The conceit, of course, is that you are in the real town of Amity and that the blockbuster film *Jaws* was not fiction but fact-based. One not unwelcome by-product of the film is that the sleepy town is now a major tourist draw, allowing Captain Jake to make a good living as the best — make that the only — sight-seeing company offering tours of the island.

As your tour boat is about to leave the dock, your friendly but cocky guide shows off a grenade launcher for effect. He points out that since the great white was killed way back in '74, Amity's been pretty peaceful. He points out Sheriff Brody's house on the left and then heads out of the harbor.

This being a Universal ride, it doesn't take long for things to go ominously amiss. A crackling, fragmented radio transmission from Amity 3, a returning tour boat, is a clear signal that danger lies ahead, but the guide assures us nothing's wrong. A turn around a rocky promontory reveals the other tour boat shattered and sinking on our left. A huge dorsal fin breaks the surface, we feel a slight bump as the shark passes beneath us, and the thrills begin.

Jaws (for that is the shark's universally agreed-upon name) breaks water on our left, showing off his gaping maw and savage teeth. Our now panicked tour guide fires off a few grenades but they go wide of the mark, sending up harmless geysers of water around his target.

A quick turn into a dark boat house promises safety, but we know better. The edgy nerves of fellow passengers provide much of the fun here until Jaws himself crashes through the wooden boat house on the right.

Back out in open water, we're in for another close call as Bridle's shoreside gasoline depot erupts in flames. The heat on the left side of the boat is intense and a wall of flame blocks our way. Our intrepid guide steers straight for the flame as our only route to safety and, mercifully, the flames die down to let us past.

Relief is only momentary, however, as Jaws lunges at the boat from the left, lifting his head high out of the water. The guide nudges the boat into a gap in a floating dock where an electrical cable has fallen into the water. Jaws lunges from our left again but this time he gets the cable before he gets us. He dies in a spectacular shower of electrified water and sparks. A little farther along, what appears to be his charred corpse bobs to the surface. But there's life in the old boy yet and he makes another attempt on the hors d'oeuvres floating by. A final volley from the grenade launcher and we are at last out of danger and glide back to the dock without further incident, barely five minutes after we left.

This is a water ride and, as you are informed several times before embarking, you will get wet. Some people just don't seem to believe it. One of the extra added amusements of this ride is watching fastidious tourists take out a tissue and carefully wipe off the damp seats before sitting down. Don't bother. There's a lot more where that came from. If you come to the park in the winter, when temperatures can be on the cool side, you might want to consider protecting yourself with a cheap plastic poncho.

***The best seats in the house.*** Where you sit can make a difference on this ride. Inveterate thrill seekers will not be satisfied with anything but the outside seat, whichever side it's on. On balance, the left side offers the most thrills, especially the furnace blast of the gas depot explosion.

The right side has the best view of Jaws' entrance into the boat house. My favorite seat is the far left of row five. Since Jaws rises from the water, those on one side of the boat will have a slightly obstructed view of his appearances on the other side. The obvious solution is to take this ride more than once. Early risers, who get to the park before the gates open, can usually cycle through the ride several times before the lines become too daunting. And if you're not concerned about getting front row seats for the *Dynamite Nights Stuntacular*, ride *Jaws* at dusk when the special effects are particularly spectacular.

While there is a certain shock value to be derived from the element of surprise, this ride is not truly scary. At least for most grown-ups. Little ones may disagree. The shark, while a masterpiece of clever engineering, always betrays its latex and aluminum origins, at least close-up. Still, this doesn't detract from the fun, especially the first few times. As you take your third, fourth, and fifth turns around the harbor, you'll probably find yourself deriving equal enjoyment by looking behind you to see the gasoline depot automatically reconstructing itself in preparation for the next boat load of happily terrified tourists.

# Earthquake — The Big One

| | |
|---|---|
| *Rating:* | ★ ★ ★ ★ + |
| *Type:* | Show and ride |
| *Time:* | 20 minutes, ride portion is 3 minutes |
| *Kelly says:* | A treat for special effects buffs |

If you've come to *Earthquake — The Big One* for yet another shake and bake thrill ride, be patient. You'll get your chills and thrills in due time, but first Universal Studios wants to teach you a thing or two about the painstaking behind-the-scenes ingenuity and craftsmanship that make film effects so special.

*Earthquake — The Big One* is actually three somewhat different attractions rolled into one — all inspired by the spectacular disaster movie that became the first film in history to win an Oscar for special effects.

The experience begins in a theater lobby displaying a fascinating collection of sepia toned photographs taken shortly after the great San Francisco quake of 1906. Also displayed here are the matte paintings used in the making of *Earthquake*. Matte paintings are painstakingly realistic paintings on glass, with a key area blacked out.

A Universal aide mounts a podium and announces that he or she is a casting director and that the good news is that all of you will be used as extras in the disaster sequence of a forthcoming film. The next order of business is to choose some in the crowd for special business. The selection process involves asking for volunteers, cajoling and, if necessary, dragooning people into service. If you're interested in becoming part of the show, standing near the podium may help. The casting director invariably selects three women to be "shoppers" (wait until the National Organization for Women hears about that!), a man to be a stunt double, and two kids to be grips.

When the three doors at the back of the lobby open, the crowd files into a long narrow room, which serves as a stand-up movie theater. There, Charlton Heston, star of the original *Earthquake*, narrates a short film describing the techniques used to conjure up the total destruction of Hollywood for the film. It's a fascinating mini-documentary that will have you shaking your head in admiration for the cleverness of those movie wizards. Most fascinating is the way high-speed photography lets the filmmaker slow down the snapping of a building and produce a startlingly realistic sequence.

When the film ends, a curtain rises on a portion of the actual model city used in the filming. The chest-high buildings are in their shattered, post-quake condition. It's worth lingering a moment to get a closer look. It took model makers six months to build and it was destroyed in six seconds. The cost: $2.4 million — and those are 1974 dollars!

As you file into the next room, you enter a larger theater, and this time you get to sit on benches. Here is where the casting session you saw in the staging area pays off. Before you is a set depicting a set. To the left, in front of an electric blue background, is an escalator that ends in mid air. To the right is a three-story high set representing the demolished stairwell of a high-rise building.

The ladies and the kids are positioned by the escalators to play their roles as shoppers and grips. The "stunt double" is issued blue coveralls and a safety harness and informed that he will be recreating the scene of an earthquake victim being lower down the stairwell shaft.

The stunt double disappears behind the scenes to take his position and our attention turns to the escalator set. Here our guide demonstrates the blue-screen process. The blue background allows the camera to electronically wash out the blue and substitute another scene. Thus two elements can be combined in one scene. On cue, the extras begin to shake, the grips pull on ropes, and columns buckle. On video screens suspended above, we see our shoppers reeling from the effects of a nonexistent quake, while Los Angeles crumbles behind them.

Attention turns next to the stunt double being prepared for his descent. The stunt is hair-raising and packs a surprise I won't reveal. When the demonstration is over, the audience is ushered in to the final phase of the *Earthquake* experience.

This is the part most people come for, a simulated ride aboard San Francisco's BART (Bay Area Rapid Transit). In keeping with the theme, we are reminded that we are going to be extras in the disaster sequence — so there's no mystery that something's going to happen. But what?

We find out soon enough. The train (with open sides and clear plastic roof) pulls out of the Oakland station, enters the tunnel under the Bay, and soon emerges in the Embarcadero station. There is an ominous rumble and the train's P.A. system announces, with the false optimism that is something of a running theme in these rides, that this is just a minor tremor and there's nothing to worry about. Hah!

Soon the earthquake reaches eight on the Richter scale and the Embarcadero station begins to artfully fall apart. Floors buckle and ceilings shatter. The car you're in jerks upward, while the car in front of you drops and tilts perilously. Then the entire roof caves in on one side, exposing the street above. A propane tanker truck, caught in the quake, slides into the hole directly towards us. The only thing that prevents it from slamming into the train is a steel beam, which impales the truck and causes it to burst into flame. Next, what looks like the entire contents of San Francisco Bay comes pouring down the stairs on the other side. And it's still not over. An oncoming train barrels into the station directly at us, but the buckled track sets it on a trajectory that narrowly misses us.

All too soon, a stage manager appears on a platform and yells "Cut!!" We are thanked for our help in filming the sequence (and, in fact, the screams were very convincing) and the train backs out of the station, returning us to "Oakland." As it backs out, you can see the Embarcadero station methodically reconstruct itself in preparation for the next "take."

**The best seats in the house.** For the first two parts of the *Earthquake* experience, it really doesn't matter where you are, although if you'd like to get a better look at the destroyed Hollywood model, you should try to get to the front. That means entering through the far left door and staying toward the back of the line.

You enter the train station through doors on the rear wall of the second theater. Those seated in the back of the theater will tend to wind up on the right hand side of the train; those seated toward the front on the left. Those seated on the right of the theater will tend to wind up toward the front of the train and those on the left toward the back. There is some room to maneuver for position left or right once on the BART platform, especially if the crowds are smaller. There is less opportunity to move from the front of the train to the back or vice versa.

The train holds about 200 people and is divided into three sections.

The first section (that is, the car to the far left as you enter the BART station), has its seats facing backwards. The other two sections have seats facing forward. This arrangement assures that people in the first section won't have to turn around to see most of the special effects the ride holds in store. The front of each section has a clear plastic panel but the view is somewhat obstructed. Avoid the first two rows of a section, if possible. I have found that the best view is to be had in the middle of the second car. The major attraction for those sitting on the right (as the train enters the tunnel) is the flood, which can get a few people wet. The more spectacular explosion of the propane tanker and the wreck of the oncoming train are best viewed from the left. As always, the outside seats are the primo location.

*Earthquake — The Big One* is unique among the thrill rides at Universal Studios in that it combines an instructional component along with the fun and games. You will emerge from the experience with a much deeper appreciation for the unseen geniuses who make the incredible seem so real on the silver screen.

# Beetlejuice's Rock-n-Roll Graveyard Revue

*Rating:* ★ ★ ★

*Type:* Amphitheater show.

*Time:* 25 minutes

*Kelly says:* Best for young and pre-teens

Beetlejuice started out as a streetside performer on the New York set and proved so popular that he was "discovered" by Universal Studios and given his own amphitheater show. The addition of a set, pyrotechnics, and what sounds like several million dollars worth of sound equipment hasn't changed the show's basic appeal, just made it louder.

The set is a jumble of crumbling castle walls, complete with a mummy's sarcophagus and a more modern coffin. The "plot" is simple. Beetlejuice, your host with the most, emerges from the mummy's tomb in a burst of fireworks that is literally blinding. He immediately gets to the business at hand, summoning the Phantom of the Opera, Wolfman, Dracula, Frankenstein, and the ever-lovely Bride of Frankenstein from their ghostly lairs for your listening pleasure. Of course, their trademark outfits just won't do for rock-n-rollers. So, in a "transfunkifying" sequence they change before your very eyes — well, behind a wall of smoke actually — into suitably hip attire. Then they begin, appropriately enough, to wail.

The premise is wafer thin, but what the show lacks in sophistication, it more than makes up for in energy and good natured fun. And noise.

The sound volume is guaranteed to wake the dead. The tender-eared and the old at heart should consider themselves suitably forewarned.

Much of the fun here comes from the matching of familiar rock and roll tunes of the past with the appropriate performer. Wolfman sings "Thank You For Letting Me Be Myself," Dracula gives a stirring rendition of "The Midnight Hour," and the Bride of Frankenstein (in a sexy little outfit that should remind the men in the audience that they're not dead yet) lets loose with "Natural Woman." The lyrics have been updated for the undead, but since with volume comes distortion, it will take a keen ear to get the jokes.

The dancing is rudimentary but energetic, and those who have yet to see their first Vegas extravaganza or Broadway musical will find it a lot of fun. Add some mildly raunchy Beetlejuice-ian humor, a few brief romps through the first few rows of the audience, regular appeals for audience participation in the form of name chanting and hand clapping, a brief foray into Calypso, and you have a recipe for cheerfully mindless entertainment.

There are really no bad seats for this one. An interesting seating choice would be next to the pit in the center of the house, where the sound and light techies run the show. If your kid has dragged you to the show for the fifth time, you can amuse yourself watching these wizards ply their high-tech trade. Seating is pretty much first-come, first-served, although at peak periods attendants may direct you to a seat to speed the flow.

## Wild, Wild, Wild West Stunt Show

*Rating:*      ★ ★ ★ +
*Type:*        Amphitheater show
*Time:*        15 minutes
*Kelly says:*  A bang-up stunt-fest

What's a Wild West show doing cheek by jowl with the *Jaws* ride in Amity? Don't ask, just sit back and enjoy yourself.

This slam-bang bit of foolishness features a handsome cowboy stunt man, his goofy sidekick, a noble steed, and a trio of villains — Ma Hopper and her "twin" boys who are evil, ornery, and stupid in approximately equal measure. Along the way, the gang gets to show off all the standard western movie stunts like falling off buildings and horses, breaking bottles and chairs over each others' heads, and generally wreaking havoc. There is also a liberal dose of pyrotechnics, with a bang-up finale that owes a debt to Buster Keaton's silent classic, *Steamboat Bill Jr.* In fact, ear-splitting explosions seem to be to Universal shows what Green Slime is to Nickelodeon — something of a corporate logo.

Despite the violence, it's hard to imagine this show offending or scaring anybody. The performances are so broad that the show reads more like a cartoon than the westerns on which the action is based. True, some of the explosions and gun shots are loud and startling, but that's all part of the fun. Another part of the fun, for some people, will be sitting in the splash zone. It's near the well, but just in case you forget, there are several announcements that point out its precise location, and like they say, you *will* get wet.

*Tip:* There are some 2,000 seats in this arena so, on all but the most crowded days, you need not arrive much before the posted show times. There are typically four shows a day which are listed in the Show Schedule section of the Studio Guide brochure you received when you entered the park.

# Selected Short Subjects

## The Amity Boardwalk

Between *Earthquake — The Big One* and *Jaws* is a winding stretch of road that offers up a typical New England boardwalk as a child might see it — bright and shining. Of course, the originals are a lot shabbier and far more weather-beaten, the games a bit more threadbare, but never mind. This is the movies, after all, and with the genius of the best set designers Universal has to offer, everything should be perfect.

Here you can try your skill at knocking over plastic glasses with a whiffle ball, tossing a softball into a farmer's milk can, or playing skeeball. If you fancy yourself a superhuman, try ringing the bell with a mighty blow of your sledgehammer. You can also test the skill of the Amazing Alonzo who bets you $2 that he can guess your weight or age. Most games cost a dollar and like the seaside attractions they mimic, the odds are heavily weighted towards the house. Universal, however, makes it easier to win at least something and the prizes, while modest (or ugly, depending on your mood), are a cut above those you'll find along, say, the Jersey shore.

Although the boardwalk is several cuts above the Arcade in New York (see below), I react in much the same way: Why bother? If you've seen all this before, you may react the same way. If, however, you hail from a part of the world where this kind of folksy seaside recreation is not part of your collective subconscious, you may want to pause and give it a whirl. Many people do. All things being equal, I'd recommend saving yourself for the more authentic (if more downscale) versions you'll encounter on your next visit to the New England seashore.

### Kodak Trick Photography Photo Spot

Just before you cross the bridge across the lagoon to Expo Center, you encounter one of those clever spots where you can use the "hanging miniature" technique to snap a unique souvenir photo. Here, you can pose your family in front of the Space Shuttle, ingeniously plunked down on top of the Institute of Future Technology in the background. Nearby is a set from the now-defunct TV series *Swamp Thing*, another good photo op spot.

## Eating in San Francisco/Amity

The San Francisco/Amity area enjoys the distinction of having the most eateries of any of Universal's six sections, thanks largely to the leisurely way it snakes along the lagoon. Here, roughly in the order you encounter them as you proceed from Expo Center around the lagoon to New York, are your choices.

### Häagen-Dazs Ice Cream

*What:*        Quick-service ice cream parlor
*Where:*      Near the entrance to *Jaws*
*Price Range:*  $

Need a quick fortifier? A sugar jolt is close at hand at this ice cream stand. Cones and sundaes are the order of the day at prices ranging from about $2.50 to $4.

### Boardwalk Snacks

*What:*        Outdoor snacking at picnic tables
*Where:*      Along the Amity boardwalk
*Price Range:*  $ - $$

Stop here for a quick al fresco snack like fish & chips ($5) or chicken fingers (about $6). There are also hot, chili, and corn dogs (in the $4 to $5 range) and the usual array of soft drinks.

All seating is outdoors at weathered picnic tables. Venture around behind the snack stand and sit by the lagoon for one of the nicest views in the park. If you stake out a spot early enough, you'll have a pretty good seat for the *Dynamite Nights Stuntacular.*

### McCann's Fruit & Beverage Co.

*What:*        Sidewalk stand
*Where:*      Along the Amity boardwalk, amid the
              pitch and skill games
*Price Range:*  $

**77**

For a change of pace, look for this quaint little stand selling fresh apples and oranges along with an array of refreshing drinks alluringly displayed in buckets of ice.

## Midway Grill

*What:* Outdoor snacking at picnic tables

*Where:* Along the Amity boardwalk, amid the pitch and skill games

**Price Range:** $ - $$

The sign says "Hot dogs • Sausage • Fries" and the menu is scarcely more elaborate than that. Grilled Italian sausage is about $6, while Philly cheese steaks are about $6.50. Hot dogs and beer are each just a bit over $4. Walk up to the window and take your snack along as you stroll the Midway, or sit at a nearby picnic table.

## San Francisco Pastry Company

*What:* Small pastry and coffee shop

*Where:* Across from *Earthquake — The Big One*

**Price Range:** $$

Right at the entrance to Lombard's Landing stands this tempting alternative. It features most of the pastries you found at the Beverly Hills Boulangerie ($2 to $3) as well as coffee, cappuccino, and soft drinks. Sandwiches are about $7 and fruit salad is about $6. There are only a few tables inside and a small outside seating area, so many customers will have to take their snacks to one of the scenic spots along the nearby waterfront.

## Lombard's Landing

*What:* Elegant restaurant evoking Fisherman's Wharf

*Where:* On the lagoon, across from *Earthquake — The Big One*

**Price Range:** $$$

Lombard's is a full-service restaurant boasting the most elegant decor at Universal and some of the best food. The main dining room exudes an industrial-Victorian aura, with brick walls, filigreed iron arches and tapestry-covered dining chairs. The room is dominated by a huge, square, centrally located saltwater fish tank like something Captain Nemo might have imagined. Windows on three sides look out over the lagoon. All in all, the atmosphere is charming.

The food here is excellent and my favorite at Universal. Only the burgers disappoint and should be avoided. Instead, splurge with the grilled or blackened seafood. The Catch of the Day menu insert lets you know what's available and gives the current market price. Expect to pay $18 or so for your fish entree, but don't expect to be disappointed.

Other entrees reflect the diverse cuisine of San Francisco, from Chinatown Chicken (about $13), to Foggy City Cioppino ($18), to Nob Hill Sirloin ($16). There's also Cape Cod Fish & Chips ($12) and Five-Cheese Ravioli ($13).

For lighter appetites, there is a selection of sandwiches (about $10), or try soup or salad. A Caesar Salad with grilled chicken breast is $12. Appetizers are in the $6 to $8 range and range from simple Chinatown spring rolls to a sumptuous shrimp cocktail.

There is an exceptional dessert served here, the San Francisco Foggie. On a bedrock of chocolate brownie rises a Nob Hill of ice cream, as a fog bank of whipped cream rolls in off the Bay. A drizzle of caramel sauce and a sprinkling of almond slivers complete this delicious creation ($5).

## Chez Alcatraz

*What:*      Outdoor stand featuring seafood snacks

*Where:*      On the lagoon, between Richter's and Lombard's Landing

*Price Range:*    $ - $$

Right at the water's edge, next to Shaiken's Souvenirs, Chez Alcatraz offers quick, upscale seafood snacks at moderate prices. Try a tuna or shrimp salad "conewich" for $5, or a turkey or ham sandwich for about $6.

## Richter's Burger Co.

*What:*      Fast-food burger joint

*Where:*      On the lagoon, across from *Earthquake —*
                  *The Big One*

*Price Range:*    $$

That's Richter as in scale, and just in case you didn't get it the first time, one glance at the damaged interior of this warehouse-like structure will let you know that the theme here is pure *Earthquake.* It's a fun environment in which to chow down on standard burger fare.

The Big One (about $6 or $7) is a burger or cheeseburger served with "a landslide of fries," while the San Andreas (about $7) is a chicken sandwich. The Trembler ($6) is a hot dog, also with a landslide of fries. Frisco shakes, chocolate and vanilla, are about $2.50.

The decor is fun and imaginative and worth more than a passing glance. At the back, you'll find tables with a lagoon view and a balcony offering a great bird's-eye view of the New York end of the lagoon.

# Shopping in San Francisco/Amity

### Bayfront Crafts
Sharing the earthquake-damaged warehouse with Richter's, Bayfront Crafts specializes in jigsaw-cut wooden letters ($1 to $2). You can buy them separately as block letters or as an entire name rendered in cursive script. Pick a sample from the shelf or, if your parents gave you an odd name like Niall or Gareth, have one made to order. One of the niftiest options is a wooden train engine ($5) pulling a string of cars carrying letters that spell out your name ($4 per letter). There are also leather belts ($17) that can be cut to size and matched with a buckle of your choice ($15 to $23).

### Shaiken's Novelties & Souvenirs
This is a souvenir shop in search of a theme. Despite the earthquake related name and its location next to Richter's, Shaiken's offers up a fairly standard selection of Universal t-shirts and other wearables, at the usual prices ($16 and up). You can, however, pick up a video of *Earthquake*, the film that inspired the ride.

### Salty's Sketches
Stop under the awning by the San Francisco Pastry Company to have one of Universal's expert caricaturists immortalize your goofy grin for posterity. These artists must all have studied under the same master because their styles are almost identical and the quality of the renderings excellent. The cost is also surprisingly moderate given the high quality of the finished product. Black and white sketches are just $12 (or $18 for a couple); color versions are $18 and $30, respectively.

### Quint's Nautical Treasures
Tucked into an old wooden lighthouse (look up as you enter), this quaint shop adopts a New England seashore theme complete with hanging nets and lobster pots. There are sea shells (40 cents to $15), some of them serving as miniature plant holders for bromeliads, the so-called "air plants" that subsist on the moisture in the air. You will also find some charming small sculptures of pelicans, dolphins, and manatees set on bases of gnarled and polished driftwood ($13 to $40).

For the kids there are plush dolls of sharks ($13) and, of course, the ever-present selection of t-shirts ($16 and up).

# NEW YORK

Compared to some others on the lot, the New York set seems downright underpopulated — with attractions, eateries, and shops, that is. Whole streets in New York are given over entirely to film backdrops. Gramercy Park, Park Avenue, the dead end Fifty-Seventh Street that incongruously ends at the New York Public Library, and the narrow alleys behind Delancey Street contain nary a ride or shop. These sets, however, provide some wonderfully evocative backgrounds for family portraits, especially the library facade, with a collection of familiar skyscrapers looming behind it. The set also includes some clever inside jokes for those familiar with the movie industry. Check out the names painted on the windows of upper story offices along Fifth Avenue and see if you can spot them.

Of course, New York does have attractions. In fact, it has two of Universal Studios' most popular draws, one of them a guaranteed blockbuster. It also serves up some of the nicest dining experiences to be had in the park, and I find it fitting that the park's one bargain-basement emporium is located here in this substitute Big Apple.

## Twister

*Rating:* ★ ★ ★ ★ +
*Type:* Stand-up theater show
*Time:* 15 minutes
*Kelly says:* Amazing in-your-face special effects

Here is an attraction that will almost literally blow you away. Based on the hit film of the same name, *Twister* is a theater show without seats that leads you through three sets for a payoff that lasts all of two minutes. But what a two minutes it is!

The journey begins as you snake though a waiting line in Wakita, Oklahoma, around large props from the film. You are entertained by two disk jockeys ("the storm chasers of rock and roll") from WNDY ("windy") who spin peppy rock songs with appropriately stormy titles. You will be kept cool by large fans that blow a fine water mist over the crowds. As you draw closer to the Soundstage on which the real adventure unfolds, the entertainment gives way to videos of actual tornadoes, some of which are really scary.

The line may seem formidable but don't despair. This show can handle 2,400 people each hour, so the line moves fairly quickly.

Once inside, the show follows a familiar three-part format. In the first chamber, themed as the prop room for the film, you watch a video in which the vivacious Helen Hunt and an oddly wooden Bill Paxton set the scene. If you missed the movie, this segment will give you all the information you need to understand what both the film and this attraction are all about.

The second chamber is themed as the ruined interior of a house. Trees and the front end of an automobile protrude through the ceiling, where a string of video monitors continue the introduction process. There is not a great deal of "edutainment" in this attraction, especially as compared to, say, *Earthquake*, but what little there is happens here. We get a brief explanation of how high-end computer software was used to re-create tornado physics and see some production shots that illustrate how some of the niftier scenes in the film were created.

Then it's on to the final chamber where the "real" show happens — live, in-person, and right before your eyes. You enter a set where you stand on a three-level viewing area under the deceptive protection of a tin roof. In front of you is the Wakita street that runs past the Galaxy outdoor movie theater where a "Horror Night" double feature of *The Shining* and *Psycho* is being shown. The street is deserted, but no sooner is everyone in place than all heck breaks loose and the inanimate objects before you take on a scary life of their own.

***The best seats in the house:*** You will have a great experience here no matter where you stand. However, die-hard thrill seekers will want to be as close to the action as possible. Stay to the right as you are ushered into this final chamber if you want to stand in the front row. Most people hug the railing, but you can form a second row and make your way to dead center if you wish.

I don't want to give too much away about what happens next but you've probably already figured out that you'll be living through the vortex of a twister. Some of the effects are versions of what you may already have seen on *Earthquake*. But when the twister arrives stage center, just feet away, you will gape in awe and wonder, "How'd they do that?"

***Tip:*** This is a wet, if not precisely soaking, experience. A poncho might be in order if you're really fussy. Otherwise, you probably will find the sprinkling fun, even refreshing. Interestingly enough, I have gotten wetter in the back row than I have in the front.

# Kongfrontation

|  |  |
|---|---|
| *Rating:* | ★ ★ ★ + |
| *Type:* | Aerial tram ride |
| *Time:* | 4.5 minutes |
| *Kelly says:* | More handsome than scary |

Pass through the huge columns of Pennsylvania Station along New York's Fifth Avenue and you will soon find yourself in a gritty re-creation of a New York subway station, specifically the Roosevelt Island aerial tram station by the Fifty-Ninth Street Bridge. As you snake your way to the tram platform, past graffiti-dense concrete walls and posters advertising forthcoming Universal films, television monitors keep you posted.

Since-departed newspeople from New York station WWOR tell us of sightings of King Kong on a rampage. When you finally board the 40-person aerial tram, the tram conductor assures you there's no danger. Somehow the padded lap bar that lowers into place suggests otherwise.

Very shortly after the tram leaves the station, the truth becomes clear. Kong is not headed for the city limits but is dead ahead and in no mood to be trifled with. What's worse, the tram cannot stop. On the left you see a subway car toppled from its elevated track, burning brightly; a police car is wrecked on a fire hydrant which sends a geyser skyward.

Turn a corner and there is Kong himself, rising threateningly out the shattered roof of an industrial building. He's close — very close — and he grabs the tram car and gives it a thorough shaking. But you escape. The next sighting of Kong is over the mist-shrouded East River. There he is, full form, hanging from the Fifty-Ninth Street Bridge, lunging for the tram which is, mercifully, just out of reach.

You reach Roosevelt Island. Are you safe at last? No such luck. Kong appears a third time, once again on the right, and gives the tram another bone-jarring shaking.

Then, less than five minutes after departure, you glide to safety in the Roosevelt Island station. Video monitors lower from the ceiling with a Channel 9 news update. There you are, high above the East River, reacting in terrified delight to the gigantic Kong.

The truth is, *Kongfrontation* is far from the scariest ride at Universal. The sudden dropping of the tram and the shaking may give you a momentary start, but the real fascination in this ride is the craftsmanship behind the mammoth figures of Kong himself. They are beautifully done and far too attractive to be frightening. I'd love to be able to run my hands through the fur, which appears luxuriant and life-like. Best of all is the full-figure of Kong hanging from the bridge. A second or third look reveals that the figure has been artfully foreshortened to make it look bigger and taller than it actually is. What's more, these huge animated figures are close enough to offer excellent photo ops. Flash photography is forbidden (although I've never seen anyone disciplined for ignoring the rule), but there's enough ambient light to pose a reasonably accomplished photographer no problem at all.

As a native New Yorker, I was especially intrigued by some of the choices that the Universal designers made in crafting this ride. Was New

York ever that graffiti-scarred? Perhaps, but recent successes by the city to combat graffiti vandalism make the setting seem vaguely nostalgic. (By the way, would be 'taggers', as graffiti vandals are called in the Big Apple, should know that Universal pores over the walls every night to "edit" the graffiti. Adding your own name is probably okay, but rude messages will be ruthlessly eliminated.)

*The best seats in the house.* If at all possible, you should ride *Kong-frontation* more than once, hoping for end row seats on both the right and the left of the car. Those on the left have a terrific view of Kong on the bridge; those on the right get to stare the magnificent beast straight in the mouth. Those on the left will also be prominent in the video news report that ends the ride.

As you exit this ride, you will have a chance to be photographed in the grip of a life-sized Kong (actually just the head and hand). It's a clever shot, the giant prop is another masterpiece of the set maker's art, and you just might find it worth a bit under $6.

# Selected Short Subjects

## Arcades

Why anyone would pay $40 to get into Universal and then waste their time in a video arcade is beyond me. On the other hand, the two Arcades in New York never seem to lack for customers, so what do I know? Perhaps the answer lies in the fact that most patrons are teenagers who probably didn't have to pay for their own admission. My advice: Skip these arcades and save your money for a visit to a much larger, more varied (and less expensive) arcade at Church Street Station's Exchange. (See *Chapter Eight: Church Street Station.*)

## The Blues Brothers in Chicago Bound!

The Dan Ackroyd-John Belushi routine that made a better Saturday Night sketch than it ever did a movie is immortalized in this peppy street show that currently holds forth from a makeshift stage on Delancey Street. The warm-up comes courtesy of a belting blues singer whose gospel-tinged renditions of blues standards are a show in and of themselves. Then, backed by a live sax player and a recorded sound track, Jake and Elwood goof and strut their way through a selection of rock and blues standards winding up with a rousing version of "Soul Man."

The genial performers, who are look-alikes only to the extent that one is tall and lanky and the other short and stout, do the material justice, and Jake's hyper-kinetic dance steps are a highlight of the show. If you like your rock straight and unadulterated, you should enjoy it. Performances are listed in the Show Schedule section of the Studio Guide brochure you were handed as you entered the park, but Jake and Elwood take no chances; they cruise the lot in their funky revamped cop car promoting the show.

# Eating in New York

## Finnegan's

| | |
|---|---|
| *What:* | Irish pub and sit-down restaurant |
| *Where:* | On Fifth Avenue across from *Kongfrontation* |
| *Price Range:* | $$$ |

Finnegan's has two parts and two personalities. The first is a full-fledged Irish pub complete with live entertainment and walls crowded with beer and liquor ads and offbeat memorabilia. Cozy up to the antique bar and order a yard of ale if that's your pleasure, or choose from a short but classy selection of domestic and imported beers. Guinness stout, Harp lager, and Bass ale are available on draught.

The other half of Finnegan's is a full-service restaurant hidden behind the false facades of the New York lot. The decor here is pared down and perfunctory, reflecting the room's other identity as a movie set. Fortunately, the food is anything but pared down or perfunctory. The theme is Irish and British Isles, with generously sized entrees to match.

Appetizers (in the $5 to $8 range) include "Irish Chicken Stingers," Cornish pasties, and Scotch eggs. London Times fish and chips is traditional, right down to the newspaper it's served in (about $11). The shepherd's pie is a juicy souvenir from the Emerald Isle, topped with perfectly browned mashed potatoes ($10). There's also bangers and coddle (sausage and boiled potatoes), Irish stew, and (of course) corned beef and cabbage. Entrees range from about $9 to $11 and are accompanied by a plate of hearty steamed vegetables.

For lighter appetites, there is a suitably authentic potato and leek soup (about $4) and sandwiches in the $10 range. Best bets for dessert are the warm bread pudding and the apple cobbler with Irish whiskey sauce (both about $4).

## Louie's Italian Restaurant

| | |
|---|---|
| *What:* | Cafeteria-style Italian restaurant |
| *Where:* | At the corner of Fifth and Canal, near the lagoon |
| *Price Range:* | $$ |

Louie's is a remarkably successful recreation of the ambiance of New York's Little Italy section — tiled floors, marble-topped tables, and cafe chairs. The only hint you're at Universal Studios is the cafeteria style serving area and the odd ceiling with its jagged edges and movie lights that remind you that the restaurant can do double duty as a film set.

The fare is standard Italian and just the basics. Pizza slices are in the $3 to $4 range ("6 slices for the price of 5") or $16 to $18 for whole pies. Entrees include chicken parmesan, lasagna, spinach tortellini, linguine with white clam sauce, and fettuccini Alfredo. They range from about $6 to just under $7. Caesar salad is $3 or $5 depending on size and a bowl of minestrone costs a bit under $3. There is imported Italian beer (about $4) as well as Bud and Lite. In one corner of the restaurant there is a counter selling coffee, cappuccino, and pastries ($1 to $3).

The quality is above average, as well, making Louie's my favorite Universal cafeteria. Louie's is quite large and makes a good place to duck in out of the sun or rain for a rest.

# Shopping in New York

### Safari Outfitters

You will find Safari Outfitters just to the right of the entrance to *Kongfrontation*. Those exiting from that ride are funneled right through this shop, so it can get crowded. While there are King Kong dolls with black leather faces and hands ($35), there are better looking (and cheaper) stuffed animals to be found here, among them lions and tigers with a cub climbing their leg ($30). Separate cubs are about $8 while single adults are about $20.

There is also a nifty line of King Kong t-shirts for $17. In keeping with the safari theme, the shop carries a small selection of straw hats and animal figurines, and, of course, you can also get videos of the original *King Kong* and its sequel. At the back of the shop is the giant Kong head, where you can have your picture taken in the monster's grasp (about $6). If you skipped this earlier, you can come back at your leisure to fill this gap in your photographic record.

### Second-Hand Rose

No real New Yorker would be caught dead paying retail, so why should you? Second-Hand Rose, located just past Safari Outfitters at the corner of Fifth Avenue and 42nd Street, is Universal's very own discount outlet. Here you'll find merchandise from around the park that, for one reason or another, is being marked down for quick sale. Sometimes the item turned out to be a loser (these are easy to spot), but sometimes the items on sale are quite nice. They may be just a little shopworn or may have been discontinued for reasons that have nothing to do with style or quality. Everything here is 25% off the marked price and most items have already been marked down. The resulting savings can go as high as 50% or 60%. Smart shoppers take note: There are some real bargains to be found here.

### Bull's Gym

Near the lagoon, you'll find Bull's Gym, dedicated to Frostbite Fall's most famous moose. The theme, of course, is athletic and you'll find a variety of t-shirts, sweats, shorts, and baseball hats graced with the Universal Studios logo. Polos are $40, tank tops $15, shorts $28 to $35, and t-shirts are $17 and up. Universal hockey shirts are $60. There is also a small selection of Blues Brothers merchandise.

# PRODUCTION CENTRAL

Production Central is modeled on a typical film studio front lot. Essentially, it is a collection of soundstages and has a resolutely industrial feel to it. But what it lacks in architectural pizzazz, it more than makes up for in entertainment value.

Production Central boasts Universal's highest concentration of attractions that teach you about movie making. It also has a very nifty simulator-style thrill ride, cleverly disguised as a kiddie ride.

### The FUNtastic World of Hanna-Barbera

| | |
|---|---|
| *Rating:* | ★ ★ ★ ★ |
| *Type:* | Simulator ride |
| *Time:* | 5 minutes |
| *Kelly says:* | For younger thrill seekers |

If you've logged any time at all in front of the television screen on Saturday morning, you are familiar with the handiwork of Bill Hanna and Joe Barbera. They are perhaps the most successful animation team outside the Disney empire and the creators of Yogi Bear, the Flintstones, the Jetsons, and Scooby-Doo and the gang. Their pared-down animation style spearheaded the explosion of mass-produced cartoons for TV.

Despite the kiddie-orientation of *The FUNtastic World of Hanna-Barbera*, this ride is not kid's stuff — at least in terms of the wallop it packs. It is second only to *Back To The Future* in its bone-jarring, inner-ear-discombobulating effects. If you were shaken up or made queasy by the former, approach the latter with care. On the other hand, if you are uncertain about your susceptibility to motion sickness, you may want to try this one before hazarding the more violent lurches of *Back To The Future.*

As you are ushered into the antechamber to this ride, Yogi Bear and Boo Boo appear on overhead screens. Before long they are joined by Hanna and Barbera themselves — the real guys, not cartoon versions. As the two animators explain some of the basics of their art, the plot thickens. The evil Dick Dastardly, accompanied by his cohort, Muttly the dog, becomes incensed when he learns that Hanna-Barbera's next feature will not be built around him. Seeking revenge, he kidnaps Elroy, the Jetson's child, and takes off into hyperspace. Now the game is afoot. We will have to take chase in our own spaceship, with Yogi himself at the controls. Ominously, we are informed that Yogi is not the best of pilots.

The interior of the spaceship is actually a movie theater divided into twelve eight-seat sections. Each section is a simulator car, very much like those in *Back To The Future.* (There is a row of stationery benches in the front for little ones and those who wish to forego the thrill ride aspect of the show.)

When the show begins, the screen in front of us becomes the windshield of Yogi's spaceship and we are off on a light-speed chase after Dastardly. Using his hyperdrive capabilities, he leads us on a merry chase through both time and space. Along the way, we roar through the streets of Bedrock, nearly collide with Shaggy and Scooby-Doo inside a haunted castle, and end up, happily but bumpily, in the future where Elroy is reunited with his grateful parents.

***The best seats in the house.*** As the line approaches the entrance to the antechamber, it divides in two. By choosing the left lane, you will wind up towards the back or middle of the theater. If you position yourself in the middle of the group in the antechamber, you stand a good chance of ending up in the middle of the theater. In my opinion, the best seats are in the middle of the house in the last, or next-to-last row. From there, you get the best, least distorted view of the screen.

After the show, the audience files out through an "**interactive area**," a large open space with imaginative cartoon-like stage settings evoking Bedrock, Jellystone Park, and the Jetson's space city. The theme is the animation process and those who pay attention can learn something about how their Saturday morning cartoon shows are created.

***Photo Op:*** There are several spots for a souvenir photo here. The best is a kid-sized version of the Flintstone's car, set against a colorful prehistoric cartoon vista. There's also a pint-sized version of a Bedrock livingroom where you can catch a shot of your loved ones lounging on a rock sofa.

Scattered about the room, in no apparent order, are illuminated signs on which Scooby-Doo outlines the process whereby an idea becomes a finished cartoon. Most people ignore these. Too bad. They are fun and informative. A fun game for older kids would be to decipher the order of the process. Offer a prize and try this one during an afternoon downpour.

Most of the kids are immediately drawn to the consoles that give the interactive area its name. In Bedrock, kids can dance along a piano keyboard painted on the floor and make a choir of prehistoric birds squawk out a tune. In Jellystone Park, they can try their hands at adding appropriate sound effects to a Yogi Bear cartoon. And in Space City, they can put outline figures of George Jetson, Rosie the robot, and Astro the dog through their animated paces.

*Tip:* The interactive area can be entered at any time through the Hanna-Barbera Store. So, if you are on a tight schedule, you might want to skip this feature. You can always come back later in the day after you have visited your must-see attractions.

## Alfred Hitchcock: The Art of Making Movies

| | |
|---|---|
| *Rating:* | ★ ★ ★ ★ |
| *Type:* | Theater show |
| *Time:* | 40 minutes |
| *Kelly says:* | A special treat for Hitchcock buffs |

This earnest homage to one of the cinema's true geniuses will be a must-see for Hitch's fans. Younger visitors may find themselves wondering what all the fuss is about. One reason is that, in the limited amount of time available in the theme park format and the need to keep up the pace, much of Hitchcock's artistry is left on the cutting room floor. The shocking images and the plot twists are here, but the clever set-ups (Hitchcock's famous "MacGuffins") and the maddeningly leisurely pace with which he built unbearable suspense are missing. Even so, there's a lot of entertainment value here. Hopefully, those unfamiliar with Hitchcock's work will be spurred to visit the video store back home and check it out.

If you have to wait, you will be entertained by interviews with Hitchcock explaining the basics of his screen philosophy. If you are fortunate enough to be able to walk right in at showtime, you may want to come back later, just to catch the pre-show video.

*Tip:* During the wait, the show's staff pick a volunteer from the line. If you're male, thin, on the tallish side, and wearing running shoes, you might get the nod.

About 250 people are cycled through the attraction at each show. You pick up a pair of 3-D glasses at the entrance and form up in an anteroom decorated with a three-dimensional collage of artifacts and stills from the master's *oeuvre*. A simulated celluloid strip winds around the room near the ceiling bearing the titles and dates of all of Hitchcock's 53 films, from *Pleasure Garden* in 1925 to *Family Plot* in 1976. If you have the time, try to count how many of them you've seen and make a list of the ones you've always been meaning to rent one of these days.

The first stop in this multi-phase show is the Tribute Theater where you see a large-screen compilation of clips from Hitchcock's films narrated by Hitch himself, thanks to the clever use of scenes from his 1950s television show and other archival sources. Those familiar with the vast scope of Hitchcock's filmography will have fun trying to identify the stars and films as they whiz by at MTV-like warp speed. Others will get some small sense of the antic humor that was always just below the surface in many Hitchcock films.

The real attraction, of course, has to do with those glasses you've been holding on to. Hitchcock's *Dial M for Murder* (1954) was originally designed to use the then popular 3-D process. However, by the time the film was ready for release, the studio decided that the craze had passed and *Dial M* was released "flat" — that is, in two dimensions.

The strangulation scene and the famous stabbing with the scissors is shown and suddenly it looks as though something has gone terribly wrong in the projection booth. But it's just part of the show, as a flock of crazed birds slashes through the screen and a newly shot sequence shows off the shock and fright possibilities of the 3-D process.

Next, you file to your left into a second theater — the *Psycho* sound stage. To the left, high on a hill, is the ghostly Bates house that has become an American icon. To the right is the Bates Motel office, its "No Vacancy" sign blinking ominously in the rain. Here, you get an all too brief lesson in how genius can transform simple elements into spine-chilling terror. Your on-screen host, Tony Perkins, who played Norman Bates in the horror classic, notes that *Psycho* was based on a true incident, one that also inspired the later *Texas Chain Saw Massacre*. How times change! Hitchcock's famous "shower scene," which is painstakingly analyzed in film schools around the world, is widely recognized as one of the scariest sequences ever put on film, yet he never shows the knife cutting skin and never shows a bloody wound.

Remember that volunteer who was chosen at the start of the show? Well here he is, all dolled up in a granny dress to play the part of Norman Bates/Momma Bates in a recreation of the shower scene. A set of Janet Leigh's motel bathroom is wheeled out, complete with "wild walls" — that is, walls that can be removed to allow access to the camera. There is also a Janet Leigh stand-in (just like in the original), a young actress in a blond wig and a flesh colored body stocking.

To illustrate how Hitchcock, over seven days, with a 40-person crew, combined 78 separate camera angles into a three-minute sequence, a grid holding several cameras, each at a different angle, is lowered into place over the bathroom set. Then the stand-ins recreate the first nine shots of the shower scene; some are from the original film, some shot live before our eyes. It's a clever idea, but one which can only hint at the complexity of the original. Universal seems to realize this, because this little exercise is followed by a screening of the entire sequence from the film, exactly as Hitch created it.

*Psycho*, of course, had a surprise ending and in keeping with tradition so does this show. I won't reveal it (and darned if I can figure out how it's done), but it involves our audience volunteer showing up in the most unexpected of places.

**The best seats in the house.** Your guides are always assuring you that every seat is a great seat. In this case, it's true. Other than trying to avoid the very first row in the Tribute Theater, don't bother jockeying for position. Dual screens on the *Psycho* sound stage make sure everyone can see the action.

For my money, the best part of *Alfred Hitchcock: The Art of Making Movies* happens after the show proper. The final component is a two-story "interactive" area with a variety of devices that are used to illustrate various aspects of Hitchcock's craft. Two of them involve audience participation.

One demonstration recreates the final sequence of *Saboteur.* This 1942 film was one of the first Hitchcock made in the United States, and what a calling card it was. Norman Lloyd, who played the villain of the piece and who later went on to direct and produce for Hitchcock's TV show, narrates a video explanation of how Hitchcock created the illusion of the bad guy falling from the torch of the Statue of Liberty. Volunteers from the crowd play the bad guy at two different points in the sequence — when he's hanging on for dear life and when he slips from the hero's grasp and falls to a grisly death. The results are combined with bits of the original on the video monitor. The cleverest part is how the "falling" villain stays in one place, while the camera pulls away from him on a vertical track.

*Photo Op:* After the demonstration, have a friend take a picture of you standing on Lady Liberty's torch!

The other live demonstration involves the sequence on the carousel from *Strangers on a Train*. John Forsythe, another Hitchcock star, narrates the explanation of this one and an audience volunteer is the victim.

Upstairs, Jimmy Stewart is your on-screen host for a discussion of two Hitchcock films in which he starred — *Rear Window* and *Vertigo*. Try your hand at peering through the binoculars as you attempt to spot the murderer in one of the windows of the apartment buildings across the way! Take it from me, it ain't easy.

One of Hitchcock's most beloved trademarks was his penchant for making a brief, silent walk-on appearance in each of his films. It was the film-making equivalent of the artist's signature on a canvas. A very entertaining video narrated by Shirley MacLaine, reprises many of these appearances, including the way he managed the seemingly impossible challenge of appearing in *Lifeboat*, a movie that takes place entirely on a small boat cast adrift in the Atlantic.

*Tip:* The interactive area is relatively small but seldom gets as crowded as it should because many people choose to skip it in their rush to get to the next attraction. Big mistake. This section will reward those who savor it at their leisure. However, if you skip the interactive displays in the interests of saving time, you can walk back into this area later by entering the Bates Motel Store from the Eighth Avenue side. The live demonstrations are geared to the exit of the crowds from the main show (about every 20 minutes), but the rest of the section can be enjoyed at any time you have a few spare moments to kill — perhaps during one of those Florida afternoon showers!

My guess is that a lot of people who have never seen a Hitchcock film go through this attraction and have a wonderful time. However, there's no escaping the fact that the more you know about the master's work the more fun you will have. On the other hand, if your curiosity is piqued by what you see, you can buy boxed sets of Hitch's greatest hits in the Bates Motel Store.

# Hercules and Xena: Wizards of the Screen

*Rating:*      ★ ★ ★
*Type:*       Theater show with volunteers
*Time:*       30 minutes
*Kelly says:*   A mini-course in digital effects

In the film industry, the executive producer is god — or perhaps a goddess — as you will discover in this entertaining overview of cutting edge special effects techniques as they are applied to *Hercules: The Legendary Journeys* and *Xena: Warrior Princess*, two syndicated TV shows from

New Zealand that have enjoyed considerable success in syndication on American airwaves.

In this show, the two legendary small screen heroes are joining forces in a "crossover episode" to be called "Magic of the Gods." We (the two hundred folks in the audience) unexpectedly become "volunteers" on the "special effects team" desperately trying to satisfy the demands of the shrewish executive producer, Kate Harrington. (Following the current trend in depicting evil incarnate, Ms. Harrington is portrayed as an up-per-class Brit, complete with plummy Oxbridge accent.) This is actually a clever way to teach us all a thing or two about the current state of the art in electronic and digital special effects.

There are four phases to this show, each lasting about seven or eight minutes. The brief introduction takes place in an antechamber decorated with production stills, costume sketches, and actual props from the TV shows. It fills in some crucial background for those whose knowledge of mythology is a bit thin and sets the "plot" in motion. Three people (male, female, and kid) are chosen to play centaurs, roles that will take them through the rest of the show. Then we are whisked through three sepa-rate theaters, arranged side by side in an arc. In the first we visit the Creature Lab where we meet Sheldon, a large bug puppet that is oper-ated by remote control by six technicians (more audience volunteers). This segment teaches us about blue-screen technique, a bit of video magic whereby actors (or bugs) shot against a blue background can be electronically dropped into existing film footage.

Then it's on to Digital Visual Effects where computers are used to remove unwanted details from existing film, turn three actors into a rag-ing horde straight out of Hades, and perform other feats of visual leger-demain. Finally, we move to Sound Effects (or the "Foley Stage") where grunts and groans, biffs and pows, and clanging swords are added to the sound track before everything comes together in a completely un-planned surprise ending engineered by the multi-faceted Ms. Harrington.

One thing the show doesn't explain is how all those New Zealand actors get their American accents. The answer (provided by a show at-tendant) is that, knowing where the *real* money is, they fake them.

***Historical note:*** Those who remember *Murder She Wrote Mystery The-ater*, the somewhat similar attraction that once occupied this space, will be intrigued to see how post-production techniques have changed since Angela Lansbury first started solving crimes on the small screen. Thanks to advances in digital computer technology, the oh-so-clever methods used not that long ago look positively primitive today.

# Nickelodeon Studios Tour

| | |
|---|---|
| *Rating:* | ★ ★ ★ |
| *Type:* | Guided tour and theater show |
| *Time:* | 25 minutes |
| *Kelly says:* | For kids 10 and under |

Nickelodeon Studios Florida is a studio within a studio. Nick (as it likes to be called) is a 24-hour cable TV network which bills itself as "the first network for kids." Its production facilities occupy two soundstages on the Universal lot, but it is otherwise a separate entity. Even its location, at the end of Nickelodeon Way, behind the Hanna-Barbera ride, sets it apart from the rest of the park.

Get in line and watch from a comfortable distance as the 17-foot-tall Green Slime Geyser in the plaza outside the studio rumbles to life. According to well-informed sources, this green Rube Goldberg-esque oddity is the world's only source of the green goo that features so prominently in Nickelodeon lore. (If you don't know what slime is, ask your kid.) Every ten minutes or so, it erupts with a roar, spewing gallons of bubbling lime green goop.

*Photo Op:* The Green Slime Geyser in full roar makes a fabulous backdrop for yet another photo of the kids. The Nickelodeon folks have also thoughtfully provided a number of other photo backdrops in the plaza.

Your wait for the tour will be a happy one, what with video games for the kids to sample and the constant barrage of clips from Nickelodeon shows. Once inside, your guide takes you on a standard walk-through guided tour of the studio facilities. When the studio was built, the architects cleverly provided a glass-walled, sound-proof walkway that lets visitors peer into Sound Stages 19 and 18 (in that order), as well as into a control room, and the wardrobe and make-up departments.

What you see depends on when you come. But even if you come on a Sunday at a time of the year when all shows are "on hiatus" (i.e. on vacation), there will be something to see on the studio floor. Just in case, they have arranged for a "director" to speak to you live from the studio below, filling you in on what's currently on tap.

During slower periods, the tour may be abbreviated, skipping any interaction with the control room or the wardrobe department, for example. However, one kid-pleasing staple of the tour is a visit with the "gak meister," a studio performer who talks about the not-so-subtle differences between gak and goo and explains that all the gak and goo produced by the studio (in enormous quantities) for its various shows is edible. After all, the gak meister points out, contestants in the sloppier game shows might accidentally eat some of this stuff. To prove his point he has an intrepid volunteer kid actually taste goo and something called "booger gak."The humor is aimed squarely at the seven or eight year old level. If you think lines like "Thank you for eating my boogers" are the soul of wit, you are in touch with your inner child.

## Game Lab

At the end of the tour, adults and kids are separated and herded into separate bleachers for Game Lab. Ostensibly, Nickelodeon tries out new stunt ideas for its game shows here. This is audience participation that pits kids against grown-ups to often amusing effect. There's a host (or hostess) and a staff of young and cheery assistants, including the inevitable joker who gets into cahoots with the grown-ups to bamboozle the kids. Volunteers are picked out of the peanut gallery to play games like firing rubber chickens into absurdly baggy pants worn by Mom or Dad. One kid has been pre-selected to be "slimed" with the green goo that has become something of a corporate logo for Nickelodeon.

The hosts of Game Lab will sometimes conduct brief candid interviews with their pint-sized guests and occasionally turn up the kind of gems that Art Linkletter made a career of in another television age. A sample from a recent visit:

*Hostess:* What's your name?

*Kid:* Brandon.

*Hostess:* How old are you?

*Kid:* Five.

*Hostess:* What do you do for a living?

*Kid:* (After a long pause) I build houses with my blocks.

You'd have to score pretty high on the curmudgeon scale not to find that adorable.

## Seeing Nickelodeon Programs

Nickelodeon, as they never tire of telling you, is a working television studio. Production goes on every day of the year except Christmas and New Year's Day. Does that mean you can see a show while you're in Orlando? The answer is a resounding "maybe."

Of course, you'll always be able to see *something* from the viewing tube as you take the tour. Something is always going on — a set is being built, a show is in rehearsal or production, a set is being taken apart and moved out. If you'd like to see television in the making as an audience member, however, you'll have to do some advance planning. Then, you'll have to keep your fingers crossed. As the folks at Nickelodeon told me, "There's a good chance that you'll be able to see something, but our production schedule is always subject to change and we don't want to make false promises."

As soon as you know the dates of your visit, pick up the phone and call (407) 363-8500 and ask them which shows that have audiences are scheduled to be in production during your Orlando stay. Usually, only the game shows have live audiences. Shows in the sitcom mold are shot on closed sets; laughs and other "audience" reactions are added later. So bear in mind that your kids' favorite Nickelodeon show may not have an audience and prepare them accordingly.

It's important to remember that all the shows on Nickelodeon are videotaped for showing at a later date. That means that none of the shows they produce absolutely has to be shot on a specific date at a specific time. The studio will usually have a pretty good idea of what it will be shooting three to four months in advance, but the schedule will not be specific as to times. In addition, production is scheduled to suit the studio's needs, not yours. If a big prop breaks just before they're ready to start taping, they'll simply stop and wait until the prop is fixed. That means you won't be able to find out that *Guts*, say, tapes every day at two o'clock and show up then.

Your chances of being in the audience of a show will also be affected by when you visit. Nick likes to schedule the taping of game shows, especially the more popular ones, during peak tourist seasons — summertime and around Christmas — because they know that people come during those times hoping to be in the audience. This guarantees that the huge audience for these shows will have a good shot at seeing them in person if they want to. Another factor that will affect your chances of seeing a particular show are the number of episodes that will be taped. Some shows are seen only on weekends. They will shoot perhaps 25 episodes during the course of the year. Other shows are "stripped." That is they are shown every day, Monday through Friday. These shows may shoot up to 40 episodes during a "season" and there may be more than one season during the course of a year. Unfortunately, it's impossible to predict when these seasons occur. Any given show will probably tape on a different schedule this year than it did last year. Again, the scheduling is determined solely by what proves to be most convenient for the studio.

Unfortunately, you won't be able to get tickets in advance, or make reservations, or have your name put on a list. There are two reasons for this. First, the studio wants to protect itself against no-shows. The last thing Nickelodeon wants is a full house that's only two-thirds full — it looks bad on TV — and in a theme park that's mobbed with kids it's not too hard to fill every seat the day of the show — especially when you're giving the tickets away. The other reason goes back to Nick's steadfast rule against making promises to its young fans that it might not be able to keep. It's perfectly possible that the show scheduled for that certain Wednesday two months down the road may have to be postponed at the last minute. As it is, everyone who walks through the front gate of Universal has an equal chance of getting into the audience of a show being taped that day.

Once you get to Orlando, call Nick again and double-check the production schedule. It may be more specific now. For example, three months ago, they might have been able to tell you that the show you wanted to see would be in production this week. Now they may be able to tell you it will be taping only on Wednesday, Thursday, and Friday. But just because you've called 363-8500, don't think you're the only one with this "inside" information. Nick puts out the word in a variety of ways when shows are in production. There may even be huge billboards along I-4 announcing current tapings! So even though you have the information, you'll still have to step lively to maximize your chances of getting a seat.

When you get to the park itself on the day of your visit, be alert for Nick staffers passing out tickets to arriving guests. If that's not happening, go immediately to Nickelodeon Studios, where people queue up to take the studio tour. Just tell the Nickelodeon staffers there that you want to see a show that day and ask them how to go about it. They'll give you the straight poop.

You will increase your chances by getting to the park as early as possible, but don't expect a ticket just because you're first on line. Nick only begins to dispense tickets an hour or two before taping begins. Apparently, they found that when they handed out tickets too early, people wound up waiting around in the hot Orlando sun and getting irritated. Still, arriving early has its strategic advantages. Some shows will tape as many as four episodes a day; if you don't get into the first taping, you'll have a shot at the others. Another strategy that might work is going to the Studio Audience Center as soon as you arrive. It's next to Lost & Found, to your right as you enter the park. I'm told they will sometimes have tickets for that day's Nickelodeon tapings. There are anywhere from 150 to 250 tickets for each show and they go quickly once distribution begins.

A word about dress codes: If you're wearing a Shamu t-shirt and a Goofy hat, you'll still be admitted to the audience of a Nickelodeon show. You can probably expect some good-natured ribbing from the person who does the audience warm-up before all Nickelodeon shows. Just don't expect to see yourself on TV when the show airs. The camerapeople know not to give the competition free advertising in the "pick-up shots" of the audience. On the other hand, outfitting yourself as a walking billboard for Nickelodeon or Universal won't garner you any special privileges.

However, if you'd like to take the next step and see your kid become a contestant on one of the shows, it will help if you pay at least some attention to junior's appearance. Nickelodeon makes a genuine effort to get a cross-section of America on its shows, but they draw the line at extreme hairstyles and odd or sloppy clothing (although they don't like to tell you as much). A few hours watching the shows themselves will give you a good set of guidelines on what Nick considers appropriate attire and grooming. My suggestion would be to avoid clothing, such as t-shirts, which openly advertise anything.

Once you've made it to the studio for the taping, the Nickelodeon staff is very good about letting you know when the episode you are watching will be aired. That way, you'll be able to tune in back home and, maybe, see yourself on the boob tube.

## What's in Studio 17?

Nickelodeon shows are taped in Studios 18 and 19. But that doesn't mean there are 17 other soundstages scattered about the lot. Movie studios like to think they are as efficient as any factory and, in keeping with this industrial mindset, all buildings at Universal Studios are numbered, regardless of their function. The two soundstages that Nickelodeon uses just happen to be buildings 18 and 19.

# Selected Short Subjects

## The Boneyard

In studio parlance, the "boneyard" is a vacant lot where set pieces, large props, and vehicles are stored after production. They wait there in hopes of a sequel or to be refurbished or cannibalized for another project. Here in Florida, this area serves as a walk-through museum of perhaps familiar items from Universal productions. Recently, you could see topiary from *Edward Scissorhands* and a variety of props from *The Flintstones* (the live-action film, not the cartoon). It's interesting to see how "chintzy" some of the props look. It's a testament to the power of the illusion created on the silver screen.

## Kodak Trick Photography Photo Spot

This is another of those spots in the park where you can take your own souvenir photo using the "hanging miniature" technique pioneered in the early days of filmmaking. Here, you can photograph your family against a fanciful New York skyline that floats above the roofs of the adjacent New York set.

### Jurassic Park Photo & Kiosk

While you wait for Universal's new theme park with an island based entirely on *Jurassic Park*, you'll have to content yourself with this preview, carved out of a corner of the Boneyard. No ride, alas, but for $5 you can have your photo taken in a re-creation of the scene from the film in which T-Rex attacks the tour jeep. Depending on your acting skills, the result will look eerily realistic or merely silly — and either result is fine.

From time to time, Universal will mount a "behind-the-scenes" exhibit about *Jurassic Park* somewhere in the park. The idea seems to be to keep the film fresh in our minds as the new theme park is being constructed.

### Universal's Studio Brass

The music is loud, the flavor is Dixieland, and the beat is infectious. This is no pickup group. These guys are really good and worth a pause on your busy schedule. Their spirited renditions of familiar (and not-so-familiar) movie and television themes will get you guessing as you tap your foot. I happen to see this brass band most often in Production Central, but they travel around the park. Their performance schedule can sometimes be found in your Studio Guide brochure.

## Eating in Production Central

### Classic Monsters Café

| | |
|---|---|
| *What:* | Buffet restaurant |
| *Where:* | Across from the Boneyard |
| *Price Range:* | $$ – $$$ |

There's nothing quite like a stroll through Dr. Frankenstein's lab to give you a monstrous appetite. Fortunately, you can satisfy it here with yummy dishes like Cauldron Soup, Monster Salads, Mummy's Pasta, and (you could've guessed) Devil's Food Cake.

Those glamorous ghouls of our collective black-and white subconscious take center stage in an eatery filled with souvenirs from zany sci-fi movies like *Abbott and Costello Go To Mars* and chillers like *Frankenstein*, *The Mummy*, and *Dracula*. The Creature from the Black Lagoon even floats in a big tank in the main dining room.

The food is served "buffeteria" style in Frankenstein's laboratory, which makes you wonder if eye of newt is among the condiments. You can take your pick of several dining areas — the Sci-Fi Room, the Crypt, and Mansion Dining — each with a different theme and all packed with life-sized statues, props, and photographs.

Universal Studios' early success was fueled by its inventive horror movies, and this gleefully ghastly gastronomic goulash is a fitting celebration of that bygone era.

# Shopping in Production Central

## Bates Motel Store

Named after the fatal motel from Hitchcock's classic *Psycho*, this small shop offers the kind of souvenirs — Bates Motel towels, soap, even shower curtains — that will make sense only to die-hard *Psycho* fans. If you are one of them, you're sure to find something to send chills down your spine every time you enter your bathroom.

Of more general interest are books about Hitchcock and videos (including some boxed sets) of his films. If the show has whetted your appetite to know more about his work, by all means browse here. If you see the Hitchcock show, you can't miss the Bates Motel Store; it's the exit. Otherwise, you'll find its discreet entrance on Eighth Avenue right around the corner from the entrance to the main show.

The cashier's counter evokes the hotel desk from the *Psycho* movies. Check out the tacky painting to the left of the cashier's desk, near Door #1. Peek behind it for a typical Hitchcockian surprise.

## The Hanna-Barbera Store

The Hanna-Barbera ride empties out into this brightly decorated toy and souvenir shop. Wearables include t-shirts and sweats at prices ranging from $8 to $25. There are some Hanna-Barbera videos to be found (mostly the Flintstones) but, surprisingly, the selection is limited. Small figurines of popular characters at $3 make a nice souvenir. Or opt for a plush doll ($7 to $21).

## Nickelodeon Kiosk

If you just can't wait, a small open-air cart sells Nickelodeon merchandise as you leave the Nick Studio area. A larger selection (and more pleasant shopping conditions) can be found just a few steps away in the Universal Studios Store on the Front Lot.

# EXTRA ADDED ATTRACTION

## The Dynamite Nights Stuntacular

*Rating:*       ★ ★ ★ ★
*Type:*         Outdoor speedboat stunt show
*Time:*         About 5 minutes
*Kelly says:*   The perfect end to the perfect day

"The Lagoon" as it is called on the official Universal Studios Florida map is an artificial lake that runs roughly north and south in the middle of the park. At the south end it is part of the New York set, to the north it is part of Amity, and in between on either side it is part of San Francisco and Expo Center.

Once a day (sometimes twice in peak season), at closing time, the lagoon becomes a gigantic film set for a razzle-dazzle action movie finale. The plot — such as it is — is standard good guys versus bad guys stuff and you can tell the two apart by the color of the speedboats they drive. You won't be able to follow the action just by watching so a helpful voice-over narration alerts you to the next likely hot spot. And "hot" is the right word.

This is yet another opportunity for Universal's pyromaniacs to show off their stuff. As the speedboats zoom back and forth at high speeds in the narrow confines of the lagoon, good guys and bad guys fire away with abandon. If you are close to the action you will feel the blast from what look to be grenade launchers as well as hear the deafening roar. With all the gunplay, it's hardly surprising that a few grenades go "astray."

There are three major explosions in this show and one minor one. First, the Texaco fuel dock at the New York end of the lagoon goes off in a spectacular blast, complete with rockets shooting high into the sky. Then the decrepit old hulk at the north end explodes, breaking dramatically in half. Finally, a fuel platform in the middle of the lagoon catches fire as the bad guy's black speedboat roars out of control and crashes through a wall of flames.

It's a fitting (and ear-splitting) finale for an action-packed day of riding the movies.

***The best seats in the house.*** If you really want to get front row seats for this one, you'll have to resign yourself to staking out your claim early — at least half an hour at the busiest times, maybe more. If you have only one shot at seeing the show (and are agile), your best bet might be to clamber on top of the rocks facing the lagoon across from Richter's. This way you will have some altitude and a fairly good view of both ends of the lagoon. The elevated grassy knoll in the park behind these rocks is also a good vantage point for latecomers.

Another primo viewing spot is from the balcony of Lombard's Landing. The second floor of the restaurant is open only during busier periods and getting there requires perfect timing, a lot of luck, and eating at this moderately priced restaurant.

Other good vantage points are along the docks on the San Francisco side of the lagoon. You will probably find, however, that no one spot is ideal. There will always be something you'll miss. Of course, if you have the luxury of coming back several times, you can see the show from a different vantage point each time. But don't drive yourself nuts worrying about getting the optimum viewing point. The show is designed to offer something for everyone, no matter where they wind up.

**Will you get wet?** Consult your map. Those little black wavy lines around the edge of the lagoon mark the "splash zones." Waves kicked up by sharply turning speedboats can drench people standing at water's edge in these locations. Plan accordingly.

*Note:* The *Stuntacular* may be preempted during certain special events such as the Mardi Gras Festival.

# CHAPTER THREE:

# CityWalk & Islands of Adventure

Cit yWalk and Islands of Adventure are the first steps in a massive expansion that will transform Universal Studios Florida into **Universal Studios Escape**, a multi-park, multi-hotel, multi-activity resort destination that will rival the fabled Disney complex down the road.

First of all, some important distinctions: **Islands of Adventure** is a full-fledged theme park, the equal in size to next-door Universal Studios Florida. Like any self-respecting theme park, it features a number of themed areas — the "islands" of the name — containing a variety of rides, attractions, restaurants, and shopping venues, all reflecting a common theme. **CityWalk** on the other hand is a more compact entertainment district that is conveniently located between Universal Studios Florida and Islands of Adventure. In fact, it will be impossible to go from one park to the other without passing through CityWalk. Here you will find a variety of themed restaurants and music clubs, along with top-notch shopping, a 20-screen movie theater, and a vibrant street scene. Comparisons will inevitably be made to Disney's Pleasure Island, Downtown Disney, and Church Street Station, all of which in some superficial respects CityWalk resembles. However, CityWalk has a very definite flavor and identity all its own. And, unlike the nearby theme parks, CityWalk has no admission charge.

At press time CityWalk and Islands of Adventure were not finished, let alone open to the general public. CityWalk is scheduled to open, gradually, in late 1998 and Universal hopes it will be completely open by the end of that year. Islands of Adventure will open in the summer of

1999, although there may be some "soft" openings before then. That means this chapter is based on informed speculation rather than concrete experience. My goal is to offer you an overview that can guide you in making decisions about where to spend your time at these two new attractions. Just keep in mind that some of what follows is speculative and that when you visit some rides and attractions may not yet be open.

## Before You Come

Presumably, Universal Studios' recorded message line at (407) 363-8000 will begin adding Islands of Adventure information as it becomes available. At least it should direct you to the correct phone number. Another source of official information is the Universal Studios web site at http://www.usf.com.

As more information becomes known and as things start to open, reviews and more detailed descriptions of the various attractions will be posted on The Intrepid Traveler's web site at

**http://www.intrepidtraveler.com**

## Getting There & Parking

To get to CityWalk and Islands of Adventure simply follow the directions given to Universal Studios in the previous chapter. Parking is in the same multi-story parking structures that serve Universal Studios and the price for parking is the same. I have heard some speculation that a new pricing structure may be introduced to decrease or even eliminate the parking fee for those arriving after a certain time of day but that remains to be seen. For those who would like to spare themselves the walk from the parking structures, both CityWalk and Islands of Adventure will offer valet parking, presumably at the same rates offered at Universal Studios ($12, or $6 for annual passholders).

Both parking structures lead to "the hub," from whence it is a short journey along a moving sidewalk to CityWalk. You can't miss it since you have no other choice; the routes to both of the theme parks lie through CityWalk. Conversely, when you are leaving the parks you have no choice but to walk through CityWalk on the way back to your car. If you are staying at a Universal Studios Escape resort, you can board a boat at your hotel and cruise to CityWalk's waterfront esplanade, which is just a short stroll from both parks.

## Opening and Closing Times

CityWalk will be open, to some extent, before the parks are. Certainly there will be places to stop for a quick breakfast before heading for

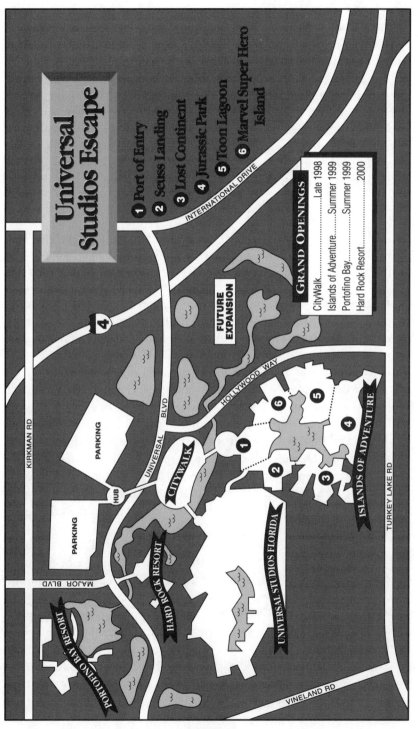

**Universal Studios Escape**

1 Port of Entry
2 Seuss Landing
3 Lost Continent
4 Jurassic Park
5 Toon Lagoon
6 Marvel Super Hero Island

**GRAND OPENINGS**

| | |
|---|---|
| CityWalk | Late 1998 |
| Islands of Adventure | Summer 1999 |
| Portofino Bay | Summer 1999 |
| Hard Rock Resort | 2000 |

FUTURE EXPANSION

KIRKMAN RD
MAJOR BLVD
UNIVERSAL BLVD
INTERNATIONAL DRIVE
HOLLYWOOD WAY
TURKEY LAKE RD
VINELAND RD

PARKING
PARKING
HUB
CITYWALK
ISLANDS OF ADVENTURE
UNIVERSAL STUDIOS FLORIDA
HARD ROCK RESORT
PORTOFINO BAY RESORT

the theme park of your choice. Perhaps some shops will be open as well. Things will be a bit more active by lunchtime, when many people will choose to leave the parks for their noontime meal. However, the main business of CityWalk won't get under way until dusk, when crowds begin to gather for an evening's entertainment. Expect CityWalk to be open until midnight most nights and until as late as 2:00 a.m. on Fridays and Saturdays.

Islands of Adventure will most likely follow the opening and closing patterns of Universal Studios Florida next door. That is, "soft" openings in the morning with closing time varying from 6:00 or 7:00 p.m. during the slower periods to 8:00 or 9:00 p.m. during the busier times.

# The Price of Admission

Good news! Once you've paid for your parking, there is no admission or cover charge for CityWalk. That's not to say it's completely free however. There will be individual admissions to the performance venues and the movie theaters. Then of course there are the restaurants, many offering entertainment along with dinner, and the posh shops. Most people will find their wallets considerably lighter after a visit to CityWalk. Nonetheless, there will be occasional free entertainment in the streets and along the waterfront and the *E! Entertainment Studios* (see below) will dispense free tickets for its shows.

As for Islands of Adventure (IOA), pricing had not been announced at press time. However, it is logical to assume that the one-day admission price will be approximately the same as that for Universal Studios Florida (USF). I have it on good authority that Islands of Adventure will be added to the Orlando FlexTicket program described in *Chapter One* although exactly how remains to be seen. For anyone spending a week or more in Orlando, and assuming that the other parks are on your must-see list, that will probably be your best deal. Among the other possibilities:

*"Park Hopper" Tickets.* Disney does it, so why not? These would allow visits to both USF and IOA on the same day. If such a ticket is offered, I would counsel against it unless and until you have visited both parks and know exactly what you will be seeing and doing in each.

*Reduced Next-Day Admission.* Under this scheme you could purchase a reduced price ticket for the next day at, say, IOA while you were visiting USF.

*Annual Passes.* It seems likely there will be annual passes for IOA as there are for USF and probably annual passes that include both parks. I already have my request in!

# CITYWALK

CityWalk is a happening enclave of heavily themed restaurants, night clubs, upscale shopping, and movie theaters that will be rocking long after the nearby theme parks have closed up for the night. Cynics might say it is Universal's attempt to mimic Pleasure Island and Downtown Disney, but then again other cynics might point out that Pleasure Island was an attempt to mimic Orlando's original sophisticated adult entertainment venue, Church Street Station (see *Chapter Eight*). Who cares? The bottom line is Orlando has yet another top-notch entertainment district to satisfy its visitors' seemingly bottomless appetite for things to do.

The layout and setting of CityWalk is ingenious. It is a 30-acre lozenge-shaped area plopped right down between Universal Studios Florida and Islands of Adventure. It is impossible to get from your car to either of the parks, or from one park to the other, without passing through CityWalk. On top of that a river runs through it — or rather a man-made waterway that separates most of CityWalk from the theme parks and will eventually link every corner of the sprawling resort complex that will comprise Universal Studios Escape.

Most of the buildings in CityWalk are arrayed along the perimeter closest to the parking structures, facing in towards the waterway. There are three major streets, a straight avenue that leads from the parking structures, a curving boulevard that leads from Universal Studios to Islands of Adventure near the waterway, and a promenade that runs past the major nightclubs. Smaller streets wind between CityWalk's few freestanding buildings. Along the waterway runs a beautifully landscaped esplanade in the middle of which is an outdoor performance space for special concerts and other events. Most of the entertainment venues in CityWalk are located across the water from the theme parks. The two exceptions are the Hard Rock Café and an NBA-themed restaurant, both of which lie along a short walk leading from the gates of Universal Studios to those of Islands of Adventure.

Just about everything in CityWalk is oriented toward a central plaza facing the water and the theme parks. To mask the backs of the buildings and their service areas, the park's designers have created an immense steel lattice work that curves up and over CityWalk enveloping it in a camouflaging green cocoon of leafy vines and other plants. Glimpsed from the parking structures, CityWalk might almost be mistaken for a small flowering hill.

Most of the entertainment in CityWalk is housed in or associated with restaurants. For this survey, I will start with the Hard Rock Café, located just outside the front gate of Universal Studios and proceed in a roughly counterclockwise direction. Little information about shopping was available at press time so the retail shops are not discussed here. Suffice it to say that the retail spaces will be filled with recognizable "brands" with an accent on the upscale.

# Hard Rock Café

The huge structure echoing Rome's ancient Coliseum is the world's largest and busiest Hard Rock Café. Those who have visited other Hard Rock's will know what to expect — just expect more of it. I refer the uninitiated to the description of the "old" Hard Rock Café in the previous chapter.

What makes this Hard Rock special, however, is not mere size but the addition of **Hard Rock Live**, the chain's first live performance venue. In its standard configuration it holds 1,700. If they pull out most of the seats on the first floor they can pack in 2,400, which still makes it "intimate" by rock standards. At the other end of the spectrum, they can use flywalls and props to shrink the performance space to the size of a truly intimate club. Given the limited capacity, it's unlikely that the real giants of rock will be able to play here (at least not too often), but the commitment has been made to make sure that, beginning in January of 1999, live rock and roll will always be on offer here.

# 'NBA Restaurant'

The name is in quotation marks because it will change before opening. What's less uncertain, however, is the theme of this trendy and sprawling sports bar — basketball. Originally, this was to have been Shaq's Place, fueled by the charisma and cash of erstwhile Orlando Magic star Shaquille O'Niell. But Shaq deserted the Magic leaving behind considerable ill will and a hole in CityWalk's lineup. Not to worry. The replacement promises to have every bit as much star power. Prices are expected to be in the moderate range.

# Jimmy Buffett's Margaritaville

After crossing the bridge from Islands of Adventure and the NBA Restaurant, this is the first place you encounter in the main section of CityWalk and a welcoming joint it is. Owned by singing star Jimmy Buffett, housing his extensive collection of memorabilia, and reflecting the easy-going themes of his popular songs, Margaritaville is a hymn to the laid-back life of the Parrot Head.

The various sections of the bar-restaurant are decorated to reflect

Jimmy's various interests and the songs he wrote about them. The Volcano Bar answers once and for all the question, "Where you gonna go when the volcano blows." In the restaurant section, the booths are styled to evoke the back end of a fishing boat. Look up and you'll see a fiberoptic map of Florida. Buffett fans will enjoy spotting the references in the decor while others will be having too much fun to care.

The cuisine is described as "island fare," with a heavy emphasis on fresh seafood and conch chowder, but rest assured that meat eaters will be able to enjoy their Cheeseburger in Paradise. Pricing is expected to be on the moderate side.

A restaurant by day, Margaritaville transforms itself after the dinner crowd thins out into a cross between a nightclub and a full-fledged performance space showcasing bands and live performers that reflect in one way or another that certain indescribable Jimmy Buffet style. A separate entrance fee will most likely be charged for nighttime entertainment.

## Emeril's Restaurant Orlando

Emeril Lagasse, the popular TV chef and cookbook author, brings his upscale New Orleans haute cuisine to Orlando in this lavish eatery decorated (if that's the word) with over 12,000 bottles of wine in climate-controlled glass-walled wine cases.

The cuisine is Creole-based but the execution and elaborate presentation is the exact opposite of down-home. This is a first-class restaurant where dining is theater and a full meal can last two and a half hours. Entrees are in the $20 to $30 range so the full cost of a meal, with wine, can be considerably to the north of $50 per person. Dining here is a special experience and Emeril's is not the kind of place where you will feel comfortable in the full tourist regalia of shorts, t-shirt, and straw hat. Stop back at your hotel to change and freshen up. Reservations are mandatory, and since it can take six months to a year to land one, plan ahead. Call Guest Services at (407) 363-8000; they should be able to direct you.

For those who take their sybaritic pleasures seriously, there is a wine tasting room, a separate cigar room, and a VIP room for private dining. Mr. Lagasse is very much the hands-on chef, I am told, so if you're lucky you might have your meal prepared by the master himself. There is even some loose talk of Emeril doing some location work in connection with the *E! Entertainment Studios* (see below).

## The Groove

This is CityWalk's dance club and it sets out to compete head to head with the legendary nightspots that have caught the public imagination in urban centers like New York, Chicago, and Los Angeles. It is also the only venue that does not come with a recognizable brand name. No Jimmy Buffetts or Bob Marleys to give this place instant name recognition. This joint will stand or fall on its own merits.

It succeeds by providing a place where a mostly young crowd can come and boogie the night away in a cacophonous atmosphere that duplicates big city sophistication. The main difference is that here you will be let in even if you don't meet some snotty doorman's idea of what is currently cool and hip. Intimate it's not, with a maximum capacity of 1,100 on multiple levels, but with crowds comes excitement.

The various areas of the club have been designed to provide ample space for those who want to thrash and writhe under pulsating lights to ear-splitting music while offering some refuge to those who just want to watch. There are even some quiet corners (50- to 80-seat bars actually) where you can get better acquainted with that special someone you just met on the dance floor. When it all becomes too much, you can repair to a balcony over the Promenade and survey the passing scene.

# CityJazz

Located in an octagonal building almost at the geographical center of CityWalk, CityJazz celebrates that most American of all musical forms with an ambitious group of venues.

*Downbeat* magazine's **Jazz Hall of Fame** pays tribute to the greats, from the founding fathers, to the red hot mamas, to the eclectic cool jazz of modern times. Twice a year, new members are inducted, offering the perfect excuse for a big party.

The **Thelonius Monk Institute of Jazz** is a non-profit organization dedicated to the perpetuation of jazz through education. Here at CityJazz promising students from around the world will have the opportunity to hone their skills under the watchful eyes and well-tuned ears of experts during the day, and at night — maybe, just maybe — get a chance to jam with the pros in the CityJazz nightclub.

For most people, the big draw will be the big-name national and regional acts who play in the **CityJazz Club**. The club's two-story design combines the intimate ambiance of a true jazz club with the great sightlines of a conventional theater. The space has also been designed to serve as a state-of-the-art recording facility, an additional draw for big-name acts looking to do a live album. Appetizers and drinks will be served, but the emphasis is clearly on the music, not food.

Outside, on a balcony overlooking the Promenade, an "E-Jockey" (that's short for Entertainment Jockey) will hold forth, playing music, announcing events and activities, and generally keeping up a high level of fun and excitement amongst the revelers passing by below.

## Bob Marley — A Tribute To Freedom

Reggae fans will appreciate this salute to Bob Marley, the king of reggae, where the infectious back-beat of Marley's lilting music mingles with the spicy accents of island cooking. Created under the watchful eye of Marley's widow, Rita, who has contributed Marley memorabilia for the project, this venue is as much a celebration of Marley's vision of universal brotherhood as it is a restaurant or performance venue. Plans are afoot to host regular festivals enshrining Marley's music, which is more popular today than it was when he was alive.

The exterior is an exact replica of 56 Hope Road, Marley's Kingston Jamaica home. Inside you will find a reggae music performance space and a place where you can sit under the stars and eat and drink. There will be jerk chicken and Red Stripe beer but, reflecting Marley's vegetarian bent, there will also be an accent on juices and healthier fare.

## Pat O'Brien's

If you can't make it to New Orleans, you can do the next best thing in this meticulous recreation of the Big Easy's fabled eatery. It's all been duplicated by Universal's scenic design wizards, right down to the cracks in the bricks.

Here, in the garden at the back, you can sit outside under the stars sipping one of Pat O'Brien's famous (not to mention lethal) Flaming Hurricane cocktails. Or step inside to the Dueling Pianos bar where the ivories are tickled stereophonically to smashing effect. Both of these trademark attractions have been copied (sometimes right here in Orlando) but these are the originals.

Lunch will be served but don't expect much of a restaurant scene at night. Pat O'Brien's is a party location with appetizer-sized portions of finger food served more to cushion the alcohol than to fill you up.

## Motown Cafe

Down home cooking and an infectious backbeat are the winning combination at this glossy eatery celebrating the Motown sound and Motown stars. In Hard Rock Café fashion, the walls are lined with photos and memorabilia of the label's greats. Soundalike vocal groups regularly take the floor in brief turns that recreate the glory days of those great groups that blended close harmony and peppy music in ways that have yet to be matched let alone surpassed.

The cuisine could be classified as soul food, but it wanders all across the African American experience, from southern fried chicken to jambalaya. The shoestring sweet potato fries, sprinkled with a dusting of cinnamon sugar, are a must.

## Universal Cineplex

This is the mall multiplex writ large. Given its 5,000 seats in 20 theaters on two stories, it's unlikely you have anything quite like it at home. Most of the theaters are comfortably large and many of them have stadium seating. Expect the usual assortment of first-run features at prices competitive with other first-run houses in Orlando, or about $6.75, with cheaper prices earlier in the day. The theater has been cleverly designed so that you enter at the plaza level but exit at the back on the upper level. From there you can either descend a narrow zigzag street lined with shops to the plaza or stroll along the Promenade, CityWalk's row of restaurants and nightclubs.

At first blush, putting what is essentially a mall movie theater, albeit a big one, in an over-the-top setting like CityWalk might seem a questionable use of valuable real estate. But it does offer the exciting possibility of staging star-studded gala premieres for major motion pictures and my sources tell me that they hope to have one or two, maybe more, such blowouts each year. One of the most exciting rumors about the Cineplex is the possibility that at least one screen will specialize in showing the great films of the past. Since Universal Studios produced films by Mae West, W.C. Fields, and the Marx Brothers, among many other greats, this is indeed something to look forward to.

## NASCAR Cafe

Described as the "next generation of restaurants," the NASCAR Cafe celebrates the lifestyle and excitement surrounding stock car racing, a sport with humble beginnings that has grown into a multi-billion dollar phenomenon with its own pantheon of stars and heroes.

It's a full-service, sit-down restaurant and reservations ( or "pole positions") are taken. You'll need them, too. Expect the restaurant to be crowded, with long waits for a table, and plan accordingly. The good news is that a typical wait is long enough to allow you, with a little planning, to do something else (maybe even see a movie!) while waiting for a table.

You could while away the wait by wandering through the memorabilia and displays on the ground floor. Laid out like a race track, the floor is sort of a NASCAR museum filled with displays about the cars and their famous drivers and providing information about the latest races. There are also interactive games and race car simulators to help you work up an appetite.

The dining room upstairs is decorated with large projection screens on which races begin every 20 minutes. There's even a starter perched overhead to call out "Gentlemen, start your engines!" and wave the checkered flag. Several times a day there is a special presentation "celebrating the NASCAR lifestyle."

Oh, by the way, there's food, too. The centerpieces of the racing-themed menu are steaks and chops, with prices in the moderate to expensive range.

## E! Entertainment Studios

Centrally located on the plaza and across the street from the Cineplex is a live broadcast television studio for E! the cable entertainment network which will bring an added level of showbiz excitement to the CityWalk mix. Not only will there be a constant need for warm bodies to fill the seats (most or all of the shows feature a live audience) but current plans call for camera crews to roam the streets interviewing guests and getting their opinions on the "hot" topic of the day.

Word is there will be one show shooting five days a week. Hopefully, the synergism offered by the CityWalk location will inspire an even more active production schedule.

## And All The Rest . . .

At press time, there were still elements of CityWalk that had yet to fall into place. There will be a few more "branded" and "themed" restaurants and performance venues joining those described above. One of the most eagerly anticipated is a "family" restaurant that will draw the kiddies. Plans had been underway to open such a restaurant based on the Marvel comics characters, but they fell through. Hopefully, a similarly themed venue will take its place, offering the younger set their very own version of Margaritaville.

CityWalk is not a completely self-contained entity. Much of what goes on here will have echoes in the two nearby theme parks and vice versa. For example, expect a jazz festival scheduled for the evening in CityWalk to be vigorously promoted with appropriate spectacle and razzle-dazzle in both Universal Studios and Islands of Adventure. Likewise, a celebration like Universal Studios' Mardi Gras parade can be expected to make its way into CityWalk after it's done its job of closing down Universal for the night.

Next to CityJazz is a small outdoor stage backed by a waterfall and featuring short sets of live entertainment throughout the day and night. Down by the waterside, there will be "sunset events" (presumably free of charge) that offer a more relaxed alternative to the high-volume entertainment venues. Here you will be able to grab a drink, sit on a bench, or stretch out on the grass, and just . . . relax.

# ISLANDS OF ADVENTURE

In the summer of 1999, with the opening of this new, 110-acre land of fantasy and adventure, Universal Studios Escape becomes the second multi-theme-park resort destination in the Orlando area. Billed as the "theme park for the next millennium," Islands of Adventure will certainly raise the competitive bar with its assortment of "next generation" attractions, thrill rides, and illusions.

Unlike Disney, Universal does not have the luxury of seemingly unlimited acreage in which to expand, but this handicap (if such it is) has its benefits. Whereas at Disney World you have to really schlepp to get from one park to another, Universal Studios Florida and Islands of Adventure are literally right next door to one another. A visitor with a multi-park pass can spend the morning in one and, after a five- or ten-minute stroll, enjoy the afternoon in the other, perhaps stopping for lunch in CityWalk on the way.

Despite the proximity, Islands of Adventure is not just more of Universal Studios. It has a separate identity and, with the notable exception of Jurassic Park, its attractions draw their inspiration from very different sources from those in its sister park. The overall effect is more reminiscent of the Magic Kingdom, with its clearly differentiated "lands."

Guests reach Islands of Adventure through the Port of Entry, a separately themed area that serves much the same function as The Front Lot at Universal. Through the Port of Entry lies a spacious lake. Artfully arranged around it are five decidedly different "themed areas" — Seuss Landing, The Lost Continent, Jurassic Park, Toon Lagoon, and Marvel Super Hero Island. The "islands" of Islands of Adventure are not true islands of course; but the central lake's fingerlike bays set off one area from the next and the bridges you cross to move from one to the other do a remarkably good job of creating the island illusion.

The flow of visitors is strictly controlled by the circular layout. If you follow the line of least resistance you will move through the park in a circle, visiting every island in turn. Or you can use the boat service to go directly from Port of Entry to Jurassic Park.

There are a number of themes, if you will, that differentiate Islands of Adventure from Universal Studios (and from other Central Florida theme parks, too, for that matter):

***Roller coasters.*** Islands of Adventure introduces to Orlando some heavy hitters in the increasingly cut-throat competition for bragging rights in the world of high-end steel coasters. It is fair to say that the two big coasters here top *Montu* and *Kumba* over at Busch Gardens Tampa (see *Chapter Ten*). *Dueling Dragons* in The Lost Continent features twin coaster tracks that intertwine and come within inches of collision, while the *Incredible Hulk* coaster on Marvel Super Hero Island zaps you to the top of the first drop with what they say is the same thrust as an F-16 jet.

***Pushing the envelope.*** Universal's designers take obvious pride in what they see as "next generation" rides and attractions that will be like nothing you have experienced before. As just one example, the *Spiderman* ride takes the motion simulator from *Back To The Future*, drops it into a simulated 3-D world right out of *T-2*, puts it on a moving track, and spins it through 360 degrees along the way.

***More for the kids.*** While Islands of Adventure provides plenty of the kind of intense, adult-oriented thrill rides for which Universal Studios became famous, it makes a special effort to reach out to kids. Seuss Landing is almost exclusively for the entertainment and enjoyment of younger children. Toon Lagoon will appeal to slightly older kids and Marvel Super Hero Island is the perfect place for adolescents to scare themselves to death.

***Less "edutainment."*** Whereas Universal Studios Florida always seems to have something to teach you about making movies, Islands of Adventure seems remarkably free of ulterior motives. This place is all about good, clean, mindless *fun!*

***More theme-ing.*** Although it hardly seems possible, Islands of Adventure promises to be more heavily "themed" than Universal and many other parks. What that means is that the park designers have made a concerted effort to stretch the theme of each island into every restaurant, every shop, indeed into as many nooks and crannies as possible. In fact, Islands of Adventure will be the first theme park to feature originally composed soundtracks — one for each island — just like a movie.

What follows is informed speculation about the rides, attractions, restaurants, and other wonders that await you at Islands of Adventure. I begin with Port of Entry and continue in a counterclockwise tour of the park. (Of course, you can also move in a clockwise direction if you prefer.) Be aware that some guesswork is involved here. Certain elements may be added, changed, or dropped altogether before your visit.

# Port of Entry

The towering lighthouse with the blazing fire at the top, modeled after the ancient lighthouse of Pharos in Alexandria, Egypt, marks the gates of Port of Entry and the beginning of your adventure. This striking structure is only the most obvious of the metaphors used in this area's eclectic blend of architecture and decor to evoke the spirit of wanderlust and adventure. At the base of the lighthouse a series of sails, like those used on ancient Chinese junks, are used to shade the ticket booths for the park. There, "customs agents" will stamp your "passport" and send you on your way.

Past the ticket booths, a semicircular array of facades around a spacious plaza house various Guest Services functions (stroller rental, will-call windows, and such) along with shops where you can pick up the sort of provisions any well-equipped explorer would need (film, sunscreen, and the like). Now that you are fully outfitted, you step through a crumbling stone archway incised with the thrilling words "The adventure begins . . . "

Through this gateway lies Port of Entry's sole street, a sort of storytelling experience that combines evocative architectural motifs to build your anticipation as you enter more fully into the spirit of discovery. It's centuries old Venice, Istanbul, Samarkand, and Timbuktu rolled into one. Here, too, you will first experience one of IOA's "next level" touches. Like all the other lands in the park, Port of Entry has its own specially composed soundtrack that unfolds as you walk along, drawing ever closer to the water.

*Note:* Port of Entry will be the first part of Islands of Adventure to open to the public, in late 1998, along with CityWalk. It will function as a sort of Preview Center for the park until the park itself opens officially in the summer of 1999.

## Island Hopper Cruises

At the end of Port of Entry, in a bustling harbor setting, you will find the area's sole attraction. Rather like the interstellar bar in *Star Wars*, this large open plaza is where characters from all the islands congregate to meet each other and greet visitors like yourself, urging them to come visit their special island.

One option is to take a cruise directly to Jurassic Park. But this is much more than a shortcut. It is an attraction in its own right and offers a pleasant way to get a preview of the entire park, if you stay on for the round trip. The boat takes a lazy, narrated tour past Seuss Landing and

The Lost Continent to its one and only stop at Jurassic Park. Then it makes its way around Jurassic Park, past Toon Lagoon and Marvel Super Hero Island, back to Port of Entry. Current plans call for on-board entertainment during the journey.

## Eating in Port of Entry

### Confisco's Grill

A major dining experience is offered by this upscale Italian restaurant serving designer pizzas, pastas, and Mediterranean-inspired entrees. It is a full-service restaurant and, like the other full-service eateries in the park, it offers cocktails and a wine list.

If you headed straight for Jurassic Park when you arrived, you may have worked your way back to Port of Entry in time for lunch here. Otherwise, this might make a good choice for dinner on days when the park is open late. Anticipating crowds, the designers have provided the adjacent **Backwater Bar** for those waiting for a table, not to mention those who see no reason to interrupt their drinking with food.

### Croissant Moon Bakery

Every theme park needs a place, strategically located near the entrance, to serve those who thought they'd save some time by skipping breakfast only to arrive at the park starving to death. Muffins and such for breakfast and light sandwiches and soup for lunch are on hand here. If you're familiar with Beverly Hills Boulangerie in Universal Studios, you'll know what to expect.

# Seuss Landing

Probably best described as a 12-acre, walk-through sculpture, Seuss Landing adds a third dimension and garish Technicolor to the wonderfully wacky world of Theodore Geisel, aka Dr. Seuss, whose dozens of illustrated books of inspired poetry have enchanted millions of kids, you and me included.

Universal designers have gone to great length to evoke the out-of-kilter world of the Seuss books, avoiding straight lines and square corners wherever possible. The horticulturists even got trees to grow in corkscrew spirals.

## The Cat In The Hat: Ride Inside

Dr. Seuss's most popular book tells the tale of what happens when two kids, home alone, allow the cat of the title to come for a visit. Inside that giant red and white striped top hat, you can get your chance to relive the adventure.

This is a "dark" ride but perhaps one of the brightest and most colorful you're likely to encounter. You and your kids climb into cars that are designed like miniature six-passenger sofas and set off through a series of 18 show scenes that recreate the story line of the book. Just don't expect the static tableaux of the older generation dark rides. One of the nicer touches on this one is something that Universal describes as "a revolving, wallpaper-peeling, perception-altering 24-foot tunnel." Oh, wow! E.T. better look to his laurels.

While you probably won't care, this ride employs never-before-available computer systems to control the flow of 1,800 guests per hour and activate the innumerable special effects along the way.

## One Fish, Two Fish, Red Fish, Blue Fish

Here's an interesting twist on an old carnival ride. You know, the one where you sit in a little airplane (or flying Dumbo) and spin round in a circle while your plane goes up and down. On this ride, based on the Seuss book of the same name, you pilot a little fishy. While you can't escape the circular route of the ride, you can steer your fish up or down in response to directions given by a rhyme that plays throughout your trip. Failure to guide your fish wisely will result in a thorough dousing from a series of "squirt posts." Presiding over the center of the ride is an 18-foot-tall sculpture of the Star Belly Fish from the book.

## Caro-Seuss-El

This is the world's first interactive carousel. Here kids can ride on the back of a beautifully sculpted Seuss-ian animal like Cowfish from *McElligot's Pool* or the Twin Camels from *One Fish, Two Fish*. There are seven different characters and a total of 54 mounts on the 47-foot diameter ride. The interactive part comes when you pull back on the reins and watch your steed's head shake, his eyes blink, his tail wag. Another fascinating feature of the Caro-Seuss-El is a special loading mechanism for wheelchairs that allows the disabled to experience the ride from their own rocking chariots.

## Sylvester McMonkey McBean's Very Unusual Driving Machines

Those clever designers have made virtually certain that kids will want to ride this one twice. That's because they've created two separate tracks for this ingenious ride, each providing a somewhat different experience. The ride is based on Seuss's popular tale of the Sneeches, which offers toddlers a gentle introduction to the adult problem of racial and social discrimination. In keeping with that theme riders choose between the Star Belly and the Plain Belly track in the loading area.

Departing from above the Circus McGurkus Café, this is an indoor-outdoor ride with little two-seater vehicles that take a five-minute ride on an elevated monorail throughout Seuss Landing and out over the lagoon. Whenever it goes inside, riders are greeted by colorfully animated show scenes where magical things happen to their vehicles as they learn the story of the Sneeches. Each track passes through the same scenes, they just take different routes to get there. When the cars enter the Circus McGurkus Café, they pass through a hanging mobile filled with Seussian characters. The drivers will be able not only to honk their horns but to control the speed of their vehicles and even bump the car ahead of them, setting off appropriately Seussian sound effects. Any right-thinking adult will let the kid do the driving.

# If I Ran The Zoo

This interactive play area is based on the charming tale of young Gerald McGrew who had some very definite ideas of what it takes to create a really interesting zoo. There are three distinct areas — Hedges, Water, and the New Zoo — each of which allows little ones to interact with or control elements like dancing snakes of water or animals that laugh when you tickle their feet. All told there are 19 different interactive elements to keep your child giggling all the way through this attraction.

# Eating in Seuss Landing

## Green Eggs and Ham Café

The eateries in Seuss Landing give new meaning to the term "fun food." The exterior of this one, for starters, is shaped like a giant green ham. Here you can order up actual green eggs (harmless food coloring let us hope) and eat your wacky meal under sunshades in the shape of giant fried — and green — eggs. For the less adventuresome, conventional breakfast-type food is also available.

## Circus McGurkus Café Stoo-pendous

Under that enormous big top is this humongous fast-food emporium themed to a fare-thee-well with circus imagery a la Dr. Seuss. The built-in entertainment comes from the little cars that choogle past overhead, courtesy of Sylvester McMonkey McBean.

# The Lost Continent

From the color and fantasy of Seuss Landing, the intrepid adventurer plunges into the mystery of The Lost Continent, which in terms of sheer size (some 20 acres) is almost a theme park in itself. There are three areas to be found here — the Lost City, an ancient Middle Eastern bazaar evoking *1,001 Nights*, and Merlinwood which may remind some of Germany's Black Forest.

The first thing you see, when you enter from Seuss Landing, is a brooding extinct volcano which hides Mythos, perhaps the most eye-popping restaurant in any Orlando theme park. A little farther along, as you approach the Lost City, you glimpse over a craggy boulder an enormous hand holding an equally enormous trident. Only when you have walked a little farther do you realize that the boulder is an enormous head of the god Poseidon and what you are seeing is the remnants of a very large and very ancient statue that fell down aeons ago.

## Escape From The Lost City

Behind the ruins of Poseidon's statue lies his temple where his devotees worshipped before Zeus banished him to the depths of the sea. With understandable trepidation, you step inside. There you are greeted by The Keeper who is extremely pleased to see you. After all, it has been hundreds, even thousands, of years since he has had any new victims . . . er, visitors.

He seizes the opportunity to tell the tale of a city that disappeared beneath the waves in the misty recesses of the past. The storytelling style is perhaps a bit too vivid because very quickly you find yourself to be a literally captive audience as you and your fellow explorers are hurled through a whirling vortex of water. There in a mysterious otherworldly chamber you find yourself in the middle of a pitched battle between Poseidon, who uses water as his weapon, and Zeus, who responds with fire. We're talking heavy artillery here, with more than 350,000 gallons of the wet stuff and 25-foot exploding fireballs.

Just when your survival looks doubtful, you are magically transported from the depths of the sea to the surface by a very thoughtful Zeus. This is yet another of Universal's "next level" experiences and is described as a major, large-scale illusion, like David Copperfield making an elephant disappear, except here the audience is the elephant.

# The Eighth Voyage of Sinbad

In a 1,750-seat theater we get to witness the eighth voyage of the legendary Sinbad (seven just weren't enough). This is a live-action stunt show that means to rival the Indiana Jones show over at that *other* movie studio park (no, not Universal).

Here Sinbad sets off on yet another search for riches untold, encountering along the way the inevitable life-threatening perils. It's an action-packed spectacular that features six "water explosions" (you *will* get wet) and 50 — count 'em, 50 — of Universal's trademark pyrotechnical effects, including a 10-foot-tall circle of flames and a 22-foot high fall by a stunt man engulfed in flames.

In front of this attraction is a bazaar straight from the ancient Silk Road which is used as a backdrop and excuse for games of chance (a la the Amity Boardwalk), street performers, and of course, shops.

# Dueling Dragons

One reason The Lost Continent is so large is to house this immense inverted steel roller coaster. Actually, it's two separate roller coasters travelling along separate but closely intertwined tracks that diverge and then converge to terrifying effect.

You enter this experience near the Enchanted Oak Tavern, past two stone dragons standing as mute sentinels to a mysterious and heavily forested world of eerie chimes and chilling sounds. At the top of a winding path lies a brooding, ruined castle. When you enter, you discover that this was once a flourishing kingdom filled with happy and prosperous people until it was overrun by two ferocious dragons — the Dragon of Ice and the Dragon of Fire.

As you make your way slowly, slowly through the castle corridors — oh, let's face it, it's the waiting line for the coaster — you receive constant warnings to turn back before it's too late. Of course, you can hardly wait for it to be too late. It's a great way to keep people entertained during the inevitably long wait and marks a new level of theme-ing in roller coasters. Finally, you are confronted by Merlin himself who bellows that the time for cowardice is past and you must now choose which of the two dragons you will attempt to slay. There's even a special line for those brave nuts, er . . . knights who want to ride in the front.

This is an inverted coaster, which means that the cars, completely dressed to look like dragons, hang from a track over your head. Your feet hang in the air below your seat. When the cars are fully loaded the passengers look as though they are dangling from the dragons' claws. Then it's off on a three-minute ride through Merlinwood and over Dragon

Lake, which is actually shaped like a dragon, a fact that few people who ride this attraction are likely to notice.

The two coasters share the same lift to the top of the first drop, but the Fire Dragon peels off to the left as the Ice Dragon swoops to the right. After that their separate trips are carefully synchronized so that, as they loop and swirl their way around Merlinwood, they meet in mid air at three crucial moments. Perhaps the scariest close encounter comes when they come straight at one another on what is obviously a head-on collision course. At the last moment, they spin apart with the cars coming within a foot of each other at nearly 60 miles per hour. At another point, both coasters enter a double helix, spinning dizzily around one another. All told there are three near misses in less than three minutes. If you've ever asked yourself what could be more terrifying than the current generation of high-speed steel roller coasters, ask no more.

# Eating in The Lost Continent

## Mythos Restaurant

This upscale restaurant is the feather in Islands of Adventure's culinary cap. Created by world-renowned restaurant designer Jordan Mozer, Mythos evokes "the alignment of the stars, the path of the sun, the sensory rapture of wind and rain." Housed (if that's the right word) in a dormant volcano, the restaurant features panoramic windows overlooking the lagoon and the other islands and indoor rainbows that materialize over the river that runs through it. Further enhancing the restaurant-as-attraction feel of the place are a series of special effects that bathe diners in swirls of multicolored sunbeams and summon up rain showers that "dance" among the diners.

The cuisine produced by the open kitchen promises to be just as spectacular as the setting, with entrees such as pepper-painted salmon with lemon cous-cous and sizzling leeks or pan-fired crab cakes with lobster sauce and basil. Expect the bill to be just as dazzling as the decor and the cuisine.

## The Enchanted Oak Tavern

The giant oak tree stump with the gnarled bark that bears an uncanny resemblance to the face of Merlin, is actually another posh restaurant. During the day, the open top of the tree serves as a skylight to the restaurant. At night, the exterior is lit to enchanting effect.

Serving is cafeteria-style and the food is "oak-fired" barbecue. Seating is amid the twisted roots of the great oak where Merlin himself materializes from time to time. Universal created its own micro-brewed beer, Dragon Scale Ale, which is served here and in the attached **Alchemist's Bar**.

# Jurassic Park

If you've seen the movie, *Jurassic Park* (and who hasn't), you will recognize the arches that greet you as you enter. Here, Universal's design wizards have re-created the theme park that the movie's John Hammond was trying to create before all prehistoric heck broke loose.

## Discovery Center

This is lifted almost straight from the film and houses a restaurant, shops and, on the ground floor, a children's science center, which is one of the few places in Islands of Adventure where edutainment rears its lofty head. Kids will certainly recognize the huge T-Rex skeleton. Nearby are the laboratories where Hammond's crew of biochemists worked to bring Jurassic Park's prehistoric attraction back to life. There's even a display in which you'll be able to watch a cute little raptor being hatched. There will also be interactive exhibits that give the kids something to do as they learn. But, careful! The exhibits mix "fun facts" with "fun fiction." Where are the thought police when you need them?

## Triceratops Encounter

This is another never-before-been-done attraction of which Universal is justifiably proud. The conceit here is that, as a visitor to Jurassic Park, you are ushered by a Jurassic Park ranger into one of several "feed and control" paddocks for an up close and personal visit with a real live triceratops. Here you meet a Jurassic veterinarian who will fill you in on the natural history and habits of this amazing beast and actually let you pet it. It's a bit like petting the giraffes at Busch Gardens Tampa (see *Chapter Ten*) except that this creature has been extinct for a good many millennia.

Lest you think that Universal has literally done the impossible, the triceratops is not a living, breathing critter but a remarkably clever counterfeit that takes the art of animatronics to a whole new level. Unlike most mechanically animated creatures, this 24-foot long, 10-foot high triceratops does not go through a fixed routine of motions, pause, then do it all over again for the next bunch of people passing by. This triceratops actually responds to stimuli provided by the guests, making each triceratops encounter a unique experience. Nor do they hedge the illusion by making you keep your distance. You can actually pet this triceratops and pose alongside it to have your picture taken. (No flash photography. She doesn't like it.)

Groups of 20 people are led into the paddocks for a five-minute visit with these remarkable animals. Just remember that triceratops are gentle creatures. If your group is quiet and respectful, she is likely to respond positively. However, if your group is loud and boisterous, she may display defensive behavior and your visit may be shortened.

## Jurassic Park River Adventure

Amazing as the Triceratops Encounter may be, this is the attraction that will draw people to Jurassic Park. Those who have experienced the current Jurassic Park ride at Universal Studios California know what to expect. This version contains some "enhancements" but it is essentially the same ride.

*River Adventure* is an idyllic boat ride that gives you an opportunity to view from close range some of Jurassic Park's gentlest creatures. Unfortunately, on the trip you take with 25 other guests, things go very, very wrong. Your first stop is the upper lagoon, where you will meet a 35-foot tall mama ultrasaur and her baby. Then you cruise past the park's north forty where you will glimpse stegosaurs and the playful parasaulopholus. A little too playful, unfortunately.

Before you know it, you're in the raptor containment area and on the lunch menu. In a desperate attempt to save you, the boat is shunted into the environmental systems building, that huge 13-story structure at the back of Jurassic Park. It is in this vast, dark, and very scary setting that the ride reaches it climax. After narrowly escaping velociraptors and those nasty spitting dinosaurs, you come face to face, quite literally, with T-Rex himself. After that, the plunge down the "longest, fastest, steepest water descent ever built" in pitch blackness will seem like a relief.

## Camp Jurassic

This 60,000 square foot interactive kids' play and discovery area is about four times the size of *Fievel's Playland* over at Universal Studios, to which otherwise it bears some similarity. Here, in a jungle on the slopes of an ancient active volcano, kids can explore amber mines and discover dinosaur bones in lava pits, while they dodge the deadly spitters.

## Pteranodon Flyers

Taking off from Camp Jurassic is this "family" ride aboard the backs of flying dinosaurs, which glide gently over the tropical terrain of Jurassic Park. It's a little more "aggressive" than the sky rides you may have encountered at other parks and offers an enjoyable soaring sensation as the flyers bank and curve.

## Eating in Jurassic Park

### Thunder Falls Terrace

This sit-down restaurant takes wonderful advantage of the Jurassic Park River Adventure, using it as both backdrop and entertainment. After you've taken your own harrowing journey on the ride, you can repair here, sit in air-conditioned comfort, and gaze through the picture windows at other happily terrified tourists as they plunge down the final 65-foot drop. There is also an outdoor seating area that receives the cooling mist from the thundering waterfall next door.

The food is casual — rotisserie chicken and ribs — but it's served on delicate china with linen napkins and formal table settings that make the dining experience something special.

# Toon Lagoon

After the intensity of Jurassic Park, the zany, colorful, high-energy goofiness of Toon Lagoon will be a welcome change of pace. Some 150 much-beloved characters are represented here, most of whom you have come to know and love through the Sunday funnies in your hometown newspaper. All of the characters will be represented, some for the first time, in life-sized, three-dimensional form. Many of them will be strolling the grounds. A visit here offers a unique opportunity to live out a child's fantasy of stepping into the pages of the comic strips and exploring a gaudy fantasy world filled with fun and laughter.

## Dudley Do-Right's Ripsaw Falls

In Dudley's home town of Ripsaw Falls, as you might expect, Nell is once again in the clutches of the dastardly Snidely Whiplash. That's all the excuse you need to take off on a rip-roaring log flume ride that, like so many other attractions in this park, takes the genre to a whole new level.

The build-up takes us through a series of scenes in which animated characters unfold a typically wacky plot that includes not just Dudley, Nell, and Snidely but Fenwick and Horse, too, as our log-boats rise inexorably to the mountainous heights where Snidely has his hideout. Anticipating victory a bit too soon, Dudley strikes a heroic pose with his foot on a dynamite plunger, precipitating a plunge through the roof of a TNT storage shack which blows to bits as the riders are plunged beneath the water surface only to pop back to the surface 100 feet downstream. This is the first log flume to pull off this little bit of wizardry and how they manage it I'll leave you to discover.

This is one ride that just may be as entertaining to watch as to take. If you'd prefer not to take the plunge and actually go on the ride, you can stand and watch others take the steep 60-foot plunge into the TNT shack, which shatters to smithereens before your eyes. Its constituent parts fly skyward, hang there in cartoon-like suspended animation for a moment, and then fall back on themselves, miraculously reassembling the shack for the next bunch of riders.

## Popeye & Bluto's Bilge-Rat Barges

You may get spritzed a bit on the *Jurassic Park River Adventure* and on *Dudley Do-Right's* flume ride, but for a really good soaking, you have to come to Sweet Haven, home to Popeye, Olive Oyl, and the gang. The barges of the name are actually circular, 12-passenger rubber rafts that twirl and dip along a twisting, rapid-strewn watercourse.

Just as Dudley has his Snidely, Popeye has Bluto. Their lifelong enmity and rivalry for the affection of Miss Olive form the basis for the theme-ing on this ride, which involves Olive, Wimpy, Poopdeck Pappy, and all the rest. Riders are sure to get hosed by the little devils (actually someone else's kids) manning the water cannons on the nearby *Me Ship, The Olive* (see below), before being swept into an octopus grotto where an eight-armed beast holds Popeye in its tentacled grip, preventing him from reaching his life-saving spinach. Before it's all over the hapless rafts have been spun into a fully operational boat wash, which is just like a car wash except it's for boats. This is the ride to take at the hottest, stickiest part of the day.

## Me Ship, The Olive

Resist the temptation to come here after the raft ride and throttle the little darlings who were squirting you with the water cannons. Instead let the kids loose in this three-story interactive play area representing the ship Popeye has named after his one true love. There's something for kids of all ages here. Wee ones can play in Swee' Pea's Playpen while their older siblings head for the Cargo Crane to soak *Bilge-Rat Barge* riders. Bells, whistles, and pipe organs, all of which can be operated by the kids, create a merry cacophony that is the perfect soundtrack for this attraction.

# Comic Strip Lane

This is a short street of shops and restaurants, including those described below, that is an attraction in itself. Nearly 80 comic strip characters call this colorful neighborhood home, including Beetle Bailey (on furlough from Camp Swampy no doubt), Hagar the Horrible, and Krazy Kat.

The concept makes for all sorts of serendipitous juxtapositions. Hagar's boat hangs over a waterfall that falls into a big pipe that bubbles up across the way at a dog fountain where all the dogs from the various comic strips hang out.

This is one place where it will pay to pay attention to the music. Like other areas of the park, this one has its own original soundtrack. What's special here is that, as you stroll along, the melody you hear changes to reflect the interpretation given it by the characters you meet. So when you pass Betty Boop, you hear Betty's version of the melody.

# Theater of the Islands

This 2,000-seat auditorium houses a Broadway-style musical that showcases all the comic strip characters of Toon Lagoon in a star-studded extravaganza with the working title of "A Cartoon Circus." From time to time, other events may be staged in this flexible venue.

# Eating in Toon Lagoon

### Blondie's Deli

This one comes with a subtitle, "Home of the Dagwood." It's a sandwich of course, and for those who don't know, it's named after Blondie Bumstead's hapless hubby, who made comic strip history with his colossal, 20-slice, clear-out-the-fridge sandwich creations. The gimmick at the Deli is that you can order your Dagwood by the inch, tailoring your sandwich to your appetite.

### Cathy's Ice Cream

In the comics, Cathy is constantly worrying about her weight. She must have taken leave of her senses, not to mention her scale, when she opened this place. Or will we get lo-cal, no-fat treats here?

### Wimpy's

Popeye's pal is as closely associated with hamburgers as it's possible to be, so it's good to see him here serving up the apotheosis of the all-American burger, along with other standard diner fare.

# Marvel Super Hero Island

It's still a comic book world, but this one is considerably darker and a lot scarier than the one you just left. Here, in a glitzy but gritty cityscape that bears some resemblance to Manhattan, Good is locked in a never-ending battle with Evil.

Those from another planet may not know that Marvel is the name of a comic book company that revolutionized the industry way back in the sixties with a series of titles showcasing a bizarre array of super heroes whose psychological quirks were as intriguing as their ingeniously conceived superhuman powers. As might be expected, this cast of characters offers rich inspiration for some of the most intense thrill rides ever created.

## The Adventures of Spider-Man

Universal's publicity powerhouse trumpets this as "the next threshold attraction," the one that takes theme park entertainment to a new level, just as *Back to The Future* and *T-2* did when they opened.

Visitors step into the offices of the *Daily Bugle* only to discover that the bad guys have used an anti-gravity gun to make off with the Statue of Liberty. Since cub reporter Peter Parker and all the rest of the staff are mysteriously absent, crusty editor J. Jonah Jameson drafts his hapless guests into a civilian force with the mission of tracking down the evildoers. Guests board special vehicles and set off through the streets of New York, where they discover Spidey is already on the case. What ensues is a harrowing high-speed chase enhanced through a variety of heart-stopping special effects.

The vehicles are simulators, much like the ones in *Back To The Future*. Underneath they have six hydraulically operated stalks which can be used to simulate virtually any kind of motion. But these cars can also move through space and they do, along tracks that allow for 360 degrees of rotation. The combination of forward motion, rotation, and simulator technology will create sensations never before possible.

Further heightening the experience is the environment through which the cars move. This is the world of Marvel comics sprung vividly to life and startlingly real. At one point, Spidey himself drops onto the hood of the vehicle. But intermixed with the solid set elements are hidden, almost undetectable, screens on which three-dimensional films are projected to add an extra measure of depth and excitement: both villains and heroes seem to leap directly at you. The ride culminates with an effect that simulates a 400-foot drop through total darkness.

# Dr. Doom's Fearfall

Near the Bugle building is Doom Alley, a part of town that has been completely taken over by bad guys with names like Dr. Octopus, The Hobgoblin, and The Lizard. Here the arch-fiend Doctor Doom has secreted his Fear Sucking Machine, in which he uses innocent, unsuspecting victims (that's you in case you hadn't guessed) to create the Fear Juice with which he hopes to finally vanquish the Fantastic Four.

The payoff is a fiendish twist on the freefall rides that have long been a staple of amusement parks and which were artfully updated in Disney's *Tower of Terror*. But whereas those rides take you up slowly and drop you, Doctor Doom, in the true Universal spirit, takes things to a whole new level.

Four victims, I mean passengers, are strapped into seats in a small chamber. Only then do they notice that the room is open to the sky and only then do they learn the hideous fate Doctor Doom has in store for them. Suddenly they are shot upwards 150 feet at a force of four G's. Then, and here's where the evil Doctor outdoes himself in wickedness, instead of simply dropping back, the vehicles are zoomed downwards creating a negative nine-tenths G force. In other words, first your heart is slammed into your belly then it is lofted into your throat.

Most people scream on freefall rides but this one happens so quickly (less than 30 seconds) and registers such a shock that most riders won't remember to scream until the ride is over.

# The Incredible Hulk Coaster

In the scientific complex where Bruce Banner, aka the Incredible Hulk, has his laboratories, you can learn all about the nasty effects of over-exposure to gamma radiation. No, it's not more edutainment, it's the warm-up for another knock-your-socks-off roller coaster.

In a high-energy video pre-ride show, you learn that you can help Bruce reverse the unfortunate effects that have so complicated his life. All you have to do is climb into this little chamber which is, in fact, a 40-seat roller coaster. This is no ordinary roller coaster, however, where you have to wait agonizing seconds while the car climbs to the top of the first drop. Thanks to an energizing burst of gamma rays you are shot at one G 150 feet upwards, going from a standstill to 42 miles an hour. From there it's all downhill so to speak as you swing into a zero-G roll and speed toward the surface of the lagoon at 58 miles per hour. This is no water ride though, so you whip into a cobra roll before being lofted upwards once more through the highest (109 feet) inversion ever built. After that it's under a bridge — on which earthbound (i.e. "sane") people are enjoying your terror — through a total of seven inversions and two subterranean trenches before you come to a rest, hoping desperately that your exertions have, indeed, helped Bruce out of his pickle. Because of the gamma radiation, the tube that shoots riders skywards glows an unearthly green, making it quite spectacular at night.

# Eating in Marvel Super Hero Island

No detailed information was available at press time but one of the restaurants here will be the **Captain America Diner**, presumably serving good old-fashioned American diner fare in hopefully heroic portions. Also on the drawing board is an eatery in the same building as *Doctor Doom's Fearfall* to be called either **Café 4** or the **Fantastic Four Café**.

# CHAPTER FOUR:

# SeaWorld Orlando

I've been to Disney," people will tell you, "But y'know what I think is the best thing they've got down there in Orlando? SeaWorld!" I heard it over and over again. In a way this reaction was somewhat surprising. After all, compared to the Magic Kingdom or Universal, SeaWorld is downright modest, with only a smattering of thrill rides.

Of course, we could simply ascribe this "I-liked-Sea-World-best" attitude to one-upmanship — that quirk of human nature that makes us all want to look superior. After all, SeaWorld is educational and how much more flattering it is to depict yourself as someone who prefers educational nature shows to mindless carnival rides that merely provide "fun." I'm just enough of a cynic about human nature to give some credence to this theory.

However, I think the real reason lies elsewhere. No matter how well imagined and perfectly realized the attractions at Universal or Disney might be, the wonders on display at SeaWorld were produced by a creative intelligence of an altogether higher order. The animated robotics guys can tinker all they want and the bean-counters in Hollywood can give them ever higher budgets and they still will never produce anything that can match the awe generated by a killer whale soaring 30 feet in the air with his human trainer perched on his snout. No matter how much we are entertained by Universal and Disney, at SeaWorld we cannot help but be reminded, however subliminally, that there are wonders in our world that humankind simply cannot duplicate, let alone surpass.

It's a feeling of which many visitors probably aren't consciously aware. Even if they are, they'd probably feel a little awkward trying to express it.

But I am convinced it is there for everyone — believer, agnostic, or atheist. It's the core experience that makes SeaWorld so popular; it's the reason people will tell you they liked SeaWorld best of all. To paraphrase Joyce Kilmer's magnificent cliché about human inadequacy,

> *I think that Walt will never do*
> *A wonder greater than Shamu.*

# Before You Come

## Gathering Information

You can get up-to-date information on hours and prices by calling (407) 351-3600 and pressing "2." Between 8:00 a.m. and 8:00 p.m. you can speak to a SeaWorld representative at this number.

For the latest on SeaWorld's animals, you can check out the Anheuser-Busch Theme Parks animal information site on the World Wide Web. The address is http://www.seaworld.org For Shamu fans there is http://www.shamu.com. Another web site provides information for both SeaWorld and Busch Gardens Tampa. The address is http://www.4adventure.com.

## Doing Your Homework

There's no real necessity to "bone up" on marine mammals before coming to SeaWorld. The park itself will give you a good introduction to the subject if you half pay attention. However, it is possible that parents might want to generate some interest in their younger children who, perhaps, might not be able to fully appreciate why they should go to SeaWorld instead of spending another day with Mickey and his friends.

There have been a number of excellent videos about SeaWorld that you may be able to find in your local library or video store. Probably easier to come by will be the video of *Free Willy*, the hit movie about a boy's struggle to liberate a killer whale from an amusement park. When your children get the idea that they can meet the star of this movie (one of his cousins actually) at SeaWorld, they should become enthusiastic boosters of the visit.

# Getting There

SeaWorld is located just off I-4 on Central Florida Parkway. If you're coming from the south (i.e. traveling east on I-4) you will use Exit 27A and find yourself pointed directly towards the SeaWorld entrance, about half a mile along on your left. Because there is no exit directly to Central Florida Parkway from Westbound I-4, those coming from the north (i.e.

traveling west on I-4) must get off at Exit 28, onto the Bee Line Expressway (Route 528). Don't worry about the sign that says it's a toll road; you won't have to pay one. Take the first exit and loop around to International Drive. Turn left and proceed to Central Florida Parkway and turn right. It's all very clearly marked. As you get close to SeaWorld, tune your AM radio to 1540 for a steady stream of information about the park. This will help while away the time spent waiting in line at the parking lot.

## Arriving at SeaWorld

Parking fees are $5 for cars and $7 for RVs and trailers and are collected at toll booths a short drive from the entrance. Mimicking Disney, the SeaWorld parking lot is divided into sections named after Shamu, Captain Kidd, and other characters familiar and unknown. The lots are not huge but it's still a very good idea to jot down a note as to which section and row you're parked in. Also like Disney and Universal, you will be ushered to your space in a very efficiently controlled manner and directed to a tram that will whisk you to the main entrance. If you arrive after noon, however, you may find yourself on your own. Fortunately, the farthest row is never too far from the park perimeter. You can orient yourself by looking for the centrally located Sky Tower; it's the blue spire with the large American flag at the summit. If you arrive late and the parking lot is full, you will have to park in the area outside the toll booths. In this case, your day's parking will be free.

Once you reach the beautifully designed main entrance, you will find a group of thoughtfully shaded ticket booths where you will purchase your admission. To the left of the ticket windows are the Guest Relations window and the annual pass center. When you purchase your tickets, you will be handed a large map of the park. On the back you will find a schedule of the day's shows. In the lower right-hand corner you will find information on any special events happening that day.

*Handicapped Parking.* Several rows of extra large spaces near the main entrance are provided for the convenience of handicapped visitors. Alert the attendant to your need for handicapped parking and you will be directed accordingly.

## Opening and Closing Times

SeaWorld operates seven days a week, 365 days a year. The park opens at 9:00 a.m. and remains open until 7:00, 8:00, 9:00, or 10:00 p.m. depending on the time of year. Unlike Universal and Disney, SeaWorld does not practice soft openings. During very busy periods, they will start admitting people at 8:30, but these early arrivals are held in the entrance plaza (or "mall") just inside the gates, until the park proper opens at 9:00. By the time the last scheduled shows are starting (about 45 minutes to an hour prior to the posted closing time), most of the park's other attractions have either shut down or are in the process of doing so.

# The Price of Admission

SeaWorld has several ticket options, including some that offer admission to its sister park, Busch Gardens, in nearby Tampa. Most visitors will be looking at either a one- or two-day admission. At press time, prices (including sales tax) were as follows:

**One-Day Admission:**

| | |
|---|---|
| Adults: | $42.14 |
| Children (3 to 9): | $33.92 |
| Seniors (55+): | $32.80 |

Children under age 3 **free**.

**Two-Day Admission:**

| | |
|---|---|
| Adults: | $47.39 |
| Children & seniors: | $44.45 |

**Adventure Passport:**

(Five consecutive days at SeaWorld and Busch Gardens.)

| | |
|---|---|
| Adults: | $67.91 |
| Children & seniors: | $59.91 |

SeaWorld participates in the Orlando FlexTicket program described in *Chapter One: Introduction & Orientation.* Prices (including tax) are as follows:

**Three-Park, Seven-Day Pass** — Universal, SeaWorld, Wet 'n Wild

| | |
|---|---|
| Adults | $105.95 |
| Children (3 to 9) | $87.93 |

**Four-Park, Ten-Day Pass** — adds Busch Gardens Tampa

| | |
|---|---|
| Adults | $137.75 |
| Children (3 to 9) | $114.43 |

## Which Price Is Right?

For most people, a one-day pass will suffice, assuming that you arrive early and stay until closing. As at Universal, you can hedge your bets. That is, buy a one-day pass and if, as the day wears on, you decide that you want to return the next day, you can pay the modest additional fee for an upgrade. Of course, if you've taken my advice and come during one of Orlando's slow periods, you'll be getting your second day free.

The major advantage of taking two days to see SeaWorld is that you can adopt a much more leisurely pace than otherwise, lingering to commune with the sharks or hanging around until something interesting happens at the killer whale observation area. At SeaWorld, second day tickets, whether purchased outright or as upgrades or received free, must be used within seven days. If you'll be visiting Tampa and you have paid separately for Universal, the Adventure Passport, offering five days at SeaWorld and Busch Gardens, is a best buy.

## Annual Passes

SeaWorld has several annual pass options:

*Sea World Annual Pass:*

|          | One year | Two years |
|----------|----------|-----------|
| Adults:  | $79.50   | $105.95   |
| Children:| $68.90   | $95.35    |

*Wild Card Passes:*

(Annual Pass to both SeaWorld and Busch Gardens)

|          | One year | Two years |
|----------|----------|-----------|
| Adults:  | $127.15  | $158.95   |
| Children:| $116.55  | $148.35   |

*Wild Card Plus Passes:*

(Adds admission to Adventure Island water park in Tampa.)

|          | One year | Two years |
|----------|----------|-----------|
| Adults:  | $153.65  | $196.05   |
| Children:| $148.35  | $185.45   |

Annual passes offer unlimited admission, free parking, and an array of discounts. I have noticed that annual passes are especially popular with local residents, so much so that during periods when SeaWorld offers its discounts to Florida residents, it can take 30 to 45 minutes to have your annual pass processed.

Annual pass holders receive a 10 percent discount at SeaWorld restaurants and shops. They also get a 50 percent discount on all guided tours. As at Universal, the annual pass is a photo ID card which is checked carefully at the gate.

## Discounts

Look for dollars-off coupons in the usual tourist throwaway publications and at the guest services desk at your hotel. A typical discount is $2.50 off per person for up to six people. Steeper discounts are available from discount ticket brokers (see *Chapter One: Introduction and Orientation*). Members of AAA, AARP, and active military personnel receive a 10% discount off regular prices. The deaf, the blind, and those with mental handicaps receive a generous 50% discount.

# Buying Tickets

You can purchase your tickets when you arrive or, to save a bit of touring time, you can come by a day or two earlier, in the afternoon when the lines are nonexistent, and buy tickets for use another day. The best way to do this is to park in the lot of the Renaissance Orlando Resort across the street and walk the short distance to the SeaWorld ticket booths.

# Staying Near the Park

If SeaWorld is your primary Orlando destination, you may want to consider staying at one of the handful of hotels that are in walking distance of the front gate. Because of their proximity, none provides shuttle service. They are listed here in order of their distance from the park.

## Renaissance Orlando Resort

6677 Sea Harbor Drive
Orlando, FL 32819
(800) 468-3571; (407) 351-5555; fax (407) 351-9991

A luxury resort hotel with a huge central atrium, first-rate restaurants, and many amenities.

*Price Range:*   $$$ - $$$$
*Amenities:*   Olympic-size pool, tennis, volleyball, health club, three restaurants, two lounges, 24-hour room service
*Walk to Park:* 5 minutes

## Sheraton World Resort

10100 International Drive
Orlando, FL 32821-8095
(800) 327-0363; (407) 352-1100; fax (407) 352-3679

An upscale motel that caters to conventioneers.

*Price Range:*   $$ - $$$
*Amenities:*   Three heated pools, two kiddie pools, lighted tennis, mini-golf, fitness center, restaurant, lounge, poolside bar
*Walk to Park:* 5 to 10 minutes

## Hawthorn Suites Hotel

6435 Westwood Boulevard
Orlando, FL 32821
(800) 527-1133; (407) 351-6600; fax (407) 351-1977

All-suite format with kitchenettes in every room.

*Price Range:* $$ - $$$
*Amenities:* Free buffet breakfast, large heated pool, kiddie pool, poolside BBQ grills, children's
play area, convenience store
*Walk to Park:* 10 to 15 minutes

## Dining at SeaWorld

Dining at SeaWorld is almost entirely of the fast-food variety. There is only one full-service restaurant. The good news, however, is that the food at the Bimini Bay Cafe (and all the other eateries for that matter) is well above average. In fact, SeaWorld's executive chef, David Nina, was named Florida's "seafood chef of the year" in 1994 and picked as the chef of the year in 1995 by the American Culinary Federation's local chapter. On top of that, the prices at all of SeaWorld's eateries are less than those you'll encounter at other area theme parks. Their lower prices on soft drinks will be especially appreciated by hard-pressed parents who felt ripped off at Universal and Disney World.

There is beer to be had, as you might expect at a park owned by Anheuser-Busch, but it seems less omnipresent than it does at Universal. Indeed, most of the fast-food establishments are alcohol-free. On the other hand, you can get a mixed drink here, at the outdoor Sunset Beach Tiki Bar next to the Bimini Bay Cafe, which you can't at Universal.

SeaWorld also lets you eat while waiting for or watching the big outdoor stadium shows; there are even snack bars (offering ice cream bars and nachos) conveniently located just near the entrances to the stands. Not all eating establishments are open throughout the park's operating hours. A "Dining Guide," listing the various restaurants, their food specialties, and operating hours, is available at the Information Desk in the Entrance Plaza.

## Shopping at SeaWorld

Of course, SeaWorld is dotted with strategically located gift and souvenir shops ready to help you lessen the heavy load in your wallet. Inveterate shoppers can soothe their conscience with the thought that a percentage of the money they drop at SeaWorld goes towards helping rescue and care for stranded sea mammals.

Most of the wares on display are of the standard tourist variety but some items deserve special mention. Many of SeaWorld's shops offer some very attractive figurines and small sculptures. They range from quite small objects suitable for a bric-a-brac shelf to fairly large pieces (with fairly large price tags) that are surely displayed with pride by those who buy them. Prices range from under $20 to well over $2,000. If you're in the market for a special gift for a friend or relative who collects this sort of *objet*, or are a collector yourself, you will want to give these items more than a cursory look.

# Good Things to Know About ...

## Access for the Disabled

All parts of SeaWorld are accessible to disabled guests and all the stadium shows have sections set aside for those in wheelchairs. These are some of the best seats in the house. Wheelchairs are available for rent at $6 per day. Electric carts are $30 per day.

## Babies

Little ones under three are admitted free and dolphin-shaped strollers are available for rent if you don't have your own. Single strollers are $7 for the day, double strollers are $13. There are also diaper changing stations in all the major restrooms (men's and women's). In addition, there are "non-gender changing areas" at *Wild Arctic*, the Friends of the Wild shop, and the *Anheuser-Busch Hospitality Center* where you will find diaper vending machines. There is also a nursing area near the Friends of the Wild shop.

## Drinking

As a reminder, the legal drinking age in Florida is 21 and photo IDs will be requested if there is the slightest doubt. Again, try to feel flattered rather than annoyed. Taking alcoholic beverages through the turnstiles as you leave the park is not allowed.

## Education Staff

It's hard to say too much in praise of the education staff at SeaWorld. There are some 60 employees whose job it is to hang around and answer your questions. They are invariably friendly, enthusiastic, and more than happy to share their considerable knowledge. Don't be shy. Taking advantage of this wonderful human resource will immeasurably increase the enjoyment and value of your visit to SeaWorld. Just look for the word "Education" on the employee's name tag. In fact, even employees who are not with the Education Department will likely have the answer to your question.

## Emergencies

As a general rule, the moment something goes amiss speak with the nearest SeaWorld employee. They will contact security or medical assistance and get the ball rolling towards a solution. There is a first aid station in a tent behind *Stingray Lagoon* in the North End of the park and another near *Shamu's Happy Harbor* in the South End.

## Feeding Times

Feeding time is an especially interesting time to visit any of the aquatic habitats. Unfortunately, there is no rigid schedule. By varying feeding times, the trainers more closely approximate the animals' experience in the wild and avoid, to some extent, the repetitive behaviors that characterize many animals in captivity. However, you can simply ask one of the education staff at the exhibit when the animals will next be fed. If your schedule permits, I would recommend returning for this enjoyable spectacle.

Of course, at some exhibits — the dolphins, stingrays, and sea lions — you can feed the animals yourself for a small fee!

## Leaving the Park

You can leave the park at any time and be readmitted free the same day. Just have your hand stamped with a fluorescent symbol on the way out; when you come back, look for the "same day reentry" line and pass your hand under the ultraviolet lamp.

## Money

There is an ATM conveniently located in the entrance area, just to the left of the ticket booths. It it is connected to the Plus, Cirrus, and Honor networks. A foreign currency exchange window is located just inside the gates.

## Pets

If you have pets, the toll booth attendant will direct you to the SeaWorld Pet Care facility, very near the main entrance, where Tabby and Bowser can wait for you in air-conditioned comfort. The fee is $4 per pet and you must supply pet food.

## Sea Gulls

If you visit from November to February, you will be joined in the park by hordes of sea gulls. These are the New Yorkers of the avian world — loud, boisterous, often rude, but very clever and with the kind of raffish personality that can be endearing. Sea gull season brings with it the increased danger of aerial bombardment, which is unpleasant but not fatal. More amusing (if you're the observer rather than the victim) are the concerted attacks the gulls make on ice cream cones.

## Smoking

Smoking is prohibited in all show and exhibit areas. The Bimini Bay Cafe has a smoking section. Most other restaurants have ample outdoor areas for smokers.

## Special Diets

Vegetarians can stop at the information counter and request the Food Services staff's list of meatless dishes and the restaurants that serve them. A similar list of low-fat selections and other dietary notes is available from the same source.

## Splash Zones

All of the stadium shows give the adventuresome the opportunity to get wet — in some cases *very* wet. One advantage of the splash zones is that they are some of the best seats at SeaWorld. But the threat is very, very real.

I am a believer in splash zones for those who come prepared. Those inexpensive rain ponchos that are sold at every major park will hold the damage to a minimum (although there is probably no real way to guard against a direct hit from Shamu!). Kids, especially young boys, will enjoy the exquisite machismo of getting thoroughly soaked.

One word of warning: In the cooler periods of the year, a full soaking will be extremely uncomfortable, and may be courting a cold, or worse. Bring a big towel and a change of clothes, or be prepared to shell out for new duds at the SeaWorld shops.

# Sailing the Sea: Your Day at SeaWorld

SeaWorld can be seen quite comfortably in a single day, without rushing madly around or otherwise driving yourself crazy. This is especially true if you've arrived during one of Orlando's slack periods. But even during the most crowded times, SeaWorld is still more manageable than other parks in the area.

# When's the Best Time to Come?

I have just mentioned the wisdom of arriving during the off-season. Crowds in January are negligible and the weather cool to moderate, perfect viewing conditions for the outdoor shows. Regardless of the time of year you visit, I would recommend arriving early and planning to stay until the park closes. There are two reasons for this. Early arrivals breeze right in; as the morning wears on, the lines at the ticket booths lengthen. As for staying 'til the bitter end, some of the best shows (including what is arguably the *best* show) are only performed in the hour before closing. Compensate for the long day with a leisurely lunch.

## What to Expect

SeaWorld is not a large park, but its comfortable layout and the large Bayside Lagoon at its center make it seem larger than it is. Much of the North End of the park is lushly landscaped with large shady trees and bird-filled pools along the walkways. The South End, on the other side of the Lagoon, is open and airy with a gently rolling landscape. In look and feel, it is quite a contrast to the more tightly crammed spaces of the Magic Kingdom and Universal Studios. Many parts of SeaWorld have the feel of a particularly gracious public park or botanical garden.

One of SeaWorld's key differentiators is the fact that the vast majority of its attractions are either shows that take place in large, sometimes huge, outdoor auditoriums or "continuous viewing" exhibits through which people pass pretty much at their own pace. My observation is that most people pass through pretty quickly so even if there's a line, the wait won't be unbearable. Once inside you can take your own sweet time.

Here, briefly, are the different kinds of attractions at SeaWorld:

*Rides.* There are just two "rides" at SeaWorld but they are doozies.

*Outdoor Auditorium Shows.* These are SeaWorld's primo attractions — Shamu, the sea lions, the dolphins, the water ski show, and some lesser events. There are plenty of seats for these shows (anywhere from 2,400 to 5,500), but even in slower periods they fill up, which should tell you something about how good the shows are. It is possible to enter these auditoriums after the show has begun if they are not full.

*Indoor Theater Shows.* Some shows take place indoors, in darkened theaters. None of them involves sea mammals and none of them falls into the must-see category. When these shows begin, the doors close and latecomers must wait for the next performance. It's also difficult to leave these shows in the middle.

*Aquatic Habitats.* This is SeaWorld's term for its continuous viewing exhibits of live marine animals. The habitats range from huge tanks like those you may have seen at aquariums to elaborate stage sets the likes of which I can guarantee you've never seen before.

# Catch of the Day

If you had very little time to spend at SeaWorld, I would venture to suggest that you could see just a handful of attractions and still feel you got your money's worth — if you picked the right ones. Here, then, is my list of the very best that SeaWorld has to offer:

The three major open-air animal shows — **Shamu, Clyde & Seamore**, and **Key West Dolphin Fest** — are the heart and soul of SeaWorld. Anyone missing these should have his or her head examined.

Close behind are the major "aquatic habitats" — **Wild Arctic** (and the ride that introduces the experience), **Terrors of the Deep, Key West at SeaWorld**, and **Manatees: the Last Generation?**. I have omitted *Pacific Point Preserve* and *Penguin Encounter* (both marvelous) only because you are likely to see their close equivalents elsewhere.

For thrill seekers, there is **Journey to Atlantis**. Finally, there is the water ski show, **The Intensity Games**, worth a visit for the sheer athleticism and excitement of the amazing stunts.

# The One-Day Stay

1. Get up early, but not as early as you would if you were heading for Disney or Universal. Remember, when SeaWorld says it opens at 9, it means it. Get there a little earlier perhaps, but no need to kill yourself.

2. After purchasing your tickets and entering the park, thrill seekers and ride freaks should head immediately to *Journey to Atlantis*. (Bear left after the entrance mall and follow the signs and the running kids.) Then plan on doing *Wild Arctic* and its exciting ride later in the day, preferably during a Shamu show when the lines for *Wild Arctic* tend to thin out.

If, for one reason or another you are taking a pass on *Journey to Atlantis*, proceed immediately to *Wild Arctic*. (Just keep bearing right until you see the Lagoon and circle it in a counterclockwise direction.) If you're not interested in taking the ride, the line for the stationary version is always a good deal shorter, so coming later may be okay. Also, if you'd like to skip the ride portion altogether, it is possible to slip quietly in through the exit in the gift shop and just see the animals.

3. Now's the time to review the schedule printed on the back of the map you got when you entered. First, check the times of the "big three" shows — Shamu, Clyde & Seamore, and the dolphins. Whatever you do, don't miss these. Don't try to see two shows that start less than an hour apart. Yes, it can be done but you will be making sacrifices.

Instead, schedule your day so you can arrive at the stadium about 20 minutes before show time, perhaps longer during busier seasons. That way you can get a good seat, like dead center for Shamu or in a splash zone for the kids. There is always some sort of pre-show entertainment starting 10 or 15 minutes before the show. It's always fun and, in the case of the warm-up to the sea lion show, often hilarious.

Arriving extra early for the water ski show is less imperative but a good idea if you really like this kind of show.

4. Use your time between shows to visit the aquatic habitats. Use the descriptions in the next section and geographical proximity to guide your choices. For example, you can leave the dolphin show and segue right into the manatee exhibit. Or you can visit the penguins just before seeing *Clyde & Seamore* and visit *Terrors of the Deep* immediately after.

5. If you have kids with you, you will miss *Shamu's Happy Harbor* at your peril. Adults, of course, can give it a miss.

6. Fill in the rest of the day with the lesser attractions or return visits to habitats you particularly enjoyed. In my opinion, several of the non-animal shows and attractions can be missed altogether with little sacrifice. If your time is *really* limited (i.e. you got to the park late), I would strongly urge you to take my advice. You can always come back another day and prove me wrong.

7. If you stay until the end, as I recommend, you will not want to miss *Shamu Rocks America* (otherwise what's the point of staying?). Then you might as well see *Red, Bright and Blue Spectacular* if only because it's on your way to the exit.

This plan should allow you to see everything you truly want to see in one day and maybe even some things you wished you hadn't bothered with.

## The Two-Day Stay

If you have the luxury of spending two days visiting SeaWorld, I would recommend relaxing your pace, perhaps leaving the park early on one day to freshen up and catch a dinner show elsewhere. With two days, even a very relaxed pace should allow you to see everything in the park, several of them more than once.

Another strategy to adopt is to use the first day to concentrate on the shows and the second day to concentrate on the rides, the animal habitats and, perhaps, take a guided tour or two.

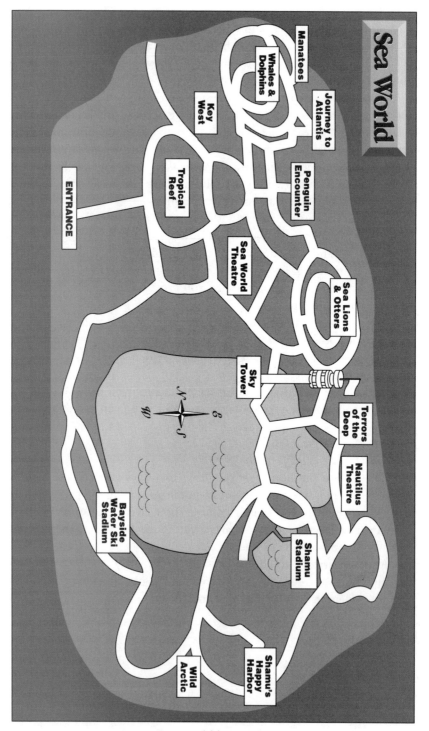

# THE NORTH END

SeaWorld is not neatly divided into "islands" (as is Islands of Adventure) or "sets" (as is Universal Studios), although the new Key West area is a step in that direction. The only geographically convenient division of the park is provided by Bayside Lagoon. If you look at the map you collected on arriving at the park, you will notice that the vertical line formed by the *Sky Tower* effectively divides the park in half: the northern half ("The North End") is to the left of the Tower; the Lagoon and the southern half ("The South End") are to the right. By the way, although Bayside Lagoon is the official name of SeaWorld's artificial lake, many SeaWorld employees have never heard the term used.

For the purposes of describing the attractions at SeaWorld I have adopted this North End/South End division. Please remember that this is *my* terminology and not SeaWorld's. If you stop a SeaWorld employee and ask, "How do I get to the North?" you may be told to get on a plane and fly to Philadelphia.

The layout and open landscaping of the southern half, combined with the sheer size of the stadiums located there, make getting your bearings relatively easy. In the northern half, however, the layout and lusher landscaping, while pleasing to the eye, can be confusing. When traveling from Point A to Point B in the northern half of the park, use the map to get you started in the right general direction. Then rely on the directional signs, which are posted at nearly every turning, to guide you to your destination.

Often, you will be able to see the distinctive blue spire of the *Sky Tower* through the trees; use it to orient yourself. In almost every case, the fastest route between the northern and southern halves of the park will be via the wooden walkway across the Lagoon.

I begin with the northern half of the park for the simple reason that this is where you enter the park past the Shamu lighthouse in the artificial harbor that graces the airy entrance area. I describe the attractions in geographical, rather than thematic order. I begin with the *Tropical Reef* exhibit, the back of which you see past the flamingos as you walk through the entrance plaza into the park. From there I proceed in a roughly clockwise direction.

## Tropical Reef

| | |
|---|---|
| *Rating:* | ★ ★ ★ |
| *Type:* | Aquatic habitat |
| *Time:* | Continuous viewing |
| *Kelly says:* | Best for fish lovers |

The *Tropical Reef* is one of SeaWorld's older aquatic habitats and suffers, perhaps, in comparison to the newer and flashier attractions. Nonetheless, it has a quiet beauty of its own and will reward those patient enough to look closely and read the back-lit identification signs.

The centerpiece of the exhibit is a 120,000-gallon circular tank containing a remarkable recreation of a Pacific coral reef. Here a profusion of tropical fish swim languidly, their names almost as colorful as their iridescent markings. There is a bewildering array of angelfish — the six-banded, the Cortez, the yellowtail, the clarion, and others. Many species sport bizarre names like the hu-mu trigger, Clark's clownfish, the singular bannerfish, the Achilles tang, and the purple square coral whose name derives from the almost perfectly formed purple square on its pinkish flank. The reef itself is entirely artificial (although it's hard to believe); the only real things in the water are the fish themselves.

Smaller tanks contain fish from other settings, including a mammoth 15-pound American lobster from the waters of New England. One of the more intriguing species, swimming in a darkened tank, is the luminescent pinecone fish which sports a bright green spot used to send a fishy sort of Morse code to others of its species.

Across from the entrance to the *Tropical Reef* is the **Tide Pool** exhibit, a shallow, open tank that mimics the rocky waters at the ocean's edge. Blue, buoy-shaped, glass-bottomed contraptions let you peer beneath the water for a closer look at starfish, anemones, and other creatures who depend on the tides to bring their meals.

# Key West at SeaWorld

*Key West at SeaWorld* is not so much an attraction as a collection of related attractions wrapped in a single theme. Shades of Disney World! The attractions here are aquatic habitats featuring the denizens of warmer waters and the theme, of course, is the casual sophistication and good times atmosphere for which Key West has become famous. On both scores, SeaWorld acquits itself admirably.

## Turtle Point

| | |
|---|---|
| *Rating:* | ★ ★ ★ |
| *Type:* | Aquatic habitat |
| *Time:* | Continuous viewing |
| *Kelly says:* | Best when a staffer is present |

Turtle Point is small by SeaWorld standards, a shallow sea water pool fringed by white sand beaches. It is home to four species — loggerhead, Kemp's ridley, hawksbill, and green sea turtles.

Turtles, it must be said, are not the most lively creatures SeaWorld has on display. No leaps and twirls here. So, for most folks, this habitat will warrant no more than a quick look. Fortunately, SeaWorld staffers are often hanging out by the pool ready to answer questions. When a group of people gathers and starts exercising their curiosity, a visit to *Turtle Point* becomes much more interesting.

## Stingray Lagoon

| | |
|---|---|
| *Rating:* | ★ ★ ★ ★ |
| *Type:* | Aquatic habitat |
| *Time:* | Continuous viewing |
| *Kelly says:* | Your best shot at touching a SeaWorld critter |

Under a shading roof lies a long, shallow pool, its edge raised to waist height. In the pool, scores of stingrays swim lazily in a counter-clockwise direction. They may look scary, but they are remarkably gentle creatures that will tolerate being petted (they feel a bit like slimy felt) and will always appreciate a free handout. Small trays of tiny fish called silversides can be purchased for $1.

Once again, SeaWorld education staffers make regular appearances here, providing a steady stream of information about these fascinating creatures. They are always ready to answer any questions you might have.

Thanks to the accessibility of the stingrays, this is a very popular attraction. If the pool edge is packed (as it well might be), be patient. Eventually you will be able to make your way to pool's edge where your patience is sure to be rewarded.

## Dolphin Cove

| | |
|---|---|
| *Rating:* | ★ ★ ★ ★ + |
| *Type:* | Aquatic habitat |
| *Time:* | Continuous viewing |
| *Kelly says:* | A spectacular SeaWorld habitat |

SeaWorld has moved its old dolphin petting pool to Key West and placed these delightful creatures in a home befitting their grace and charm. (The old facility now serves as a dolphin nursery.) If you liked the old pool, you will love the new one.

This extensive habitat allows petting and feeding on one side; on the other is a raised viewing platform, under which is an underwater viewing area. This underwater observation post is the highlight of the new habitat and, not incidentally, a wonderful place to wait out those afternoon summer thunderstorms for which Orlando is famous.

Dolphin feeding is carried out by paying customers. A small tray of smelt-like fish is $1 and there is a two-tray limit per person. Having fish to offer will definitely increase your chances of touching a dolphin, although they will occasionally swim close enough to the edge to allow a foodless hand to sweep along their flanks. If touching a dolphin is a priority for you or your child, I would advise checking out feeding times and arriving a bit early to get on line for food. Otherwise, there is a good chance you will be disappointed.

While touching these cousins of Flipper seems to be the first order of business for most visitors, you should not overlook the underwater viewing area (as many people obviously do). It offers a perspective on these graceful beasts that you just don't get from above. It will also give you a deeper appreciation of the skill and craft that went into designing the reef-like pool in which the dolphins live. To get there from the petting and feeding area, walk around the pool to your left.

As at all the habitats, SeaWorld staffers make occasional educational presentations. There is usually a staffer sitting on a life guard's raised chair on the beach across from the petting area. Feel free to hail him or her from the sidelines if you have any questions.

# Entertainment at Key West

*Rating:*    ★ ★ ★ ★
*Type:*      Smorgasbord of live street performers
*Time:*      Irregular and unpredictable
*Kelly says:*  Great fun

Part of the Key West theme is a steady stream of live entertainment. At its most formal, it takes the form of live musical sets performed in a gazebo by Captain Pete's Island Eats, across from *Stingray Lagoon.* The music, light and easy, has an island slant to it, with Beach Boys and calypso standards much in evidence.

Outside the Coconut Bay Trader shop, a small, open-air performance area plays host to fire-eaters, jugglers, and wire walkers, who sometimes may be the same person. At other places in the Key West area, you may encounter a comic prestidigitator luring you with card tricks or a unicyclist juggling. All of these performers observe the traditions of street performance. That is, they keep up a steady stream of amusing patter and shamelessly solicit applause and praise from the crowd. They also make effective use of pint-sized "volunteers" from the audience. If you enjoy the conventions of street performance, you are not likely to be disappointed here.

Performances take place on a somewhat irregular basis, more frequently in the afternoon hours. There is no posted schedule. However, there is a **Sunset Celebration** every day during which all of Key West's performers will be holding forth. Sunset time should be listed on the map and entertainment schedule you picked up at the park entrance.

# Key West Dolphin Fest (at Whale & Dolphin Stadium)

*Rating:* ★ ★ ★ ★
*Type:* Live water show with dolphins
*Time:* 25 minutes
*Kelly says:* A crowd-pleaser

This show, which rounds out the Key West experience, is Shamu in miniature. Instead of giant killer whales we have the far more approachable Atlantic bottlenosed dolphins, familiar to generations of TV viewers from the *Flipper* show. The setting is also homier. Instead of the high-tech setting of Shamu Stadium, we have a smaller pool and a warm looking stage set, dominated by a lighthouse and looking rather like a cross between New England and the Florida Keys.

The Key West flavor extends to the pre-show entertainment by a singer who turns out to be the show's host. One of the nicest touches of this show is the way it uses its audience volunteer — a four- or five-year-old, pre-selected before the show starts and waiting on the porch of a little house on the set. The lucky child gets to pet a dolphin, feed it, and give it some simple hand signals. The child is also invited to leap into the pool, where the dolphin will pick him (or her) up and carry him around the pool as he waves to the crowd. The audience knows it's a joke but, of course, the kid doesn't, and some kids show a remarkable eagerness to dive right in.

There is the usual deft mix of conservation education and entertainment here, although the accent is definitely on the graceful athletic agility of these most charming of marine mammals. At one point, a dolphin leaps a seemingly impossible 30 feet out of the water and over a rope. Especially lovely is a behavior in which the dolphins rise high out of the water and seem to walk across the surface on their tails.

Making a brief appearance in the show are the pseudorcas or "false killer whales," Shadow and Streak. Of course, by this time we're Shamu experts, so it's a bit difficult to see how anyone could confuse these animals for killer whales. In any event, they do a few leaps, making for a satisfying cameo appearance.

*Tip:* To reach the *Manatees: The Last Generation?* exhibit after the show, walk down the steps, toward the stage, and exit to your right, then bear left. To reach *Key West at SeaWorld,* walk toward the stage and exit to the left.

# Manatees: The Last Generation?

| | |
|---|---|
| *Rating:* | ★ ★ ★ ★ ★ |
| *Type:* | Aquatic habitat |
| *Time:* | 20 to 30 minutes |
| *Kelly says:* | For everyone in the family |

You don't expect a natural history exhibit to pack an emotional wallop, but this one sure does — and does it very deftly. It is unlikely that anyone in your family will emerge from this experience unaffected.

The manatee is a large, slow-moving marine mammal that favors the shallow brackish waterways along the Florida coast, the very same areas that have become a recreational paradise for boaters and fishermen. As man's presence in their habitat has increased, the manatees' numbers have dwindled. A sign in the entrance to this exhibit informs us that there are only about 2,000 manatees left in Florida and that about 10 percent of this number die each year. Far fewer are born. It doesn't take a mathematical genius to figure out that at this rate the manatee will be extinct (in the wild, at least) in the very near future.

The message takes on an additional poignancy when we realize that all of the small manatees in the exhibit are orphans and that some of the larger animals have been grievously wounded by their encounters with civilization. One has lost most of its tail, another a front flipper. One of the themes of this exhibit is SeaWorld's on-going rescue efforts of manatees and other marine mammals. On video, we see a seriously wounded adult nursed back to health and released back into the wild. The news that at least one released manatee has reproduced in the wild cheers us like a major victory.

After viewing the manatees from above — in a pool that recreates a coastal wetland, with egrets and ibises looking on — we pass into a circular theater for a short and highly effective film containing a plea for conservation and protection of the manatee. From there, we pass into the underwater viewing area where the majesty and fragility of this odd beast become even more apparent. Their slow, graceful movements and their rather goofy faces make the manatee instantly appealing. The aquatic setting is lovely too, shared as it is by a variety of native fish. There are glistening tarpon here and a variety of gar, including one large specimen of the alligator gar, a large black beast that hovers just under the surface, the reasons for its name instantly apparent. In an interesting bit of verisimilitude, the pool contains tilapia, a fish that is not a native but imported from Africa. It competes with and threatens some native species.

Interactive touch-screen video monitors provide a self-guided wealth of additional information about manatees and the problems they face from habitat destruction and pollution. Staffers from SeaWorld's education center stroll the viewing area ready to answer your questions.

I found this a profoundly moving experience and one to which I returned eagerly. As you leave, you can pick up more information about how to be a responsible boater, diver, and snorkeler in manatee areas. You will also be challenged to make a personal commitment to help the manatee. What will *you* do?

*Photo Op:* As you leave the exhibit, look for the sculpture of the manatee cow and her calf floating artfully above the pavement. It makes an excellent backdrop for a family photograph.

## Journey to Atlantis

| | |
|---|---|
| *Rating:* | ★ ★ ★ ★ |
| *Type:* | Combination flume ride and roller coaster |
| *Time:* | About 6 minutes |
| *Kelly says:* | Wet *and* wild |

It just goes to show you: always heed the warnings of crusty old Greek fishermen, no matter how crazy they seem. Of course, the tourist hordes ignore Stavros's sage advice and set sail on a tour of the ancient city of Atlantis which has mysteriously risen from the Aegean.

Rising some 10 stories, Atlantis looks gaudily out of place at Sea-World, but it sure looks pretty in the golden glow of the setting sun. But it's not the architecture that draws us here. It's the dizzyingly steep water flume emerging from the city walls and the happy screams of those plunging down it to a watery splashdown. Wend your way through the Greek-village-themed waiting line and be entertained by the news coverage of this eerie phenomenon as you wait for your boat.

The voyage gets off to a peaceful start, but after a benign and quite lovely interlude, the boat is seized by the evil Allura, who I gather is a vengeful ancient spirit of some sort. You are winched higher and higher before being sent on a hair-raising journey that combines the scariest elements of a flume ride and a roller coaster. It's a nifty engineering feat but most people probably won't care as they plunge down the 60-foot flume into a tidal wave of water. Another slow ascent gives you a chance to catch your breath before you zip through a fiendishly hidden mini roller coaster to another splashdown, as Allura cackles gleefully. It's all over quickly — too quickly for my taste — but you can always head immediately for the end of the inevitably long line for another go.

*Tip:* This is a *very* wet ride, especially if you are in the front row of the eight-passenger boat that serves as the ride vehicle. An inexpensive poncho (which you can get at any of the theme parks) provides pretty good protection. Expensive cameras and other items that might not survive a soaking can be checked as you enter the boat, but they are placed in unlocked lockers and no guarantees are provided. Pay lockers are available near the entrance to the waiting line.

As you exit the ride, don't miss the lovely **Jewels of the Sea** aquarium, just off the inevitable gift shop. Hammerhead sharks swim above you in a domed aquarium, while stingrays and angelfish inhabit the aquarium beneath your feet. Around the walls, don't miss the sea nettle jellyfish which glow enchantingly when you press the light button. Just outside the aquarium and gift shop, playful hidden fountains await to soak the unwary.

*Photo Op:* Just outside the Jewels of the Sea aquarium is a plaza with a splendid view of the 60-foot flume plunge. If you don't want to take your own pictures, shots of every boatload of happily terrified cruisers are on sale at the ride exit.

## Penguin Encounter

| | |
|---|---|
| *Rating:* | ★ ★ ★ ★ |
| *Type:* | Aquatic habitat |
| *Time:* | Continuous viewing (5 to 10 minutes) |
| *Kelly says:* | Kids love this one |

This is the only exhibit at SeaWorld that you smell first. It hits you the moment you enter but, for some reason, you get used to it very quickly. Soon you are facing a long glass wall behind which is a charming Antarctic diorama packed with penguins. If you bear to the right as you enter, you are funneled onto a moving conveyor belt that takes you at a steady pace past the viewing area; bearing to the left takes you to a slightly raised, and stationary, viewing area. Don't worry if you get on the conveyor belt and discover you want to dawdle; you can get back to the stationary section at the other end.

As you ride the conveyor, water level is about at chest level, so you get an excellent view of the underwater antics of these remarkable birds as they almost literally "fly" through the water. On land, their movements are considerably less graceful, but their slow waddling has its own kind of grace, especially in the case of the larger emperor penguins with their yellow-accented faces. Overhead, artificial snow sprinkles down from hatches in the roof. The water temperature, an electronic readout informs us, is 45 degrees Fahrenheit, while the air temperature is maintained at 34 degrees. Chilly for us, perhaps, but these highly adapted creatures are used to a much deeper freeze, as we learn in the Learning Center immediately past the penguins.

Here, interactive teaching aids provide a wealth of additional information about gentoos, rockhoppers, and chinstraps for the curious. Here, too, you can watch informative videos about the hand-rearing of penguins and how they molt, the Antarctic environment and penguin predators, and Isla Noir, a Chilean island that is especially popular with penguins.

Just past the Learning Center is a smaller habitat featuring alcids, a group of birds, including the puffins and murres, that is the northern equivalent of the penguin. Unlike their Antarctic cousins, these birds fly in the air as well as beneath the sea. Like the penguin exhibit, the alcid viewing area is equally divided between land and sea and, if you're in luck, you will see murres "flying" to the bottom to scavenge smelt.

As you leave the exhibit, you will have an opportunity to circle back to the penguin viewing area for another look if you wish.

## Pacific Point Preserve

*Rating:*  ★ ★ ★ ★
*Type:*     Outdoor aquatic habitat
*Time:*     Continuous viewing
*Kelly says:*   Don't miss feeding the sea lions

Over 50 sea lions roar and bark with delight in this two-and-a-half - acre, open-air, sunken habitat. SeaWorld's design team traveled to the Pacific Northwest to take molds of the rock outcroppings along the coast to build this remarkable re-creation. Adding to the verisimilitude is a wave machine, similar to those used in the water theme parks, that creates waves of anywhere from a few inches to two feet in height. The viewing area extends entirely around the exhibit, and while the sea lions (and a smaller number of harbor seals) are safely out of reach, it's almost as if you can touch them.

But if you can't pet them, you can feed them. Eight hundred to a thousand pounds of capelin (a variety of smelt imported from Iceland) are set aside each day for sale to the public. You get just two six-inch capelin for a dollar and they will very quickly disappear down a sea lion's gullet. It's all great fun and, if you aren't careful, you can very quickly squander your lunch money. The sea lions, for their part, have learned how to part you from your smelt and will bark furiously and even leap decoratively up onto the edge of the pool until their hunger is satisfied, which it never is. Fortunately, watching other people feed the sea lions is almost as entertaining as doing it yourself. The feeding stations are open continuously and it is only on extremely crowded days that the allotted ration of capelin is sold out before closing time.

While their feeding behavior might lead you to believe these animals are tame, they are not. The sea lions you see perform in the

*Clyde & Seamore* show just around the corner live separately from their cousins in *Pacific Point.* They have been trained for years and habituated to interacting with humans. The animals in *Pacific Point Preserve* are wild and like all wild animals unpredictable. In other words, don't dangle little Susie over the edge to get her within smelt-tossing range.

*Tip:* You might want to ask someone on the education staff when the main feeding will take place that day. While the public certainly helps with the feeding, the staff has to make sure that their charges are adequately fed. They do this by serving up fish by the bucketful at least once a day. This is a highly entertaining ritual so it's worthwhile to check the schedule. Also, the handlers have to hand-feed some of the older sea lions and seals who don't compete well for food with their younger rivals. You and your kids will undoubtedly find this part of the feeding particularly touching.

# Clyde & Seamore Take Pirate Island (at Sea Lion & Otter Stadium)

| | |
|---|---|
| *Rating:* | ★ ★ ★ ★ |
| *Type:* | Live water show with sea lions, otters, and walruses. |
| *Time:* | 25 minutes |
| *Kelly says:* | The funniest show at SeaWorld |

Forget about education. This one's all about high spirits and low humor and it's a sure-fire crowd pleaser. Clyde and Seamore are sea lion versions of Laurel and Hardy, or Ralph Kramden and Ed Norton, or maybe two of the Three Stooges. In any event, they're bumblers.

There's a plot about a search for gold (and fresh fish), a treacherous otter, and (of course) pirates, but it's almost beside the point. The real point of this show is watching Clyde and Seamore cavort up, down, and around the multi-level set and into and out of the pool that rings the lip of the stage. The humor is broad and the little kids love it. One thing that makes the show such a hoot is the slapdash way in which the human performers carry it off, bloopers and all. Some of the gaffes are due to the unpredictability of the animals but other boo-boos seem to be written into the script, although few will suspect as much unless they see the show several times.

If you are lucky, you might get to see some walruses make a cameo appearance. Walruses, I am told, are nowhere near as tractable as sea lions and, given their considerable bulk and potential for wreaking havoc, they only appear when they're in the mood. Even then, they may balk at performing, just like a Hollywood star, and the trainers know better than to argue with several tons of balky blubber. As usual, a small child is summoned from the audience to help out (and shake Clyde's flipper). And, of course, there are the usual dire warnings about splash zones, although the wetness quotient is far lower here than at the Shamu show.

*Tip:* If you arrive more than about 10 minutes early, you will be entertained by "The SeaWorld Mime." If you arrive fewer than 10 minutes before show time, you may become one of his victims. This is not mime in the cutesy Marcel Marceau tradition — there's no getting trapped inside an invisible box or walking against an imaginary wind. This is mime with an attitude, that mimics, mocks, and plays pranks on the steady stream of people arriving for the show. Those familiar with the work of David Shiner, the clown prince of this genre, will know what to expect. For others, I don't want to give too much away. This is, far and away, the best of SeaWorld's pre-show entertainments. It is an attraction in its own right and not to be missed.

## Pets on Stage (at SeaWorld Theatre)
| | |
|---|---|
| *Rating:* | ★ ★ ★ + |
| *Type:* | Indoor theater show |
| *Time:* | 25 minutes |
| *Kelly says:* | A must for pet lovers |

If you saw *Animal Actors Stage* at Universal Studios, you might be tempted to skip this one. However, if you are a pet lover, you'll want to put this charming show on your list.

The SeaWorld twist here is that almost all the animals in the show were found in Central Florida animal shelters and rescued from an uncertain fate. As a result, the cast list runs heavily to cats and dogs, although there is an amusing little potbellied pig and even a mouse.

Ace trainer Joel Slaven (of *Ace Ventura: Pet Detective* fame) has done an amazing job here, especially with the cats. Not only do Slaven's pussycats do every doggie trick and do them better but there is a cat who does a tightwire act and one who bounds across the audience, jumping across a series of tiny platforms.

The pre-show warmup consists of old silent movies featuring the likes of Laurel and Hardy, making this show a pleasant break from the hot Florida sun.

## Dolphin Nursery
| | |
|---|---|
| *Rating:* | ★ ★ ★ |
| *Type:* | Small shaded outdoor pool |

*Time:*          Continuous viewing

*Kelly says:*    Not much to see but hard to resist

This is where dolphin moms get to enjoy a little maternity leave with their newborns during the bonding process. A barrier fence prevents you from getting right to the pool's edge, so at best you will just be able to glimpse the little ones as they swim by in close formation with mom.

Still, even a glimpse of a baby dolphin is a hard lure to resist and you will probably want to pause here for a look. Education staffers are on hand to answer your questions. Feedings usually take place in the morning and late afternoon, making those the best times to visit.

# Hawaiian Rhythms

*Rating:*        ★ ★ +

*Type:*          Indoor theater show

*Time:*          25 minutes

*Kelly says:*    For the easily entertained

The rhythms of the title are not just Hawaiian but also Samoan and Tahitian, at least according to the host and lead singer. Actually some of the rhythms seem to have strayed through Harlem on their way to this harmless bit of time-passing fluff.

The show takes place in the Luau Terrace, next to the Bimini Bay Cafe. A singer, backed by two electric guitars and drums, sings some songs that smack vaguely of the islands and introduces four attractive dancers who don a variety of costumes to do a variety of dances from a variety of South Seas cultures. I have no idea how authentic the dances are but strict ethnographic accuracy is hardly the point here.

The real high point of the show is the audience participation and, as always, it's a sure-fire crowd pleaser and laugh getter. Four men are selected from the audience by the dancers and put through the paces of the hula. One of them (the best or the worst?) is selected for a grand finale of hip wiggling that invariably reduces the audience to gales of laughter.

It's easy to look down your nose at a hokey show like this but very hard not to enjoy the good fun it offers. From my observation, this show is most popular with seniors and foreign tourists (who are the most eager volunteers).

# Walk-By Exhibits

In addition to the larger, more formal aquatic habitats and stadium and theater shows, SeaWorld is dotted with a number of smaller, "walk-by" exhibits, typically showcasing the birds who live by the sea. They blend in so well with the landscaping that they seem almost like set decoration, and many people simply breeze by. Most of them are to be found in the northern end of the park.

Certainly some of them, like the sand sculpture exhibits, don't deserve more than a cursory look. Others, like the flamingo exhibit, will reward those who pause for closer inspection and perhaps a photograph. These exhibits are more elaborate and more thoughtfully designed versions of what you might see at the bird house of an old-fashioned zoo. In addition to the flamingos, you will find ducks, pelicans, and spoonbills. Signs identify each species and provide interesting tidbits of information about their habitat, range, and habits.

# Eating in the North

Most of SeaWorld's eating establishments, including its sole full-service restaurant, are located in this end of the park. I will describe them geographically, beginning in the entrance plaza and then proceeding in a roughly clockwise direction.

## Polar Parlor

*What:*          Small ice cream parlor
*Where:*         In the entrance plaza
*Price Range:*   $

This compact, rather bare ice cream dispensary serves up some tasty sundaes in waffle cones (about $3). There is a small outdoor seating area. Or you can carry your sundae out into the park and take your chances with the dive-bombing sea gulls, who have obviously developed a sweet tooth.

Polar Parlor also serves up regular ice cream cones and "Shamu bars" in the $2 range, as well as soft drinks and coffee. In the early mornings, a continental breakfast is served here.

## Cypress Bakery

*What:*          Compact bakery with outdoor seating
*Where:*         In the entrance plaza
*Price Range:*   $

Cypress Bakery, a perfect choice for that missed breakfast, serves muffins, cakes, pies, pastries, and enormous cookies along with coffee, tea, and orange juice. Or try the Cypress Cooler ($2.50 or $2.95), a frosted concoction of espresso, chocolate, and milk. Seating is all al fresco at shaded tables.

# Captain Pete's Island Eats

| | |
|---|---|
| *What:* | Outdoor fast-food eatery |
| *Where:* | In Key West, near *Stingray Lagoon* |
| *Price Range:* | $ - $$ |

This walk-up, window-service fast-food joint carries off its Key West theme deftly. Spicy conch fritters and sweet coconut and pineapple fritters are $3. You can wash them down with a non-alcoholic "Frozen 'Rita" or an "Island Fruit Smoothie" in a variety of flavors ($2 each). There are also Bud, O'Doul's, and the usual range of soft drinks. On the sweeter side are funnel cakes ($2), which can be had with hot fudge or strawberry toppings for about $3. Seating is outdoors, some of it shaded, near the gazebo where the musicians play.

# Buccaneer Smokehouse

| | |
|---|---|
| *What:* | Barbecue joint |
| *Where:* | Behind SeaWorld Theatre |
| *Price Range:* | $$ |

This is the larger of two barbecue "joints" at SeaWorld and the only one serving beef. Otherwise, the menus and prices are much the same as at the Dockside Chicken & Ribs (described in Eating in the South, below). The barbecue chefs here, who slowly smoke their meats over hickory and oak and then finish them with mesquite, assure me that their version is superior to their counterpart's. I can't tell the difference; to my mind they're equally scrumptious.

This is a cafeteria type stand with all seating outside in a patio protected from dive-bombing seagulls by thin wire string overhead or in a sheltered seating area. No alcoholic beverages are sold.

# Mama Stella's Italian Kitchen

| | |
|---|---|
| *What:* | Cafeteria-style Italian |
| *Where:* | Near *Penguin Encounter* |
| *Price Range:* | $$ |

This is one of the larger fast-food restaurants in the park. Here you can get pizza for about $5. For a bit more you can have fries with it. The rest of the menu is limited to just a couple of dishes. Chicken parmesan is about $6 and a simple spaghetti with meat sauce is about $5. Just outside Mama Stella's, a walk-up window dispenses "soft serve ice cream."

# Chicken 'n' Biscuit

| | |
|---|---|
| *What:* | SeaWorld Fried Chicken |
| *Where:* | Across from the SeaWorld Theatre |

*Price Range:*   $$

This is SeaWorld's version of KFC and other fried chicken fast-food chains. All chicken dinners come with french fries and a biscuit. The two-piece dinner is priced at about $4 and the three-piece at about $5. Corn on the cob or BBQ bean side orders are just under $2. Beer is available here in $2 and $3 sizes. There is a smallish indoor seating area. Outdoor seating is in a sun-baked and rather charmless square.

## Waterfront Sandwich Grill

*What:*          Fast-food burgers
*Where:*         On Bayside Lagoon, near the *Sky Tower*
*Price Range:*   $ - $$

This brightly painted eatery serves up standard burger and fries fare at moderate prices. Burger platters, which include fries, are about $5. Only slightly more expensive are the ham and cheese sandwich and a "California Light" sandwich of smoked turkey breast served with potato salad. Fries by themselves are just over $1 or $2 depending on size. No alcoholic beverages are served here. The scrumptious desserts, including carrot cake, cheesecakes, and chocolate pudding, are about $2.

There is a largish indoor seating area; outside, the Waterfront Sandwich Grill shares a patio with the Smokehouse next door. The view looks out over the Lagoon and is charming.

## Bimini Bay Cafe

*What:*          Caribbean-flavored sit-down restaurant
*Where:*         On Bayside Lagoon, turn right at the flamingos
*Price Range:*   $$ - $$$

SeaWorld has only one full-service restaurant and, hence, only one chance to get it right. Thankfully, they succeed. For those who enjoy something better than standard fast-food fare, the Bimini Bay Cafe will be a welcome oasis. The decor evokes a breezy, pastel-drenched Caribbean bungalow, complete with a verandah. The dining, however, is strictly indoors, since the verandah is reserved for the bar next door. The menu is short but tasty and the prices are surprisingly moderate, with the most expensive entree (the filet mignon) just $13.

Starters are limited to salads, from a simple Caesar to a more elaborate chicken fajita supreme. Salads range from about $8 to about $10. Sandwiches are $7 to $8 and include Nassau Chicken (with Muenster cheese and bacon) and a fried grouper sandwich with a tangy tartar sauce. All sandwiches are served with french fries.

Among the entrees, my favorites are the Mahi Mahi Martinique ($11), napped in a slightly sweet piña colada sauce and garnished with toasted coconut and almonds, and the Key West Pasta ($10), featuring spicy shrimp in a fontinella pesto sauce. Also available is the Neptune's Seafood Platter ($12), a feast of grouper, shrimp, and scallops (broiled or fried to your order) served with a vegetable medley. Vegetables at Bimini Bay Cafe are especially well prepared, steamed until perfectly crisp-tender and attractively presented.

Most soft beverages are $1.25. Order iced tea and you get a bottomless carafe. Domestic beers are $2.25 and imported Carlsberg only slightly higher. Wine, red and white, is about $3 by the glass and $12 for a bottle. Desserts consist of a variety of cakes and pies in generous portions for just $3. On a recent visit, a towering chocolate layer cake, strawberry cheesecake, and key lime pie were prominently featured on the dessert tray.

The wait here can be daunting during the lunch time rush (usually about noon to 3:30). Reservations are not accepted.

# Shopping in the North

Just as most of the restaurants are concentrated in the North End of the park, so are most of the shops. What follows are brief descriptions of SeaWorld's shops, beginning with those in the entrance plaza and continuing in a roughly clockwise direction. While the accent of the merchandise changes from shop to shop, the good folks at Kodak have made sure that you can get film everywhere.

### Shamu's Emporium

If you'd like to leave your souvenir shopping until the end of the day you can stop at this large shop on your way out of the park and be reasonably sure of finding something suitable for yourself and the folks back home. You have to pass right by it to get to the exit so don't worry about missing it.

There are some beautiful small sculptures by John Perry. This artist works in resin to depict dolphins, orcas, sharks, and other sea creatures which he then mounts on decorative burlwood bases. They range in size from small pieces depicting an individual to larger ones with several individuals of varying sizes. The price range is from about $16 to $100.

Of course, the usual selection of t-shirts is to be found here, some of them quite stylish. Prices range from $15 for the standard variety to $28 for the fancy models. In addition, there is a nice line of SeaWorld polo shirts starting at about $45.

Also prominently displayed is a wide selection of plush toys in a variety of sizes at prices ranging from about $6 to about $30. Here your kids will find cuddly killer whales, seal pups, polar bears, sharks, walruses, manatees, even king penguins. In my opinion, the polar bears and penguins offer the best value for the dollar, although the $6 seal pup is sure to be a winner with any small child.

Before leaving, make sure to check out the selection of books and videos about some of the creatures you've visited during your stay.

## Shamu Souvenir Shop

Just a few paces away you will find this small square shop, hardly more than a kiosk really. It is aimed squarely at kids and features small toys, gifts, and t-shirts for tots ranging from about $8 to about $22. You can also pick up a straw hat and film here should you need either.

## Discovery Cove

This small shop at the entrance to Key West features educational books, videos, toys, and treats for children. The display is helpfully broken down by theme, from glow in the dark, to undersea life, to creepy critters.

## Sandcastle Toys .n. Treats

Nearby and part of the Key West area is a somewhat larger shop with a larger range of merchandise and less of an educational emphasis (although there is a Sesame Street section here). Plush toys and toddler-sized clothing can be found here. There are also some toddler-sized tables where the little ones can try out the wind-up toys before pestering Mommy and Daddy to buy them.

## Coconut Bay Trader

This is Key West's largest and poshest shop. There is a good selection of resort wear and swimwear for women, at moderate prices, as well as a small selection of tabletop sculptures of dolphins. It also provides plush versions of sea turtles and, yes, stingrays.

## Antique Photo

Not shown on the SeaWorld map, this shop near *Key West at Sea-World* purveys old timey costumed photos, letting your family see what it might have looked like circa 1900. There is an extensive selection of good quality costumes, much better than those offered in a similar shop at Universal Studios surprisingly enough. The cost of the photo depends on how many people are in it: one person for $20, two for $22, and three for $25. Group photos of four to six are $29. Additional prints are $10 each. A computerized system lets the shop archive your photos, just in case you decide you need more prints months later.

## Manatee Cove

This small circular shop is at the top of the ramp leading out of the manatee exhibit. Here you'll find a selection of t-shirts commemorating the sluggish sea mammal ($17 to $27) and a large variety of manatee collectibles, including some very well executed small figurines. Manatee plush dolls range from $6 to $16 and there's a large plush sea turtle on display for about $50. This shop has a good range of manatee books for all ages in case you or someone in your family would like to learn more about the endangered critter. This is also probably a good place to remind yourself that a portion of your purchase price will go towards helping rehabilitate injured manatees.

## Friends of the Wild

Near the exit to *Penguin Encounter* and just across from Mama Stella's, this spacious, airy store serves up a fairly representative cross section of SeaWorld souvenirs.

Unique at this location is a jewelry section featuring moderately priced gold bracelets, earrings, brooches, and pendants, some bearing semi-precious stones and many with a dolphin or sea shell motif. This section also features various types of small, delicate glass sculptures, the most interesting of which feature frolicking dolphins with gold tipped fins and snouts.

There is a nice selection of the John Perry art pieces described above as well as a variety of porcelain collectibles, mugs, and glasses. The kids haven't been forgotten. There is a good selection of toys and books aimed at the younger crowd.

## O. P. Otter's Souvenir and Gift Shop

This small kiosk, tucked away directly behind Chicken 'n' Biscuit, is pretty much limited to kiddie merchandise. There are some plush dolls, t-shirts, and toys, as well as a line of clothes for infants and toddlers.

## Crosswalk Gifts

If you file out of the *Clyde & Seamore* show from the top of the auditorium, it will be hard to miss this small shop; it's just at the bottom of the hill. The accent here is on cuddly plush toys with a large selection at the usual prices ($6 to $30).

## Cruz Cay Harbor

The emphasis here is on clothing, specifically the type of clothing that is usually referred to as "resort wear." Attractive tops for women are priced from about $25 to over $40, and there is a nice selection of SeaWorld's classier t-shirts. What's more, it's actually possible to find something to wear here that doesn't say "SeaWorld" on it, including sundresses and swim suits. Cruz Cay also features a line of inexpensive jewelry, including earrings, pins, and coral bead necklaces ($3 to $10).

## Flamingo Point

The focus at this small kiosk is on t-shirts, most of them for women. There is also Bud gear for the guys. In keeping with its namesake, the shop offers pink plush flamingos with long ribbony legs for about $12.

## Sweet Sailin'

With this colorful candy store we've come full circle, back to the entrance plaza and Shamu's Emporium. Creamery fudge and caramel apples are on sale here along with an extensive selection of candies sold in bulk (about $2 a quarter pound). You can also get a fancy cup of coffee here ($2 to $3).

## Exit Gifts

Just in case you have second thoughts after leaving the park, SeaWorld has thoughtfully provided this vest-pocket shop for your convenience. Unfortunately, you'll have to do with a limited selection of souvenirs.

# THE SOUTH END

The southern half of SeaWorld lies across the wooden walkway that takes you over Bayside Lagoon to Shamu Stadium. The whole feel of this end of the park is quite a bit different, with its large open spaces between huge modern stadiums and buildings.

Once again, I describe the attractions here in geographical rather than thematic order, beginning with the *Sky Tower* and continuing in order in a clockwise direction around Bayside Lagoon.

## Sky Tower

| | |
|---|---|
| *Rating:* | ★ ★ + |
| *Type:* | Bird's-eye view of Orlando |
| *Time:* | Six and half minutes |

*Kelly says:*  For those who've seen everything else they want to see at SeaWorld

Riding the *Sky Tower* will set you back an additional $2.50, unless you have an annual pass, in which case it's free. You'll have to decide whether the six-and-a-half-minute glimpse of Orlando from on high is worth the extra charge. I regularly see people answering that question in the negative.

The *Sky Tower* is a circular viewing platform that rotates slowly while rising from lagoon level to a height of 400 feet. From there you can see the dome of *Spaceship Earth* at EPCOT and *Space Mountain* at the Magic Kingdom, as well as some of the Orlando area's other high-rise buildings. There are two levels, each offering a single row of seating that circles the capsule. You pick the level of your choice as you enter. The upper level would seem the better choice, and most people head that way, but it only gives you a 10-foot height advantage which doesn't really affect your enjoyment of the experience.

Riding the *Sky Tower* is an enjoyable enough way to kill some time if you aren't eager to see anything else and don't mind paying the extra charge. Seeing SeaWorld from the air can be fascinating, especially if the water ski show is going on at the time. You will also gain an appreciation for the cunning way the park is laid out and see why you were having difficulty navigating from place to place.

The *Sky Tower* ride is at the mercy of the elements. Any hint of lightning in the area closes it down, as do high winds, which might buffet the top of the tower even when it's perfectly calm on the ground.

# Terrors of the Deep

*Rating:*  ★ ★ ★ ★

*Type:*  Aquatic habitat

*Time:*  15 - 30 minutes

*Kelly says:*  Up close and personal with some scary fish

In *Terrors of the Deep*, SeaWorld has very cleverly packaged an aquarium-style display of some of the seas' scariest, ugliest, and most dangerous creatures. What kid could resist a title like that? They'll be so excited and grossed out that they won't even notice that they've learned a thing or two in the process. Adults will appreciate the ingenious and informative ways in which the specimens are displayed and explicated.

The tone and lighting of this exhibit is dark and foreboding, with appropriately ominous soundtrack music, but you needn't worry about any unpleasant surprises. When you get right down to it, it's fish in tanks and far too fascinating to be truly scary to any except perhaps the most suggestible kids. This is a very popular attraction and, with long lines in mind, the interior has been cleverly designed to offer space for the line to back up, while keeping the crowds entertained with informative videos and educational displays.

You enter this habitat via a bridge over a shallow pool in which some of the smaller and less threatening shark specimens are displayed. Here are small hammerheads and nurse sharks along with a variety of rays, including the jet-black bat ray. A long dark corridor, leads us to a clear acrylic tunnel through an artificial tropical reef. This is home to the moray eels — nasty-looking snake-like fish. The moray's coating of yellow slime over its blue flesh gives it a sickly green tint. At first all you see is the many varieties of reef fish swimming about, but closer inspection reveals the morays poking their heads out of their holes. The more you look the more you see. There are dozens and dozens of the creatures hidden in the crevices of the reef. From time to time one swims free, undulating its long body right overhead. Looking up you see the surface of the water. The tank has been designed to mimic the natural habitat as closely as possible; the lighting comes from a single overhead source, standing in for the sun.

The tunnel curves around and into a viewing area in which several tanks hold specimens probably best kept separate. First is the delicate and intricately camouflaged lion fish. Looks are deceiving here, because the lion fish's feathery appendages are actually poisoned spines which are highly toxic to swimmers unfortunate enough to come in contact with them.

Tried any *fugu* at your local sushi bar? You may want to reconsider after viewing the puffer fish on display here. Fugu, as the fish is known in Japan, is one of the world's most poisonous fish. The Japanese consider its edible portions a delicacy and licensed fugu chefs carefully pare away the poisonous organs. Despite their precautions, several people die each year from fugu poisoning. Swimming unconcernedly with the puffer fish are surgeon fish, a pretty species that carries the marine equivalent of switchblades concealed near their tails. When attacked (or grabbed by unwary fishermen), they lash out with their hidden weapon, inflicting a nasty gash. Across the way are barracuda, looking every bit as terrifying as when I first encountered them while snorkeling in the Caribbean. Had I been to SeaWorld first, I would have known that an attack was unlikely and probably would have made less of a fool of myself.

Fascinating as all this is, it is merely a warm up for the main feature of *Terrors of the Deep* — a 660,000-gallon tank filled with six species of shark. As you walk down a sloping tunnel to the shark viewing area, videos and wall displays fill you in on little known shark facts. For example, did you know that a shark's liver takes up nearly 90 percent of its body cavity and accounts for nearly a quarter of its weight? Scientists theorize that, since the liver contains a great deal of oil and since oil is lighter than water, the shark's huge liver may contribute to its buoyancy.

The shark viewing area is large with three rows of benches for those who want to take a break and watch these spooky creatures float by the huge picture windows in front of them. Back-lit signs identify the species in the tank: small toothsaw sharks, brown sharks, nurse sharks, bull sharks, lemon sharks, and sandpiper sharks. A video plays on a continuous loop, offering up shark facts and profiling some of the sharks on display. There are no giants here but what the specimens lack in size they more than make up for in number. If you ever encounter sharks in the wild, hopefully there will be nowhere near this many of them.

Your shark encounter is capped off by a ride on a conveyer belt through a 124-foot tunnel that takes you right down the middle of the shark tank. About a foot thick, the clear acrylic walls of the tunnel are supporting 450 tons of man-made salt water over your head. Don't worry, you're perfectly safe; the acrylic can withstand a tromping by 372 elephants (as you are informed on exiting).

*Tip:* You will pass one of the best viewing spots for the shark tank on your right as you exit. From here, you look back along the tunnel through which you just passed. This is also a great place to observe the twice-weekly shark feedings. At press time, they were feeding the sharks on Tuesdays and Thursdays, sometime between the hours of 10 a.m. and noon, but check with an attendant to get the latest information on the feeding schedule.

# Cirque de la Mer (at Nautilus Theatre)

*Rating:*      ★ ★ ★
*Type:*        Indoor stage show
*Time:*        30 minutes
*Kelly says:*  An amiable time-passer

Why this show is called Cirque de la Mer is beyond me. It is neither a circus, of the sea, nor French. But why be picky? What we get, in fact, is a talented Peruvian troupe that combines mime comedy, acrobatics, and ballet in an amiable vaudeville that, true to the genre, has something for everyone.

The sets and costumes draw on themes and imagery from Peru's Nazcan and Incan past but this show is pure twentieth century entertainment. Our master of ceremonies is an engaging, shaggy haired mime who uses a whistle much as Harpo Marx used his tooting horn. In his best bit, he creates a bizarre boxing match, using six volunteers from the audience to splendid comic effect. Two bare-chested acrobats perform a slow motion series of poses that highlight their sense of balance and superb physical conditioning. If they decide to stay in the States, they have a future at Chippendales. A lovely dance number showcases a lithe acrobat representing (I think) a condor who soars aloft on wings of white cloth; it's a simple effect but mesmerizing nonetheless.

# Clydesdale Hamlet & Anheuser-Busch Hospitality Center

*Rating:*  ★ ★ +
*Type:*  Horse stables and free beer
*Time:*  As long as you want
*Kelly says:*  For horse lovers and Bud fans

Since Anheuser-Busch, the brewing giant, purchased SeaWorld a few years back, you probably can't hold it against them for blowing their own horn a bit. And even if you find this sort of blatant self-promotion distasteful, you'll probably have to admit they do a pretty good (and fairly tasteful) job of it.

There are really two attractions here, Clydesdale Hamlet, the home of Budweiser's trademark Clydesdale beer wagon team, and the Anheuser-Busch Hospitality Center. **Clydesdale Hamlet** is actually a very upscale stable, impeccably clean and not in the least aromatically offensive. This is where the Clydesdales hang out between appearances elsewhere in the park.

This breed, from Scotland, was specially bred for the heavy work of hauling man's stuff from place to place, and while they may not have the magnificent grace of their racing cousins they are pretty impressive in their own right — all 2,000 pounds of them. They are also pampered, beautifully groomed, and obviously well-cared for. There are stable attendants always close at hand to make sure you don't slip them a sugar cube or a contraband carrot and to regale you with horse lore. Did you know, for example, that if you hold down the jaw of a supine Clydesdale, it will be unable to stand up? Seems they have to be able to raise their heads off the ground first before they begin the process of standing up.

Next door, is the **Anheuser-Busch Hospitality Center,** a large, airy pavilion whose architecture reflects that of the stable. It's a lovely building with a comfortable outdoor seating area overlooking a crystal clear lake, fed by a babbling waterfall, and surrounded by immaculate lawns. It's the nicest place in the park to just sit and take your ease.

Inside you'll find The Deli (a fast-food restaurant) and the Label Stable (a souvenir shop), which are described elsewhere. The centerpiece of the

Center, however, is the free beer dispensing area that faces the main entrance and is backed by huge copper brewing kettles. That's right, *free* beer. The cups are on the small size (about 10 ounces) and there's a limit (one sample at a time, two per day), but it's still a gracious gesture. Most of Anheuser-Busch's brands are available, including the non-alcoholic O'Doul's.

You can take your free brewski and stroll around behind the copper kettles and into the information center featuring an outline of the beer brewing process and a huge block of crushed aluminum cans. There is also the Color of Life Theater where a continuously running, seven-minute film, narrated by Walter Cronkite (once called "the most trusted man in America"), unfolds on five screens to a heart-warming song about rainbows. The theme is Anheuser-Busch's commitment to the environment (it's the world's largest recycler of aluminum cans) and the good life. The imagery is gorgeous and doesn't miss the chance for a few well-placed plugs for the company's other theme parks. Propaganda? Absolutely, but well done and quite restful. This might be a good place to hide out from the rest of your group or escape the heat of the midday sun.

## Arcade and Midway Games

| | |
|---|---|
| *Rating:* | ★ + |
| *Type:* | Video and "skill" games arcades |
| *Time:* | As long as you want |
| *Kelly says:* | For video addicts |

I feel the same way about these money-siphoning operations, located near the Shamu Stadium, that I feel about the arcades and Amity games at Universal Studios Florida — why bother? The main reason you paid good money to come to SeaWorld is just paces away and everything you can do here, you can do elsewhere for less money. That being said, these venues are clean and attractive and the prizes at Midway Games are better than most.

## The Shamu Adventure

| | |
|---|---|
| *Rating:* | ★ ★ ★ ★ ★ |
| *Type:* | Live stadium show |
| *Time:* | 25 minutes |
| *Kelly says:* | The acme of the SeaWorld experience |

Could there be a better job than being a killer whale trainer and being shot 30 feet into the air off the nose of a 5,000 pound orca? You won't think so after seeing this razzle-dazzle demonstration put on by the dashing young SeaWorld staffers who spend their time teaching the Shamu family some awesome tricks.

Actually, they aren't "tricks" at all in the common sense of the term. They are simply extensions of natural behaviors that have been reinforced with patient attention and liberal handfuls of smelt. Nor is *The Shamu Adventure* mere entertainment. In keeping with SeaWorld's commitment to conserving the marine environment and saving endangered species, this show teaches important lessons about the realities of nature (including its darker sides) and the importance of the marine mammal husbandry practiced at SeaWorld Orlando and its sister parks.

The stars of the show are members of the family orsinus orca, commonly known as killer whales and affectionately known by nearly everyone who visits SeaWorld as Shamu. We are introduced to Shamu, her calf Baby Shamu (born in late 1995) and Namu. The first killer whale ever captured was named Namu after a town in British Columbia. Shamu means "mate of Namu" in the language of British Columbia's native people.

The "stage" is a huge seven million-gallon pool filled with man-made salt water kept at a chilly 55 degrees (although the whales are used to much chillier water in their natural habitat) and completely filtered every 30 minutes. At the back is a small island platform for the trainers, above which looms a large screen on which a film and live video of the show in progress are displayed. The front of the stage is formed by a six-foot high Lucite wall, which gives those in the first several rows an underwater view. Downstage center is a shallow lip which allows Shamu to "beach" herself for our enjoyment.

On film, TV's "animal expert" Jack Hanna introduces us to killer whales in their natural habitats around the world, but the real focus of the show is the awe-inspiring and absolutely delightful interaction of the whales and their trainers. The whales leap, glide, dive, and roll with a grace that belies their huge size. The trainers ride on their charges' bellies, surf the pool on their backs and, in the most breathtaking moments, soar high aloft, propelled off a whale's snout.

One of the show's more amusing moments comes when the trainers attempt to answer the burning question, "Who make better trainers, men or women?" A male and female volunteer are selected from the audience and, as so often happens in battles of the sexes, the man completely loses his dignity and gets wet.

And speaking of getting wet, the warnings that precede the show's grand finale are in deadly earnest. If you're sitting in the first 14 rows, you'll get very, very, *very* wet. Actually, it's possible to sit in this section and escape a drenching — I've done it. But if you happen to be in the direct line of one of the salvos of chilly salt-water hurled into the audience by the cupped rear fluke of a five-ton whale, you will be soaked to the skin. It's pretty much a matter of luck.

Some of the biggest laughs come when people who have fled the "splash zone" for the higher ground of the first promenade get nailed anyway by a particularly forceful fluke-full of water.

*The best seats in the house.* Many kids (especially 9- to 13-year-old boys) will insist on sitting in the splash zone and will feel cheated if they don't get soaked. But adults should consider sitting here as well. If you wear a rain poncho (which you may already have from a visit to another park) you can protect yourself relatively well, and these seats do offer an excellent view, especially underwater. But the seats higher up offer excellent sightlines and the video coverage of the show assures that you won't miss anything.

# Shamu Rocks America

| | |
|---|---|
| *Rating:* | ★ ★ ★ ★ ★ |
| *Type:* | Live stadium show |
| *Time:* | 20 minutes |
| *Kelly says:* | Shamu and trainers at play |

The last show of every day in Shamu Stadium is somewhat shorter and different in tone but no less exciting and enjoyable. In fact, they seem to save the best for last.

This time around, there's little or no attempt to "educate" you. Instead, the focus is on fun and the amazing feats of which these sea-going behemoths are capable. For fun, there's a showing of *SeaWorld's Funniest Home Videos* featuring stunts that didn't quite go off as planned. For amazement, there's the wonderful spectacle of watching the trainers romp and play with their multi-ton partners. Also, whereas the daytime shows tend to showcase the female trainers, the men tend to take over at night. Maybe they're just trying to make up for the male-bashing of the earlier shows, but whichever gender takes the stage at night expect the highest leaps and the biggest splashes in this version of the Shamu show.

Some things don't change, however. The show still ends with a barrage of water to the lower seating area. Why tamper with success?

*Tip:* The *Red, Bright and Blue Spectacular* show (the last show of the day) is usually scheduled to begin about 20 minutes after *Shamu Rocks America* ends. If you sit to the left-hand side of the stadium, near an exit, you'll be well positioned for the dash over to the Bayside Water Ski Stadium that inevitably follows.

# Shamu: Close Up!

| | |
|---|---|
| *Rating:* | ★ ★ ★ ★ |
| *Type:* | Aquatic habitat |
| *Time:* | As long as you wish |
| *Kelly says:* | For everyone in the family |

Before or after the stadium show, why not pop backstage and visit with the stars in their dressing room? That's essentially the opportunity afforded by *Shamu: Close-Up.* While its not as elaborately decorated as some of SeaWorld's other "aquatic habitats," this large pool with its underwater viewing area gives you a chance to observe these graceful beasts as they relax and unwind between shows.

There's usually not a great deal to see on the surface, unless it's feeding time or the trainers are performing some "husbandry" procedures. At these times, the trainers will appear on the other side of the pool from the public viewing area and, using microphones, explain the procedures they are carrying out, such as washing the whales' teeth, drawing blood, or collecting a urine sample (now *there's* an attraction for you!). During these presentations, they will also have the whales do a few "tricks" for your amusement, like swimming around the pool waving at you. A member of the education staff will usually be prowling the area to answer any questions. If nothing's happening when you come by, ask this person when the staff is likely to be doing something next. Schedules are erratic, but the education staffer may be able to suggest a good time to return.

During sea gull season (roughly November through February) you may get to see the whales hunting for these pesky birds. They bait the surface of the water with chewed up bits of fish and when an unwary gull swoops down for a free morsel, the whale strikes from below. They seldom actually eat the birds but tend to "play" with their injured prey much as a cat will with a mouse. The battered gulls are fished out of the water by the training staff and are, we are assured, carefully nursed back to health by the aviculture staff. Sometimes, the staff will place a whale sized version of a "tubby toy" in the water for the whales to play with, which also tends to make surface viewing more interesting.

If nothing is happening up top, you can still get a great look at the whales through the three large underwater viewing windows. Just follow the edge of the pool in a clockwise direction to locate the ramp to the Underwater Viewing Area. This is a not-to-be-missed perspective on these magnificent creatures. Especially enchanting is the opportunity to watch Shamu and her much smaller calf, Baby Shamu, swimming gracefully in tandem. The whales are rotated through this viewing pool, so there's no guarantee that a specific whale will be there when you drop by. There are benches in front of the acrylic picture windows and if the crowds are thin enough you can watch while you rest. During presentations upstairs, the trainers will some-times give a whale the "go see the people at the viewing window" signal. It consists of forming a large rectangle in the air.

*Photo Op:* Plastic replicas of killer whale snouts and dorsal fins poke out of the asphalt near the pool as if it were the Pacific Ocean. They make good props for photos of the little ones.

# Shamu's Happy Harbor

| | |
|---|---|
| *Rating:* | ★ ★ ★ ★ + |
| *Type:* | Play area |
| *Time:* | 30 minutes to an hour |
| *Kelly says:* | Great for young kids, toddlers, and their long-suffering parents |

If *Wild Arctic* represents an attempt to reach out to the thrill-seeking segment of the tourist population, *Shamu's Happy Harbor* seeks to appeal to the youngster too antsy or uninterested to sit still for a fish — no matter how big it is. Here is a way for even very young children to be entertained in that most effective of ways — by doing things for themselves.

*Shamu's Happy Harbor* is dominated by a four-story, L-shaped, steel framework painted in bilious shades of sea green and pink. At first glance it looks like a construction site gone very wrong. Closer inspection re-veals it to be an intricate maze of cargo netting, plastic tubes, and slides that kids can climb through to their heart's content. Some chambers in this maze contain tire swings, just like the ones in backyards across America, except that these are two stories above ground level. The cargo netting is completely enclosed in smaller-mesh black netting. While there's no danger of falling, the upper reaches of the structure are quite high and some smaller children may become frightened.

It's not just for kids, either. Adults can join in, too, although some of the parents I watched obviously wished they weren't allowed. While the corridors of netting are big enough to accommodate anyone, the tubes are designed with smaller people in mind. Thus, the average sedentary grown-up will get quite a workout going through them. You're allowed to climb up but stairs are provided for the trip down. Too many middle-aged sprained ankles is my guess.

The larger structure of *Shamu's Happy Harbor* is complemented by any number of lesser activities, called "elements," all of them action-ori-ented, that will keep kids busy for hours unless you can drag them away to the next show at the Sea Lion and Otter Stadium. There are four-sided, canvas "mountains" that kids can climb with the help of knotted ropes and then slide down, "ball crawls" that are rooms filled with small plastic balls to a depth of a few feet in which children can jump and "swim," and large inflated rooms in which kids can bounce and tumble. There is also an area featuring remote-controlled cars and tugboats. There is an additional charge for this activity. Nearby vending machines dispense tokens for the remote controls — one token for $1, seven for $5. Each token yields about two minutes of play.

Standing in front of it all is a kid-sized schooner, the **Wahoo Two**, armed with water cannons. Mercifully they don't have sufficient range to pose a threat to passersby, but they can be aimed at targets in the small pond in which the fun ship sits. **Pete's Water Maze** offers a jumble of tubes and netting which is constantly splashed with jets of water. Off to one side is **Boogie Bump Bay**, a play area within a play area which has been very specifically designed for kids shorter than 48 inches. Here the little ones can do most of the activities available in the larger area but on a scale of their own and without having bigger kids to intimidate them and hog all the fun. One unique feature here is a "fence maze," tall enough to keep little ones perplexed but short enough to allow parents to peer over and shepherd the little ones through. Also in Boogie Bump Bay is a fabulous sandbox area, the kind you wish you had at home, that should prove popular with the preschool set. Nearby, you'll find **Shamu's Splash Attack**, where you can pay to sling water bombs at a friend. Buckets of eight water-filled balloons are $3, two for $5.

*Shamu's Happy Harbor* is an ideal place for parents to take the squirmy baby of the family when he or she gets restless with the more grown-up attractions at SeaWorld.

**Photo Op:** Just opposite *Shamu's Happy Harbor* is a made to order photo backdrop. It's a life-sized model of Shamu and Baby Shamu perfectly posed under a sun awning (to protect your shot from that annoying glare). Place your kid on Shamu's back and click away.

# Wild Arctic

| | |
|---|---|
| *Rating:* | ★ ★ ★ ★ ★ |
| *Type:* | Simulator ride plus a spectacular habitat |
| *Time:* | 5 minutes for the ride; as long as you want for the habitat |
| *Kelly says:* | A SeaWorld must-see |

That large, techno-modern, warehouse-like building near Shamu Stadium houses one of SeaWorld's most popular attractions — a devilishly clever combination of thrill ride with serene aquatic habitat. All in all, this is one of the most imaginative attractions in Orlando. Mercifully, the waiting line snakes through an area that is shielded from the blazing sun, because the lines can get long.

During the wait, we are entertained by a fascinating video presentation on the lifestyle of the Inuit peoples who inhabit the frozen realm of the Arctic. And during our slow journey through the line, we are asked to make an important decision: Do we want to take the helicopter ride to the base station or do we want to go by land? It's a choice between "motion" and "non-motion" and it can be important.

## The Wild Arctic Ride

With the ride portion of *Wild Arctic,* SeaWorld goes head to head with simulator-based attractions like Universal's *Back To The Future* and Disney's *Star Tours* and *Fantastic Voyage.* And by some standards, SeaWorld may have come out on top. Certainly if my experience is anything to go by, this is the most stomach-churning ride of the bunch. Of course, that might just be because I naturally associate the sea with sea-sickness.

You begin your journey by crossing a metal bridge into the vehicle itself. Once you and your 58 fellow voyagers are strapped in, the staff exits, the doors close, and the ride begins.

The ride, which lasts all of about five minutes, simulates a flight aboard an amphibious (not to mention submersible) helicopter to a research station deep within the Arctic Circle. Despite the gale warnings crackling over the radio, our friendly pilot can't help doing a little sight-seeing, including putting the rotors into "whisper mode" so we can drop in on a polar bear family, and dipping below the waves for a glimpse of a narwhal. But his unscheduled detours exact their price and soon we are caught in that gale. At first the pilot prudently puts down on a glacier to await a better reading on the weather but the glacier gives way and we plummet headlong towards the waters below. At the last second, the pilot gets the rotors whirling and we zoom away from certain death. Next, he decides we'll be safer flying through a crevasse, away from the howling winds, but we fly straight into and through an avalanche. Finally, we break through into the clear and the Arctic base station lies dead ahead.

Like I said, it's a real stomach-churner and remarkably realistic. As I write these words I realize that I'm becoming a little queasy just remembering it all. The action is fast, abrupt, and violent. You'll find yourself being tossed from side to side as you grip the armrests and scream — in excitement or terror, depending on your mood.

Those who choose the "non-motion" alternative for their voyage to the Wild Arctic, are escorted past the three simulators to a stationary room where they watch the same video, before entering the Arctic base station.

*Tip:* The non-motion line moves much, much faster than the line for the simulator ride. If you are pressed for time you might want to consider making the ultimate sacrifice (or use this as an excuse for missing what can be a very scary ride).

## The Wild Arctic Aquatic Habitat

Once you wobble off the simulator ride, you enter SeaWorld's most elaborately conceived aquatic habitat, one that would have been a five-star attraction even without the exhilarating thrill ride that proceeds it.

The conceit here is that scientists have discovered the wrecked ships from the expedition of John Franklin, a real-life British explorer who disappeared in 1845 while searching for the nonexistent Northwest Passage. The wreck, it seems, has drawn a wide variety of wildlife seeking shelter and prey, so the scientists "stabilized" the wreck and constructed their observation station around it.

The first "room" of the habitat simulates an open-air space, with the domed ceiling standing in for the Arctic sky. A sign informs us that we are 2,967 miles from SeaWorld in Florida. Gray beluga whales (the name is derived from the Russian word for "white") are being fed in a pool directly in front of us. Thankfully, SeaWorld has not attempted to mimic Arctic temperatures.

From here we enter the winding tunnels of the research station proper. The walls alternate between the ancient wood of the wrecked vessels and the corrugated steel of the modern structure. We view the animals through thick glass walls; on the other side, temperatures are maintained at comfortably cool levels. Art imitates reality here in the form of the SeaWorld research assistants, clad in their distinctive red parkas. They are here to answer guests' questions but they are also carrying out valuable scientific research by painstakingly recording the behavior patterns of the polar bears and other animals in the exhibits in an attempt to find ways to short-circuit the repetitive motion patterns that befall many animals in captivity. One strategy has been to hide food in nooks and crannies of the habitat, encouraging the animals to use true-to-nature hunting behaviors to find their food. By the way, the fish swimming with the polar bears usually avoid winding up on the dinner table, although the younger bears sometimes just can't resist taking a swipe at them.

For most people, the highlight of this habitat will be the polar bears, including the famous twins Klondike and Snow, born in the Denver

Zoo, abandoned by their mother, nursed through infancy by their zookeepers, and then placed with SeaWorld as the facility best equipped to nurture them to adulthood. Klondike and Snow alternate in the main viewing area with two adult bears. Polar bears are solitary animals so the two pairs are kept separate to avoid any unpleasant scenes. As brother and sister, Klondike and Snow enjoy playing together, but eventually they, too, will answer the call of their instincts and have to be separated.

There are also enormous walruses swimming lazily in a separate pool. Harbor seals are represented only via a video presentation showing the animals in their natural habitat. The narration is cleverly disguised as the radio transmissions of the scientists gathering the footage for research purposes.

After viewing the animals on the surface, we walk down a series of ramps to an underwater viewing area for a completely different and utterly fascinating perspective. Video monitors show what's happening on the surface and simple controls allow visitors to move the cameras remotely to follow the animals when they climb out of the pool. The set decoration below the surface is every bit as imaginative as it is above, simulating the Arctic Sea beneath the ice shelf.

There's much to explore here, including displays that let kids crawl through a simulated polar bear den or poke their heads through the ice, just like a seal. Dotted throughout the exhibit are touch-sensitive video monitors that let us learn more about the animals we are viewing and the environment in which they live. Just before the exit ramp, a small room offers a variety of interactive entertainments. One lets you plan a six-week expedition to the North Pole, selecting the mode of transportation, date of departure, food supply, and wardrobe. Then you get to find out how wisely you planned. Another computer offers up a printout that tells, among other interesting facts, how many people have been born since the date of your birth.

*Tip:* The exit is through the Arctic Shop and a prominent sign says "No Re-Entry." However, late in the day, it appears to be easy to sneak back in through the back door if you'd like another peek at this fabulous habitat.

## The Observation Bay

Many people leave *Wild Arctic* through the gift shop and disappear into the Florida sun without realizing they have missed what I think is one of the best features of this attraction. Don't make the same mistake.

As you come into the shop, look to your right for the lettering on the wall that marks the location of the *Observation Bay*. The *Observation Bay* is a small, stand-up viewing area that gives you a "backstage" look at the technology you experienced en route to the habitat. Through the glass window of the bay you can see the room in which the simulated chopper sits. It's a large, darkened, two and a half story, industrial-looking space. Suspended in the center is the "cabin" of the simulator — a 22-by-30-foot metal box that looks like a large crate. It is poised delicately on four hydraulically operated struts; two flexible yellow tubes carry ventilation into the cabin. Underneath, you can barely make out the wiring that provides power and audio to the interior. The side of the simulator facing you is painted in day-glo fluorescent paint glowing under black light.

You watch as a new group of passengers enters the simulator from the left. When the doors have been sealed, the drawbridge over which they entered raises and the cabin is cut off from any escape. Television monitors in the *Observation Bay* show the same video you watched in the simulator and you settle back to relive the journey from a unique perspective that is guaranteed to give you a much deeper appreciation of the technology that goes into providing a few minutes of edge-of-your-seat thrills. No other theme park has realized that putting this technology on display can be an attraction in its own right.

As the ride begins, the cabin of the simulator lurches into motion. The hydraulic limbs beneath allow the computer-guided simulator to move the 35,000-pound box along six separate axes — yaw (left and right), pitch (nose up and down), roll (banking left and right), heave (up and down vertically), surge (forward and backward horizontally), and sway (side-to-side) — and the ride must go through all of them a dozen times at least. I was amazed at how far and how fast the system bounced that box around. From the inside, I would have guessed that the actual motion was far less. In some directions, the simulator system can move the cabin as much as nine feet at speeds of up to 24 inches per second. Watching from the security of solid ground, you really have to feel for the people inside. When the ride ends, the cabin returns to its neutral position, the drawbridges descend from either side, and the deep sea voyagers emerge to allow another group of victims ... er, guests, to take their place.

The great thing about the *Observation Bay* is that you can get to it without having to take the ride itself. Simply walk through the gift shop. There's no line and you can walk right in. If you have any doubts about whether you want to experience the ride portion of *Wild Arctic*, the *Observation Bay* gives you everything you need to make a rational and informed decision. Even if you are unfortunate enough to miss *Wild Arctic* altogether, the *Observation Bay* provides an enjoyable and educational experience that is better than that offered by a lot of other attractions elsewhere.

*Tip:* *Wild Arctic,* with it combination of thrill ride and polar bears is one of SeaWorld's most popular offerings. You will be well advised to see it early in the morning. The waiting line fills up very quickly when the Shamu show next door empties out.

# The Intensity Games

| | |
|---|---|
| *Rating:* | ★ ★ ★ + |
| *Type:* | Outdoor water ski show |
| *Time:* | 25 minutes |
| *Kelly says:* | Super stunts |

Twenty of the best water skiers the country has to offer go mano a mano in a hypercharged competition played out to the accompaniment of the kind of pulse-pounding rock anthems that are a staple of the modern sports arena.

Sea-Doo racers speed through a slalom course of buoys, and barefoot skiers scorch their soles at 40 mph. The long-distance jumpers hit the ramps at twice the speed of the boats pulling them and leap more than 120 feet before splashing down. Best of all are the waveboarders, who zip across the wake of the boats pulling them to perform dizzying aerobatic feats of skill and daring. If this is the only water ski show you get to see on your Florida trip, you will be more than satisfied.

*Note:* I am told that this show is the result of the water skiers' complaints that they didn't have enough to do in earlier versions of the water ski spectaculars staged here. We owe them a vote of thanks.

**The best seats in the house.** This show benefits from some height. The best seats are on the upper level, dead center, in the small section just below the show's control room.

# Red, Bright and Blue Spectacular

| | |
|---|---|
| *Rating:* | ★ ★ ★ |
| *Type:* | Nighttime multimedia show |
| *Time:* | 15 minutes |
| *Kelly says:* | A rousing finale |

*Red, Bright and Blue* is the grand finale to your day at SeaWorld. It is shown just once a day and takes place at the Atlantis Bayside Stadium about 45 minutes before the park's scheduled closing time. Since it's scheduled immediately after *Shamu Rocks America* and is on the way to the park exit, most people check it out and I would recommend that you join them.

The show is an odd multimedia mixture of elements with no spoken narration, making it ideal for non-English speakers. One of the neatest elements of the show is a curtain of water spray that rises from the Lagoon to serve as a screen on which film is projected. Most of the show, however, consists of bursts of laser light from behind the audience and from across the lake, cute cartoons projected in the same laser light against the ski show backdrop, and (best of all) copious fireworks. All of this is accompanied by a loud up-tempo medley of all-American music celebrating all-American themes and motifs — from Broadway musicals like *West Side Story* and *On The Town* to "Orange Blossom Special" and "Pop Goes the Weasel." The show ends with a rousing gospel rendition of "God Bless America." Hear, hear!

# Eating in the South

Of SeaWorld's 12 daytime eateries, just four are located at the South End of the park. I will describe them in geographical order, starting with the Dockside Chicken & Ribs and continuing clockwise around the Bayside Lagoon.

## Dockside Chicken & Ribs

*What:* Walk-up barbecue stand

*Where:* Near *Terrors of the Deep* and the walkway across the Lagoon

*Price Range:* $$

That mouth-watering smell that's been making you feel hungry ever since you entered the park comes from this vest-pocket barbecue stand (and its cousin, the Buccaneer Smokehouse not too far away). Here you can get succulent barbecued chicken and pork ribs that are comparable in quality, quantity, and price to the fare available in local barbecue restaurants. That makes the Smokehouse one of the better deals at SeaWorld.

The generous chicken-and-ribs combo platter, with french fries, is about $7. Ribs by themselves are only slightly more expensive, while chicken comes in quarter or half portions for about $5 and $6 respectively. A "lunch-size" ribs option is also about $6. Side dishes of fries, cole slaw, corn on the cob, and BBQ beans are in the $1.50 to $2 range.

Seating is all al fresco and the patio, which is shared by the Waterfront Sandwich Grill, can get crowded at meal times. If you can't find a seat outside, take your tray into the Waterfront Sandwich Grill next door (but reviewed above in "The North End").

# The Deli

| | |
|---|---|
| *What:* | Cafeteria-style sandwiches |
| *Where:* | In the *Anheuser-Busch Hospitality Center* |
| *Price Range:* | $$ |

Tucked into a corner of the *Anheuser-Busch Hospitality Center*, The Deli serves up thick sandwiches in the $5 to $6 range. Among them are an open roast turkey sandwich, top round of beef, German sausage, and the Hospitality Club sandwich. All are served with potato salad.

Interestingly enough, no beer is served here, but you can take your tray to the lovely outdoor patio and walk back in to the free sample line to pick up a small cup of frosty brew.

## Coconut Cove Snack Company

| | |
|---|---|
| *What:* | Quick snacks with kids in mind |
| *Where:* | At *Shamu's Happy Harbor* |
| *Price Range:* | $ |

This walk-up stand is dedicated to the proposition that what a kid playing at *Shamu's Happy Harbor* needs is a sugar rush, not healthy food. Churros, the sugared fried dough from Mexico, is about $2. Apple juice for little ones is a little less. There is also a variety of sugary snacks, drinks, and ice cream bars, all in the $2 to $3 range.

## Mango Joe's Cafe

| | |
|---|---|
| *What:* | Cafeteria-style fajitas and sandwiches |
| *Where:* | Near *Wild Arctic* |
| *Price Range:* | $ - $$ |

Chicken and beef fajitas or fajita sandwiches are featured here for about $6 and very tasty they are indeed. There is also a huge smoked turkey sandwich for about the same price. Mango Joe's serves some specialty salads, too, including one of crab meat and tiny bay shrimp and a fajita salad served in a tortilla "bowl" (both about $7). In addition to the usual soft drinks and iced tea (about $1.50), Bud is served here in $2 and $3 sizes. In the mornings, Mango Joe's serves a full breakfast.

# Shopping in the South

There are a limited number of shopping opportunities in the South End of the park, but some nice merchandise if you're a shark freak or polar bear fancier. What follows are brief descriptions of the South's shops, starting with Ocean Treasures, near *Terrors of the Deep*, and continuing in a clockwise direction around Bayside Lagoon.

## Ocean Treasures

SeaWorld obviously figures you'll have sharks on the mind as you exit from *Terrors of the Deep* because fully half the space in this nearby store is devoted to the finny predator. There are sharks on t-shirts, sharks on ties, sharks on mugs, polo shirts, baseball caps, towels, magnets, calendars, books, and videos (including the Discovery Channel's excellent series of shark fests). There are shark sculptures, shark toys, shark models, shark dolls, and shark puppets. Prices are inexpensive to moderate.

## Gulf Breeze Trader

A short walk away, on the way to the Nautilus Theater, you'll find this small shed-like store. The accent here is on moderately priced t-shirts and Budweiser merchandise. There is also a display of inexpensive straw hats for men and women ($9 to $15).

## Label Stable

This vest-pocket souvenir shop is in the *Anheuser-Busch Hospitality Center* and, naturally, is aimed at those who want to wear their beer on their sleeve. T-shirts run from about $8 to about $23, with caps in the $6 to $12 range. If you really like your Bud, you can get a very nice $150 denim jacket with the Clydesdales on the back. Beyond that there is the usual assortment of logoed key rings, mugs, refrigerator magnets, and such.

## Shamu Stadium Gift Shop

This shop is literally a hole in the wall of the massive Shamu Stadium. The wares here are mostly Shamu oriented and strictly for kids. There is a line of Shamu clothing for infants and toddlers (about $10 to $20) as well as Shamu school supplies. The pink ones, which include cosmetic bags, are just for little girls. There are some cute inflatable Shamu pool toys and a small assortment of small Shamu and seal pup plush dolls.

## Wild Arctic Gift Shop

The *Wild Arctic* attraction is sure to put you in an upbeat mood, so hang on to your wallets as you pass through the gift shop on your way out. This shop has some of the most attractive (and most expensive) stuff you'll see at SeaWorld. The clothing is especially attractive, with shirt prices approaching $60 and windbreakers for about $75. Even t-shirts are on the pricey side here, coming in at around $28 to $30. There is a good selection of Arctic plush dolls from $6 to $30. A bit more expensive are polar bear moms with an attached cub (about $35). There is also a section featuring books and videos about the animals of the frozen north. Art lovers may want to check out the polar bear sculptures by John Perry ($8 to $80).

# GUIDED TOURS

SeaWorld offers a number of guided tours and other special events worth noting. All of them carry an additional charge, over and above your admission price. But depending on your time constraints and interests, you may find one or more of them of interest.

At this writing there are two guided tours offered on a regular basis. The tours last approximately one hour each and cost $6 ($5 for children 3 to 9). Annual pass holders get a 50% discount. The schedules are somewhat erratic depending on the number of people expected that day and other factors. The tour desk is almost directly ahead as you pass through the turnstiles and enter the park. The guides are members of the education staff and are all extremely knowledgeable, personable hosts.

Since all tours limit the number of participants, signing up early is advisable. Perhaps the best way to plan your tours is to call the education department the day before your visit to inquire about tomorrow's schedule. Their number is (407) 363-2398. Failing that, stop at the information counter as soon as you arrive to check the schedule and sign up for the tour or tours that interest you. When you purchase your tours, you will be given a stick-on label to wear when you are on the tour. This serves as your "ticket" and lets the guide know who belongs to the tour and who doesn't.

## Polar Expedition

This tour cleverly capitalizes on the rush of interest in things polar that followed the addition of the spectacular *Wild Arctic* attraction. The tour has two stops. The first takes you "backstage" at *Wild Arctic*, past the huge filtration tanks that keep the artificial salt water in the attraction sparkling clean, to the hidden "den" of Klondike and Snow, brother and sister polar bear twins. Whether you will actually see the two bears depends on your luck with timing. Nothing happens on a rigid or even regular schedule with these animals. Their keepers don't want them to become habituated to a set routine and, so, try to keep the daily sequence of events just as it is in the wild — fairly random.

Even if you don't get to see Klondike and Snow through the one-way glass in their den, you can see them on the remote video camera that is focused on their public habitat. You will also get a wealth of fascinating information about polar bears in the wild and the behind-the-scenes world of *Wild Arctic*. You might be told, for example, that the water in the exhibit is kept at 45 to 55 degrees Fahrenheit, just warm enough to prevent ice from forming on the bears' fur. When keepers must enter the water, they wear three wet suits and then can only stay in the water 10 minutes before hypothermia starts to set in. You'll even get to pet polar bear fur (courtesy of a deceased bear whose pelt remains behind for its educational value).

The next stop is the chilly confines of the Avian Research lab. Penguin mothers have a spotty record when it comes to parenting skills. Abandoned or abused chicks are brought here to be reared in a more caring environment. The center even hatches orphaned eggs. Depending on when you visit, you may see young chicks covered in their downy gray baby coats or molting into the more recognizable sleek black and white of their mature feathers. Penguins are gregarious and curious birds and they will take great interest in your visit, waddling over for a closer look and eyeing you with apparent curiosity. Careful of your fingers!

## Sharks!

Here's a great chance to find out more about those cartilaginous carnivores we all love to hate and actually pet a shark. And for those who don't like to read, taking this tour can serve as an alternative to reading all that informational signage in the *Terrors of the Deep* exhibit.

What you can't get from the signs, however, is a visit to. the inner workings of the shark tank, where you can gain some appreciation of the water filtration system. Then comes a chance to examine shark jaws, shark skins, and saw fish bones up close.

The piece de resistance is a close encounter with a shark — a small, docile critter, but a shark nonetheless. Reach out your hand and enjoy bragging rights back home.

## To The Rescue

SeaWorld is far more than "just" a theme park. This engrossing and entertaining tour highlights SeaWorld's role as a rescuer and rehabilitator of aquatic mammals.

What you see on this tour will depend on which animals are currently in the park's care, but you will likely get to see manatees, dolphins, and sea turtles who have been injured, typically by the carelessness of Man. Thanks to its reputation, SeaWorld is sometimes given injured animals that are not part of its usual stock in trade — like snakes, rabbits, and exotic birds. These, too, are on display.

One of the more amusing moments of the tour comes during a stroll past rows of parrot cages, where you are greeted by a chorus of avian "hellos." On your way back, the birds squawk "goodbye."

# TAKE A DIP

Imagine seeing a great Broadway show and then getting to go out on a date with the star. Thanks to the Dolphin Interaction Program (DIP) you can do just that with Atlantic bottlenosed dolphins just like those you saw performing in the Whale & Dolphin Stadium.

The two-hour program begins with an instructional session during which you will learn how SeaWorld trains and cares for its sleek grey stars. Then it's into wet suits and non-slip footgear for your up-close and personal encounter with Flipper's cousins. This takes place in a shallow, three-foot wading area of the Whale & Dolphin Stadium where you will be able to tickle, cuddle, and shake fins with these lively and intelligent creatures. You'll also be able to play trainer and give a few simple commands. What you won't be able to do, alas, is actually swim with the dolphins. Blame the lawyers. The actual in-the-water part of the experience lasts an all too brief 30 to 45 minutes.

Children must be at least 10 years of age and 52 inches tall to participate. Kids under 18 must be accompanied by a parent or guardian.

None of this comes cheap. The fee for all participants (regardless of age) is $159, plus tax. Each participant can bring along one observer for $55. If it makes you feel any better, those rates include one day's admission to the park. Annual passholders are charged $119 to participate and $10 to observe. Holders of Orlando FlexTickets will also be offered the $10 observer's fee. Observers can take photographs but they will not be close to the action. For up close photos, you will have to turn to SeaWorld's photographer, who charges $40 for three photos or $50 for five.

DIP sessions take place at 7:00 a.m. daily and at 10:30 a.m. Monday through Friday, although the availability of the later session may vary with the season. Since there is a maximum of eight participants daily, slots fill up quickly and well in advance. Reservations are mandatory and can be made by calling (407) 370-1385 to request a registration form. Return the form by mail or fax only, with payment (check or credit card). Cancellations must be made 48 hours in advance if you wish to obtain a refund.

# CHAPTER FIVE:

# Cypress Gardens

This is where it all began. Yes, it's true, Silver Springs was running glass bottom boats before the turn of the century, but that was simply a matter of capitalizing on a ready-made attraction. In the opinion of many, the Central Florida theme park phenomenon actually began when Dick Pope carved a man-made paradise out of a patch of swampy cypress forest along the east shore of Lake Eloise to create Cypress Gardens in 1936. Today, Cypress Gardens is world-renowned for its spectacular botanical gardens and its innovative water ski spectaculars. As theme parks boomed in the 1970s, Cypress Gardens added other attractions to meet the competition, but it still retains the easy-going, leisurely air that has characterized it since its early days.

The story of Cypress Gardens' development and of Pope's single-minded boosterism is almost as entertaining as the park itself. When he launched his enterprise on little more than a dream and a hunch, most people thought he was nuts. One newspaper called him "the Swami of the Swamp." Opening day brought in gate receipts of $38. Hardly a propitious sign. Fortunately, Pope, whom the *Orlando Sentinel* calls "the flamboyant father of Florida tourism," was blessed with an instinct for publicity that P.T. Barnum would have admired. Within five years, Cypress Gardens was drawing half a million visitors a year.

Pope did it with publicity — free publicity. He staged photo shoots of pretty girls in his picture perfect park and mailed copies by the thousands, in gardenia-scented envelopes, to newspapers and magazines throughout the country. The media took the bait. One photograph of a skyborne water skier appeared in 3,670 publications. Of course, Cypress Gardens was mentioned in the caption. Pope lured filmmakers and television stars to Cypress Gardens. Esther Williams, Mike Douglas, and scores of others used Cypress Gardens as a backdrop. He staged outrageous stunts like playing the piano for a ballerina while both of them were being towed behind a speedboat, she on water skis, he on a piano-sized platform. Taking a cue from the Miss America pageant, he started crowning a new queen of something or other on an almost daily basis. All of it became grist for Pope's voracious publicity mill. Pope and his wife were also inspired improvisers, creating new marketing strategies on the spur of the moment. Some of Cypress Gardens' most revered traditions, like the water ski shows and the Southern Belles, came about almost by accident.

When Dick Pope's health began to fail in the mid-eighties, Cypress Gardens was sold, first to the publisher Harcourt Brace Jovanovich, then to the Busch Entertainment Corporation (of SeaWorld and Busch Gardens fame). It is now owned by a group of former Busch executives who are preserving Pope's legacy.

Cypress Gardens has long had a reputation as a park for senior citizens. While that perception may not accurately reflect the breadth and scope of the park's appeal, the fact remains that on the typical day you will see a majority of silver-haired guests. I wouldn't let that dissuade younger readers from coming and bringing the kids. There's plenty here to enchant visitors of all ages, just so long as they don't come expecting another Universal Studios or SeaWorld.

## Before You Come

If you'd like to get advance information on what will be going on at Cypress Gardens during the time of your visit, give them a call at (800) 282-2123 or fax (941) 324-7946. They'll be happy to fill you in on the floral calendar or send information. Cypress Gardens also maintains a web site at http://florida.com/cypressgardens.

## Getting There

Cypress Gardens is a leisurely one-hour drive from Orlando (less, if you drive like the locals who take the 65 miles per hour speed limit as a suggested minimum). The easiest way to get there is to follow I-4 to Route 27 South. Turn right off Route 27 at State Route 540 (it is well marked). Cypress Gardens is a bit less than four miles along on your left.

## Parking at Cypress Gardens

Cypress Gardens' general parking is **free**, on grass, in an area dotted with shade trees. You will never be terribly far from the front gate, so no transportation is provided. "Preferred Parking" is also available for $4 ($3 for annual pass holders). This allows you to park in a two-tiered, sunken circular lot formed by a sinkhole. The Preferred Parking lot is close to the main gate but it is still possible to be parked in this area and be farther from the gate than the early birds who snared the best spots in the free parking area.

## Opening and Closing Times

Reflecting the laid-back tempo preferred by its core clientele, Cypress Gardens does not open early and boogie late. The park is open every day of the year from 9:30 a.m. until 5:30 p.m. Hours are extended until 7:00 p.m. during the warmer months and sometimes until as late as 9:00. Periodically, there will be special nighttime events that require a separate admission and may run later.

It's a shame the hours aren't a bit longer since the early dawn hours would be an ideal time to avoid the heat of a stroll through the botanical gardens and the sunsets over Lake Eloise are spectacular.

## The Price of Admission

Cypress Gardens sells admission by the day and by the year; reflecting its popularity with seniors, there is special pricing for those 55 and older.

At press time, prices (including tax) were as follows:

***One-Day Pass:***

| | |
|---|---|
| Adults: | $32.81 |
| Seniors (55+): | $27.88 |
| Children (6 to 17): | $22.21 |

One child (6 to 17) enters **free** with each paying adult.
Ages 5 and under **free**.

***Annual Pass:***

| | |
|---|---|
| Adults: | $68.85 |
| Seniors (55+): | $58.25 |
| Children (6 to 17): | $37.05 |

The annual pass carries a number of benefits, among them:
- A 10 percent discount at all shops and restaurants.
- A 15 percent discount on admissions for friends and family.
- A frequent diner program. Purchase five entrees at the Crossroads Restaurant, Cypress Deli, or Food Fair and receive a sixth free.
- A frequent shopper program. Make 20 $5 purchases in Cypress Gardens' gift shops and get $20 credit towards your

next purchase. There are also occasional specials on merchandise that are offered exclusively to passholders.

A quarterly newsletter for passholders will keep you posted on special events and special passholders-only deals.

Considering the discounts, the annual pass pays for itself if you visit the park more than once during the year. Still, the pass will probably make the most sense for Florida residents or others who find themselves in the Winter Haven area on a regular basis. If you decide you want one, step into Guest Relations; they will take your picture and have your photo ID pass ready when you leave the park.

## Discounts

You will find dollars-off coupons for Cypress Gardens in all the usual places (see *Chapter One*). The park also runs frequent promotions — kids free with an adult, Moms free on Mothers' Day, and so forth — so you may want to call ahead to see what's available. Discounted tickets are often available from hotel Guests Services desks and ticket brokers in the Orlando area.

Active duty members of the military receive a 15% discount off posted admission prices, while members of AAA get 10% off.

## Staying Near the Park

If Cypress Gardens is your primary destination, or if you just want to spare yourself the drive back to Orlando, you may want to stay just outside the main gate.

### Best Western Admiral's Inn

5665 Cypress Gardens Boulevard
Winter Haven, FL 33884
(800) 247-2799; (941) 324-5950; fax (941) 324-2376

Standard mid-range motel.
*Price Range:* $$
*Amenities:* Pool, restaurant, lounge
*Walk to Park:* 2 minutes

Other moderately priced motels can be found three to four miles west along Route 540 (Cypress Gardens Boulevard) in the town of Winter Haven. None is within walking distance.

## Special Events

Cypress Gardens offers a growing number of themed special events throughout the year. Most of these are elaborate floral displays that fill the International Gardens section of the park and are geared to the changing seasons. Here are the major events, with their approximate dates. A recorded message at (800) 324-2123 offers a listing of upcoming events. A complete list can be obtained by calling (941) 324-2111 and asking for extension 213, 215, or 290.

*Spring Lights* (February to April). A twinkling extravaganza involving over 100 animated pieces bedecked with lights and displayed beside the moss-draped oaks, babbling brooks, and waterfalls of Cypress Gardens. A "Fantasy on the Lake" laser show is presented every evening.

*Spring Flower Festival* (Mid-March to mid-May). Huge topiary animals covered in bright flowers fill the lawns of the park for this salute to the resurgence of life in the spring.

*Victorian Garden Party* (June to early September). Nearly 100 ivy-covered topiary figures with floral accents recreate the ambiance of 1860s America, complete with a topiary riverboat at the lake's edge.

*Fourth of July*. Celebrate the nation's birthday with special water ski shows and the largest fireworks display in Polk County. There is a nominal charge for admission after 6:00 p.m.

*Mum Festival* (November). Mum's the word — chrysanthemum, that is — in this cornucopia of autumn flowers. More than two and a half million blooms are displayed in cascades, columns, cones, spheres, even bonsai trees.

*Glitter, Glisten and Glow Holiday Festival* (November 28 to early January). Get in the Yuletide spirit with this riot of lights on just about everything in the park, including animated displays. Every year the number of lights seems to increase. It's now two million and counting.

*Poinsettia Festival* (Late November to early January). A huge indoor display of this delicate and lovely Christmas favorite helps celebrate the holiday season.

Cypress Gardens also plays host to some major musical acts, with the accent on swing. Among the acts playing two-day stands during recent years were the Glenn Miller Orchestra, Guy Lombardo and His Royal Canadians, the Lettermen, and Bobby Rydell. Each act performs several times each day. Call for details.

## Dining and Shopping at Cypress Gardens

Your dining choices at Cypress Gardens are limited. Fortunately, the one full-service restaurant is a winner, especially when you choose to dine al fresco, overlooking the main floral display area. In addition to the eateries reviewed in this chapter, there are a number of small refreshment stands that operate seasonally.

Like the dining, the shopping is not a reason in itself to visit the park. There are some nice things to be found at the Butterfly Shop and the "country crafts" store, Plantation Emporium.

For those who keep track of such things, soft drinks are $1.40, $1.60, and $1.80 for small, medium, and large sizes.

# Good Things to Know About...

## Access for the Disabled

Almost all of the park is wheelchair accessible, although some of the inclines are best climbed with the help of a companion. The exceptions are the boat rides which may not be able to accommodate all disabled guests. Both wheelchairs and electric carts can be rented at the Bazaar Gift Shop in the entrance arcade. Wheelchairs are $5 per day. Electric carts rent for $6 an hour with a minimum of three hours; the maximum rental charge is $30.

A brochure, *All Are Welcome,* containing "helpful hints for guests with special needs" is available at Guest Relations in the main entrance arcade.

## Babies

Strollers can be rented at the Bazaar Gift Shop. Single strollers are $5 per day, doubles $6. Diaper changing stations can be found in most restrooms, men's and women's.

## Emergencies

Medical personnel are available during park hours. If you or someone in your party has a problem, contact the nearest park employee. If you lose a child, do the same; park staffers are far better able than you to comb the underbrush for your little ones.

## Leaving the Park

You may leave the park and return during the day. Just make sure to have your hand stamped as you leave.

## Lockers

Coin-operated lockers (50 cents for each use) can be found in the entrance arcade near the Bazaar Gift Shop.

## Mail

A tiny branch post office is located just outside the main gate, but plan to get there early. The window is open only from 9 a.m. to 10 a.m.,

Monday through Friday. Otherwise, stamps can be purchased at the Bazaar Gift Shop. Cards and letters posted here will receive a special "Cypress Gardens" postmark. If you're there when the window is open, ask them to use the hand cancellation stamp; it's easier to read.

## Merlin's Messages

An audio tour of the park is available via credit-card sized "smart cards" that you insert in special boxes scattered around the park. They activate a short recorded message with interesting information about the immediate surroundings. Merlin's Messages Smart Cards are available at all shops in Cypress Gardens for $3.18 including tax. They are computer coded to work only on the day of issue. Annual pass holders can get a year-long card for $10.60 including tax.

## Money

There is an ATM located in the entrance arcade, just before you reach the ticket windows. It is connected to the Plus, Cirrus, Honor, and Exchange networks. It will also provide cash advances on Visa and MasterCard.

## Pets

A self-service pet kennel will be found near the south parking area. The small, glass-fronted lockers (which look a bit like wall-mounted microwave ovens) cost $1.00 while the larger, dog-sized ones below cost $1.50. Quarters are required; change can be obtained from the shops in the nearby entrance arcade. Disposable food bowls and a wash-up sink are also provided.

## Safety

Cypress Gardens is open to all the birds and animals who take it into their minds to pay a visit. The park warns people not to feed the birds or other little critters because they are wild and unpredictable and may become aggressive. That's good advice, but the squirrels are hard to resist. It's unlikely that you'll see an alligator during your visit but, if you do, remember that feeding wild alligators is not only stupid but illegal.

## Special Diets

If you have special dietary needs, your best bet is the Crossroads Restaurant, which offers a number of special meals on request.

# Smelling the Flowers: Your Day at Cypress Gardens

Cypress Gardens can easily be seen and appreciated in a day. You may not see everything, but as you read through the descriptions that follow, you will probably find there are some things you won't mind missing.

## When's the Best Time to Come?

The size of the crowds is not a factor in picking the date of your visit; Cypress Gardens is rarely mobbed. And thanks to the wizardry of the horticultural staff, there's always something to see. If you're a true gardening buff, you may want to call ahead for the "Floral Calendar" to help guide your planning. Simply dial (941) 324-2111 and ask for extension 213, 215, or 290. Otherwise, I recommend spring and fall. The floral festivals at these times are spectacular and the weather is close to ideal; the summer can be stifling and winter is unpredictable, with temperatures ranging from pleasant to quite chilly.

## What to Expect

Cypress Gardens' fame rests primarily on its flowers and spectacular gardens. Many guests are also attracted by its reputation as the Water Ski Capital of the World. But the park has developed an eclectic blend of attractions. The major themes are:

*The Gardens.* Not only are "the original gardens" (so called to distinguish Pope's original creation from later innovations) still growing, but there are also regular floral festivals, the formal *Plantation Gardens*, and special garden-themed presentations.

*Water Skiing.* The Cypress Gardens water show is the original and, in the opinion of many, still the best.

*Variety Entertainment.* Cypress Gardens presents a regular schedule of family-style entertainment, from singers in the *Cypress Gazebo* to an ice show, to clowns and acrobats.

*Nature Shows.* In addition to the gardening shows already mentioned, Cypress Gardens presents show-and-tell presentations starring some of nature's most interesting birds and reptiles.

*Rides.* Cypress Gardens is not and never has been a "ride" park. Yet there are *some* rides, most of them for little ones. The only thing that qualifies as an adult ride is the fun aerial viewing platform, *Island in the Sky.*

This is not a large park, although when you take into account the meandering paths through the many garden areas, you can walk a fair distance during your visit. The park comprises 200 acres and runs north to south along the shore of Lake Eloise; it is divided into three areas, the "original" gardens, International Gardens, and Southern Crossroads.

# The One-Day Stay

As you enter the park, pick up a copy of the "Cypress Gardens Entertainment Schedule," a large one-sheet flyer with a map of the park and a schedule of shows and events. Scan this for the show times of the entertainments you most want to see and plan accordingly. In my opinion, the water ski show, "*Hot Nouveau Ice*," and "*Make 'Em Laugh*" are must sees. You should also choose one of the animal shows in *Nature's Theater*.

If you arrive at opening time, the Southern Crossroads area won't be open yet and the first water ski show will be a few hours away. So a visit to the nearby botanical gardens is a logical first step. This is also a good time to see them, before the heat of the day. Depending on how long it takes you to see the gardens, you may have time for both the *Botanical Boat Cruise* and the half-hour *Pontoon Lake Cruise*. If so, you may finish up just in time to catch the first performance of the water ski show. If you have a little time to kill, wander over to the International Gardens and check out the current floral show.

Now you have the afternoon to tour the attractions in Southern Crossroads and enjoy a leisurely lunch. In addition to the shows recommended above, don't miss *Wings of Wonder*. *Island in the Sky* is a fun diversion that can be squeezed in just about anytime you like; it only takes five minutes.

Another option is to save your visit to the botanical gardens for late in the day. Photographers, especially, may find the afternoon sun and the lengthening shadows a plus. You can linger until the staff starts to shoo you out at closing time.

## Attractions at Cypress Gardens

At the north end of the park, where you enter, is what I call "The Gardens," which comprises what the management refers to as "the **original gardens**" and the water ski arena. Proceeding south, you enter the **International Gardens**, a gentle valley that extends from the water ski arena to the entrance to Southern Crossroads. This is the area of the park in which the major floral festivals are held. (The exception is the Poinsettia Festival which is held in the Crossroads Pavilion, a large tent-like structure at the south end of the park.) In International Gardens you will find the lovely **Italian Fountain** and the **Mediterranean Waterfall**. The waterfall is artificial and fed by thousands of gallons of recycled lake water; the stream that flows from its base to the lake marks the approximate centerline of the park.

Finally, there is **Southern Crossroads**, a melange of shops, eateries, and attractions arranged along a pleasant tree-shaded promenade that

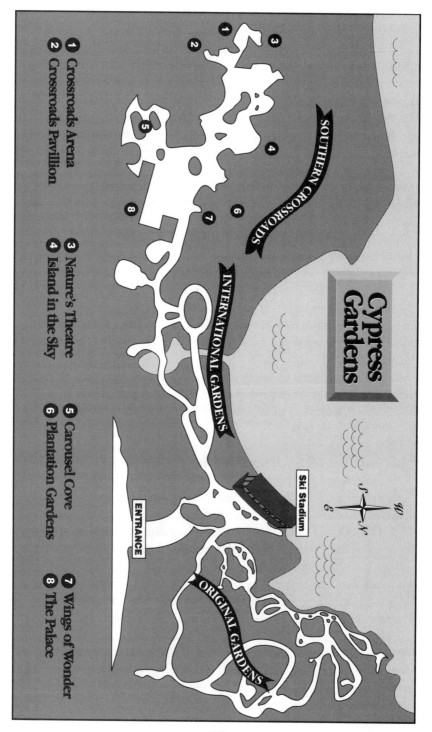

**Cypress Gardens**

SOUTHERN CROSSROADS

INTERNATIONAL GARDENS

ORIGINAL GARDENS

Ski Stadium

ENTRANCE

1 Crossroads Arena
2 Crossroads Pavillion
3 Nature's Theatre
4 Island in the Sky
5 Carousel Cove
6 Plantation Gardens
7 Wings of Wonder
8 The Palace

evokes the antebellum Deep South. Most of the park's attractions are located here.

For this survey of Cypress Gardens attractions, I will start at the north end of the park, describing the botanical gardens and their surrounding attractions, and then move directly to Southern Crossroads at the opposite end. I have not attempted to describe International Gardens simply because it is constantly changing with the seasons. See the list of Special Events above to get an idea of what you will find there at the time of your visit.

For those with sufficient time, starting at the north end of the park and slowing wending your way southward is a highly efficient way in which to see the entire park. Assuming that there will be a few attractions you will pass up, the entire tour can be done in a day. Those who want to be absolutely thorough will probably have to return a second day to complete their survey.

# "The Gardens"

The Gardens area contains relatively few attractions but they are the ones for which Cypress Gardens is justly famous. The two marquee attractions, the ski show and the botanical gardens, are doozies.

The water ski show area with its twin stadiums is the first thing you see as you enter the park, so we'll start there.

## Ski Stadium: "Ski Xtreme"

*Rating:*　　★ ★ ★ ★ ★
*Type:*　　Water ski spectacular
*Time:*　　20 minutes
*Kelly says:*　　The original and still the best

An entire industry was born here at Cypress Gardens when Dick Pope inaugurated regular water skiing shows. The story goes something like this: During the early forties, Pope staged a water skiing exhibition for a photographer as part of his on-going campaign to get free publicity for his park. This time he got something else. A group of soldiers was touring the park after the photo appeared and asked, "What time's the water ski show?" Thinking quickly, Pope quoted a show time that gave him just enough time to round up some water skiers and put on the first show.

Since then the water ski shows have become a Cypress Gardens trademark, one Pope promoted tirelessly. In a never-ending effort to improve the shows and stay one or more steps ahead of the inevitable copycats, Pope and his crew kept dreaming up new, bigger, and better stunts.

As a result, Cypress Gardens boasts 51 world-record water skiing firsts, the most recent (an eight-man flip off a single ramp) in 1993.

One result of all this striving is that Cypress Gardens doesn't have to resort to gimmicks to put on a good show. They simply showcase talented athletes who, by dint of hard work, have become the best in the world at what they do. The show has a theme, of course — currently it's a "competition" of water ski daredevils — but the structure of the show remains the same in all its incarnations — a display of water skiing artistry that moves deftly from the pretty nifty to the truly amazing.

True to the Pope tradition, the show doesn't ignore the possibilities of attractive young women (none dare call them girls) in bathing suits. The Cypress Gardens AquaMaids specialize in looking pretty but they are a lot more than cheesecake. These women are accomplished athletes who combine balletic grace with impeccable balance and split second timing in a series of appearances that punctuate the show.

The heart of the show is the stunt skiing, and that is the province of the men. Barefoot water skiing seems amazing enough to me but these guys do it in more ways than you'd imagine possible, from starting out face down and backwards in the water to jumping off regular water skis at 45 miles an hour. On a variety of skis and ski boards, they twist and flip and dismount spectacularly at the foot of the stands.

There is also an interlude of "adagio" skiing, male-female teams on a single pair of skis who engage in a series of graceful lifts as they speed along at 40 miles an hour. The form was borrowed from ice skating and adapted to water skis in the early seventies; I can't help feeling it's a lot harder on water.

In the guise of "The Rampmasters," four guys put on a display of gutsy ramp jumping that involves aerial spins over the heads of their colleagues, back and front flips in unison, and something called a "gainer," a sideways flip at nearly 50 miles an hour. A wonderfully corny circus clown interlude provides an opportunity for some good-natured high jinks and derring-do that may not be pretty but is still pretty amazing.

As a sort of bonus, they throw in something that has little to do with water skiing, except perhaps that the hang glider involved gets his initial lift by being towed behind a boat. The announcer points him out off in the distance and then, via a wireless mike, the high flying daredevil narrates his own descent and pinpoint landing on the shore between the two stadiums. Pretty neat if you've never seen it done before.

The climax of the show is one of Cypress Gardens' famed human pyramids — a four-level extravaganza in which a bottom row of six men hoist six AquaMaids aloft, the top one waving Old Glory as they zoom in review past the stands. Cypress Gardens skiers have actually created a five-level pyramid (there are photographs to prove it) but the trick is apparently too dangerous to attempt in public.

*The best seats in the house.* In this case there are two houses, twin stadiums separated by a grassy slope. You can also sit on the grass; the park provides simple cardboard mats to protect your tush from grass stains. My feeling is that the best seats are in the right-hand stadium. The hang glider zips right past you and the human pyramid heads directly towards you on its final run.

The stadiums' overhangs offer some protection from the sun, although the lower seats become exposed about midday. Seating is on simple aluminum benches. Signs painted on them warn that the first five rows may become a splash zone, but there seems less of an effort made here to soak you than at, say, SeaWorld. A splash or two does find its way into the seats but it's usually fairly localized.

*Extra added attraction:* If you have at least some level of water skiing experience, why not take advantage of your presence at Cypress Gardens to get some tips from the pros? Thanks to **Extreme Experience** you can. For $75, plus tax, you get a behind-the-scenes tour of the ski arena, a coaching session with a certified instructor, and the thrill of skiing in the show arena of the "Water Skiing Capital of the World." You must be at least six years old and sessions fill up on a first come, first served basis. Call (941) 324-2111 or inquire at the Information Booth in front of Landings Snack Bar near the ski stadium.

## Botanical Gardens

| | |
|---|---|
| *Rating:* | ★ ★ ★ ★ ★ |
| *Type:* | Beautifully landscaped gardens |
| *Time:* | 40 to 45 minutes or as long as you wish |
| *Kelly says:* | Among the best of its kind in the world and a photographer's paradise |

By definition, botanical gardens are a sort of museum. Most botanical gardens seem to strive for order. Succulents here, pines there, palms over there. Tropical plants in this area, temperate plants in that area. That way people can study them better. Completeness is also a goal, trying to have more epiphytes than the next botanical garden, for example. The aesthetics of display, while important, often seem to be a secondary concern, except in the more formal gardens.

The designers of Cypress Gardens, however, seem to have started by asking a simple yet powerful question — "How can we produce the most stunning visual spectacle possible?" — and letting everything else follow from there. The result is a remarkable blend of over-the-top land-scaping hyperbole and serene beauty.

These 16 acres contain over 8,000 different kinds of plants, trees, and flowers collected from 90 different countries. There are over 60 varieties of azaleas alone. I have no idea whether that means the collection is un-usually complete (I mention azaleas only because it's a flower I recog-nize). Nor do I know if the designers have carefully segregated tropical plants from the temperate varieties (I suspect they have not). I don't know if the Oriental Gardens contain only oriental plants or the French Garden only flowers indigenous to France. But I can't imagine anyone will care.

Here the purely aesthetic experience is paramount. A leisurely stroll, with open eyes and a receptive soul, will yield abundant treasures. And if you're a typical vacation photographer, bring along a few more rolls of film than usual. You'll find ample use for them.

As large as it is, the garden is not a maze and there's little likelihood of getting lost. The map on the *Cypress Gardens Entertainment Schedule* that you picked up at the park entrance, while schematic, is adequate and the trails are well marked. Real gardening enthusiasts may want to invest in a copy of *Cypress Gardens Botanical Walking Tour* (about $4), which can be purchased in the Bazaar Gift Shop in the entrance arcade and at other shops in the park. It contains a somewhat better map with a suggested route through the gardens marked in red arrows. It also contains a refer-ence to some of the many plants and flowers to be found in the gardens, including tips on which ones make good house plants.

Many plants in the gardens are identified by marker signs. The col-ored dots on the signs correspond to sections in the *Walking Tour*, al-though it's probably faster to look up the plant name in the index. The book contains close-up pictures of the plants it describes but unfortu-nately doesn't include any panoramic views of the garden's many stun-ning vistas.

*Tip:* The garden is dotted with wooden benches. Bring a handker-chief or paper towel, as many of them are wet in the morning hours, before the sun has had a chance to dry them off.

As you enter the gardens, you cross a bridge onto a chain of man-made islands. To your left is Lake Eloise, its shore often guarded by stately cypress trees emerging from the shallow water. To the right is a man-made canal. Must-see sights along this archipelago are the **Big Lagoon**, across which you will see a pretty Southern Belle gracing one of Cypress Garden's loveliest vistas. At the end of the island is a typical Dick Pope inspiration, the **Florida Pool**. This is a swimming pool in the shape of the state of Florida, nestled right against the lake shore. It's fenced off now and used primarily for publicity shots. Its main claim to immortality is its appearance in the 1953 Esther Williams film, *Easy To Love*.

The **Oriental Gardens** are an oasis of cool serenity presided over by a towering gold Buddha. A wooden "Japanese tea house" offers a place to sit in the shade and survey the scene. Even those seemingly immune to Nature's wonders will be startled by the massive **banyan tree**. This behemoth began its tenure at Cypress Gardens as a 50-pound sapling in a bucket. Today it's larger than your average castle, with its aerial root system creating a charming maze of paths through its very heart.

There are two formal gardens nestled here, the **Rose Garden** and the **French Garden**. The former pays homage to two saints: St. Francis of Assisi, better known as an animal lover, was also a devoted gardener. St. Fiacre, a seventh-century Irish monk who created a renowned monastery garden outside Paris, is the patron saint of gardeners. Interestingly, he is also the patron saint of taxi drivers, because in the 17th century the horse-drawn carriages that ran between Paris and his suburban shrine were nicknamed *fiacres*. The French Garden is a charming sunken brick oval with a perfectly symmetrical floral arrangement and a wooden bench under the spreading arms of a red silk cotton tree.

*Tip:* Near these two gardens is **Banyan Terrace**, a rental facility for meetings and banquets. When it is not otherwise engaged, the place is pretty much deserted, but you can find a bench on the broad terrace overlooking Lake Summit (where the ski team practices). It makes a nice quiet getaway from the heat and the sun.

Perhaps the most beautiful spot in the entire gardens is the **Gazebo**. This is no rustic wooden affair but a resplendent white-domed structure supported by eight fluted Greek columns and flanked by gently bubbling fountains. Also known as the "Love Chapel," it is the site of the over 300 weddings that take place at Cypress Gardens each year. The Gazebo stands at the top of a rise that looks down across the Big Lagoon and out to Lake Eloise; the view from here is as fine as the reverse view from below. An ingenious **photo op** has been provided near the French Garden. You stand facing a large mirror with your back to the Gazebo. Place your camera on the small platform provided, set the timer, and smile. You'll get a lovely shot of yourself with the Gazebo in the background and the words "Cypress Gardens" floating on the mirror.

The gardens are dotted with a rotating display of **wildlife sculpture**. Some are on permanent display but most are on loan from the artists. The display changes once a year, in November. If you take a fancy to one of these works of art, you can buy a copy. The smaller ones are almost cheap ($2,500 or so) but the larger pieces cost tens of thousands of dollars. If it makes the buying decision easier, five percent of the proceeds goes to support the work of the National Wildlife Federation.

## The Southern Belles

The Southern Belles deserve a special note. Although the botanical gardens seem to be their "natural habitat," they will be seen in all areas of the park. The story of their origins is another example of the wonderfully ingenious and utterly benign hucksterism that characterizes the history of Cypress Gardens.

It seems that in 1940 a devastating winter freeze killed the colorful but delicate flame vines that framed the entrance at that time. The interior of the park had been saved by the heat of many oil heaters and looked just fine. Visitors didn't know this, however, and when they saw the wilted entrance they assumed the worst and kept on driving.

Noticing this, Julie Pope, Dick's wife, rounded up a bevy of local high school girls and outfitted them in colorful antebellum hoop-skirted gowns. She then placed them strategically in front of the damaged flame vines to wave at approaching cars. Not only did attendance pick up, but the visitors were so enchanted by the girls that another Cypress Gardens tradition was born. Today, the Southern Belles take turns sitting decorously in the hot Florida sun to serve as beautiful props in tourists' photos. In typical Cypress Gardens hyperbole, they are billed as "the most photographed women in the world." Their bright and fanciful gowns are another Cypress Gardens trademark. All of them are made by hand at the park. Each one takes some 13 yards of fabric, 5 yards of lining, over 63 yards of lace, and more than 45 hours to complete. Since that moment of inspiration in 1940, over 800 of them have been created. Thanks to the *Junior Belle Program* (see *Shopping in Southern Crossroads*, below), visiting moms and daughters can live out this cheerful fantasy.

# Botanical Boat Cruise

*Rating:*      ★ ★ ★ ★
*Type:*       Guided boat tour
*Time:*       15 minutes
*Kelly says:*  Another perspective on these magnificent gardens

Near the entrance to the botanical gardens you will spot a lakeside landing for the boat cruise. This is a leisurely, short guided tour past the lake shore cypresses and back through the gardens' man-made canal aboard an 18-passenger motor launch.

It is not, I hasten to add, a substitute for a stroll through the gardens themselves but it does offer a different perspective and a few sights you can't see from the land.

As you cruise north along the shore and enter the canal that links Lakes Eloise and Summit you will see to your left a patch of untouched, dense cypress swamp that stands as a sort of "before" to the botanical gardens' "after." It makes you appreciate the magnitude of Pope's accomplishment.

Then you enter a man-made canal laboriously dug out of the muck by dollar-a-day laborers between 1936 and 1938. Later, you can see photos of the canal under construction in the *Cypress Roots* display at the other end of the park. Cruising through the canal you will pass the **Chairman of the Board**. With an estimated age of 1,600 years, it is the oldest cypress tree in the gardens. The canal cruise also offers an excellent look at the gardens' 27 varieties of palm trees, including a "one-in-a-million" two-headed palm tree. This botanical rarity is one of just four in the entire state of Florida.

The tour is capped off by a brief stop in the Big Lagoon for yet another look at the beautiful, flower-fringed greensward sloping up to the Gazebo.

## Pontoon Boat Cruises

*Rating:* ★ ★ ★ ★
*Type:* Boat cruise on the lake
*Time:* 30 minutes or 1 hour
*Kelly says:* Bird watching and real estate envy

There is an additional charge for these relaxing excursions, but it's worth the price. Tickets can be purchased at a booth in front of the Landings Snack Bar. You will be given a specific departure time; seating is limited so you may not always be able to get on the next sailing.

The **half-hour Lake Cruise** ($3.50, $2.50 for annual pass holders) takes you on a counterclockwise, seven-mile circumnavigation of Lake Eloise, never getting more than a few dozen yards off shore. Aside from the warm sun and the cool breeze, there are two major attractions of this ride. First is the nature. Be prepared to see lots of birds, or at least their nests. Ospreys have established a prominent place among the lakeside birds and their large nests and distinctive markings make them readily identifiable. You will also most likely see heron, cormorants, and anhinga, all of which your tour guide will point out. Depending on the time of the year, you may glimpse a gator or two or three, some sunning themselves placidly on residents' boat docks. One reason for the increase in raised sun decks around the lake was the gators' penchant for pulling themselves up alongside startled sunbathers. You'll also no doubt be treated to local lore about the 200-odd gators who call Lake Eloise home — the 14-footer that was captured and relocated to a remote area, the rogue gator that was shot and whose belly yielded nine dog collars.

The tour also serves as a ready-made real estate tour for those in the market and those who wish they could afford to be. Homes by the lake start at about $500,000 for places that would be hard to sell elsewhere to several million for the grander manses, including one that is a replica of Tara from *Gone with the Wind*. On a recent tour, a large house complete with mother-in-law apartment over the boathouse was on the market for $1.2 million. You'll learn that those huge screened-in pools and patios, called "Florida rooms," keep out not just the bugs but alligators as well. Apparently, once a gator gets into your pool, the fire department will have a tough time hauling him out.

*Tip:* During the spring, the last departure is a lovely "sunset cruise." Times vary, but it's generally around 6:30 p.m.

The **one-hour Eco-Tour** ($6, $4 for annual pass holders) covers much the same territory and subject matter but adds Lakes Lulu and Summit to the itinerary. The lakes are reached via narrow canals which link a total of 14 lakes in the Winter Haven area. On Lake Lulu you can glimpse the spring training home of the Cleveland Indians and on Lake Summit a section of Cypress Gardens that is open to the public only for special events.

## Swan Boat Adventure

*Rating:*       ★ ★ +
*Type:*        Paddle boat rentals
*Time:*        15 or 30 minutes
*Kelly says:*   If you must

Here you can rent two-seater paddle boats in the shape of large swans and take a short spin around the water ski arena. The rental fee is $6 for 15 minutes and $10 for half an hour. It's unlikely you'll need more time. For those who would rather not expend the calories paddling, each boat has a small electric motor. If you'd like to give it a go, inquire at the small stand in front of the Landings Snack Bar.

## Eating in "The Gardens"

Your dining choices here are strictly fast-food and strictly of the sweet and salty snack variety. All of these stands are conveniently located in or near the ski stadiums. Feel free to carry your snacks in to sustain you as you watch.

## SuperCone

This ice cream parlor specializes in waffle cone sundaes with your choice of hot fudge, strawberry, or caramel topping for under $4. Chocolate-dipped cones are a bit more. There is also the usual range of beverages. A sit-down counter along the picture window lets you watch the ski show in air-conditioned comfort.

## Lakeview Terrace

This stand is actually in the left ski stadium, up at the top of the stands. The featured snack here is turnovers, both apple and cherry ($2). Muffins, cookies, cotton candy, and soft pretzels are about the same price. There are a few small tables but most people eat in their seats.

## Landings Snack Bar

Located between the right ski stadium and the boat landing, this snack bar features funnel cakes (fried dough) with powdered sugar (about $2.50) or fruit (about $3). Also on hand are cookies, strudel, and muffins, all for about $2, along with the usual array of beverages. Seating is outdoors at small tables with awnings.

# Shopping in "The Gardens"

There's really only one shop in "The Gardens." That is Resort Wear. All the other shops described here are in the entrance arcade, before the ticket booths. They can be visited without paying admission to the park.

## Resort Wear

The Entertainment Schedule you picked up at the gate calls this shop the Ski and Surf Shop, but the sign outside says "Resort Wear." Inside you'll find an extensive selection of t-shirts, polos, and sweats in a variety of styles, patterns, and colors, from kiddie models at about $10 to more elaborate adult styles for about $38. Most are in the $14 to $20 range. There is also a goodly selection of ladies swim wear and a variety of straw hats for both men and women.

## Rainbow Wax Works

This small booth sells multicolored, carved, and intricately twisted candles. Prices start at about $10 and go up to about $30 or so.

## Baker's Dozen

This bakery and coffee shop is a place to stop for breakfast on the way into the park or to load up on goodies for the drive back to the motel or for tomorrow's in-room breakfast. Turnovers, muffins, Danish, and giant cookies are $2 to $3. You can also pick up Cypress Gardens' award-winning key lime pie by the slice or, better yet, pick up a whole pie for about $12. There are stools and a counter inside and shaded outdoor tables.

## Bazaar Gift Shop

Perhaps the largest gift shop at the park, the Bazaar focuses on items that feature the Cypress Gardens name and logo on every imaginable surface, from shot glasses to t-shirts. There's also a kids' section and a nice assortment of collectible figurines and wall hangings. You will find some beautifully elaborate old-fashioned dolls with prices to match.

## Photo Memories

This photo shop sells film and frames and also offers "olde time" photos with its small collection of period costumes. Its main business, however, is providing the photographic support for the *Junior Belle Program* (see below).

## Sweet Creations

This is a standard-issue candy store featuring eight varieties of fudge ($4 for half a pound), honey, and an assortment of candies ($5 a pound).

## Camelot Crystal

Small, delicate glass sculptures are made before your eyes in this shop. Prices start at about $10 and go up from there.

# Southern Crossroads

At the South end of the park, Southern Crossroads evokes a make-believe antebellum Southland that probably never existed in quite this quaint a form. The long promenade (which dead-ends at the park's Southern extremity) is accented by flowers and shaded by oaks dripping theatrically in Spanish moss. Off this central corridor is artfully arranged a collection of shops, restaurants, and entertainments in gracious white clapboard buildings. The area is actually quite compact, yet it seems wonderfully spacious and contains a multiplicity of things to see and do.

The following attractions are described in roughly the order in which you will encounter them as you walk through Southern Crossroads:

# The Palace: "Hot Nouveau Ice"

*Rating:* ★ ★ ★ +
*Type:* Ice show
*Time:* 25 minutes
*Kelly says:* Tame but tasty

The Palace evokes an old Southern playhouse, complete with faux marble columns at the entrance. Inside is an 800-seat auditorium with a standard proscenium stage. The stage area has been converted into an ice rink but, given, the shallowness of the performing area, some compromises have been made. Don't expect the electrifying leaps you may have seen in other ice shows where the skaters have the advantage of larger arenas.

That being said, the 10 Russian performers who grace this show do the most with the space available. The show uses a celebration of earth and its peoples as a thread on which to string a quick succession of smoothly elegant dance numbers. Visits to Scotland, India, Italy, and America's own Broadway offer plenty of opportunities for aestheticism and grace. Best of all are the adagio acts in which the man lifts his graceful female partner high overhead as they glide gracefully across the stage. Another standout is a solo ballet to the strains of "Don't Cry For Me, Argentina." *Hot Nouveau Ice* performs about four shows a day. If this sort of thing appeals, check the schedule to make sure you don't miss it.

# Tampa Electric's Bright House

*Rating:* ★
*Type:* Exhibit
*Time:* Continuous viewing
*Kelly says:* Can be missed

This vest-pocket exhibit, just outside the entrance to The Palace, is a self-administered pat on the back for its sponsor. Best part: the black and white photos of Tampa Electric's early days.

# Wings of Wonder

*Rating:* ★ ★ ★ ★ +
*Type:* Butterfly-filled conservatory
*Time:* Continuous viewing
*Kelly says:* One of Cypress Gardens' best

What an inspired idea this is! Build a 5,500 square foot Victorian style glass conservatory and run a stream through it. Keep the glass walls and roof sparkling clean. Plant the conservatory with the kinds of trees, plants, and flowers that butterflies love. Then fill the space with over

1,000 free-flying butterflies, exotic waterfowl, and a few iguanas.

The result is pure enchantment and an experience that will reward patient viewing. The more you look, the more butterflies you will see. Some of them are so ingeniously camouflaged, it may be many minutes before you realize they are there at all. A looping path takes you through this wonderland, past babbling waterfalls and quiet ponds as butterflies flutter all about you. At the back, you can see butterflies in the pupal stage, just before they emerge in all their splendor; with a bit of luck, you may see one break through to the light. Somewhere between 700 and 1,000 butterflies are hatched each week in this fashion to keep the conservatory well stocked.

# Plantation Gardens

| | |
|---|---|
| *Rating:* | ★ ★ ★ |
| *Type:* | Formal gardens |
| *Time:* | Continuous viewing |
| *Kelly says:* | Best for serious gardeners |

Past *Wings of Wonder* a large open area with a stunning view of the lake has been set aside to showcase themed formal gardens. The **butterfly garden** has been designed to attract the local species. The **herb and scent garden** invites you to touch, rub, and taste. If you've never seen a vegetable in the wild, you may spot one of your favorites in the **vegetable garden**. The **rose garden** offers another chance to display this perennial favorite. Looking back you will have a lovely view of Magnolia Mansion. Or stroll across the lush green lawn to the lake's edge, a spot rarely visited by guests.

# Crossroads Gazebo

| | |
|---|---|
| *Rating:* | ★ ★ + |
| *Type:* | Live solo entertainers |
| *Time:* | About 20 minutes per show |
| *Kelly says:* | If you must |

The gazebo in question is a small structure in the middle of the Southern Crossroads promenade. Here, about every hour throughout the afternoon, earnest young singers accompanied by a synthesized rhythm section attempt to entertain an audience of resting seniors old enough to be their grandparents. It's got to be the toughest job in show business.

Sometimes the performers are quite good. At other times they uncomfortably resemble Bill Murray's goshawful lounge singer on *Saturday Night Live*. My advice: Give it a try. If you aren't having fun, just get up and head for the shops.

## Carousel Cove

*Rating:* ★ ★ ★
*Type:* Kiddie rides
*Time:* As long as you (and junior) can stand
*Kelly says:* Head here with squirmy kids

You enter *Carousel Cove* near the *Crossroads Gazebo*. On your right is the colorful carousel with its gaily painted wooden horses. To the left is a putt-putt golf course and a small video arcade. The golf costs extra (about $2), as do the arcade games, but the carousel and the half dozen or so kiddie rides you will find farther back cost nothing.

The gaudy carousel seems to appeal to kids up to about 10 or 11. The other rides will probably seem déclassé to anyone much over five. At the very back of *Carousel Cove* is a regular old playground with a climb-up, crawl-through, slide down structure in wood and plastic, a welcome refuge for tired moms (or grandparents) with active kids.

## Cypress Junction

*Rating:* ★ ★ ★ ★
*Type:* Model railroad exhibit
*Time:* Continuous viewing
*Kelly says:* A treat for the model railroad buff

Maintained by a volunteer staff of locals, the HO-gauge train set on display here is one of the nicest I've seen. Others may be larger or have more trains, or more "miles" of track, or more levels and tunnels and switchbacks, but surely there are few that are as exquisitely designed as this. Especially enthralling are some of the smaller touches, like the airliner flying past the thunderstorm (complete with thunder and lightning). The trains travel through "six identifiable areas of the United States" beginning in what looks like Miami Beach, visiting the Southwest and Chicago before ending in the "mountains of Maine." Be sure to pick up the one-page flyer in the small wooden box near the entrance for all the facts and figures on this astonishing labor of love.

## Kodak's Island in the Sky

*Rating:* ★ ★ ★ ★
*Type:* Aerial platform ride
*Time:* 5 minutes
*Kelly says:* A too-short bird's eye view

Tucked away behind Magnolia Mansion is a 370 ton counterbalance which is used to loft a circular platform 153 feet in the air (roughly 16 stories high), where it rotates to give its passengers a panoramic view of

Cypress Gardens and Lake Eloise. Off in the distance, you can see the silhouette of stately Bok Tower, 11 miles away. Seating is single-file around the edge of the platform and once the platform is airborne, you can stand and move to the rail for a better look. The center of the platform is gussied up to resemble a snow-capped volcanic mountain.

This is a fun way to get another perspective on the park, and the lofty vantage point offers photographers many wonderful **photo ops**. At five minutes from start to finish, this ride is a bit too short for my taste, but it's free and you can ride as often as you wish (or until your film runs out). The location of this attraction and the mobile platform itself have been cleverly hidden behind trees and buildings. You can see the raised platform from elsewhere in the park, but you could spend all day in Southern Crossroads and never suspect it was there.

# Antique Radio Museum

*Rating:*      ★ ★
*Type:*        Exhibit
*Time:*        Continuous viewing
*Kelly says:*  A blast from grandpa's past

This hodgepodge display of old radios and radio components will probably appeal most to people who will experience a wave of nostalgia when they see the very console on which they listened to FDR's fireside chats or the old crystal set on which they heard news of the Hindenberg disaster. I had that very experience with a snazzy 1950s plastic Westinghouse table model on which I heard the first, seminal chords of rock and roll. For younger visitors these may be the first radios they've seen outside a car or a Walkman.

# Cypress Roots

*Rating:*      ★ ★ +
*Type:*        Exhibit
*Time:*        Continuous viewing
*Kelly says:*  Cypress Gardens memorabilia, and worth
               a peek

This small exhibit houses bits and pieces of Cypress Garden's family album, everything from vintage water skis to a "celebrity wall" of stars who have visited (there's a key in case you don't recognize Tiny Tim). A vintage television console plays clips from movies and television shows that were shot at Cypress Gardens. Photos and newspaper clippings provide a fascinating, if somewhat spotty, history of Cypress Gardens and its founder's prodigious penchant for publicity.

Check out one of Dick Pope's gaudy sports jackets, a flowered model looking like it was cut from upholstery fabric. Pope explained his eye-popping sartorial style by pointing out that he was a short man. Unless he dressed conspicuously, he claimed, people might mistake him for "a short fire plug."

# Gardens Theatre

| | |
|---|---|
| *Rating:* | ★ ★ |
| *Type:* | Slide show and talk |
| *Time:* | 15 minutes |
| *Kelly says:* | Strictly for gardeners |

Under the title "Why Do Plants . . . ? (And Other Botanical Mysteries)," this show presents a brief slide presentation about the wonderful world of plants. A typical presentation may discuss the variety of ways in which plants adapt to meet the special circumstances of their environments. These presentations will appeal most to those who have a serious interest in gardening or botany. Others may find them a bit dull.

# Crossroads Arena: "Make 'Em Laugh"

| | |
|---|---|
| *Rating:* | ★ ★ ★ |
| *Type:* | Circus-style show |
| *Time:* | 20 to 25 minutes |
| *Kelly says:* | An entertaining interlude |

"*Make 'Em Laugh*" presents a changing lineup of Russian circus performers who entertain several times a day in this domed tent at the back of Southern Crossroads. While perhaps not of the first rank, these performers are never less than genial and at least some acts are guaranteed to catch your fancy. I especially liked the lady clown with a trained white cat. Yes, you read that right — a *trained* cat, who runs around his trainer's body while she performs rolls on the floor. In keeping with the theme, a pair of droll clowns punctuate the acrobatic and tumbling acts with inspired bits of insanity. Younger kids will really enjoy this show and their elders will not be bored.

# Nature's Way

| | |
|---|---|
| *Rating:* | ★ ★ ★ |
| *Type:* | Small zoo |
| *Time:* | Continuous viewing |
| *Kelly says:* | Worth a stroll-through en route to the shows in Nature's Theatre |

This vest-pocket zoo is tucked away in a corner of the park under an attractively shaded canopy of moss-draped oaks. Most animals are held in roughly circular sunken pits, eliminating the need for bars.

Most of the animals are Florida natives (although there is a growing collection of "exotic" animals such as rheas, emus, and wallabies). Best of all are the injured birds of prey for which Cypress Gardens cares; some of them appear in the presentations in *Nature's Theatre*. There is also a magnificent Indian rock python, all 17 feet and 225 pounds of him.

Along the shores of Lake Eloise you will find **Nature's Boardwalk**, a charming area offering a chance to feed the emus and such (50 cents for a small handful of food pellets) and delightful views across the lake. Also in this area is the **Birdwalk Aviary**, a walk-in exhibit of birds and a few tiny Muntjac, or barking, deer. The big draw here are the chattering, multi-hued lorys and lorikeets which you can also feed ($1).

Near the exit to *Island in the Sky* is the **Florida Historical Garden Railway**. Created by architect and railway enthusiast Paul Busse, it features some 5,000 feet of G-scale train tracks snaking though a lush landscape dotted with clever models of historic Florida buildings cunningly made from natural materials like acorns, leaves, bark, and seed pods.

With the possible exception of the python, you can see more, larger, and better displayed specimens at other zoo-type attractions in the Orlando area. Still, this makes a pleasant time-killer as you wait for the nature shows to begin.

# Nature's Theatre

*Rating:*    ★ ★ ★
*Type:*    Nature show
*Time:*    15 minutes
*Kelly says:*    Too short

Nature's Theatre is a simple tarp-covered amphitheater that serves as the venue for a series of educational nature shows hosted by Cypress Gardens' staff members. Check the schedule for show times. In what may be a sad commentary on the attention span of its guests, Cypress Gardens has combined separate 15-minute shows on birds of prey and reptiles into one 15-minute show about both, entitled **"Raptors and Reptiles."**

The raptors are Cypress Gardens' lineup of injured birds of prey that can never be released back to the wild and are living out their lives in the comfort and security of the Gardens. They earn their room and board by posing for your photos during this informative presentation. At a typical show you will see two birds of prey, perhaps a red-tailed hawk and a barred owl. For each bird, the handlers present a fascinating sampler of natural history tidbits. The bird is then paraded in front of the audience for those who wish to take close-up photos. Interestingly, despite their phenomenally keen eyesight, these raptors are not fazed by popping flashes.

The reptile portion features the show's true star, an albino Indian rock python with the rather cruel nickname "Banana Boy." The snake retains the camouflage markings of his species but with a pronounced yellow hue. It's a beautiful animal. Also on the program is a small gator. Once again, the presenters fill us in on fascinating factoids about each species and bring them forward for a closer look and a snapshot or two.

# Eating in Southern Crossroads

For anything more substantial than a snack, you will have to head for Southern Crossroads. Here you will find a small but good selection of eateries. I have described them in rough order as you encounter them on entering the Southern Crossroads section of the park.

## Crossroads Restaurant & Terrace

*What:*　　　Full-service restaurant with lovely terrace
*Where:*　　　Near entrance to Southern Crossroads
*Price Range:*　$$ - $$$

This is Cypress Gardens' only full-service restaurant and, given its moderate pricing, it shouldn't disappoint. The interior decor is simple and tasteful but, on a fine day, the better choice is to dine al fresco. The tree-shaded outdoor terrace overlooks the International Gardens area where the annual flower festivals are held. Overhead fans keep the air circulating. All in all, a perfectly delightful dining experience.

The food may not win any awards (the exception is noted below), but it is fresh and attractively presented in generous portions at modest prices. Among the appetizers, the sumptuous basket of light and feathery Diablo onion rings (about $3) and the seafood stuffed mushroom caps (about $3.50) are good choices.

Entrees are in the $8 to $9 range and include standbys like carved roast beef au jus and fried shrimp. I particularly liked the creamy chicken in puff pastry and the Alpine chicken with cheese and mushrooms. All entrees come with a small side salad and a choice of french fries or rice pilaf. Main course salads — chicken, seafood, and fruit — are about $7 or $8, as are the sandwiches, which include Cypress Gardens' version of a club sandwich, a French dip sandwich, and the usual burgers.

The desserts ($2 to $3) are special. In fact, the key lime pie was chosen as the best in the region by a local newspaper. Also worth checking out is the chocolate pecan pie with vanilla ice cream. Treat yourself to a dessert on the Terrace.

## Carousel Ice Cream

*What:*     Ice cream stand
*Where:*    At entrance to *Carousel Cove*
*Price Range:*  $

A basic walk-up ice cream stand dispensing cones and floats in the $2 to $3 range, along with the usual range of beverages.

## Cypress Deli

*What:*     Fast-food BBQ
*Where:*    In the plaza near the *Crossroads Gazebo*
*Price Range:*  $$

Barbecue ribs and chicken (about $6 to $7) are the featured items here, although "deli sandwiches" (about $6) are also on the menu. The BBQ is quite good actually, although the takeout style presentation doesn't tend to raise one's expectations. Key lime pie is also available here at about $2.50 the slice.

Service is fast-food style at a walk-up window and the eating area is largely outdoors. Time your meal to one of the regular shows at the Gazebo and you can be entertained as you eat.

## Magnolia Mansion

*What:*     Drinks and snacks in a posh setting
*Where:*    Overlooking *Plantation Gardens*
*Price Range:*  $

Magnolia Mansion is another Dick Pope inspiration. It is a heavily re-modeled former private home that evokes the stately white-columned splendor of antebellum plantations. All that is served here is beer and soft drinks with a few salty snacks. You can sit indoors in a country-club setting or (better) outside on a terrace overlooking the gardens and Lake Eloise.

## Ice Cream Parlor

*What:*     Ice cream specialties
*Where:*    Near *Island in the Sky*
*Price Range:*  $

Deep-dish fruit cobblers with ice cream are the specialty here, along with the usual sundaes, for a bit over $3. There is very little indoor seating available here.

## Village Fare Food Court

*What:*     Take-your-pick selection of fast-food windows

*Where:*          Near exit of *Island in the Sky*
*Price Range:*   $$

Village Fare is a large circular eatery with a semicircular array of fast-food windows along the back wall. The number of windows operating at any given time is a function of the crowds the park is drawing.

Choices range from deli sandwiches, to roast beef or fried chicken dinners, to burger platters and baskets with fries. The typical main course will run about $5 to $6. Beer is served here for about $2, along with the usual array of soft drinks.

# Shopping in Southern Crossroads

The shops in Southern Crossroads are less cluttered with Cypress Gardens souvenirs than one might expect. Instead, there is a nice selection of craft-type gifts and gardening paraphernalia, along with some more touristy fare.

### Ole Woodcutter

This small shop specializes in die-cut wooden names. You have your choice of plain ($5) or mirror-coated ($10) wood. Names mounted on themed wooden backgrounds cost upwards of $30.

### The Bear Bungalow

There is a bewildering variety of teddy bears on display here, from simple little bears, to elaborately dressed up Southern Belle bears, to truly humongous bears that will dwarf a small child. Prices range from about $12 all the way up to about $350. Also available are bear figurines and bear prints.

### Butterfly Shop

Located at the exit to *Wings of Wonder*, this shop is impossible to miss. Not surprisingly, the theme is butterflies. There are butterfly stickers, pins, magnets, books, t-shirts, jewelry, even a little motorized butterfly that will flutter tirelessly around your potted plants. At the upper end of the price range are mounted butterflies and other insects in acrylic display cases for up to $100.

### The Garden Shop

Across the promenade from the Butterfly Shop, this outlet features garden accessories and gifts for your gardening friends. Whimsically painted garden furniture will set you back several hundred dollars, but there are many moderately priced choices, from garden sculpture and fountains to wind chimes, books, and seeds. One of the more unusual gift items is Zoo Doo, small animal sculptures of clay and "organic zoo manure." Place them in your garden and they slowly dissolve, releasing their nutrients into the soil.

## Plantation Emporium

"Country crafts" are the theme at this spacious shop, which means quilt-patterned wall hangings, rag rugs, baskets, teddy bears, and other stuffed animals, as well as a broad selection of decorative objects with a country flavor. You can pick up Cypress Gardens salad dressing and condiments, too. There is a small selection of works by local artists, most of whom are accomplished amateurs. Prices are moderate.

## Junior Belle Boutique

This is headquarters for the **Junior Belle Program**, a brilliant gimmick of which Dick Pope would have most assuredly approved. For just $28.57 (tax included) you can have your daughter dolled up and dressed up just like one of the real Southern Belles for a one-hour stroll through the park grounds and a free photograph. Perfect! Cypress Gardens gets more adorable atmosphere and *you* pay for it! On top of that, they give you a press kit to send to your local newspaper along with a picture of your little angel, the perfect Pope touch.

Cynicism aside, the results are absolutely adorable and you might find it hard to resist. There's also a deluxe package for $42.35, which offers a two-hour stroll and the use of the perfect accessory, a parasol. If you really want to go whole hog, Mom can dress up too. The program is officially for girls three to 12, although they will bend a bit on either end of the age spectrum. Annual pass holders receive a 10 percent discount.

## Historical Research, Inc.

This shop is one outlet in an international chain with over 500 locations. For about $16 their computer will spit out a history of your family name on acid-free paper in ink that will not fade in the light. You can gussy it up with framing and a variety of coats of arms if you wish. If you can't rein in your family pride, you can easily spend several hundred dollars here.

# CHAPTER SIX:

# Gatorland

Those born during World War II or earlier, may remember the road
side attractions that dotted the tourist landscape. Half carnival side-
show, half shanty town, these entrepreneurial "attractions" served as
living proof of Mencken's maxim that "no one ever went broke underes-
timating the taste of the American public." Trading on actual freaks of
nature ("See the two-headed calf!") or objects of less certain provenance
("Mummified Indian chief!"), the typical roadside attraction tended to
spread incrementally along the highway as the owner figured out new
ways to lure the passing parade of cars with stranger wonders or larger
souvenir shops featuring the latest in joy buzzers and whoopee cushions.
Each year, it seemed, the advertising budget would finance a few more
garish billboards, a few more miles away, until tourists knew hundreds of
miles in advance that something extraordinary lay ahead. The old roadside attractions were a blight on the landscape. They were tacky, low-
brow, often smelly, and altogether marvelous. They represent one of the
most cherished memories of my youth and I wish they were still around.

At Gatorland, they still are — in a way. Gatorland is a modern and
evolving nature-themed attraction. It is well-run, clean, and in spite of
the 5,000 alligators crammed into its 55 acres, remarkably smell free. But
its roots are firmly in the roadside attraction tradition. In fact, that's how
it started out back in 1949.

Owen Godwin was a local cattle rancher — Florida was once
America's second-biggest cattle producer, after Texas — who decided to
turn a liability into an asset. Alligators were the Florida cattleman's nemesis. They would hunker down in water holes and kill unsuspecting

calves. This intolerable loss of income prompted a vendetta against the gator and cattlemen became adept at capturing and killing the scaly predators. Godwin realized not only that there was a market for the hides and meat of the gators he killed but that few of the tourists who whizzed past on highway 441 had ever seen an alligator and might pay for the privilege. So Godwin rounded up some gators and a passel of the snakes that thronged his property and the "Snake & Reptile Village" was born, beckoning to the southbound tourist traffic. Even today, in spite of Orlando's phenomenal post-Mickey growth, Gatorland's location seems a bit out of the way. In 1949, it really must have seemed in the middle of nowhere.

Gatorland has come a long way since its early days, not so much in its look and feel as in its focus and attitude. For a while Godwin followed the pattern of many roadside attractions. As he prospered, he traveled farther afield, adding "exotic" animals to his collection. Those days are past and only a few holdovers from that era remain.

Today the emphasis is on alligator farming — the park is a working farm sending over 1,000 gators to market each year — and the conservation of Florida species. Gatorland is also a partner with the University of Florida in alligator research and is the only place on earth where alligators are bred through artificial insemination.

Compared to the big attractions in town — Universal Studios and SeaWorld — Gatorland is downright modest. Many of the exhibits are made of simple cinder block construction painted white and green, and I'm sure the appearance of much of the park hasn't changed a whole lot since the sixties. Rather than a being a drawback, I find this homey quality to be a large part of Gatorland's charm. If you don't come with exaggerated expectations fueled by Hollywood scenic artists and are willing to accept the park on its own low-key terms, you won't be disappointed.

## Getting There

Gatorland is located at 14501 South Orange Blossom Trail, also known as US Routes 441, 17, and 92, in the southern fringes of Orlando. It is seven miles south of the Florida Mall and 3.5 miles north of US 192 in Kissimmee. To reach Gatorland from I-4, take either the Bee Line Expressway (SR 538) or Central Florida Parkway East to Orange Blossom Trail and turn right.

Gatorland will be on your left as you drive south, made prominent by its trademark alligator jaws entrance. There is parking for about 500 cars, which gives you an indication of the size of the crowds they expect. Parking is free and all spaces are a short walk from the entrance.

# Opening and Closing Times

Gatorland is open from 9:00 a.m. until dusk. In winter that means until 6:00 p.m., in spring and fall 7:00 p.m., and in summer 8:00 p.m. The park, which is largely out of doors, operates rain or shine.

# The Price of Admission

At press time, admission prices (including tax) were as follows:

| | |
|---|---|
| Adults: | $14.79 |
| Juniors (10-12): | $9.49 |
| Children (3 to 9): | $6.87 |

One child is admitted **free** with each paying adult.

Annual passes are $29.65, $21.18, and $15.88 (tax included), for adults, juniors, and kids, respectively. You can upgrade to the annual pass before leaving the park on the day of your visit. If you think you will return more than once, this is a good deal. I suspect it will appeal most to bird watchers and nature photography buffs who will find plenty to keep them occupied at various times of the year. Gatorland's annual pass is good only for admission to the park. It does not give you a discount at the restaurants or gift shop, nor does it allow you to bring in guests at a discount.

Members of AAA, CAA (the Canadian Automobile Association), AARP, and the military receive a 20% discount on admission. These discounts cannot be combined with any dollars-off coupons.

# Good Things to Know About . . .

## Access for the Disabled

The entire park is accessible to the disabled (with the exception of the third level of the Observation Tower in the Alligator Breeding Marsh) and wheelchairs are available on a rental basis for $3.71 per day, plus a $10 refundable deposit.

## Babies

Strollers are available on the same terms as those for wheelchairs. Diaper changing facilities will be found in all restrooms.

## "Crackers"

You'll hear the words "Cracker" and "Cracker-style" a lot at Gatorland. The term "Cracker" refers to Florida's version of the cowboy. Using ropes to snare recalcitrant and wandering cattle was the norm in the West but it was not an option in the thick palmetto groves of Central Florida. So the cowboys took to using whips which they would crack over the heads of the cows to get them moving. Gradually, they came to be known as "Crackers" for the sound the whips made as they plied their trade and they adopted their nickname with pride.

Today, the word is used at Gatorland to refer to any native-born Floridian. The term "Cracker-style" is used to describe anything with the look or feel of turn of the century Florida. Thus, "Cracker-style architecture" refers to wooden buildings with peaked tin roofs and wide verandahs on all four sides. Be aware, however, that the word "Cracker" is a term of opprobrium in some quarters, carrying connotations of racism and ignorance. I wouldn't advise using it in casual conversation.

## Leaving the Park

When you pay your admission, your hand will be stamped with a gator symbol that allows you to leave the park (for lunch perhaps?) and return on the same day.

## Money

An ATM hooked up to the Honor System is located in the gift shop.

## Safety

Alligators may look like they never move a muscle but they can move with surprising speed when a meal is in the offing. And to an alligator your toddler looks an awful lot like lunch. The railings over the alligator lake have been fitted with green mesh guards to discourage leaning over the sides. Nonetheless, I have seen people lift their children onto the railings and lean them over for a closer look or to help them feed the gators.

**DON'T DO THIS!** You will not only give people like me heart failure but if your child wriggles loose and falls he or she could very well be killed.

## Special Diets

Gatorland restaurants are not equipped to handle special diets. However, Gatorland welcomes picnickers, so feel free to bring your own meals. In fact, feel free to bring an entire cooler. There are several nice areas to eat your own meals; just ask a park employee. No alcoholic beverages are permitted and Gatorland requests that you do not bring any glass containers into the park.

# Swamp Thing: Your (Half) Day at Gatorland

Gatorland recommends four hours as a comfortable time in which to see the park. That seems about right to me. Many people stay for a shorter period and it's doubtful you will stay longer unless you are an ardent bird watcher or a wildlife photographer willing to wait for that perfect shot. In any event, you can take your time here. There is never any need to rush madly from place to place to avoid long lines or crushing crowds.

## When's the Best Time to Come?

Even at the height of the tourist seasons, Gatorland will be far less mobbed than the larger attractions. The best time to visit, then, is dictated more by the patterns of the animals than those of the people who come to see them.

Alligators are cold blooded and derive their warmth from the sun and surrounding atmosphere. Thus, in the winter they tend to be slow moving and sluggish, not that they're particularly lively in the best of circumstances. April and May is breeding time and if you visit then you will be entertained by the bellowing of amorous males attracting their mates. It sounds a bit like a lovesick Harley if you can imagine such a thing. Alligators lay hard-shelled eggs in nests on the ground. So by June you may be able to see nests in the *Breeding Marsh*. The hatchlings emerge in late August and early September, when visitors will be treated with dozens of joyous events in the *Gator Grunts Nursery*. Birds have their own migratory and mating patterns. Nesting in the *Alligator Breeding Marsh* begins in January or February, hits its peak in April and May, and continues through the summer, as various species arrive to raise their young.

## What to Expect

As I mentioned before, Gatorland is modest in both scale and execution. Unlike the bigger parks, it's not filled with attendants and hosts; you are pretty much on your own, although you can certainly feel free to collar one of the "Crackers" with your questions.

The park is an elongated rectangle divided into three main parts. The first is a huge alligator-clogged lake that stretches the entire length of the park. When you enter the park from the Gift Shop after paying your admission you step onto a large wooden platform over this lake. The platform is honeycombed with open areas filled with sunbathing and swimming gators. One of these openings is the site of the *Gator Jumparoo* show, Gatorland's signature attraction. Also on this platform is the loading area for the Gatorland train ride.

Across the wooden platform, you will find *Alligator Alley*, the second major area of the park. It is a long, narrow, shaded concrete walkway that runs north and south through the middle of the park. It is instantly recognizable by the wavy, blue-green, snake-like line down its middle. Along this walkway you will find a variety of displays, animal pens, and scientific work areas, as well as (at the southern end) the *Gator Wrestlin'* arena and Pearl's Smokehouse.

On the other side of *Alligator Alley* is the third major area, a 10-acre *Alligator Breeding Marsh*, with its wooden walkway and Observation Tower. The *Swamp Walk*, reached through a gate at the south end of the park, comprises a separate fourth area.

## The Half-Day Stay

When you pay your admission you will be given a sheet of paper with a Gatorland map on one side and a schedule of the day's shows on the other. Check to see the starting time of the next show. If you have more than half an hour before show time, head straight for the *Gatorland Train Station* (keep bearing right) and take the short but informative train ride. This will give you a brief orientation to the park and the first bits of the considerable amount of alligator trivia you will collect during your visit.

The next order of business will be the live shows. It doesn't much matter in which order you see them. You may want to consider seeing the wrestling show twice. In between shows, you can check out the smaller exhibits dotted along the spine of the park.

Give yourself at least 20 uninterrupted minutes or more to take in the *Alligator Breeding Marsh and Bird Sanctuary*, more if it's nesting season. You'll probably want to spend some time at the highest level of the Observation Tower for a great bird's-eye view and then take a leisurely stroll along the water level walkway for a closer look. The *Swamp Walk* is restful but not a must-see unless you're a bird watcher.

## Attractions at Gatorland

There are three live shows at Gatorland, each presented several times a day, and they form the heart of the Gatorland experience. The shows let us get close — but not too close — to critters that alternately fascinate and repel us. Since alligators and other reptiles are a natural source of curiosity for most of us, it's easy for these shows to jump right in and start answering our unasked questions about these scaly creatures. The result is that staple of the modern-day theme park: effortless "edutainment."

A group of about five young men, all Florida natives, or "Crackers" in Gatorland parlance, take turns starring in these exhibitions. They have mastered an easy, laid back, aw-shucks, country boy style that is most ingratiating. The humor — and there's lots of it — is self-deprecating while at the same time letting us city slickers know who's got the really cool job. These guys are the living embodiment of Gatorland and I think you'll find it hard not to like them.

## Gator Jumparoo

*Rating:* ★ ★ ★ ★
*Type:* Outdoor show
*Time:* 15 minutes
*Kelly says:* As close as it gets to performing alligators

This show is simplicity itself. The scene is a large open square in the wooden platform over the alligator lagoon. A walkway leads to a small platform in the middle where our host stands and dangles plucked half chickens from a metal cable over the shallow waters below. The audience stands at a railing along the sides of this watery alligator pit.

Alerted by the clanging of a large bell, mammoth gators swim lazily into view. Slowly, they zero in on the morsels over their heads. They begin to lunge upwards at the bait, urged on by cheers from the crowd. Alligators jump by curling their tails on the shallow bottom and thrusting upwards. A successful leap is something to see and will make a great snapshot for the photographer with good timing.

One thing this show teaches is that alligators are none too bright. They have brains the size of a lima bean (about the size of the tip of your thumb, the host tells us, knowing perhaps that we are probably as familiar with vegetables in the wild as we are with gators). Their aim is none too good either. They regularly seem to over- or undershoot their targets.

After the gators have snared the half chickens, the host ups the ante by grabbing whole chickens and hand feeding them to the now-excited gators. The thick leather belt around his waist, attached to a thick chain, ensures that while a gator might get an arm, the rest of the host will be spared.

This show appeals to some of our most primordial fascinations with animals and it's an appeal that's hard to deny. Most people find this show very entertaining. Precisely how exciting the show is will depend to some extent on when you visit. During the cooler months, alligators tend to be sluggish. Under optimum conditions, the gators leap lustily, flashing their pale undersides and gaping maws as they snare lunch.

*The best seats in the house.* First of all, there are no seats, just a railing along which you stand. If you're not in the first row, your view will be somewhat impaired. The best view is to be found along the side directly facing the small gazebo in which the host stands. Arrive about 10 minutes early to secure a spot by the rail.

# Cracker-Style Gator Wrestling

| | |
|---|---|
| *Rating:* | ★ ★ ★ ★ ★ |
| *Type:* | Outdoor show |
| *Time:* | 15 minutes |
| *Kelly says:* | Best show at Gatorland |

Gatorland's best show takes place in an open-air arena next to Pearl's Smokehouse. Four covered bleachers face a sunken sandy platform surrounded by a small moat and a raised border which (we hope) keeps the gators from getting out. Eight gators, about seven or eight feet long, lie on the sand sunning themselves.

This is a two-man show. Ostensibly one is the host and the other the gator wrangler but I suspect the second man is there in case the wrangler gets in trouble. This show is obviously for real and there's no disguising the fact that it's hard work. ("I never finished school," the wrangler says. "So you kids out there study real hard or you might wind up doin' this.")

Alligator wrestling began, we are told, as a matter of necessity. Alligators would hide in water holes and take the occasional calf. The cattle boss would order the Crackers to get that gator out. Their courage bolstered by a little moonshine, the Crackers would oblige. Eventually, the practice became a competitive sport that gave Crackers a chance to show off their courage and prowess. Which is exactly what happens in this show.

The show begins with the wrangler kicking the gators off their sunny perch into the moat. They hiss their annoyance. Then a kid picked from the audience carefully picks out the biggest one for the wrangler to wrestle. Resigned to his fate, the wrangler drags the wriggling, hissing and none too cooperative beast onto the sandy platform.

Along with an informative patter about alligators, often made breathless by the exertion of keeping a 150-pound gator motionless, the gator wrangler shows off a few of the tricks of the trade — like pulling back the gator's head and placing his chin across its closed jaws. Despite his assurance that it doesn't take much pressure to hold a gator's jaws closed, you respect and admire his gumption. At one point, the Cracker pries the gator's jaws apart to show us his teeth. "If this works, it's gonna make you a pretty nice little snapshot," he says and then adds with perfect backwoods *sang froid,* "If this don't work, it's gonna make you a pretty nice little snapshot."

Maybe there's less to wrestling gators than meets the eye, but I wouldn't bet on it. The casual machismo and sly good humor with which these fellows put their charges through their paces makes for a thoroughly entertaining 15 minutes. After the show, the stage area is mobbed with audience members eager to ask questions ("Didja ever get bit?") and shake the hand of someone with the guts to wrestle a gator.

# Snakes of Florida

| | |
|---|---|
| *Rating:* | ★ ★ ★ + |
| *Type:* | Outdoor show |
| *Time:* | 15 minutes |
| *Kelly says:* | Poisonous snakes on parade |

If this show is less spectacular than the others, it probably has to do with the fact that while snakes may grow to be 12 feet long they never weigh much over six or seven pounds. Snakes, of course, have their own fascination, especially the ones on display here.

Actually, this show might more accurately be called Poisonous Snakes of Central Florida. The state is host to 69 species of snakes, of which only six are dangerous, of which only four are to be found in the Central Florida region around Gatorland, of which just three are profiled in the show. The other poisonous snake of Central Florida (the pygmy rattlesnake) is safely behind glass elsewhere in the park, along with a goodly selection of his nonpoisonous cousins.

The host meticulously takes visitors through his repertoire of both poisonous and nonpoisonous snakes (the yellow rat snake, we are told, makes an excellent pet). The highlight of the show comes when the host coaxes a rattlesnake into striking at a large red balloon. Photographers with fast film and reflexes to match may be able to get a great shot here.

The venue is the aptly named Snake Pit, a sunken rectangle surrounded by a chest-high cinder block wall. While you wait for the show to begin, amuse yourself by looking around the "empty" pit. It's not empty.

# Gatorland Express Railroad

| | |
|---|---|
| *Rating:* | ★ ★ ★ |
| *Type:* | Kiddie train ride |
| *Time:* | 7 minutes |
| *Kelly says:* | Easy intro to gator lore |

The *Gatorland Express Railroad* leaves about every 20 minutes from a small station on the wooden platform over the main alligator pond. It's a scaled-down steam engine with five cars and child-sized seating that takes you on a lazy loop around the southern end of the park. While not the most exciting of experiences, it provides a painless introduction to Gatorland and alligator lore.

The engineer/narrator is a Cracker taking a break from his more strenuous chores at the live shows. He points out sights of interest along the route and fills you in on Gatorland's purpose and the range of its attractions. The train makes one stop, near Pearl's Smokehouse, the *Gator Wrestlin'* arena, and the southern entrance to the *Alligator Breeding Marsh*.

# Alligator Breeding Marsh and Bird Sanctuary

*Rating:*     ★ ★ ★ ★ +

*Type:*       Observation platforms and walkways through a wildlife sanctuary

*Time:*       As long as you wish

*Kelly says:*  Bring your binoculars

This is one of Gatorland's more recent attractions and one of its most successful, in its own low-key way. The concept was ingenious: Build a natural setting in which some 100 female and 30 male alligators would feel free to do what comes naturally and provide a steady stream of new alligators to enthrall visitors and serve the growing market for gator meat and hides. (Gatorland is a working alligator farm, remember.) But because birds like to nest over alligator holes for the protection they provide against predators like raccoons, opossum, snakes, and bobcats, Gatorland hoped for a bonus population of wild birds. They built it . . . and they came.

Today there are over 1,000 bird nests in active use at Gatorland. Here you will find the magnificent, bright white great egret with its majestic plumage alongside the more dowdy green and blue herons. There are also snowy egret, cattle egret, and tricolor egret. With a bit of luck you might also spot an osprey perched high in a pine tree, surveying the alligator pool below and weighing his chances for a fish dinner.

The *Alligator Breeding Marsh* has three entrances. To the north near the Snake Pit and to the south near Pearl's Smokehouse you can gain access to the wooden walkway that runs the length of the alligator lake. In the middle of the park is a bridge that takes you directly to the Observation Tower. Starting in June you will be able to see alligator nests, some remarkably close to the walkway. Shortly after the eggs have been laid, Gatorland staffers remove them to an incubator to insure hatching. Signs left behind document the date of laying and the number of eggs.

Large, shaded gazebos with wooden benches offer a chance to rest, relax, and contemplate the serenity of the preserve. It's hard to believe some of Florida's scariest critters are basking just feet from where you sit. You'll see plenty of gators from the walkway. They wallow in the mud, float almost submerged in the water, and sun themselves on logs and the opposite shore. But for a really great look, you'll want to climb the Observation Tower.

The **Observation Tower** is a three-story affair located in the center of the walkway. It is accessible from the walkway, of course, but you can also reach the second level via a bridge directly from the park's central spine. An elaborate zigzag ramp next to the bridge makes the tower's middle level accessible to wheelchairs.

If you brought binoculars to Florida, don't forget to bring them to

Gatorland. Climb to the top level, where signs point out the direction and distance to major Florida landmarks. Look straight down at the alligator lake and you will see dozens of 10-footers clustered around the base of the platform. Look across at the opposite shore and you will see more gators amid the foliage; the longer you look, the more you'll see. Look at the trees and you will see dozens of white egrets tending their nests. Look closer and you will see the drabber species well camouflaged amid the leaves. A quarter will get you a brief look through a telescope mounted on the railing but when a hawk appears in the high branches, the line gets long.

## Jungle Crocs

| | |
|---|---|
| *Rating:* | ★ ★ ★ ★ |
| *Type:* | Walk-by animal exhibit |
| *Time:* | Continuous viewing |
| *Kelly says*: | Come for lunch |

It's not quite equal time but this exhibit gives the alligator's crocodilian cousins a chance to bask in the sun. Down a wooden walkway at the southern end of the *Alligator Breeding Marsh,* Gatorland has assembled one of the largest collections of crocodiles, which can be distinguished from alligators by their pointy snouts and snaggly, protruding teeth. There are saltwater crocs from Australia and Southeast Asia, Nile Crocs from (where else?) the Nile, as well as a representative cross section of American and Cuban crocodiles.

*Tip:* It's best to time your visit to one of the regular feeding sessions. These critters are more active feeders than alligators and the sound of their two-inch teeth slamming down on 20 pounds of red meat is something to hear.

## Swamp Walk

| | |
|---|---|
| *Rating:* | ★ ★ ★ |
| *Type:* | Wooden walkway through a cypress swamp |
| *Time:* | Five minutes or as long as you like |
| *Kelly says*: | Best for bird watchers |

Through an iron gate, across a swinging wooden bridge over a moat with yet more alligators, lies what Gatorland bills as the headwaters of the Everglades. From here, so the sign says, water flows through the Kissimmee lake system to Lake Okeechobee and, thence, to the Everglades.

What we see on this leisurely walk is a wilderness setting with a quiet calm and a very special type of beauty, made all the more enjoyable because we don't have to wade through the muck and the cottonmouth moccasins and the poison ivy to appreciate it. Much of the Orlando area looked just like this before people started draining the wetlands to farm and, later, build shopping malls. Only the soft whoosh of traffic on nearby highway 441 reminds us that we are in modern, not primordial, Florida.

# Grow Out Areas

| | |
|---|---|
| *Rating:* | ★ ★ ★ |
| *Type:* | Walk-by exhibit |
| *Time:* | 10 minutes |
| *Kelly says:* | The working end of Gatorland |

At the northern end of the park, at the end of *Alligator Alley*, you will get to see the commercial side of Gatorland. These gators are not here for entertainment but are being "grown out" for their hide and meat. They are fed a high protein diet of red meat, chicken, liver and supplements, at the rate of about 2,000 pounds a week, until they are ready to be harvested. That time comes when they are about 18 to 24 months old and have attained a length of about six feet. If you stop by at feeding time, you may get to see a buzzard drop in for a free meal.

# World of Alligators Education Center

| | |
|---|---|
| *Rating:* | ★ ★ |
| *Type:* | Educational display with diorama |
| *Time:* | 5 minutes |
| *Kelly says:* | Worth a peek |

This small self-guided exhibit near the *Jumparoo* show is notable for its diorama depicting a mother gator protecting her brood of just hatched "grunts," as baby alligators are called. Here you can also peruse grisly newspaper clippings about fatal gator attacks and photographs outlining the steps in alligator propagation by both natural and artificial means.

*Photo Op:* Just outside this display a large plaster model of an alligator makes a good prop for a photo of your fearless kids.

# Giant Gator Lake

| | |
|---|---|
| *Rating:* | ★ ★ ★ ★ |
| *Type:* | Huge alligators in huge observation area |
| *Time:* | As long as you wish |
| *Kelly says:* | Rewards patient viewing |

This is the huge lake that lies right next to the gift shop and park entrance. The place is home to Gatorland's largest specimens, giant 12-footers who are truly awesome, whether in catatonic repose in the sun or cruising ominously through the murky waters.

Other than feeding them (see below), there's not much to do here except watch. At first it will seem that there's nothing much going on. It may even seem that some of these critters are statues. But your patience will be rewarded. As you continue looking you will be able to sort the alligators from the crocodiles and start to notice those nicely camouflaged gators lurking in the shadows or lying submerged and motionless.

*Photo Op:* If you've got a video camera try for a shot of a white heron hitching a ride on the back of a floating gator.

## Feed the Gators

| | |
|---|---|
| *Rating:* | ★ ★ + |
| *Type:* | Audience participation |
| *Time:* | A few minutes |
| *Kelly says:* | Fun for the kids |

Near the train station is a stand selling half a dozen fish for $2.25 to those who'd like to feed a gator. Don't expect to be able to dangle your hand down like the Cracker in the Jumparoo show. The trick to feeding gators is to loft the fish gently so it lands to either side of the gator's head. They can't see directly in front. Many of the fish wind up in the beaks of the ugly wood storks that patrol this area. Resist the temptation to hand feed these scavengers; their beaks can draw blood.

*Tip:* Take your fish over to the *Alligator Breeding Marsh* and feed the gators from the Observation Tower. The gators over here are not as well-fed as those in the Giant Gator Lake and will show more interest in your free handouts.

## Alligator Alley Animal Exhibits

| | |
|---|---|
| *Rating:* | ★ ★ |
| *Type:* | Zoo-like walk-by exhibits |
| *Time:* | 15 to 30 minutes |
| *Kelly says:* | Worth a stroll by; kids will enjoy feeding the lorikeets, goats, and deer |

*Alligator Alley* is lined with a hodge-podge of cages, pens, and glass-walled displays that hearken back to the days when Gatorland was building its collection of "exotic" animals. Today, most of the animals on display are Florida natives like "Judy" the black bear and a small group of white-tailed deer, along with a variety of turtles, gators, and crocs. You can visit Monty the Python, a 16-foot Burmese python who lives in ducal splendor with three smaller females. The **Snakes of Florida** display is one of the more elaborate, housing a representative sample of Florida's 69 snake species behind glass windows and accompanied by helpful bits of written information. Also of interest, especially in late August and early September, is the **Gator Grunts Nursery** where just-hatched young from the Alligator Breeding Marsh are nurtured in optimum conditions. The walk-through **Very Merry Aviary** houses a scruffy band of lorikeets whom you can feed ($1 with two refills); it is open for half-hour periods on a regular schedule posted on the door.

Many of the animals, like the macaws and emus (*not* Florida natives), and the farm animals in **Allie's Barnyard** can be fed. Convenient dispensers contain appropriate treats (at 25 cents a modest handful) for the kids to feed to their favorites. A sign next to the dispenser at **Deer Park** says, "The buck stops here."

## Lilly's Pad

| | |
|---|---|
| *Rating:* | ★ ★ + |
| *Type:* | Kiddie play area |
| *Time:* | As long as you wish |
| *Kelly says:* | For toddlers unimpressed by alligators |

Located behind the Gator Jumparoo arena, *Lilly's Pad* offers refuge for squirmy toddlers. There are two separate play areas here, wet and dry. For cooling water play, there is a large rubberized mat with sprinklers, fountains, and surprise spritzes. The adjacent playground is filled with colorful wooden, plastic, and metal play structures and is carpeted with a layer of soft wood chips. In between, a small shaded area gives parents some relief from the sun.

## Eating at Gatorland

### Pearl's Smokehouse

| | |
|---|---|
| *What:* | Fast-food stand featuring BBQ gator ribs |
| *Where:* | At the south end of the park, next to *Gator Wrestlin'* arena |
| *Price Range:* | $ - $$ |

Pearl's Smokehouse is a wood-sided, tin-roofed, Cracker-style fast-food stand. Nearby is a screened-in smokehouse where the signature dish is prepared in a big black oven. You get your food at one of several serving windows and eat at umbrella-shaded picnic tables. There is a white sand play area with a rustic cabin for little ones to climb in, around, and over under Mom and Dad's watchful eyes. A few steps away is a covered seating area, closer to the *Alligator Breeding Marsh*. In this area, you can sit at a small counter facing a pen holding a white-tailed deer buck who will cruise by looking for a handout.

The featured attraction at Pearl's is alligator served up in two ways: as breaded, deep-fried "nuggets" or (my personal choice) as barbecued ribs, both for about $6 a serving. It would really be a shame to come to Gatorland and not sample this local delicacy. The ribs are lightly sauced and succulent. They look a lot like small pork ribs but the bones are much lighter, some no bigger than fish bones. So nibble with care. The taste lies an indefinable somewhere between pork and chicken. The gator nuggets are chewier versions of the chicken nuggets you get at McDonalds. Any gator-y taste is pretty well masked by the breading, spices, and deep frying. There is barbecue sauce available for those who want to mask the taste even further. Whichever version you choose, my advice is to go for it. At these prices you can afford the gamble. At least get one order for the members of your group to sample — if they dare! Who knows, you may turn out to be a gator fan.

My observation, however, is that many people are not yet ready to take the plunge. If you are one of them, you needn't worry about going hungry. Good old reliable hot dogs are about $2 and turkey subs, ham and cheese, and smoked chicken breast sandwiches are about $4. A side order of fries is under $2 and a variety of soft drinks are served for $1.35 and $1.75 in small and large sizes only. No alcoholic beverages are available. Desserts, mostly of the ice cream bar variety, are all less than $2. Coffee, tea, and milk are under a dollar. You can eat hearty at Pearl's for well under $10 a head.

*Tip:* Pearl's is right next door to the *Gator Wrestlin'* arena. Consider taking your lunch over there and eating while you grab a good seat and wait for the show to begin.

### Ice Cream Churn

> *What:*  Snack bar
> *Where:*  Near the *Gator Jumparoo* attraction
> *Price Range:*  $

The name pretty much says it all. In addition to ice cream treats in the $2 range, you can get the same sandwiches available at Pearl's (no gator though) at the same prices. A full range of drinks is also available here. Two smaller snack stands, one near the Snake Pit and another near the entrance to the *Alligator Breeding Marsh* Observation Tower, are open seasonally as the crowds warrant. They serve a limited selection of snacks and drinks.

## Shopping at Gatorland

No self-respecting theme park would be complete without offering its visitors regular opportunities to part with their cash in the name of souvenir hunting. Gatorland is no exception, although the number of shops and kiosks is mercifully limited.

## Gator-Themed Souvenirs

What better way to commemorate your visit to Gatorland than with a photo of yourself with a real, live alligator. No, you don't get a chance to pose with any of the 12-foot whoppers you saw in the pool, but you can have your picture taken while holding a small gator whose jaws have thoughtfully been taped shut. If gators aren't your cup of tea, you can also have a boa constrictor draped decoratively over your shoulders. The cost is just $6, including tax, and the stand can be found right next to the *Gator Jumparoo* area.

## The Gift Shop

For such a modest park, Gatorland has a surprisingly upscale gift shop. The big attraction, as you might expect, is the extensive range of alligator skin products. The price tags are truly heart-stopping but if you've done any serious comparison shopping you will realize there are some real bargains to be had here.

Full alligator boots, which retail for $2,000 and up in places like New York, are available here for $1,100. Men's loafers, handmade in Italy, are $598 here; they cost $900 in downtown Orlando. Alligator "vamp" boots (that is, half alligator, half leather) are $550; they can be found for $800 at the boot outlets in Kissimmee.

Nice wallets for men and women $109 to $290. Women's purses are in the $1,500 range. Men's and women's belts range from about $125 to $200. If you're really cheap, you can settle for an alligator key chain ($12.50) or money clip ($35). Far less expensive than alligator skin is snake skin. Wallets run from $45 to $120.

A very nice line of denim shirts, jackets, and windbreakers with embroidered logos ranges from $60 to $140. The usual array of t-shirts is in the more economical $15 to $25 range. There are also some intriguing 'natural history' gifts including skulls and mounted rattlesnakes in strike position.

In addition to the pricier items, the gift shop carries a full assortment of standard tourist souvenirs, from mugs and refrigerator magnets to alligator claw backscratchers and games for kids. There's lots to see here and you can always return to shop another day without paying admission to the park.

# CHAPTER SEVEN:

# Splendid China

As you drive up the landscaped but strangely deserted boulevard that leads to Splendid China you might think you were headed for a new subdivision of luxury homes. In fact, if you drive past the Splendid China entrance, you will find several are sprouting in the immediate area. But nestled in this nursery of suburban developments is one of the Orlando area's newest — and oddest — attractions.

Coming up with the perfect label for Splendid China is difficult. While there, I overheard a bewildered, tow-headed moppet whine, "Mummy, I thought this was a *theme* park."

"It *is* a theme park," Mum replied, a bit testily.

But if you think of a theme park as a series of rides, with long lines and furry-costumed critters circulating amongst the crowds, you will be disappointed.

Splendid China might more accurately be called "Miniature China." It is, in fact, a travel agent's brochure sprung to life — or at least rendered in three dimensions. Not too surprising considering that this outdoor museum park is a collaboration of a Hong Kong-based travel company and the government of the People's Republic of China.

According to its founders, Splendid China seeks to provide "Americans and overseas visitors the most extensive and authentic close-up of China possible without actually visiting China itself." It does this through two primary media. First, there are the more than 50 miniature reproductions of China's most popular man-made tourist attractions. These are no tabletop dioramas but ambitious outdoor recreations, almost photographic in their detail, rendered in one-third to one-fifteenth scale. Many of them are impressive, indeed. The miniature Great Wall of China stands five and a half feet tall in places and snakes along for more than half a mile. Less obvious, but just as effective in promoting China as a destination, are the entertainments and cultural shows that take place throughout the park on a regular basis during the day. For many people, the shows will be the highlight of the visit.

Who then is most likely to enjoy Splendid China? On several visits, the crowd has been heavily weighted towards senior citizens, who seem to like the leisurely pace and gentle entertainments. There are also young children in evidence, usually in groups, suggesting that they have been brought here for "cultural enrichment." Beyond that, Splendid China should appeal to serious photographers. The extreme detail with which the models are executed offers many opportunities for cunning trompe l'oeil photos. A telephoto lens and a good selection of filters will probably come in handy in heightening the illusion of having traveled to China for these shots.

## Getting There

To reach Splendid China, take I-4 to Exit 25 and drive 3.3 miles east on route 192. The entrance sign to the park will be on your left, two golden dragons rampant around a circular sign. The park entrance is a little more than half a mile up this side road. Parking is free.

## Opening and Closing Times

The park opens every day at 9:30 a.m. Closing time varies with the season, from 6:00 p.m. during the winter to 9:00 p.m. in the summer. The Chinatown section is open until 10:00 p.m. and the Suzhou Pearl Restaurant until 11:00 p.m. even when the park itself closes earlier.

## The Price of Admission

At press time, admission prices, including tax, were as follows:

| | |
|---|---|
| Adults: | $28.88 |
| Children (5 to 12): | $18.88 |
| Seniors (with AARP): | $25.99 |
| Children 4 and under **free.** | |

You may purchase separate admission to the evening show, *Mysterious Kingdom of the Orient*, which is included in the above prices. The show-only prices, including tax, are:

| | |
|---|---|
| Adults: | $16.00 |
| Children: | $10.65 |
| Seniors: | $13.85 |

Children 4 and under **free.**

A recorded message at (407) 397-8800 provides current hours, admission prices, and information on special events.

An **annual pass** is available for $49.76 including tax ($30.50 plus tax for children). You may upgrade to an annual pass on the day of your first visit. To do so, you must pay the full price and then take your original admission receipt to Guest Services for a refund.

Splendid China runs frequent promotions featuring discounts. Two-for-one promotions crop up with some regularity. In addition, you should be able to find dollars-off coupons in the usual places.

## Special Events

During January or February of each year, Splendid China celebrates the Chinese lunar New Year with a week-long party that includes special performances and special menus in the restaurants.

## Good Things To Know About. . .

### Access for the Disabled

The entire park is wheelchair-accessible. Wheelchairs can be rented for $5 a day. Electric scooters are available for $30 a day.

### Babies

Strollers are available for rent at Guest Services, in the Harmony Gardens building to your right as you enter the park. Single strollers are $5 a day, double strollers $7. You will find diaper changing stations in the restrooms.

### Guest Services

Guest Services is located at the back of Chinatown, next to the turnstiles where you enter the park proper. It provides most of the services outlined in this section as well as reservations (seldom actually needed) to the Suzhou Pearl Restaurant. There is a small first aid station at the main entrance.

### Lockers

A limited number of small storage lockers are available for 50 cents. If you add to your stash during the day, it will cost you another 50 cents to relock your locker.

## Tours

Guided tours can be arranged through Guest Services. One-hour tours via motorized golf carts are $48.15 including tax and can accommodate up to five people. Walking tours, also about an hour, are $9.63 per person, tax included.

# Scaling the Wall: Your (Half) Day at Splendid China

Splendid China has perhaps more than its fair share of detractors. Some have ideological bones to pick with the Chinese government. Others simply find the park "boring." True, the serene spectacle of acre upon acre of meticulous scale model buildings that is the park's centerpiece seems oddly out of place in hyperkinetic Orlando, but the park also offers some of the best live entertainment to be found in Central Florida. It may not be to everyone's taste, but I would urge you not to dismiss Splendid China out of hand. Even if you only come for the spectacular evening show, *Mysterious Kingdom of the Orient*, this park is worth a look.

# When's the Best Time to Come?

The short answer is whenever you're in town. Crowds are not an issue at Splendid China. However, if you're a photographer, I would advise waiting for a nice, sunny day.

# What to Expect

You enter Splendid China through a spectacular traditional archway 44 feet high and 82 feet wide. It is apparently the largest such structure ever built outside China. Through this gate lies "Chinatown" a 63,000-square-foot re-creation of the legendary gardens of the city of Suzhou as it looked some 700 years ago. The square is dominated by a lovely water garden accented with dramatic Tihu stones. These gnarled and weathered limestone rocks were prized by the ancient Chinese for their ability to mimic mountains in miniature. The setting is airy and peaceful and forms a lovely backdrop for martial arts and tumbling demonstrations. Suzhou is one of China's "water cities" which, like Venice, are crisscrossed with canals. A more extensive model of a water city can be seen elsewhere in the park (number 42 on the map provided by the park).

The Chinatown section contains all of Splendid China's souvenir shops as well as two restaurants, and Guest Services. Best of all, Chinatown is open free of charge to all comers. You only have to ante up the price of admission if you decide to pass the turnstiles at the far end of Chinatown to explore the scale models and gardens beyond. Several shows are presented in this part of the park, along with the overview film that introduces the park. So a visit here can help you make up your mind about visiting the whole park or serve as a pleasant interlude in its own right, especially in the evening when the area is illuminated with thousands of tiny lights.

Most of the park's 76 acres are beyond the turnstiles and are given over to meticulously built models of China's man-made wonders (with a few examples of nature's handiwork thrown in for good measure). Through the use of clever landscaping and strategically placed trees and shrubbery, the designers have created a constantly changing scenic experience that unfolds artfully as you stroll the grounds, allowing each exhibit to be appreciated on its own. This large "back" area of the park is also dotted with restaurants and performance venues, but the emphasis is squarely on the scale models that await you around each turn.

## The (Half) Day Stay

When you purchase your tickets, you will be given an admirably designed and easy-to-use full color map of the park and a schedule of the day's entertainments. If you are arriving early in the day, there will probably be a show starting in the Chinatown courtyard shortly and this is a very good way to start your visit. My suggestion would be to construct your visit around the show schedule, taking in the sights between performance venues as you move from show to show. Not every show will be to everyone's taste. Use the descriptions below to guide you. However, I can't imagine anyone not liking the acrobatic and magic shows. These are definite must-sees.

The color map you receive names and numbers each scale model exhibit. If you follow the map in numerical order, you will make a leisurely, spiraling circumnavigation of the park, ending up approximately in the middle of the large back section. A notation on the map estimates that it will take about four hours to view the park in this fashion and I have found this to be a reasonable estimate. For others with less time and patience, the map thoughtfully highlights in yellow eleven "must-see" exhibits.

Diehard tourists may want to jump right in and do it all, but others may want to get a quick overview first by catching the **tram ride** that runs regularly from in front of the Stone Forest at the front of the park. While not precisely a tour, there is a host who will point out some of the highlights of the park along the way. The tram ride circles the park in a clockwise direction and the whole trip takes about 20 minutes.

In summary, then, I would advise seeing most if not all of the shows and as many of the scale model exhibits as you have either the time or inclination for. It is quite possible to spend a full, unhurried day at Splendid China with a leisurely lunch thrown in. Most people, however, spend about four hours.

## Attractions at Splendid China

In a sense there is only one attraction at Splendid China with nearly 60 variations on the theme.

## Scale Models

*Rating:* ★ ★ ★ ★
*Type:* Self-guided outdoor museum/park
*Time:* As long as you wish; at least two hours for a good look
*Kelly says:* Great phun for photogs

The original Splendid China is in Shenzhen, a city near Hong Kong. It was conceived as "a 10,000 mile journey through 5,000 years of Chinese history and culture." Florida Splendid China is a near carbon copy of that park. It was constructed over three years at a reported cost of $112 million. The models were painstakingly created by a team of 125 artisans brought over from China and assisted by 280 Americans. The models range in scale from one-fifteenth to one-third the size of the originals.

The attention to detail is astonishing. The **Great Wall of China** re-creation, for example, contains some six million tiny bricks, each laid by hand using real mortar. The miniature versions of the distinctive Chinese roof tiles were all individually cast and glazed. The scale model streets were paved in precisely the same manner as the originals. Even the trees have been carefully crafted by bonsai artists to match the scale of the model they are decorating.

Most models incorporate small porcelain figures giving each scene a charming "lived in" look. At various points along the Great Wall we can observe tiny workmen busy constructing the only man-made object visible from space and, a little farther along, an army undertaking the considerable challenge of attacking this mammoth defensive system. At Beijing's **Forbidden City** we see an elaborate official ceremony under way, and at the fabled **Shaolin Temple** we see the monks in the courtyard practicing their kung fu. One model even features some modern-day tourists sporting video cameras!

The brochures boast of more than 60 scale models. I only count 56, but no matter. What's here is impressive enough. These little scenes are spread out over an ingeniously landscaped park-like setting. You observe these miniature marvels from broad avenues that wind their way through the park and, thanks to the cunning of the landscapers, you seldom find your attention to one diorama interrupted by another in the distance. The avenues are thoughtfully punctuated by "shade structures," long roofed benches decorated with Chinese lanterns and hanging plants, their superstructures cooled by nearby foliage and climbing vines. Here and there you will find a kiosk at which you can slake your thirst.

At each display you will find a sign containing a brief description of the site and a map of China pinpointing its location. The signs also tell you the date of completion and the scale of the model. Especially interesting is a time line at the bottom of the sign that tells you what was happening elsewhere in the world. For example, the **Temple of Confucius** was completed about the time Hippocrates was born in Periclean Athens. When the magnificent golden-roofed **Yellow Crane Tower** was built, Christians were being persecuted by the Romans. It's a wonderfully effective way of putting the accomplishments of Chinese culture in perspective for a Western audience.

Near each sign is a green metal box with two buttons. Push them and you can hear the text on the sign read in either English or Spanish. Don't be afraid that people will think you can't read. These spoken signs let you peruse the model while being told about it. I found it a very enjoyable way to take in the sights. They are also a ready-made sound track for your home video camera.

A closer examination of the variety of scale models reveals that there are several different types. Most successful are the single buildings and temple groups. There are also scenes of entire villages depicting the distinctive architecture of China's various ethnic minorities. Somewhat less successful are the grottoes grouped near Chinatown. They reproduce statues and temples carved out of living rock. They never quite match the realism of the buildings modeled elsewhere. An exception is the **Midair Temple**; a good photograph of this fairy-tale temple will convince people you actually traveled to Shanxi for the shot. Least successful are the re-creations of natural scenery. The **Stone Forest**, while a lot of fun, has an unfortunate way of reminding us of the mountains of one of the many miniature golf courses that dot the Orlando landscape.

Carping aside, many of the exhibits are truly beautiful. The **Summer Palace**, viewed across an artificial lake, is especially evocative. And the **Terra Cotta Warriors** of Xian will have you plotting a trip to see the originals. Reproduced in one-third size here are just a fraction of the more than 8,000 life-sized sculptured soldiers created to accompany the Qinshihuang emperor to the afterlife. Each sculpture is different, reflecting a very specific individual with a very identifiable personality. When all this was happening in far-off Xian, Rome was busy conquering the lands that would later become Spain.

One of the more controversial displays, but nonetheless arresting, is the **Potala Palace** of Tibet. When the park opened, this model drew protests over China's brutal occupation of Tibet and suppression of the Tibetan people and their religion. Like the original, this one-fifteenth scale model sits high on a landscaped hill. Photographed against the blue Florida sky, it looks remarkably real.

*Photo Op:* Splendid China offers opportunities for the amateur and professional photographer that are . . . well, *splendid*. Through careful framing and composition, it is possible to capture some remarkably realistic views of a China you have never visited. In many cases it is possible to set your subject against a backdrop of blue sky creating an almost perfect illusion. A telephoto lens and the artful use of filters will enhance the shots you take here. One of the nicest angles can be found in the shade structure behind the **Lijiang Scenery** model (number 39 on the Splendid China map). From here you can shoot through the greenery and the sculpted mountains of Lijiang to the Potala Palace in the near distance.

# Entertainment at Splendid China

Just as fascinating as the scale models — perhaps more so for some people — are the various entertainments that take place at various venues throughout the park during the course of the day. You will never have to wait long for the next show to begin. On a recent visit, there were 22 performances of nine different shows scheduled.

Performances take place at venues scattered around the park, ranging from large theaters, to covered amphitheaters, to tents, to intimate pavilions, to the great outdoors. The major venues are the $2 million Golden Peacock Theater; the Temple of Light Theater, a covered amphitheater with open sides; the tent-like Pagoda Garden show area; and the Harmony Hall theater where the introductory *Splendid China* film is usually shown. What happens at which venue and when is subject to change.

Since most of the entertainment involves live performances by artists from China, and since these folks like to get home every now and then, exactly what you will see when you visit is hard to predict. However, even though the performers may rotate, the general shape of the entertainment provided remains much the same. What follows, then, are descriptions of the shows I have seen on my visits. They will give you some flavor of the entertainment experience that awaits you. Just be aware that when you visit the lineup may be somewhat different.

# The Film of Splendid China

*Rating:*     ★ ★ +
*Type:*     Orientation film to the Splendid China experience
*Time:*     15 minutes
*Kelly says:*     Good mood setter

This brief film offers an introduction to Splendid China, its history and goals. It contains some hints on how to best experience the park and some words of welcome from Chairman Ma — that's Ma Chi Man, the founder of Splendid China.

Much of the material in the film is covered in this chapter but that's no reason not to see it. The film itself cites the ancient Chinese proverb, "Better to have seen once than to have heard a hundred times." The color photography in the film is breathtaking and provides a look at the real attractions that are reproduced in miniature outside.

The film is shown in the Harmony Hall theater near the park entrance and is an excellent starting point for your tour of the park.

# Chinese Folk Dance and Costume

*Rating:*     ★ ★ ★
*Type:*     Theater presentation
*Time:*     25 minutes
*Kelly says:*     Lovely to look at

This show gets off to a slow, if colorful, start as the cast members appear in a variety of traditional and ethnic costumes. They parade about the stage and strike poses reminiscent of socialist realism posters of the fifties and sixties. The regions and ethnic groups represented by the costumes are not identified. If your curiosity is aroused, a costume display in the building next door can satisfy you after the show.

The pace picks up with a selection of dances from various ethnic groups, with Mongolia and other Northern areas prominently represented. Whatever rough edges these dances might have in their home settings seem to have been smoothed with a polite balletic quality and the dances remain picturesque without ever becoming truly exciting. The most interesting dance, to this untrained eye at least, was the least Chinese — a very Russian-looking number from Chinese Siberia.

The real highlight of this show is an acrobat who builds dizzying towers of glassware and candles on a rod balanced on the bridge of her nose and then proceeds to lie down and roll over and over while balancing other objects with her hands and feet.

# Imperial Bells Music Show

*Rating:*    ★ ★ ★
*Type:*    Chamber concert
*Time:*    20 minutes
*Kelly says:*    Enchanting

This enjoyable show offers a painless introduction to Chinese music offered up by a gracious ensemble playing a variety of traditional instruments. Most prominent are the eponymous bells, cast in bronze and forming a sort of giant xylophone. Smaller versions of these bells are sold in the Ancestral Artifacts shop in Chinatown.

A representative selection of Chinese tunes is played on Chinese versions of the hammered dulcimer, wooden flute, and lute. Oddest of all are the two-stringed fiddles with their small snakeskin-covered sound boxes and eerie high-pitched sound which is the hallmark of Chinese music. The ensemble ends the show with a spirited rendition of "Oh, Susanna," which proves to be a real crowd-pleaser.

# Jiang Family Acrobats

*Rating:*    ★ ★ ★ ★ +
*Type:*    Acrobats and jugglers
*Time:*    25 minutes
*Kelly says:*    Fabulous

This show features a number of brief turns presented in almost kaleidoscopic fashion. A young girl balances glasses of water in increasingly unbelievable ways while twirling a hula hoop and two fans. A man juggles knives and catches a bouncing ball on the end of what looks like a wooden kitchen spoon. A hoop dancer entwines his body through increasingly intricate patterns formed by 20 some iridescent red hoops. A lithe young man does a series of handstands on a tower of tables and wooden blocks. All very impressive.

But the real show stopper is a young woman who specializes in foot juggling. Lying on her back on a specially designed stand she twirls, tumbles, and spins a large earthenware pot overhead. Then out comes her itsy-bitsy six-year-old sister made up like a China doll. She climbs atop the jug and, miming giddy terror in the cutest imaginable way, proceeds to do a handstand. In an instant, the jar flies away and the recumbent foot juggler is tumbling the moppet head over heels and spinning her around at dizzying speed. This is a truly jaw-dropping act made especially delectable by the canny performance of the pint-sized pro who serves as a human projectile.

# Wuhan Acrobats

| | |
|---|---|
| *Rating:* | ★ ★ ★ ★ |
| *Type:* | Acrobats and jugglers |
| *Time:* | 30 minutes |
| *Kelly says:* | Another winner |

Only slightly less spectacular than the Jiang Family troupe are these talented performers. Five beautiful young women, each of them spinning eight plates on the ends of long thin poles, go through a stately, choreographed routine that deftly blends dance and acrobatic skill. A trio of jugglers demonstrate their skill by passing spinning tridents back and forth, above and behind themselves, and while standing on each others' shoulders. Another beautiful young woman, an acrobatic contortionist, balances plates and bowls on her head and then removes them with her feet, while twisting her body into positions that you would swear are impossible except that you are seeing them in front of you. Then the jugglers are back, this time as the "Chinese Chefs," for a lighthearted routine that combines cooking gear and hot potatoes and then branches out to include tennis balls and hats. The closing bit, in which they shuffle an endless stream of hats from head to head while strutting across the stage, is wonderfully droll.

# Magical Snow Tiger Adventure

| | |
|---|---|
| *Rating:* | ★ ★ ★ ★ |
| *Type:* | Animal show with big cats |
| *Time:* | 45 minutes |
| *Kelly says:* | A true crowd-pleaser |

This show follows the familiar formula of all the other animal nature shows you are likely to see in the Orlando area. A steady parade of interesting critters is trotted out while your host keeps up a running patter filled with educational facts and figures about their habits and peculiarities.

Several things set this show apart, however. For one thing, the host is an attractive and utterly self-assured young woman who goes out of her way to terrify the volunteers brought from the audience to hold the tarantulas, snakes, and alligators who make up the first part of the show. The results are often hilarious, so think twice before you volunteer.

For another thing, this show offers the chance to get up close and personal with some of God's most beautiful creatures — the big cats. Among the beasts you are likely to see are the lion who served as the life model for Disney's animated *Lion King*, a leopard (and his black coated offspring), a Florida panther (which you may get to pet) and the white snow tigers of the show's title. The snow tigers are another father–son team, Samson and Taj.

At the end of the show, you can have your picture taken with one or more of the big cats for $5. If you buy a $15 tiger t–shirt, they throw in the picture for free. Since the proceeds go to animal conservation, the decision is pretty much of a no–brainer and they get a lot of takers.

# Mysterious Kingdom of the Orient

| | |
|---|---|
| *Rating:* | ★ ★ ★ ★ ★ |
| *Type:* | Stage spectacular |
| *Time:* | 85 minutes |
| *Kelly says:* | Not to be missed |

Missed the acrobat shows in the park during the day? Not to worry. This spectacular stage show, which plays every evening except Monday at 6:00 p.m. in the 750-seat Golden Peacock Theater, reprises most of the best acts. In fact, it adds new layers of complexity to many of them — something that hardly seems possible. On top of that, it showcases even more astonishing feats of skill and balance. There are aerialists performing high overhead atop tall poles balanced on the stout shoulder of a man below. Six agile men and women do handstands on a teetering tower of chairs. There is even a bicycle built for twelve. And the acrobatic acts are just one element of this extravaganza.

*Mysterious Kingdom of the Orient* provides a framework on which to string a series of lavish costume spectacles, lively or graceful dance routines, and displays of acrobatic, juggling, and magic skills.

The dancing is vaguely balletic with martial arts grace notes. At its most energetic, the choreography leans heavily to heroic poses, dashing leaps, and waving banners which make for some startlingly beautiful stage pictures. In its more reflective moods, it features beautiful women, gorgeously costumed, floating across the stage as water lily blossoms or courtesans of the Imperial court.

Usually, saying that the costumes are one of the best things in the show is a decidedly backhanded compliment. Not in this case. Even better is that many of these costumes are worn by some of the most beautiful women China (or any other country) has to offer.

The show changes about every six months or so, which means that the shape, length, and quality varies somewhat. The shows I have seen have varied from the truly astonishing to the merely wonderful. Still, this is quite simply one of the best shows to be seen in Orlando. Anyone who pays the price of admission to Splendid China and misses this show should have his head examined. The separate admission charged for the show alone makes it an attractive option for those who have no particular interest in visiting Splendid China itself. A combination ticket that includes dinner at the Suzhou Pearl Restaurant and the show ($34.95) makes *Mysterious Kingdom of the Orient* a serious contender in Orlando's dinner attraction sweepstakes.

# Eating at Splendid China

Splendid China misses a sure bet in the food department. While you certainly won't starve on a visit to the park, neither will you get a chance to savor the best of what China's culinary tradition has to offer. Of all the food choices in the park, I found the most interesting to be a soft drink. Jan-li-bo is advertised as an "energy replenisher...with a burst of honey." This "official drink of the Chinese National Sports Teams" comes in exotic flavors like mandarin orange, kiwi, mango, and pear. It's available throughout the park and, at just $1.25 a can, it's worth a try.

## Suzhou Pearl Restaurant

| | |
|---|---|
| *What:* | Elegant full-service restaurant |
| *Where:* | Chinatown, by the pool |
| *Price Range:* | $$$ - $$$$ |

This is Splendid China's attempt to bring fine Chinese dining to Central Florida. Considering that the prices are expensive by Orlando standards, the food is a bit of a disappointment. Still, the extensive menu offers Chinese specialties you are not likely to find elsewhere in the area. The wine list features some very interesting American varietals at prices ranging from $15 to $24 a bottle.

## Seven Flavors

| | |
|---|---|
| *What:* | Fast-food Chinese style |
| *Where:* | In Chinatown |
| *Price Range:* | $ - $$ |

If you've ever had Chinese food at a shopping mall food court, you know what to expect here. The food is undistinguished but cheap. "Combos," which offer a choice of entree and varying side dishes are priced between $5 and $7. On a recent visit, the entrees offered were Buddha's Delight (a vegetarian dish), sweet and sour chicken, and spicy kung pao chicken. Ordered separately, entrees are about $6. Yang-Zhou fried rice and Beijing lo mein are about $3.50. Soft drinks are available in three sizes from about $1 to $1.50. Imported Tsingtao beer is also available here for a little over $3. All seating is indoors in a setting devoid of atmosphere.

## Wind and Rain Court

| | |
|---|---|
| *What:* | Fast-food Chinese style |
| *Where:* | Near the Temple of Light Theater |
| *Price Range:* | $ - $$ |

This restaurant, which sits on bleached weathered wooden poles, is a series of pavilions, covered but open to the breezes. It's a lovely setting. Unfortunately, the food is the same as that served up at Seven Flavors. There are also a few concessions made to American palates. Burgers are available for about $6.

## Pagoda Garden

| | |
|---|---|
| *What:* | American fast-food |
| *Where:* | At the very back of the park |
| *Price Range:* | $ - $$ |

Surrounded by palm trees and with a simulated thatched roof, this restaurant looks almost Polynesian. The food is strictly shopping mall American, however, featuring Italian hoagies, ham and cheese, BLTs, and chicken and tuna salad sandwiches in the $5 to $6 range. You can also get a simple green salad or a more elaborate chef's salad or chicken or tuna salads at prices ranging from about $2 to a little over $4. Desserts are also featured here, with cheesecake for about $3. A range of domestic, imported, and draft beer is to be had here ($2.50 to $3.50) as well as wine coolers ($2).

You can eat in the small cafeteria serving area or take your food outside to one of several shaded pavilions, a much better choice.

### Other Eating Options

The handsome Great Wall Terrace restaurant, located appropriately enough behind the Great Wall model, has been closed on every visit. Perhaps it will open as attendance improves.

An impromptu, and unnamed, food concession in Chinatown serves such non-Chinese delicacies as tiramisu and espresso. Small kiosks scattered around the park serve ice cream and other goodies, and you will find soft drink vending machines at the various performing venues.

# Shopping at Splendid China

All of the shopping at Splendid China is cleverly and conveniently located in the Chinatown area at the front of the park, to your left as you enter the main gate. The shops, all fairly small, are interconnected so you can enter at one end of the courtyard and shop 'til you drop out at the other. Those of you who like Chinese style pottery and decorative items will find some hard-to-resist bargains here. Best of all, you can visit the shops for free, without paying the admission to the miniature displays.

## S.W. Books

If you took a fancy to the lilting Chinese music piped throughout the park, you can pick it up on cassette or CD at this small shop. Also here is a goodly selection of books from and about China. Cookbooks are prominently displayed as you might expect, but there are also translations of the great Chinese philosophers and upscale guidebooks to China.

## Ancestral Artifacts

Some of the nicest decorative objects and small furniture pieces to be found at Splendid China are right here in Ancestral Artifacts. There are few actual antiques; these are mostly reproductions. The prices seem quite reasonable and it's unlikely you'll be able to cut a better deal back home, unless perhaps home is in China.

Large pottery vases are a standout here. Elaborately decorated pieces standing four feet high and adorned with gaily colored birds and flowers are $300. Smaller vases and urns can be had for less than $200 and occasional half-price sales can create some terrific bargains.

A small selection of jade objects features a pretty bowl for just $130 and pendants for $120 while bracelets go for $1,000. Dong Yang yellow wood carvings, which are amazingly light for their size, depict elaborate scenes such as a group of horses galloping across what look to be sea waves. There is also furniture to be found here. A lovely four piece nested set of black lacquer tables with mother-of-pearl figures set under glass is just $450 while an elaborate four-panel dragon screen is about $1,000.

## Buddha Gifts I & II

The usual theme park souvenirs are the order of the day in these cheerful little shops. A selection of magic tricks that comes with a demonstration and personal instructions is $25. Bamboo boats, some of them quite large, range from $10 to $130. Abacuses are $7 to $11. A martial arts section features a good selection of books on the subject, kids' kung fu outfits ($20), and toy num chuks and other martial arts implements, some of them quite nasty looking. The second half of this store features Splendid China t-shirts in a variety of colors and styles (some of them quite nice) for prices ranging from $12 to $30. You can also find a wide variety of glassware and mugs bearing the Splendid China logo. Prices range from $3 for shot glasses to $11 for tumblers and old-fashioned glasses. A souvenir shop wouldn't be complete without mugs bearing your name and they can be found here for about $6. Rounding out the collection are small Splendid China souvenirs (key chains, refrigerator magnets, and such) and postcards. Other inexpensive Splendid China souvenirs are also available.

## Golden Treasures

This is a jewelry store with most selections in the inexpensive to moderate category. There are also some very pretty lacquerware jewel boxes and cabinets. Along with the usual array of gold chains, jadeite and amethyst beads, cloisonné, and costume jewelry, you will find Chokin 24 karat gold metal carvings on small plates for just $20 and more elaborate ladies' fans from $36 to $72.

## Loomed Creations

Despite its name, this shop concentrates on figurines at surprisingly low prices. Some very attractive porcelain figures of Chinese fishermen are just $7 to $15. There are also imitation jade Buddhas, calligraphy sets, and willowy white porcelain Guan Yin statuettes for under $40. A beautiful waist-high rosewood altar table on display on a recent visit was just $450.

## Marco Polo Silk

The selection is limited in this vest-pocket boutique but the prices are attractive. There are cotton batik print shirts for men and buttery silk shifts designed by Paloma Picasso for women.

## Suzhou Embroidery

Silk and cloth are the themes here and the selections range from Yunnan batik to inexpensive linen towels, to hand-embroidered doilies and placemats. There is clothing, too, all of it for women. Traditional Manchu qi pao dresses, ankle length and close-fitting, in a variety of colors are about $60. A very pretty white woven nightgown is $76. Colorful women's robes with gaily embroidered dragons are just $22.

## Dragon Teas — Asian Super Market

This is a smaller version of the Asian food markets you see in ethnic neighborhoods around the country and features a wide variety of fresh and canned goods that will seem strange to Western tastes. In keeping with the name, imported teas can be found here, ranging from Special relaxing Tea, to Ginseng-Oolong, to Chrysanthemum, to the more familiar Jasmine and green teas. Gift-boxed assortments are also available.

# CHAPTER EIGHT:

# Church Street Station

C hurch Street Station is an urban renewal success story. In the 1970s this little corner of downtown Orlando, like many similar inner city locations around the country, had fallen on hard times. The 1880s vintage buildings (including a charming old railroad depot) that survived were derelict and seemingly destined for the wrecker's ball that turned many American downtowns into large parking lots during that era.

Fortunately for us, a group of forward-looking entrepreneurs moved in and turned four blocks into a perfectly smashing eating, shopping, and nighttime adult (yet family-friendly) entertainment complex that quickly became an Orlando landmark. Through a clever combination of restoration and new construction, they have created a showplace. Make no mistake, even in the best of the good old days, Orlando never looked like this. What has been created at Church Street Station is an elegant, good-times, gay nineties America that exists in the imagination if not the history books. In my humble opinion it matches or beats anything that Disney's designers have come up with and it contains some of the most spectacular interior spaces to be found in Orlando — or anywhere else for that matter.

The charming rabbit's warren of restored and extensively renovated buildings and arcades that is Church Street Station is right next to Interstate 4. At night, the buildings are outlined in thousands of tiny lights, the brick-paved street is blocked off and Church Street becomes one long street party. Antique cars and Keystone Kops fill the streets, Scottish pipers and jugglers hold forth on the sidewalks, and music pours from the doorways. Three "Showrooms," as Church Street calls its entertainment venues, get rolling with live entertainment in the early evening and roar on into the early morning hours. A disco cranks up its ear-splitting entertainment a little later while fine restaurants and ice cream parlors beckon the hungry.

Much of this ambiance can be enjoyed for free. Admission is required only in the evenings and only for the three Showrooms featuring live entertainment. Even if you don't catch the shows, Church Street is worth a late afternoon (or evening) visit just for a quick look around. If you come for a peek, you may not be able to resist buying a ticket and staying all evening.

By the way, there are cynics who claim that Disney, taking note of Church Street Station's growing popularity, created Pleasure Island just to siphon off the market for this kind of adult-oriented evening entertainment. Could Mickey be that kind of a rat? Perish the thought.

While there are some obvious points of comparison between the two operations — a single admission to a variety of shows, the street party atmosphere, and so forth — I think it's really an apples and oranges kind of comparison. Pleasure Island is much more youth oriented, whereas Church Street Station will appeal to an older and more sophisticated audience. That being said, some parents may find that there is less to shield their younger children from at Church Street Station. Pleasure Island, with its in-your-face rap-style concerts and gyrating teens in brief, skin-tight costumes, can get downright raunchy compared to Church Street.

## Gathering Information

Church Street Station is located at 129 West Church Street, Orlando 32801. The general information number is (407) 422-2434. You can call ahead and ask for information to be sent to you. Allow about four to six weeks.

You can also access Church Street Station's home page on the World Wide Web at http://www.churchstreetstation.com. This will fill you in on current prices and upcoming special events. While there, you can fill out a form requesting further information.

## Getting There

Take I-4 to Exit 38, the Anderson Street exit. If coming from the east, turn left at Boone Street. If coming from the west, the exit ramp will feed you right onto Boone. Go one block north and turn left on South Street then right on Garland. Valet parking is one block ahead of you at the corner of Church Street.

# Parking at Church Street Station

Valet Parking costs $6 (plus tip) and is by far the most convenient alternative. However, you have other options. Just past the valet parking booth, you will find municipal parking on your left under the Interstate. This is metered parking and the trick is to have the right change in quarters and adequately estimate your length of stay. Those who underestimate often find a ticket awaiting them on their return. The maximum the meters accept is $4, which will cover you for the evening. There are other parking lots, covered and uncovered, in the immediate area. One of the most convenient lies directly ahead of you as you come down Boone Street to South Street. It charges $5 for the evening. The Church Street Parking Garage at Bob Snow Lane and Hughes Street (just under the Interstate) charges just $3 for 12 hours. All parking is within easy walking distance of the Church Street Station complex.

# The Price of Admission

As noted earlier, much of Church Street Station requires no admission at all, at any time of the day. Admission (more of a cover charge, really) is required only in the evening and only for entrance to the live shows at Rosie O'Grady's, Orchid Garden, and the Cheyenne Saloon, as well as the disco in Phineas Phogg's. The street performers, the shops, the restaurants, Apple Annie's, The Exchange, and Commander Ragtime's arcade (all described later) are open to all, free of charge, at all times.

At press time, admission prices, including tax, were as follows:

| | |
|---|---|
| Adults: | $19.03 |
| Children (4 to 12): | $12.67 |

Children under four are admitted **free** and all entertainment is suitable for little ones.

If you plan to be in the Orlando area on a regular basis — and especially if you are a local resident — Church Street Station's annual pass options will be very attractive indeed. They are:

| | |
|---|---|
| Single Annual Pass: | $24.95, plus tax |
| Dixie Double (for two): | $44.95, plus tax |
| V.I.P. Annual Pass: | $74.95, plus tax |

(Admits you and up to 3 guests)

Since the acts, especially those in the Orchid Garden and Cheyenne Saloon, change periodically you will be seeing fresh entertainment throughout the year. And if you are a family with two teenagers, the V.I.P. Annual Pass means that the entire family's second visit costs about $8. Many locals have V.I.P. passes and find them very handy for entertaining visiting guests. Annual passes also put you in line for a host of discounts from local merchants, including rental cars, hotels, area attractions, and shops, including many Church Street Exchange merchants.

Dollars-off coupons for Church Street Station can be found in all the usual places and tickets are usually available through discount ticket brokers. (See *Chapter One* for more information on discount coupons and brokers.) In addition, if you log on to the Church Street Station home page (listed above), you can print out a coupon good for $3 off the admission price for each of up to six people.

## Special Events

Church Street Station has a never-ending series of promotions going on, all of them aimed at luring folks in the afternoon and early evening in hopes that they'll wind up staying all night, as many of them do. Typical promotions include Nickel Beer Night at Phineas Phogg's, Longneck Night at the Cheyenne Saloon, featuring bottle beer for $1, and afternoon Country Dance lessons, also at the Saloon.

Throughout the year, there are themed street parties geared to the calendar. From New Year's Eve, to Carnival, to Saint Patrick's Day, to Thanksgiving Day, to lighting the Great American Christmas Tree, there's always some celebration on the horizon. Call ahead or check out Church Street's home page on the World Wide Web to see what's on tap at the time of your visit.

## Street Party: Your Evening at Church Street Station

Church Street Station and the nearby Exchange open at 11:00 a.m. each day. Nighttime entertainment gets under way shortly after 7:00 p.m. and continues until 2:00 a.m. There's plenty to do at Church Street Station and the immediate area to keep you busy from mid-afternoon until after midnight, especially if you want to spend some time shopping (or at least browsing) in the many shops in The Exchange and the next door Church Street Market. Most people, however, come for dinner and the shows, followed perhaps by a few more drinks and some disco dancing. In that case, plan to arrive by 7:00. Night owls can come a bit later (especially on weekends when late shows are added), but arriving by 7:00 allows for a leisurely tour of the Showrooms and a nice dinner while still leaving time to explore your other options.

When you purchase your ticket at the box office on Church Street, you will receive a small brochure with a map of the complex, a listing of the various shops, restaurants, and Showrooms, along with a schedule of show times. Check out the schedule and devise a plan for seeing all three shows (and they are *all* worth seeing!). You might want to ask for a copy of the free *Good Time Gazette*. It's a newspaper style informational puff piece about Church Street, filled with fascinating facts. It makes a great souvenir.

When you're ready to start show hopping, just hand your ticket to the doorman at the first Showroom you enter after 7:00 p.m. and have your hand stamped. Thereafter, just pass your hand in front of the ultra-violet lamp at each Showroom for admittance.

The shows are timed in such a way that, if you begin at Rosie O'Grady's, you can move seamlessly to the Orchid Garden and then to the Cheyenne Saloon, arriving at each in perfect time for the next show. If you start at 7:15 you'll be done by about 9:30 and ready for a hearty meal to soak up all the beer and booze you've been downing. After that, take to the disco, revisit your favorite show, or head down the street to some of the other bars in the neighborhood offering live entertainment.

## Church Street Station's Showrooms

The Church Street Station brochure you receive with your ticket lists six Showrooms, of which only four require payment for admission and only three of which are actual show rooms in the sense that they offer live entertainment. Rosie O'Grady's, the Orchid Garden, and the Cheyenne Saloon present live entertainers. Phineas Phogg's is a discotheque that rocks to the recorded taste of the DJ on duty. The other "showrooms," neither of which requires payment for admission, are Apple Annie's Courtyard, which is essentially a bar in an open arcade, and Commander Ragtime's, a gussied-up video arcade at the top of The Exchange, the shopping mall that is part of the complex.

## Rosie O'Grady's Good Time Emporium

Step into a raucous Gay Nineties saloon suspended somewhere between New Orleans and the Bowery in the romantic American imagination. You have arrived at Rosie O'Grady's Good Time Emporium where good times is exactly what they serve up in heaping portions.

Like all of Church Street's performance venues, Rosie's is a large open space with a balcony level that rings the room. And like the others, it is beautifully realized, with antique bars, pressed tin ceiling, chandeliers, and red Victorian bunting.

The entertainment is infectious, high-octane Dixieland jazz complete with a "Red Hot Mama" and the "Baron of Bourbon Street." The waiters sing and the waitresses slide down a fire pole and do the cancan on the top of the bar. There's plenty of opportunity to sing along and at least one audience member is made part of the show. There's even a soul-stirring patriotic finale, complete with waving flags and Uncle Sam on stilts.

Big draft beers will set you back almost $7 or you can go whole hog and for about $10 order up Church Street's trademark "Famous Flaming Hurricane," an appropriately lethal pink combination of rums and fruit juices which arrives blazing merrily away. The glass and the garter which rings it are yours to keep. The non-flaming Orange Blossom Special and other fancy multi-shot drinks are about $5 to $6. Teetotalers can opt for $2 soft drinks.

Rosie's serves a limited and moderately priced "deli sandwich" menu. Hot dogs are a bit over $2 or a bit more than $3 with all the fixings. The most expensive sandwich platter is about $6. The place is also open for lunch from 11:00 a.m. to 4:00 p.m. with a "Good Time Banjo Man" performing every hour or so. No admission is required during this time.

# Orchid Garden Ballroom

After your Dixieland extravaganza at Rosie O'Grady's, walk across the swirling street scene of Church Street and into the Orchid Garden, a drop-dead gorgeous room that evokes an elegant Victorian crystal palace. The resplendent bars are green and white marble with golden Art Nouveau chandeliers and tall golden statues holding up the ceilings between the broad expanses of mirrors. The room soars to two stories with lacy steel arches curving overhead. Above the bandstand is a circular dance floor and behind that a huge wall of stained glass. Across the top of the elegant design runs the inspiring motto: "While music and dance do fill the night, rise up my heart in lofty flight with wings of joy and spirits light."

And that's very likely what will happen if your tastes run to the old-ies but goodies that made the fifties and sixties such a special time in which to come of age. Various bands, none of whose members could have been born much before 1970, do an excellent job of evoking the era in their leather jackets, ponytails, and crinoline skirts. The repertoire varies somewhat from band to band but there is always at least one song that allows the lead vocalist to show off his considerable solo talents.

By the way, if you make it up to the dance floor, you may notice another elaborate stained glass window across the courtyard out back. That's the Presidential Ballroom in the new Private Parlour Rooms, which are used for conventions, meetings, and private functions.

No food is served in the Orchid Garden, but an extensive drink menu of "Rock & Roll Classics" and frozen specialty drinks is offered. Most of them come in at about $6. The Flaming Hurricane and a selection of alcohol-laced coffee drinks are also available here.

# Cheyenne Saloon & Opera House

If you go to the second level of the Orchid Garden, at the back, you can open a discreetly mirrored door in the corner and step smack into the middle of the roaring, Wild West hoe-down taking place at the Cheyenne Saloon. You can also enter from the street or by walking out of the main entrance to the Orchid Garden and turning left, but I enjoy the feeling of being shot through time and space that comes with the second story route.

Totally different in look and feel from Rosie O'Grady's and the Orchid Garden, this is Church Street's most spectacular interior space and worth walking through during the day even if you have no plans to come for the evening shows. It is a wild fantasy of a frontier saloon by a talented designer with a few million to spend on decor. Made entirely of oak in the old-world mortise and tenon fashion — not a single nail was used in its construction — it rises majestically, like a grand old opera house, in three levels. Where there isn't wood, there's intricate and elaborate stained glass with a western theme, some of the niftiest art glass I've seen in a good long while. The room took 50 craftsmen two and a half years to build; it was worth the effort.

Then there's the decoration. Sprinkled around are 15 sculptures by famed western artist Frederick Remington. The walls are lined with displays of antique derringers, pistols, and rifles. Up top there are stuffed Kodiak bears and moose heads hanging on the walls. It's all topped off with a magnificent stained glass dome

The ingenious layout allows you to see the stage from every level or to step back from the railing and enter a separate world of food and entertainment. Tucked away at the back of the second level is a full-service barbecue restaurant. On the top level you can sit on barrels and play checkers, shoot a round of eight ball, or play blackjack with Church Street supplied funny money.

Or you can watch the show, which is a high-octane Grand Ole Opry-style blend of country and western numbers. There's a bit of everything here, from bluegrass fiddlers to twangy laments about love gone awry. In front of the stage, the dance floor offers a chance for folks to try out the line dancing they learned at the free dance sessions hosted here in the afternoon. As at Orchid Garden, the bands change regularly here, but whichever group is holding forth when you visit, you will be guaranteed a toe-tappin', foot-stompin' good time. Most customers opt for beer in keeping with the down-home atmosphere but if you can't do with out a fancy drink, try the Gunslinger (about $6).

The Cheyenne Saloon also boasts the only full-service eatery in

Church Street's performance venues. You'll find the **Cheyenne Barbeque Restaurant** on the second level serving up a very respectable menu of beef, pork, chicken, and ribs barbecue dinners. Most entrees are in the $13 to $15 range with steaks rising to about $20. There are some tasty home-style cobblers and pies for dessert, all under $5. Less expensive barbecue sandwiches, platters, and appetizers ($4 to $7) can be ordered from the railing seats if you'd prefer to eat while watching the show. The Cheyenne Barbeque Restaurant is open for dinner from 5:00 p.m. to 11:30 p.m. (midnight Friday and Saturday). On Fridays, the restaurant is open for lunch from 11:00 a.m. to 3:00 p.m., when there is an all you can eat "Backyard Barbeque" for just $7.

This is Church Street's most popular Showroom, so if you want to snare a seat at the railing, you'll have to show up early. The Cheyenne's cleverly designed tiered seating offers lots of seats but you'll get a great view of the entertainment even if you have to stand.

## Phineas Phogg's Balloon Works

This is Church Street Station's own discotheque with a hot air ballooning theme. Balconies on the second level mimic the heavy wooden gondolas from old-time hot air balloons like those made famous in the movie version of *Around the World in Eighty Days*. Ballooning exhibits and memorabilia ring the walls.

Most of Phineas Phogg's customers, however, are far more interested in the here and now than in history. Dancing and loud, loud music are the order of the day (or rather, the evening, since the place doesn't start hopping until around 9:00 p.m.). The music, selected by a rotating roster of DJ's, leans heavily to recent rock tracks. You know instantly that it's good, though, because you feel it in your sternum as soon as you enter the room. Phineas Phogg's is the only Showroom that requires (and rigorously enforces) a 21 year minimum age requirement.

## Apple Annie's Courtyard

This small but attractive bar occupies a broad corridor that runs from Church Street to The Exchange, between Rosie O'Grady's and Lili Marlene's. The decor evokes a flowery Victorian garden, right down to the wicker chairs. There's no entertainment or food served here, just some more of those wonderful specialty drinks. In addition to the Flaming Hurricane and the usual range of frozen tropical drinks, Apple Annie's offers its own line of sweet but deadly ice cream-based drinks. They're all about $6 and most of them can be ordered in a non-alcoholic version for the young or timid.

# Commander Ragtime's Midway of Fun, Food & Games

At the top of The Exchange (see below), and a world away from the glitzy Showrooms of the rest of Church Street Station, is Commander Ragtime's. In simplest terms, this is a video arcade, just like the ones at Universal Studios or SeaWorld (in fact, this one is run by NAMCO, the same company that manages the arcades at Universal). But the similarity ends there. Commander Ragtime's wildly imaginative layout and decor make this the best video arcade in Orlando — and you don't have to pay a nickel to get in.

In true Church Street Station fashion, great attention has been paid to decorating this large, open space. Three replicas of World War I fighter planes do silent aerial battle overhead. Antique canoes, racing sculls, and smaller model planes hang from the ceiling. In the pool hall, there's a mammoth scale model of the old Queen Elizabeth ocean liner occupying an entire wall. The games on hand are all state of the art, arrayed along comfortably wide aisles, and with the volume turned down to a reasonable level. This might not be to every teen's taste but the adults who accompany them will appreciate it.

All games take tokens only, which can be purchased from vending machines. The more you buy, the better the deal. A dollar bill nets three tokens (33 cents each), while a $10 bill gives you 40 tokens (25 cents each). The best deal is 90 tokens for a $20 bill, or about 22 cents each. The most expensive games, which use high quality virtual reality video screens, cost four tokens; garden variety video games are just one token.

Food of the hot dog, burger, and popcorn variety is also to be had here. If the kids are bugging you to let them play the video games at high-priced Universal or SeaWorld, buy them off with a promise to bring them here.

*Tip:* You can buy your tokens here and use them at Universal.

## Eating at Church Street Station

In addition to the deli menu at Rosie O'Grady's and the Cheyenne Barbeque Restaurant, Church Street Station offers a number of other dining options, among them two of the most attractive restaurants in Orlando. If you are traveling with small children, check out the $7 children's menu offered at Crackers, Lili Marlene's, and the Cheyenne Barbeque Restaurant.

### Crackers Seafood Restaurant

This brick-walled, casually elegant space is to be found right next to the Orchid Garden. Brass accents the brick walls very nicely, and large screen televisions featuring professional sports add a sports bar touch to the atmosphere. Belly up to the seafood bar for oysters Rockefeller and steamed shrimp, or select a table for a complete seafood dinner.

The accent is on freshness and daily specials are always a wise choice. They range from about $15 to about $20, with steaks (if you insist) running somewhat higher. For an interesting appetizer that you're not likely to find at home, try the blackened gator tail ($8). The lunch menu is less expensive.

Crackers is open for lunch from 11:00 am to 4:00 p.m. and for dinner from 4:00 p.m. to 11:30 p.m. (midnight Friday and Saturday).

## The Wine Cellar

Right in the middle of Crackers, and roped-off so you don't fall into it, is a narrow, winding staircase that leads 12 feet underground to a 5,000-bottle wine cellar, one of the largest in Florida. It's not a restaurant per se, although wine-tasting parties are sometimes held here at a long narrow table that completely fills the available space. A small bar, a friendly sommelier, and a constantly changing menu of wines by the glass make this a relaxing place to escape the hustle and bustle upstairs. The selection leans heavily to American varietals with France scarcely represented.

## Lili Marlene's Aviator's Pub and Restaurant

This dark, wood-paneled room that hovers somewhere between tweedy club and hearty pub is perhaps Church Street's most elegant restaurant. The decor is sumptuous yet understated with the occasional antic touch. Check out the elaborately carved wooden phone booth which once saw service as a confessional in a nineteenth century Catholic church. The wood paneling, fireplaces, and other decorative accents were salvaged from clubs, banks, and townhouses from Atlanta to London to Paris.

The menu is vaguely "Continental" in tone and prices are moderately expensive by Orlando standards. Fortunately, the quality justifies the cost in this case. Appetizers run $5 to $9 with salads $4 to $6. Entrees range from $15 to $20 with some very nice steaks somewhat higher. Vegetables are served a la carte for an extra charge of $2 to $3. Lunch is somewhat less pricey.

Lili Marlene's is open for lunch from 11:00 a.m. to 4:00 p.m. and for dinner from 5:30 p.m. to 11:30 p.m. (until midnight Friday and Saturday). A sumptuous $13 brunch buffet ($7 for kids) is served Sunday from 10:30 a.m. to 3:00 p.m.

## William J. Sweets

This charming spot, with its fresh-faced and friendly young staff, evokes the look and feel of a turn of the century ice cream parlor and candy shoppe. The ice cream is homemade and excellent. Cones are in the $2 to $3 range and scrumptious sundaes are $4 to $5. A full range of tempting chocolate candies and fudge is also available here.

# Shopping at Church Street Station

If you come to Church Street Station just to shop, you can spend a very full day browsing and buying, not just at Church Street Station's shops but at others that have opened up nearby. (See "Beyond Church Street Station," below.)

## The Bumby Emporium

This shop takes its name from a hardware store that once occupied the space, but its wares are a long way from homespun. This is headquarters for all your Church Street Station souvenirs, including a video tape that will save you the trouble of trying to describe its many wonders to folks back home (about $22). Most of the space, however, is given over to clothing with various Church Street Station logos emblazoned boldly or subtly on the fronts and backs. The line of western wear bearing the Cheyenne Saloon logo is especially attractive.

## Buffalo Trading Company

Hang onto your wallet as you enter this upscale Western emporium next door to Bumby's. They have everything from furniture made from cowskin and bulls' horns to fringed leather jackets and doeskin dresses. Even if you don't walk out with a pair of cowboy boots or a Stetson, there's great entertainment value in browsing here.

## The Historic Railroad Depot

Part of the property that Church Street Station took over included the derelict old train depot. Now it's been all gussied up and is currently home to a garden-variety souvenir shop and some t-shirt emporiums. The real reason for straying across the train tracks to the depot, however, is to take a gander at "Old Duke," a 1912-vintage, 140-ton steam engine from the Baldwin Steam Engine and Iron Works in Ohio. Railroad buffs will recognize it as an "0-6-0" locomotive.

Besides being just plain gorgeous, the locomotive's main claim to fame was its central role in the John Wayne flick *Wings of Eagles*, shot in Florida in 1960. Today it sits on a siding, pulling a string of passenger cars that serve as offices for the Church Street Station staff. By the way, those are working railroad tracks you're crossing. Freight trains rumble through on a regular basis, so stop and look both ways before stepping out onto the tracks.

### The Exchange

Past Rosie O'Grady's and Lili Marlene's, through Apple Annie's Courtyard, lies The Exchange, a three-story shopping mall with that special Church Street Station touch. The theme of understated Victorian elegance continues here in tones of brass and cream. There are elevators and escalators as well as cleverly cantilevered stairways, but the overall impression remains turn of the century and utterly charming.

The 50-odd shops are an eclectic and generally upscale mix. A few of the shops (like Victoria's Secret and Sam Goody's) may be familiar, but most are boutique style enterprises offering everything from women's fashions (The Casual Place) to refrigerator magnets (Stuck On U). An International Food Court on the second level offers a less-expensive alternative to the eateries to be found elsewhere in Church Street Station. The top level is given over to Commander Ragtime's, described above.

The Exchange is open daily from 11:00 a.m. to 11:00 p.m.

## Beyond Church Street Station

One measure of Church Street Station's success is the way in which other players have moved into the neighborhood to capitalize on the crowds that Church Street Station draws to downtown. Just across the railroad tracks, wrapping around the Railroad Depot is a new, two-story shopping and dining arcade called **Church Street Market**. Here you will find a range of upscale specialty shops like **Brookstone** and **Sharper Image** as well as moderately priced eateries like **Pizzeria Uno**, **Jungle Jim's**, **The Olive Garden**, and **Hooters**. Church Street Market is also home to two virtual reality attractions, **Virtual Reality** and **Venturer**, that are described in *Chapter Thirteen*.

A few paces farther up Church Street, the street party atmosphere continues with **Sloppy Joe's** and **Mulvaney's Irish Pub**, both featuring live music of the rock and roll variety and no cover charge. Also on this block is a branch of **Pebbles**, Orlando's home-grown and highly recommended upscale restaurant chain.

# CHAPTER NINE:

# Kennedy Space Center

About an hour from Orlando (and Disney's Tomorrowland) is a place where the fantasy drops away, replaced by awe-inspiring reality. It is here, at the John F. Kennedy Space Center, smack in the middle of a wildlife refuge, that real people, riding real live spaceships, are blasted into outer space on a variety of scientific, military, and commercial missions. On the fringes of this very serious enterprise is a sort of mini theme park that lets us earthbound types get a peek at this very special world and imagine — just for a moment — what it must be like to be on the cutting edge of tomorrow. If you time your visit just right, you can even see the actual space shuttle roaring into the heavens towards another rendezvous with the future.

The Kennedy Space Center (or "KSC" for short) is immense, one-fifth the size of the state of Rhode Island. Only 6,000 of its 140,000 acres are used for operations; the rest is a wildlife refuge. Most people are amazed to learn that this monument to high-tech is home to more endangered species (15) than any other place in the United States except the Everglades. There are also 310 types of birds flitting between the launch pads. Yet over the years, the complex has logged some 3,000 launches. As you might expect, you will only get to see a small sliver of Kennedy Space Center's vastness but the access you are granted is remarkable.

For those who care about such things, I should note that no taxpayer money is used to support the visitor facilities, tours, or other tourist activities at Kennedy Space Center. All of these are run by a private company and are entirely self-supporting.

# Before You Come

Doing homework for your visit to Kennedy Space Center is not absolutely necessary, but it helps if you have at least some background knowledge of the space program. A painless way to get that background is to head down to the video store and rent *The Right Stuff* and *Apollo 13*. Both films are a lot of fun to watch and offer great insight into the human as well as the technical dimensions of the space program. Somewhat harder to find but worth looking for is the Discovery Channel special *The Space Shuttle*.

For information about the Kennedy Space Center itself, call (407) 452-2121; in Florida only, you can call (800) 572-4636 ("KSC-INFO"). Ask for brochures and they will patch you into a voice mail system where you can record your name and address. The brochures are free and take about three weeks to arrive. The Visitor Complex brochure, with its schedule of tours and films, can help you plan out your day in advance. Readers with an Internet connection can log on at http://www.kscvisitor.com and follow the prompts.

Another way to get an advance look at the Center is to call either the (407) number above or (800) 621-9826 and order the *Kennedy Space Center Visitor Complex* tour book. It is $5.95, plus $4 shipping and takes about a week to arrive. It doesn't provide tour and film times but it will certainly whet your appetite and help you decide how to focus your time during your visit.

If you are interested in seeing a shuttle launch, see the discussion on getting tickets and the best view later in this chapter.

# Getting There

The easiest way to reach KSC from Orlando is to get on the Bee Line Expressway (SR 528) headed east. The tolls will set you back $2.50 but it's the fastest route (about an hour or so). Turn off onto SR 407 North, and then onto SR 405 East, which will lead you directly to the Visitor Complex.

You can also take SR 50 (Orlando's East Colonial Drive) to route 405. It takes a bit longer but it's free and passes attractions like Back To Nature Wildlife Refuge and Jungle Adventures (both described in *Chapter Fifteen*) which you might want to visit en route.

# Opening and Closing Times

Hours for the Visitor Complex vary throughout the year. Opening time is invariably 9:00 a.m. but the closing time changes to keep pace with sunset. From late October through January, closing time is 6:00

p.m. In February and March, closing time is 7:00 p.m. From early April to late June, closing is at 7:30 p.m.; from late June to late August at 8:30 p.m. From late August until early October, KSC closes at 7:30 p.m., then, briefly, at 7:00 p.m. until it returns to 6:00 p.m. in late October. These dates and times are approximate. Please call for exact times.

Tours and IMAX films begin at 9:30 a.m. Tours stop departing about three hours prior to the closing time of the Visitor Complex. The last showing of the IMAX films is usually about two hours prior to closing. Some attractions at the Visitor Complex also close early.

## The Price of Admission

Admission to the Visitor Complex is **free**. The main attractions — the tours and the IMAX films — require the purchase of tickets and are priced a la carte, as follows (plus tax):

Bus Tours:          Adults $14, Children (3 to 11) $10
IMAX films:        Adults $7.50, Children (3 to 11) $5.50
Crew Pass:          Adults $19, Children (3 to 11) $15

The Crew Pass combines the bus tours with admission to one IMAX movie and represents a $2.50 savings on an adult admission.

There are no discounts extended to groups such as the AARP, AAA members, or the military.

The typical visitor will take the tours and see one film, which makes the Crew Pass the logical choice. If you see it all, the cost becomes $34 for adults and $26 for children.

Parking, in lots with sections named after shuttle craft, is **free**.

## Good Things to Know About . . .

### Access for the Disabled

All of Kennedy Space Center is wheelchair accessible. Free wheelchairs may be obtained at the Information Central counter in the Main Entrance building. The IMAX films are equipped with devices for the hearing impaired.

### Babies

Strollers are **free** at KSC (at the Information Central counter in the Main Entrance). Diaper changing tables are located in some restrooms, including the men's room at the Orbit Restaurant.

### Cameras

Forgot your camera? No problem. Stop at the Information counter in the Main Entrance area and exchange your drivers license for a free loaner 35mm camera to use during your visit. Film is not included but is readily available in shops at the Visitor Complex.

### First Aid

There is a well-equipped first aid station with a nurse on duty from 9:00 a.m. to 5:00 p.m. It is located near the bus depot.

### Leaving the Park

Since there is no admission to the Visitor Complex or parking fee, you may come and go as you please during the day.

### Money

There is an ATM on the wall of the Space Shop across from the Ticket Pavilion. It is hooked into the Honor System and Exchange Plus. It also accepts Visa cards.

### Pets

Pets will be boarded free of charge during your visit. The pet kennel is to your right as you approach the main entrance to the Visitor Complex.

# Blast Off: Your Day at Kennedy Space Center

I have found that it is impossible to see everything at Kennedy Space Center in one day. It is, however, possible to see most of it — including all the ticketed attractions — if you get there early and step lively for the next 8 to 10 hours. Even a delay of a few hours will decrease your chances of seeing everything.

# When's the Best Time to Come?

To a great extent, attendance at KSC reflects the seasonal ebb and flow of tourists described elsewhere. However, attendance is also greatly affected by the launch schedule at the Kennedy Space Center.

The days before and after a launch tend to be busier than usual; the day of a launch, the Visitor Complex will also be busy, although I am told that on some launch days the crowds are thinner than on a "typical" day. In addition, the Visitor Complex is closed on the day of a launch until approximately one and a half hours after launch. Given the fact that launches are frequently delayed, that could mean the Visitor Complex will be open for just a few hours or not at all.

So even though seeing a launch is one of the neatest things to do while you're in Florida, a visit to Kennedy Space Center at that time may not be an ideal choice — unless you don't mind missing some things or will be able to spend more than a day on the Space Coast.

## What to Expect

When you arrive at Kennedy Space Center, you will stop first at the Visitor Complex. Don't worry about finding it. You can't miss the life-size replica of the space shuttle and its twin booster rockets that grace the entrance.

Kennedy Space Center and the adjacent Cape Canaveral Air Force Station cover a great deal of territory. The Visitor Complex, by contrast, is quite small; you can walk from one end to the other in about five minutes. Your visit to Kennedy Space Center will be centered here — *except* when you leave on one of the two bus tours. Your activities at KSC, then, will be divided into two categories:

First are the free attractions and activities offered at the Visitor Complex; these are either museum-like exhibits or film or video presentations. Second are the attractions that require the pre-purchase of tickets — the three IMAX films, which have their own theater at the Visitor Complex, and the two bus tours which venture out of the Visitor Complex. You must purchase these tickets at the Visitor Complex on the day of your visit.

## The One-Day Stay

When you arrive at the KSC Visitor Complex and enter the Main Entrance building, virtually the first thing you see is a counter called "Information Central." This is **not** where you purchase your tickets. Your day will get off to a much smoother start if you walk straight through the Main Entrance building, pausing only to pick up the Visitor Complex brochure which contains a map and a schedule of tours and IMAX films. As you emerge on the other side, the Ticket Pavilion will be directly ahead of you.

If you got a brochure ahead of time, you may have already mapped out your day. Otherwise, use your time in line at the Ticket Pavilion to orient yourself with the map and plan your day with the schedule. You will notice that the schedule favors the bus tour of the "Kennedy Space Center Tour" over the "Historic Cape Canaveral Tour" and the IMAX film *The Dream Is Alive* over the other two. So if you have your heart set on taking the Canaveral Tour and seeing the other two IMAX films, plan your day around them. Given the continuous departures for the main tour and frequent screenings of *The Dream Is Alive*, they should then be easy to fit into your schedule.

If you plan on doing all or most of the ticketed attractions, you will discover that once you have mapped out your schedule, you will have a half hour or an hour here and there during the day to see what's left and eat. I suggest grabbing your food on the run if you want to maximize your touring time. There are plenty of free-standing kiosks scattered about, making this a viable strategy.

You can use the descriptions below and your own taste to determine which of the "what's left" will most appeal to you. I strongly recommend the Launch Status Center and the Gallery of Space Flight. The free film showing in the Main Entrance building (not open at press time) may also be worth a look.

## The Two-Day Stay

If you'd rather not run yourself ragged trying to see all the ticketed attractions, or if you have more than one day to allocate to visiting the Space Center, your task becomes much easier. If you are planning a two-day visit, I would recommend taking the Kennedy Space Center Tour and seeing *The Dream Is Alive* on the first day, spending the remainder of the time touring the Visitor Complex. Then, on the second day, you can do the Historic Cape Canaveral Tour (if it's available), and catch the other two IMAX films if you wish.

## Attractions at Kennedy Space Center Visitor Complex

As noted earlier, all the attractions at the Visitor Complex, with the notable exception of the IMAX films, are free. Most are available for continuous viewing, except the film- and video-based exhibits which have frequently scheduled showings throughout the day.

The exhibits range from the compelling to the easy to miss. They are described here starting from the Main Entrance to the Visitor Complex, and proceeding in a somewhat erratic path to the back of the Center.

## Main Entrance

*Rating:*       ★ ★ ★
*Type:*         Variety of exhibits housed under one roof
*Time:*         Continuous
*Kelly says:*   A grab bag of time killers

At press time, Kennedy Space Center announced a major overhaul of its main entrance, designed to improve traffic flow and provide guests — via large video monitors — with a quick overview of what awaits them within. Scattered through the building will be a number of displays, some of them interactive and some of which are still tentative as I write this. Although this is the first building you enter, you may want to pass through quickly en route to more interesting fare. You can always return here later.

The **Information Central** counter, mentioned above, is the place to come with general questions about the Space Center and NASA. The staff here can also offer sound advice on how best to allocate your time at the Center. This is where you can get a wheelchair, a loaner camera, or postage stamps.

The **Merritt Island National Wildlife Refuge** display consists of "immersive" dioramas depicting the wildlife and natural scenery that surround the Space Center. Also in the Main Entrance building is a **tourist information counter** should you decide to spend some more time on Florida's "Space Coast." Still uncertain is the fate of several **interactive displays** that provide information on the current or next scheduled shuttle mission, every astronaut who has flown for NASA, and the history of various space missions. These may remain in the Main Entrance building or be moved elsewhere in the Visitor Complex.

The major attractions in the Main Entrance building will be a **300-seat theater** showing an as yet untitled million dollar film about the search for life on other planets and throughout the universe, and the tentatively titled multimedia presentation, **Robot Pioneers.**

*Robot Pioneers* begins with a short film about the use of remotely controlled devices like Sojourner, which recently explored the surface of Mars. Then you walk through a series of animated dioramas that expand on and further illustrate the theme.

The new Main Entrance is scheduled for completion in the Spring of 1999. Check for updated information on its attractions on the Intrepid Traveler's web site:

http://www.intrepidtraveler.com

## Rocket Garden

| | |
|---|---|
| *Rating:* | ★ ★ ★ |
| *Type:* | Outdoor display of rockets |
| *Time:* | Continuous viewing |
| *Kelly says:* | Great photo backdrops |

This may remind you of a sculpture garden at a museum of modern art. Indeed, some of the tracking antennas on display look just as arty and a lot prettier than some modern art. The stars of the show, however, are the big rockets. A plaque gives the vital statistics for each object for the technically inclined, but most people will be content to gawk and have their pictures taken in front of these amazing machines.

The Rocket Garden can be appreciated from a distance, but the Apollo-Saturn service arm, once part of the gantry that served the giant Saturn rockets, lets you follow in the footsteps of the astronauts who walked down this metal walkway to enter their space capsules. Also worth a closer look is the mammoth Saturn 1B rocket lying on its side on the far side of the garden; this behemoth generated a thrust of 1.3 million pounds as it lofted Skylab astronauts into orbit back in the seventies.

Guided tours of the area are available from time to time, but I always seem to miss them.

## Children's Play Dome

*Rating:* ★ ★ +
*Type:* Kids' play area
*Time:* Continuous
*Kelly says:* Strictly for wee ones

Harried parents who want to rest while their active youngsters burn off a little excess energy can repair to this shaded geodesic dome. Here, under the canvas cover, is the kind of play area you'd find at an Orlando area McDonalds. This one has a space theme, including a kiddie-sized space shuttle.

## Gallery of Space Flight

*Rating:* ★ ★ ★ +
*Type:* Space program museum
*Time:* Continuous viewing; about 20 minutes
*Kelly says:* An eye-popping encounter with history

In this building are some amazing artifacts of the space era. Among others, you will see the first unmanned Mercury spacecraft launched in 1960, a Gemini capsule from 1966, the Apollo-Soyuz capsule used in the first international rendezvous and docking in space in 1975, and the actual suit worn by Neil Armstrong on the moon. Equally impressive are some of the models on display, especially a remarkably detailed cutaway of the 363-foot Apollo-Saturn V rocket that shot the astronauts to the moon and a model of Skylab.

The museum is designed to take you on a leisurely, looping tour of space history, letting you out where you entered. Along the way, you can pause to get a picture of yourself sitting in a lunar rover or 'wearing' an official NASA space suit. It's a fun and painless way to get a quick grounding in space history.

# Galaxy Center Exhibits

*Rating:*    ★ ★ +
*Type:*    Various displays
*Time:*    Continuous viewing
*Kelly says:*    If you have the time

A number of exhibits and displays are scattered about the Galaxy Center building that houses the IMAX film theaters (see below). If you have a few moments to spare before or after the show — or have ducked inside to escape a rain shower — you might want to take a quick look around.

At one end of the building is an **art gallery** featuring works commissioned by NASA to commemorate the space program. They range from hyperrealism to the surreal to the completely abstract and are worth at least a quick look. At the other end is a life-sized, walk-through **space station module**, specifically the laboratory module from the forthcoming space station. Here protein crystals "of incredible purity and uniformity" will be fashioned for optical and electronic devices. Nearby, and in sharp contrast, is a hydroponics "farm" where plain old lettuce will be grown for the astronauts' dinner table. In a passage between the two theaters you will find two **interactive displays**. One explains the process whereby shuttles are prepared, launched, retrieved, and prepped yet again for another flight. The other is an entertaining overview of the scientific, medical, and consumer spin-offs that have resulted from the massive investment in the space program.

# Astronaut Memorial (Space Mirror)

*Rating:*    ★ ★ ★
*Type:*    Memorial to fallen astronauts
*Time:*    Continuous viewing
*Kelly says:*    Intricate, intriguing, and moving

At first this monument to those who have lost their lives in the space program struck me as a bit of overkill. But as I examined the intricate mechanism that uses the sun's beams to illuminate the 16 names on this massive memorial, I came to realize how fitting it is to blend the high-tech and the heavenly to honor these special people. The entire memorial tilts and swivels to follow the sun across the sky as mirrors collect and focus the sun's rays onto clear glass names in a huge black marble slab. From the opposite side the effect is startling. The memorial is handsomely sited at the end of a large pool at the back of the Gallery Center; a small kiosk on the side of that building houses computers that offer background information on the astronauts honored on the memorial.

# Shuttle Plaza/Explorer

*Rating:*       ★ ★ +
*Type:*         Full-scale shuttle model
*Time:*         Continuous viewing with the possibility
                of long waits
*Kelly says:*   If you have time

The full-scale model of the space shuttle is certainly impressive. But don't be surprised if you find a visit a bit of a let down, especially if you've had to wait 40 minutes or an hour for a glimpse inside. The line spirals up an elaborate exterior superstructure (which also contains an elevator for the disabled). You can step in on two levels — the cockpit and, immediately below it, the crew compartment. To your left is the huge empty cargo bay. What stuck me most was how cramped the space allotted to the crew is. Not even a New York landlord would have the gall to call this a studio apartment. This attraction closes down when lightning is spotted within 30 miles of the Center. Guided tours of the Shuttle Plaza area, which also contains two booster rockets, are offered from time to time.

# Launch Status Center

*Rating:*       ★ ★ ★ ★ +
*Type:*         Live briefings and educational displays
*Time:*         Briefings last about 20 minutes
*Kelly says:*   The best thing at the Visitor Complex

The modest looking, almost anonymous, white geodesic dome near the Explorer mock-up in Shuttle Plaza houses what is, in my opinion, the best thing at the Visitor Complex. There are models and displays here of the retrievable solid rocket boosters and their motors, a manned maneuvering unit, even an outer-space soft drink dispenser. Perhaps the most fascinating artifact is an actual solid rocket booster nose cone from the 66th shuttle mission; usually these sink to the bottom of the ocean and are replaced, but this one remained afloat long enough to be retrieved.

The main attractions here, however, are the live briefings that occur every hour on the hour from 11:00 a.m. to 5:00 p.m. Held in front of a set of simulated mission control panels like those used in astronaut training, they feature a live "communicator" and live shots from remote video cameras strategically stationed around the working heart of the space center, including the Vehicle Assembly Building and the launch pad itself.

No matter when you visit, there will always be something going on at the Space Center and this is your opportunity to get the inside scoop. Obviously, the most interesting time to come here is in the days and hours before a launch and during an actual mission, when you'll get to see the live video feed from the shuttle itself. However, a visit is worthwhile no matter where they are in the launch cycle. The communicators are veritable encyclopedias of information about the space program, and I would urge you not to be shy about asking questions once the formal briefing is over.

## Center for Space Education

*Rating:*   ★ ★ ★
*Type:*   Hands-on science displays open to the public
*Time:*   Continuous viewing
*Kelly says:*   For teachers and budding astronauts

On the opposite side of the Visitor Complex grounds from Shuttle Plaza, set well away from the other attractions, this large building houses the educational outreach component of the Kennedy Space Center. Inside, teachers will find a library and resource center just for them. Special programs for visiting school groups are also held in this building. The Exploration Station is open to the general public. It is a largish room filled with hands-on, interactive exhibits that demonstrate basic principles of science. This will probably most appeal to younger kids.

## The Bus Tours

The only way to see the working end of the Space Center is by taking a guided bus tour. Two tours are offered, representing the past and the present of the space program. One tour visits the Kennedy Space Center on Merritt Island. This is where the shuttle launches take place; you will get a fairly close look at the major sites in the vast complex and get an awe-inspiring close-up look at the largest rocket ever built.

There are three stops on this tour and you can stay as long at each of them as you wish because the buses run continuously. This system has obvious advantages but the downside is that crowds can build up, making the bus loading process slow and chaotic. So it's best to take this tour early in the day.

The KSC tour is quite clearly the star of the show, with continuous departures starting at 9:30 a.m. and continuing until about three hours prior to closing.

The other tour visits Cape Canaveral, site of the original U.S. space program. On this tour, you get to enter sites where history was made. Unfortunately, this tour runs only a few times a day and is frequently unavailable because of the steady stream of commercial launch activity at Cape Canaveral. Unlike the Kennedy Space Center tour, the Canaveral tour requires that you depart and return with the same group on the same bus.

All tours leave from an efficient bus terminal at one end of the Visitor Complex. Most buses are comfortable 100-seat double deckers designed for sightseeing. I prefer the upper section. No food is allowed aboard the buses and the only beverage allowed is bottled water, which is available for purchase at the Visitors Complex. It's not a bad idea to bring some, especially in the warmer months.

Both Kennedy Space Center and Cape Canaveral Air Force Station are working spaceports, which means that the itinerary of these tours may be modified to accommodate launch and other activities. Another element of unpredictability comes from the wildlife at the Center. Alligators, sometimes jokingly referred to as part of the security system, are sighted frequently and there are bald eagle nests along the tour routes.

Both tours feature recorded narration, which will be supplemented — or interrupted — whenever the driver feels it's time to add his or her own commentary or release a late-breaking news bulletin ("Wild hogs on the left!"). Foreign language narration, in French, German, Spanish, and Portuguese, is available on tape on a first-come, first-served basis.

# Kennedy Space Center

*Rating:*          ★ ★ ★ ★ ★
*Time:*           2 to 4 hours
*Kelly says:*     This is the next best thing to becoming
                    an astronaut

Now that the Apollo/Saturn V Center is open, the bus tour of Kennedy Space Center has become yet another "must-see" stop on the Central Florida tourist circuit. And no wonder. This tour takes you to the sites where the space shuttle is prepared and launched. It also gives you an opportunity to gape and gawk at an actual Saturn V rocket. It's as close as you'll come to being launched into space without joining the astronaut corps.

There are three stops on this tour — the LC-39 Observation Gantry, the Apollo/Saturn V Center, and the International Space Station Center. You will also get to drive by the Vehicle Assembly Building, where the space shuttle is mated with its immense fuel tanks prior to each launch.

The **LC-39 Observation Gantry** ("LC" stands for "launch complex") is a four-story tower that offers a bird's-eye view of launch pads 39A and B, from which all shuttle flights depart. If you visit close to a launch, you'll see the support structure that completely surrounds the shuttle. It is only removed a few hours prior to launch. You may also get a chance for an up-close photo of the massive crawler transporters that carry the shuttle from the Vehicle Assembly Building (VAB) to the launch pad. These 6-million-pound vehicles roar along at one mile per hour when fully loaded and get an incredible 35 feet per gallon.

You'll also get close to the VAB itself. One of the largest buildings in the world, its roof covers five acres. It encloses so much space that it has its own atmosphere and it has actually rained inside. It was here that the gigantic Saturn V rockets used in the Apollo program were assembled. The shuttles seem tiny by comparison.

The undisputed highlight of this tour is a visit to the **Apollo/Saturn V Center**. The building is massive — and it has to be to house a refurbished, 363-foot-tall Saturn V moon rocket, one of only three in existence. Before you get to see the star of this show, you enter the **Firing Room** where the actual mission control consoles used during the Apollo missions form a backdrop for a video and audio re-creation of the launch of Apollo VIII, the first manned lunar mission.

Then you step into the massive building that houses the Saturn V, suspended horizontally in one long open space. No description can prepare you for just how immense this thing actually is. The word "awesome" moves from hyperbole to understatement. Arrayed around, alongside, and under the rocket are interpretive displays filled with astounding facts about this magnificent achievement.

Before you leave, visit the **Lunar Surface Theater** where you will see a recreation of the first landing on the moon and be reminded of just how touch-and-go this mission was up to the very last second. After the show, you step into the **New Frontiers Gallery** for a preview of space missions yet to come.

The final stop is the **International Space Station Center** where the components for this ambitious multinational, multi-year construction project are meticulously examined and tested before being lofted into orbit aboard the space shuttle. An observation window lets you view activities in the "clean room" where this painstaking work is carried out. A guide fills you in on what's going on below.

If you don't linger at the various stops, you can complete this tour in about two hours, but rushing through is a mistake. Take your time, invest three or four hours and enjoy yourself. There are places to eat at each stop and the Saturn Center even boasts the **Moon Rock Cafe**, the "only place on earth where you can dine next to a piece of the moon."

This tour is an exciting experience for anyone. For Americans, it should be a source of deep patriotic pride.

*Tip:* On this tour, try for a seat on the right side of the bus as you shuttle from stop to stop.

# Historic Cape Canaveral Tour

*Rating:*       ★ ★ ★ ★
*Time:*       Approximately 2 hours
*Kelly says:*    Stirring history

Perversely, I slightly prefer this tour to the other. The main reason is that on this one you actually get to enter the places where space history was made. It was from Cape Canaveral that the first Americans were launched into space.

You can walk through the blockhouse that housed mission control for the early Mercury missions and stroll out to the pad from which puny looking Redstone rockets launched the first Americans into space using a gantry jury-rigged from an old oil drilling rig. The room-sized computer used for these launches could be replaced by a modern laptop, with plenty of room left over on the hard drive for games. Next door is a small museum with a collection of artifacts relating to the early days of the space program. Much of the launch pad area has been turned into a sort of outdoor sculpture garden displaying two dozen or so rockets and missiles, including my personal favorite, the sleekly magnificent and rather sexy Snark.

Later, you can stand in the former press and VIP viewing area of the Mission Control building used during the later Mercury and Gemini missions. A film recounts the history of the ground-breaking (or should I say space-breaking) efforts of these programs. I found this small room, which looks a bit like a set from a low-budget 1950s television series, absolutely fascinating. It bears mute testimony to the speed at which our technology is exploding. And standing where President Kennedy once stood to witness a launch adds an extra level of excitement to an already special experience.

Cape Canaveral entered the space age in 1950 with tests of captured German V-2 rockets. But it is far from being a dusty museum or a monument to the past. It is a bustling modern spaceport from which a wide variety of unmanned scientific and commercial satellites are launched into orbit, including many of the satellites that provide our telephone communications and weather forecasting. As you drive around, you may catch glimpses of preparations for upcoming launches. Much of the land here has been leased back to the farmers who occupied the area before the space age; now orange groves and launch pads sit side by side in incongruous harmony.

The recorded narration for this tour may get a little portentous for some tastes, but it's a minor fault. Either side of the bus is okay since you get to walk up to and into the most interesting sights.

*Tip:* The early Mercury program blockhouse and the adjacent Air Force Space Museum are open to visitors **free** of charge. If you didn't have time during the bus tour's short stop to read all the material accompanying the displays in these buildings (and you won't), you may want to return. The catch is, you have to enter through the gate of Cape Canaveral Air Force Station between 10:00 a.m. and 2:00 p.m. on weekdays or 10:00 a.m and 4:00 p.m. on weekends. To get there, take SR 528 East towards Cocoa Beach; turn left on SR 401 which will take you right to the gate of the Air Force base. Tell them you want to visit the museum and you will be given a pass. You must exit the way you entered; there is no access from the Air Force Station directly to Kennedy Space Center.

## The IMAX Films

If you've never seen an IMAX film, this is an excellent place to remedy that situation. IMAX is an ultra-large film format, 10 times larger than standard 35mm film and three times the size of the 70mm films you see at your local movie theater. It is projected on a screen some five and a half stories high and 70 feet wide. The sound system is equally impressive, producing bass tones you will feel in your bones.

The Galaxy Center at the Visitor Complex contains two back-to-back IMAX theaters, the only such IMAX "multiplex" in the world. The auditoriums are small relative to the size of the screen, so I would recommend showing up early so you can grab a seat towards the back of the house. There are doors on five levels and I find the seats in the middle of the third level to be just about ideal.

Of the films reviewed below, *The Dream Is Alive* will almost certainly be playing when you visit. The other films change from time to time.

## The Dream Is Alive

*Rating*:  ★ ★ ★ ★ +
*Time:*  37 minutes

Of the three IMAX films, this one offers the best overview of what the shuttle program is all about. It takes you step by step through the process of refurbishing and readying a shuttle for the next mission. It features spectacular footage of the shuttle in action, including enthralling sequences on the training of astronauts to service an orbiting satellite and the subsequent successful completion of the mission. Best of all are the sequences shot by the astronauts far above the planet's surface. Walter

Cronkite narrates with his trademark aplomb. If you can see just one of the IMAX films, I recommend this one.

# Mission to MIR

*Rating:* ★ ★ ★ ★
*Time:* 40 minutes

Now that the "Evil Empire" has collapsed, the long-time dream on international cooperation in space is becoming a reality, as this film amply demonstrates. It features glimpses of the Russian space program's facilities that most Westerners have never seen. Compared to what you will see at KSC, the Russian space program looks downright low-tech and dingy. But the real attraction here is the footage shot high above the earth's surface during the lengthy visit by American astronaut Shannon Lucid to MIR, the aging Russian space station. The scenes of life aboard are interesting but they only seem to detract from the beautiful shots of the space station docking with the space shuttle or just drifting serenely through space.

# L5: First City in Space

*Rating:* ★ ★ ★
*Time:* 33 minutes

3D is the gimmick in this short film fantasy about a space city of the future that captures a comet to serve as a source of water and other useful raw materials. Some of the footage is fun, especially the sequence in which an intrepid astronaut lands a small craft on the comet to repair the robot engines that will power this chunk of space ice back to L5. But for the most part this film is a disappointment. IMAX seems to work far better in recording actual reality than in creating computer animated fantasy.

# Eating at Kennedy Space Center

While you won't have to subsist on the powdered drinks and squeeze-tube dinners that were once standard fare for astronauts, neither can you expect a gourmet dining experience at KSC Visitor Complex. The eateries here are geared to processing hundreds of generally young diners in a quick and efficient manner, and the food quality seldom rises above fast-food or cafeteria level, although the desserts in The Orbit are delicious. One of the management's best inspirations has been to dispatch dozens of free-standing food carts to various points in the Visitor Complex. They offer everything from ice cream snacks to fruit to more substantial fare like hot dogs. Given the difficulty of squeezing everything into a one-day visit to the Center, it makes a lot of sense to eat on the run from these carts and save the big sit-down meal for later in the evening.

The only full-service restaurant at the Center is **Mila's Roadhouse**, overlooking the Space Mirror. The decor is vaguely fifties or sixties in feel (there are a few outdoor tables) and the menu runs to home-cooked meat-and-veg meals. Hot dogs and burgers are only offered to the small fry. Most entrees cost less than $10.

Next door is **The Orbit**, a large, noisy fast-food emporium with a modern metallic high-tech decor. Service is cafeteria style, with a large central carousel dispensing beverages, salads, sandwiches, and desserts. On one side of the carousel, you can get pizzas and pasta dishes for about $6 to $8. On the other side, a steam table offers roast beef, turkey, chicken, and fried fish dinners with a choice of vegetables. Prices range from $5 to about $10. A whole chicken or a slab of ribs is $11. Beer and wine is served here ($4).

Another cafeteria, **The Lunchpad**, is located near the bus depot. This is the place to come for breakfast first thing in the morning or for burgers and fries or fish and chips later in the day. There is also a decent Greek salad available here, one of the healthier food choices to be found at the Visitor Complex. A standard meal of entree and soft drink should cost well under $10.

Food is also to be had on the Kennedy Space Center Tour. The LC-39 Observation Gantry and the International Space Station Center both have hot dog stands where a quick meal will cost about $5. The Apollo/Saturn V Center features the **Moon Rock Cafe**, a cafeteria where you will find hot dogs, Polish sausage, and cheeseburgers served with fries for $4 to about $6. Individual pizzas are about $5 and desserts are in the $2 to $3 range. If you are trying to pack as much as possible into a one-day visit, grabbing a hot dog on this tour and eating it while waiting for the shuttle bus is a good strategy.

# Shopping at Kennedy Space Center

The largest selection of KSC souvenir and outer-space themed merchandise to be found anywhere is yours to browse through in the mammoth, two-level **Space Shop**, which lies between the ticket pavilion and the bus depot. Here you will find everything from t-shirts priced well under $20 to leather bomber jackets with the NASA logo for over $200. There are also buttons, badges, patches, and medallions commemorating every shuttle mission. Some of these collectibles are issued in limited editions of just one million copies, so snatch yours up before they're gone! Among the best souvenirs are the videos, available in all international formats, and the space shuttle and rocket model kits. A video version of *Destiny in Space* (about $35) makes a nice memento. The official Kennedy Space Center tour book (about $6) also makes an excellent (not to mention inexpensive) souvenir.

If you want stuff but don't want to spend your time at the Visitor Complex shopping, call the mail order department at 1-800-621-9826 and wade through the automated answering service.

## Seeing a Launch

You've probably seen film clips of shuttle launches on TV. You've probably seen them dozens of times. But, to quote Al Jolson, you ain't seen nothin' yet! Seeing a shuttle launch live and in person is one of the truly great experiences a Florida vacation has to offer. Catching at least a glimpse of a launch is surprisingly easy. On a clear day, the rising shuttle is even visible from the Orlando area. Getting a closer look, however, requires a bit of planning.

First, you must understand that you don't have to be close to the launching pad to get ringside seats. In fact, *no one* can be close to the launching pad. The greatest danger a launch poses to bystanders is, surprisingly, the noise generated by the awesome engines. It is, I am told, the loudest man-made sound next to the explosion of a thermonuclear device. An elaborate sound suppression system clicks in at launch time, spewing 300,000 gallons of water on the escaping gases from the rocket engines. Were it not for this system, the observers in the press and VIP section, some three and a half miles away, would permanently lose their hearing.

Unless you're a credentialed reporter, a relative of an astronaut, or have some inside pull at NASA, you will be a good bit farther way. But you can still have an excellent view and an experience you will remember for the rest of your life.

The best viewing venue for the general public is along the NASA Causeway that runs from Merritt Island to Cape Canaveral Air Force base across the Banana River. This puts you approximately seven miles from the launch pad. There's nothing fancy about the viewing area; cars simply pull off the road and are parked tightly on the grass with the help of parking attendants. A narrow area next to the water is left free for picnickers. Many people bring folding chairs, beach blankets, and elaborate repasts. The shuttle will be visible to the naked eye across the water to the north, but a pair of binoculars will allow you to see the vapor pouring off the fuel tanks.

There are two ways to get here; both require advance planning:

The first way is absolutely free but requires the most advance planning. Write a short note to the Public Affairs Office, PA-PASS, Kennedy Space Center, FL 32899, requesting a Launch Viewing Car Pass. They recommend that you write two to three months in advance. In practice, it seems, they will simply send you a pass for the next launch for which passes are available.

The pass itself takes the form of a heavy paper card, about 5 by 8 inches, in a bright day-glo color keyed to the number of the launch. (Launches are numbered sequentially, STS-90, STS-91, and so on.). Place it on the dashboard of your car and it will grant you access to the Space Center and the viewing area on the day of the launch. After the launch, save it as a souvenir.

The second way will cost you some money but may work better for those who don't (or can't) plan ahead. The Kennedy Space Center Visitor Complex sells approximately 1,500 tickets for a bus trip to the viewing area. The cost is $10 for visitors of all ages. Tickets go on sale five days before launch date only at the Visitors Complex. There are no phone sales and no reservations are taken. The demand for these tickets is unpredictable. On at least one occasion, they sold out within an hour of first being offered. For other launches, the demand has been considerably less intense. If you find that the launch is sold out, there is still a slim chance you may be able to get tickets. Very occasionally a few tickets go back on sale on launch day. So if you arrive bright and early that morning, you just may be able to buy a ticket. No guarantees, of course, but for a sold-out launch it's your best bet.

Given the uncertainty of the actual launch date, you will have to check back regularly to plan your visit. A recorded message at (407) 867-4636 provides the very latest in launch schedule information.

## On Launch Day

If you are driving to the viewing area, plan on pulling on to SR 405 (from the west) or SR 3 (from the south) several hours before the scheduled flight time. I arrived for one launch about three hours prior to the scheduled time and got a nice spot in Section Delta, a bit past the bridge in the middle of the causeway. Take note of the section in which you are parked and be aware that if you wander far from your car you may have a hard time finding it again. I recommend using a nearby RV or motorcoach (they are parked closest to the road) as a landmark.

You are on government property and in a wildlife refuge to boot, so there are a few simple rules. Cooking and fires are prohibited, as are alcoholic beverages. You are not allowed to fish, wade, swim, or feed the wildlife (there are some manatee holding pens along the causeway viewing area). If you have a pet, you'll have to make arrangements to leave it behind.

Dotted along the viewing area are NASA Exchange trailers selling snacks and souvenirs. The prices for food and drink are surprisingly cheap, especially considering they have a captive audience. Coffee and tea are just 50 cents, cold drinks are 75 cents. Few snacks are more than a dollar. The most expensive items on the menu are sandwiches (usually ham and cheese) at $2.50. On top of that, there's no tax.

The atmosphere at the viewing area is infectiously cheerful and friendly. People seem to instantly become one happy family. At the launch I attended, a professor of astronomy from a nearby university was letting passersby take a peek at the shuttle through his eight-inch telescope.

A public address system mounted on poles carries live announcements from NASA mission control. As launch time approaches, you will hear the actual conversations between mission control and the shuttle crew. A few minutes before the launch, several local radio stations begin live coverage. Among them are 580AM, 90.7FM, and 107.1FM.

At the actual launch, you will see a flash of light a second or two before blast-off. Then the shuttle disappears in a towering cloud of white exhaust only to emerge a moment later, its engines spewing a blinding flame. The shuttle will be well up into the air before you hear the sound, but when it arrives at your viewing point you will feel the land tremble beneath your feet as well as hear the throaty rumble of the booster rockets. As it continues its eight minute journey to orbit, arcing gracefully to the east, the shuttle looks like a tiny toy atop a massive column of white clouds. About two and half minutes into the flight, the booster rockets drop away. (If you have binoculars, you may be able to spot the parachutes that lower them to the sea for recovery by NASA ships.) At this point, the shuttle becomes a star-like point of light hurtling into the history books.

I was lucky. The launch I observed went up on the dot. But you should be aware that, more often than not, the shuttle doesn't go up on schedule. If there are delays for weather or technical glitches, you will be kept posted. If the launch is scrubbed (that is, canceled) you will be asked to leave. However, you can use the NASA-issued dashboard cards again when the launch is rescheduled.

# CHAPTER TEN:

# Busch Gardens Tampa

B usch Gardens is a somewhat schizophrenic mixture of zoological park and amusement park, with a dash of variety show thrown in. Given the seemingly disparate demands of these elements, the designers have done an admirable job of creating an attractive whole. Aesthetically, a stroll through Busch Gardens is one of the most pleasing in Central Florida.

Like any good theme park, Busch Gardens has one. In this case it's Africa, the mysterious continent so linked in the popular imagination with wild animals and adventure. Borrowing a page from the Disney manual, the park is divided into nine "lands," or as Busch calls them, "themed areas." With few exceptions, they take their names from countries or regions in Africa. The metaphor works wonderfully for the zoo side of things, although it results in the occasional oddity (Bengal tigers in the Congo? Dolphins in Timbuktu?). It is largely extraneous to the park's other elements. A roller coaster is a roller coaster, whether it's named after an Egyptian god (Montu) or in a Congolese dialect (Kumba). Switch the locations of these giant coasters and no one would know the difference. On the other hand, who cares?

Since the focus of this book is on the Orlando area, the question naturally arises: Why schlep to Tampa for another theme park? There are two main answers: the animals and the roller coasters. Disney's Animal Kingdom has created some competition to Busch's great apes and white Bengal tigers, but it has no mammoth roller coasters. There are other reasons, as well. For early risers at least, Busch Gardens is a very doable day trip from the Orlando area. The addition of Busch Gardens to the

Orlando FlexTicket program (see "The Price of Admission," below) adds just another incentive to make the trip.

Finally, Busch Gardens has a personality and an allure all its own. The innovative animal habitats temper the frenticism of the rides, and the rides give you something to do when just sitting and watching begins to pale. The park is beautifully designed with some absolutely enchanting nooks and crannies. While it's a great place to *do* things, Busch Gardens is also a delightful place simply to *be*.

My only caution would be that the amusement park side of the equation can tend to overshadow the zoo. Many of the animal exhibits reward quiet, patient observation, but the excitement generated by the smorgasbord of giant roller coasters and splashy water rides will make it hard to cultivate a contemplative state of mind, especially for the younger members of your party. Perhaps the best strategy is to use exhibits like the *Myombe Reserve* (great apes), the walk-through aviary, and the air-conditioned koala habitat and monorail ride to cool out and cool down between bouts of manic activity. Another approach is to devote one visit to the amusement park rides, another to the zoo.

## Gathering Information

By dialing (800) 4ADVENTURE (423-8368) you can hear some very general information about the Busch family of theme parks and short sales pitches about individual parks. You can also leave your name and address to have general information about all their parks sent to you (in about two to three weeks). In Tampa, call (813) 987-5082 for a recorded message that provides current operating hours and admissions prices for one-day tickets and the various annual pass options. This recording tends to be rather general; more specific information can be obtained from Guest Relations at (813) 987-5212.

For the latest on Busch Gardens' zoo animals, you can check out the park's animal information site on the World Wide Web. The address is http://www.buschgardens.org.

Another web site provides information for the amusement park side of Busch Gardens Tampa. The address is http://www.buschgardens.com.

## Getting There

Busch Gardens is roughly 75 miles from Universal Studios, about 65 miles from the intersection of I-4 and US 192 in Kissimmee. You can drive there in about one and a quarter to one and a half hours depending on where you start and how closely you observe the posted speed limit. Drive west on I-4 to Exit 6 (US 92 West, Hillsborough Avenue). Go about 1.5 miles and turn left on 56th Street (SR 583); go another two miles and turn left on Busch Boulevard. Busch Gardens is about two miles ahead on your right.

## Parking at Busch Gardens Tampa

You know you're almost at Busch Gardens when you see the giant roller coaster Montu looming overhead. You'll probably also hear the screams as you pull into the parking lot. Actually, there are a series of parking lots with room for 3,400 vehicles. Lots A and B are near the park entrance and there are several more across the street. If you find yourself turning into the lots across the street from Montu, you'll know the park is beginning to fill up. Trams snake their way back and forth to the entrance, but if you're in A or B it's just as easy to walk.

Motorcycles are $4, cars $5, campers and trailers $6, tax included. If you have a Busch Gardens Wild Card or other annual pass, parking is free. Preferred Parking gets you into Lot A, the closest to the entrance, and costs $10 ($5 for annual pass holders).

## Opening and Closing Times

The park is usually open from 9:30 a.m. to 6:00 p.m. every day of the year. However, during the summer months and at holiday times the hours are extended, with opening at 9:00 a.m. and closing pushed back until 7:00, 8:00, or 9:00 p.m. The Morocco section stays open a half-hour or so later than the rest of the park to accommodate last-minute shoppers. Call Guest Relations at (813) 987-5212 for the exact current operating hours.

## The Price of Admission

Busch Gardens sells only one-day admissions. There are no two-day passes, although you can receive a discount for the next day's admission while you are in the park. If you're interested, make sure you ask before you leave for the day. The following prices include tax.

### One Day Admission:
| | |
|---|---|
| Adults: | $41.55 ($29.50 after 3:30 p.m.) |
| Children (3 to 9): | $34.10 ($24.50 after 3:30 p.m.) |
| Ages 2 and under **free**. | |

A *Combination Pass* that lets you visit Adventure Island, Busch's water park, on the same day is $48.35 ($41.60 for kids).

Visa, MasterCard, and Discover credit cards are accepted. While you are in the park, you can purchase a ticket for admission the next day for $10.66, including tax. This makes a two-day visit to Busch Gardens a very good buy.

*Orlando FlexTicket*

Busch Gardens participates in the Orlando FlexTicket program described in *Chapter One: Introduction & Orientation*. The Four-Park, Ten-Day pass grants admission to Universal Studios Florida, SeaWorld, and Wet 'n Wild (all in Orlando), as well as to Busch Gardens, and is priced as follows:

| | |
|---|---|
| Adults: | $137.95 |
| Children (3 to 9): | $114.65 |

## Annual Passes

### The Busch Gardens Annual Pass

Unlimited access to Busch Gardens Tampa.

| | |
|---|---|
| Adults: | $101.35 ($128.00 for two years) |
| Children & Seniors (55+): | $80.00 ($117.40 for two years) |

### Surf n' Safari Pass

Annual pass to both Busch Gardens and Adventure Island.

| | |
|---|---|
| All ages: | $117.40 ($154.70 for two years) |

### Wild Card Pass

Annual Pass to both Busch Gardens and SeaWorld.

| | |
|---|---|
| Adults: | $128.05 ($160.10 for two years) |
| Children & Seniors: | $117.40 ($149.40 for two years) |

### Wild Card Pass Plus

Annual Pass to Busch Gardens, Adventure Island, and SeaWorld.

| | |
|---|---|
| Adults: | $160.10 ($197.45 for two years) |
| Children & Seniors: | $144.05 ($186.75 for two years) |

The amount of a one-day admission can be applied to these passes, but only if you upgrade on the day you buy it.

## Discounts

You will find dollars-off coupons for Busch Gardens in all the usual places (see *Chapter One*). Discounted tickets are also available from hotel Guests Services desks and ticket brokers in the Orlando area. In addition to the discounts accorded to senior citizens purchasing annual passes, AAA cardholders can get a 10 percent discount on one-day admissions at the ticket booths. Special deals are offered to Florida residents during the off-season (fall to spring); call for details. Annual pass holders receive a 10 percent discount on merchandise in park shops and at the larger eateries as well as a 15 percent discount on admission to other Busch theme parks.

## Buying Tickets

Tickets can be purchased as you arrive, at ticket booths immediately in front of the park entrance. However, you can save yourself a bit of time by purchasing your tickets the day before, in the afternoon, when there are no lines. If you are based in Orlando, you can purchase a discounted combination ticket when you visit SeaWorld. You can also purchase Busch Gardens tickets at SeaWorld even if you are not visiting SeaWorld.

I am told that Busch Gardens tickets are available through several local Tampa hotels, so you might want to check with the concierge or the front desk if you are staying nearby. Another option is to purchase tickets through your travel agent before you leave home.

## Staying Near the Park

If you'd like to spend a few days at Busch Gardens or just want to avoid doing the round trip from Orlando in one day, you may want to consider staying at one of the motels within walking distance of the park. Look for discounts on these motels in the throwaway coupon books given away at many locations along Florida's major highways.

There is a not very well marked pedestrian entrance on Busch Boulevard (about midway between 30th Street and McKinley Street) that takes you right to the main entrance. If you're on foot, I recommend using this rather than the automobile entry on McKinley. Walking times listed below are to this entrance.

### Days Inn
2901 East Busch Boulevard
Tampa, FL 33612
(813) 933-6471
> A standard mid-range motel.
> **Price Range:** $$ - $$$
> **Amenities:** Pool, restaurant
> **Walk to Park:** 10 minutes

### Budgetel
9202 North 30th Street
Tampa, FL 33612
(813) 930-6900; fax (813) 930-0563
> Newly built budget hotel.
> **Price Range:** $$
> **Amenities:** Pool
> **Walk to Park:** 10 minutes

### Howard Johnson
4139 East Busch Boulevard

Tampa, FL 33612
(813) 988-9191; fax (813) 988-9195
   A standard mid-range motel.
   **Price Range:**   $ - $$$
   **Amenities:**   Pool
   **Walk to Park:** 10 minutes

## Red Roof Inn
2307 East Busch Boulevard
Tampa, FL 33612
(813) 932-0073; fax (813) 933-5689
   A nice, clean budget motel.
   **Price Range:**   $$
   **Amenities:**   Small pool
   **Walk to Park:** 15 to 20 minutes

## Special Events

Other than an alcohol-free New Year's Eve celebration for young people, Busch Gardens doesn't go in for the kind of razzle-dazzle events keyed to the calendar that are a staple at Disney and Universal. So if the Halloween festivities in Orlando's parks start to pale, you can come to Tampa and enjoy a "theme-less" theme park.

## Dining at Busch Gardens Tampa

On the whole, the dining experience at Busch Gardens is a step down from that at its sister park, SeaWorld, in Orlando. However, the single full-service restaurant (Crown Colony House) has some very tasty dishes and, if you can wangle a window seat, the views are spectacular. Also worth noting is that the barbecue at Stanleyville Smokehouse is on a par with that served up at SeaWorld. Most disappointing is that Busch Gardens has not chosen to extend its African theme to its restaurant menus. I found myself wishing for something akin to the first-rate Moroccan restaurant at EPCOT.

Parents of thirsty kids will be pleased to know that soft drinks are a relative bargain here with small, medium, and large sizes priced at 99 cents, $1.39, and $1.59, plus tax, respectively. (An interesting note: No straws are served at any of the park's restaurants or fast-food outlets in deference to the safety of the animals.) Those on really tight budgets should bear in mind that there is a McDonald's across the street from the park's main entrance. Other cheap eats are just a short stroll away. Get your hand stamped for re-entry.

# Shopping at Busch Gardens Tampa

The souvenir hunter will not leave disappointed. There are plenty of logo-bearing gadgets, gizmos, and wearables from which to choose. The t-shirts with tigers and gorillas are especially attractive. Tiger fanciers will also be drawn to the beach towels with the large white Bengal tiger portrait.

Best of all are the genuine African crafts to be found here and there around the park. Look for them in Morocco, Crown Colony, and Stanleyville. The prices can be steep for some of the nicer pieces, but there are some very attractive (and attractively priced) smaller items to be found.

# Good Things To Know About ...

### Access for the Disabled

Handicapped parking spaces are provided directly in front of the park's main entrance for those with a valid permit. Otherwise, physically challenged guests may be dropped off at the main entrance.

The entire park is wheelchair accessible and companion bathrooms are dotted about the park. Some physically challenged guests may not be able to experience certain rides due to safety considerations. An "Access Guide" is available at Guest Relations near the main entrance.

Wheelchair and motorized cart rentals are handled out of a concession next to the Jeepers and Creepers shop in Morocco. Wheelchairs are $6 a day (which includes a refundable $1 deposit). Motorized carts are $30 (including a $5 deposit). Motorized carts are popular, so plan to get there early to be sure you get one.

### Babies

Diaper changing tables are located in restrooms throughout the park. A nursing area is located in Land of the Dragons.

If you don't have your own, you can rent strollers at the concession next to Jeepers and Creepers in Morocco. Nifty looking Jeep Strollers are $7 for the full day, which includes a $1 deposit. Double strollers are $11, which also includes a $1 deposit.

### Drinking

As a reminder, the legal drinking age in Florida is 21 and photo IDs will be requested if there is the slightest doubt.

### First Aid

The first aid station is located next to Das Festhaus restaurant in Timbuktu. If emergency aid is needed, contact the nearest employee.

## Getting Wet

The signs say, "This is a water attraction. Riders will get wet and possibly soaked." This is not marketing hyperbole but a simple statement of fact. The water rides at Busch Gardens are one of its best kept secrets (the mammoth roller coasters get most of the publicity), but they pose some problems for the unprepared. Kids probably won't care but adults can get positively cranky when wandering around sopping wet.

The three major water rides, in increasing order of wetness, are *Stanley Falls Log Flume, Congo River Rapids*, and the absolutely soaking *Tanganyika Tidal Wave.* (The *Mizzly Marsh* section of Land of the Dragons can also get tykes very wet.) Fortunately, these three rides are within a short distance of each other, in the Congo and Stanleyville, allowing you to implement the following strategy:

First, dress appropriately. Wear a bathing suit and t-shirt under a dressier outer layer. Wear shoes you don't mind getting wet; sports sandals are ideal. Bring a tote bag in which you can put things, like cameras, that shouldn't get wet. You can also pack a towel and it's probably a good idea to bring along the plastic laundry bag from your motel room.

Plan to do the water rides in sequence. When you're ready to start, strip off your outer layer, put it in the tote bag along with your other belongings, and stash everything in a convenient locker. There are lockers dotted throughout the Congo and Stanleyville. A helpful locker symbol on the map of the park will help you locate the nearest one. Now you're ready to enjoy the rides without worry.

Once you've completed the circuit, and especially if you rode the *Tidal Wave,* you will be soaked to the skin. You now have a choice. If it's a hot summer day, you may want to let your clothes dry as you see the rest of the park. Don't worry about feeling foolish; you'll see of plenty of other folks in the same boat, and your damp clothes will feel just great in the Florida heat. In cooler weather, however, it's a good idea to return to the locker, grab your stuff, head to a nearby restroom and change into dry clothes. Use the plastic laundry bag for the wet stuff.

The alternative is to buy a Busch Gardens poncho (they make nice souvenirs and are readily available at shops near the water rides) and hope for the best. This is far less fun and you'll probably get pretty wet anyway.

## Lost Children

If you become separated from your child, contact the nearest employee. Found children are returned to the Security Office next to the Marrakesh Theater in Morocco.

## Leaving the Park

Just have your hand stamped at the exit for readmittance on the same day. Your parking stub will get you back into the lot free.

## Money

There is an ATM located to your right in the plaza just before the admission booths. There is another in Das Festhaus restaurant in Timbuktu. They are connected to the Plus, Honor, and Cirrus systems. In addition, you can get cash advances on your American Express, Visa, MasterCard, or Discover card.

## Pets

There is a **free** Pet Care Center located between parking lots A and B. The simple facility has large and small chain-link-fence kennels. They provide locks for the kennels — if you're lucky enough to find an attendant on duty when you arrive. Food bowls and a wash-up sink are also available.

## Special Diets

A "Dining Guide" is available at the Information Booth just inside the main entrance. It will alert **vegetarians** to restaurants in the park where they can request special meals. Those with other dietary needs (low-fat, no-salt, etc.) will have to use their judgment to pick and choose from the standard menus.

# On Safari: Your Day at Busch Gardens

The bad news is that it's difficult — probably impossible — to see all of Busch Gardens in a day. The good news is that most people will be happy to forego some of the attractions. The more sedate will happily pass up the roller coasters to spend time observing the great apes, while the speed demons will be far happier being flung about on Montu than sitting still for a sing-along in Das Festhaus.

# When's the Best Time to Come?

Plotting the best time of year at which to visit is less of a consideration than with, say, Universal Studios or SeaWorld. According to the trade paper *Amusement Business*, Busch Gardens gets less than half the visitors Universal hosts each year and less than a third of those who show up at the Magic Kingdom. On the other hand, attendance grows each year and on several recent visits large groups of foreign tourists and American high school kids were much in evidence.

# What to Expect

In many respects, Busch Gardens is a "typical" theme park. Each area of the park is decorated and landscaped to reflect its particular "theme," which is also reflected in the decor of the shops and restaurants (although not necessarily in the merchandise and food being offered). The attendants wear appropriate uniforms and a variety of rides, exhibits, attractions, and "streetmosphere" compete for your attention. If you've been to any of the other theme parks, it's unlikely you'll find anything radically different about Busch Gardens.

As I noted earlier, Busch Gardens combines a number of seemingly disparate elements into an eclectic whole. Here, then, are some of the elements in the Busch Gardens mix:

*The Zoo.* Home to 3,000 animals, representing 340 different species (the numbers will probably have risen by the time you visit), Busch Gardens is one of the major zoological parks in the nation. It is also a highly enlightened zoo, embodying the latest thinking about how animals should be housed and displayed to the public. You will receive an understated but persistent message about the importance of conserving and protecting the planet's animal heritage. Like its sister park, SeaWorld in Orlando, Busch Gardens boasts a zoological staff that is friendly, visible, approachable, and more than happy to answer questions.

*Animal Enrichment.* One way in which the staff helps spread the conservation message is through regular "shows" built around feeding and caring for the animals. The presence of food means that the animals are usually at their most active during these shows; the attendants also attempt to coax their charges into appropriate poses for those with cameras. The schedule for these "Animal Enrichment" events is printed along with the Entertainment Guide; pick it up at the Information Booth just inside the main entrance.

*Roller Coasters.* Busch Gardens boasts one of the largest concentrations of roller coasters in the nation. They range from the relatively modest Python to the truly awesome Montu. Even the smallest of these rides features elements, like loops, that are not to be found on just any roller coaster. You will be well advised to take advantage of the coin-operated lockers located near every roller coaster to store your loose gear. Anyone who is serious about their roller coasters will definitely want to put Busch Gardens on their must-see list for their Central Florida vacation.

*Water Rides.* Busch Gardens is also home to a group of water rides that are designed to get you very, very, very wet. They are great fun, but require some planning and strategizing. Unless, of course, you're a young boy, in which case you simply won't mind walking through the park sopping wet from the top of your head to the toes of your $100 sneakers. See *Good Things to Know About ... Getting Wet*, above.

**Live Shows.** There is a regular schedule of entertainment throughout the day in open-air amphitheaters and indoor, air-conditioned theaters. A few are animal-oriented, but most are pure variety entertainment shows that change periodically. Most shows don't gear up until 11:30 a.m. or noon. Thereafter, they run pretty regularly until closing time.

# Big Game

For those with limited time or who just want to skim the cream of this multifaceted park, here are my selections for the trophy-winning attractions at Busch Gardens:

For coaster fans, **Montu** and **Kumba** are musts. Of the water rides, **Congo River Rapids** is my favorite and the **Tanganyika Tidal Wave** is highly recommended for those who want to get totally drenched. The best theater show is **Hollywood Live on Ice.** If you won't be going to SeaWorld, add **Dolphins of the Deep** to the list.

Animal lovers will not want to miss the chimps and gorillas in **Myombe Reserve** or the tigers on **Claw Island. Edge of Africa** is another must-see animal habitat, but the **Serengeti Safari Tour** (for an extra charge) is the best way to get close to the animals. The **World of Birds** show is the best of the animal shows. And finally, if you have preschoolers in tow, you will not want to miss the spectacular **Land of the Dragons**.

# The One-Day Stay for Ride Fans

1. Plan to arrive at the opening bell. As soon as the park opens, grab a map and an Entertainment Guide at the Information Booth (just inside the turnstiles) and proceed directly to *Montu* in Egypt (keep bearing right).

2. After *Montu*, retrace your steps to Crown Colony and take the *Skyride*, a shortcut to the Congo. Once there, head for *Kumba* and then cool off with a ride on *Congo River Rapids*.

3. Now head south, pausing to admire the tigers on *Claw Island* and ride *Stanley Falls* and the *Tanganyika Tidal Wave*. By now, you will be soaking wet. It may also be close to noon. Check your Entertainment Guide. The *Ballet D'Afrique* and the dolphin show are nearby, or you could catch the *Skyride* again and head back to the Moroccan Palace Theater to catch *Hollywood Live on Ice*.

4. After lunch, you have several choices. You can hit your favorite rides again, try the lesser rides, or (my personal suggestion) visit the various zoo

attractions, perhaps catching another show at some point in the afternoon. Don't forget to check the schedule of Animal Enrichment shows.

## The One-Day Stay for the More Sedate

1. If you are not a ride fanatic you don't have to kill yourself to get there at the minute the park opens, although a full day at Busch Gardens, taken at a moderate pace, is a full day well-spent. For now, I'll assume you are arriving early. Grab a park map and the Entertainment Guide and bear to the right as you stroll towards Crown Colony. En route, peruse the times for the variety shows and the Animal Enrichment sessions.

2. If you plan to take the *Serengeti Safari Tour*, sign up now. After a leisurely tour of *Edge of Africa*, take the *Monorail* for another look at the Serengeti. If you're interested and the lines aren't too long, you might want to walk to Egypt and pop into *King Tut's Tomb*. Otherwise, stroll to Nairobi for a visit to *Myombe Reserve* and the *Nairobi Nursery*.

3. Now board the *Trans-Veldt Railroad* at the Nairobi Station for the journey around the Serengeti. Disembark in the Congo and visit the tigers at *Claw Island*. Check the Animal Enrichment schedule for those times when the wart hogs, orangutans, and tigers are fed 15 minutes apart. If you start with the wart hogs, you can follow the same attendant as he makes his rounds of all three enclosures. You may even be able to grab a quick barbecue lunch at Stanleyville Smokehouse.

4. Now you're ready to see some shows. You can walk to Timbuktu for the dolphin show and *International Celebration* at Das Festhaus (and have lunch if you haven't grabbed a bite yet) or you can take the *Skyride* again to catch *Hollywood Live on Ice*.

5. Round out your day with a visit to Bird Gardens and the *World of Birds* show. If you have little ones in tow, don't forget to let them have their own special time in Land of the Dragons.

# Attractions at Busch Gardens

Busch Gardens is divided into nine "themed areas," most of them named after a country or region of Africa. Each area is relatively compact but the entire park is quite large (335 acres) making covering the entire place a bit of a challenge, especially on foot.

In describing the nine areas, I will start with Morocco, the first area you encounter as you enter the park, and then proceed clockwise around the park, ending with the newest themed area, Egypt. I am not suggesting that you tour the park in this order (although this would be the most direct route if you were to walk the entire park). Use the descriptions that follow, along with the suggestions given above, to pick and choose the attractions that best suit your tastes and that you can comfortably fit into the time available. Remember that you can use the *Skyride* between the Congo and Crown Colony, and the *Trans-Veldt Railway* with its three stops to cut down on the walking.

In addition to the attractions listed below, Busch Gardens features a number of strolling musical groups playing peppy music designed to put a bit of bounce back in your step as you stroll the grounds. The **Mystic Sheiks of Morocco** are a brass marching band outfitted in snappy red and black uniforms that make them look like a military band from a very hip African nation. They are most frequently sighted in Morocco and Crown Colony. **Sounds of Steel**, a four-man steel drum band marches through Stanleyville and the Congo from time to time, and the **Men of Note** offer up the kind of close harmony, a capella doo-wop music more associated with the streets of Philadelphia than the souks of Morocco. Still, they can often be found entertaining departing guests there.

There are two television series — the new *Captain Kangaroo* show and the syndicated *Jack Hanna's Animal Adventures* — that film segments at Busch Gardens. Hanna's set is located in Bird Gardens and shoots on an erratic schedule from fall through early spring.

# Morocco

There's only one entrance to Busch Gardens and Morocco is your first stop in the park, so some of the available space is given over to housekeeping. Here you'll find Guest Services and, directly ahead of you as you pass through the gates, an Information Booth where you can pick up an indispensable park map, a schedule of live entertainment and "Animal Enrichment" shows and, for hard-core foodies, a dining guide. Also in Morocco, just around the corner to your right, is the stroller and wheelchair rental concession. Since Morocco is also the *exit* to the park, a fair amount of space is given to souvenir and other shops, the better to lure those on the way out.

Otherwise, the main business of Morocco is stage shows of one sort or another. There are three theaters here, all reviewed below. There is also an **alligator pond**, where several times a day an Animal Enrichment show takes place. It's a zoologically correct version of the more popularized shows you get at Gatorland or other gator-themed attractions in the Orlando area.

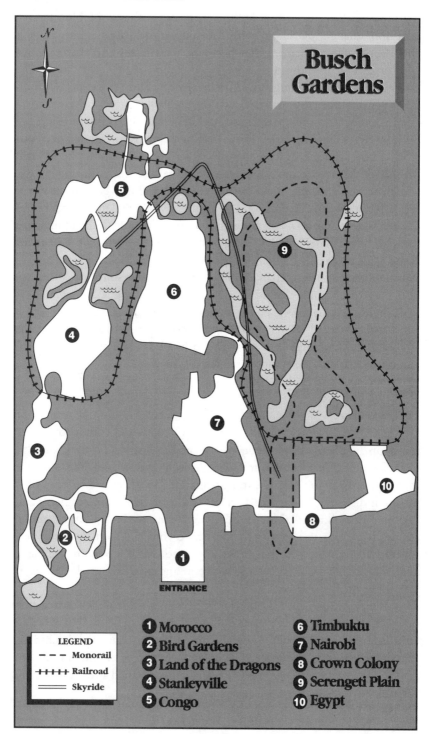

N
S

# Busch Gardens

**5** Congo
**9** Serengeti Plain
**6** Timbuktu
**4** Stanleyville
**7** Nairobi
**3** Land of the Dragons
**10** Egypt
**8** Crown Colony

**7** Nairobi

**1** Morocco

ENTRANCE

LEGEND
- - - Monorail
+++++ Railroad
═══ Skyride

**1** Morocco
**2** Bird Gardens
**3** Land of the Dragons
**4** Stanleyville
**5** Congo

**6** Timbuktu
**7** Nairobi
**8** Crown Colony
**9** Serengeti Plain
**10** Egypt

# American Jukebox (Marrakesh Theater)

*Rating:* ★ ★ ★ +
*Type:* Live stage show
*Time:* About 25 minutes
*Kelly says:* American pop through the ages

Using the invention, in the 1940s, of the jukebox as a thread, this peppy revue traces American popular music from the teen-rock of the fifties, through the electric country music of the sixties, through the disco craze of the seventies, to the current vogue for techno-pop music videos.

Ten energetic singer-dancers do double, triple, and quadruple duty in this infectious romp, changing from one set of gaudy costumes to another, sometimes in full view of the audience. There are some very competent pop voices in the ensemble and the dancing makes up in showbiz pizzazz what it lacks in precision. After the show, some of the performers mingle with the audience for **photo ops**.

The Marrakesh Theater is a shaded area across the plaza from the Zagora Cafe, which means you can escape the sun but not the heat.

# Hollywood Live on Ice (Moroccan Palace Theater)

*Rating:* ★ ★ ★ ★
*Type:* Indoor theater show
*Time:* About 30 minutes
*Kelly says:* A nifty ice show

The 1,200-seat Moroccan Palace Theater is a nice re-creation of those movie palaces of the distant past which often drew on exotic locales for the inspiration for their lavish interiors.

Currently holding forth here is a tuneful tribute to Hollywood films. All of the familiar icons make an appearance — Bogie and Brando, Chaplin and Monroe — all on ice skates. Just in case you don't immediately pick up on the references, film clips are run on either side of the stage.

Some of the numbers — like an extended celebration of horror flicks complete with a whizzing and whirling werewolf — are a lot of fun. And the "Singing in the Rain" number features real rain and twirling umbrellas that could make this the only stage show with a splash zone.

# Sultan's Tent

*Rating:* ★ ★
*Type:* Open air snake show
*Time:* About 10 minutes
*Kelly says:* Much ado about touching a snake

A belly-dancing snake charmer holds forth in the plaza outside the Tangiers Theater on a regular schedule. After a brief and wordless introduction in which she shimmies and drapes a python over her head, she gets down to the main order of business which is sitting at the edge of the stage and letting you touch and photograph her slinky friend.

If your kids are snake fanciers, it's worth a look should you happen on a show in progress.

# Eating in Morocco

## Boujad Bakery

*What:*        Sweet baked goods
*Where:*     Near Tangiers Theater
*Price Range:*  $ - $$

If you forgot breakfast, or just want a sugar rush before pressing into the park interior, this is a good place to stop. The limited menu features sweet baked goods like turnovers and awesomely syrupy cinnamon rolls. There are also croissants and muffins, along with coffee. Baked goods are all in the $2 range. Coffee, cappuccino, and espresso is $1 to $2. You can also pick up a soft serve sundae in a waffle cone for about $3. All of the seating is outdoors under canopies; it's a very pleasant place to sit and take in the passing scene.

## Zagora Cafe

*What:*        Fast-food burgers and sandwiches
*Where:*     Near Tangiers Theater
*Price Range:*  $ - $$

This spacious fast-food eatery looks out across a lovely palm-accented plaza to the Marrakesh Theater. About half of the seating is under a large colonnaded porch decorated with the stuffed heads of African game animals, including a trumpeting elephant. The plaques identifying each beast take care to note that the specimen in question died of natural causes. The other half of the seating is outdoors on a semicircular terrace; only some of these seats have awnings.

The menu is basic: turkey sandwiches, burgers, and fajita sandwiches for about $5 to $6. Kids' safari meals (a hot dog and fries) are about $3. Desserts — carrot cake, chocolate cake, strawberry and blueberry cheesecake — are quite good at about $2. Bacon and egg breakfasts (about $5) are served here until 10:30 a.m.

## Ice Cream Parlor

*What:*        Just what the name says
*Where:*      Near Marrakesh Theater
*Price Range:*  $

A small fast-food style ice cream parlor that gets crowded when shows at the next-door Marrakesh Theater let out. Single and double scoops are about $1.70 and $2.50 respectively. A waffle cone sundae will set you back about $3 to $4. The usual range of soft drinks is also served here.

# Shopping in Morocco

## Casablanca Outfitters

Expedition and travel attire are the order of the day here. The moderately priced wares are quite nice, especially the African spiced outfits for women. For men there are some nice fishing and safari vests as well as some way cool men's leather hats for under $50.

## Tangiers Taffy House

A vest-pocket candy store selling by-the-piece saltwater taffy and wrapped candy for about $2.25 for half a pound. A "Busch Gardens Safari Sampler" of various taffies is about $5. A variety of your favorite candies is also available.

## Rabat Label

This is a much larger version of the small Label Stable at SeaWorld. You will find Anheuser-Busch logos on a wide variety of clothing and other merchandise. If your bowling ball positively must have the Bud logo on it, this is the place to come.

## Professor Bloodgood's Olde Time Photo

Turn of the century style photos in period costumes run from $19 to $45 depending on the size of the print and the number of people.

## Safari Central

Despite the name, there's little in the way of safari gear here. Instead, it's a good place to come for a wide selection of branded souvenirs, everything from key chains, mugs, and refrigerator magnets to t-shirts. The best buy in t-shirts (in my opinion) are the black shirts with the large brooding portraits of gorillas, white tigers, and other wildlife stars (about $12 to $17). In the same vein are beach towels with the white tiger ($17).

Another good souvenir is the video "Safari Adventure," the official souvenir of Busch Gardens.

## Jeepers and Creepers

Actually an extension of Safari Central, this kids' store has a wide variety of clothing and toys for the younger crowd. Worth checking out (especially if you have little ones) are the plush toys. An adorable white tiger mom with two cubs goes for $40.

## Nature's Kingdom

Located near the Tangiers Theater, this shop has an environmental theme and features gardening accessories, rocks and crystals, mounted butterflies, natural cosmetics, science toys, rustic baskets and pottery, and the obligatory t-shirts.

## Sidi Kacem African Curios

One of the nicer touches, shopping-wise, in Morocco is the way in which the designers have evoked the *souks* of Fez and Marrakesh. Sidi Kacem's is actually a mini-Moroccan bazaar comprising an indoor shop and a number of outdoor stalls that surround it.

Here you'll find crafts such as soapstone carvings and boxes, pottery from the Moroccan city of Safi, hand-painted in traditional patterns ($8 to $450), carved wooden animals from Kenya ($3 to $100), hand-crafted Moroccan leather goods ($40 to $100), and brassware ($10 to $500). My favorite brass pieces were the urns and kettles decorated with inlaid bone ($100 to $450). You may even get to meet some of the actual craftspeople responsible for these attractive wares; they staff the stalls on an irregular schedule.

Inside you'll find a goodly selection of African-style baubles, bangles, and beads ($20 to $40) along with some very attractive women's clothing.

## Safari Trader

This shop is actually just outside the entrance to the park, allowing for those all-important last-minute purchases. There is a small and somewhat haphazard selection of souvenir t's and merchandise here. However, the Safari Trader also unloads discontinued and overstock merchandise at discounts of up to 50%. Depending on when you visit, you might find some real bargains here.

# Bird Gardens

As the name suggests, Bird Gardens houses most of the birds in the Busch Gardens zoo collection. In addition to the few larger displays mentioned below, the area is dotted with flamingos and other exotic water fowl, their wings obviously clipped, in beautifully landscaped open settings with ponds and streams. They are joined by a rotating group of visiting Florida species. Some of the walkways are lined with gaudy parrots in free-hanging cages. Over all, the effect is enchanting, rather like the private gardens of a rich and tasteful eccentric.

## Busch Gardens Bird Show

*Rating:* ★ ★ ★ ★ +
*Type:* Live amphitheater show
*Time:* About 30 minutes
*Kelly says:* Fascinating birds and lore

This show is perfect theme park edutainment. A parrot talks and even sings on cue. A variety of multi-colored parrots and raptors fly through hoops, swoop low over the heads of the audience, and land on volunteers brought up from the audience. The odd-looking South American serijama, nicknamed the lizard smasher, demonstrates its unique technique. There is even an international all-raptor lineup, including a magnificent bateleur eagle from Africa. Then there is Abe, an old and battered, one-eyed American bald eagle, rescued by hikers in Alaska. This crusty old survivor manages to look majestic despite his battered face and ruffled feathers. All of this is accompanied by a steady flow of fascinating facts and lore about the birds on display. The show is fast-paced and professionally presented by an energetic team of handlers and trainers. Some of the birds are brought out into the audience to give you a closer look and a chance for snapshots. All in all, one of the best animal shows in the park.

## Hospitality House Stage

*Rating:* ★ ★ +
*Type:* Live music
*Time:* About 20 minutes
*Kelly says:* Diverting with lunch

On a small outdoor stage near the Hospitality House (see below), a cheerful ragtime band holds forth on a regular schedule. The selections are all likely to be familiar and they are all certified toe-tappers put over with a great deal of good-humored élan. If you find yourself near here at show time, why not grab a free beer inside and give a listen?

# Budweiser Beer School

Rating: ★ ★
Type: An edutainment commercial
Time: 45 minutes
Kelly says: Best for the air conditioning

This is a pleasant enough way to kill some time and perhaps get answers to those questions that have been tormenting you for years. Why is it called Budweiser? Who was Anheuser? However, I suspect most people are lured here by the beer tasting that follows some videos about the history of Anheuser-Busch and the art of brewing beer. At the end you get a certificate attesting to your newfound status as a "Beermaster."

# Koala Habitat

Rating: ★ ★ ★
Type: Animal habitat
Time: Continuous viewing
Kelly says: Cute and cuddly

A long, snaking walkway leads across a bridge over a pond filled with a variety of water fowl (bird feed dispensers thoughtfully provided) to a vaguely Chinese-style building with a series of antechambers. The building originally housed pandas and was designed to accommodate large crowds. The current occupants, while cute and cuddly in their own right, obviously don't have quite the same cachet, so it's unlikely you'll find a line here.

Inside is a spacious and wonderfully air conditioned two-level viewing area. The lower level is a conveyer belt that takes you at a stately pace past the animals; the upper level allows for more leisurely contemplation.

The display area features koalas at one end and Dama wallabies at the other. The koalas, about the size of a large, tubby housecat, calmly munch eucalyptus leaves, while the wallabies (equally small) are a bit more lively. If there's a new "joey" (or baby) in the koala family, a sign will direct you to the Nairobi Nursery (see the Nairobi section).

Compared to other habitats in the park, this one seems a bit underdecorated. If you've never seen one of these little critters up close, it's worth at least a quick visit. On a hot day, the air conditioning might also be a draw. Visiting Australians, on the other hand, will probably not want to bother.

# Aviary

Rating: ★ ★ ★ +
Type: Walk-through animal exhibit
Time: Continuous viewing

*Kelly says:*     A lovely place to pause

This is a smallish habitat compared to others in the park, but its size belies its enchantment. Essentially a large tent made of a dark mesh fabric, the aviary lets you visit a wide variety of tropical birds in a remarkably realistic setting, instead of peering at them through the bars of a cage. Benches allow for long and leisurely viewing and a large illustrated guidebook lets you tell one species from another. Some, like the roseate spoonbill, may look familiar but others, like the odd Abdim's Stork and a beautiful blue Victoria Crowned Pigeon that thinks it's a peacock, will probably be new to you.

I have discovered that the longer you sit and relax here, the more the mesh tent fades from your consciousness. What remains is a charming encounter with some very lovely birds.

# Eating in Bird Gardens

## Hospitality House

| | |
|---|---|
| *What:* | Deli sandwiches and free beer |
| *Where:* | Near the Bird Show |
| *Price* | Range: $ - $$ |

Like its counterpart at SeaWorld, the Anheuser-Busch Hospitality House is a beautiful modern building in a knock-your-socks-off setting. The main draw is the free (albeit small) beer samples. The limit is one at a time per person and two per person per day. There is also a small fast-food counter, the Hospitality House Cafe, featuring sandwich platters and pizza for about $4 to $6. Salads are less than $3.

Your best seating choice is outside on the two-tiered terrace overlooking the duck-filled pond. The vista is, quite simply, one of the loveliest at Busch Gardens. Also outside is an area where kids can try their skill at piloting remote-controlled tugboats. A token (1 for $1, 6 for $5) gives you about two and a half minutes of play.

## Bird Show Snacks

Next to the entrance to the Bird Theater, this little kiosk sells popcorn and cotton candy for a bit under $2, plus the usual selection of soft drinks.

# Shopping in Bird Gardens

## Bird Gardens Gift Shop

If you visit the koalas, it will be hard to miss this shop which is right by the exit. It carries a broad range of cuddly plush toys including, inevitably, some koalas. A furry mother and child runs about $25. The rest of the shop is given over to what is collectively known as collectibles — figurines, frames, mounted butterflies, and the like — all at moderate prices.

### Gulf Wind Trader

This shops sells a variety of decorative objects, such as wall-mounted artificial floral arrangements, and women's t-shirts.

### Wilde and Wonderful Gallery

Next door to the Hospitality House stage, this vest-pocket shop sells some very nice wildlife photos and paintings. Most of the art on display is the work of Walter and Cheryl Kuck, although other artists are represented. Some pieces were done at Busch Gardens and others in East Africa. The prices are quite moderate for the obvious quality of the work. A very nice series of animal photos framed with an African postage stamp featuring the same animal are about $40. Otherwise, unframed pieces range from $45 to $95.

### The Pearl Factory

This small shop sells Japanese cultured pearls, in five basic colors and 120 shades, in a variety of settings at prices that begin at about $20 and rise sharply from there. For $12 you can pick an oyster and, if you like the pearl you find inside, have it set in a variety of settings for $16 and up.

# Land of the Dragons

Sandwiched between Bird Gardens to the south and Stanleyville to the north, is a play area just for the preschool set. Other theme parks in Central Florida have similar kiddie areas but nowhere will you find the concept pulled off with as much wit and verve as the Land of the Dragons. Here, the clever design of *Fievel's Playland* at Universal and the size of *Shamu's Happy Harbor* at SeaWorld come together to create the only five-star kiddie attraction in this book.

There are animals to be seen here, too, of course. At one end are the iguanas, monitor lizards, and komodo dragon that give the area its name. At the other, in a separate circular area, is Lory Landing described below. But the emphasis is on fun in the Land of the Dragons and the little ones will not be disappointed.

# Interactive Play Areas

| | |
|---|---|
| *Rating:* | ★ ★ ★ ★ ★ |
| *Type:* | Hands-on activity |
| *Time:* | As long as you want |
| *Kelly says:* | The best of its kind in Central Florida |

Most of the Land of the Dragons is given over to a series of loosely connected climb-up, crawl-through, slide-down play areas that can keep little ones occupied for hours. I have given them the rather cumbersome name of "interactive play areas," but each has its own identity and special attractions, as we shall see.

Dominating the north end of the area is the **Dragon's Nest**, an elaborate two-story structure colorfully painted and shaded by a large tarp covering. On the lower level, it features a net climb, an "air bounce" (a large inflated floor on which kids can jump to their heart's content), and a "ball crawl" (a pit filled with colored plastics balls into which kids can literally dive). The upper level is reached either via the net climb or, for less agile adults, a stairway. There you will find a two-level, kids-sized, climb-through, maze-like environment forming a delightful obstacle course. No one higher than 56 inches is allowed in this one, so Mom and Dad are excused.

From this upper level extend two rope bridges. Both go to the **Tree House,** one directly and the other via an intermediate tower, from which kids can slide though a corkscrew slide to ground level. The Tree House, itself, is a kid's fantasy of a humongous old tree girdled by a spiral wooden staircase leading to a "secret" room at the top. Along the way, you can detour off into jungle gym-like environments that snake off through the Land of the Dragons. Kids will love it; nervous parents may find it hard to keep track of their little ones.

At the foot of the Tree House lies **Mizzly Marsh**, a watery play area where kids can really get soaked. The marsh leads through and around the old tree and comes complete with a dragon whose snake-like body appears and disappears beneath the water.

Set apart and surrounded by a fence is the **Dragon Diggery**, a large sandbox with adorable playhouses, one in the shape of a giant mushroom.

The overall effect of these interlocking entertainments is pure delight. Not only is virtually every activity conceived by the preschool mind represented here, but the design and attention to detail are wonderfully imaginative. Even the trash cans are part of the theme. They're called Gobblety Goop, and let you shove your candy wrappers and soda cups down a dragon's throat.

*Tip:* If your kids are old enough to be turned loose in the Land of the Dragons, you can draw some comfort in the knowledge that there is only one way out, at the southern end. There is no entrance at the north end, near *Lory Landing*.

# Kiddie Rides

*Rating:* ★ ★ ★
*Type:* Mechanical rides for toddlers
*Time:* A few minutes each
*Kelly says:* Variations on a single theme

Sprinkled around Land of the Dragons are small kiddie rides. You know the kind of thing: tiny vehicles that go round and round in a tiny circle with tiny little people sitting in them. The ones here are better designed and executed than most, with cutesy names like Eggery Deggery, Chug-A-Tug, and Dapper Flappers.

# A Dragon's Tale

*Rating:* ★ ★ ★ +
*Type:* Live outdoor show
*Time:* About 15 minutes
*Kelly says:* Politically correct fairy tale for tots

This a delightful little singalong and audience participation show for the kids. Adults should check their sophistication at the door.

Your host with the most is Gordon the Dragon who introduces a tale about how the weak-at-the-knees Sir Bumbly the Knight wanders into the Land of the Dragons and encounters the equally frightened Dumphry Dragon. Their initial fright gives way to wary acceptance and then to fast friendship. By the end they are singing about how "being different" is perfectly okay.

There is an adult mindset, with which I am afflicted, that finds this sort of "P.C." pabulum a bit on the cloying side. Fortunately, the kids don't have these silly hang-ups and seem to enjoy the show immensely. And, besides, the dragons in the show have better costumes than Barney.

# Lory Landing

*Rating:* ★ ★ ★ +
*Type:* Walk-through animal exhibit
*Time:* As long as you'd like
*Kelly says:* Close encounters with inquisitive charm-
ers

Lorys and lorikeets are the main attraction in this aviary within an aviary. About halfway between parakeets and parrots in size, lorys are as curious as they are colorful. As you walk through their jungle-themed aviary, they are likely to land on your head, shoulder, or arm to check out your shiny jewelry or cadge a handout. Busch Gardens encourages this by selling "lory nectar" ($1) just in case you forgot to bring your own.

This is great fun for kids (grown-ups, too!) and well worth a visit. In the antechamber to the lorys' dig are large cages displaying their larger cousins — cockatoos, macaws, and the like.

## Eating in the Land of the Dragons

Fine dining is not on the menu in the Land of the Dragons and heaven forbid that there should be anything healthy on hand. But the cleverly named **Snack Dragon** kiosk features ice cream and strawberry bars for about $2, plus popcorn and soda.

# Stanleyville

Stanleyville is a compact, heavily shaded area with plenty of places to sit and survey the passing scene. The theme is African exploration and a lot of the window dressing includes piles of crates, cargo netting, and other expedition gear. In the middle is a shaded amphitheater flanked by two enjoyable water rides and at the southern end are some very entertaining animals like the **wart hogs**, which aren't reviewed here, and the orangutans, which are. This area also offers some excellent shopping for African curios.

## Trans-Veldt Railroad

> *Rating:* ★ ★ ★
> *Type:* Steam railroad journey
> *Time:* 30 minutes for a complete circuit
> *Kelly says:* Shuttle with a view

Board a reconstruction of the type of steam railroad that served as mass transit in turn-of-the-century Africa, rest your weary feet, and get some great views of the animals of the Serengeti Plain. This is one of three vehicular viewing venues for the Serengeti (the *Monorail* and the *Skyride,* described in the Crown Colony section below, being the other two). It makes a leisurely circuit of the park in a generally counterclockwise direction with stops in Nairobi (the closest stop to the main entrance) and the Congo (near Timbuktu). Since you can board or exit at any stop, the *Trans-Veldt* is a great way to cut down on your walking time.

As you travel from Nairobi through Egypt to the Congo, you will see the Serengeti stretching out to your left and get your only chance to see Busch Gardens' baboon troop. Too bad you can't stop for a longer look. After the Congo stop, the train loops around the Congo and back to Stanleyville. The portion of the journey from the Congo to Nairobi is the least scenic, although it does provide some intriguing "backstage" glimpses of the park, including close-up looks at three roller coasters.

## Stanley Falls Log Flume

| | |
|---|---|
| *Rating:* | ★ ★ ★ + |
| *Type:* | Water ride |
| *Time:* | About 2 minutes |
| *Kelly says:* | The last drop is a doozy |

This is a log flume ride, one of the longest in the nation, they say. The car in which you ride is a log-shaped contraption with two seating areas scooped out of it. Each car holds four adults (although at less busy times you can ride two to a car).

Your log rumbles along at a moderate pace in a water-filled flume, takes a few turns, and then climbs slowly to a modest height. The first small drop is merely preparation for the finale, a slow ride up yet another steep grade and an exhilarating drop to the bottom in full view of the passing crowds. Like all water rides, this one has a warning about getting wet, but the cars, with their scooped out fronts, seem designed to direct the wave generated by the final splashdown away from the passengers. It's unlikely that you'll get seriously wet on this one.

As you exit, pause for a moment to commune with the Colobus monkeys with their beautiful shaggy black and white coats.

## Tanganyika Tidal Wave

| | |
|---|---|
| *Rating:* | ★ ★ ★ ★ |
| *Type:* | Water ride |
| *Time:* | About 2 minutes |
| *Kelly says:* | A first-class soaking |

If the nearby *Stanley Falls Log Flume* lulled you into a false sense of security about staying dry, this one will dispel and such notions. Like the log flume ride, this one is all about the final drop. In fact, until then, this ride is far tamer. It snakes lazily through a narrow waterway past stilt houses, whose porches are piled high with Central African trade goods, before taking a slow climb to the top.

Then, all bets are off as the 25-passenger car on which you're riding plunges wildly down a sharp incline into a shallow pool of water, sending a drenching wave over not just the passengers but the spectators who have eagerly gathered on a bridge overhead. No two ways about it. This one really soaks you. Even with a poncho you'll still be pretty darned damp. Since you're probably soaked to the skin anyway, why not top the ride off by standing on the bridge and waiting for the next car to come by? For those who don't want to take the ride or get soaked on the bridge, there is a glassed in viewing section that offers the thrill of a wall of water rushing at you, without the soaking effects.

See *Good Things to Know About... Getting Wet*, earlier in this chapter, for some tips on negotiating Busch Gardens' water rides.

## Ballet D'Afrique Djoniba (Stanleyville Theater)

| | |
|---|---|
| *Rating:* | ★ ★ + |
| *Type:* | African dance troupe |
| *Time:* | About 30 minutes |
| *Kelly says:* | So-so |

It's a great idea: bring real African performers to Tampa so they can share the rich and rhythmical traditions of their homelands. This engaging troupe from West Africa serves up drumming and dances from the Ivory Coast, Senegal, and other countries but, despite some exciting moments, the effect is less than overwhelming.

The show certainly doesn't skimp in the rhythm department. The drumming is loud, compelling, and non-stop. The dancing has less to recommend it, however. Most numbers are more energetic than elegant, more frenetic than flowing. Still, the eight performers are ingratiating, especially the handsome leader of the troupe who has great fun teaching volunteers from the audience the basics of African dance.

## Orangutans

| | |
|---|---|
| *Rating:* | ★ ★ ★ ★ + |
| *Type:* | Animal habitat |
| *Time:* | Continuous viewing |
| *Kelly says:* | Best at feeding time |

You can catch the wonderfully anthropomorphic orangutans any time. They hang out on a small island with plenty of climbing structures to keep them amused. (By the way, the cables stretched around the island provide the orangutans, who hate the water and can't swim, with hand holds should they accidentally fall in.) The stairway that leads to Land of the Dragons provides a nice viewing area, especially if one of the apes has climbed to the top of the tallest wooden tower in the habitat. But I would recommend timing your visit to one of the "Animal Enrichment" feedings when these natural born comedians of the South Asian jungle ham it up for their supper.

They applaud, gesture, and even put on t-shirts — a skill they "just picked up" the attendant told me. The t-shirts do double duty as bedding, after the hairy apes tear them in strips and knot them together (yes, they ties knots!) into a chaotic but presumably comfy tangle. Photographers should position themselves near the presenter, who will coax the old male orangutan into offering a series of comical facial expressions that make for the perfect picture.

*Tip:* The attendant who does this show, starts his rounds with the nearby wart hogs and then moves on to the tigers in the Congo. Tagging along with him is a good way to guarantee the best views, as well as being an efficient way of seeing three entertaining shows. The Entertainment Guide you picked up at the Information Booth in Morocco lists times.

# Orchid Canyon

| | |
|---|---|
| *Rating:* | ★ ★ |
| *Type:* | Floral display with monkeys |
| *Time:* | Continuous viewing |
| *Kelly says:* | For orchid fanciers |

Tucked away behind the *Tanganyika Tidal Wave* is its complete antithesis. The canyon in question is a tall, narrow, winding maze of artificial rock punctuated with artificial waterfalls and dotted with a wide variety of beautiful, multicolored orchids. Along the way, there is a large compound filled with spider monkeys. Kids may be tempted to explore this area but, aside from the monkeys, there's little to hold their interest. Orchid fanciers, however, may enjoy coming across unfamiliar species.

# Eating in Stanleyville

## Stanleyville Smokehouse

| | |
|---|---|
| *What:* | Fast food barbecue |
| *Where:* | Next to the wart hogs |
| *Price Range:* | $$ - $$$ |

This is Busch Gardens' barbecue joint and as an aficionado of this cuisine I can report it ain't half bad. A rib dinner is about $7 with chicken about $6. A combination of the two is $7. Those with less of an appetite can get a small chicken dinner for about $5. Desserts are $2 and there is the usual array of soft drinks. Service is at walk-up windows and all seating is outdoors.

# Shopping in Stanleyville

### Tropical Wave

Strategically located next to the *Tanganyika Tidal Wave*, this kiosk offers (in addition to $4 ponchos) t-shirts celebrating not just the Tidal Wave but also Adventure Island, Busch Gardens' next-door water park (which is covered in the next chapter).

### Stanleyville Bazaar

This long shed-like building offers an unusually wide range of Busch Gardens t-shirts, along with mugs, names plates, key chains, pens, in short the whole panoply of things that can be stamped with a logo and sold for a profit.

### Air Africa

This "African Goods Trading Post" just opposite the Stanleyville Bazaar is one of the best shopping venues in the park, featuring some arresting crafts from sub-Saharan Africa. There are Kenyan Kisi stone carvings, reproductions (I assume) of tribal masks and ceremonial stools, and a wide variety of carved wooden objects. Some of this is quite inexpensive but the masks cost $75 to $350 or more and one stunning, six-foot high carving of a giraffe was listed at about $1,000. There are carvings of Masai tribesmen fashioned by members of the neighboring Akamba tribe ($23 to about $100). The Akamba started making these lovely decorative objects as a gesture of friendship after a long-standing animosity between the two tribes was put to rest. There is a small selection of men's safari clothing, leather bags, and canvas back packs. But the main attraction here is the wide selection of African crafts. Anyone interested in a gift that's out of the ordinary should head here bearing money.

# The Congo

The Congo is another compact, cleverly-designed area with twisting tree-shaded walks and a number of spectator bridges over rides and animal habitats. Most of the space is given over to some of Busch Gardens' premiere thrill rides, although the Congo is also home to the park's ravishing and much-ballyhooed white Bengal tigers. The predominant architectural motif is round buildings with conical wooden stick roofs.

In addition to the major attractions profiled below, the Congo contains a bumper car ride (**Ubanga-Banga Bumper Cars**), a trio of kiddie rides (**Pygmy Village**), and remote control trucks and boats. There is also a stop for the **Trans-Veldt Railway** (described in the Stanleyville section, above).

# Kumba

| | |
|---|---|
| *Rating:* | ★ ★ ★ ★ ★ |
| *Type:* | Steel roller coaster |
| *Time:* | Just under 3 minutes |
| *Kelly says:* | The next best (i.e. scariest) thing to *Montu* |

Before *Montu* opened (see Egypt, below), *Kumba* was Busch Gardens' blockbuster ride. It's still pretty amazing and is the largest of its kind in the southeastern United States.

*Kumba* means "roar" in a Congolese dialect, the P.R. people say, and it's well named. Riders are braced with shoulder restraints into 32-seat vehicles (eight rows, four abreast) that roar along almost 4,000 feet of blue steel track that winds up, around, over, and through the surrounding scenery. There are loops, camelbacks, and corkscrews to terrify or thrill you, as the case may be. One of the more disorienting maneuvers takes you on a "cobra roll" around a spectator bridge, which is a great place for the faint of heart to get an idea of what they're missing. Remember to wave to Aunt Martha as you whiz by.

# Claw Island

| | |
|---|---|
| *Rating:* | ★ ★ ★ ★ ★ |
| *Type:* | Animal habitat |
| *Time:* | Continuous viewing |
| *Kelly says:* | Time your visit to the "Animal Enrichment" schedule |

*Claw Island* is the Hollywood-ish name for an intriguing habitat housing three of Busch Gardens' most beautiful residents. Here, in a deep pit, on a small, green, palm-dotted island, you'll find three magnificent Bengal tigers. One bears the tawny coat we are all familiar with, one has dark stripes on a white background, and the third is completely white. These rare white tigers were prized by Indian royalty, and no wonder. They are truly awe-inspiring.

*Claw Island's* pit is surrounded by gazebo viewing areas and a wooden spectator bridge, all of which have heavy rope netting to make doubly sure that no one climbs or falls in. By walking around the perimeter you should be able to get good views of the tigers.

Most of the time, they are just lounging around (these are cats, after all). That's why it's a good idea to time your visit to one of the "Animal Enrichment" presentations during which the tigers rouse themselves from their customary torpor to get a light chicken snack. The Entertainment Guide you collected at the Information Booth has the times.

The attendant who conducts these sessions moves around the enclosure and makes sure the tigers give photographers plenty of chances for a good shot. At the finale of the short presentation, he tries to get all three big cats in a row for a group portrait. This is one of the few enrichment shows that draws sizable crowds. You may want to position yourself in the middle of the spectator bridge or on the opposite side of the enclosure near the Pygmy Village kiddie rides for the best photo ops.

*Tip:* The staffer who conducts these sessions begins his rounds with the wart hogs in Stanleyville, then moves to the orangutans, and finishes up with the tigers. Following him is an efficient way to catch all three shows.

## The Python

| | |
|---|---|
| *Rating:* | ★ ★ ★ ★ |
| *Type:* | Small roller coaster |
| *Time:* | About a minute and a half |
| *Kelly says:* | Roller coasters 101A |

Along with *The Scorpion* in Timbuktu (see below), this is one of Busch Gardens warm-up coasters for *Kumba* and *Montu*. It's hard to differentiate the two lesser coasters, but I rate this as slightly more advanced than *The Scorpion* if only because it has two up-and-over loops. It's also a good place to test your resolve before braving the bigger coasters. The business end of the ride, between the slow climb to the top and the slowdown before returning to the start, lasts just 30-some seconds. You can hold your breath for the entire trip.

## The Congo River Rapids

| | |
|---|---|
| *Rating:* | ★ ★ ★ ★ |
| *Type:* | Water ride |
| *Time:* | About 3 minutes |
| *Kelly says:* | The best of the water rides |

It doesn't have the steep drops of the flume rides in Stanleyville, but for me *Congo River Rapids* provides the most enjoyable overall water ride experience in Busch Gardens.

Here you climb aboard 12-seater circular rafts which are then set adrift to float freely along a rapid-filled stretch of river. The raft twists, turns, and spins as it bumps off the sides and various cunningly placed obstacles in the stream. In addition to the raging waters, which periodically slosh into the raft, the course is punctuated with waterfalls and waterspouts all of which have the potential to drench you to the skin. The most insidious threat of all comes from your fellow park visitors who are encouraged to spray you with water cannon (at 25 cents a shot) from the pedestrian walkway that skirts the ride.

Despite all the white water, the raft proceeds at a relatively stately pace and the "river" drops only several feet over its quarter-mile course. The real excitement is generated by the ever-present threat of a soaking. How wet you get is purely a matter of chance it seems. One person on the raft may emerge virtually unscathed while another will get sopping wet.

See *Good Things to Know About... Getting Wet*, earlier in this chapter, for some tips on negotiating Busch Gardens' water rides.

# Eating in The Congo

## ViVi Storehouse Restaurant

*What:* Sandwiches
*Where:* Near *Claw Island*
*Price Range:* $$ - $$$

This cafeteria-style eatery (open seasonally) specializes in sandwiches. Club sandwich platters and fajita sandwiches are both about $6. There are also salads and the usual array of desserts. Seating is outdoors at trestle tables under circular wooden-roofed pavilions.

## Python Soft Serve

For those who missed (or lost) lunch while riding the nearby roller coaster of the same name, Python Soft Serve offers a quick sugar jolt in the form of soft ice cream waffle-cone sundaes for about $3 to $4.

# Shopping in The Congo

## The Roar Store

As you might have guessed, this shop is just outside the exit to *Kumba*. Here you can get "I survived *Kumba*" t-shirts ($13 to $16) as well as *Kumba* mugs, key chains, and the like.

## Congo River Rapids Outpost

Also called the Kinshasa Outpost, this large open-sided building, with its heavy wooden supporting posts and tin roof, mimics a trading warehouse deep in the jungle. They advertise "Dry Goods and River Gear," which means, among other things, you can pick up a poncho for about $4. You'll also find sports sandals, t-shirts (about $13), sun hats, and beach towels.

### Tiger's Den

This open-sided kiosk celebrates the nearby Bengal tigers in a bewildering variety of media, from beach towels to posters to bookmarks. There are also some lovely t-shirts ($9 to $20) and a plush doll of a mother tiger with two cubs for a very reasonable $40.

# Timbuktu

Timbuktu is, of course, the legendary sub-Saharan trade crossroads that figures prominently in the popular imagination of adventure and exploration. It is, in fact, a dusty remnant of its past glory. Here at Busch Gardens, Timbuktu is an open, sun-drenched plaza dotted with palm trees and featuring architecture that mimics the mud towers of its namesake. There is precious little shade here unless you venture indoors.

The attractions in Timbuktu are a mismatched assortment, having little to do with either Timbuktu or even Africa. But then, Timbuktu is emblematic of far-flung trade, so perhaps it's not so farfetched that it contains an eclectic grab bag of themed attractions from around the world.

There are no zoo animals here, but there are dolphins and a sea lion in the large amphitheater at the north end. At the opposite end you'll find, of all things, a German restaurant! In between there is a variety of typical **amusement park rides**, including Busch Gardens' only **carousel** and several other **kiddie rides**.

Also at hand are a collection of **midway games**, cleverly disguised as a sub-Saharan marketplace, and a **video arcade** housed in a vaguely Saharan edifice with a vaguely Saharan name, The Sultan's Arcade. The major rides and attractions are described below.

## The Scorpion

| | |
|---|---|
| *Rating:* | ★ ★ ★ + |
| *Type:* | A "baby" roller coaster |
| *Time:* | About a minute |
| *Kelly says:* | Roller coasters 101 |

This is the place to come to decide if you have what it takes to tackle the bigger coasters in the park. In my estimation, *The Scorpion* is the tamest of the lot, although it does have one up-and-over loop. So if you've never been "inverted," this is as good a place to start as any. Otherwise, it's no more terrifying than, say, Disney's *Thunder Mountain*.

# Dolphins of the Deep (Dolphin Theater)

*Rating:*      ★ ★ ★ ★

*Type:*        Live show

*Time:*        About 30 minutes

*Kelly says:*  A reprise for SeaWorld visitors

This entertaining show will seem familiar to those who have visited SeaWorld and, if you fall into this category and are pressed for time, you may want to skip it here. On the other hand, it still ranks as one of Busch Gardens' most enjoyable experiences. It's a tough call.

In this version, two dolphins named (what else?) Mich and Bud are put through their paces in a show that follows the edutainment formula — fascinating facts interspersed with even more fascinating "behaviors." This show even features a pint-sized version of Shamu's tail-splashing stunt. Adding a touch of humor is an interloping sea lion who hopes to land a spot in the show with an audition. It's all great fun and is topped off by a spectacular leap.

The show takes place in an open amphitheater with a roof for us and a sun shade for the dolphins. In the distance, you can see *Kumba*'s roaring loops. If you're hungry, you will find popcorn, ice cream, and soft drinks at the back of the auditorium.

# The Phoenix

*Rating:*      ★ ★ ★

*Type:*        Amusement park ride

*Time:*        5 minutes

*Kelly says:*  Only if you haven't done it before

This is a very familiar amusement park ride. A curved boat-like car seating 50 people, swings back and forth, gaining height. At the apex of its swing, it pauses and the passengers hang briefly upside down, screaming merrily. Then on the next swing it goes completely up and over.

Chances are, there's a ride like this at an amusement park somewhere near your home, which leads to the question: Ride this one or spend the time doing things you *can't* do near home? I'd recommend the latter.

# International Celebration (Das Festhaus)

*Rating:*      ★ ★ ★

*Type:*        Musical variety show

*Time:*        About 20 minutes

*Kelly says:*  Best with a meal

Backed by a 10-piece band with an accent on brass, a sunny ensemble of young performers (Are there any other kind at these parks?)

takes you on a musical tour of the world — or at least selected portions thereof. According to my count, the show visits France, Mexico (for a hat dance featuring a six-foot tall hat), Germany, Italy, and Ireland.

It's all great fun and there is some audience participation built in, which is a big hit with the younger members of the crowd. If your child is the outgoing type, grab a seat near the wide central aisle. After the show, the performers linger to mingle, making for a great **photo op**.

One of the best things about this show is that the busy tourist can combine it with a hearty lunch from the Festhaus cafeteria (described below).

## Eating in Timbuktu

### Das Festhaus

| | |
|---|---|
| *What:* | German beer hall |
| *Where:* | South end of the plaza |
| *Price Range:* | $$ - $$$ |

It must be hard to make every shop and every restaurant fit into the right theme at a park this size. And at the Festhaus they don't even try. At least the theme at this cavernous restaurant harkens back to Anheuser-Busch's German origins. The dining area of this "German Festival Hall" seats 1,000 at trestle tables. To the front is a stage for the variety show and high overhead is a mammoth chandelier hanging from the tent-like ceiling. The walls are decorated with painted panels that conjure up a Bavarian town square and the air conditioning is like a fresh breeze from the Alps.

To your left as you enter, tucked away, is the cafeteria line. The menu, in a nod to American tastes, offers both German and Italian entrees. You can stick with the theme and have a German sampler platter ($6) of wursts and sauerkraut or opt for the Italian dinner ($5). The oven-roasted turkey sandwich at $6 is juicy and tender and Das Alpine ($6) is a "mile-high" corned beef on rye. Beer is served here for $2 to $3 depending on the size and the brand. Desserts are about $2.

After the Crown Colony Restaurant (see below), Das Festhaus offers Busch Gardens' most enjoyable dining experience, largely because of the chance to be royally entertained while eating.

### Oasis Juice Bar

At the other end of the plaza, next to the midway games, this small kiosk serves fresh-squeezed fruit juices and churros, Mexico's tasty version of the doughnut.

## Shopping in Timbuktu

### West Africa Trading Company

Echoing Timbuktu's mercantile roots, this shop focuses on small decorative objects and gifts from a variety of far off sources. Preeminent among them are a variety of brass crafts — gold- and silver-finished, brown-lacquered, and inlaid with mother of pearl — from India. Prices start at under $10 and go up. You should be able to find a lovely gift here for under $30. There is also an ever-changing variety of crafts from around the world. For other tastes, the shop offers a walk-in cigar humidor, with imported stogies from Honduras and the Dominican Republic as well as the handiwork of Tampa's own hand rollers.

Outside, in a setting that mimics a bazaar in a dusty sub-Saharan crossroads, you will find a variety of crafts including Ugandan baskets, Moroccan leather goods, Kenyan wood carvings and other decorative objects, straw hats, and the ever-present Busch Gardens t-shirts. Prices on the crafts here are modest to moderate.

# Nairobi

This is Busch Gardens' most zoo-like themed area. To the East, the plains of Serengeti stretch as far as the eye can see. On the other side are a string of animal exhibits ranging from the merely interesting to the truly wondrous. There are no rides here to distract from the main attractions, which are some of the zoo's most intriguing creatures.

In addition to the attractions listed below, Nairobi is home to the **Show Jumping Hall of Fame and Museum**, a small display of memorabilia from the United States Equestrian Team. It will be of interest primarily to aficionados of this upper crusty sport. There is also a display of **Aldabra tortoises**, with regular "Animal Enrichment" sessions.

## Myombe Reserve: The Great Ape Domain

*Rating:*    ★ ★ ★ ★ ★
*Type:*      Ape habitat
*Time:*      Continuous viewing
*Kelly says:*  The zoo's crown jewel

Of all the animal habitats at Busch Gardens, this is the hands-down winner. The beautifully imagined setting here would be almost worth the visit without the chimps and gorillas. But it is these fascinating primates that we come to see, and the scenic designers and landscape architects have given them a home that provides plenty of variety for the animals while making it easy for us to spy on them. The achievement is remarkable and ranks right up there with the spectacular habitats at SeaWorld.

The habitat is divided in two, with the first area given over to a band of nine chimpanzees in a rocky, multi-leveled environment complete with spectacular waterfalls, calm pools, and a grassy forest clearing with plenty of climbing space. Best of all is a glassed-in viewing area that allows us to eavesdrop on the chimp's private behavior.

Passing through a tunnel, we arrive at the lowland gorilla habitat. There's a wonderful theatricality to this entrance as we pass through a simulated jungle fog to "discover" the gorillas grazing on our left. Talk about gorillas in the mist! In addition to a glassed viewing area, this habitat features a small amphitheater for extended observation and video cameras that allow us to observe individuals in the far reaches of the habitat.

There's plenty of explanatory information provided on blackboards (the conceit here is that we are visiting a jungle outpost of a scientific expedition), drawings in large, plastic-covered notebooks that we can leaf through, and voice-over narration in the hidden viewing area. If you only have time for one zoo exhibit between roller coaster rides, make it this one. The entrance to *Myombe Reserve* is opposite the Moroccan Palace Theater; the exit leads you into the rest of the Nairobi section.

## Nairobi Station Animal Nursery

*Rating:* ★ ★ ★ ★
*Type:* Newborn animal exhibit
*Time:* Continuous viewing
*Kelly says:* Lifestyles of the cutest and cuddliest

One of the main missions of today's enlightened zoological parks is the propagation of species, especially threatened and endangered ones. Busch Gardens takes this responsibility very seriously and, rather than leave things to chance, they scoop up newborns, bring them here, and give them the kind of tender loving care that will best ensure their survival. What you see here will, naturally, depend on who's been giving birth in the days and weeks prior to your visit.

## Asian Elephants

*Rating:* ★ ★ ★ ★
*Type:* Animal habitat
*Time:* Continuous viewing
*Kelly says:* Come at show time

A small herd of female Asian elephants is housed in a spacious, if rather barren, habitat at the northern end of Nairobi. The "Animal Enrichment" shows featuring these enormous creatures are highly entertaining and invariably feature one of the ponderous pachyderms getting a bath. The attendant will also make sure that photographers get a good shot of the elephant in an alluring pose. Happily, these shows are presented more frequently than the other animal presentations in the park.

# Petting Zoo

| | |
|---|---|
| *Rating:* | ★ ★ ★ + |
| *Type:* | Hands-on exhibit |
| *Time:* | Continuous viewing |
| *Kelly says:* | Interesting twist on an old idea |

Ever notice how aggressive those cute little goats get at children's petting zoos? It's because of the constant supply of rich food pellets you buy for your kids to dole out. Busch Gardens has solved the problem by banning free goodies. Instead, your child can pick up a stiff plastic brush and groom the goats to their hearts content. The result is some very happy kids and some of the tidiest goats you're likely to see.

Besides the African pygmy and Nubian goats (which are clearly the main attraction and have the run of the place), there are bunnies, chickens, and such in small pens.

# Curiosity Caverns

| | |
|---|---|
| *Rating:* | ★ ★ + |
| *Type:* | Walk-through exhibit |
| *Time:* | Continuous viewing |
| *Kelly says:* | A real "Bat Cave" |

Decorated to evoke a prehistoric cave, complete with wall paintings, this darkened walk-through tunnel displays, behind plate glass windows, a variety of critters that most people thing of as "creepy," although the nocturnal marmoset is positively cuddly. Aside from the snakes and reptiles, the main attractions here are the bats. Fruit bats cavort in a large enclosure decorated with bare trees artfully draped with bananas, apples, and other yummy treats. Nearby, in a smaller display, are the vampire bats (yes, they really exist!), the animal blood on which they thrive served up on dainty trays.

# Eating in Nairobi

## Kenya Kanteen

| | |
|---|---|
| *What:* | Quick snacks |
| *Where:* | Between the elephants and the tortoises |
| *Price Range:* | $ |

Popcorn, nachos, cotton candy, and waffle cone sundaes are the order of the day here, with nothing costing more than $4. You can sit at umbrella-shaded tables and observe the red-necked ostriches in the Serengeti across the way. Nearby are some attractive, slightly smaller than life size hippo sculptures that make a great place to take yet more pictures of your kids.

## Shopping in Nairobi

### J.R.'s Gorilla Hut

Just outside the Myombe exit, this outdoor kiosk sells, you guessed it, t-shirts, dolls, and other souvenirs that celebrate our primate relatives. Best of the lot are the t-shirts with white on black gorilla portraits ($16). This is one of the few shops in the park where you can pick up truly first-rate books on the subject at hand. Here you'll find Dian Fossey's *Gorillas in the Mist* and several books by chimp maven Jane Goodall.

# Crown Colony and the Serengeti Plain

This area takes its theme from the great British colonial enclaves of East Africa, where the well-heeled lived the good life and played cricket and polo while being waited on by the unshod. A real British Colonial would probably not recognize the place, but for the rest of us it'll do just fine. The overall impression is one of casual elegance and good taste and it serves as a comfortable home to several attractions, like *Akbar's Adventure Tours* and the Clydesdale stables, which stretch the African metaphor a bit. It is also the home of Busch Gardens' only full-service sit-down restaurant.

## Edge of Africa

| | |
|---|---|
| *Rating:* | ★ ★ ★ ★ ★ |
| *Type:* | Brilliant animal habitat |
| *Time:* | Continuous viewing |
| *Kelly says:* | Up close and personal with lions and hippos |

With *Edge of Africa*, Busch Gardens has created an animal habitat to rival *Wild Arctic* at SeaWorld. Here, on a looping trail that evokes a number of African themes, are displayed a compact colony of adorable meerkats, a pride of lions, a pack of hyenas, a few hippos, and a troop of baboons. The genius of the design is in the glass walls that allow you, literally, to come nose to nose with some of these animals.

The lion display is built around the metaphor of a scientific encampment on the Serengeti that has been invaded by a pride. Two Land Rovers are built into the glass wall that separates you from the lions, allowing you to climb into the vehicles and recreate an actual safari experience. At feeding time, the handlers drop meat morsels into the lion enclosure from above the Land Rovers, encouraging the lions to climb into the backs and onto the hoods of the vehicles. The effect is breathtaking as you sit a hand's breadth away from a snarling lion.

The hippo exhibit evokes an African river village with the huts raised over the water on stilts. The viewing area is nicely shaded by the huts and the extensive glass wall allows a terrific underwater perspective on these beasts. While they may seem lumbering on land, under water they are surprisingly graceful as they lope past swarms of freshwater tropical fish. One visitor compared them to flying pigs.

The key to really enjoying *Edge of Africa* is to come at feeding time when the animals will be at their most active and most visible. At other times they will most likely be off relaxing in the shade somewhere. The attendants doing the feeding are all experienced animal handlers who are more than happy to share their extensive knowledge with you, so don't be shy about asking questions. Unfortunately, there is no regular feeding schedule. Feeding times are varied to mimic, to some small extent, life in the wild, where animals can never predict when their next meal is coming.

The solution is to ask the attendants at the attraction when feeding time will be. You may have to be persistent and you must also be willing to drop whatever you're doing elsewhere in the park to return for feeding. Take it from me, it's worth it.

*Note:* The main entrance to *Edge of Africa* is in Crown Colony but you can also reach the attraction from Egypt.

## Serengeti Safari Tour

*Rating:* ★ ★ ★ ★ ★
*Type:* Guided tour
*Time:* 30 minutes
*Kelly says:* A safari for those who can't get to Africa

First the bad news: There is a hefty extra charge for this attraction of $20 for everyone five and older (annual pass holders get a 10 percent discount). That will probably be a budget-buster for many families, but if the cost doesn't scare you off this one will provide experiences you'll remember for a good long time. And if it's any consolation, it's a lot cheaper than going to Africa.

The tour takes you, aboard a converted flat-bed truck, into the Serengeti Plain for some up-close encounters that offer unique **photo ops**. The first stop is the hippo pen. Not the one in *Edge of Africa* but the dressing room, if you will, where the animals relax during their time off. An attendant will attempt to coax one of their ponderous charges to the fence of the enclosure where you can get a good look into its gaping mouth.

Then it's off to the interior of the Plain for the real highlight of the tour — a chance to hand feed the ostriches and giraffes. The adult giraffes tower over you, while the youngsters just get their heads over the edge of the truck. They are remarkably tame and will let you pet their stiff, tawny necks and soft muzzles. You may also get a demonstration of how they use their long black tongues to pluck the dainty leaves off thorny acacia bushes. It's quite a treat.

***The best seats in the house.*** The back of the truck is standing room only with a padded rail around the rim. I suggest positioning yourself at one of the back corners since giraffes will often trail after the slow-moving vehicle looking for another handout.

***Tip:*** The trucks have a maximum capacity of 20 people and on a typical day there are just five tours. While the high price keeps the crowds down, tours do fill up quickly. You can reserve ahead for the first tour of each day only, which departs at 10:00 or 10:30 a.m., and is the only morning tour. The morning tour also offers the advantage of beating the heat of midday. Call (813) 987-5212 to make your reservation. When you arrive at the park, go to *Edge of Africa* and turn right. Follow the signs to the Safari Tour. There, at a small booth you can pay for your tour with cash or credit card. If you don't reserve ahead, you must sign up in advance for one of the afternoon tours; it is wise to do so early.

## Serengeti Plain

*Rating:* ★ ★ ★
*Type:* Extensive animal habitat
*Time:* Continuous viewing but access is limited
*Kelly says:* Takes persistence to see it all

This is one of Busch Gardens' major zoological achievements. A 50-acre preserve that evokes the vast grasslands of Eastern Africa. (Serengeti is a Masai word meaning "plain without end.") Here, Busch displays a representative cross-section of African plains dwellers, from major predators like lions taking a break from *Edge of Africa*, to charming curiosities like giraffes and the endangered black rhinoceros, to the herd animals — lithe gazelles and lumbering wildebeest (or gnus).

It's a brilliant idea and, by and large, well executed, although it still looks far more like Florida scrub land than the real Serengeti. The concept and the design involve a number of tradeoffs. By mimicking nature, the designers have made the animals hard to see — just like in the wild. Although you can see into the Serengeti from Nairobi or the terrace of the Crown Colony House, the only way to get a good look is to go inside. Unless you are willing to pay the stiff extra fee for the *Serengeti Safari Tour*, that can be accomplished only by the *Monorail*, the *Skyride*, and by the *Trans-Veldt Railroad* (see the Stanleyville section, above) which circles the perimeter. So your routes through the Serengeti are predetermined as are the lengths of your visits. This creates a number of minor problems. There's no guarantee that the animals will be in prime viewing position (or even visible) when you pass by, although it's unlikely that you will miss much. And, if an animal catches your fancy or is doing something particularly interesting, your vehicle simply keeps on going; you don't have the luxury of stopping. You also have no control over how close you can get to the animals (with the notable exception of the *Serengeti Safari Tour*).

That being said, the Serengeti Plain remains a major feather in Busch Gardens' zoological cap. The animals enjoy a much more spacious and natural environment than they would have in a more "traditional" zoo and we probably shouldn't complain too much about the compromises we must make for their comfort.

Those who want to make the investment of time and money can visit the Serengeti many times — on the two rides over the plain, the train ride around it, the truck tour, and from vantage points in *Edge of Africa* and around the perimeter. The nature of the park experience, however, suggests that most people will glimpse the animals briefly on the short rides. And that's too bad.

## The Monorail

*Rating:*        ★ ★ ★
*Type:*          Round trip through *Serengeti Plain*
*Time:*          About 12 minutes
*Kelly says:*    Best view of the Plain

The best view of the *Serengeti Plain* — and the *only* view of some of its denizens — is to be had aboard this sleek, suspended train-like ride. The *Monorail* dips to just feet off the ground and rises over fences as it completes a circumnavigation of Busch Gardens' largest animal exhibit. You ride in air-conditioned comfort in 12-person cars as your guide reads a script about the animals you are passing. You'll have to look quickly to catch glimpses of some of them and don't be too disappointed if the hippos are submerged when you pass overhead. The train hangs a U-turn over the parking lot before returning to its starting point.

*Tip:* If you jump the low rails along the exit ramp you can take a shortcut to the *Skyride*, which departs from the same terminal.

## The Skyride

| | |
|---|---|
| *Rating:* | ★ ★ ★ |
| *Type:* | Suspended gondola ride |
| *Time:* | 5 minutes |
| *Kelly says:* | Shortcut with a view |

If you've been on the sky ride at Disney World you know what this one's all about. This isn't intended as a tour of the *Serengeti Plain*, although it does pass over it. Rather, this is a one-way shortcut from Crown Colony to the Congo, or vice versa. Your vehicle is a small four-seat gondola suspended from an overhead cable. You can board at either end, but you cannot stay aboard for a round trip. The ride dips down for a dog-leg left turn at a checkpoint on the northern end of the Serengeti. This is not a disembarkation point but is used primarily to adjust the spacing between gondolas to assure a smooth arrival.

You can get some good views of the Serengeti from this ride, although most people will take the opportunity to check out the action on *Montu* and *Kumba* or perhaps to spot the towers of Adventure Island, Busch Gardens' water park, down the road.

## Akbar's Adventure Tours

| | |
|---|---|
| *Rating:* | ★ ★ ★ + |
| *Type:* | Simulator ride |
| *Time:* | 10 minutes |
| *Kelly says:* | Not bad of this kind |

Join the intrepid, if slightly desperate, Akbar as he tries to fend off the repo man and save his failing Egyptian tour operation with a "home-made simulator" operated by his baby brothers. That's the premise of this dotty exercise in simulated insanity. Amazingly enough it works pretty well.

After you snake through the line to the attraction's doors, groups of 60 are led into a pre-show area where Akbar (played with manic abandon by comedian Martin Short) explains his ingenious idea, only to be interrupted by a sleazy collection agent bent on repossessing everything Akbar owns. Akbar begs, pleads, and finally kidnaps this nemesis to show how his brilliant idea can make them both rich.

That's your cue to enter a simulator that seems to be the twin of the ones used at SeaWorld's *Wild Arctic* ride; only the interior decoration is different. We get to sample three of Akbar's tours, a ride through an Egyptian market on camel-back, a visit to the Sphinx that succeeds in destroying the ancient wonder, and a visit to a mummy's tomb that goes seriously awry and occasions a truly scary response from the owner.

If this is your only shot at a simulator ride, it's well worth the trip. Otherwise, you might agree with me that *Wild Arctic* does much the same thing better.

**The best seats in the house.** As you line up along the illuminated circles on the floor to enter the simulator, be aware that the screen (or front window of Akbar's homemade simulator) will be on your left as you enter. Your best view will be towards the back in the center. Attempt to arrange yourself accordingly.

# Clydesdale Hamlet

> *Rating:* ★ ★ +
> *Type:* Horse stables
> *Time:* Continuous viewing
> *Kelly says:* For horse lovers and Bud fans

This is a smaller version of the *Clydesdale Hamlet* at SeaWorld. The horses are magnificent; there may be a foal on view during your visit. Even if you aren't a horse lover, the stroll through the stables makes a convenient shortcut to *Akbar's Adventure Tours*. The Clydesdales also pose for **photo ops** several times a day. Check the Entertainment Guide you picked up at the Information Booth for exact times.

# Eating in Crown Colony

## Crown Colony House

> *What:* Full-service restaurant
> *Where:* Opposite the *Monorail*, overlooking the Serengeti
> *Price Range:* $$ - $$$$

The only full-service restaurant at Busch Gardens is the 240-seat Crown Colony House restaurant, a droll evocation of a posh East African club during the heyday of British colonialism. It was founded, so they would have us believe, by an eccentric group of explorers, including Sir Edison Fitzwilly who unearthed the only known sphinx skeleton in addition to the Crystal of Zed. The walls are decorated with old cricket bats, polo mallets, and tennis racquets, as well as antelope horns and buffalo heads.

If the decor is British Colonial a la East Africa, the menu is standard American. Standouts include the Chicken Fettucini and the Captain's Choice, a platter of broiled or fried shrimp, scallops and grouper served with grilled vegetables. In the salad department, check out the large and beautifully presented Grilled Chicken Salad and, for vegetarians, the vegetable or fruit salad platters. Entrees range from $10 to $13; salads are about $8 and sandwiches about $7. The big bargain offered here is the family-style dinner (fried chicken or fish) for $9, or $4 for those 12 and under.

*Tip:* In addition to the luxury of being waited on, the main draw here is the great view of the Serengeti Plain. No reservations are accepted so you can't call ahead and reserve a table by the great semicircular sweep of window overlooking *Edge of Africa*, but you can request one and wait until it becomes available. If you're not on a tight schedule I highly recommend doing so. The view alone makes this one of the nicest places to eat in Central Florida.

## Anheuser-Busch Hospitality Center

Downstairs in the Crown Colony House is another dispensary of free beer samples. Nearby, is **Provisions**, a fast-food eatery serving up sandwich platters and pizza for about $4 to $6.

# Shopping in Crown Colony

## Trader Jim's

This stone building with its wooden stick roof is located at the juncture where Morocco and Nairobi meet and Crown Colony begins. The merchandise leans heavily to plush animal toys, animal themed t-shirts (about $13 to $20), and Busch Gardens baseball caps in a wide variety of styles (about $8 to $12).

## Expedition Africa

After you make your way past the obligatory t-shirts with *Edge of Africa* themes and logos ($12-$20), you will find some very nice upscale clothing for both men and women. Multi-pocket safari vests are $65 and nice polo shirts with understated *Edge of Africa* logos are $40. In the back you will find tops for women ($20-$25) and men ($25-$35) and a line of simulated exotic animal skin purses and luggage ($28-$50). Also available here are lightweight pants that convert to shorts thanks to strategically placed zippers.

## Crown Colony Gift Shop

This upscale boutique is a sort of yuppie version of the Rabat Label Stable. It's for those who wouldn't be caught dead wearing a Budweiser logo — unless it cost a small fortune. That being said, some of the polo shirts and jackets sold here are very attractive.

# Egypt

This is Busch Gardens' newest "land" and one of its smallest, at least in terms of strolling space and amenities. Its primary purpose is to give the mega-coaster *Montu* a home. The *King Tut* attraction seems a bit of an afterthought, and the only eatery here is a kiosk dispensing snacks. The shopping is a bit more elaborate but not much.

The design evokes upper Egypt as it might have looked about the time Howard Carter was unearthing King Tut's treasure. The scale is appropriately grandiose but the statuary and wall carvings fall well short of the originals. Still, it's pleasant enough. There's a clever "archaeological dig" that is, in fact, a shaded sand box in which little ones can uncover the past. A strolling juggler decked out as King Tut entertains the passing crowd.

For most people, however, Egypt will be glimpsed briefly en route to the massive temple gates at the end, beyond which lurks the terrifying *Montu*.

## Montu

| | |
|---|---|
| *Rating:* | ★ ★ ★ ★ ★ |
| *Type:* | Inverted roller coaster |
| *Time:* | About 3 minutes |
| *Kelly says:* | The cutting edge of roller coaster design |

This one is truly terrifying. It is also, for those who care about such things, the tallest and longest inverted steel roller coaster in the world.

*Montu* (named for a hawk-headed Egyptian god of war) takes the formula of *Kumba* and, quite literally turns it on its head. Instead of sitting in a car with the track under your feet, you sit (or should I say "hang") in a car with the track overhead. Once you leave the station, your feet hang free as you pass over a pit filled with live crocodiles and climb to a dizzying 150 feet above the ground before being dropped 13 stories, shot through a 360 degree "camelback loop" that produces an eternity of weightlessness (actually a mere three seconds), and zipped, zoomed, and zapped along nearly 4,000 feet of track that twists over, above, and even into the ground. Fortunately, when you dip below ground level you do so in archaeological "excavation trenches," in keeping with the Egyptian theme. There's not much to see in these trenches, but then you don't spend much time in them and you'll probably have your eyes jammed shut anyway.

Each car holds 32 passengers. At maximum capacity, 1,700 guests can be pumped through this attraction each hour. Nonetheless, lines can be formidable. If this is your kind of ride, plan on arriving early during the busy times of the year.

The best (and scariest seats) are in the front row. Otherwise, the outside seats are the ones to hope for. Given the overhead design of this ride, the interior seats offer a very obstructed view, which may not be a problem if you tend to ride with your eyes shut most of the time. Getting the front seats is pretty much the luck of the draw, although every once in a while you may be able to step in when the faint of heart opt out of the front row.

Even if you can't or don't ride roller coasters, *Montu* is worth a visit for a close-up view of the crazy people who are riding. Position yourself at the black iron fence that you see as you pass through the massive temple gates that lead to the ride. Here you'll get an exhilarating close-up look of 32 pairs of feet as they come zipping out of the first trench.

If you do ride, don't forget to look for your terrified or giddy face on the instant photos they sell. It's $9 for a photo, $13 for two key chains, and $14 for your mug on a mug.

# King Tut's Tomb

*Rating:*      ★ ★ +
*Type:*        Walk-through attraction
*Time:*        About 10 minutes
*Kelly says:*  A "spirited" guide to an ancient tomb

Here's your chance to walk in the footsteps of Howard Carter, the legendary archaeologist who discovered King Tut's tomb in the 1920s. As you wait in the darkened entrance to the tomb, old newspaper headlines and period newsreels recreate the excitement and wonder of the discovery. Then, the projector jams, the film melts and, as you enter the tomb proper, the spirit of Tut himself takes over as tour guide.

What you see is a re-creation of the tomb as it looked at the time of discovery, the many treasures and priceless artifacts piled in jumbled disarray. As lights illuminate specific artifacts, Tut tells us about his gilded throne, his golden chariot, and his teenage bride. Moving to the burial chamber, we see his solid gold sarcophagus and the golden goddesses who guarded the cabinet containing alabaster urns filled with his internal organs.

For newcomers to Egyptology, this attraction will serve as an intriguing introduction. The marvelously air-conditioned tomb also makes for a pleasant break from the burning Florida sun. Those who are more familiar with Tut, and especially those who saw the resplendent Tut exhibition that toured the world in the eighties, may want to skip this one.

# Eating in Egypt

**Pyramid Joe's** is a snack kiosk with a limited menu of refreshments. Strawberry bars and Shamu bars are about $2. If you need anything more substantial, the Crown Colony House restaurant is just a short stroll away.

# Shopping in Egypt

## The Golden Scarab

Located at the exit to King Tut's Tomb, this shop specializes in Egyptian-themed curios and statuettes of so-so quality that struck me as over-priced. Far more attractive are the costume jewelry and the hand-blown Egyptian glass objects in ancient designs. Just outside is a stand selling attractive paintings on papyrus. It's a family-owned business that claims to have rediscovered the ancient Egyptian formula for making this earliest of all papers. Prices range from $2 for bookmarks to $110 for framed paintings.

## Montu Gift Shop

You walk through this gift shop on your way out of *Montu,* so you may be tempted to stop for something tangible to commemorate your survival. One of the "I Survived *Montu*" t-shirts ($15 to $16) should do the trick nicely. Another nifty souvenir is a mug that features your name in heiroglyphs as well as Roman letters.

# CHAPTER ELEVEN:

# Water Parks

Orlando is the home of the water park as we know it today. George D. Millay, a former SeaWorld official, started it all in 1977 with the opening of Wet 'n Wild. Since then, the concept has been copied, most noticeably by Disney, whose nearby complex has three water-themed parks — Typhoon Lagoon, Blizzard Beach, and River Country — all of them beautifully designed in the Disney tradition. Despite its deep pockets and design talent, Disney hasn't buried the competition. Wet 'n Wild is still the most popular water park and nearby Water Mania has its fans. To the west, the folks at Busch have built Adventure Island, right next to Busch Gardens Tampa. All of these water parks offer plenty of thrills at a competitive price.

An often overlooked selling point of these non-Disney water parks is that they all have numerous hotels and motels just a short drive away. Wet 'n Wild has many hotels within walking distance. This makes them especially easy to visit. If you are staying near one of these parks, there is little need, in my opinion, to trek all the way to Disney for a water park experience.

Like any self-respecting theme park, a water park has rides. But the rides here don't rely on mechanical wonders or ingenious special effects. Indeed they are the essence of simplicity: You walk up and then, with a little help from gravity and a stream of water, you come down. The fun comes from the many variations the designers work on this simple theme.

## Slides

These are the most basic rides. After climbing a high tower, you slide down a flume on a cushion of running water, either on your back, on a rubber mat, in a one- or two-person inner tube, or in a raft that can carry anywhere from two to five people. Virtually every slide will have a series of swooping turns and sudden drops. Some are open to the sky, others are completely enclosed tubes. All slides dump you in a pool at the bottom of the run.

## Speed Slides

Speed slides appeal to the daredevil. They are simple, narrow, flat-bottomed slides; some are pitched at an angle that approaches the vertical, others descend in a series of stair steps. Most culminate in a long, flat stretch that allows you to decelerate; a few end in splash pools. They offer a short, intense experience.

## Wave Pools

These large, fan-shaped swimming pools have a beach-like entrance at the wide end and slope, to a depth of about eight feet at the other. A clever hydraulic system sets waves running from the wall to the beach, mimicking the action of the ocean. Most wave pools have several modes, producing a steady flow of varying wave heights or a sort of random choppiness. Sometimes rented inner tubes are available for use in the wave pool.

## Good Things To Know About . . .

### Dress Codes

Swimsuits are de rigeur at water parks. Most parks prohibit shorts, cut-off jeans, or anything with zippers, buckles, or metal rivets, as these things can scratch and damage the slides. Those with fair skin can wear t-shirts if they wish. Some rides may require that you remove your shirt, which you can usually clutch to your chest as you zoom down. Most people go barefoot, as the parks are designed with your feet's comfort in mind. If you prefer to wear waterproof sandals or other footwear designed for water sports, they are permitted.

### Leaving the Park

All the parks reviewed here let you leave the park and return the same day. Just make sure to have your hand stamped before leaving.

### Lockers

All water parks provide rental lockers and changing areas. Most people wear their swimsuits under their street clothes and disrobe by their locker. At day's end, they take their street clothes to a changing area, towel down, and get dressed, popping their wet suits into a plastic bag. The plastic laundry bag from your hotel room is ideal for this purpose.

## Safety

Water park rides are safe, just as long as you follow the common sense rules posted at the rides and obey the instructions of the ride attendants. You are more likely to run into problems with the sun (see below) or with physical exertion if you are out of shape. You will climb more stairs at a visit to a water park than most people climb in a month. If you're not in peak condition, take it slow; pause from time to time and take in the sights. Remember that after a few hours in the sun, your body will start showing signs of wear and tear.

## The Sun

The Central Florida sun can be brutal. If you don't have a good base tan, a day at a water park can result in a painful sun burn, even on a cloudy day. Use sun block and use it liberally. Most overlooked place to protect: your feet. The sun also saps your body of moisture. Be sure to drink plenty of liquids throughout the day.

## Towels

At Wet 'n Wild and Water Mania you can rent towels for a modest fee. Adventure Island, at my last visit, was not renting towels but said they were considering doing so, "because we get so many requests." It's easy (not to mention cheaper) to bring your own, even if it's one borrowed from your hotel.

# Eating at the Water Parks

Water parks are an active, wet, and sometimes sandy experience — just like a day at the beach. Consequently, dining (if that's the right word) at the parks is a pretty basic experience. The eateries at these parks are pretty modest, both in terms of size and food quality. Most of them offer walk-up window service, paper plates, plastic utensils, and outdoor seating, some of it shaded. The bill of fare seldom ventures out of the hot dog, hamburger, pizza, barbecue, and ice cream categories. The prices are modest as well. You really have to work hard to spend more than $10 per person for a meal. In short, food at the water parks has been designed with kids and teenagers in mind, so I have not covered the restaurants in the reviews which follow. Suffice it to say that you won't go hungry.

However, in my opinion, the best way to eat at the water parks is to bypass the fast-food eateries altogether and bring your own. All of the parks offer picnic areas, some with barbecue pits, some of them quite enchanting. If you are the picnicking type, I don't have to tell you what to do. Others should be aware that Florida supermarkets are cornucopias of picnic supplies. The folks at the deli counter will be more than happy to fix you up with a sumptuous repast. Many supermarket meat departments offer marinated or stuffed meat entrees ready for the grill. You can even pick up an inexpensive cooler while you're there along with ice to keep things cool. All of the parks prohibit alcoholic beverages and glass containers.

Most people simply find a suitable picnic bench when they arrive and stake it out with a beach towel and their cooler, returning at lunch time. If you feel uncomfortable doing this, you can leave your cooler in the car and retrieve it at lunch time. (Don't forget to get your hand stamped!) Another option would be to use one of the rental lockers.

## Shopping at the Water Parks

The casual attitude of these parks toward eating is echoed in the shopping. Don't worry, you'll be able to get that nifty t-shirt or the key chain with the park's logo if you must. But the shops are fairly basic even at their most spacious. The best thing about them is the canny selection of merchandise. If you get to the park and find yourself saying, "Oh no, I forgot my . . ." chances are you'll be able to find it in the shop.

In addition to the usual gamut of souvenirs and t-shirts are swim suits (some of them quite snazzy), sandals, sun block and tanning lotions, film, combs, brushes and other toiletries, towels, sunglasses, trashy novels — in short everything you need for a day at the beach. Forgetful picnickers will also be pleased to know that they can find soft drinks, snack foods, and candy bars at most of the shops.

## Which Park Is Best?

We all have our favorites. My personal favorite of the parks covered in this chapter is Wet 'n Wild. However, if you have never been to a water park, I can virtually guarantee you will have a wonderful time at any of these parks. Then, too, comparing these parks is always something of an apples and oranges exercise. Each park has its unique attractions. Wet 'n Wild has the tow rides in its large lake. Water Mania has its simulated surfing ride. Adventure Island has the Everglides.

If you have a choice of parks, use the descriptions below to help decide which will most appeal to your tastes. Otherwise, pick the most convenient for your touring plan or the one that's offering the tastiest discount at the time of your visit.

# Wet 'n Wild

6200 International Drive (at Republic Avenue)
Orlando, FL 32819
(800) 992-WILD; (407) 351-1800

The original Orlando water park is still the best. Add to that its location in the heart of Orlando's tourist country and its partnership in the Orlando FlexTicket program and Wet 'n Wild is a shoo-in as the most popular water park in the area. In fact, you may be surprised to learn (as I was) that, according to *Amusement Business*, Wet 'n Wild's attendance figures outstrip all of the nearby Disney water parks (1.33 million visitors in 1995) and have since the trade paper started tracking attendance.

The park layout is compact and efficient with little wasted space. The style is sleekly modern and the maintenance is first rate — even though Wet 'n Wild is the oldest water park in the area, it looks as if it opened just last week.

## Getting There

Wet 'n Wild is located in the heart of Orlando's prime tourist area on International Drive at the corner of Republic Avenue. It is less than a half mile from I-4 Exit 30A.

## Opening and Closing Times

Thanks to heated water on its slides and in its pools, Wet 'n Wild is open year-round, although it can get plenty chilly in the winter months. The hours of operation vary from 10:00 a.m. to 5:00 p.m. from late October to late March to 9:00 a.m. to 11:00 p.m. at the height of the summer. Call the information lines above for information on park hours during your visit.

## The Price of Admission

The following prices include tax:

| | |
|---|---|
| Adults: | $27.50 |
| Children (3 to 9): | $22.20 |
| Children under 3 **free.** | |
| Seniors (55+): | $13.76 |
| Annual Pass (all ages): | $84.80 |

Parking is $4.

Wet 'n Wild participates in the Orlando FlexTicket program described in *Chapter One: Introduction & Orientation*. Prices (including tax) are as follows:

   ***Three-Park, Seven-Day Pass*** — Universal, SeaWorld, Wet 'n Wild
   Adults:      $105.95
   Children (3 to 9):   $87.93
   ***Four-Park, Ten-Day Pass*** — adds Busch Gardens Tampa
   Adults:      $137.75
   Children (3 to 9):   $114.43

In addition, the park offers discounts for entry in the afternoon throughout the year. Call for details.

## Rentals

The following are available for rent or loan at the round kiosk located to your right as you enter the park:

Lockers are $4, plus a $3 deposit.

Inner tubes are $4, plus a $1 deposit.

Towels are $2, plus a $1 deposit.

Life vests are **free** but require a $1 deposit.

# Rides and Attractions at Wet 'n Wild

Wet 'n Wild is a compact and tightly packed park that somehow avoids feeling cramped. For the purposes of describing its attractions I have divided the park into three slices. I will start on the left-hand side of the park (as you enter the front gate), then proceed to the center section, and finally describe the slides and such on the right-hand side.

# Kid's Playground

This delightful, multi-level water play area is a sort of Wet 'n Wild in miniature for the toddler set. At the top, there are some twisting water slides that can be negotiated with or without tiny inner tubes. On the other side is a mini-version of the Surf Lagoon wave pool surrounded by a Lilliputian Lazy River. In between are shallow pools with fountains, showers, water cannons, and a variety of other interactive play areas, all watched over by vigilant lifeguards. Rising above the pools is a blimp into which kids can climb; once aboard they can use a battery of water cannons to spray those below. Surrounding the Kid's Playground is a seating area filled with shaded tables and chairs where Mom and Dad can take their ease while junior wears himself out nearby.

# Mach 5

The massive tower that houses Mach 5 and two other rides looks like a giant pasta factory after a nasty explosion, with flumes twisting every which way. At the entrance, you grab a blue toboggan-like mat; the front end curves up and over two hand holds. Then there is a very long climb to the top where you will find three flumes labeled A, B, and C. They all seem to offer pretty much the same experience, but you'll probably want to try all three anyway. I sure did. You ride belly down on your mat and take a few gently corkscrewing turns. But then there is a quick drop followed by a sharp turn followed by another drop and so on until you zip into and across the splashdown pool. Keeping your feet raised will decrease the coefficient of drag and give you a slightly zippier ride.

## Raging Rapids

This inner tube ride shares the tower with Mach 5 but starts about halfway up. Once again, you pick up your bright pink inner tube at the bottom and carry it up. This is a comparatively gentle ride with a series of short slides into shallow pools, in each of which there is an attendant to send you over the next drop-off. The excitement comes when you find yourself going down backwards, unable to see what's ahead. One slide takes you under a delightfully drenching waterfall, and there is a sharp drop to the final splashdown. If you hit the bottom pool just right (or just wrong) you may find yourself unceremoniously dumped from your tube. It's a great way to end a fun ride.

## Fuji Flyer

This newer ride also shares the Mach 5 tower and, while it starts at about the same height as Raging Rapids, it's a much faster, scarier ride. This time there's nothing to drag to the top with you; your vehicle awaits at the launching area. It's a bright green two-, three-, or four-person raft (no single riders), with built-in hand grips. Hang on tight because the turns are sharp and the raft gets thrown high up the curved side walls as you zoom quickly to the bottom. This is a justifiably popular ride with a lot of repeat riders.

## The Surge

The Surge has a tower all to itself. One reason is the size of the rafts, large five-person circular affairs. You sit in the bottom of the raft, facing toward the center, and grab hand holds on the floor. Then the attendant gives the raft a good spin as he sends you on your way down the first fall. The flumes are larger versions of those at Mach 5 and the descent seems somewhat slower. The turns, however, are deceptive. Depending on where you're sitting as the raft enters a turn, you can find yourself sliding high on the curved walls, and when you hit one of the frequents drops backwards you'll feel your tummy do a little flip.

# Fountain Pool

Near the exit to The Surge is a small, shallow play area with waterfalls and fountains for the younger set, a good place for the littler members of your party to wait for you while you ride The Surge.

# The Black Hole

The last slide ride on this side of the park, The Black Hole works an interesting variation on the theme. Here you ride a two-person, Siamese inner tube down completely enclosed black tubes. It's not totally dark, however; a thin line of light at the top gives some illumination and lets you know which way the tube will twist next. Although the darkness adds a special thrill, The Black Hole is not especially scary or fast, especially compared to, say, Mach 5. If you choose the tube to your right as you enter the launch area, you'll get a few extra bumps. A single person can ride alone, occupying the front hole in the inner tube.

# Knee Ski

Rounding things off on the left side of the park is something completely different — a modified water-skiing experience. You kneel on a small surfboard specially designed for this sort of thing; molded rubber impressions make it easy to stay on and a mandatory life-jacket protects you if you fall off. And instead of a speedboat, your tow line hangs from a sort of cable-car arrangement that tows you in a long circle around a lake. The entire course is surrounded by a wooden dock and, should you fall, you are never more than a few strokes from the edge. Ladders like those in swimming pools are provided at regular intervals, making this a very safe ride.

Dunkings are rare, however. Given the special design of the board, the low center of gravity, and the moderate speed of the tow line, most people complete the circuit easily. So don't let a lack of experience with water skiing keep you from enjoying this ride.

# Surf Lagoon

Moving to the center section of the park we find, appropriately enough, the centerpiece of Wet 'n Wild. This is an artificial ocean. Well, actually, it's a fan shaped swimming pool with a hydraulic system that sends out pulsing waves in which you can jump and frolic. You can also bounce around on top of them in an inner tube. At the "beach" end of the pool, you'll find plenty of lounge chairs for soaking up the sun.

# Volleyball Courts

Squeezed between the back of the wave pool and the arcade are two side-by-side volleyball courts. The surface is soft beach sand. Balls can be obtained free of charge at the Courtesy Counter at the front of the park. If there are people waiting, you are asked to limit games to 15 minutes or 11 points, whichever comes first. The courts are occasionally reserved for the use of private groups visiting the park.

## Arcade

A video arcade. 'Nuff said.

## Wild One

Head past the volleyball courts on to the dock and hang a right. Down at the end is Wild One, the only ride at Wet 'n Wild that requires an additional charge over and above the admission to the park. You need to buy a $3 ticket to ride and unfortunately you can't buy it at the ride itself. At press time, tickets were sold at the entrance booth to the Congo River miniature golf course (see below). The booth is located near the base of the tower for Der Stuka and Bomb Bay, a bit of a walk from Wild One itself. Be sure to check the large announcements sign at the entrance to the park, in case they change the location.

The ride itself is worth the hassle of buying tickets and the small extra charge. You are towed in a large inner tube behind a jet ski as it races around the Wet 'n Wild lake. The fun here is in the turns as the two inner tubes being towed accelerate sharply in wide arcs to keep up with the jet ski's tight turns. The ride lasts about two minutes.

## Bubble Up

As you move to the right side of the park, you encounter Bubble Up. This attraction is just for kids. Too bad, because it looks fun. In the center of a pool stands a large blue and white, rubber mountain; at the top is a circular fountain producing a steady downpour. The object is to grab the knotted rope hanging down from the summit and pull yourself to the top up the slippery sides. Once there you can slide back down into the pool.

## Lazy River

Circling Bubble Up and the Bubba Tub is a swift-moving stream, about 10 feet wide and three feet deep. There are a number of entrances and you can enter or exit at any of them. Grab one of the floating tubes or, to assure you'll have one, bring your rented tube and float along with the current; it takes about five minutes to make one complete circuit. It is also possible to swim or float down Lazy River unaided, and many people choose this option.

# Bubba Tub

This is a deceptively simple ride that packs a wallop. Five-person circular rafts zip down a broad, straight slide that features three sharp drops on the speedy trip to the bottom. The ever-helpful attendant gives the raft a spin at takeoff so it's hard to predict whether you'll go down backwards or not. It's a short ride, almost guaranteed to raise a scream or two, and a lot of fun.

# Der Stuka

Behind the Bubba Tub, you will find a high tower housing three speed slides — Der Stuka, Bomb Bay, and Blue Niagara — billed as the tallest and fastest in the world. Like all speed slides, Der Stuka is simplicity itself. You lie down on your back, cross your ankles, fold your arms over your chest, and an attendant nudges you over the edge of a precipitously angled free fall. You'll reach speeds approaching 50 mph before a long trough of shallow water brings you to a halt.

# Bomb Bay

Bomb Bay is right next to Der Stuka. Its slide is precisely the same height, length and angle of its neighbor. So what's the difference? Here you step into a bomb-shaped capsule which is then precisely positioned over the slide. The floor drops away and you are off to a literally flying start down the slide. Thanks to the gravity assisted head start, speeds on this slide are even faster than on Der Stuka, or at least they seem that way.

# Blue Niagara

After Der Stuka and Bomb Bay, Blue Niagara, which shares the same tower with the two speed slides, seems tame by comparison. But looks are deceiving.

Blue Niagara, which takes off from a point slightly below the top of the tower, consists of a pair of blue-green translucent tubes that corkscrew around each other at a seemingly modest angle.

You enter feet first, riding on your back. If you're wearing a t-shirt, you'll be asked to remove it. The reason quickly becomes clear. The speed you pick up as you hurtle down the ride could wrap a t-shirt around your face very quickly. As it is, you may get a nose-full of water as you splash down at the end of this exhilarating twist-a-rama.

# Hydra Fighter

This clever little bit of fun is billed as the "first interactive water ride." Essentially, it is a series of tandem swings in which the riders sit back to back with a high power water cannon between their legs. With a bit of teamwork, riders can use their water cannons to swing themselves higher and higher. Or they can just squirt anyone in range while they bounce around aimlessly. Before hopping on yourself, take some time to observe the proper technique.

There are two towers with three arms, at the end of which dangle the two-seat gondolas; so the three-minute ride can accommodate 12 people at a time.

# Water Mania

6073 West Irlo Bronson Highway
Kissimmee, FL 34747
(800) 527-3092; (407) 396-2626

Water Mania is Kissimmee's answer to Orlando's Wet 'n Wild. It's slightly larger than its Orlando neighbor (36 acres), but it has only six slides (as opposed to nine) and doesn't have the lake and tow rides that Wet 'n Wild boasts. It is, however, the only water park in Florida with a "continuous wave form" allowing surfers a chance to hone their skills on the boogie board.

Water Mania positions itself in the Orlando water park sweepstakes as a park for families; they see Wet 'n Wild as more for teenagers. The park is right next to bustling route 192 but, unless you are right at the front fence, you'll hardly notice. The picnic area at the other end of the park, in fact, is an oasis of cooling shade and you will find it hard to believe you're in the heart of Kissimmee's tourist belt. The rest of the park is very nicely landscaped, too, with more green areas than you're likely to spot at Wet 'n Wild.

## Getting There

Water Mania is easy to find, just a half mile east of I-4 Exit 25A on US 192, between Markers 8 and 9. The park will be on your left. Parking is at the back.

## Opening and Closing Times

Water Mania is open year-round with the water heated during the cooler months. Hours vary throughout the course of the year, from 11:00 a.m. to 5:00 p.m. at the beginning and end of the season to 9:30 a.m. to 8:00 p.m. on summer weekends. Call for the current schedule.

# The Price of Admission

The following prices include tax:

| | |
|---|---|
| Adults: | $26.70 |
| Children (3 to 9): | $19.21 |
| Children under 3 **free.** | |

Annual Pass $53.45 for all ages.

Parking is $4 per vehicle. You can come and go during the day; simply show your parking receipt when you return.

In addition, the park offers discounts for entry in the afternoon throughout the year. Call for details.

## Rentals

The following are available for rent or loan at the Rental Warehouse, located to your left as you enter the park:

Small lockers are $4, plus a $3 deposit, for a total of $7.28 when tax is added. Small lockers are cramped but doable for two people unless you are schlepping a great deal of stuff.

Large lockers are $6, plus a $3 deposit, for a total of $9.42.

Single tubes $5, plus a deposit of $1, for a total of $6.35.

Double tubes $7, plus a deposit of $1, for a total of $8.49.

Basketballs and volleyballs are free, but require a deposit of $5 and an ID.

Life vests are free, but require a deposit of $10 *or* an ID.

Towels $2, plus a $1 deposit, for a total of $3.14.

# Rides and Attractions at Water Mania

As you enter the park and turn right, you will see (on your right) a large wall-mounted map of the park that you can use to get your bearings. All of the rides are to the right as you enter the park. I have described them in the approximate order in which you will encounter them as you walk around the park in a counterclockwise direction.

# Twin Tornadoes

This is the first of four slides sharing the same tower. Grab a blue mat and climb about halfway to the top. There you can choose from two flumes, A and B, for a 320-foot twisting ride to the bottom. The B flume gets off to a quicker start with an early drop but thereafter it's hard to distinguish the two. Both send you through a series of tight, fast turns to the final splashdown. Twin Tornadoes strikes me as being faster and more dizzying than Wet 'n Wild's Mach 5; otherwise, the two rides are very similar.

# The Abyss

Right next to the Twin Tornadoes flumes is the jump-off point for The Abyss. This ride requires a two-person inner tube (no single riders). You find your tube at the bottom and tote it up the stairs.

The Abyss is a bit longer (380 feet) than Twin Tornadoes and the turns are even tighter. On top of that, the entire journey is enclosed in deep blue darkness. This is a really exhilarating ride, much more fun than The Black Hole, which is Wet 'n Wild's equivalent.

# The Screamer

Leave the tubes and mats at the bottom and climb all the way to the top of the tower to reach Water Mania's speed slides. The Screamer offers a sheer drop of 72 feet into a lengthy deceleration area. Lie on your back cross your arms and ankles and scream your way to the bottom.

# The Double Berzerker

Right next to The Screamer, but kicking off from a few feet lower down, are two identical slides that descend in three stages rather than one. To my mind, they offer an added twist to the speed slide experience. There is a millisecond of weightlessness (is it imagined?) as you go over each drop. Some people "cheat" on this one by riding sitting up and holding the sides, which slows their descent.

# Wipe Out

Surf's up!

This is Water Mania's premiere ride and worth the trip if you're a surfer or would like to become one. A "continuous wave form" machine sends a swift cascade of water into and over a shallow trough, which you enter on a body board (a sort of truncated surf board) via a small angled slide from the side. Once into the trough, those who know what they're doing assume a kneeling position on the board and "ride" the artificial wave, weaving, swooping, even spinning completely around, all the while maintaining their position relative to the sides of the fast flowing stream of water. The real hot-doggers can ride forever but the attendant whistles them to give others a chance after they have shown off long enough.

Most people, of course, don't know what they're doing, making for a short but exhilarating ride. They loose their balance, the board, or both as they attempt to mimic the more advanced riders. When this happens you are either dumped out the far side or swept over the rear of the artificial wave into a long spillway that dumps you unceremoniously into Cruisin' Creek. The water here is quite turbulent and fast-moving, so prepare yourself for a dunking. If you don't have a firm grip on the board, it will be ripped from your grasp.

This is a must-do ride, even if you've never surfed. If you have the patience to wait in line and stick at it a bit, you can start to get the hang of it. The only downside to this ride is that the waiting line is right next to the wave, giving everybody a perfect view of your form, such as it is. It's a good test of your ability to maintain your self-esteem in the face of adversity.

# Rip Tide

This short but sweet ride takes advantage of the spillway from Wipe Out to Cruisin' Creek. You can ride on your tush or (more fun) on an inner tube down a short slide, down the spillway, and back into the rough and tumble entrance to the creek. If you decide after watching Wipe Out for a while that you'll wind up in the spillway, you might decide to come straight here.

# Cruisin' Creek

This is a circular stream like Lazy River over at Wet 'n Wild. It circles past Wipe Out and under the speed slides over an 850-foot course. If you want to float through on a tube, you can grab one of the complimentary ones floating by. Be aware, however, that the complimentary tubes go fast. You may find it more convenient to rent one for the day. The complete circuit takes about five minutes.

# The Rain Forest

This kiddie pool varies in depth from nine inches to two feet. There are baby sized slides and a pirate ship in the middle, as well as floats and water cannons to keep the kids busy. There's also plenty of lounging space (much of it shaded) to keep Mom and Dad happy.

# The Anaconda

This 420-foot slide starts 50 feet up and brings you to splashdown through a series of gently swooping curves. The flume is 14 feet wide to accommodate a variety of vehicles. You have your choice of a single inner tube, a double tube, or a four-person circular raft, all of which you must collect at the bottom and carry to the top. As you slide down, watch out for a cascade of water halfway down that can drench those lucky enough to pass beneath it.

# The Banana Peel

This is a sort of speed slide with training wheels. Two people in a

Siamese inner tube swoop down a 176-foot slide in a single sharp drop to a bumpy landing. Screams galore and a good way to "test the waters" before tackling The Screamer.

## Squirt Pool

The second kiddie play area is a slightly less elaborate version of The Rain Forest. Next door is a white sand play area with a large climb-up, clamber-through, slide-down locomotive for little ones.

## Barnacle Bill's Bumper Boats

The newest part of this section of "fun for the very young" is a bumper boat pool. Kids must be between the ages of 2 and 9 and weigh no more than 90 pounds to ride. They can spend 10 to 15 minutes cruisin' around.

## Whitecaps Wave Pool

By now, you have come full circle to the park's front entrance, in front of which is this 720,000 gallon wave pool surrounded by scores and scores of chairs and lounges for the sunbathing set. The wave machine runs in 10-minute cycles, kicking up rocking waves just crying out for you and your inner tube. Peppy rock music plays constantly as you splash about. There is a stage behind the pool and on special occasions entertainment is laid on.

## Big Chipper

Behind the shaded rest area to the left of the pool is a vest-pocket 18-hole miniature golf course. Just pick up a putter and ball at the Rental Warehouse. The course is pretty flat and the holes are quite short — nothing here to rival the mega-mini-golf courses just a short drive away — but it makes a good break from the water park routine.

## Volleyball

Water Mania boasts half a dozen sandy volleyball courts, scattered about the grounds. All are well-maintained, but the ones towards the rear of the park seem to me to be preferable if only because they are not smack in the middle of all the crowds. Balls may be obtained, free of charge, at the Rental Warehouse with a $5 deposit.

## The Woods

This is not an ride but your best bet for fine dining al fresco. It's not a fancy restaurant with a clever name; it is just what the name suggests

— a heavily wooded, gloriously shady three-acre picnicker's retreat at the rear of the park. The management guarantees that, in summer, it will be at least 10 degrees cooler here than on the pool deck. Most people bring their own food. However, Water Mania has a catering staff for groups of all sizes; call (407) 396-2626 and ask for the sales department to make arrangements. The Woods offers spacious picnic tables and plenty of barbecue pits. Volleyball and basketball courts are just a short stroll away. Even if you're not eating here, it's worth a peek.

# Adventure Island

10001 McKinley Drive
Tampa, FL 33674
(813) 987-5093
http://www.4adventure.com

Busch's entry into the Central Florida water park market is a winner, and if your only shot at a water park is during a visit to Tampa, it's the obvious choice. While I give a slight edge to Wet 'n Wild, Adventure Island, with its artful design and pleasing layout, runs a close second. I don't think you'll be disappointed.

## Getting There

Adventure Island is right next to Busch Gardens Tampa, two miles west of I-75 and two miles east of I-275. Drive past the Busch Gardens parking lots and keep a sharp lookout for the entrance on your right. The main gate is not very conspicuously marked and it's easy to over-shoot it if you're not careful.

## Opening and Closing Times

The park is open daily from mid February to early September and then weekends only to late October. It is closed the rest of the year. Park hours are generally 10:00 a.m. to 5:00 p.m. with closing time extending to as late as 8:00 p.m. during the warmer months. Call for the exact schedule, or request a brochure that has a calendar chart with operating hours.

## The Price of Admission

The following prices include tax:

| | |
|---|---|
| Adults: | $23.50 |
| Children (3 to 9): | $21.35 |
| Children under 3 **free**. | |
| Annual Pass (all ages): | $63.85 |

A "Surf 'n Safari" annual pass, good for Adventure Island and adjacent Busch Gardens, is $117.40. A Combination Pass for a one-day visit to each of the parks is $48.35 ($41.60 for kids). These prices include tax.

In addition, the park offers discounts for entry in the afternoon throughout its season. Call for details.

Parking is $3 per vehicle, motorcycles **free**. If you hold any Busch Gardens annual pass, parking is **free**.

### Rentals

Small lockers are $3, plus a $2 deposit.

Large lockers are $5, plus a $2 deposit.

Beach umbrellas are $3, plus a $1 deposit.

The admission price includes free use of inner tubes in designated areas of the park and life vests for all guests.

# Rides and Attractions at Adventure Island

Adventure Island is laid out in a sort of figure eight. I have described its attractions in the approximate order you would encounter them on a counterclockwise circumnavigation of the park.

# Beach Areas

As you move from the entrance plaza and walk down the steps into the park proper, you see a delightful sandy expanse in front of you. It's ideal for sunning and relaxing (although not for picnicking) with its many lounge chairs. Many people prefer to spread a beach towel on the pristine white sands. The entire area is ringed by an ankle-deep stream so as you exit you can rinse the sand off your feet. Similar areas are dotted around the park.

# Runaway Rapids

This series of five water slides is so ingeniously snaked through a simulated rocky canyon that you are hard pressed to spot the flumes as you wend your way to the top. To the left are two child-sized slides on which parents and tots can descend together. To the right and higher up are the three adult flumes. Here, as at other slides in the park, red and green traffic lights regulate the flow of visitors down the slides.

You ride these slides on your back or sitting up; there are no mats or tubes used. As a result, they can get off to a slow start but they pick up speed as you hit the dips and turns about a third of the way down. Of the three adult slides, the one on the left seems the zippiest, while the one in the middle is the tamest. None of them are super scary, however, and most people should thoroughly enjoy the brief ride to the shallow pool below.

# Paradise Lagoon

This is a swimming pool with pizzazz. At one end, two short tubes (one slightly curved) let you slide down about 15 feet before dropping you from a height of about three feet into 10-foot deep water. A short distance away, you can leap from an eight-foot high rocky cliff, just like at the old swimmin' hole. Although the pool seems deep enough (10 feet), head-first dives are not allowed. At the pool's narrowest point, you can test your balance and coordination by trying to cross a series of in-flated stepping stones while holding on to an overhead rope net.

# Endless Surf

Adventure Island's 17,000 square-foot wave pool generates five-foot-high waves for body surfing as well as random choppiness for what is billed as a "storm-splashing environment." This is the smallest of the wave pools at the three parks reviewed here, with a correspondingly small lounging area at the beach end. Waves are set off in 10-minute cycles, with a digital clock at the deep end counting down the minutes 'til the next wave of waves.

# Fabian's Funport

Adventure Island's kiddie pool follows the formula to a "T." The ankle- to calf-deep pool is abuzz with spritzing and spraying water foun-tains, some of which let kids determine when they get doused. A raised play area features mini water slides and water cannons with just enough range to spray unwary adults at the pool's edge. A unique touch here is an adjacent mini version of the wave pool, scaled down to toddler size. A raised seating area lets grown-ups relax while keeping an eagle eye on their busy charges.

# Rambling Bayou

Adventure Island's version of the continuous looping river is de-lightful, with a few unique touches — a dousing waterfall that is marvel-ously refreshing on a steamy day, followed by a gentle misting rain pro-vided by overhead sprinklers.

# Spike Zone

This is by far the nicest volleyball venue at any of the water parks reviewed in this book. In fact, these 11 "groomed" courts have hosted professional tournaments. Most of the play, however, is by amateurs. Even if you're not into competing, the layout makes it easy to watch.

# Water Moccasin

Three translucent green tubes descend from this moderately high tower. The center one drops sharply to the splashdown pool, while the two other tubes curve right and left respectively for a corkscrew descent. This is a body slide (i.e. you ride lying down on your back) that offers the thrill of a speed slide in the middle tube and a rapidly accelerating descent through the two others.

# Key West Rapids

The tallest ride at Adventure Island attracts long lines due in part to slow loading times. Fortunately the wait is made easier to take by the spectacular view of next-door Busch Gardens. In the distance, past the loops and sworls of *Montu*, you can see the downtown Tampa skyline.

Here you pick up a single or two-rider tube at the bottom and climb up for a looping and swooping descent on a broad open-air flume. The ride is punctuated twice by rapids-like terraces where attendants (I call them the Rapids Rangers), regulate the flow of riders. Thanks to the two pauses, this ride never attains the speed of similar rides at the other parks, but it offers an enjoyable descent nonetheless.

# Splash Attack

This is a more elaborate version of *Fabian's Funport* and draws an older crowd — kids from 8 to about 15. The multi-level play area (much like that found in Land of the Dragons at nearby Busch Gardens) is alive with spritzes, sprays, spouts, and hidden geysers that erupt to catch the unwary. A variety of ingenious hand-operated devices lets kids determine to some extent who gets doused and when. A huge bucket at the summit tips over every now and then soaking everyone below.

# Caribbean Corkscrew

This ride is almost identical to Blue Niagara at Wet 'n Wild, although to my untutored eye the angle of descent seems slightly narrower. You probably won't care as you spiral down and around one of these two tubes, twisted around each other like braided hair, picking up speed until you are deposited in the long deceleration pool. Holding your nose is highly recommended for this one.

# Tampa Typhoon

These twin speed slides are the park's highest at 76 feet. The ride down is fast and seems more like falling than sliding. Riding on your back is recommended but some thrill seekers come down sitting up.

# Gulf Scream

Right next to the Tampa Typhoon, these two slides offer a toned down speed slide experience and, by comparison, the ride down is leisurely. If you're uncertain about tackling the Typhoon, test your mettle here.

# Aruba Tuba

Aruba Tuba shares a tower with the Calypso Coaster. As with Key West Rapids, you pick up your single or double tube at the entrance and climb to the top. This ride, as the name implies, descends through a tube which is mostly enclosed with a few brief openings to the sky. Periodically, you are plunged into total darkness adding to the excitement generated by the speed, sudden turns, and sharp dips of the ride. All in all, one of Adventure Island's zippiest experiences. You emerge into a pool with a convenient exit into Ramblin' Bayou, just in case you feel a need for a marked change of pace.

# Calypso Coaster

Unlike its sister ride, Aruba Tuba, Calypso Coaster is an open flume. It is also wider, allowing for more side-to-side motion at the expense of speed. But there's no drop-off in excitement as you are swooped high on the sides of the flume in the sharp turns you encounter on the way down. Of the two, I give Aruba Tuba slightly higher marks in the thrills department, but it's a very close call.

# Everglides

This ride is unique among the parks reviewed in this book. It is a slide — a speed slide in fact — but instead of descending on your back or in a tube you sit upright on a heavy yellow, molded plastic gizmo that's a cross between a boogie board and a sled. As you sit in the ready position, held back from the steep precipice by a metal gate, you might start to have second thoughts. But then the gate drops, the platform tilts, and you are sent zipping down the slide. The best part of the ride is when you hit the water. Instead of slowing down quickly, you go skimming across the surface for about 20 yards before slowing to a stop. If you're doing it right, you'll hardly get wet. The major error to be made on this ride is placing your center of gravity too far back. If you do, you're liable to be flipped over backwards for a very unceremonious dunking.

# CHAPTER TWELVE:

# Dinner Attractions

The concept of the "dinner attraction" is not unique to Orlando, but surely there can be few places on earth where there are so many and such elaborate examples of the genre. A dinner attraction differs from a dinner theater, nightclub, or supper club in a number of important respects. For one thing, the dinner is an integral part of the evening, not a separate component; the meal and the theme of the show are closely intertwined and usually something will be going on as you eat. Beer and wine (along with soft drinks) are poured freely from pitchers throughout the evening. The shows have been created specifically for the attraction; everything from the decorations on the wall to the plates you eat off reflect the theme. By and large, the shows are permanent, whereas a dinner theater or nightclub changes shows on a regular basis.

Dinner attractions are unabashedly "touristy." You'll have plenty of opportunity to buy souvenir mugs, a photo souvenir (often in the form of a key chain), and other tourist paraphernalia. There is plenty of audience participation; in fact, sometimes it's the best part of the show. Many (but by no means all) dinner attractions have an element of competition built in, with various sections of the audience being assigned to cheer on various contestants. And finally there is the matter of scale. With the exception of the murder mystery shows, Orlando's dinner attractions are huge productions put on in large arenas and halls, some of which seat over 1,000 people. You will find exceptions to these rules in individual attractions but, by and large, they describe the dinner attraction experience.

In this chapter, I have reviewed all the non-Disney dinner attractions (and one true dinner theater) in the Orlando area. For pageantry and large-scale spectacle there are American Gladiators, Arabian Nights, Medieval Times, and Pirates Dinner Adventure. For musical entertainment there are Aloha! Polynesian Review, Capone's, King Henry's Feast, the Mark Two Dinner Theater, and Wild Bill's. Finally, for comedy/mystery fans there are Capone's (again), MurderWatch Mystery Theater, and Sleuths. I have tried to give you an good idea of the nature of each experience, bearing in mind that not everyone shares the same taste.

You should also be aware of the combination ticket offered by Splendid China (see *Chapter Seven*) for dinner and their evening theatrical extravaganza, *Mysterious Kingdom of the Orient*. This is yet another excellent choice for dinnertime entertainment.

In my opinion a trip to Orlando is not complete without a visit to one of these attractions. If you have the time (and the stamina), catch two or more shows representing different genres. I don't think you'll regret it.

*Tip:* Discounts to most of the dinner attractions are readily available, either in the form of dollars-off coupons or reduced price tickets obtained through discount ticket brokers (see *Chapter One*).

## Aloha! Polynesian Luau
In the SeaWorld park
(407) 363-2559

| | |
|---|---|
| *Prices:* | Adults $35.95, juniors (8 to 12) $25.95, children (3 to 7) $15.95. Prices do not include tax or tip. |
| *Times:* | Daily at 6:15 p.m. |
| *Directions:* | In the SeaWorld park, in an annex to the Bimini Bay restaurant |

If you liked the *Hawaiian Rhythms* show during your visit to SeaWorld (see *Chapter Four*), you'll *love* this nighttime version. It's larger, longer, splashier and they feed you.

In a low ceilinged room adjacent to the Bimini Bay restaurant, you are transported to the lush South Seas. Family-style tables radiate out from the semicircular stage, and tropical flowers and large green leaves hang down from the rafters.

The show, which begins as the crowd settles in, is hosted by a suave crooner in the manner of Don Ho. It takes us through a leisurely history of Hawaii, as the islands move from the worship of volcano gods to the coming of the missionaries, to the bustling, pulsating Hawaii of today. As with the daytime show, there is time for a tour of the pageantry and dancing of other Pacific islands, Samoa and Tahiti prominent among them.

Backed by a small band, most of the show is given over to the dancers, four bare-chested men and four lissome young women who constantly reappear in new and ever more colorful costumes to evoke a variety of styles and moods. The dancing is a bit more suggestive than the daytime version, which seems to offend no one. In fact, the loudest hoots and cheers come from the women in the audience when the male dancers leer, grind their hips, and grab their buttocks. How times change! Most of the evening is far more genteel than that, however. Indeed, this is a rather stately show compared to other dinner attractions, much like what you'd expect in a fairly upscale Hawaiian nightclub.

The singing by our host is mellifluous and soothing, ranging from Hawaiian language songs (including a "Hawaiian yodel"!) to the more familiar "Stranger in Paradise" from *Kismet*. The dancing is never less than enchanting and in the war chant numbers rather exciting. Volunteers are dragooned from the audience to dance the hula, which is always good for a laugh. The finale is literally incendiary, as a dancer wearing nothing but a brief loincloth twirls a flaming baton and rests the burning ends on his tongue and the soles of his feet.

The food may not be quite as good as the show, but there is plenty of it, all served family style. First comes a selection of fresh fruit and salad. Among the three entrees, the mahi-mahi in piña colada sauce is a standout. The sweet and sour chicken and roast pork loin are okay, as are the mixed steamed vegetables. Dessert is a tasty cheesecake accompanied by coffee. The admission price includes the meal, a complimentary drink (alcoholic or non), and unlimited iced tea. For the drinkers in the crowd, a cash bar is available.

All in all, this show is a real crowd-pleaser, but I can't keep from wondering just how authentic it all is. Am I seeing the real thing or the Hawaiian equivalent of Pat Boone singing a Little Richard song?

## American Gladiators

5515 West Irlo Bronson Highway, Kissimmee 34746
(800) 228-8534

| | |
|---|---|
| *Prices:* | Adults $19.95, children (2 to 12) $14.95. Show only: $9.95 (adults and children). Prices do not include tax or tip. |
| *Times:* | Nightly at 7:30. During July, the first half of August, and Christmas week there are shows at 6:30 and 9:00 nightly. |
| *Directions:* | I-4 to Exit 25A, then east on Route 192 for 2 miles. The theater is on your left, at Mile Marker #10. |

In many ways, American Gladiators is the ideal Orlando dinner show. It has no plot; it requires no knowledge of English; it has a built-in reason to get the audience cheering; there's plenty of action. Best of all, there's a tie-in with a TV show seen around the world, which means that the bulk of the audience arrives primed to have a good time.

For those of you who may have managed to miss the television version, American Gladiators pits somewhat anonymous contenders against much larger, sleeker, pumped-up super-athletes in a series of athletic events that are a sort of cross between the Olympics and *Star Wars*. Here in Orlando, there are two-coed teams, Red and Blue, each cheered on by half of the 1,600-seat arena. The contenders are on the payroll, but that doesn't mean the games are rigged. I'm told there's a bonus pool up for grabs, so each contender is motivated to do his or her best.

Pitted against the contenders are the Gladiators. Someone has done an excellent job of casting these paragons of pumped-up power and pulchritude. The men are all handsome, the women all gorgeous, and they give every impression of being genuinely likeable personalities when they work the crowds during the show. They look like cartoon super-heroes sprung to life, which is appropriate since they have cartoon names like Laser, Ice, and Titan.

The show has been over-produced with a great deal of verve and wit. There are fireworks, smoke effects, laser lights, a series of spectacular set changes, and a corps of dancing cheerleaders, the Energy Force. Through it all, a team of hyper-efficient stagehands scurries about to keep things moving smoothly. The athletic events are wonderfully silly and great fun, ranging from high-tech battles with guns that shoot tennis balls to high-touch encounters reminiscent of Greco-Roman wrestling. Two co-hosts work on whipping the crowd into a frenzy (not too difficult), the Gladiators mix and mingle with the audience, and the competition continues through six events. Finally, the winners are crowned.

While all this is going on, you get dinner — which isn't half bad. There's roast chicken, with stuffing and a tangy Béarnaise sauce, for the grown-ups and mini-pizzas for the kids. Beer, wine, and cola flow freely, and the apple pie dessert is the perfect accompaniment to the show's rousing red, white, and blue finale.

# Arabian Nights

6225 West Irlo Bronson Highway (Route 192), Kissimmee 34746
(800) 553-6116; (407) 239-9223; fax: (407) 239-9622

**Prices:**  Adults $36.95, children (3 to 11) $23.95, seniors (55+) receive a 10% discount.

|  | Prices do not include tax or tip. |
|---|---|
| **Times:** | Daily. Show times vary, so check. Matinees sometimes available. |
| **Directions:** | I-4 to Exit 25, then east on Route 192 for less than a quarter of a mile. The entrance road is on your left, with the theater itself set well back from the highway. |

Orlando residents have voted Arabian Nights their favorite dinner attraction year after year, and it's easy to see why. Beautiful horses, impeccably trained and put through their intricate paces by a young and vivacious team of riders, are hard to beat. The show may appeal most to horse lovers and riders, but the old clichés "something for everyone" and "fun for the whole family" are not out of place here.

Arabian Nights is huge and it has to be to accommodate the 20,000 square foot arena the horses need to strut their stuff. Each side of the arena is flanked by seven steeply banked rows of seats; all told, the house can hold 1,200 spectators and every seat provides a good view of the action.

The "seats" are actually a series of benches, each seating 12 people at a small counter on which you will be served your dinner. The fare is simple but satisfying — soup, a slab of roast beef with vegetables, and dessert. Vegetarian lasagna is also available. Unlimited beer, wine, and soft drinks are included in the price. Carafes of fancier wine can be ordered separately for about $18, as can mixed drinks.

On most nights, seating begins at about 7:00 and the show gets underway shortly after 7:30. We are guests at a feast celebrating the marriage of the Sultan's daughter, Scheherazade, to Prince Khalid. But the real emcee is the sultan's genie, a wisecracking sprite who smacks more of the Borscht Belt than Baghdad. It's just enough of a "plot" on which to string a series of scenes that show off the beauty and skills of Arabian Nights' $4 million stable of horses. More than 50 appear in each show.

While there are plenty of stunts involved in this show, the main emphasis is on the horses themselves, with their trainers and riders playing important supporting roles. Much of the evening involves intricate dressage and group riding in which the training of the horses and the precision of the riders are essential. Horses dance, prance, and strut to the music. They even do a square dance. Snow-white Lipizzans, the imperial breed of Austria, leap in the air and do a tricky double kick. One of the evening's most stunning moments comes when a magnificent, riderless black stallion performs an intricate series of movements in response to the subtle signals of his trainer.

Action fans won't be disappointed here. A circus sequence offers a chance for daring bareback riders to show their stuff and contains a hilarious comedy bit. There are cowboys and Indians with stunts straight out of the movies. Riders race around the arena standing up on the backs of two horses. There is even a Roman chariot race, complete with a spectacular "accident."

All of this is performed by a remarkably small cadre of talented performers who change costumes and wigs with amazing rapidity to reappear over and over in new guises. In the end, however, it is the horses that command our admiration. At show's end, many of the equine performers romp about spiritedly in the arena; many people linger just to watch them play. If you still haven't had enough, private VIP stable tours can be arranged.

## Capone's Dinner & Show

4740 West Highway 192, Kissimmee 34746
(800) 220-8428; (407) 397-2378

| | |
|---|---|
| *Prices:* | Adults $39.03, children (4 to 12) $20.73. Prices include tax and partial gratuity. |
| *Times:* | 8:00 p.m. nightly |
| *Directions:* | On the south side of 192, a short distance east of the junction with SR 535, between Mile Markers 12 and 13. |

Somewhere along the tawdry, commercial strip of Route 192 in Kissimmee you'll find an innocent ice cream parlor. But as with so much in the Orlando area, there's more here than meets the eye. For you see, the ice cream parlor is just a front for a speakeasy, Prohibition style. Yes, we've gone back in time again to 1930s Chicago, where the action owes a lot to Damon Runyon via *Guys and Dolls* and the Chicago accents sound straight outta Brooklyn.

Capone's Dinner & Show is a cheerfully amateurish mishmash of Broadway show, nightclub cabaret, sketch comedy revue, and all-you-can-eat buffet — that's *buffet*, as in Warren or Jimmy.

The fun begins when you arrive and pick up your tickets at the box office. You're instructed to knock three times at the secret door and give a password. Then you get in line outside, where black-vested waiters warm up the crowd with the wisecracking rudeness that is to become the evening's hallmark.

Once the show's ready to begin, each party is led to the secret door, knocks three times, and gives the password — and they don't let you in until you get it right. Once inside, you're in a spacious nightclub with a large stage. The waiters — with names like Babyface — take drink orders and keep up a cheerful patter laced with film noir gangster patois. Much of the seating is in long rows of tables, so you'll have a chance to chat with the folks on either side of you; it's a fun way to get an idea of the wide cross section of types and nationalities drawn to Orlando.

The show, which has a weak plot about star-crossed lovers and even weaker dancing, is like the buffet — not great but hearty and lots of it. As with most amateur productions, some performers are better than others and, with the exception of some minor characters, they give it the old college try. At the show we caught, the biggest laughs came from a child in the audience who joined in an over-long bit about whether a gangster was going to be able to think of an opera to sing.

Still it's hard not to like this bunch, even if they don't always shoot straight.

# King Henry's Feast

8984 International Drive, Orlando 32819
(800) 883-8181; (407) 351-5151

| | |
|---|---|
| ***Prices:*** | Adults $36.95, children (3 to 11) $22.95. Prices do not include tax or tip. |
| ***Times:*** | Vary with the season; twice a night during busier periods |
| ***Directions:*** | From I-4, use Exit 29 (Sand Lake Road). Go east on Sand Lake one block to International Drive. Turn right. King Henry's is a short way down on your right. |

Tired of being a nobody? Then, step through the castle gates of King Henry's Feast and become milord or milady, slip on a paper crown, call for your serving wench, and shout "Wassail" as you loft your goblet on high at a royal feast celebrating the birthday of King Henry VIII.

The theme here is updated English Renaissance. The music is a blend of old and modern standards from the British Isles, and the musicians are splendid. A violin and guitar duo do yeoman service and take the spotlight for a wonderful rendition of the infamously difficult fiddle tune, "The Devil's Hornpipe." A supple soprano offers marvelous interpretations of old favorites like "Greensleeves" and "Danny Boy."

The seating is family style and the service harkens back to olden days when manners weren't quite what they are today. The various courses (or "removes" as they are called in the old English style) arrive to musical accompaniment in buckets to be dished up by the guests. Leek and potato soup is followed by salad and a main course of succulent sliced pork and roast chicken with vegetables and buttery red potatoes. Beer, wine, and soft drinks flow freely, followed by an ice cream cake dessert.

Entertainment is the real main course, however, and with King Henry himself and his able jester as your hosts, you won't be disappointed. In keeping with the theme, the entertainment leans towards the kind of aerialists, jugglers, and prestidigitators that might have amused the original King Henry. In our post-vaudeville age, we would call them specialty acts.

A beautiful girl spins and twirls high above the raised central platform that serves as the stage. Another, truly awesome act combines sword swallowing and fire eating. Adding a high-tech touch to the old standby of swallowing a 30-inch sword to the hilt, this practitioner of the art also downs a 15-inch lighted glass tube; you can see the lights glowing through his throat as they slide down.

Audience participation plays an amusing role in the proceedings, with both adults and little ones called to the stage to dance and generally make fools of themselves. Periodically, King Henry canvasses the audience in search of a suitable queen. They all turn him down though, presumably having read too much English history.

King Henry's Feast is affiliated with Wild Bill's Wild West Dinner Extravaganza (see below). If you think you might be interested in seeing both shows, ask about their attractive discount offer.

# Mark Two Dinner Theater

3376 Edgewater Drive, Orlando 32804
(800) 726-6275; (407) 843-6275; m2orlando@aol.com

| | |
|---|---|
| *Prices:* | $28.50 to $36 (matinees), $33.50 to $41 (evenings). Prices include tax but not tip. Children under 16, $10 off. Seniors (55+) $1 off. |
| *Times:* | Performances Wednesday through Sunday; matinees Wednesday, Thursday, and Saturday. Matinees: Dining 11:15 a.m., Curtain 1:15 p.m. Evenings: Dining 6:00 p.m., Curtain 8:00 p.m. Sundays: Dining 4:30 p.m., Curtain 6:30 p.m. |
| *Directions:* | I-4 to Exit 44, then west on Par Street, which deadends into Edgewater. The theater is at the back of the mall in front of you. |

Of all the dinner attractions in Orlando, this is the only one that is a "dinner theater" in the classic sense of the term — you have dinner and then watch a Broadway musical or play. It is also a fully professional theater, employing only members of Equity, the actors' union.

The Mark Two is somewhat off the beaten tourist track, tucked away in the College Park neighborhood of Orlando's northeast. It is open year-round and presents about eight shows a year, each running about six weeks. Most of the shows are familiar Broadway musicals, although the occasional British sex farce or Broadway comedy creeps into the repertory.

The theater is at the back of a none-too-prosperous looking retail mall. While the space was obviously intended for other uses, it has been cleverly converted to a 320-seat theater with tables arrayed on tiers around three sides of the stage floor; ramps slope gently down to the stage, which doubles as the buffet line for the pre-show dinner. (Thanks to the use of ramps, every part of the theater is wheelchair accessible.) The entire space is gaily decorated in accents of valentine red, with large Broadway posters ringing the walls. The tiny lamps on each table add a touch of elegance and intimacy.

The all-you-can-eat buffet will appeal primarily to the meat and potato lovers in the crowd. Typically, there are a chicken and a fish entree on the steam table, but the line culminates in a carving board where roast beef and ham are sliced to order. The food, while hardly exceptional, is abundant and you are encouraged to return again (and again, if you must). There is an extra charge for desserts and specialty coffee, but the key lime pie is worth it.

Dinner is served for about an hour and a half, with the line closing a half hour before show time to allow for the removal of the food and setting of the stage. Dessert is served during the intermission. There is a bar in the lobby and drinks are also served at your table.

The play I saw was enjoyable and the performances sturdily professional if perhaps not quite up to Broadway standards. The Mark Two compares favorably to other dinner theaters I have visited. If you arrive with modest expectations, you are not likely to be disappointed. In any event, the live performance of first-class musicals offers a refreshing change of pace from Orlando's usual evening fare for tourists. And considering the huge meal, the price is a bargain.

*Tip:* Tables have two or four seats. If you are a couple, request a two-seat table. If none is available, you will be seated at a four-seat table and may be joined by another couple (unless you purchase every seat at the table).

## Medieval Times

4510 Highway 192, Kissimmee 34746
(800) 229-8300; (407) 396-1518; from Orlando: (407) 239-0214

| | |
|---|---|
| *Prices:* | Adults $37.95, children (3 to 12) $22.95. Prices do not include tax and tip. 10% discount for seniors (55+). |
| *Times:* | Daily in evenings. Show times vary from month to month. Call for current schedule. |
| *Directions:* | On the south side of 192, between Mile Markers 14 & 15 |

Back in time to the year 1093 we go as we cross a drawbridge across a murky moat and enter a "climate-controlled castle," guided by wenches and squires with a decidedly nineties look about them. Medieval Times, in Kissimmee, is a cheerfully gaudy evocation of a time most of us know so little about that we'll never know if they've got it right — although I strongly suspect that Ethelred the Unready wouldn't recognize the joint.

Actually, Medieval Times tells us more about American tourist history than it does about eleventh century Europe. The emphasis here is more on showing visitors an old-fashioned good time than on chivalry and historical accuracy. The medieval theme is merely a convenient excuse on which to hang a display of horse-riding skills.

Medieval Times is a bit like a large ride at one of the nearby theme parks. As you enter, you are issued a color-coded cardboard crown and have your picture taken for the inevitable (and optional) souvenir photo of yourself in chivalric garb. The large, banner-bedecked anteroom in which you wait for the show to begin does a brisk trade in tourist items and souvenirs, including some lovely goblets and very authentic looking swords.

A burly bearded knight is your host. His booming voice, with its idiosyncratic mock-formal cadences, will become familiar over the course of the evening as he explains the seating process, exhorts you to be of good cheer, introduces you to the players, and chides you for not having enough fun.

The dinner show itself takes place in a long, cavernous room in which guests are arrayed on six tiers of seats flanking a 70-yard-long, sand-covered arena. Each row consists of a long bench and counter arrangement so that everyone can eat and have a good view of the show. Each side of the arena has three color-coded sections which correspond to the color of the crown you have been given. Where you sit determines which of the color-coded knights you cheer for during the festivities.

The meal and the show unfold simultaneously. The meal is simple — soup, a small, whole roasted chicken, a pork rib, a roasted potato — but the herbed chicken is roasted to perfection and the ribs melt off the bone. In addition, you get to eat with your fingers: It's 1093, remember. I can't explain the psychology, but it helps put you in a suitably barbaric mood to cheer on your knight. (Vegetarians will be accommodated on request.)

The show begins slowly and builds to a climax of clashing battleaxes and broadswords that throw off showers of sparks into the night. Demonstrations of equestrian skills and a demonstration of falconry give way to our six mounted knights, young men who race back and forth on their charging steeds, plucking rings from the air and throwing spears at targets. Successful knights are awarded flowers which, in the spirit of chivalry, they share with young women in the crowd who have caught their eye. These guys are good at what they do and you may find yourself wondering if there's a career in this and, if not, what their day job is.

The show is wrapped in twentieth century showbiz, with swooping computer-guided lighting, pyrotechnics, and a sound system that just might blast you back into the eleventh century. The main event is the joust in which the knights compete against each other, charging full tilt down the lists, shattering their lances on their opponents' shields, and taking theatrical falls to the soft earth beneath. The battle continues on foot with mace and sword and at least as much verisimilitude as you get from professional wrestling.

All of this is narrated with much portent and hokum by your host. The victorious knight chooses a "princess" from the crowd, who is escorted to the throne at the end of the hall for investiture.

This ain't art but it's a lot of fun. And the folks putting on the show obviously know their business. On the night we caught the show, the sold-out house, tepid at first, grew more and more enthusiastic until, by the end of the show, they were pounding the tables and cheering lustily for their champions.

This is a major production with a huge cast and considering the overhead, the cost is moderate. Medieval Times supplements its box office by selling souvenirs (remember that photo that was taken when you came in?) and they find a lot of takers.

## MurderWatch Mystery Theater

1850 Hotel Plaza Boulevard, Lake Buena Vista 32830
(in Baskerville's Restaurant in the Grosvenor Resort Hotel)
(800) 624-4109; (407) 827-6534

| | |
|---|---|
| *Prices:* | Adults $34.95, children (3 to 9) $17.95. |
| | Prices include tax but not gratuity. |
| *Times:* | Saturdays only at 6:00 p.m. and 9:00 p.m. |
| *Directions:* | I-4 to Exit 27, west on SR 535 (Apopka- |

Vineland Road), then left on Hotel Plaza Boulevard (opposite the Crossroads Shopping Center). The Grosvenor Resort is on the right just before Disney's Village Marketplace.

In the elegant confines of Baskerville's Restaurant, decorated with etchings of scenes from the works of Sir Arthur Conan Doyle, a sumptuous buffet is being served. A cabaret act has been laid on for the entertainment of the guests but, as is so typical of the underbelly of show biz, jealousies and intrigue are waiting just off stage. Before long, murder most foul has reared its ugly head and the game is afoot.

This entertaining dinner party cum murder mystery features a female hostess-detective — "My name is Holmes, *Shirley* Holmes" — who clues us in on the rules of the game, keeps track of the body count, and catalogues the growing number of clues.

The action, which cleverly involves the professional and personal jealousies of the lounge-singing act that is the evening's nominal entertainment, takes place throughout the large dining area. While it is always possible to *see* what is happening, it's not always possible to *hear*, given the distance of your seat from the action of the moment. Audience members are encouraged to get up, move around the room, eavesdrop, and ask pointed questions, but good manners seem to keep most people in their seats. Nonetheless, by the time the evening winds to its conclusion, you will know all the dramatis personae, their relationships with each other, and have your own suspicions about who dunnit.

As amateur detectives, the audience's task is to solve the crime by listening to four widely divergent versions of "what really happened" and then voting with their feet by gathering in different corners of the room with the cast member they believe to be telling the truth.

In this show the action is virtually continuous throughout the meal and wraps up shortly after everyone has had dessert — about two and a half hours. The cast is smoothly professional, good singers and expert kibitzers with the audience (some of whom wind up becoming suspects in the final line-up). Virtually every table in the restaurant is visited by one or more cast members during the course of the evening, giving you a chance to size up the suspects at close range. The humor, while sometimes on the racy side, is strictly PG and the kids seem to love it. In fact, there is a special kids' version of the show which is used when the number of children in the audience reaches critical mass. After the show, you can have your picture taken with cast members in a nearby room decorated to re-create Sherlock Holmes' study at 221B Baker Street.

One of the drawbacks of the show is that it only takes place on Saturdays. On the plus side is that it takes place in Baskerville's, a lovely restaurant at the upscale Grosvenor Resort Hotel, which probably explains why the food here is the best of any Orlando area dinner attraction. It's an all-you-can-eat affair, with at least three entree choices in addition to carved-to-order roast beef au jus and Yorkshire pudding. The dessert array is especially bountiful and of the highest quality. Unlimited beer and wine and full bar service are available for an additional fee.

Finding the show can be a bit tricky if you're not familiar with the hotel's layout. Perhaps the simplest way is to avail yourself of the valet parking at the hotel entrance ($4) and have the doorman direct you to the staircase in the lobby that leads upstairs to the restaurant. Dreamland Productions, which puts on MurderWatch Mystery Theater, may have other shows taking place at other venues in the area during your visit.

## Pirates Dinner Adventure

6400 Carrier Drive, Orlando 32819
(800) 866-2469; (407) 248-0590

| | |
|---|---|
| *Prices:* | Adults $39.17, children (3 to 11) $22.42, tax included |
| *Times:* | Nightly except Monday at 7:30 p.m. |
| *Directions:* | From I-4 Exit 29, drive east on Sand Lake Road, one block past International Drive to Canada Drive and turn left. Entrance to parking is on Canada. |

If there were Academy Awards for Orlando dinner shows, Pirates Adventure would have to get the best set award. This cheerful melange of old-time Technicolor pirate movie, Broadway musical, and big top circus unfolds in a fog-shrouded domed arena dominated by a towering and ghostly pirate vessel a-sail on the watery deep (into which not a few of the performers take some spectacular falls).

The fun starts in a large antechamber where a Festival, celebrating the arrival of Princess Anita, welcomes arriving guests with Gypsy fortune tellers, face painting for kids, hors d'oeuvres, and a cash bar. There's even a tiny arcade for die-hard video game freaks. The show proper gets under way with the explosive entrance of a band of oddly friendly pirates who kidnap the princess and a comely gypsy wench. For good measure, they shanghai the entire audience, shepherding us to their outlaw realm.

We know these pirates can't be all bad when they announce that they will serve us a sumptuous meal, just to prepare us for the torture, maiming, and certain death that will follow shortly. The meal, served by the pirate crew, is a hearty one. Yellow rice with sliced beef and spicy chicken barbecued to a turn on pirate swords.

Then we settle back for a celebration of swashbuckling derring do on the high seas. In a plot that defies rational explication, we find ourselves caught up in a story that involves crew rivalries, the love of a young pirate lad for a princess, long dead pirates, trampolines, basketball, and — would you believe? — a circus aerial act. There is also a delightfully droll and smarmy pirate captain, complete with black beard and a wig of cascading ringlets; his wife is a brassy blonde with a voice like cannon fire. They make a highly entertaining couple.

Punctuated by song, the fast and furious action moves left and right, up and down, comes from behind us and soars high over our heads. The "Golden Gypsy" dances high above, the pirates compete in wacky games of skill, and kids from the audience are taken aboard to be sworn in as swashbuckling buccaneers. All too soon it seems, the King's army arrives to save the day. There will probably be times during all this when you don't know what the heck is going on, but you'll probably be enjoying yourself too much to care.

All of this cheerfully chaotic mayhem is carried forward by a game and talented young cast. The male pirate chorus is especially fine. Don't be surprised if your find yourself singing along to the refrain of "Drink, Drink, Drink." And speaking of drinking, beer, wine, and soda flow freely during the meal and afterwards.

For those who care to linger after the show, there is a "Pirates' Buccaneer Bash" where crew members lead the crowd (kids mostly) in silly song and dance routines.

## Sleuths Mystery Show & Dinner

7508 Universal Boulevard (Republic Square), Orlando 32819
(800) 393-1985; (407) 363-1985

| | |
|---|---|
| *Prices:* | Adults $35.95, children (3 to 11) $22.95. |
| *Times:* | Varies. Call for current schedule. |
| *Directions:* | Exit 30 off I-4, south on Kirkman Road and right on Carrier Drive. The theaters are in the Republic Square mall at the corner of Carrier and Universal. |

Nestled incongruously in a suburban-style strip mall just past Wet 'n Wild is one of Orlando's most enjoyable attractions. Sleuths presents a rotating menu of hilarious whodunits served up with relish before, during, and after dinner.

You may find yourself invited to Lord Mansfield's Fox Hunt Banquet or discover yourself one of the alumni attending a reunion at genteel Luray Academy. Whatever the premise, the hilarity is virtually guaranteed, thanks to an ensemble of accomplished (and wonderfully hammy) local actors with a gift for improvisation and the quick comeback. Most of the fun and the biggest laughs come from the unscripted interactions with the "guests" who are made to feel very much part of the action.

As you arrive for dinner, you will meet some of the cast members ushering guests to their tables and passing hors d'oeuvres. After the salad course, the murder mystery proper unfolds on a minuscule set at the front of the house. Don't be surprised if you're called from your seat to participate in some bit of lunacy. At one show I saw, four people found themselves galloping through the house on make-believe horses while the rest of the audience bayed like hounds. But, if you're shy, don't fret; cast members seem to have an uncanny knack for not disturbinbg those who'd rather not be chosen for "stardom."

The humor is broad, with a healthy dose of double entendre. The cast members throw themselves into their parts but occasionally drop out of character in gales of suppressed laughter. And the audience never hesitates to pitch in, gleefully pointing out telltale clues that those on stage have missed. Before long, someone turns up dead and everyone in the cast seems to have a motive.

Now it's your turn to play detective. Each table of eight is asked to name a spokesperson. During dinner, each table mulls over the clues and tries to come up with one telling question that will uncover some yet-unknown fact that will point to the murderer. Each audience member is asked to write down their solution to the crime— who dunnit, with what, and why.

Another bit of good news is that the food, while simple, is quite tasty. The choices are limited — Cornish hen, prime rib (for an extra charge), and vegetarian or meatball lasagna. I'd recommend the Cornish hen. Beer, wine, and soft drinks are poured freely.

After dinner, the cast reappears and submits itself to the interrogation of the audience. This is no dry exercise in forensic logic. Thanks to the expert kibitzing of the cast, the laughter continues virtually nonstop. Ultimately, the wrong-doer is identified and audience members who guessed right win a prize.

One indicator of the success of the Sleuths experience is that, by show's end, the audience feels part of the family. The cast members graciously thank you for your attendance and point out the valuable service you perform in helping a local business survive and thrive without being owned by Disney or ABC. Hear! Hear!

# Wild Bill's Wild West Dinner Extravaganza

5260 US 192, Kissimmee 34746
(800) 883-8181; (407) 351-5151

| | |
|---|---|
| *Prices:* | Adults, $36.95, children (3 to 11) $22.95. Prices do not include tax or tip. |
| *Times:* | Vary with the season. Twice a night during busier periods |
| *Directions:* | I-4 to Exit 25, then east on Route 192 to Liberty Village. The complex is on your right and hard to miss. |

Get ready for a rip-roarin', rootin'-tootin', foot-stompin' good time when you enter the massive portals of Fort Liberty in the far west of Kissimmee to take in Wild Bill's little shindig. The setting is Liberty Village, a shopping center with wooden sidewalks and western-style storefronts. Stroll to the end of the street and you'll find the log facade of the fort where the cavalry is busy keeping the wild west safe for settlers.

The fun begins as soon as you enter the fort's parade grounds as a gaggle of lissome saloon dancers entices guests to try their hand (or their feet) at the old-fashioned two-step and the currently popular country line dance. Or shop in one of the many western-themed shops that ring this courtyard.

Step inside to the Wild West of America's collective subconscious in a cavernous paneled room with rough-hewn timber rafters draped in patriotic bunting. The walls are decorated with portraits of the original Wild Bill Hickock and Abraham Lincoln, along with an impressive collection of western memorabilia. There's even a stuffed bison tucked away in the corner. Seating is family style at tables for 10 and your waiters are "mess sergeants" decked out in the familiar cavalry blue uniforms with yellow stripes.

The food, served military-family style, from large buckets onto pewter dinnerware is copious and a cut above the dinner show standard. Each course arrives accompanied by a rousing song from the cast — from the vegetable barley soup, to the fried chicken and pork ribs with baked potato and corn, to the ice cream cake dessert. Pitchers of beer and soft drinks and carafes of wine keep everybody in a good mood as the nonstop entertainment unfolds on a raised stage in the center of the room.

The show itself is a razzle-dazzle combination of song, dance, vaudeville derring-do, and hilarious audience participation. Wild Bill himself and the alluring Miss Kitty are your hosts, backed up by the attractive and energetic Centennial Dancers. This is some of the best dancing to be seen in Orlando and the cancan number may help unclog some arteries among the older male members of the audience. The music is country-western in flavor with some steel guitar and fancy fiddle accents, and the performances smooth and energetic.

There is a father-son knife throwing and arrow shooting act that's scary and funny in equal measure. Exhibitions of Native American dances by tribal dancers culminate in a swirling presentation of fast-paced dances from three Native American cultures by spectacularly costumed dancers. The evening ends with a display of rope twirling artistry by a man whose skills have earned him a place in the *Guinness Book of World Records*.

But perhaps the highlight is a Romeo-and-Juliet story of ill-fated love between a sheepherder lass and a cattle punching buckaroo acted out by "volunteers" dragooned from the audience. The Wild Bill cast members have discovered the comic possibilities of enlisting those from distant lands with limited (or nonexistent) English skills. The results are truly hilarious and never mean-spirited, proving that laughter is indeed the universal language.

It's all packed into an hour and a half of nonstop fun that continues even after the audience files out of the theater. Out on the parade grounds, mingle with cast members for one last souvenir photo.

If you've seen King Henry's Feast, which is operated by the same company, you will see a remarkable similarity in the formula used here at Wild Bill's. Yet in spite of the similarities, these are two very different shows. If you haven't seen King Henry's Feast and think you might like to, ask about their very attractive discount offer.

The night I caught the show, two families at my table were repeat visitors. It's easy to see why Wild Bill and Miss Kitty enjoy this kind of loyalty.

## Other Ways to Be Amused While Eating

As the dinner attraction scene continues to expand, other Orlando entrepreneurs continue to provide less elaborate but nonetheless diverting ways of making meal times do double duty. All the phone numbers listed below are in the 407 area code.

Two venues in the Mercado Mediterranean Village on International Drive are worth mentioning. **Bergamo's** (352-3805) is an upscale Italian restaurant featuring singing waiters and waitresses. These are people with superbly trained voices who can fill a room without the aid of mikes and amplifiers. The repertoire is concentrated on old favorites from the Italian opera canon, Verdi arias prominent among them, and the more operatic musical composers like Andrew Lloyd Webber. Entertainment begins about 7:00 p.m. Bergamo's is expensive by Orlando standards (most entrees are in the $16 to $30 range) but the food is excellent. A few steps away, you'll find **Blazing Pianos** (363-5104), an infectiously enjoyable boîte where three pianists at red baby grands pound out a repertoire of rock 'n' roll favorites with ample audience participation. The action is continuous from 8:00 p.m. until midnight (or 1 a.m. on Fridays and Saturdays). The menu is limited and there is a $5 cover charge.

Not too far from the Mercado, and also on International Drive, are two other eateries featuring entertainment. **Ran-Getsu of Tokyo** (345-0044) Japanese restaurant offers up demonstrations of Nihon Daiko percussion Thursdays through Saturdays at 7:30 and 9:00 p.m. The performers are outside on a platform over a fish pond but, don't worry, you'll be able to hear their pounding rhythms just fine. Farther down the street, **Friday's Front Row Sports Grill** (363-1414) offers a nonstop menu of professional sports on dozens of televisions hanging from the ceiling. The huge, open, two-decker restaurant is reminiscent of a baseball park, complete with concrete ramps, metal railings, and stadium-style seating. Call ahead to find out what games will be featured on any given night.

# CHAPTER THIRTEEN:

# Another Roadside Attraction

Earlier, I mentioned the great American tradition of the roadside attraction — those weird, often wacky, always wonderful come-ons that beckoned from the highway's edge, all designed to amuse or entertain or mystify, all designed to part the tourist from his money and keep him happy while they did it. Fortunately for us, the tradition is alive and well and flourishing in the fertile tourist environment of Central Florida. Gathered together in this chapter is a cornucopia of museums, monuments, mysteries, and amusements that, in my opinion, partake of this noble legacy of American showmanship and hucksterism. Enjoy!

## Astronaut Hall of Fame

6225 Vectorspace Boulevard, Titusville 32780
(407) 269-6100

*Admission:*  Adults $13.95, children (6 to 12) $9.95.
Prices do not include tax

*Hours:*  Daily 9:00 a.m. to 5:00 p.m. (6:00 p.m. in summer)

*Location:*  On SR 405, just off US 1, on the way to Kennedy Space Center

Just before you reach Kennedy Space Center you pass the home of U.S. Space Camp, a residential camping program for kids. Attached to the camp, and open to the general public, is a beautifully designed museum/simulator attraction called the U.S. Astronaut Hall of Fame. It's no substitute for a visit to the Space Center but, if you have an extra day, it makes for an enjoyable supplement.

The museum portion of the experience pays homage to the seven Mercury and 13 Gemini astronauts who worked in the days when space travel was new enough (and the space capsule small enough!) that we could all keep track of who was who. More recently, 22 Apollo and Skylab astronauts were added to the Hall of Fame. Also on display are actual Mercury, Gemini, and Apollo capsules. There is even a Mercury model into which you can squeeze yourself — or try to. If you ever wondered why the early astronauts referred to the Mercury program as "man in a can," this experience will explain it all.

Probably of more interest to most visitors, especially the younger ones, will be the variety of simulated experiences this attraction has to offer. They range from the mildly interesting to the rather spectacular. At the lower end of the spectrum is **Shuttle to Tomorrow**, a film shown in the cargo bay of the model Space Shuttle. The film offers a brief overview of current and future space activities. Also in this category are **Virtual Zero G**, which superimposes your floating video image on a shot of the Shuttle interior, and **To Explore**, a somewhat ponderous 10-minute salute to the astronauts in the Hall of Fame.

Things get more interesting with the **Shuttle Landing Simulator**, a sort of video game in which you use a joy stick to guide the Shuttle to a safe landing. The best experiences are the true simulators. The **G Force Trainer** puts you in a centrifuge that simulates 4-Gs of acceleration. A video screen in front of you shows what a jet pilot might see while zooming through the wild blue yonder. Amazingly, there is no sensation of spinning, just eight minutes of the rather uncomfortable pull of rapid acceleration. The **Mission To Mars** simulation takes you on a bumpy ride across the surface of the Red Planet. The 16-seat **3D-360** takes you for a flight on what's billed as "the most realistic flight simulator ever created." They're probably right because this one takes you on actual barrel rolls, two in a row at one point, as the entire simulator rotates rapidly through 360 degrees. This 7-minute ride is not for the squeamish but is a lot of fun. The less intrepid will probably have just as much fun watching their friends and family on the video monitors of the interior and seeing the simulator buck, roll, and spin. The video serves a double purpose; if you decide you can't take any more, you can wave your arms and the attendants will stop the ride to let you off.

The **U.S. Space Camp** is a residential program lasting one week. Tuition is $700 to $900 depending on the program, and I am told that many parents drop their kids off while they take a Florida vacation on their own. You can get a look at the Space Camp Training Center as you return from the film aboard the shuttle mock up.

Allow about two to three hours to fully experience this attraction. If you just want to hit the highlights, it will take far less time. A snack bar, the Cosmic Cafe, serves inexpensive breakfasts from 9:00 a.m. to 11:00 a.m. Lunch is served from 11:00 to 4:00 p.m. There is, of course, the obligatory Right Stuff Shop where you can pick up the Honorary Astronaut certificate included in the admission.

# Fantasy of Flight

P.O. Box 1200, Polk City 33868
(941) 984-3500

| | |
|---|---|
| *Admission:* | Adults $18.95, seniors (55+) $16.95, children (5 to 12) $9.95. Annual pass $59.95 |
| *Hours:* | Daily 9:00 a.m. to 5:00 p.m. |
| | Restaurant open 8:00 a.m. to 4:00 p.m. |
| *Location:* | Exit 21 off I-4, about 50 miles west of Orlando |

Vintage aircraft collector Kermit Weeks has turned his avocation into an irresistible roadside attraction that is definitely worth a visit if you are traveling between Orlando and Tampa. Just off I-4, Fantasy of Flight, with its Compass Rose restaurant, makes a great place to take a breakfast or lunch break. You can tour the exhibits and have a meal in less than two hours.

There are three major sections to Fantasy of Flight. The first is a walk-through history of flight, with an accent on its wartime uses. Using dioramas, sound, film, and life-sized figures, it's the equivalent of a Disney World "dark ride" without the vehicles. You start your journey in the hold of an old war transport. Suddenly, the jump master is ushering you out the open door of the plane. The engines roar, the cold wind whistles through your hair, you step out into the pitch blackness of the nighttime sky; all you can see is stars. Soon you find yourself at the dawn of flight, as a nineteenth century hot-air balloon is preparing to take off. Then you are in the trenches of World War I, a tri-plane about to crash into your position. Next you are at a remote World War II airstrip. As a new replacement in the 95th Bomber Group, you receive a briefing and then step aboard a restored B-17 Flying Fortress. As you walk through the aircraft you hear the voices of the crew during a mission over Europe, anti-aircraft fire bursting all around you. Stepping across the bomb bay catwalk, you see the doors open beneath you as 500-pound bombs rain down on the fields and cities below. All of this is beautifully realized. The sets are terrific, the lighting dramatic, the soundtrack ingenious, the planes authentic in every detail. I found the B-17 mission to be truly moving.

The second section is a large, spotless, sun-filled hangar displaying Weeks' collection. There are reproductions of the Wright brothers' 1903 flyer and the Spirit of St. Louis. There are a few oddities, like the 1959 Roadair, an attempt to build a flying automobile. But most of the planes are the real thing. The oil leaks, captured in sand filled pans, tell you that many of these planes still fly. You'll see the actual 1929 Ford Tri-Motor used in the film *Indiana Jones and the Temple of Doom*. There are World War II immortals as well, the B-24J Liberator, a heavy bomber, and the Grumman FM2 Wildcat, the U.S. Navy fighter that shone in the early days of the war. There's even a Nazi short-take off and landing plane, the Storch, that once saved Mussolini's neck by plucking him from a remote mountain resort.

By this time, you may wish you were able to get behind the controls of one of these great machines. Fortunately the price of admission includes unlimited flight time aboard the eight simulators in Fightertown, Fantasy of Flight's third main section. Past a wrecked Zero and a restored Corsair, lies a land of virtual reality fantasy where you can strap yourself into a Wildcat and go gunning for Zeroes over tropical islands in *Battle over the Pacific*. Each sortie lasts seven minutes.

The experience is surprisingly realistic. A flight instructor monitors your progress and provides helpful hints — like don't fly upside down. You can fly against the computer or against another pilot in a different simulator. It's also possible for teams to fly against each other. After your own flight, you'll probably want to go to the control tower to see how things look from the flight instructor's point of view.

When you leave the hangar area, you find yourself back where you began. If you'd like to walk through the dioramas again (and you might), help yourself. Otherwise you can visit the gift shop (leather bomber jackets just $300!) or stop into the Compass Rose restaurant, a beautifully designed re-creation of the kind of Art Deco restaurant you might have found at a fancy airport in the 1930s. The Compass Rose opens at 8:00 a.m. and makes a good choice for breakfast. The regular menu features burgers, sandwiches, and salads (all named after aircraft) in the $5 to $8 range. Daily specials are about $7 and the desserts are scrumptious.

# Flying Tigers Warbird Air Museum

231 North Hoagland Boulevard, Kissimmee 34741
(407) 933-1942

> *Admission:* Adults $8, plus tax, seniors (60+) and children (6 to 12) $6, plus tax. Children 5 and under **free**

*Hours:*       Daily 9:00 a.m. to 6:00 p.m. (to 5:30 p.m.
              on Sundays). Closed Thanksgiving and
              Christmas

*Location:*    About half a mile south of Highway 192

That's not a pile of junk behind that hangar. That's history.

The dusty hangar at the end of a runway at the Kissimmee Airport is home to the very serious (and expensive!) business of restoring battered and crumpled warplanes to flying trim once again. Fortunately, owner Tom Reilly and his wife Sue couldn't bear to keep this labor of love all to themselves, so they opened their treasure trove of restored planes, historical oddities and, well, junk to the general public.

You can wander through the hangar on your own but unless you're a real military aviation expert, it will probably make little sense to you. Far better to wait for one of the regular tours that take you around, through, and under the hodgepodge of planes and into the workshop where once proud fighting machines are being resurrected by dedicated craftsmen.

Tours last about half an hour but the length varies depending on the number of people and the number of questions they ask. Feel free to give your curiosity free rein. The guide will be more than happy to explain the intricacies of what goes on here. The style of these tours is wonderfully lacking in theme park polish and long on easy-going macho anecdotes about mid-air crashes and 400-degree-per-second spin ratios. These guys know what they're talking about and obviously love what they do.

And of course there are the planes. Everything from a wood and canvas 1909 "pusher" (so called because the engine sits behind the pilot and pushes the plane through the air) to an A4 Skyhawk (made famous by the movie *Top Gun*) to a MiG 21 (once part of the Latvian air force and confiscated from an arms dealer). The shop is in the process of renovating not one but two B-17s as well as two Corsairs. Don't worry, they'll still be there when you visit. It takes about five years to restore one of these babies. There are occasional visitors, too, like the nifty little French-built Israeli fighter trainer that lost its canopy on takeoff and was in for repairs when I visited.

There are also some poignant reminders of what war is all about. On exhibit, "as a war memorial," is the fuselage of a World War II P-40 that crashed into a Florida swamp on a training mission. It was discovered 40 years later, the pilot still strapped into his seat. Some 2,000 aviators lost their lives in Florida while training for World War II; in fact, Kissimmee Airport was a U.S. Army Air Corps base, maintained by a crew of German and Italian POWs.

A lot of old-timers pay a visit here and I'm told that it's not unusual for tears to be shed. It's not surprising. After spending an hour or so poking your head into the cramped spaces of these old war machines, you'll have a deeper appreciation of the special breed of men who took them aloft to fight for our freedom. If you're really lucky, you may arrive in time to see a B-25 bomber rumble down the runway and make a flyover escorted by a Mustang fighter, just as in its heyday. If you attend the monthly, week-long vintage aircraft restoration course ($995), you'll be treated to a spin in a B-25 on your graduation.

There is a small, rather helter-skelter, collection of military aviation memorabilia on display in the Museum's office. A few items are for sale, as are aviation books and souvenirs.

*Nearby:* Fighter Pilots USA, Green Meadows Farm, Skate Reflections.

## Fun World at Flea World

4311 North Highway 17-92, Sanford 32771
(407) 330-1792

| | |
|---|---|
| *Admission:* | **Free** admission; rides about $2 |
| *Hours:* | Friday and Saturday 10:00 a.m. to midnight; Sunday 10:00 a.m. to 10:00 p.m. |
| *Location:* | From I-4 Exit 50, drive east on Lake Mary Boulevard, then south on Route 17-92 |

For most kids, a visit to Fun World will be like a history lesson. This is what amusement parks looked like before Disney and others started turning this homey business into a twentieth century art form. Of course, Fun World suffers from the comparison but I find something refreshing about the decidedly down-scale look and feel of the place.

The park is a tightly packed jumble of rides and attractions. In addition to a selection of carnival-style rides there are several go-kart tracks, bumper cars and boats, mini-golf, and the inevitable video arcade. A separate Kid's World is reserved for the preschool crowd. Rides are paid for in tickets purchased at booths for 50 cents each or 25 for $10. There are also a number of combination deals that might prove attractive. The typical ride costs about four tickets. If your kids are old enough to be set loose on their own, this is a good place to park them while you explore Flea World next door (see *Chapter Twenty: Shop 'Til You Drop*).

## Grand Citrus Tower

North US 27, Clermont 34711

| | |
|---|---|
| *Admission:* | (Elevator to top of tower) Adults $3.50, children (3 to 15) $1 |

*Hours:*          Daily 8:00 a.m. - 5:00 p.m.

*Location:*      Half a mile north of SR 50

The Florida Citrus Tower is a monument to a vanished industry. While I was visiting, another tourist told of coming here as a child in the fifties. "All you could see was miles and miles of orange trees," he remembered. "There's not much to see now." A series of devastating freezes over the past two decades has forced Florida's citrus industry farther south. Today, the fields around the Tower are more likely to hold Christmas tree farms or a new subdivision. Most of them are empty.

From the observation platform at the tower's top you can see 35 miles in all directions. You can even make out downtown Orlando and the taller buildings at Disney World in the hazy distance. Later, you'll be able to argue that you were as high as it is possible to get in the state of Florida. (The Bok Tower in Lake Wales also claims this distinction.) The brochures claim the 226-foot tower is 22 stories high but the numbers in the elevator only admit to 15. I am told a new owner plans changes.

*Nearby:* House of Presidents, Lakeridge Winery.

## Haunted Mansion

4710 East Irlo Bronson Highway, Kissimmee 34746

(407) 396-6661

*Admission:*    Adults $9; children (under 12) $6

*Hours:*         Daily 12:00 noon to 12:00 midnight

*Location:*      On Route 192 about 1 mile east of SR535

This is one of several attractions using the haunted house format pioneered in the Orlando area by Terror on Church Street (below). Fortunately, Haunted Mansion is up to the competition. A 20-minute stroll through these darkened corridors snaking through two floors takes you past all the stock monsters, from aliens to vampires. Unlike the other haunted houses, Haunted Mansion doesn't wait for a group of eight to 10 to form before dispatching them to their doom. You can wander through alone if you happen to be the only one there.

The tour empties out into a large gift shop, with a difference. If you really want to see a two-headed calf, here's your chance. It's part of the ghoulish and grisly collection of the attraction's owner. It includes a nineteenth century horse-drawn hearse, a fifteenth century South American mummy, human skeletons, and more modern Halloween memorabilia. None of it is for sale but a lot of other stuff is, including a sizable collection of gory Halloween masks priced from $25 to $40.

*Neraby:* Jungleland, Kartworld, Medieval Times.

# House of Presidents

123 U.S. 27 North, Clermont 34712

(352) 394–2836; in Orlando: (407) 394–2836

| | |
|---|---|
| *Admission:* | Adults $8.95, children (4 to 13) $4.95 |
| *Hours:* | Daily 9:30 a.m. to 6:00 p.m. |
| *Location:* | About half a mile north of SR 50, next to Grand Citrus Tower |

Next to the Grand Citrus Tower (see above) sits a small porticoed house that houses an even smaller porticoed house. This is home to House of Presidents, a meticulous scale model of the White House that has been the life's work of Orlando resident John Zweifel and his wife Jan. Anyone who's into modeling or anyone who's helped a child build a doll house will want to visit this astonishing work.

Parked right outside the entrance is the presidential limo in which Gerald Ford was riding when Lynette "Squeaky" Fromme took a pot shot at him. Inside you'll find life-sized wax museum-style statues of all the U.S. presidents from Washington, right down to Clinton. They will remind you of just how few presidents you can recognize by sight. They also form a fascinating chronicle of the evolution of upscale American male clothing over the past 200 years or so.

In the first of the two display rooms in this small museum is a 16-foot square diorama depicting the building of the White House as it might have looked in 1797, three years before its completion. At a scale of three-quarters of an inch to one foot, we can watch the dozens of stonemasons, carpenters, and laborers ply their trade while George Washington himself surveys their progress. Washington, by the way, was the only president not to live in the White House, even though he supported the project.

The *piece de resistance*, however, awaits in the much larger second room. Here you will find the 60- by 22-foot model of the White House executed in a scale of one inch to the foot. It took Zweifel, his wife, and hundreds of volunteers over 500,000 man-hours to bring the model to its present state and apparently they're not done yet, since the work is billed as an on-going project. The result is impressive indeed. They have re-created not just the main building but the East and West wings as well, all in astonishing detail.

As you enter the room, you see the front of the building. Peek through the windows and you can glimpse details of the rooms inside. But walk the length of the model and around to the back and the entire White House will be revealed to you. In doll house fashion, there is no rear wall and here the full extent of the Zweifels' accomplishment becomes apparent.

The scope of the re-creation and the attention to detail are astounding. You can spot pens and pencils on the tables, cigar burns on the table-tops, even the occasional gravy stain. The clocks tick, the phones ring, the television sets are on and working (picking up Orlando stations oddly enough). Along the wall behind you are dioramas of the Oval Office as decorated by a series of recent presidents.

The gift shop offers a surprising number of books about the White House and the presidents who have lived in it along with an assortment of more traditional souvenirs. A few items (not for sale) are worthy of Ripley's Believe It or Not! You can see, through magnifying lenses, the flags of all nations painted on a grain of wheat or a portrait of the Kennedys, John and Jackie, executed on the head of a pin. What possesses people to do this sort of thing?

Periodically, the White House model is broken down and loaded aboard the 40-foot semi-trailer parked outside and taken on tour. You might want to phone ahead just to make sure the model is home before you take the drive out to Clermont.

*Nearby:* Citrus Tower, Lakeridge Winery.

## Lakeridge Winery Tour

19239 U.S. 27 North, Clermont 34711-9025
(800) 768-WINE; (352) 394-8627

| | |
|---|---|
| *Admission:* | **Free** |
| *Hours:* | Monday to Saturday 10:00 a.m. to 5:00 p.m.; Sunday 11:00 a.m. to 5:00 p.m. |
| *Location:* | About 5 miles north of SR 50 and 3 miles south of Florida Turnpike exit 285 |

Believe it or not, American wine making began in Florida, thanks to some French Huguenot settlers who started fermenting the local wild Muscadine grapes near present-day Jacksonville in about 1562. Viticulture was a thriving Florida industry until the 1930s, when a plant disease wiped out most of the grapes. Now, thanks to Lakeridge, the only winery in Central Florida, wine making is starting to make a comeback in the Sunshine State. Lakeridge currently produces some 50 thousand gallons a year with plans for expansion. Perhaps one day it will fill up all the acres abandoned by the citrus industry. (See Citrus Tower, above.)

The attractive Spanish-style building that sits atop a small hill on a bend in the highway has been cleverly designed to serve as both a working winery and a welcome center for passing tourists. Despite its out-of-the-way location and low-key promotion, Lakeridge attracts a steady stream of visitors. I wonder if it's the lure of free wine?

Tours run constantly, as long as there are people arriving, and take about 45 minutes. After a short video about the history of wine making in Florida and Lakeridge's operations, you are taken on a short tour. It leads you, via an elevated walkway, over the compact wine making area at the back of the building, onto a terrace that overlooks the vineyards and the rolling, lake-dotted countryside of the Central Florida Ridge, and back over the U-shaped wine making room.

After the tour, there is a 15-minute wine tasting that lets you sample five of Lakeridge's 11 wines, including Crescendo, their *methode Champenoise* sparkling wine. You will also get to taste their mulled wine and, if you like, purchase a bag of spices to make your own. And speaking of purchases, all of Lakeridge's wines are available for purchase. In addition to a varying menu of specials, full cases are sold at a 20% discount. Buy three cases and get 25% off. Lakeridge also sells its own line of salad dressings, sauces, mustards, jams, and jellies.

The winery throws special events on a regular basis throughout the year, ranging from "Jazz at the Winery" to vintage auto shows. There is an admission of $1 to $5 for most of these events, although some are free.

*Nearby:* Citrus Tower, House of Presidents.

# Medieval Life Village

4510 West Irlo Bronson Highway, Kissimmee 34746
(800) 229-8300; (407) 396-1518

| | |
|---|---|
| *Admission:* | Adults $8, children (3 to 12) $6. |
| | **Free** with tickets to Medieval Times |
| *Hours:* | Daily, for two hours before each show at Medieval Times |
| *Location:* | At the Medieval Times dinner attraction |

What's a medieval castle without a village to supply all its needs? Fortunately, the owner of Medieval Times, the popular Kissimmee dinner attraction, is a Spanish count. So it wasn't too much of a stretch for him to clear out the attics and barns of his estates, buy up an old village on Majorca, and ship the whole lot to Central Florida.

The result is an intriguing re-creation of a twelfth century village complete with a cadre of artisans and craftspeople plying their trades in much the way their medieval predecessors did. The buildings are modern construction, but the doors, the wooden windows, the furniture, and many of the other objects to be found in the village are all originals, some as many as 800 years old.

The small village is set around a small courtyard and cobblestone street. Much of it is given over to a series of workshops and ateliers, including a basket shop, a carpenter's workshop, a metalsmith, and a blacksmith creating chain mail armor one link at a time. There is also a cloth weaver working at an 800-year-old loom. Many of the items produced here can be purchased in the gift shop.

One of the more intriguing displays is "The Dungeon," a collection of implements of torture. There is an additional $1 fee for this section. A sign outside cautions that the display may not be suitable for small children and it's advice well worth heeding. The implements themselves (all apparently genuine) are ghastly enough but, for those with poor imaginations, mannequins have been added to illustrate the hideous uses to which these bizarre inventions were put. It may not be the best thing to see before sitting down to a meal and a night's entertainment.

Admission to the village is included in the price of your ticket to the dinner attraction, which is one of the best in the Orlando area. Whether the village is worth the admission if you are not seeing the show will depend on your interest in things medieval. There is a fair amount to see here, but much of it is unidentified and unexplicated. The artisans who "inhabit" the village, however, are friendly and knowledgeable and are a great source of information about the strange objects you'll encounter.

**Nearby:** Airboat Rentals U-Drive, Haunted Mansion, Jungleland.

## Movie Rider

8815 International Drive, Orlando 32819,
5390 West Irlo Bronson, Kissimmee 34746
(407) 352-0050

| | |
|---|---|
| *Admission:* | Adults $8.95, children (12 and under) $6.95, plus tax |
| *Hours:* | Daily; hours vary by location |
| *Location:* | In Orlando, near the Mercado; in Kissimmee, near Mile Marker 8 |

Movie Rider is an attempt to cross simulator technology like that used in Universal Studio's *Back To The Future* with the neighborhood movie theater. The result illustrates the pitfalls and potential of the idea.

The price of admission gets you a double feature. The two "movies" are short on length (about five minutes each) and even shorter on plot. Most of the films consist of one extended chase scene (if you can call five minutes "extended"). Like the simulator attractions at the theme parks, these movies use the conceit that you, the audience, are in a vehicle being driven through a virtual world. The movies change from time to time but all of them seem to have titles like *Dino Island, Temple of Doom, Super Speedway,* and *Red Rock Run.*

If you come expecting a movie, you're likely to be disappointed. However, if you approach the experience as another theme park ride, you may find the experience a lot of fun. (The expense is a separate issue.)

The main difference between Movie Rider and other simulator attractions is the movie theater-like setting. The International Drive location uses four-seat modules and has a capacity of 36 people on three levels. The Kissimmee venue uses larger 12-seat modules. Choosing a seat up front helps prevent other modules or guard rails from spoiling the illusion. The two theaters show different films, so you can see all four by visiting both. All seats have seat belts and hand grips; wedging your knees against the sides of the seat is not a bad idea since the ride does get bumpy.

Of course, Movie Rider begs comparison with *Back To The Future*. On balance, the Universal ride does a better job of fooling you with the motion. Movie Rider, on the other hand, offers more jolts for your buck. The film quality is excellent, considering that Movie Rider obviously didn't have the mega-budget enjoyed by the *Back To The Future* crew.

# Mystery Fun House

5767 Major Boulevard, Orlando 32819
(407) 351-3355; (407) 351-3359

|  |  |
|---|---|
| *Admission:* | About $20 for all three main attractions |
| *Hours:* | Monday through Thursday 11:30 a.m. to 9:00 p.m.; Friday and Saturday until 10:00 p.m. Sunday 10:00 a.m. to 9:00 p.m. All closing hours are one hour later during the summer months. |
| *Location:* | Off Kirkman Road across from the main entrance to Universal Studios |

Mystery Fun House is a bit like those computer programs that combine word processing, spreadsheets, and a database. In exchange for the three-for-one convenience and a somewhat lower price you accept a tradeoff in features. At the fun house, the three attractions are a haunted house, a laser tag game, and a miniature golf course; you can find superior examples of all three elsewhere in the area. Although you can purchase admission on an a la carte basis, the best deal is the Wizard's Super Combo which gives you all three for $19.95, a savings of about $5.

The Mystery Fun House ($10.95 separately) that gives the attraction its name is similar to that found at Old Town (see below), a walk-through, pitch dark maze punctuated by "scary" encounters. "Starbase Omega" ($9.95) is a laser tag game played in a large room dotted with obstacles. Electronic targets on the space-themed vest players are issued register "hits" from their opponents' laser guns. Each game lasts about 10 minutes and players receive a score from the electronic scorekeeper. The "Jurassic Era" mini-golf course ($4.95 for 18 holes, second round for $2.50) is decorated with plaster dinosaurs (coincidentally the same ones seen in the movie *Jurassic Park*) as well as alligators and turtles. Otherwise it's a pale reflection of the more elaborate mini-golf courses to be found a short drive away.

The Mystery Fun House also houses a rambling video arcade (only quarters are accepted by these machines), a discount ticket outlet, and a snack bar. During the day, the clientele is decidedly on the young side. At night, the place becomes a hangout for young teenagers.

*Nearby:* Universal Studios Escape, Wet 'n Wild.

# Old Town

5770 West Irlo Bronson Highway, Kissimmee 34746
(407) 396-4888

*Admission:* **Free**. Rides are extra.
*Hours:* Daily 10:00 a.m. to 11:00 p.m.
*Location:* About 1 mile east of I-4

Take away the window dressing and Old Town is just a mall filled with gift, novelty, and souvenir shops. But the window dressing is fun and obviously popular with the crowds that make Old Town a lively place to visit and shop during those sultry Florida evenings.

Behind a small, brightly lit amusement park facing route 192, a vaguely Western Main Street stretches through a few blocks of 70-plus shops, cafes, and entertainments to a tiny carousel on the edge of the Kissimmee night. It's pedestrians only, with frequent benches for weary strollers and a constant swirl of visitors from around the world.

The rides are of the carnival midway variety and are paid for with tickets purchased from a booth at the front ($1 for one, $20 for 22). Most rides cost two tickets, with the gut-churning Mixer and the mini roller coaster requiring three. A tiny go kart track collects a separate fee of $5 for a 13-lap, four-minute ride. Old Town also boasts a haunted house, the **Haunted Grimm House**. Admission is $5 ($3.50 for kids 10 and under) for a five to 10 minute stroll through 20 rooms of shocks and surprises courtesy of special effects and a handful of live actors. If you don't plan on visiting the more elaborate Terror on Church Street in downtown Orlando, and absolutely must visit a haunted house, the Grimm establishment is a satisfactory substitute.

**Lazer Blast**, the resident laser tag game, works an interesting variation on the theme — the floors are inflated and the walls padded, allowing the shoeless players to dive and roll like action movie heroes as they fire off their laser weapons at all and sundry. For the fearless (or foolhardy, depending on your point of view), the **Human Slingshot** beckons. For $20 you can be shot into the sky in a seat powered by a giant rubber band.

Old Town lays on a number of free events to draw crowds and keep them entertained between bouts of shopping. An outdoor stage down one of the side streets offers musical entertainment on an irregular schedule. More predictable is the 8:30 p.m. **Saturday Night Cruise** of vintage automobiles. Over 300 cars show up on the average Saturday and Old Town claims it's the largest such event in the world. Live rock 'n' roll adds the perfect musical accompaniment to the nostalgia.

Also in Old Town is the radio station **AM 1220**, "the vacation station." Between 6:00 p.m. and midnight, you can watch deejays ply their trade behind the station's picture windows.

*Nearby:* Paintball World, SkyCoaster, Water Mania.

# Ripley's Believe It Or Not

8201 International Drive, Orlando 32819
(407) 363-4418

| | |
|---|---|
| *Admission:* | Adults $9.95, children (4 to 12) $6.95, plus tax |
| *Hours:* | Daily 9:00 a.m. to 11:00 p.m. |
| *Location:* | Next to the Mercado |

Is that an ornate Italian villa sliding into a Florida sinkhole on International Drive or is it just Ripley's Believe It Or Not? It's Ripley's, of course, and the zanily tilted building is only one of the illusions on display here (and one of the best).

Robert Ripley was a newspaper cartoonist whose series on oddities and wonders, man-made and natural, made him a very wealthy man and an American institution. The Orlando Ripley's is one of several monuments to Ripley's weird and wonderful collections, gathered in the course of visits to some 198 countries at a time when such globe-trotting travel was still a challenge. On display here are *objets* collected by Ripley himself, along with others gathered after his death, and a series of show-and-tell displays illustrating a variety of optical and spatial illusions.

Where else are you going to see a real two-headed calf? Or the Mona Lisa recreated in small squares of toasted bread? Or a three-quarter scale Rolls Royce crafted from over a million matchsticks? Most displays here are fascinating, although a few are not for the squeamish and some may strike you as tasteless. Best of all are the show-and-tell displays, like an elaborately tilted and skewed room in which the balls on a pool table seem to roll uphill. There is also a giddily disorienting catwalk through a rock-walled tunnel. From the outside, it is obvious that the walls are moving, but step inside, onto the catwalk, and suddenly the walls seem to be rock solid and it is the catwalk that seems to be rotating.

A combination ticket that also admits you to one of the two Movie Rider attractions in the area (see above) is available for $14.95.

*Nearby:* Amazing Animals, King Henry's Feast, Movie Rider.

## Skull Kingdom

5931 American Way, Orlando 32801
(407) 354-1564

| | |
|---|---|
| *Admission:* | Adults and children $9.95 |
| *Hours:* | Daily 11:00 a.m. to 12:00 midnight |
| *Location:* | Across from Wet 'n Wild. |

This is yet another attraction copying the format of Terror on Church Street (below), Orlando's oldest haunted house attraction. Located on International Drive's gaudy tourist strip, Skull Kingdom enjoys a competitive advantage over its older rival simply because of its location. Skull Kingdom also has a spiffy new building, a brooding castle with an enormous skull shaped entrance, and it uses a bit more technology than Terror on Church Street — film, mechanical monsters, voice-over recordings, and the like. Otherwise, the experience is much the same. Connoisseurs of the haunted house genre will probably still give Terror on Church street the edge, but if you'd rather not take the time to go downtown, Skull Kingdom should suit you just fine.

*Nearby:* Wet 'n Wild, Shooting Sports, Universal Studios Escape.

## Spook Hill

| | |
|---|---|
| *Admission:* | **Free** |
| *Hours:* | 24 hours |
| *Location:* | South on 27 to 17A (before Lake Wales), turn left (east) and follow signs |

I don't get it. A sign at this "attraction" (which is just a line drawn on a road in the small town of Lake Wales) talks about a legendary Indian chief, an epic battle with an alligator, and the belief of early pioneers that the place was somehow haunted. Then you are instructed to stop your car on the white line painted in the street, place it in neutral, and then marvel as the car mysteriously rolls backwards *uphill!*

The only problem with this scenario is that it seems to me screamingly obvious that your car is rolling *downhill.* Maybe I'm perceptually challenged. Or maybe the locals are hiding in the bushes laughing at tourists making fools of themselves on Spook Hill. But what the heck, it's a local legend, it's free, and it's on the way to Bok Tower Gardens if you're heading that way. Maybe you can explain it to me.

# Terror on Church Street

135 South Orange Avenue, Orlando 32801
(407) 649-FEAR

| | |
|---|---|
| ***Admission:*** | Adults $12, children 17 and under $10, plus tax; $2 discount for Florida residents |
| ***Hours:*** | Sunday to Thursday 7:00 p.m. to midnight; Friday and Saturday until 1:00 a.m. |
| ***Location:*** | At the intersection of South Orange and Church Street, near Church Street Station |

"Wait inside. If you touch anything, I'll kill you!"

Hospitality like that is a dying art, but it's alive and decomposing at Terror on Church Street, a wonderfully entertaining haunted house in the heart of downtown.

If you associate "haunted houses" with amateurish Halloween fundraisers, think again. Terror on Church Street is run by professionals who are deadly serious about their art. The sets are first rate and the live (or at least undead) actors do it just right.

The show is simplicity itself. You, and a group of eight to 12 other victims, are formed into a sort of conga line, each person holding the shoulders or waist of the person in front. Then you are set loose to negotiate a lugubrious labyrinth that snakes up, down, and around the 22,450 square feet of a former Woolworth's store. Along the way you will meet a grab bag of horror movie stalwarts, from the Wolfman and Hannibal Lechter, to Freddy Kreuger and Norman Bates' mom. All this as you shuffle and scream your way past moldering graveyards, haunted bedrooms, torture chambers, and (my personal favorite) a gruesome morgue filled with cadavers just dying to meet you. It all takes about 15 minutes filled with piercing screams and self-conscious laughter. For those who find that the experience is too intense, the management has thoughtfully provided an escape hatch at the halfway point. If it's any comfort, the ghouls and goblins may scare the dickens out of you, but they never actually touch you.

Shows are continuous, although you may have to wait a bit during slower periods for a quorum to arrive. After the show, browse through the Little Shop of Terrors. Terror on Church Street has one of the neatest logos in Orlando and t-shirts are about $18 with tax.

*Nearby:* Church Street Station, Venturer, Virtual Reality, Lake Eola Swan Boats.

## Trainland
Altamonte Springs Mall, Altamonte Springs 32701
(407) 260-8500

| | |
|---|---|
| *Admission:* | For museum only: Adults $6.95, children, $4.95, seniors $5.95 |
| *Hours:* | Monday to Saturday, 10:00 a.m. to 9:00 p.m.; Sunday 11:00 a.m. to 6:00 p.m. |
| *Location:* | Just east of I-4 Exit 48 |

If you think your old HO-gauge model train set was pretty nifty, you may want to do a reality check at Trainland. This combination train store/museum boasts one of the largest G-gauge layouts in the world — and G-gauge is four times bigger than HO.

The layout occupies 4,000 square feet of space in its own room and required more than 3,000 feet of track and some 4,700 man-hours to complete. The result is impressive, rising high overhead and twisting and turning through mountain passes, quaint small towns, industrial zones, and idyllic farm valleys. There's even a spur line to Santa-Land. The elaborate landscape is microscopically imagined with a wealth of telling details. The rivers have fish in them and the mountain tops are home to Bigfoot and the Abominable Snowman.

Trainland is a labor of love, as you will quickly discover if you fall into conversation with managers Bob Schuster or Tony D'Avino. They take great pride in their creation and obvious joy in sharing its wonders with visitors. Model train devotees will find them a virtually inexhaustible font of modeling tips and train lore.

Trainland spices up the fun of visiting the train layout with a scavenger hunt. Collect the form as you enter and circle your sightings of the Lone Ranger, the Laundry Lady, and other inhabitants of the make-believe world you are touring. The scavenger hunt may appeal most to young children, but grown-ups have a good reason to participate as well. Drop off your completed scavenger hunt form, with your name and address, as you leave and you will be automatically entered in Trainland's monthly prize drawing. The winner receives either $100 in merchandise (shipped anywhere in the world) or a $100 gift certificate. Getting the scavenger hunt 100% correct is not a prerequisite to winning, but Trainland does require that you make a good faith effort and they say they can tell who's done that and who's just circled things at random.

The museum contains a small break area where you can grab a **free** coffee or buy a soda from the vending machine and watch a never-ending showing of movies about trains, ranging from documentaries to Buster Keaton's silent classic *The General*. The area is also used for frequent birthday parties — bring your own refreshments or have Trainland cater.

By the way, if you're so taken with the layout that you just can't live without your very own, Trainland will reproduce it on your premises for a mere $125,000. Trains will run you about $8,000 extra.

*Nearby:* Fun World at Flea World.

# Venturer

55 West Church Street, Orlando 32801
(407) 843-2600

| | |
|---|---|
| *Admission:* | Adults $5, children (12 and under) $4. Discounts for groups of 8 or more |
| *Hours:* | Daily 10:00 a.m. to 2:00 a.m. |
| *Location:* | On the second level of Church Street Market, near Church Street Station |

It looks like a blue mini-van without windows. It is, in fact, a cousin of the full-motion simulators used in *Back To The Future* at Universal and *Wild Arctic* at SeaWorld. Climb into this 12-seater and you enter a virtual realm of thrills, as the image on the screen in front of you is synchronized with the lurching and jarring of your virtual vehicle.

These four-minute adventures are short on narrative and long on thrills — those screams you hear on the speakers are coming from inside the bouncing vehicle. You can ride a scary roller coaster on what looks like an asteroid, go downhill skiing, or try out an Olympic bobsled. If these begin to pale, try *Muggo the Space Pig* ("One of our least favorite," the attendant confided.) Each of the eight adventures offered requires a separate admission fee.

*Nearby:* Church Street Station, Terror on Church Street.

# Virtual Reality

55 West Church Street, Orlando 32801
(407) 849-9968

| | |
|---|---|
| *Admission:* | $5 per game; discounts for multiple games and for groups |
| *Hours:* | Monday to Thursday 11:00 a.m. to 12:00 midnight; Friday and Saturday to 1:00 a.m.; Sunday noon to midnight |
| *Location:* | On the second level of Church Street Market, near Church Street Station |

Just down the corridor from Venturer, you will find another application of virtual reality technology. Rather than rides, Virtual Reality offers interactive games in which you call the shots, or at least try to. Strap on a space cadet helmet that replaces your normal line of vision with a computer-generated virtual world. Rotating your body changes what you see in the helmet. Hand-held controls allow you to "move" forward and backward and fire your weapon.

The virtual worlds you enter here are still rather angular and jerky, a function of limited computer power. That doesn't mean they aren't a lot of fun, although those prone to motion sickness should approach with caution.

*Nearby:* Church Street Station, Terror on Church Street.

# WonderWorks

9067 International Drive, Orlando 32819
(407) 351-8800

| | |
|---|---|
| *Admission:* | Adults $12.95, children (4 to 12) and seniors (55+) $9.95, plus tax |
| *Hours:* | Daily 10:00 a.m. to 11:00 p.m. |
| *Location:* | On International Drive, next to Pointe★Orlando |

If you liked the subsiding building that houses Ripley's Believe It Or Not, wait 'til you see WonderWorks. The fantasy here is that a mysterious neo-classical building has crashed out of the sky, upside down, right in the middle of Orlando's glitziest tourist strip. Inside, the normal laws of physics are likewise turned upside down. The exterior of WonderWorks may be the attraction's best feature; it has become Orlando's most-photographed building.

In fact, WonderWorks is packed with the kind of games and gimmicks (over 75) used by science museums to teach basic principles of physics and it turns them into a highly enjoyable interactive amusement arcade. Here, on two noisy levels, you can experience an earthquake or a hurricane and get some idea of what it would be like to be fried in the electric chair. Then test your reflexes, your pitching arm, the strength of your grip, and your visual acuity. Or maybe you'd just prefer to play around with soap bubbles as big as you are. There's plenty more to keep you amused and entertained for as long as you'd like to hang out.

Plans are afoot to open the "world's largest" laser tag game on a third level. Next door is Pointe★Orlando, an elaborate shopping, dining, and movie venue that is an attraction in its own right.

*Nearby:* Amazing Animals, King Henry's Feast, Movie Rider.

# World of Orchids
2501 Old Lake Wilson Road, Kissimmee 34747
(407) 396-1887

| | |
|---|---|
| *Admission:* | Adults $8.95, children under 16 **free** |
| *Hours:* | Daily 9:30 a.m. to 5:30 p.m. |
| *Location:* | From I-4, take US 192 West and turn left on Old Lake Wilson, about one mile |

If the last orchid you saw was on a corsage at the high school prom, a visit here may remind you why this delicate bloom is the symbol of choice for proms and other events. World of Orchids is actually a working greenhouse that will ship its orchids and other plants nationwide. To educate and enchant the public, they have constructed a vast greenhouse covering some three-quarters of an acre. In the carefully controlled warm, humid air some 5,000 orchids are displayed in a natural jungle setting, complete with waterfalls, babbling streams, and squawking parrots. The total varies seasonally and can double at certain times of the year.

You can wander through this wonderland on your own, but I would highly recommend timing your visit to one of the guided tours. They take place Monday through Friday at 11:00 a.m. and 3:00 p.m. On Saturday and Sunday there is an additional tour at 1:00 p.m.

The tours, which are aimed primarily at the experienced gardener ("Do you grow?" I was asked pointedly), are chatty, straight-from-the-mulch affairs. On the tour I took, our trusty guide kept pointing out how hardy orchids are and how they thrive in seemingly inhospitable places. The unmistakable inference was that the avid gardeners in the group were mollycoddling their houseplants. "Let them live!" he trumpeted. The tours are also a lot of fun for non-gardeners and ignorant questions are tolerated gracefully. One of the most enjoyable aspects of the tour is a running guessing game to figure out what some of these orchids smell like — everything from baked goods to a cobbler's shop. This helps make the point: "Orchids don't smell like flowers."

*Nearby:* Splendid China.

# CHAPTER FOURTEEN:

# Do It!

A vacation in Orlando doesn't mean always being a spectator. There are plenty of activities that will put you right in the middle of the action. In this chapter, I will discuss some of them. Of course, there are more sports oriented activities as well. They are discussed in *Chapter Nineteen: Sports Scores.*

## Airboat Rentals U Drive

4266 West Irlo Bronson Highway, Kissimmee 34746
(407) 847-3672

| | |
|---|---|
| *Cost:* | $5 to $25 an hour |
| *Hours:* | Daily 9:30 a.m. to 5:00 p.m. |
| *Location:* | East of Medieval Times, near Mile Marker 15 |

Just east of the Medieval Times dinner attraction, highway 192 crosses Shingle Creek. You'd never notice if it weren't for this unassuming rental operation. Here in the middle of Kissimmee's major commercial strip is a little fragment of old Florida wetlands that you can explore in that most traditional of vehicles, the airboat.

The four-person airboats, which rent for $25 an hour, are so easy to drive that even a child can pilot them (as long as an adult is present). The driver sits in a slightly elevated seat right in front of the shielded, rear-facing propeller. A lever, operated with the left hand, steers the boat right and left; the throttle is on the right.

You can explore upstream (under the highway bridge) for about a mile and a half before the water gets too shallow for even the low-draught airboats. Or you can head downstream for about two miles toward Lake Kissimmee. Since the airboats do about 8 to 10 miles per hour, this makes a comfortable hour's outing.

There are other boats available. A six-seat rowboat powered by a tiny electric outboard is $20 an hour or $45 for the day; rent a fishin' pole for another $5. Two-person paddle boats are $5 an hour or $15 a day, as are canoes. Alligators are spotted here occasionally; river otters are seen more frequently: A family of six or seven frequents the area near the dock.

*Nearby:* Jungleland, Laser Action, Medieval Times.

## Fighter Pilots USA

4010 Fourth Street, Kissimmee, 34741
(800) 568-6748; http://travelassist.com/tcd/fighter.html

| | |
|---|---|
| **Cost:** | $895 and up |
| **Hours:** | Daily, by appointment, weather permitting, October through May |
| **Location:** | At Kissimmee Municipal Airport |

Earlier in this book I ventured the opinion that *Back To The Future* at Universal Studios is the best thrill ride in Orlando. Allow me to rephrase that: *Back To The Future* is the best thrill ride in Orlando that costs less than $895. If you have the big bucks, you might just want to enlist for an adventure that could quite literally be the thrill of a lifetime.

For a mere $895 (plus tax, of course), Fighter Pilots USA will put you at the controls of a real fighter-trainer and let you shoot it out against another Top Gun wannabe high over the Florida countryside. The planes are SF260 Marchetti's, Italian built prop planes used by the air forces of 23 countries to train fighter pilots. Astonishingly enough, you don't need a pilot's license or any prior aviation experience to fly these things. Of course, you will have a real pilot sitting next to you to get the plane aloft and keep you from doing something real stupid, but otherwise you're on your own in your own personal dogfight, zooming along at 250 miles per hour, pulling G's and shooting laser bullets at a real opponent who's shooting back at you.

And speaking of Top Guns, the guys who run this operation and serve as the co-pilots look like they just stepped out of a movie themselves. They are all military veterans, many of them with impressive combat records, and the right stuff seems to ooze from every pore. A big part of their job seems to be to transfer their calm assurance, gung-ho attitude, and Chuck Yaeger cool to you. They do this through an extensive pre-flight briefing during which you discuss tactics ("Speed is life.") and the airman's code of honor when discussing a mission ("Lie, lie, lie.").

Then it's into the wild blue yonder to practice for a while before they turn you and your opponent loose to fight it out. Laser guns trigger bursts of smoke from your opponent's tail when you score a hit. On a typical mission, you get to fly three to five fights, all of which are captured by three on-board video cameras.

When you land, you review the tapes from both planes and get a critique from the aces. Then you're assigned your very own "tactical call sign" and an Air Combat Certificate. The video is yours to keep as well. If you catch the fighter pilot bug, there are 'post-graduate' courses that can lead to exciting multi-pilot contests like the "Red Baron Flyoff" or bankruptcy, whichever comes first.

*Nearby:* Flying Tigers, Skate Reflections, Green Meadows Farm.

## Fun 'n Wheels

6739 Sand Lake Road, Orlando, 32819
(407) 351-5651
3711 West Vine Street, Kissimmee, 34741
(407) 870-2222

| | |
|---|---|
| *Cost:* | $1 to $5 depending on the ride |
| *Hours:* | Mid-February to Labor Day, 10:00 a.m. to 11:00 p.m., Monday to Thursday; until midnight Friday and Saturday. The rest of the year, the parks open at 4:00 p.m. |
| *Location:* | Orlando location is near the intersection of International Drive and Sand Lake Road; the Kissimmee venue is in the Osceola Square Mall. |

The two Fun 'n Wheels locations offer go karts and other diversions. Payment is by tickets, with each ride costing from one to five tickets. Tickets are $1.25 each. Florida residents can get discounts.

There are three different kart tracks, all of them on the small side. The Fast Track (5 tickets) is a twisting figure eight track with an overpass featuring bare-bones, 22 mph go karts. Drivers must be at least 14 to ride this track. The Slick Track (4 tickets) is a small oval course with specially treated asphalt that lets more experienced riders spin out as they take the curves at either end. The Family Track (3 tickets) offers larger two-seater karts that let parents and kids ride together. A ride on any of the tracks lasts about four minutes or less.

The Orlando location also boasts a 65-foot high ferris wheel (two tickets) and an 18-hole, water-themed miniature golf course (five tickets for adults, four for children).

# Fun Spot

551 Del Verde Way, Orlando, 32819
(407) 363-3867

| | |
|---|---|
| *Cost:* | $2 to $6 depending on the ride |
| *Hours:* | Daily 10:00 a.m. to 11:00 p.m.; to midnight on Friday and Saturday |
| *Location:* | Just off International Drive near the intersection of Kirkman Road and International |

Fun Spot easily wins the Orlando go-kart sweepstakes with its intriguing, twisting, up and down, multi-level tracks. There are four of them here, with the 1,375-foot, three-level QuadHelix the most popular.

There are also bumper cars, bumper boats, and a 101-foot high ferris wheel that offers a panoramic view of the upper end of International Drive and Universal Studios across the Interstate. A 10,000 square foot video arcade (tokens at 25 cents each) and a snack bar round out the offerings at this compact amusement park.

Rides are paid for with tickets that cost $2.50 each, although most people will opt for the 10 tickets for $20 package deal. The QuadHelix requires three tickets for a four-minute, four-lap, one mile ride. The other go-kart tracks cost two tickets each and all the other rides are one ticket each.

*Nearby:* Wet 'n Wild, Universal Studios Escape.

# Kartworld

5370 International Drive, Orlando, 32819
(407) 345-9225
4708 West Irlo Bronson Highway, Kissimmee, 34746
(407) 396-4800

| | |
|---|---|
| *Cost:* | $3.50 per lap |
| *Hours:* | Daily usually 11:30 a.m. or noon to 11:00 p.m. but varies slightly by location |
| *Location:* | Orlando: on the north end of International Drive, near the large outlet malls; Kissimmee: 1 mile east of SR 565 at Mile Marker 13 |

Kartworld has two almost identical locations. The layouts differ slightly and the Kissimmee location has an extra kiddie track. Go karts come in three sizes — a large and a small single-seater and a two-seater. Prices are $3.50 per lap, with 4 laps for $12 and 10 for $20; the price is the same for all sizes of kart. Tickets for the go kart track can also be used on the bumper boats, which are like large truck inner tubes with a motorized center. The almost one-mile track snakes around three loops with a bridge and overpass arrangement allowing the karts to end up where they started. The bumper boat pool and a small kiddie-sized track are nearby.

Inside you'll find a video arcade (tokens 25 cents each, 25 for $5) and a vendor selling discounted tickets to area attractions. Nothing fancy here, just go karts convenient to the Orlando area's two main tourist centers.

*Nearby:* Haunted Mansion, Jungleland, Medieval Times.

## Lake Eola Swan Boats

Lake Eola Park, Orlando
(407) 839-8899

| | |
|---|---|
| *Cost:* | $7 per half hour, including tax |
| *Hours:* | Daily 11:00 a.m. to 5:30 p.m., to 8:30 p.m. in summer |
| *Location:* | Downtown, near the intersection of Rosalind Avenue and Robinson Street |

Right in the heart of Orlando's super-serious business district is this charming bit of whimsy. Lake Eola is Orlando's signature park, with its spectacular floating fountain. Along its shore, at a tiny kiosk called the Lake Eola Cafe, you can rent paddle boats decked out as graceful white swans and take them for a spin on this picture postcard lake. Since Lake Eola is just a short stroll away from Church Street Station and other downtown attractions, a sunset cruise on a swan makes a lovely way to get your evening off to a flying . . . er, floating start.

*Nearby:* Church Street Station, Terror on Church Street, SAK Theatre Comedy Lab.

## Malibu Grand Prix/Malibu Castle

5863 American Way, Orlando, 32819
(407) 351-4132 (Grand Prix); (407) 351-7093 (Castle)

| | |
|---|---|
| *Cost:* | $3 and up per lap |
| *Hours:* | Monday to Thursday noon to 10:00 p.m.; Friday noon to midnight; Saturday 10:00 a.m. to midnight, and Sunday 10:00 a.m. to 10:00 p.m. |
| *Location:* | Off International Drive, near Wet 'n Wild |

This three-quarter-mile go-kart track boasts the only "Virage" cars in the Orlando area. They are 27 horsepower, single-seater, three-quarter scale versions of the race cars run at the Indy 500. Capable of speeds up to 50 mph, they require that drivers have a valid driver's license; drivers under 18 must also have a parent present. For the younger or less adventuresome, Malibu Grand Prix offers 5 horsepower Mini-Virages and two-seater Grand Virages. The former can be driven by anyone over eight years old and four feet six inches tall, while the latter require a driver over 18 with a driver's license.

All cars roar around a flat, elaborately twisting track next to Interstate 4. Prices range from about $3 to $4 per lap depending on the vehicle, with the Mini-Virage the least and the Grand Virage the most expensive. However, a single lap is rarely enough, so you'll probably want to opt for a multi-lap package. For the Virage, the packages range from about $14 for four laps to about $23 for 10; the other vehicles are similarly priced. If you buy an optional Malibu Grand Prix Photo Driver's License for about $3, you get one free lap, so it makes a nice souvenir. The track opens at noon, but the indoor video arcade is open from 10:00 a.m.

Next-door to the Grand Prix is Malibu Castle. It features yet another noisy video arcade, this time with some skee-ball and pool tables thrown in for good measure. The games operate on 25-cent tokens, with no discount for bulk purchases unless you buy 100 for $20. Kids, however, can bring in their report cards and get two free tokens for every A and one token for every B.

Behind the Castle are two 18-hole miniature golf courses. Compared to the more elaborate courses in the area, they are a bit of a letdown. But the cost of playing is moderate (about $4.50 for one round, second round $1) and an entire day of unlimited play can be had for about $5 ($6 on weekends).

Would-be major leaguers can test their skills in one of eight batting cages; five are for baseball, three for softball. A single round of 13 pitches is just $1. A half-hour of practice (300 pitches) goes for $12, an hour (600 pitches) for $18.

*Nearby:* Wet 'n Wild, Shooting Sports, Universal Studios Escape.

# Maze World

4623 West Irlo Bronson, Kissimmee, 34746
(407) 397-7111

|  |  |
|---|---|
| *Cost:* | Adults $6.98, children (12 and under) $5.98; second run $3.00, plus tax |
| *Hours:* | Daily 10:00 a.m. to 10:00 p.m. |
| *Location:* | About 2 miles east of the intersection of SR 535 and Highway 192; half mile west of Medieval Times |

Tired of being run ragged by theme parks? Then come here and run *yourself* ragged in an infuriating rat's maze under the blazing sun. This odd and rather anonymous-looking attraction is hard to spot (which may explain the lack of crowds). Behind that blank white wall is an open-air maze constructed of white and blue plastic panels mounted on poles on a concrete base. Climb to the free observation platform to get the lay of the land and decide if you want to submit yourself to this challenge. Or just stay for a while and amuse yourself watching those who have.

Maze runners, who are working against the clock, are given a card with eight countries marked on it. The object is to negotiate the maze, locate the flags of the countries, stamp your card at each location, and find your way to the end of the maze. The average time to complete the maze is about 20 minutes. I'm told one fellow did it in less than five, but they think he cheated by crawling under the panels.

If you'd like a hint, a map outlining the route through the maze is visible on the rear wall where you buy your tickets. Another tip: Come at night during the warmer months; it gets hot in there during the day.

*Nearby:* Jungleland, Medieval Times.

## Naskart Family Raceway

5071 West Irlo Bronson Highway, Kissimmee, 34746
(407) 397-7699

| | |
|---|---|
| **Cost:** | $5.35 for a 5-minute ride, including tax |
| **Hours:** | Daily 10:00 a.m. to 12:00 midnight |
| **Location:** | Across from Wild Bill's |

There are no video arcades or other distractions at Fastrack. Go karts are the central, and only attraction, at this small venue on the busy 192 tourist strip. There are two fairly short tracks. The "Naskar" track features fully enclosed stock car like karts (the roof closes over your head) and an oval track, while the "Indy" track offers one- and two-seater karts and a winding course. Buy four rides and get the fifth ride free ($21.40).

*Nearby:* Wild Bill's, American Gladiators, Movie Rider.

## Paintball World

2701 Holiday Trail, Kissimmee, 34746
(407) 239-4199
http://www.paintball-world.com

| | |
|---|---|
| **Cost:** | $25, plus tax, plus paintballs |
| **Hours:** | Wednesday, Saturday and Sunday 10:00 a.m. to 4:00 p.m., year round; Wednesday and Friday 6:00 p.m. to 10:00 p.m., June through August; other times by appointment |

*Location:*        Behind Old Town, about 2 miles east of
                   I-4 off Highway 192

Hunkered down behind a sandbag bunker with a remorseless "enemy" bearing down on you or running like mad through the scrub forest from barricade to barricade, with bursts of gunfire going off all around, you begin to understand why the owners of this paintball field call it "the ultimate adrenaline rush."

Paintball World lets you play John Wayne (or Rambo, or Chuck Norris) in refereed "battles" that last about nine or 10 minutes and pit two teams of five to eight players against each other. In "Attack and Defend," one team defends a bunkered jungle compound, while their opponents attempt to storm it and seize the flag. In "Capture the Flag," both teams have flags to defend as they advance against each other down a long narrow field dotted with fences, barrels, and other barriers. The first team to seize its opponents' flag and return it to its territory wins.

The challenge — and the fun— comes in the form of the tiny paintballs that give the game its name. Fired from small $CO_2$ powered guns, they zip along at 190 miles an hour, splatting against whatever they come in contact with, leaving a tell-tale mark. They hit with quite a sting and raise a lovely red welt so when you get hit, you'll know it. Hit players must cry out "I'm hit!" and leave the playing area for the rest of the 20-minute game. The paintballs and their contents are biodegradable, non-toxic, non-staining, and washable, which is a good thing because inexperienced and unwary players are liable to get hit quite a few times.

The games are highly structured with an emphasis on good sportsmanship and safety. Those flaunting the rules will be removed from the game. According to the management, paintball causes fewer participant injuries than bowling and golf. And, lest you think paintball is a game just for young boys and grown men who act that way, a surprising number of women play here — and make formidable opponents.

All games are played outdoors on a 60-acre championship course comprising nine separate game areas. The sections I have played are very imaginatively designed, well executed, and meticulously maintained. Game sessions last about four or five hours and you can play as long as you wish during any session.

Much of the play at Paintball World is by organized local groups with regular playing schedules, so drop-ins must plan their visit with some care. "Open play" takes place on Wednesday and weekends from 10:00 a.m. to 4:00 p.m. As the term suggests, it's open to everyone who shows up. Night games are especially exhilarating and are available to tourists from roughly June to August from 6:00 p.m. to 10:00 p.m. on

Wednesday and Friday. During other times of the year, night games are for private groups. If you have, or can assemble, a group of 10 or more players, you can schedule a private game session, day or night, and get some discounts. Schedules are somewhat loose and there's always a possibility that you'll be able to join a private group, so it's worth dropping by or calling in to check. Kids as young as 10 may play with signed parental approval.

The basic entry cost is $25, plus tax, which includes admission, a paintball gun, and the mandatory face mask. If you bring your own equipment, you pay only a $12.50 admission fee. Paintballs are extra and cost $6 per hundred. Prices decrease with volume, with price breaks coming at 500, 1,250, and 2,500 balls. Most novice players can budget about 200 balls for a four-hour session; more aggressive players will use more. Make sure to dress down for your game and make sure to wear the required footgear, either boots or athletic shoes. The optional jumpsuits ($5 rental), many of them camouflaged, are highly recommended. They provide concealment and some protection from the sting of a direct hit.

*Nearby:* Old Town, Million Dollar Mulligan, SkyCoaster, Water Mania, American Gladiators.

If paintball catches your fancy or if you're a diehard player, you may also want to check out **Orlando Paintball**, a 300,000-square-foot, air-conditioned, indoor playing area housed in a former shipping warehouse well off the tourist track on the northeast side of Orlando. Indoor paintball is a different experience and is best in the cooler months or when it's raining. The floor here is well cushioned with sawdust and the low-tech layout of plywood and rubber tire barricades is imaginative and challenging with many dangerous cul de sacs to trap the unwary. This is sort of the urban guerilla version of paintball and vaguely reminiscent of those post-apocalypse shoot-em-up movies. A game called "Siege Camelot Castle," played in and around a two-story crusader's castle complete with turrets and parapets, is especially challenging.

Orlando Paintball is located at 7215 Rose Avenue, Orlando 32810. The phone is (407) 294-0694. Call for directions.

# Rock on Ice
7500 Canada Avenue, Orlando, 32819
(407) 352-9878

| | |
|---|---|
| *Cost:* | $4.50 to $6, plus $2 skate rental, per session; call to check on specials |
| *Hours:* | Daily 7:30 a.m. to about midnight |

*Location:*        Near Pirates Dinner Adventure

This Olympic-sized ice rink offers skating in sessions of varying lengths, themes, and prices. On a typical day, there will be early morning "freestyle" sessions lasting about an hour, followed by an open skating session from roughly 11:00 a.m. to 4:00 p.m. Then it's back to more short sessions until about 7:30 or 8:00 p.m. when various music-filled sessions, with names like "Cool Zone," hold forth. A complete schedule can be picked up at the box office.

The rink draws a young and sometimes boisterous crowd in the evenings and on the weekends, which may explain the rather strict rules of conduct prominently posted on the premises. Next door is the World Bowling center (see below).

*Nearby:* Fun 'n Wheels, Pirates Dinner Adventure, Wet 'n Wild.

# Shooting Sports
6811-13 Visitors Circle, Orlando, 32819
(407) 363-9000

*Cost:*        Averages $35 to $37
*Hours:*       Daily 10:00 a.m. to 11:00 p.m.
*Location:*    Off International Drive, opposite Wet 'n Wild

Go ahead. Make your day.

For most people, one of the most unusual things to do while in Central Florida is to empty a clip of ammo into a paper silhouette 25 yards down the shooting range, and you can do it here, right in the heart of tourist Orlando.

No experience is necessary to work off your aggression at this indoor shooting range, and kids as young as seven can claim their rights under the second amendment as long as they are accompanied by a parent. (In fact, anyone under 18 must bring a parent.) Just walk in, show your driver's license or passport, plunk down your range fee of $12 ($6 for those under 13), rent eye and ear protectors for $1.25, and select the weapon of your choice and the appropriate ammo. You're also welcome to bring along your own weapon.

According to Shooting Sports, "First-time shooters are welcome. If you are a shooter with no equipment, the average cost per person shooting a .38 or .45 caliber [handgun] is $35.00. The average cost per person shooting a .22 caliber [rifle] is $26.00." Those figures assume you are using just one box of ammo.

*Nearby:* Fun Spot, Wet 'n Wild, Malibu Grand Prix.

# Skate Reflections

1111 Dyer Boulevard, Kissimmee, 34741

(407) 846-8469; (407) 239-8674 (from Orlando)

| | |
|---|---|
| *Cost:* | $3.50 to $5; skate rentals $1 |
| *Hours:* | Vary by day |
| *Location:* | Just south of Highway 192 |

This roller skating rink specializes in good clean fun with strict rules against smoking and gum chewing and a dress code that bans such things as "muscle shirts" and "obscene wording" on clothes. Tuesday night is "Christian Night" with contemporary Christian music piped over the disco loudspeakers. The large rink is impeccably maintained with subdued disco lighting and a small snack bar area with seating. Wednesday and Thursday nights are reserved for private parties.

*Nearby:* Flying Tigers, Fighter Pilots USA, Green Meadows Farm, and the many attractions along US 192.

# SkyCoaster

2850 Florida Plaza Boulevard, Kissimmee 34746

(407) 397-2509

| | |
|---|---|
| *Cost:* | $29.95 |
| *Hours:* | Daily noon to midnight |
| *Location:* | On US 192 near Old Town, between Mile Markers 9 and 10 |

Those odd looking white towers, floodlit at night, that stick up over the Kissimmee tourist strip will lead you to SkyCoaster where for about $30 a head you can swing high and low over an artificial lake. The experience begins when you are strapped into a full body harness, on your stomach, in a prone position. Two friends can ride with you, but there is no discount for multiple riders.

Next you are hoisted 300 feet in the air to the rear tower and . . . well, dropped. But this is not bungy jumping. There is no gut-wrenching jolt at the bottom. Instead you glide suspended on stainless steel airline wire along a path mathematicians call an "arcuate curve" between the other two towers. The result is a remarkably smooth and — once you recover from the initial shock — relaxing ride.

After about three swings of ever decreasing arc, you are lowered to a platform and released. For $15 you can have your adventure immortalized on video.

*Nearby:* Million Dollar Mulligan, Old Town, Paintball World, Water Mania, American Gladiators.

# SkyVenture

6805 Visitors Circle, Orlando, 32819

(407) 903-1150

| | |
|---|---|
| *Cost:* | $35 |
| *Hours:* | Daily noon to midnight |
| *Location:* | Off International Drive, opposite Wet 'n Wild |

The folks that brought you SkyCoaster bring you this free-fall sky-diving adventure housed in an odd looking tower that packs quite a punch. Inside is a powerful fan that creates a 120 mile per hour rush of air in a vertical wind tunnel.

Following a course of instruction in the fine art of skydiving, you are suited up and walked high into the tower where, along with your instructor, you step out into mid air and learn to fly. The upwards rush of air keeps you aloft as your instructor takes your hand and shows you how to negotiate the updraft. Around you, a 360 degree virtual reality display heightens the sensation of free falling thousands of feet above the ground below. The entire experience takes about an hour, although the free fall portion lasts only about two minutes, which they say is about as much as first-timers can take.

*Nearby:* Fun Spot, Haunted Mansion, Shooting Sports, Wet 'n Wild.

# World Bowling Center

7540 Canada Avenue, Orlando, 32819

(407) 352-2695

| | |
|---|---|
| *Cost:* | $1.25 to $3 per game |
| *Hours:* | Daily 9:00 a.m. to 11:00 p.m., until 11:30 p.m. or midnight on weekends; Sunday until 10:00 p.m. |
| *Location:* | Near Pirates Dinner Adventure |

Here is a moderately-priced, basic 32-lane bowling alley right in the heart of the I-Drive district. Prices vary according to time of day, with day games running $2.25 ($1.75 for children and seniors) and evening games (after 5:00 p.m.) $3.25. The best deal is on Sunday morning when games are just $1.25. Shoe rental is $1.75. The Rock on Ice ice skating rink (see above) is next door.

*Nearby:* Wet 'n Wild, Pirates Dinner Adventure, Fun 'n Wheels.

# CHAPTER FIFTEEN:

# A Who's Who of Zoos

A nimals have always held a fascination for us humans, especially the younger members of our species. So it's hardly surprising that in a tourist-saturated area like Orlando, you'd find a number of attractions built around this ancient allure. The attractions I describe in this chapter run the gamut from a true zoological park, to roadside attractions, to Gatorland clones, to conservation and preservation efforts. Other animal-themed attractions such as SeaWorld, Busch Gardens, and Gatorland are described in separate chapters.

## Amazing Animals
8990 International Drive, Orlando 32819
(407) 354-1400

| | |
|---|---|
| *Admission:* | Adults $7.95, children (3 to 12) $4.95 |
| | Children under 3 are **free** |
| *Hours:* | Daily 10:00 a.m. to 7:00 p.m. |
| *Location:* | Next door to Race Rock, just down the |
| | street from the Mercado |

Right in the middle of Orlando's premiere tourist strip you'll find this modest zoo-like attraction. The collection of animals may not be the best in the area, but it's hard to beat the convenience of the location. The animals are a sideline for Air Orlando, whose helicopter tours take off from the helipad just outside (see *Chapter Eighteen*).

Inside you'll find a catch-as-catch-can collection of "exotic" animals including camels, reindeer, a Florida panther, and a number of reptiles including a beautiful Emerald tree boa and a Burmese python sitting, rather ominously, in a kiddie wading pool. At the back of the circular building is a "petting farm" with bunnies, goats, a llama, a number of dwarf horses, and a huge Clydesdale.

In the center of the single room are a number of old circus calliopes and wagons. Out back is a pool filled with young gators and a number of parrot cages.

*Nearby:* King Henry's Feast, Movie Rider, Ripley's Believe It Or Not.

# Back to Nature Wildlife Refuge
18515 East Colonial Drive, Orlando 32820
(407) 568-5138

> *Admission:* **Free.** Donations requested
> *Hours:* Daily 9:00 a.m. to 4:00 p.m.
> *Location:* East of central Orlando

Located incongruously next to an auto repair shop, with which it shares an office, this non-profit organization is dedicated to the four R's — Rescue, Raise, Rehabilitate, and Release. In the average year, it plays host to some 1,500 critters, but unlike Birds of Prey (see below), Back To Nature Wildlife Refuge takes on all comers, except common household pets like dogs and cats. The ultimate goal is to release their charges back into the wild, a goal which often proves illusive. What you will see when you visit are the animals that, for a variety of reasons, will be living out their lives in captivity. Many of the cages are marked with the nicknames and histories of their occupants.

The tales told about these animals are a litany of abuse, abandonment, stupidity, and the random cruelty of nature and (more often) mankind. There's a fox presumably abandoned by its owner, but not before he lopped off its tail for a souvenir. There are "throw away" pets sold by unscrupulous dealers and abandoned when their owners discovered that porcupines, raccoons, and wild African cats don't make the charming pets they'd imagined. Then there are the birds and beasts damaged by pesticides or wounded by bullets. There are also many animals orphaned in the wild or born with disabilities that would have quickly killed them had they not been rescued first. Among the more impressive residents here are cougars, bobcats, bald eagles, a hybrid wolf, and a serval. A small nursery looks after the littlest guests, including baby raccoons and fledgling birds.

Back To Nature is a labor of love of David and Carmen Shaw and a dedicated group of volunteers. Donations are requested subtly via donation boxes scattered throughout the property. Many of the animal enclosures bear the names of donors who made them possible. It is unlikely that you will leave without becoming a donor yourself.

*Nearby:* Fort Christmas Historical Park, Jungle Adventures.

# Birds of Prey Center

1101 Audubon Way, Maitland 32751
(407) 644-0190

*Admission:*    Adults $5; children (6 to 12) $4; children under 6 are **free**

*Hours:*    Tuesday to Sunday 10:00 a.m. to 4:00 p.m.

*Location:*    East of I-4, between exits 46 and 47

One of the most enchanting animal encounters to be found in the Orlando area is also one of the cheapest. The Center for Birds of Prey is an endeavor of the Florida Audubon Society. It takes in wounded and orphaned raptors from all over Florida, tends to their wounds, and nurses them back to health with the ultimate goal of releasing them back into the wild. They take in some 600 birds a year and succeed in returning about 40 percent to the wild.

You won't be able to see the rehabilitation process; these birds are shielded from public view lest they become habituated to humans, thus lessening their odds for survival back in the wild. What you will see at the Center are birds whose injuries are so severe that they cannot be released to the wild. Here they lead the good life (at least they eat well and regularly) and perform a useful role in educating Florida school children and others about the wonders of wildlife and the need to protect it.

There are about 32 different species of raptors housed here. They range from tiny screech owls to crusty old bald eagles. On a recent visit, a large cage held nine of these magnificent birds, from immature specimens lacking the distinctive white hood to battered old survivors. There are also a fair number of ospreys, red-tailed hawks, kites, and others. There are even three species of vultures.

A visit here can be an educational as well as an uplifting experience. While here, I learned for the first time of the 1916 Migratory Bird Treaty Act, which makes it illegal to own or transport even a single feather from these birds. The Center collects every feather from molting birds, as well as feathers from specimens that don't survive. They are turned over to the government which in turn distributes them to Native American tribes for whom the feathers of eagles and other species have ritual significance.

A boardwalk leads down to a charming gazebo set in the wetlands along the shore of Lake Sybelia. Guided tours are available by reservation for groups of 10 or more and it's a good idea to call ahead to find out when volunteers will be on hand to answer questions. Finding Birds of Prey is a little tricky but it's worth it. Call ahead for detailed directions.

# Central Florida Zoological Park

3755 NW Highway 17-92, Sanford 32747
(407) 323-4450; fax (407) 323-2341

| | |
|---|---|
| *Admission:* | Adults $7, children (3 to 12) $3, seniors (60+) $4 ($2 on Tuesdays); **free** parking |
| *Hours:* | Daily 9:00 a.m. to 5:00 p.m. Closed Thanksgiving and Christmas |
| *Location:* | From I-4 Exit 52 drive south on US 17-92 and follow signs, less than a mile. |

The Central Florida Zoo can't hold a candle to its bigger cousins in the Bronx and San Diego, but it does wonders with what it has. The collection is small, with an understandable strength in local species, many of which will be found in the excellent herpetarium (snake house). Among the more "exotic" species are two elephants, a hippo, a clouded leopard, and cheetahs in a lovely habitat viewed through one-way glass.

What makes this zoo special is its design and layout. A series of lovely boardwalks carries you between exhibits that are graciously arrayed under a sheltering canopy of oaks. Especially nice is the Florida Nature Walk that snakes through a wooded and swampy area of the zoo grounds. Signs along the way do an excellent job of explicating Central Florida fauna and explaining the way in which minor differences in altitude produce major differences in plant life. There are many similar "nature walks" in the Orlando area; this one does the best job of making a stroll both an aesthetic and educational experience.

On weekends and holidays there are animal demonstrations involving the elephants and alligator snapping turtles. Volunteer "docents" also roam the park with one of some 40 species used for educational purposes. You may get a chance to hold a boa or pet a Madagascar tenerec. The zoo has a bare-bones snack bar, serving inexpensive hot dog and burger fare, with a lovely outdoor seating area nearby. Across from the entrance there are sheltered picnic tables and barbecue pits.

# Green Meadows Farm

1368 South Poinciana Boulevard, Kissimmee 34741
(407) 846-0770

| | |
|---|---|
| *Admission:* | $15, plus tax, for all those 3 years old and up; Florida residents $13; annual pass $30 |
| *Hours:* | Daily 9:30 a.m. to 4:00 p.m. |

*Location:*      Six miles south of Highway 192

This is where kids meet kids — and piglets, and ducklings, and chicks. If you have little ones between the ages of three and seven, this cleverly conceived and well-run petting farm is sure to be a favorite memory of their Orlando visit. Better yet, let their grandparents take them! Green Meadows is an ideal place for this sort of trans-generational bonding experience. Meanwhile, you and your spouse can take the in-room jacuzzi out for a spin.

The ethos of Green Meadows Farm is pretty well summed up by the quote from Luther Burbank that greets you on your arrival:"Every child should have mudpies, frogs, grasshoppers, waterbugs, tadpoles, mud turtles, elderberries, wild strawberries, acorns, chestnuts, trees to climb, animals to pet, hay fields, pine cones, rocks to roll, lizards, huckleberries, and hornets. Any child who has been deprived of these has been deprived of the best part of their education."

Green Meadows Farm is spread out over 40 acres under the dappled shade of moss-draped Southern oaks. The farm is experienced via a guided tour that lasts about two hours. If the park is busy, you may be asked to wait until the next tour begins but on slower days you'll be escorted to the tour in progress. ("When you get back to the chickens, you'll know the tour's over.") If you like, you can simply stay with the tour and repeat it over and over.

The tour includes a short ride on a miniature railway and a bumpy tractor-powered hayride, but the real stars of the show are the animals. This is not a working farm but more of a "farm zoo" with widely spaced pens holding a fairly representative cross section of American farm animals. There are also a few more exotic species, like llama, buffalo, and ostriches, that are showing up on your trendier farms. Visitors can enter most of the pens for a close-up encounter. This is the city kid's chance to hold a chicken, pet a baby pig, feed a goat, milk a cow, chase a goose, and meet a turkey that has yet to be served at Thanksgiving. Squawking guinea hens and stately peacocks (including a stunning all-white specimen) roam freely about the grounds. And, of course, there is a pony ride. The little ones love every minute. For doting parents and grandparents, it's a photographic field day.

The tour guides are the antithesis of theme park attendants. There are no spiffy uniforms or carefully rehearsed spiels here. These folks look and talk like they're down on the farm, dirty jeans and all. It's truly refreshing. But don't expect to escape the edutainment. You'll be treated to spot quizzes ("Who can tell me what a baby goose is called?") and little known facts ("The pig is a very clean animal.") as the guide shepherds you from pen to pen. Thanks to this tour I now know that the gestation period of a Vietnamese pot-bellied pig is three months, three weeks and three days.

Of course everyone's favorites are the farm babies, and you can increase your odds of seeing them by visiting during the spring or around harvest time. During October there is pumpkin picking and in November there are cowboys and Indians, featuring Indian dances and trick roping.

There's little in the way of food here. At the General Store (or the Chuck Wagon during busier months) you can get sandwiches for about $3 and ice cream bars for about half that. Soft drinks are available from vending machines. You can also bring a cooler and have a picnic. Judging from the number of tables provided, quite a few people do just that.

Remember to wear sensible shoes — this is a farm, after all, and after a rain it can get muddy. The tour is long and covers a fair amount of ground. You can rent a "little red wagon" for $3 in which to lug the kids.

*Nearby:* Water Mania.

# Jungle Adventures

26205 East Colonial Drive, Christmas 32709
(407) 568-2885

> *Admission:*     Adults $11.50, children (3 to 11), seniors (60+) $9.50, all plus tax
>
> *Hours:*     Daily 9:00 a.m. to 6:00 p.m.
>
> *Location:*     On SR 50, about 17 miles east of Orlando

It's hard to miss Old Swampy. He's a 200-foot foam and cement alligator stretched smilingly alongside SR 50 on the way to the Space Coast. Step into (or more precisely, around) his jaws and you enter Jungle Adventures, a small attraction that has many things in common with Gatorland but a few unique surprises of its own.

At its most basic, Jungle Adventures is a small zoo with a familiar cast of characters — two black bears (Boris and Natasha), some spider monkeys, some crocs, macaws and cockatoos, and a small collection of injured birds of prey. The zoo's most distinguished specimens are its four Florida panthers and two western cougars; especially handsome is a large panther named Roman. But mostly there are alligators. Like Gatorland, Jungle Adventures is part of a larger alligator farming operation. There are some 200 gators living in the 20-acre park but just a stone's throw away are 10,000 more being grown out for their skin and meat.

What sets Jungle Adventures apart, and makes a visit worth consideration, are its fascinating setting and its shows. The setting is in the midst of a swamp, with the main zoo across a bridge and completely surrounded by water fed from a sulfurous spring. At first it seems that there's something terribly wrong with the water; it's completely covered by what looks like a chartreuse slime. Actually, it's duckweed, a tiny four-leafed water plant that grows in the billions. It adds a marvelously primordial touch to the alligators that swim through it, coating their horny hides with gooey green.

The shows at Jungle Adventures are refreshingly low key, one might almost say amateurish, although in the very best sense of the term. There are three shows and a boat ride that are timed so that you can move seamlessly from one to the next. A complete cycle takes about one and a half hours and there are four cycles each day.

The 10-minute **pontoon boat ride** circles the island zoo as gators swish thorough the duckweed, leaving a tell-tale trail in the green coating on the water's surface. Along the way, your guide tells tales of Jungle Adventures' past and present, and its future plans. An eclectic **animal show** features a small alligator which everyone gets a chance to hold while their picture is taken. Next comes a passel of snakes, draped languorously on the presenter's shoulders. But the *piece de resistance* is the appearance of a young Florida panther. The animal I saw was dropped off mysteriously on the park's doorstep in the dead of night, so its exact parentage is unknown. The animal, however, shows characteristics of both the panther and the Western cougar. The staff surmises that it was an illegal pet until its erstwhile owners got annoyed when it ate the leather sofa, a scenario they pieced together from the animal's spoor in the days after its arrival. After a brief show and tell, the audience is invited up to pet the panther — as far as I know, the only show in Central Florida offering this special type of close encounter.

Next comes a tour of the **Indian Village**, a re-creation of a Calusa settlement. The Calusa were a tribe that predated the Seminole, who are actually a Creek people driven from Georgia by white settlers. The Calusa were an advanced and warlike seafaring culture. They were decimated by the European diseases brought by the colonizers and have completely disappeared. On a recent visit, I was treated to a spellbinding description of how Calusa warriors killed giant alligator-crocodiles (a mutant hybrid species now extinct, they tell me) with a sacred pole. Neat stuff.

Finally, there is an **alligator feeding** show reminiscent of the *Jumparoo* at Gatorland, although the main course of choice here is fish. Sometimes, the gators are fed from a dock-like platform over the water but from time to time the handler chooses to work the shore, drawing the enormous reptiles from the green waters to leap and snap just a few feet away from the audience. Even for those who have toured Gatorland, this will be an exciting spectacle.

The staff is young and wonderfully free of the heavily rehearsed spiels that some parks insist on using. Also, Jungle Adventures doesn't draw the larger crowds that the Orlando attractions have to deal with, so there's more occasion for an easy give and take between the staff and the visitors. It can be a lot of fun.

*Nearby:* Fort Christmas Historical Park, Midway Airboat Tours.

# Jungleland

4580 West Irlo Bronson Highway, Kissimmee, 34746
(407) 396-1012

| | |
|---|---|
| *Admission:* | Adults $11.95, children (3 to 11) $6.95, seniors (55+) $9.95, all plus tax; AAA, AARP, and military discounts |
| *Hours:* | Daily 9:00 a.m to 6:00 p.m. |
| *Location:* | 6 miles east of I-4; 2 miles east of SR 535 |

The 120-foot plaster alligator outside might make you think this is a Gatorland clone but, while Jungleland has a first-rate gator wrestling show, it is primarily a small zoo specializing in "exotic" animals. Still, it's the gator show you'll probably remember.

Plan your visit around the schedule for the **"Bushmasters Gator Show"** which takes place at noon, 2:00 p.m., and 4:00 p.m. every day. This 25-minute display is first-rate "edutainment" and well worth the price of admission. Jungleland compresses all its gator lore and trivia into this single show, whereas Gatorland spreads it out over your entire visit. Otherwise the shows are very similar, although I'd have to give the edge to Jungleland.

The show takes place in a 300-seat outdoor amphitheater with shaded seating areas. If you drop by early, you may be able to see the gator wrangler lasooing a likely looking co-star from the nearby gator pond. Once inside the arena, the barefoot wrangler puts the uncooperative gator through its paces, showing off its teeth and gaping maw. He also holds the gator's jaws shut with his chin, the *piece de resistance* of every gator wrestling show.

This show offers a different version of the origin of gator wrestling than the one I heard at Gatorland, attributing the practice to the Seminole Indians who hunted gators in this fashion for their skin and meat. Hunters usually worked in pairs, with one getting on the gator's back and clamping its jaws shut while his partner tied the jaws shut for the trip back to market. The trick of pulling back the gator's head and holding its jaws with the chin was developed, according to this version, by lone hunters who didn't want to share the sale price with a partner. By holding the jaws with their chin, they were able to free their hands to tie the gator's jaws shut single-handed. All in all, the Jungleland version has the ring of truth to it.

After the show, stroll back along the half-mile looping path through **Jungleland's zoo** which houses some 300 specimens. You can get closer to the animals here than at most zoos, and Jungleland is far less concerned about your feeding the animals than many. In fact, there are 25-cent food dispensers dotted along the route just for that purpose. There are some lovely members of the big cat family here, ranging from African leopards and lions, to brother and sister Bengal tiger cubs, to an older Siberian tiger. The North American cats — cougars, lynx, and bobcats — are also represented. There are some unusual felines, too, like the African caracol with its distinctive ears and the dog-sized serval, once the house cats of Egyptian royalty.

Monkeys are another well-represented family. My favorite is **Radcliffe**, the zoo's only large primate and a bona-fide movie star. He was one of the orangutans who played Clyde in the Clint Eastwood film, *Every Which Way But Loose*. Radcliffe will respond to simple hand signals — waving your hand over your head, placing it on your forehead as if you have a headache, sneezing with your hand over your nose. He also seems to respond to the verbal command, "Smile." Like any good actor, he performs more willingly if you bribe him with food.

Most people seem to spend about an hour and a half at Jungleland — half an hour for the gator show and about twice that long to visit the other animals. Don't forget to take a family snapshot by the big gator outside before you leave. A helpful sign tells you the best place to stand.

*Nearby:* Haunted Mansion, Kartworld, Medieval Times.

## Reptile World Serpentarium

5705 East Irlo Bronson Highway, St. Cloud 34771
(407) 892-6905

| | |
|---|---|
| *Admission:* | Adults $4.55, students (6 to 17) $3.48, children (3 to 5) $2.41; prices include tax |
| *Hours:* | Tuesday to Sunday 9:00 a.m. to 5:30 p.m. |
| *Location:* | East of St. Cloud, about 9 miles east of Florida Turnpike exit 244. |

This unassuming cinder block and stucco building houses an impressive collection (over 50) of snakes from around the world, ranging from the familiar and innocuous to the exotic and deadly. Here you'll find the Australian taipan, considered by some to be the world's deadliest snake, as well as a splendid 18-foot king cobra. There are also snakes you may never see elsewhere, like the brilliant pea green East African green mamba and its less startling but nonetheless beautiful West African cousin. The snakes are housed in modest glass-fronted pens along a darkened corridor. Snakes are the main course, but there are also a 14-foot gator sulking in a shallow, murky pool, a passel of iguanas, and a pond full of turtles.

If all Reptile World had to offer was its snake displays, it might be recommended only to the certified snake fancier. But this is a working venom farm (if that's the right term). Though there may be only 50 snakes on public display, behind the scenes are hundreds of venomous snakes just waiting to be milked for their valuable venom. Reptile World ships this precious commodity world-wide for use in medical and herpetological research. The regular milking of these dangerous snakes is done in public and makes Reptile World more than just another snake house.

Venom shows are scheduled at 3:00 p.m. on weekdays. On weekends they are scheduled at 11:00 a.m., 2:00 p.m., and 5:00 p.m., although the two earlier shows tend to start late. The wait will quickly be forgotten, however, once the show starts. After bringing out a large snake for guests to hold, owner George VanHorn retreats behind a glass wall to take care of business. About half a dozen snakes are plucked from their boxes and coaxed into sinking their fangs through a clear membrane stretched over a collection glass. The glasses range in size from small test tubes used for coral snakes to hefty pilsner glasses used for large rattlers and cobras. The view can't be beat; you are just three feet away from these fanged wonders and will be thankful for the glass window between you and the snakes.

The entire show is fascinating but the large snakes are the most impressive. The Eastern diamondback rattlesnake, the largest of its kind, bares huge fangs and spits copious venom into the collection glass. The black and white spitting cobra requires special care. As its name suggests, it spits its venom into its victim's eyes and the recommended treatment is to wash the eyes with urine. The monocled cobra, so called because of the eye-like marking on the back of its head, emerges from its box with hood flaring and head darting rapidly about. This is serious, not to mention dangerous business. VanHorn once received a near-fatal bite from a king cobra while 30 school children looked on enthralled, convinced it was part of the show.

Reptile World is on the extreme outer fringe of the Orlando tourist circuit. For anyone who has ever been fascinated by snakes, it's well worth the detour. By all means time your visit to the venom shows.

# CHAPTER SIXTEEN:

# Gardens & Edens

For those who feel the Orlando theme park experience is "so plastic!," help is at hand. Within the Orlando metropolitan area, or just a short ride away, are private gardens, public parks, and wilderness tracts where cool waters, fresh breezes, and quiet forests await to soothe the simulation- and stimulation-weary tourist.

The most famous man-made garden in the area, Cypress Gardens, is described in *Chapter Four*. Here I describe the Harry P. Leu Gardens, right in the heart of Orlando, and the spectacular Bok Tower Gardens in Lake Wales, a short drive from Orlando and not too far from Cypress Gardens. Of course, these attractions involve the cunning hand of man and are, in a way, just as artificial as any theme park — although some would argue they are a good deal more beautiful.

Then there are the state, county, and city parks, many of which have been only slightly modified by humans. It comes as a surprise to many visitors that the "real Florida" (to use a phrase pushed by the state's public relations campaigns) lies all around them. Just a short drive from your motel, you can hike miles and miles of pristine trails and never see another human, or swim in a crystal clear spring bubbling up from deep in the earth, or canoe down a river that still looks much as it did when the first Europeans arrived in this part of Florida.

This is nature, let us not forget, so in addition to sunscreen a good bug repellent will come in handy for hikers. Be aware too that deer ticks carrying Lyme disease are found here. Common sense precautions should be used with wildlife — don't pick anything up and don't feed the alligators (it's against the law!). The words to live by when visiting these beautiful areas are: "Take nothing but pictures, kill nothing but time, leave nothing but footprints."

The parks listed here are just the beginning. If this type of unspoiled recreation is to your taste, you may want to venture farther afield — to Blue Springs State Park to the north, where manatees come to warm up in the winter, or to Homosassa Springs State Park to the west, or to Lake Kissimmee State Park to the south. An excellent (and **free**) guide to Florida's state parks is available from the Department of Environmental Protection, Division of Recreation and Parks, MS#535, 3900 Commonwealth Boulevard, Tallahassee, FL 32399-3000. Or ask for *Florida State Parks . . . the Real Florida* at the ranger station of any state park.

## Big Tree Park

General Hutchinson Parkway, Longwood 32750
No phone

| | |
|---|---|
| *Admission:* | **Free** |
| *Hours:* | Daily 8:00 a.m. to sunset |
| *Location:* | Take I-4 Exit 49, drive east on SR 434; turn left on Route 17-92 and left on General Hutchinson |

Pay a brief visit to this small Seminole County park to gawk at the oldest cypress tree in the U.S. "The Senator" (nicknamed to honor the senator who donated the land) stands 126 feet high and measures 47 feet around. It's estimated that the behemoth is some 3,500 years old. A boardwalk leads from the parking area to the tree. The park is part of the Spring Hammock Nature Reserve, a sylvan oasis in the midst of Orlando's suburban sprawl. Picnic tables and grills invite you to stay a while.

## Bok Tower Gardens

1151 Tower Boulevard, Lake Wales 33853
(941) 676-1408

| | |
|---|---|
| *Admission:* | Adults $4, children (5 to 12) $1 |
| *Hours:* | Daily 8:00 a.m. to 6:00 p.m. (last admission at 5:00 p.m.) |
| *Location:* | Off Burns Avenue in Lake Wales. Take US 27 South, turn left on 17A (Masterpiece Road) and follow signs about 6.6 miles |

Once upon a time, before the age of Leona Helmsley and Donald Trump, the wealthy knew how to spend their money. One such individual was Edward W. Bok, a Dutch immigrant born in 1863 who came to the United States at the age of six and made his fortune as a writer and magazine publisher. In the twenties, after his retirement, he set out to create an Eden on an unprepossessing patch of land whose only claim to fame was that it was the highest point on the Florida peninsula. He enlisted the creator of New York's Central Park, Frederick Law Olmstead, to do the landscaping and hired noted architect Milton B. Medary to build a setting for a very special musical instrument. In 1929, he presented the result as a gift to the American people. The "result" is the Bok Tower and its magnificent carillon that stands majestically in the midst of an artfully designed wooded park, specifically conceived as a refuge from the bustle of "the world."

Bok Tower Gardens is a very special and a very quiet experience. Unlike nearby Cypress Gardens, where the landscaping is over-the-top and in-your-face, the effect here is far more subtle, almost ethereal. The bark-chip covered paths through the woods are meant for leisurely strolls and quiet moments alone with one's thoughts. The vistas, powerful as they are, are contemplative and softly romantic.

Olmstead's design is devilishly clever in the way he leads you to the tower. He only lets you see it when he wants you to. Your first glimpse is across a reflecting pool, framed by palm fronds and Spanish moss. Then it vanishes as you walk through a palm-fringed glade to approach more closely. Suddenly, the tower rises above you, standing on an island barely larger than its base, surrounded by a moat crossed by marble bridges and guarded by massive wrought iron gates. It's as if you have come upon a magical remnant of an ancient city in a storybook land, part cathedral, part castle keep.

The storybook aspect is heightened by the pink and gray Georgia marble that forms the tower's base and accents its flanks, the odd and complex sundial mounted on the side of the south wall, the highly polished brass door on the north, the mysterious red door behind the ornately carved balustrade above the sundial, by the very fact that you cannot cross the moat for a closer look. It must be a wondrous experience on a foggy morning.

The tower was never intended to welcome guests; the only way to get a look inside is to see the slide show orientation screened at the Visitors Center on a regular schedule. The tower exists solely to house the 57 precisely tuned bronze bells operated by a massive keyboard played with the fists. The carillon occupies the upper third of the structure. The unique sound produced by this massive instrument rolls out across the surrounding woods through 35-foot high grilles in the form of Art Deco mosaics of drooping trees and animals in colorful shades of turquoise and purple.

Every afternoon at 3:00 there is a 45-minute carillon recital. Many of the pieces played were composed specifically for carillon, others have been adapted to the unique requirements of the massive instrument. A schedule of "Daily Carillon Music" lists the day's program, everything from old folk tunes to opera. It's a wonderful experience on a warm, sunny day and, unless you're a carillon connoisseur, probably unlike any other concert you've ever heard.

*Tip:* Most people sit on the grass or on benches under the shady oak trees near the tower's base during the recitals. You will have a better musical experience if you move somewhat farther away. Stroll down the slope away from the tower until the tower's mosaic grilles reappear over the tops of the oak trees. Then find a spot with an unobstructed view of the top of the tower. This way, the music will roll over the tree tops and cascade down the slope towards you.

Don't leave without exploring the rest of the grounds. Past the reflecting pool that marked your approach to the tower lies an "exedra," a semicircular marble bench that looks out from the top of Iron Mountain to the west. At the northern edge of the grounds is a recent, and ingenious, addition, the **Window By The Pond Nature Observatory**. It's a small wooden building on the lip of a pond. You sit behind a large picture window, unseen by the wildlife outside. A sign notes that this is nature's show and that the performance schedule is erratic. On the back wall are drawings of the local animals you might glimpse from your hiding place.

From here you can take a three-quarter mile hike through one of the few remaining fragments of the sort of longleaf pine forest that once covered millions of acres of the Southeastern United States. Preserving this patch of woods is not as easy as it may sound. A carefully orchestrated series of controlled burns is used to mimic ageless natural processes. Otherwise, evergreen oaks would invade the habitat and eventually kill the pines with their shady branches. An informative brochure that explicates the habitat can be found at the trailhead.

The Visitors Center houses a modest cafeteria-style restaurant serving simple sandwich platters and hot-dogs. A meal will cost about $5 or $6. There is also a tasteful gift shop where you can get cassettes and CDs of Bok Tower carillon recitals. They have a good selection of books about gardening, wildlife, conservation, and Florida's natural wonders. Framed photos and posters of the gardens make nice souvenirs.

*Nearby:* Spook Hill, Cypress Gardens.

# Katie's Wekiva River Landing

190 Katie's Cove, Sanford 32771

(407) 628-1482 (from Orlando); (407) 322-4470 (from Sanford)

| | |
|---|---|
| *Cost:* | Adults $15 to $18.50, depending on canoe route; children (3 to 11) half price |
| *Hours:* | Daily 8:00 a.m. to sunset |
| *Location:* | Take I-4 Exit 51, go west on SR 46 for 5 miles, then right onto Wekiva Park Drive for 1 mile |

What easier way to appreciate the pristine wilderness of the "real Florida" than to glide gently past it in a canoe? Katie's is a small RV and camper resort along the banks of the Wekiva River that offers canoe excursions along some of Central Florida's most beautiful waterways. There are four expeditions to choose from.

The Little Wekiva River Run is their most popular and it's easy to see why. The scenery is drop-dead gorgeous and there are plenty of turtles and birds to be seen. You might also glimpse an alligator. The shoreline varies from well-manicured backyards to impenetrable jungles. They estimate four to five hours for this nine-mile trip, although inexperienced paddlers may take longer. The Rock Springs Run is a 19-mile marathon and paddlers have the option of making it an overnight trip, with primitive camping in Wekiva State Park. For these trips, you are driven to drop off points upstream and end your trip back at Katie's.

Two other trips head downstream from Katie's and require that you arrive at pick-up points by specified times. They are the St. John's River Run (6 miles, 2 to 3 hours) and the Blue Springs Run (12 miles, 5 to 6 hours). The latter involves some six miles on the St. John's River with its motorized traffic and is recommended for experienced canoers only. Both these trips require a minimum of four adults.

*Nearby:* Rock Springs Run State Reserve, Wekiva Falls Resort.

# Kelly Park, Rock Springs

Kelly Park Drive, Apopka

(407) 889-4179

| | |
|---|---|
| *Admission:* | Adults $1, children under 12 **free** |
| *Hours:* | Daily 9:00 a.m. to 7:00 p.m. in summer; 8:00 a.m. to 6:00 p.m. in winter |
| *Location:* | Take Rock Springs Road north from Apopka, then left onto Kelly Park Road and follow signs |

This small Orange County park is built around one of the Apopka area's crystal clear springs. As its name suggests, Rock Springs bubbles up from a cleft in a rock outcropping and, instead of spreading out into a pool, becomes a swiftly running stream that quickly slows to a meander. The activity of choice here, and the major reason for the park's obvious popularity, is riding down the stream in an inner tube or on a float.

Kids, and not a few grown-ups, jump into the head waters by the dozens and bob and splash their way downstream for about a mile. There are exits from the river along the way and an excellently maintained network of boardwalks (with flooring designed to protect the barefooted) let you carry your tube back to the beginning for another go. You can also go down without a tube but, for most adults at least, the stream is too shallow for swimming during most of its course. At the middle of the one-mile tubing course, the stream blossoms into a series of lagoons and pools that form the centerpiece of the park. This is the place to come for a cooling, if somewhat crowded, swim. Or join the sunbathers thronging the shores and islands. This is a great park for kids and, if you don't have any, you may feel a bit overwhelmed by other people's.

Tubes are not available in the park, so unless you bring your own, stop at one of the tube rental shops near the park entrance. The cost is modest, about $3 for a day's rental.

Most of the rest of the park is given over to nicely shaded picnic tables, most with a barbecue nearby. The park also offers camping sites ($11 a night, $7 for residents); electricity is another $3. Your admission receipt lets you leave the park and return the same day.

## Leu Gardens

1920 North Forest Avenue, Orlando, 32803
(407) 246-2620; fax (407) 246-2849

|  |  |
|---|---|
| *Admission:* | Adults $4, children (grades K-12) $1 |
| *Hours:* | Daily 9:00 a.m. to 5:00 p.m. (to 8:00 p.m. April to October); Sunday 9:00 a.m. to 6:00 p.m. |
| *Location:* | Take I-4 Exit 43 (Princeton Street), go east to Mills (US 17-92) and turn right. Turn left on Virginia Drive and follow signs |

Strolling through Harry P. Leu's magnificent formal gardens on the shores of Lake Rowena, it's hard to believe that you're in the heart of the city, just a short drive from the bustling "Centroplex" as Orlando rather inelegantly refers to its central business district. There's nothing inelegant about this luxurious estate, however. Deeded to the city by a local industrial supplies magnate and amateur botanist, the 50 acres of manicured grounds and artfully designed gardens offer a delicious respite from the cares of the workaday world.

Camellias were Harry Leu's first love and the place is full of them — over 2,000, making this the largest documented collection of camellias in North America. But there are many other trees, flowers, and ornamental plants to catch the fancy of amateur gardeners, who will appreciate the meticulous signage which provides the full scientific name for the thousands of species represented. They can flag down a passing staff member, who will be more than happy to answer their questions. The rest of us will simply enjoy strolling through this artfully constructed monument to the gardener's art, stopping now and then to smell the roses.

The estate is given over to a number of gardens which blend seamlessly one into another. Camellias bloom under tall Southern oaks dripping with Spanish moss in the North and South woods, while the palm garden allows botanists to test the hardiness of various species during the nippy Central Florida winters. In the center is a formal rose garden that is at its best from April through October. By the lake, the aquatic wetland garden is home to swamp hibiscus, lizard's tail, loblolly, and dwarf wax myrtle, all under the shade of stately cypress trees. And don't miss the small hothouse tucked away in a corner of the estate. There you will find orchids, ferns, aroids, and other cold-sensitive plants.

Another not-to-be-missed highlight is the 50-foot floral clock. The mechanism was purchased in Scotland and now sits on an intricately planted sloping hill at the foot of a formal garden. Later, a stroll down to the lake takes you past the Ravine Garden, lush with tropical plants. At the water's edge a spacious wooden terrace offers a peaceful spot to sit and admire the wading birds. Benches and a gazebo encourage you to sit and stay awhile. Your patience may be rewarded with a glimpse of Lake Rowena's resident eight-foot alligator.

Every half hour from 10:00 a.m. to 4:00 p.m., volunteers conduct tours through the Leu house. Don't miss it. You'll be treated to a wonderfully gossipy recounting of the building's evolution, through several changes of ownership, from humble farm house to rich man's estate, spiced with tales of a sheriff gunned down in the line of duty and a home-wrecking New York actress. (That's her as Cleopatra in the photo in the living room.) Nearby is a cemetery in which the unfortunate lawman lies buried with many of his kin.

The ante-bellum-style Garden House, where you pay your modest admission to the gardens, houses a 900-volume horticultural library (open to visitors) and spacious meeting rooms. The terrace at the back of the building offers a stunning view of the lake. There are frequent arts and crafts exhibits in the Garden House, as well as a regular schedule of musical events. Wheelchairs are available free of charge.

A small gift shop offers a tasteful array of floral themed merchandise, including birdhouses, garden tools and accessories, and other small items. Leu Gardens t-shirts, sweats, and polo shirts range from $10 to about $35. There is a small selection of educational toys aimed at awakening a youngster's interest in gardening and nature. There are also hundreds of gardening books on sale here.

# Orlando Wetlands Park

Wheeler Road, Christmas
(407) 246-2288

| | |
|---|---|
| *Admission:* | **Free** |
| *Hours:* | Daily 7:00 a.m. to half an hour before sunset, January 21 to September 30 only |
| *Location:* | East on SR 50, then left on County Road 420 (Ft. Christmas Road); go 2.3 miles and turn right onto Wheeler Road. |

Tucked away on the far eastern fringes of Orlando, is an ingenious combination of the practical and the aesthetic. To the untrained eye, the "Iron Bridge Easterly Wetlands" that comprise this park look like a preserved sliver of the "real" Florida. It is, in fact, part of the City of Orlando's wastewater treatment system. Every day, 16 million gallons of highly treated reclaimed wastewater from parts of Orange and Seminole counties are pumped into this 1,200-acre, man-made wetlands where aquatic plants continue the process of removing nutrients as the water slowly makes its way to the St. John's River. If visions of open sewers spring to mind, banish them. The result is enchanting, combining open fields, gently rolling woods, a small lake, and a thick forest.

In the parking area, go to the wooden announcement board. There you can sign in (don't forget to sign out!) and pick up a park map and a "Field Checklist of Birds." The best way to get acquainted with the park is to walk (or jog) the four-mile "walk/jog loop." If you'd like, you can veer off onto a more primitive hiking trail through the woods; it eventually rejoins the main trail. The map thoughtfully points out the best bird-watching spots along the park's 18 miles of raised roads. More than 150 species frequent the park. The Checklist lists them and the seasons in which they visit and notes whether they are common, uncommon, or rare.

Biking is permitted on the berm roads and there is a sheltered picnic area in a broad grassy area near the parking lot. The Florida Trail skirts the property, allowing serious hikers to extend their explorations. The Orlando Wetlands Park is a bit out of the way (it is about a 40-minute drive east of the city), but a visit will reward bird watchers and those looking for a more exciting jogging trail than the motel parking lot.

*Nearby:* Jungle Adventures, Fort Christmas Historical Park, Back to Nature Wildlife Refuge, Tosohatchee Reserve.

# Osceola District Schools Environmental Study Center

4300 Poinciana Boulevard, Kissimmee, 34758
(407) 870-0551

| | |
|---|---|
| *Admission:* | **Free** |
| *Hours:* | Saturday 10:00 a.m. to 5:00 p.m. |
| | Sunday 12:00 p.m. to 5:00 p.m. |
| *Location:* | 13 miles south of Highway 192 |

During the week, this 19-acre patch of Reedy Creek Swamp serves as an educational resource for the school children of Osceola County. On weekends, it's open to the public and well worth a visit from the wildlife-loving tourist.

Begin at the Visitors Center, which houses one of the best introductions and reference guides to Central Florida wildlife you are likely to find. If you've spotted some critter that you couldn't identify, you'll probably find it here. Most impressive are the taxidermy of birds like the bald eagle and osprey. There are also stuffed panthers and black bears. Most of these specimens were killed accidentally, typically by an automobile. Now they help teach school kids. These three-dimensional examples are supplemented by quite lovely color photographs of the native species taken right here at the Study Center. On another wall are photos of the local flora. Add to this charts of bird silhouettes and animal tracks and you have a remarkably complete resource for enjoying the Florida wilderness. Pick up a free copy of *The Reedy Creek Swamp Nature Guide* and the trail guides to guide the rest of your visit.

There are three short trails to explore. An 1,800-foot raised walkway takes you into Reedy Creek Swamp and its 400-year-old cypress trees. At the end, an observation platform lets you eavesdrop on the osprey nests. The short Pine Woods Trail features a reconstruction of the portable logging railroads that once ferried felled trees out of the swamp. The rails were made by Krupp, the famous German industrial giant. Another trail leads to a modest Indian mound formed by snail shells discarded by the aboriginal inhabitants. A small picnic area is available.

*Nearby:* Green Meadows Farm.

# Rock Springs Run State Reserve

SR 433, Apopka

(407) 884-2008

| | |
|---|---|
| *Admission:* | $2 per vehicle |
| *Hours:* | Daily 8:00 a.m. to sunset |
| *Location:* | From I-4 (Exit 51), take SR 46 West about 7 miles; turn left onto route 433. |

This park is bounded by Rock Springs Run and the Wekiva River, which might suggest that water activities abound. Not so. There is no water access and a sign at the gate directs you to nearby resorts and parks if that's what you have in mind.

What the Reserve has to offer, in abundance, is solitude and well-maintained hiking trails that meander through 8,750 acres of the kind of terrain that's referred to as "Florida's Desert." Depending on how far you trek, you'll see sand pine scrub, pine flatwoods, bayheads, hammocks, and a few swamps. Depending on how lucky you are, you may glimpse a black bear. (If you do, report the sighting by calling (407) 884-2008.)

There is one "primitive" camping site in the Reserve for those hardy enough to backpack to the far side of the park. If this is your cup of tea, make reservations at the number above.

*Nearby:* Katie's Wekiva River Landing, Wekiva Falls Resort.

# Sylvan Lake Park

845 Markham Road, Sanford 32771

(407) 322-6567

| | |
|---|---|
| *Admission:* | **Free** |
| *Hours:* | Daily 8:00 a.m. to sunset |
| *Location:* | From I-4 Exit 51, drive west on SR 46 3.2 miles, turn left onto Markham. Park is less than a mile on left |

This Seminole County park offers cut-rate tennis and racquetball. Tennis courts are $2 an hour before 5:00 p.m. and $4 per hour thereafter; racquetball courts are $4 an hour at all times. Use of the courts is open to all, even to tourists.

Otherwise, the park offers picnicking and an intricate network of boardwalks that take you through the woods and across the swampy fringes of Sylvan Lake, where you can sit in a spacious gazebo and bird watch or just while away the time. A small dock offers fishing or a place to launch your own canoe or other non-motorized boat.

# Tosohatchee State Reserve

3365 Taylor Creek Road, Christmas, 32709
(407) 568-5893

*Admission:*   $2 per vehicle
*Hours:*   Daily 8:00 a.m. to sunset
*Location:*   3 miles south of SR 50 in Christmas

If you really want to get away from it all, this mammoth (28,000-acre) state park is an excellent choice. I visited one Wednesday afternoon and was the only person there. The park borders 19 miles of the St. John's River and includes wetlands, pine flatwoods, and hammocks. The name is a contraction of Tootoosahatchee, an Indian word for "chicken creek," and the eponymous stream flows through the northern portion of the park.

Hiking, biking, and horseback riding are the activities of choice here. If you want the purest experience of this enchanting and sometimes spooky ecosystem stick to the primitive Florida Trail, marked with white (or sometimes blue) blazes. The trails marked with rectangular or diamond-shaped orange blazes allow bikes and horses. Walking softly and quietly will increase your chance of spotting wildlife. There are white-tailed deer, bobcat, gray fox, and several varieties of raptors to be seen here. The Florida panther is said to put in a rare appearance. More likely, you will flush large vultures or hawks as you proceed through the semi-gloom of the forest past tea-dark streams and pools, their still surfaces like obsidian mirrors.

If a casual visit is not enough, why not spend a few days? The camping here is "primitive," that is no recreational vehicles or pop-up tent trailers are allowed. Most of the campsites have nearby parking areas but for the truly adventuresome there are two backpacking campsites, one of them seven miles from the nearest road. Campers must make reservations by phone at least two weeks (but no more than 60 days) in advance. There is a fee of $3 per person per night ($2 for those under 18).

When you arrive, sign in and pay your vehicle fee (envelopes are provided). You must also sign out to let the park caretaker know that you are not lying wounded in some far flung corner of the wilderness. Also, be aware that hunting is allowed in this park. The deer season runs from late September to about Thanksgiving. The wild hog (yes, wild hog) season is in January and wild turkey have their turn in March and April. All of these hunting seasons have gaps, that is, periods of three days to two weeks when hunting is not allowed. Being in the woods when trigger happy hunters start thinking that deer wear orange vests is never a great idea; call to check the schedule, which is also posted at the sign-in area.

*Nearby:* Jungle Adventures, Fort Christmas Historical Park, Back to Nature Wildlife Refuge, Orlando Wetlands Park.

## Turkey Lake Park

3401 Hiawassee Road, Orlando 32835
(407) 299-5594

| | |
|---|---|
| *Admission:* | Adults $2, children (3 to 12) $1 |
| *Hours:* | Daily 9:30 a.m. to 7:00 p.m.; winter hours 9:00 a.m. to 5:00 p.m. |
| *Location:* | From I-4 Exit 30 take Kirkman north, turn left onto Conroy then right onto Hiawassee to park entrance, about 4 miles total |

Just a stone's thrown from the hurly-burly of Universal Studios Escape, the city of Orlando has created a 300-acre oasis along the shores of Turkey Lake. This beautifully landscaped and maintained park offers picnicking, hiking along seven miles of nature trails, biking along a three-mile bike path, and a number of other diversions. The picnic areas are close to the lake with beautiful shaded tables and "picnic pavilions" (additional charge). There are nearby kiddie play areas and sandy "beaches" but no lake swimming. Instead there is a large pool overlooking the lovely lake. A fishing pier lets you test your angling skills against large-mouth bass and other species.

Across the park, an "all children's" playground offers an enormous wooden and car-tire wonderland that will offer little ones hours of exploration and fun. Shaded gazebos nearby keep Mom and Dad out of the sun. No eating here, however, as food draws rats and other not-so-welcome wildlife. Next door is a "Cracker" farm featuring an authentic 100-year-old barn, to give kids an idea of what pioneer Florida looked and felt like.

There's camping here, too. "Family" camp sites for trailers and RVs are $14.38 per night including tax, electricity, and water. If you need a sewer hookup as well, the price is $16.60. The area is beautifully shaded, with picnic tables and barbecue pits. A "primitive" camping area nearby is less shady but at $6.61 per tent the price may be right. Camping requires reservations and there is a 21-day time limit.

*Nearby:* Universal Studios Escape, Mystery Fun House.

## Wekiva Falls Resort

30700 Wekiva River Road, Sorrento 32776
(407) 830-9828

| | |
|---|---|
| *Admission:* | Adults $5, children (2 to 11) $3, seniors (65+) $4, pets $3. Prices include tax |
| *Hours:* | Daily 8:00 a.m. to 6:00 p.m. |
| *Location:* | From I-4 Exit 51, drive west on SR 46 5.5 miles, turn left on Wekiva River Road; entrance is 1.4 miles on left |

This homey camping resort welcomes day guests for picnicking, ca-noeing, and swimming. For most visitors the centerpiece of the resort will be Mastodon Springs, where slightly sulfurous but crystal clear wa-ter bubbles up from a 68-foot-deep well forming a long, narrow pool that's ideal for splashing and wading. The pool is flanked by steep grassy slopes ringed on top by shaded concrete picnic tables. (Bring your own grill if you want to cook.) Another ring of tables is at the bottom of the slope at the edge of the sandy beach that surrounds the spring. A struc-ture in the middle of the water lets kids climb up and slide down six tu-bular slides into the cool water. The pool spills out into a shallow stream for wading or tubing; about 100 yards downstream a wooden bridge blocks passage. This is very much a kids' place; most adults hang out on the shore or tend to the barbecuing. Pets must be on leashes and are not allowed in the swimming and concession areas.

On the other side of the bridge the stream opens into an small la-goon from which canoes depart. Canoes rent for a modest $5 for the day or $3 for two hours.

If you'd like to stay here, camping fees start at $18 a day with weekly and monthly rates available. The resort's glossy brochure recounts the owners' running battle with local government authorities over water rights. It makes for interesting reading.

*Nearby:* Rock Springs Run State Reserve, Katie's Wekiva River Landing.

## Wekiwa Springs State Park
1800 Wekiwa Circle, Apopka 32712
(407) 884-2009

| | |
|---|---|
| *Admission:* | $3.25 per vehicle (maximum of 8 people) |
| *Hours:* | Daily 8:00 a.m. to sunset |
| *Location:* | From I-4 (Exit 49) take route 434 West to Wekiva Springs Road, then about 3 miles to the park entrance. |

This gem of a park boasts what must be the most beautiful spot in all of Central Florida to take a swim. The spring that gives the park its name bubbles up at the base of an amphitheater of greensward, forming a crystal clear circular pool of pure delight. The water is a steady 72 degrees year-round, making for a bracing dip in the heat of summer and a heated pool for snow birds in the winter. The pool is fairly shallow, seldom more than five feet deep. Bring a snorkel and mask for a peek down into the spring itself.

The spring is one source of the Wekiva River which flows from here northeast to the St. John's River. You can rent a canoe to explore this lovely stretch of river. Rates (including tax) are $14 for two hours, $16 for three, $18 for four, $22 for six, or $25 for the entire day. Trail bikes can be rented for $5 for one hour, $9 for two, $12 for three, $15 for four, or $18 for the day.

The river is gorgeous from a canoe but some daring souls snorkel it. The park police tell me this is a foolhardy venture given the population of large alligators who have lost their fear of man, thanks to being fed by ignorant tourists. Shortly before one of my visits to the park, an 11-foot gator was pulled from the waters of nearby Wekiva Marina. Because of its aggressive behavior and total lack of fear of humans, the trapper was forced to kill it.

If you get hungry after your swim, there's a bare-bones snack bar at the top of the hill. But a better choice might be the picnic area at the other end of the park, where you'll find a couple of dozen picnic tables artfully sited around the shores of Sand Lake. There are alligators here, so be careful.

In between there are some beautifully maintained trails. If you begin from the spring-fed swimming pool, a boardwalk takes you from the swampy jungle of the river's edge to the sandy pine forest of the drier uplands. This is one of the nicest spots I found in Central Florida for a visitor to get a quick appreciation of just how different Florida's ecosystems are. There's plenty of wildlife, too. I've spotted white-tailed deer fawns leaping through the woods and armadillos grubbing in the underbrush.

# CHAPTER SEVENTEEN:

# Artful
# Dodges

T hose who assume that Orlando, with its high concentration of theme parks and "mindless" entertainments, is a cultural wasteland have got it dead wrong. In fact, the Orlando area boasts some world-class museums, a lively and growing theater scene, and a number of modest local history museums.

## HISTORICAL & SCIENCE MUSEUMS

### Fort Christmas Historical Park & Museum

1300 Fort Christmas Road, Christmas 32709
(407) 568-4149

| | |
|---|---|
| *Admission:* | **Free** |
| *Hours:* | Museum is open Tuesday to Saturday 10:00 a.m. to 5:00 p.m.; Sunday 1:00 p.m. to 5:00 p.m. |
| | Park is open daily 8:00 a.m. to 6:00 p.m. (9:00 a.m. to 7:00 or 8:00 p.m. during daylight savings time) |
| *Location:* | Two miles north of route 50, a major artery between Orlando and the Kennedy Space Center |

This is not the actual Fort Christmas but a re-creation. The original was built a short distance away in 1837 during the Second Seminole Indian War (1835-1842) and has long since rotted away. The re-created fort, with its log cabin-like blockhouses and pointed palisades, is remarkably evocative of a frontier that most Americans associate with the West, not the South.

Display cases in the blockhouses provide a fragmentary history of the Seminole Wars, the culture they destroyed, and the early days of white settlement. In the nearby Visitors Center, which is built in the style of a "Cracker" farm house, you can get a pamphlet that explicates the museum's exhibits and provides a short history of the Seminole Wars. Scattered about the property is a small but apparently growing collection of original Cracker architecture. Yesterday, disreputable shacks. Today, cherished history.

Fort Christmas is also a county park complete with picnic tables (many with barbecues), a shaded playground, a baseball diamond, and tennis, volleyball, and basketball courts.

*Nearby:* Orlando Wetlands Park, Jungle Adventures, Tosohatchee Reserve, Back to Nature Wildlife Refuge.

# The Holocaust Memorial Resource & Education Center

851 North Maitland Avenue, Maitland 32751
(407) 628-0555

*Admission:* **Free**

*Hours:* Monday to Thursday 9:00 a.m. to 4:00 p.m.; Friday 9:00 a.m. to 1:00 p.m.

*Location:* At the intersection of Maitland Boulevard and Maitland Avenue, about a mile east of I-4 Exit 47

Someone once observed that for there to be peaks there must be valleys. The reference was to art, but the metaphor holds true for history too. This modest and moving museum commemorates one of the darkest valleys of human experience — the martyrdom of the six million Jews who, along with homosexuals, Gypsies, and other "undesirables," were ruthlessly exterminated by the Nazis in the 1930s and 1940s.

A small chapel-like room houses "The Holocaust in History," a permanent collection of multimedia displays documenting the horrors of institutionalized hate. A separate room houses rotating exhibits on aspects of the Holocaust; these change every three to four months. A 4,000-volume library is devoted exclusively to Holocaust history.

A visit here can be a profoundly disturbing experience, which is not to say it is something to shy away from. Stepping out once again into the Florida sunshine, we are reminded that we are blessed to live on one of history's peaks — a lesser peak, it might be argued, but a peak nonetheless. A visit here will put the pleasures of your Orlando vacation in a richer perspective.

*Nearby:* Maitland Art Center, Maitland Historical Museum, Waterhouse Residence, Birds of Prey Center.

# Maitland Historical Museum

221 West Packwood Avenue, Maitland 32751
(407) 644-2451

| | |
|---|---|
| *Admission:* | Donations requested |
| *Hours:* | Thursday to Sunday noon to 4:00 p.m. |
| *Location:* | From I-4 Exit 47 go east on Maitland Boulevard, then turn right onto Maitland Avenue and right onto Packwood. |

This modest museum, housed in a former residence next to the Maitland Art Center (see below), houses memorabilia of the tiny town of Maitland, which began its life as Fort Maitland in 1838, serving as a way station between larger forts in Sanford and Orlando. There are photographs of old houses and early residents along with the contents of Maitland's attics — old radios, cameras, glassware, and household implements. A small room houses old desks and class photos from the turn of the century, when children would row through Lakes Faith, Hope, and Charity to reach the Maitland School.

The real attraction here, however, is the telephone museum housed in a building out back. Telephone service in this part of Florida began in 1909, when the Galloway family grocery store installed 10 phone lines so their good customers could order by phone. The service mushroomed into what came to be known as the Winter Park Telephone Company, which remained independent and family-owned until 1976 when it was sold to the company that became Sprint. There are several old magneto switchboards here, dating back to 1900, and a large collection of phones, from the old-fashioned, wall-mounted, hand-cranked varieties to a sleek one-piece 1970 Swedish Ericofon. Also on display are samples of copper wiring and other telephony paraphernalia, including wooden conduits once used to snake wire beneath city streets. Some more recent switching equipment is housed here and volunteers hope to get it working again for demonstration purposes.

There are very few explanatory labels, so ask for a guided tour. On my visit, I was escorted by a charming lady who once worked for the Galloways themselves.

*Nearby:* Maitland Art Center, Waterhouse Residence, Birds of Prey Center.

# Orange County Historical Museum

812 East Rollins Street, Orlando 32803

(407) 897-6350

*Admission:*    Adults $4, children (6 to 12) $2, seniors (55+) $3

*Hours:*    Monday to Saturday 9:00 a.m. to 5:00 p.m.; Sunday 12:00 noon to 5:00 p.m.

*Location:*    In Loch Haven Park, east of I-4 Exit 43

Unlike most county historical museums, which are dusty hodgepodges of miscellaneous objects, housed in a donated and thread-bare house of "historical" interest, Orange County's museum is housed in a handsome modern building, its collection attractively and professionally displayed. This is one of the best looking local history museums I have visited.

The main collection is small but ranges widely from some 12,000 years ago to the recent past (with some considerable gaps in between). Beginning with ancient arrowheads, the collection lurches forward to the nineteenth century, featuring some fascinating photos of Central Florida from the 1880s to the early 1900s. One of the most attractive exhibits is a Victorian parlor, recreating bourgeois interior design as it existed in the gay nineties. "Uncle Neil's Gen'l Mdse." evokes an old country store with men's detachable collars, women's bonnets, and display cases set on barrels. Incongruously rounding out the first room are two standing stuffed polar bears once used as advertising devices by a local TV and stereo dealer named Baer.

The second room houses rotating exhibits and, in the back of the room, the actual *Orlando Sentinel* hot type composing room, with machinery dating from 1900 to 1978. If you've forgotten how profoundly the computer has transformed our lives, just take a look at how newspapers were put together not that long ago. There is a small exhibit on the citrus industry and a series of photographs called "Orlando: Then and Now." Most interesting are the photos of the Church Street Station area before and after the extensive renovation.

The highlight of the museum, however, and the major reason for a visit, is **Fire Station No. 3**. This 1926 two-story brick firehouse, which was moved to this site, houses a fascinating collection of old fire engines and assorted fire fighting memorabilia. The most spectacular object on display is the 1911 American LaFrance "Metropolitan" steam powered fire engine. This ornate pumper was horse drawn, the steam being used to power the pump which sucked water from nearby streams and lakes (there was a filter to keep fish from gumming up the works) and sprayed it on the fire. Nearly as wonderful are the two motorized vehicles on display, a 1915 fire engine and a 1917 ladder truck. Antique car buffs will definitely want to swing by for a look.

Surrounding the old fire engines and in several rooms upstairs are a collection of objects and photographs which form the collective memory of the Orlando Fire Department. There's even a signed photograph from Miss Flame of 1972, a 16-year-old local lass named Delta Burke who went on to other things.

*Nearby:* Orlando Museum of Art, Orlando Science Center, Leu Gardens.

## Orlando Science Center

777 East Princeton Street, Orlando 32803
(407) 514-2000

| | |
|---|---|
| *Admission:* | Adults $8, seniors (55+) $7, children (3 to 11) $6.50 |
| *Hours:* | Monday to Thursday 9:00 a.m. to 5:00 p.m.; Friday and Saturday 9:00 a.m. to 9:00 p.m.; Sunday noon to 5:00 p.m. |
| *Location:* | From I-4 Exit 43, drive east and follow Loch Haven Park signs; about one quarter mile |

The Orlando area is gaining a reputation as another high-tech business corridor with specialties in laser and simulation technologies. The Orlando Science Center's smashing new home is a fitting monument to the technological explosion going on around it and should serve as a launching pad for future generations of scientists. The accent is on kids and science education but, thanks to its ingenious hands-on approach, the Center offers plenty to keep even the dullest adult occupied.

The Center's 42,000 square feet are crammed with eye-catching exhibits that illustrate the many faces of science and how it interacts with our everyday life. Power Station teaches about energy, LightPower about lasers and optics, The Cosmic Tourist about earth and the solar system, and Body Zone about health and fitness. There's even a section, ShowBiz Science, that explains the technology underlying some of the man-made wonders you've been gaping at during your Orlando visit.

The 310-seat CineDome features IMAX movies, planetarium shows, and, late at night, 3-D laser light shows set to the music of groups like Metallica. There is an additional admission charge for these shows. The Double Adventure Pass ($12 adults, $11 seniors, $9.50 children) gives you one "CineDome experience" in addition to basic admission.

The Triple Adventure Pass ($14 adults, $13 seniors, $11.50 children) offers a choice of two CineDome shows. The laser shows have a separate admission structure; call for schedule and show details. This is the largest such theater in the world and seeing an IMAX movie on the vast curved screen is an experience not easily duplicated elsewhere.

There's a spacious cafeteria so you can plan a visit around lunchtime and then spend the rest of the day exploring the wonderful world of science.

*Nearby:* Orlando Museum of Art, Leu Gardens.

## Spence-Lanier Pioneer Center

750 North Bass Road, Kissimmee 34746
(407) 396-8644

| | |
|---|---|
| *Admission:* | **Free** (Donations requested) |
| *Hours:* | Thursday to Saturday 10:00 a.m. to 3:30 p.m. |
| *Location:* | Half a mile south of Irlo Bronson Highway (Route 192) |

Sometimes referred to as the Pioneer Museum, this open-air museum is a labor of love of the Osceola County Historical Society. The highlights are two old wooden buildings, rescued from oblivion and moved to this site as reminders of Central Florida's not too distant but nonetheless vanished past.

The Lanier House is a 1905 Cracker-style residence made from broad cypress boards which have aged to a lovely cafe au lait shade of beige. The broad, shaded porches and airy central breezeway, or "possum trot," were designed to let air circulate through the four rooms. The spare interior rooms, including a kitchen with a wood stove, touchingly evoke the rhythms of life in a simpler time. Next door is the smaller, two-room 1890 Tyson Home, now used to re-create a turn of the century general store. Books of local history and locally produced crafts are sold here.

A nearby modern prefab building holds a growing and random collection of antiques and memorabilia donated by the local community. Many of these touchstones to the past seem to have been passed from generation to generation before finding their way here. This is the living, collective memory of Osceola County and reflects not just Florida history but the many ways in which foreign and national events impinged on small towns like Kissimmee.

Across the street from the four-acre site of the museum is the **Mary Kendall Steffee Nature Preserve**. This 7.8-acre patch of wilderness lies in the very heart of tourist Kissimmee and yet remains remarkably isolated. A short walk on marked trails brings you to a raised boardwalk that juts out into Shingle Creek Swamp. A shaded seating area beckons the footsore. Aside from the intermittent drone of small planes landing at the nearby Kissimmee Airport, this is an oasis of tranquillity where you can glimpse the occasional eagle or other large raptor. The numbers on the trail markers correspond to a trail guide which the museum will lend you. Or you can purchase a copy for $2.

*Nearby:* Flying Tigers Warbird Air Museum, Kissimmee Rodeo, Medieval Times, and the many other attractions along Route 192.

# Waterhouse Residence & Carpentry Museum

820 Lake Lilly Drive, Maitland 32751
(407) 644-2451

| | |
|---|---|
| *Admission:* | Donations requested |
| *Hours:* | Thursday to Sunday noon to 4:00 p.m. |
| *Location:* | From I-4 take Exit 47 East onto Maitland Boulevard, then turn right onto Maitland Avenue and right onto Lake Lilly Drive |

William H. Waterhouse, a home builder and cabinet maker by trade, came to Central Florida in the early 1880s and put his obvious skills to use building a handsome family residence overlooking tiny Lake Lilly. Today, it serves as a monument to gracious living in a simpler, less stressful time.

Lovingly restored and maintained by volunteers, the house contains many items of furniture fashioned by Mr. Waterhouse in the carpentry shop behind the home. The home itself is furnished throughout and looks as if the Waterhouse family had just stepped out for a moment. Do-it-yourselfers will marvel at the fine detail work and the lavish use of heart of pine, a favorite of builders of the period because it was impervious to termites. It is rare today because few loggers are patient enough to let pines go unharvested long enough for this prime lumber to develop.

Tours are conducted by knowledgeable volunteers who will provide you with many insights into this charming home and the people who lived here. If you arrive when a tour is in progress, you may find the door locked. Just take a seat in the comfortable chairs on the porch; a volunteer will be with you shortly. Tours last about 30 to 40 minutes.

*Nearby:* Maitland Art Center, Maitland Historical Museum, Birds of Prey Center.

# Winter Park Historical Association Museum

200 West New England Avenue, Winter Park 32790
(407) 647-8180

*Admission:*  **Free** (Donations requested)

*Hours:*  Thursday 11:00 a.m. to 3:00 p.m.; Saturday 9:00 a.m. to 1:00 p.m.; Sunday 1:00 p.m. to 4:00 p.m.

*Location:*  In downtown Winter Park next to the park

This fledgling historical museum is housed in one room around the corner from the building in which Winter Park's Saturday Farmer's Market is held. The display is simple, relying heavily on photographs of now-vanished buildings and assorted household items and artifacts that speak less of Winter Park than of American consumerism.

The best part of this museum is the central display area, a sort of room within a room, that houses changing exhibits artfully put together by a local architect and interior decorator using donated and loaned furniture and artifacts. A Victorian parlor decked out for a Christmas celebration will give way to an upper middle-class kitchen circa 1932. The exhibit changes every six months or so.

While perhaps not worth a special trip, this museum is worth visiting if you are touring the many other attractions in Winter Park.

*Nearby:* Morse Museum, Cornell Museum, Albin Polasek Galleries, Winter Park Scenic Boat Tour.

# ART MUSEUMS & GALLERIES

## Albin Polasek Galleries

633 Osceola Avenue, Winter Park 32789
(407) 647-6294

*Admission:*  **Free**

*Hours:*  Wednesday to Saturday 10:00 a.m. to 12:00 noon and 1:00 p.m. to 4:00 p.m.; Sunday 1:00 p.m. to 4:00 p.m.; closed July and August

*Location:*  From I-4 Exit 45, follow SR 426 East about 3 miles

The studio-home and gardens of the late Czech-American sculptor, Albin Polasek, have been turned into a loving memorial by his widow. The quietly luxurious home was designed by Polasek himself and constructed in 1950 overlooking Lake Osceola. Today it houses some 200 of his works. The paintings are originals while most of the sculptures are reproductions.

Polasek was a devout Roman Catholic and a self-taught wood

carver who, as a young immigrant, found work carving religious statues in the Midwest. Later, he received formal art training and eventually became a highly respected academic artist. The work on display here ranges from the mawkish to the quite impressive. He was a better sculptor than painter and some of his bronzes, like *The Sower* and *Man Carving His Own Destiny*, possess real power. The former is a classically inspired bronze, the latter depicts a muscular figure in the process of carving itself out of stone.

One of his most affecting pieces is *The Victorious Christ*, a larger than life sculpture of the crucified Christ gazing heavenward. The original hangs in a cathedral in Omaha, Nebraska. There are two reproductions here. One dominates his two-story studio but the real stunner is the bronze version in the back garden. Mounted on a large wooden cross and sited under a theatrically towering oak tree, facing the lake, it is a powerful work.

*Nearby:* Cornell Fine Arts Museum, Morse Museum of American Art, Winter Park Scenic Boat Tours.

## Cornell Fine Arts Museum

1000 Holt Avenue, Winter Park 32789
(407) 646-2526

| | |
|---|---|
| *Admission:* | **Free** (Donations accepted) |
| *Hours:* | Tuesday to Friday 10:00 a.m. to 5:00 p.m.; Saturday and Sunday 1:00 p.m. to 5:00 p.m. |
| *Location:* | On the campus of Rollins College, at the foot of Holt Avenue |

Travel guru Arthur Frommer lists the Cornell Fine Arts Museum as one of the top 10 free attractions in the world, but don't come here just to save money. The collection's emphasis is on European and American painting of the last three centuries. It boasts a permanent collection of some 6,000 objects, ranging from Old Masters to twentieth century abstractionists, making it the largest public museum collection in Florida.

The Cornell is also the oldest in the state, having recently celebrated its centennial. The current museum building, a handsome Spanish style villa, was dedicated in 1978 and is shortly to undergo a much-needed expansion to provide more gallery space.

Typically, the lion's share of the gallery space is given over to a special exhibition, while a smaller gallery features some choice examples from the permanent collection. Many exhibits are locally curated and draw either from the permanent collection or from private and public collections in Florida, offering the art lover the opportunity to view works that would otherwise be impossible to see. For other exhibits, the Cornell joins forces with other smaller museums across the country to mount distinguished traveling shows. Exhibits, which run from six to eight weeks, range from retrospectives of a single artist, to highlights of distinguished private collections, to surveys of important movements, to themed shows illuminating genres and techniques.

In addition to its exhibits, the Cornell offers a generous selection of other free programs including lectures by prominent artists, chamber music recitals, and showings of art-related films. Call for details.

*Nearby:* Albin Polasek Galleries, Morse Museum, Winter Park Scenic Boat Tours.

# Frank Lloyd Wright Buildings at Florida Southern College

111 Lake Hollingsworth Drive, Lakeland 33801
(941) 680-4110

| | |
|---|---|
| *Admission:* | **Free** |
| *Hours:* | 24 hours but best in daylight |
| *Location:* | On the shores of Lake Hollingsworth |

Devotees of Frank Lloyd Wright (and they are legion) will want to make a pilgrimage to Lakeland, about 54 miles west of Orlando, to marvel at the largest group of Wright-designed buildings in the world. Wright designed 18 buildings for Florida Southern, a liberal arts college affiliated with the Methodist Church. Twelve were built.

To get there from Orlando, drive west on I-4 and take Exit 18. Follow US 98 South. From Tampa take Exit 14 and follow US 92 East. The two routes join in downtown Lakeland. When they part ways again, follow route 98 and, shortly, turn right onto Ingraham Avenue. Follow Ingraham until it dead-ends at Lake Hollingsworth Drive (you'll see the campus of Florida Southern College on your right).

Turn right onto Lake Hollingsworth, then right again onto Johnson Avenue. Look for the parking lot on your right opposite the William F. Chatlos Journalism Building. In front of you will be a red and white sign; on it is a small red box containing brochures that outline a self-guided walking tour that circles the grounds.

The buildings were designed for a tight budget (much of the early construction was done by students in the forties) but the results are impressive. Many buildings are unlocked and open to the casual visitor. Inside, look for the tiny squares of colored glass embedded in the exterior walls — a delightfully whimsical touch. Take a moment to sit in the quiet splendor of the

Annie Pfeiffer Chapel; the smaller but equally arresting Danforth Chapel is nearby. One of the most interesting buildings to be seen here is the only planetarium Wright ever designed.

The buildings are starting to show their age, but Wright's designs are so idiosyncratic, his decorative elements so unique, that this extensive example of his "organic architecture" seems to exist outside the time/style continuum we carry around in our heads. Instead, it is easy to imagine you are in a city built a long time ago in a galaxy far, far away.

The buildings are linked by one and a half miles of covered esplanades which Wright, in his charmingly perverse way, scaled to his own rather short height. "It makes it kind of difficult to recruit a basketball team," a college executive confided. But for those who fit underneath the effect is rather cozy and Florida Southern students must say a silent prayer of thanks to Wright as they scurry between classes during an afternoon downpour.

## Maitland Art Center

231 West Packwood Avenue, Maitland 32751
(407) 539-2181

| | |
|---|---|
| *Admission:* | **Free** |
| *Hours:* | Monday to Friday 9:00 a.m. to 4:30 p.m.; Saturday and Sunday noon to 4:30 p.m. |
| *Location:* | From I-4 take Exit 47. Go east on Maitland Boulevard, then turn right onto Maitland Avenue and right onto Packwood |

The Maitland Art Center is both a gallery and a working art school. It was founded in the late 1930s by the artist and architect André Smith as a "laboratory" for the study of modern art. Smith built a charmingly eccentric complex of tiny cottage/studios for visiting artists. He decorated the modest buildings with cast concrete ornaments and detailing heavily influenced by the art of the ancient Aztecs and Maya.

Today the gallery plays host to a regular succession of exhibits by local and national artists as well as exhibits of private collections. After visiting the gallery, take some time to stroll the grounds. The place must have been idyllic in its heyday, before Maitland became quite so built up. Across the street from the gallery and studios is a roofless outdoor concrete chapel with a lattice-work cross. Shaded by oaks dripping in Spanish moss and surrounded by lush vegetation, the chapel offers a peaceful corner for contemplation. Right next to it is an open courtyard whose exuberant decoration owes a debt to the boisterous paganism of pre-

Columbian Mexico; it makes for quite a contrast.

The Maitland Art Center hosts occasional half-day and day-long workshops on topics such as papermaking as a sculptural art and casting silver jewelry, with tuition ranging from $35 to $100. Artists may want to call ahead for a schedule. There are also regular lectures and gallery talks.

*Nearby:* Maitland Historical Museum, Waterhouse Residence, Birds of Prey Center.

# Mary, Queen of the Universe Shrine

8300 Vineland Avenue, Orlando 32821
(407) 239-6600

| | |
|---|---|
| *Admission:* | **Free** |
| *Hours:* | Daily 7:30 a.m. to 5:00 p.m.; museum 10:30 a.m. to 4:00 p.m. (closed Wednesday) |
| *Location:* | Near I-4 Exit 27 |

This Roman Catholic shrine had humble beginnings as a tourist ministry; today it is a large modern cathedral named by the Pope as a "house of pilgrimage." There is some striking architecture and religious art to be seen here, especially a lovely, abstract, blue stained-glass wall in a chapel dedicated to Our Lady of Guadelupe. A small museum off the gift shop hosts rotating exhibits of religious art from around the world, such as a recent exhibit of Russian crosses and icons.

*Nearby:* SeaWorld, Arabian Nights.

# Morse Museum of American Art

445 Park Avenue North, Winter Park 32789
(407) 645-5311

| | |
|---|---|
| *Admission:* | Adults $3, children and students $1 |
| *Hours:* | Tuesday to Saturday 9:30 a.m. to 4:00 p.m.; Sunday 1:00 p.m. to 4:00 p.m. |
| *Location:* | On Park Avenue, just past the fancy shopping district |

Could the Charles Hosmer Morse Museum of American Art be the best museum in Central Florida? Well, for my money, it's hard to beat the world's largest collection of Tiffany glass. That's Louis Comfort Tiffany, the magician of stained glass who flourished at the turn of the twentieth century. The works on display here are absolutely ravishing and, if you have any interest in the decorative arts, your visit to Orlando will be poorer for not having found the time to visit this unparalleled collection.

When most people think of Tiffany glass they think of those wonderfully organic looking table and hanging lamps with the floral designs. Those are here, of course, as are some stunning examples of his large-scale decorative glass windows and door panels. But there's much else, some of which may come as a surprise.

As brilliant a marketer as he was an artist, Tiffany saw the World's Fair of 1893 as an opportunity to spread his fame world-wide. So he put his best foot forward by creating an enormous chapel interior for the exhibit. Everything in it, from a massive electrified chandelier, to a baptismal font, to intricate mosaic pillars to stunningly beautiful stained glass windows was of Tiffany design. The chapel has been lovingly restored by the Morse.

The faces on Tiffany's glass pieces were painted with powdered glass that was fused to clear glass, but much of the other detail and molding is created by the rich colors and tonal fluctuations in the glass itself. Tiffany is less well known as a painter, but several of his paintings, including some very deft watercolors from his world-wide travels, are to be seen here. There are also miniature glass pieces, vases in delicate, psychedelic-colored favrile glass, inkwells, jewelry, and other decorative objects.

In a rear gallery there are some lovely examples of American painting of the last century, including a deft portrait by John Singer Sargent and one by Samuel F.B. Morse, a distant cousin of the man for whom the museum is named and better known as the inventor of the telegraph and the code that bears his name.

The Morse's collection focuses on the decorative arts and is extensive, comprising some 4,000 pieces. In addition to the permanent displays, the museum dips into its collection to mount special exhibits illuminating various aspects of American decorative arts, including "vignettes," small rooms in which interior designers show off the museum's collection of furniture and decorative objects as they might have looked in the well-to-do homes for which these lovely objects were created.

*Nearby:* Albin Polasek Galleries, Cornell Fine Arts Museum, Winter Park Scenic Boat Tours.

# Orlando Museum of Art

2416 North Mills Avenue, Orlando 32803
(407) 896-4231; fax (407) 896-9920

| | |
|---|---|
| *Admission:* | Adults $4, children (4 to 11) $2; more for special exhibits |
| *Hours:* | Tuesday to Saturday 9:00 a.m. to 5:00 p.m.; Sunday 12:00 noon to 5:00 p.m. |

*Location:*      In Loch Haven Park, near I-4 Exit 43

The Orlando Museum of Art (OMA) was founded in 1924 to present local, regional, and national artists and develop art education programs for the community. Today, its handsome modern building with its arresting circular hub houses a permanent collection of nineteenth and twentieth century American paintings. There is also a distinguished collection of pre-Columbian art housed in its own gallery.

On any given day, the galleries may host a special exhibit, a selection of works on loan, and a selection of works from the permanent collection. The museum also offers regular video, film, and lecture series, most of which require an additional admission charge. Wheelchairs and lockers are provided free of charge.

A small gift shop offers a tasteful range of small art objects, reproductions, calendars, and glossy art books. You can even get an Orlando Museum of Art t-shirt.

*Nearby:* The Orange County Historical Museum, Orlando Science Center, Leu Gardens.

## Osceola Center for the Arts

2411 East Irlo Bronson, Kissimmee 34744
(407) 846-6257

*Admission:*      **Free**

*Hours:*      Monday to Friday 8:00 a.m. to 4:00 p.m.;
            Saturday 10:00 a.m. to 4:00 p.m.

*Location:*      A mile east of Florida Turnpike exit 244

This community-based arts organization mounts exhibits of Florida artists. Based on what I've seen, the standards for exhibition are quite high. Exhibits change monthly on the first Friday. The Center also hosts special events, such as a recent exhibition of a Mexican artist sponsored by the Mexican consulate in Orlando.

In addition, the Center hosts a regular schedule of theatrical and musical presentations, including local tours by the Southern Ballet Theatre and the productions of a local community theater group.

## Zora Neale Hurston National Museum of Fine Arts

227 East Kennedy Boulevard, Eatonville 32751
(407) 647-3307

*Admission:*      **Free**

*Hours:*      Monday to Friday 9:00 a.m. to 4:00 p.m.

*Location:*      From I-4 Exit 46 take Lee Road east and
            turn left almost immediately on Wymore;

at the next light turn right on Kennedy
for about a quarter mile

The tiny African-American enclave of Eatonville is the hometown of the writer Zora Neale Hurston, one of the shining lights of the Harlem Renaissance of the 1920s. Her namesake museum is a small gallery hosting rotating exhibits of African-American artists from Florida and around the nation. The shows change about every six weeks.

# THEATER

Orlando and the surrounding communities have an extremely active theater scene. In addition to the companies listed here, you should be aware of the Mark II Dinner Theater, reviewed in *Chapter Twelve: Dinner Attractions*. There are also a goodly number of community theaters, as well as touring Broadway shows. You will find complete listings of current theatrical offerings in the "Calendar" section of the Friday *Orlando Sentinel*, as well as in the free weekly papers, *Orlando Weekly* and *artsLink*.

## Annie Russell Theatre

1000 Holt Avenue, Winter Park 32789
(407) 646-2145

The drama department of Rollins College holds forth in this lovely, 377-seat Spanish Mediterranean style theater, offering an eclectic season of modern classics, a contemporary musical, and an old farce or Shakespearean play. The season runs from October to May and ticket prices are a bargain — $8 to $15 a seat.

The Annie, as it's known locally, also presents touring dance companies of international renown. Pilobolus and the Paul Taylor Dance Company are among the troupes they have hosted.

## The Civic Theatres of Central Florida

1001 East Princeton Street, Orlando 32803
(407) 896-7365

From September through June, The Civic Theatres produce an eclectic season of musicals and classic, contemporary, avant garde, and children's plays. This institution is a non-Equity professional repertory company. That is, they don't employ members of Actors Equity, the actors' union. Nonetheless, the quality is quite high and Civic productions regularly garner enthusiastic reviews from the local critics.

There are three performance spaces. The 350-seat MainStage hosts five major productions of important plays and musicals. The 90-seat

SecondStage is more on the model of Off-Broadway, presenting four small-cast, offbeat productions each season in a simple three-quarters round space with folding chairs. The third space is the 350-seat Theatre for Young People, which hosts the children's theater productions, many of which are given during the afternoon hours. Ticket prices range from $8 for the children's shows to $15 for the SecondStage to $18 for MainStage productions. The box office is open Monday to Friday from 10:00 a.m. to 6:00 p.m.

## Mad Cow Theater Company

146 Orange Place, Maitland 32751
(407) 599-7119

This is Orlando's version of New York's Off-Off Broadway or London's Fringe. In a tiny theater in a building used by a local acting school a dedicated group of non-Equity actors put on mostly contemporary plays. The fact that these performers aren't being paid is no slight to their seriousness and judging from what I've seen here the standards are quite high.

The selection of plays is eclectic, everything from Coward's *Blithe Spirit* to Fugard's *Master Harold and the Boys*. Don't expect Broadway-style production values or Broadway comfort. The budget for these shows ranges from the minuscule to the modest. The small audience seating section varies from 59 to 80 folding seats on risers. But for those with an adventuresome taste in theater-going, Mad Cow will be well worth checking out.

## Orlando International Fringe Festival

120 North Orange Avenue, Suite B, Orlando 32801
(407) 648-0077

If you're in Orlando during April and your tastes run towards experimental theater, you won't want to miss this theatrical feast. For 10 days, from noon to midnight, the streets of downtown are given over to an international smorgasbord of traditional theater, cabaret, performance art, and street acts. A typical Festival will see over 500 performances by more than 50 groups representing 10 or more countries. Most of the shows are indoors, but there is one outdoor performance venue and many acts simply use the streets.

To attend, you must first purchase a $4 button, which serves as a sort of cover charge for the Festival's indoor shows. You may pay an additional $1 to $8 for each show you see, although some shows are free and the street performances don't even require the purchase of a button. A printed program lets you know what's coming up next, and since the Festival is geographically compact, it's easy to dash from site to site. Veteran Festival-goers suggest quizzing others making the round of shows for suggestions on what's worth seeing and what should be avoided like the plague. Call the number above for the exact dates and location of this year's bash.

# Orlando Opera

1111 North Orange Avenue, Orlando 32804
(407) 426-1717

Dedicated to bringing the piercing sounds of Italians in pain to Central Florida, the Orlando Opera offers a season of three mainstage productions and two minor productions. The major productions feature the heavyweights (you should excuse the term) of the opera world; Pavarotti, Domingo, and Sills have all performed here. The minor productions feature resident artists. There is also at least one recital or concert performance featuring a major artist during the season.

The season runs from September to May. Prices for tickets to individual performances range from $15 to $55; half-priced tickets are available to students with a valid ID.

# Orlando Theatre Project

Seminole Community College
100 Weldon Boulevard, Sanford 32773
(407) 328-4722, ext. 3323

After a decade of presenting plays in makeshift and temporary theaters throughout the area, the Orlando Theatre Project has settled into residence at Sanford's Seminole Community College, to the north of Orlando. This small Equity company (all of its actors are based in the Orlando area) presents primarily American plays by playwrights such as Arthur Miller and A. R. Gurney. They also produce original scripts by local playwrights.

The three-play season runs from September to May, with each production running for three to four weeks. Tickets are $15, with students and seniors (65+) receiving a $2 discount. OTP also presents a series of **free** play readings.

# Orlando-UCF Shakespeare Festival

30 South Magnolia Avenue, Orlando 32801
(407) 317-7800

The Bard of Avon is alive and well in Orlando, thanks to this up and coming professional theater company. In the fall, the OSF presents three plays, which may or may not have a Shakespearean connection. One of their on-going projects is to present faithful stage adaptations of classic novels, such as Bram Stoker's *Dracula*. These plays are presented at the Orange County Historical Museum Theater in Loch Haven Park and each runs four weeks.

In the spring, the company presents two Shakespeare plays in repertory, that is, they alternate performances over a period of about six weeks. These shows are presented in the open-air Walt Disney amphitheater at Lake Eola. The casts for both these series, so they tell me, are about equally divided between New York actors and local talent, although in the show I caught all the performers were equally polished.

Throughout the season, OSF presents a series of readings, *Shakespeare Unplugged*, on the second or third Monday of the month. These events are **free**. Otherwise, ticket prices range from $6 to $35.

## Osceola Players

2411 East Irlo Bronson Highway, Kissimmee 34744
(407) 846-6257

In addition to its fine-arts endeavors, the Osceola Center for the Arts is the home of the Osceola Players, a community theater troupe that presents a six-play season of contemporary comedies and musicals with the occasional Shakespeare play thrown in for good measure. The season runs from September to May and tickets range from $12 to $15. The Center also presents touring performances by the Southern Ballet Theatre, two local dance studios, and the Orlando Opera.

## SAK Theatre Comedy Lab

45 East Church Street, Orlando 32801
(407) 648-0001

In the heart of downtown, just a short stroll from Church Street Station, you'll find the Orlando home of improvisational comedy. "Improv," as its practitioners invariably call it, involves a group of agile and quick-witted actors creating a coherent and hilarious sketch based on frequently bizarre suggestions from the audience. More often than not, they succeed.

Typically, what you will see is *TheaterSports*, which is described as "two teams of improv comedy stars . . . in an all-out battle for laughs with Olympic judges, official referees, the pink shoe of salvation, help from the audience, and free candy!!!" From time to time, they present "plays" based on improv principles, such as *Blank: The Musical* and *Sus-*

*pect*, a murder mystery in which the audience gets to decide whodunit. Popcorn and soft drinks are served.

The SAK is open year round, Tuesday to Sunday. There is one performance on Tuesdays and Wednesdays at 9:00 p.m., and two on Thursdays at 8:00 and 9:45 p.m. Fridays and Saturdays there are three performances at 7:30, 9:30, and 11:30 p.m. There is one show Sunday at 9:00 p.m. Tickets are $13 for adults, but Florida residents with photo ID, and all students, seniors, and military personnel with ID, get in for $8 ($10 for the 9:30 shows).

## Southern Ballet Theatre

1111 North Orange Avenue, Orlando 32804
(407) 426-1728

From September to May, this home-grown ballet company mounts three-performance runs of four ballets, ranging from "timeless classics to innovative contemporary works." They draw on a permanent company of 22 professional dancers and 19 apprentices, occasionally presenting guest artists and visiting choreographers. Each year during the Christmas season they present the ever-popular *Nutcracker*, in association with the Orlando Philharmonic; it runs for 12 performances.

All performances are given at the Bob Carr Performing Arts Center downtown (I-4 Exit 41). Single tickets range from $15 to $37 ($15 to $39 for *The Nutcracker*). Call the number above to purchase tickets.

## Theatre Downtown

2113 North Orange Avenue, Orlando 32803
(407) 841-0083

Here is another Off-Off Broadway-style theater offering contemporary classics, like *Twelve Angry Men*, and the occasional classic, like Sheridan's *The Critic*, at moderate prices. The theater, a converted industrial building, has two performing spaces — a 125-seat main stage with the audience on three sides of the stage and the more informal "dramarama," a space which doubles as the lobby for main stage productions. The rock musical I saw here was vastly entertaining thanks to a spirited cast that made up in energy whatever they may have lacked in the talent department. Shows run for about a month with performances on Thursday, Friday, and Saturday evenings; there is an occasional Sunday matinee. Tickets are $12 ($10 for students and seniors) on Friday and Saturday and $8 ($6 for students and seniors) on Thursday and Sunday.

# FILM

Orlando has the usual quota of mall-based multiplex movie theaters offering the latest Hollywood entertainment. The typical admission price is about $6.75 for adults. Some theaters have lower prices ($3.50 or $4) for all showings prior to 5:00 p.m. or for one late afternoon screening each day. The "Calendar" section in Friday's *Orlando Sentinel* lists the show times of every movie showing in the greater Orlando area (which extends to the Atlantic coast) along with helpful capsule reviews.

Several local movie houses deserve special mention:

The **Enzian Theater** (1300 South Orlando Avenue in nearby Maitland, (407) 629-0054), is the local art house. It shows subtitled European imports and the more adventuresome independent American films. From time to time, it runs special series built around a specific theme. Best of all, the films are screened in a 225-seat movie theater cum restaurant. You can have a full meal, washed down with beer or wine, while soaking up culture. Appetizers run about $2 to $6, sandwiches are $5 to $6, and pizzas run from $7.50 to $13, with toppings extra. Beer is sold by the pitcher from about $9 to $13. Tickets are $4 for matinees and $6.50 for evening performances.

In June of each year, the Enzian hosts the Florida Film Festival, screening as many as 150 films in four venues. Many filmmakers journey to Orlando for the event and give seminars. Single tickets are $6 and $100 buys a pass that lets you see every film in the Festival.

The **Southchase**, (407) 856-9409, **Park 11**, (407) 644-6000, and **Favorite Cinemas,** (407) 352-2601, are second-run houses showing slightly older films for $1.50 or $2. These theaters show a steady stream of lesser hits and box-office failures but they show their share of Oscar contenders as well. It's a great way to catch up on your movie-going at bargain basement prices.

Most centrally located is the Favorite, at 7488 Universal Boulevard, behind Wet 'n Wild, in the same strip mall as Sleuths dinner show. The Southchase is located not too far from Gatorland, on Orange Blossom Trail, in the Southchase Village Shopping Center, just north of SR 417, the Central Florida Greeneway. The Park 11 is in Winter Park in the K-mart Shopping Center, at the corner of Lee Road and Orlando Avenue (US 17/92), not far from I-4 Exit 46.

# CHAPTER EIGHTEEN:

# Moving Experiences

Not only are there a lot of things to see in the Orlando area, there are a lot of ways to see them. If walking or driving around begins to seem a bit boring, why not try some of these alternate modes of taking in the sights? There are some sights you will be able to see in no other way. Then again, some of these experiences are ends in themselves, with the passing scenery merely a backdrop.

Gathered together in this chapter, then, are the many and varied ways to get up in the air or out on the water during your Orlando vacation.

## Balloon Rides

Up, up, and away in a beautiful balloon. It's a great way to start the day and, if floating along on a big bubble of hot air appeals to you, that's when you'll have to go — at dawn. The weather's capricious in Orlando and at dawn the winds are at their calmest. A number of companies offer ballooning experiences in the Orlando area, and they all operate in much the same fashion, providing much the same experience.

Typically, you will make your "weather-permitting" reservation by phone; your flight will be confirmed (or called off) the night before. Then it's up with the birds to meet at a central location in the pre-dawn twilight for a ride to the launch site, which will be determined by the prevailing weather conditions.

Most balloon operators let their passengers experience the fun (or is it the hard work?) of unloading and inflating the balloon. When the balloon is fully inflated, you soar aloft on a 45-minute to one-hour flight to points unknown. Of course, the pilot has a pretty good idea of where he'd *like* to put down, but the winds have a way of altering plans. After landing, once the balloon is packed away, a champagne toast is offered. With photographs and certificates, the passengers are inducted into the confraternity of ballooning. Some excursions include breakfast. The whole experience takes anywhere from three to four hours.

The balloons — or more properly the baskets that hang beneath the balloons — hold anywhere from two to 20 people, with six- to eight-passenger baskets being the most common. Usually, then, you will be riding with other people. If a couple wants a balloon to themselves (a frequent request), the price goes up. A few balloon operators try to float over Disney World whenever the winds cooperate, but it's hard to guarantee. The Disney folks are (understandably) less than happy about balloons landing on their property, so pilots must plan with care. Typically, your flight will be over the less-populated fringes of the metro area.

Hot-air ballooning is not cheap (most accept credit cards). Figure on about $150 to $170 per person for the brief flight and the attendant hoopla. Still, for those looking for a very special way to celebrate a birthday or an anniversary, the ballooning experience is not quite like any other. As one brochure puts it, "the ballooning adventure will last three to four hours, the memories will last a lifetime!"

## AirSports Aviation

11475 Rocket Boulevard, Orlando 32824
(407) 438-7773

Cost is $150 per person, $95 for children under 12, with groups of six or more receiving a 10% discount. Private flights for couples are $600. Prices include a champagne toast and a continental breakfast on landing, as well as a number of souvenirs of your flight.

## Orange Blossom Balloons

P.O. Box 22908, Lake Buena Vista 32830
(407) 239-7677

Cost is $160 per person, $85 for children 10 to 16, with younger children riding **free** with a paying adult. There are no private flights. Meets at Travelodge in Disney Village, where an all-you-can-eat breakfast buffet is served after the flight.

## Painted Horizons Hot Air Balloon Tours

7741 Hyacinth Drive, Orlando 32835
(407) 578-3031

Cost is $145 per person, $260 per couple on private flights, which are available only on weekends. I'm told the couples-only flights book up fast.

## Rise & Float Balloon Tours

P.O. Box 620755, Orlando 32862-0755
(407) 352-8191

"For Lovers Only" flights are $395, which includes an airborne champagne party. Regular flights are $165 per person, children (4 to 12) $85, and couples $325. An "introductory" flight for $85 involves groups of up to 20 people; half the group flies for half an hour, while the other half follows in the chase van; the two halves then switch places for another half hour flight. Meets in the parking lot of Mystery Fun House, across from Universal Studios Escape.

## SkyScapes Balloon Tours

5755 Cove Drive, Orlando 32812
(407) 856-4606

Specializes in "couples only" private flights for $350 per couple. No credit cards.

# Boat Rides

As you can easily see when you fly into Orlando, Central Florida is dotted with lakes, from the tiny to the fairly large. It also boasts its fair share of spring fed streams and rivers, as well as acre upon acre of swamps. It should come as no surprise, then, that the Orlando area offers the visitor plenty of opportunities to get on the water.

The signature Central Florida boat ride, of course, is aboard an airboat. These cleverly designed craft were created to meet the challenges of Florida's swamps and shallow estuaries. The pontoons allow the craft to float in just inches of water, the raised pilot's seat allows the driver to spot submerged obstacles (like alligators) before it's too late, and the powerful (if rather noisy) airplane propellers that power them let the boats skim across the water at a remarkable clip. The airboat is a raffish, backwoods sort of vehicle and it is used to give tourists a taste of what the old Florida of trappers and hunters was like. The "prey" is much the same — gators and such — but these days the only thing that gets shot is photographs.

Of course, there are other ways to cruise Central Florida's waters. One of the most popular is the pontoon boat, a flat rectangle set on two buoyant floats and designed for leisurely lake cruising. For many of Florida's lakeshore residents, they serve as sort of floating patios; for the tourist trade, they make excellent sightseeing vessels. Central Florida even lays claim to a sort of cruise ship that takes passengers out on the broad St. John's River for an elegant dinner. All these options are listed below, along with the major airboat excursion companies.

## A-Awesome Airboat Rides

P.O. Box 333, Christmas 32709
(407) 568-7601

| | |
|---|---|
| *Cost:* | Adults $30, children (3-12) $15, under 3 **free** |
| *Hours:* | Daily, 24 hours |
| *Location:* | Meets on SR 50 at the bridge over the St. John's River |

"Captain Bruce" runs one of two operations offering private airboat tours of the St. John's River ecosystem near Christmas, to the east of Orlando. (The other is Old Fashioned Airboat, below.) The 90-minute tours offer a close-up look at alligators, bald eagles (September through May), and other denizens of this starkly beautiful landscape.

You can take a trip in the middle of the night if you wish but you are better advised to consult with Captain Bruce on the best time to go to see what you want to see. There are two six-passenger airboats but if you have a large group, Captain Bruce can round up enough boats to accommodate 30 people.

## Adventures in Florida

1250 South 17-92, Suite 110, Longwood 32750
(407) 331-0991

| | |
|---|---|
| *Cost:* | $49 to $95, discounts available to children 5 to 10 |
| *Hours:* | Daily |
| *Location:* | Picks you up at your hotel |

Mike Kelley's innovative tour operation specializes in showing off the offbeat and natural Florida that all too many tourists never see. Many of his tours feature airboat, pontoon, and canoe trips, so I have listed them here.

The menu of tours ranges from four-hour outings to event-filled 12-hour expeditions. The "Cowboys and Indians" tour, for example, features a morning of horseback riding followed by an afternoon of canoeing, while other tours feature airboat and pontoon boat alligator hunts.

One of the wackier offerings combines a nighttime "gator hunt" with a midnight visit to Church Street Station.

All tours pick you up from your hotel and are limited to 28 people (the capacity of their mini-buses). The price includes all transportation, a professional guide, and (on the longer tours) lunch. Many of the tours take you to places and use the services of companies listed elsewhere in this book. You may find the added convenience of door to door service, the quirky combination of experiences, and the knowledgeable guides worth the additional expense. Call ahead and request their brochure, which describes their tours in detail; or ask at the Guest Services desk in your hotel.

## Aquatic Wonders Tours

101 Lakeshore Drive, Kissimmee 34741
(407) 973-4549

| | |
|---|---|
| *Cost:* | Adults $18.95, children (12 and under) $12.95, plus tax |
| *Hours:* | 9:00 a.m. to dusk |
| *Location:* | Departs from Big Toho Marina on the Kissimmee waterfront |

"Captain Ray" runs this friendly tour operation offering a terrific variety of water-borne experiences on Kissimmee's Lake Toho. You cruise aboard the 30-foot pontoon boat "Eagle Ray," and since all tours are limited to just six people, there's plenty of elbow room. Most tours last two hours and are offered both during the day and at night.

The "Eagle Watch Tour" goes in search of bald eagles and ospreys. The "Sunset Sounds" and "Starlight Wonders" tours can be taken separately or combined for a full evening of entertainment. Other tours concentrate on Native American and local settler history, fishing for kids, and nighttime gator safaris. The half-day "Aquatic Wonders" tour ($35 for all ages) concentrates on the lake's ecology and features experiments and demonstrations in the boat's "on-board wet lab." Snacks and beverages are served on board and you are encouraged to bring along your own picnic cooler. Captain Ray will even put together a custom tour just for you and your family. Call ahead and ask him to send you his informative brochure, which describes all the tours in detail and lets you make an informed decision.

## Boggy Creek Airboat Rides

Boggy Creek Road South, Kissimmee 34744
(407) 344-9550

| | |
|---|---|
| *Cost:* | Adults $16, children (8 and under) $8 |
| *Hours:* | Daily 9:00 a.m. to dusk |
| *Location:* | About 8 miles from East Irlo Bronson Highway on the north shore of East Lake Tohopekaliga |

Boggy Creek Airboats operates both 6- and 18-passenger boats on half hour tours of the northern shore of East Lake Tohopekaliga and the nooks and crannies of Boggy Creek, which is one of the few habitats of the endangered snail kite. Also on the wildlife menu are alligators, turtles, and a multitude of water fowl. Deer and bobcat are sighted, too, although this is rare. At night, by reservation only, they run "alligator hunts." The rides last about an hour and cost $25 for all.

Boggy Creek Airboats is located at East Lake Fish Camp, a lovely camping and fishing resort. Several fishing guides operate from this base. You might want to consider spending a day (and perhaps a night) here.

## Midway Airboat Tours

28501 East Highway 50, Christmas 32709
(407) 568-6790

| | |
|---|---|
| *Cost:* | Adults $14, children (11 and under) $7 |
| *Hours:* | Monday to Saturday 9:00 a.m. to 5:00 p.m.; Sunday 10:00 a.m. to 6:00 p.m. |
| *Location:* | At the St. John's River, just past Christmas |

The cheerfully ramshackle set of buildings perched on the edge of a swampy backwater in the middle of nowhere give Midway Airboat Tours the look of a movie set for some post-apocalyptic Mad Max adventure. But the featureless desolation of the immediate surroundings is deceptive because a short distance away, over the swamp grass, are the wide expanses of the St. John's River.

Midway runs economical 30- to 40-minute tours through the edges, nooks, and crannies of this fascinating ecosystem aboard 20-passenger airboats. Each trip covers about six or seven miles with gator sightings the primary goal. During the spring, this is also prime bald eagle habitat. Night tours are $25 for adults and $15 for children, with a minimum of $100 per boat; 24-hour advance reservations are required. The night tours use spotlights to point out unwary gators.

## Old Fashioned Airboat Rides

24004 Sisler Avenue, Christmas 32709
(407) 568-4307
http://www.airboatrides.com

| | |
|---|---|
| *Cost:* | Adults $30, children (12 and under) $15 |
| *Hours:* | By appointment |
| *Location:* | Meets at SR 50, opposite Midway Airboat Tours |

John "Airboat John" Long runs this boutique operation from his home, specializing in private airboat tours on three six-passenger boats. Make your arrangements by phone and then meet John at the St. John's River bridge on State Route 50. Make sure you bring along lunch or a snack.

John's 90-minute nature trips are leisurely by the standards of most airboat tours. They explore a 40-mile-round-trip swath of river and swamp. There's plenty of gators and bald eagles to be seen along this remote stretch. On one side is the Tosohatchee Preserve, on the other large swaths of private ranch land. You can stop at a small island cabin or an ancient Indian mound for lunch and a great **photo op** of the boat on the water. In the warmer months, John runs night trips in search of alligators. Gators have a reputation for being stupid but they avoid the blistering summer sun, making them smarter than the average tourist in some people's estimation.

These tours are run just for you and your family. If two couples want to take a tour at the same time, they go out on different boats. Single passengers are charged $60. "Those boats burn a lot of gas," John explains. John doesn't recommend the trips for very young children, but if you insist and the child sits on your lap, they go **free**. Payment is strictly in cash; no credit cards.

## Ride the Gator

551 Del Verde Way, Orlando, 32819
(407) 716-2285

| | |
|---|---|
| *Cost:* | $8 for all, but one child under 12 rides **free** for each adult |
| *Hours:* | Wednesday to Friday 5:00 p.m. to midnight; Saturday and Sunday noon to midnight |
| *Location:* | In the Fun Spot parking lot, near International Drive |

This one's only partially a boat ride, but thanks to a converted military amphibious vehicle, you can journey from the Fun Spot amusement park to Sandy Lake, behind Wet 'n Wild, moving from land to water and back several times along the way before returning to the starting point. Once designed to haul 10,000 pounds of live ammo, the impressive looking vehicle now hauls up to 47 happy tourists. If there's sufficient interest, the driver will stop at Congo River Golf on International Drive, where you can alight and feed the alligators for an additional fee. The fare can also be paid using four Fun Spot tickets (see *Chapter Fourteen*).

# Rivership Romance

433 North Palmetto Avenue, Sanford 32771
(800) 423-7401; (407) 321-5091

*Cost:*       $35 to $50, tax included, plus drinks and tip

*Hours:*     Cruises at 11:00 a.m. daily; 7:30 p.m. Friday and Saturday; year-round

*Location:*   From I-4 Exit 51, 4 miles east on SR 46

The Rivership Romance is a refurbished, 100-foot, 1940s Great Lakes steamer that plies the waters of Lake Monroe and the St. John's River for leisurely luncheon and dinner cruises. It's not quite the Love Boat, but for a nice change of pace from landlocked dining, it will do quite nicely.

There are three-hour luncheon cruises on Wednesday, Saturday, and Sunday; four-hour luncheon cruises on Monday, Tuesday, Thursday, and Friday; and three-and-a-half-hour dinner cruises on Friday and Saturday. Live entertainment is featured on the longer luncheon cruise and there is dancing to a sophisticated combo on the evening cruises. Reservations are required and all major credit cards are accepted.

The dinner menu is short but sumptuous and, in true cruise line tradition, the portions are generous. After starting off with plump chilled shrimp, you can choose from glazed chicken breast, a chicken Caesar salad, or vegetarian lasagna. The roast prime rib, however, seems to be the favorite.

The scenery's nothing to sneeze at either. The St. John's is one of just two larger rivers in the world that flow north and during the four-hour luncheon cruise, you'll get to see some 25 miles of its history-steeped shores. There's not much to see at night, of course, except for the stars. And for the romantic couples who take these cruises that's the whole point.

# St. John's River Cruises

4255 Peninsula Point, Sanford 32771
(407) 330-1612

*Cost:*       $12 to $49, plus tax

*Hours:*     Daily 8:00 a.m. to sunset, except Monday; 2-hour cruises at 11:00 a.m. and 1:30 p.m.

**Location:**  From I-4 Exit 51, follow SR 46 through
Sanford, then turn left on SR 415

Bob and Evie Hopkins are waiting to take you on a nature cruise aboard the Native II, a 50-foot, 48-passenger shaded pontoon boat, along the densely wooded shores of the St. John's River. There are two two-hour cruises daily (sometimes reduced to one in the off-season) that head south on the winding river for a 15-mile round-trip journey. Thanks to the river's many islands, estuaries, and bayous, the boat never traverses the same stretch of waterway twice. Much of the territory covered is wilderness, although there are a few homes to be seen. Wildlife is plentiful and the boat's leisurely six-mile-per-hour pace makes critter-spotting easy. Prices for these cruises are $12 for adults, $10 for seniors (60+), and $6 for children under 12.

If you can round up at least 20 people, you can book the Native II for an all-day cruise across Lake Monroe and north on the St. John's to beautiful Blue Springs State Park, the winter home to many of Florida's manatees. This cruise, which leaves at 8:00 a.m. and returns around 5:00 p.m., includes continental breakfast, lunch, and afternoon snacks. The flat deck of the boat is outfitted with moveable tables and chairs, making for a comfortable and homey day's enjoyment. The cost is a surprisingly modest $49 per person. On days when an all-day outing is scheduled, there are no two-hour cruises. Advance reservations are essential for the all-day cruise and highly recommended for all cruises.

## Two Rivers Outpost
4650 East SR 46, Geneva 32732
(407) 349-1110

**Cost:**  Adults $15, children (8 and under) $8, including tax

**Hours:**  Daily 6:00 a.m. to 10:00 p.m.

**Location:**  From I-4 Exit 51, follow SR 46 East about 24 miles; 12 miles from I-95

It's a bit of a drive to Two Rivers, but once you arrive you'll know you've left tourist civilization miles behind. There's not a house to be seen for miles out here, just unspoiled, pre-settler Florida wilderness. The half-hour airboat jaunts into the wild from this lonely outpost are filled with sightings of deer, eagles, ospreys, pelicans, and alligators. Nighttime gator hunts are arranged by appointment (call at least six hours ahead) and cost $25 for all. They last 45 minutes to an hour and offer a wonderfully spooky backwoods experience. You can also rent fishing boats here for $45 a day, $25 a half day, or $15 an hour.

# Winter Park Scenic Boat Tour
312 East Morse Boulevard, Winter Park 32789
(407) 644-4056

| | |
|---|---|
| *Cost:* | Adults $7, children (2 to 11) $3, with tax |
| *Hours:* | Daily 10:00 a.m. to 4:00 p.m. on the hour |
| *Location:* | At the foot of Morse Boulevard, a short stroll from Park Avenue's fancy shops |

The little town of Winter Park has 17 lakes. Thanks to the operators of these modest, flat pontoon boats, you can visit three of them on a leisurely one-hour cruise. You slip between the lakes through narrow canals originally cut by logging crews in the 1800s and barely wide enough to accommodate the tour boat. It's not quite Venice but it makes for an unusual and relaxing outing.

There's plenty of bird life to be seen on this tour and your guide will dutifully point out the wading herons, muscovy ducks, and ospreys nesting high in the cypress trees. Less frequently sighted, but there nonetheless, are alligators, some of them quite large. There's also a bit of local history to take in, from the campus of Rollins College to the palatial 1898 Brewer estate, the only Winter Park home on the National Historic Register.

But, this tour is really about real estate envy. As you glide past one gorgeous multi-million dollar home after another, their impeccably landscaped backyards cascading down to boathouses that coyly echo the architecture of the big house, you will find yourself asking, "Why them and not me? Why, why, why?"

# Helicopter Tours
Small operations offering guided aerial sightseeing by helicopter pop up (and disappear) with some regularity. If the ones listed here are closed by the time you arrive, you'll probably spot new ones as you drive around the tourist areas. They all seem to offer much the same menu of tours, ranging from short five- to seven-minute hops for about $20 to half-hour surveys for about $125. Some offer extended trips that take in Kennedy Space Center for $400. Typically, these operators require a minimum of two passengers, although some offer special one-person rates.

*Tip:* The farther they have to fly the more expensive the trip. So if you especially want to see Universal Studios, pick a helipad on International Drive; if Disney World is on your must-see list, try a tour that leaves from Kissimmee. You might save some money.

## Air Orlando Helicopters

8990 International Drive, Orlando 32819

(407) 354-1400

| | |
|---|---|
| *Cost:* | $20 to $395 per person, with discounts for children under 12 on some of the longer flights |
| *Hours:* | Daily 10:00 a.m. to 9:00 p.m. |
| *Location:* | At Amazing Animals, next to Race Rock |

## Orlando Helitours

5519 West Irlo Bronson Highway, Kissimmee 34746

(407) 397-0226

| | |
|---|---|
| *Cost:* | Adults $20 to $125, children (under 11) $20 to $65 |
| *Hours:* | Daily 9:00 a.m. to sunset |
| *Location:* | Just east of I-4 |

# Plane Rides

## Air Florida Charter

Orlando Executive Airport, Orlando 32803

(407) 888-4114

| | |
|---|---|
| *Cost:* | Adults $40, children (under 10) $25 |
| *Hours:* | By appointment |
| *Location:* | At the Orlando Executive Airport, near Fashion Square Mall on East Colonial Drive |

This on-demand air charter service will fly you to the Bahamas or Key West if Orlando's attractions begin to pale. They also offer a 45-minute aerial sightseeing tour of Orlando aboard 3- or 4-seater fixed wing aircraft such as a Cessna 172. The narrated tour covers the major theme parks (Disney, Universal, SeaWorld) and includes a souvenir photo.

## Seminole-Lake Gliderport

P. O. Box 120458, Clermont 34712

(352) 394-5450

http://www.soarfl.com

| | |
|---|---|
| *Cost:* | $50 to $110, including tax |
| *Hours:* | Tuesday to Sunday 9:00 a.m. to dusk |

*Location:*     Just south of Clermont, at the intersection of SR 33 and SR 561

If you look up in the sky and see puffy cumulus clouds against a warm blue sky, it's perfect gliding weather. You might just want to pop over to the Clermont area for an air-powered glider ride. The folks at Seminole-Lake Gliderport will put you in a high-performance glider with an FAA-certified instructor, tow you into the wild blue yonder — and let you go.

The price depends on the altitude at which the flight starts and, hence, its length. A $50 flight starts from 2,000 feet and last 15 to 20 minutes. At $90 and 4,000 feet they'll throw in some aerial maneuvers and the flight will last about 35 minutes. The $110 flight takes you to 5,300 feet, offering a spectacular view of Central Florida on the nearly one-hour glide to landing.

Flights begin about 11:00 a.m., with the last flight about 4:00 p.m. Visa and MasterCard are accepted. Instruction is also offered; rated pilots can pick up a gliding add-on to their license in about three or four days.

# CHAPTER NINETEEN:

# Sports Scores

## PART I: PARTICIPANT SPORTS

The mild climate of Central Florida is an open and on-going invitation to the active life. Sportsmen and women will find a wide array of choices to fit every taste and every budget.

## Golf Courses

For golfers, Central Florida is a sort of demi-paradise, with 123 courses within a 45-minute drive of downtown Orlando. With that many, choosing one can be a daunting task. You can simplify matters by using the services of Tee Times USA, (800) 347-8633. They will help you pick a course and make the reservations for you; they'll even fax driving directions to your home or hotel. It's a free service and you will pay the regular greens fees. You'll get the best choice of courses and times if you book several months in advance but they will arrange next-day tee times as well.

I have listed here golf courses in Orange and Osceola counties on the theory that most of my readers will be staying in Orlando (Orange County) or Kissimmee (Osceola County). If you want to explore farther afield, call (800) 864-6101 before you leave for Florida and order a copy of *Golfer's Guide* for the Orlando and Central Florida area. There is a $3 charge which can be paid for over the phone with a credit card. Or call the Orlando Convention and Visitors Bureau, (407) 363-5831, to find out where you can pick up a free copy in the Orlando area. You will also find an extensive listing of golf courses of all types in the Yellow Pages in your hotel room.

All these courses are in the (407) area code.

## Municipal Courses

Dubsdread Golf Course, Orlando, 246-3636
Winter Park Municipal, Winter Park, 623-3339

## Public Courses

Crystalbrook Golf Club, Kissimmee, 847-8721
Forest Lake Golf Course, Ocoee, 654-4653
The Greens Golf Club, Orlando, 351-5121
Hunters Creek Golf Club, Orlando, 240-4653
Remington Golf Club, Kissimmee, 344-4004
Walk-N-Sticks Golf Club, Kissimmee, 348-9555
Winter Pines Golf Club, Winter Park, 671-3172

## Resort Courses

Eagle Pines (WDW), Lake Buena Vista, 939-4653
Falcon's Fire Golf Course, Kissimmee, 397-2777
Grand Cypress Resort, Orlando, 239-4700
International Golf Club, Orlando, 239-6909
Marriott's World Center, Orlando, 239-4200
Orange Lake Country Club, Orlando, 239-1050
Poinciana Golf and Racquet Club, Kissimmee, 933-5300

## Semi-Private Courses

Buenaventura Lakes West, Kissimmee, 348-4915
Cypress Creek Country Club, Orlando, 351-2187
Eastwood Golf Club, Orlando, 281-4653
Kissimmee Bay Country Club, Kissimmee, 348-4653
Kissimmee Golf Club, Kissimmee, 847-2816
Meadow Woods Golf Club, Windermere, 850-5600
Metro-West Country Club, Orlando, 299-1099
The Oaks, Kissimmee, 933-4055
Rosemont Golf and Country Club, Orlando, 298-1232
Ventura Country Club, Orlando, 277-2640
Wedgefield Golf and Country Club, Orlando, 568-2116
Zellwood Station Country Club, Zellwood, 886-3303

# Fishing

The best time to go fishing, the conventional wisdom has it, is when you can. And you can go fishing in Central Florida. Boy, can you ever. If you just want to throw a line in the water and drift into a semi-trance, you can do that just about anywhere. If you'd like to do some *real* fishing, I strongly suggest you hire a guide. There are a number of reasons for this:

- A guide has the in-depth local knowledge you lack.
- A guide may be your only means of access to private lakes that have not been over-fished.
- A guide will provide tackle and bait, saving you the hassle of schlepping it with you.
- Many of Orlando's fishing guides are attractions in themselves, practitioners of a lifestyle that has all but disappeared in our homogenized fast-food culture.

Throughout much of the American Southeast bass fishing is virtually a state religion, and most of the Orlando area fishing guides seem to specialize in this feisty game fish. There are, however, other fish to be caught hereabouts. Here is a list of Central Florida species, with notes on their seasons:

*American shad:* Optimum, February and March, so-so January, April, and May.

*Bluegill:* Optimum, April to June, so-so the rest of the year.

*Channel catfish:* So-so all year.

*Crappie:* Optimum, December to March, so-so April and May.

*Largemouth bass:* Optimum, January to March, so-so the rest of the year.

*Shellcracker:* Optimum, May to July, so-so the rest of the year.

*Sunshine bass:* Optimum, December to February, so-so March, April, October, and November.

*Striped bass:* Optimum, December to February, so-so March, April, October, and November.

What you go after, then, will be a function of the time of your visit and your guide's predilections. Where you go will depend to a fair extent on the guide you hire and his location; each has his favorite (or even exclusive) areas. Among the more popular fishing spots are the Clermont chain of lakes (west of Orlando), the Wekiva River and the St. John's River (north of Orlando), and West Lake Tohopekaliga (in Kissimmee). Serious fishermen will want to pick up a copy of Kris Thoemke's *Fishing Florida* (Falcon Press, $18.95), which provides lake by lake, stream by stream commentary.

Guides do not come cheap; $200 for a full day and $125 for a half day is fairly standard, although some services charge as much as $275 for a full day and $180 for a half. The price covers two people, plus tackle and, sometimes, bait. If all you have time (or money) for is a half-day, make it the morning. Of course, you will also need a Florida State fishing license. A 7-day license for a non-resident is $16.50, an annual one is $31.50. You can get one at any fishing camp, or your guide will help you obtain one.

**A #1 Bass Guide Service**
P.O. Box 421257, Kissimmee 34742
(800) 707-5463

**A-Action Bass Guide Services**
P.O. Box 701625, St. Cloud 34770
(800) 936-7398; (407) 892-7184

**A Pro Bass Guide Service**
398 Grove Court, Winter Garden 34787
(407) 877-9676

**Bass Anglers Guide Service**
6526 SR 535, Windermere 34786
(407) 656-1052

**Bass Brothers**
P.O. Box 120459, Clermont 34712
(800) 883-6415

**Bass Challenger Guide Service**
P.O. Box 679155, Orlando 32867
(407) 273-8045

**Bass Fishing Unlimited, Bob Lawson**
(407) 931-3130

**Big Toho Marina**
101 Lake Shore Boulevard, Kissimmee 34741
(407) 846-2124

**Lake Charters Guide Service**
1820 Henry Street, Kissimmee 34741
(407) 933-2021

**Richardson's Fish Camp**
1550 Scotty's Road, Kissimmee 34744
(407) 846-6540

**Shiner King Bass Guide Service**
P.O. Box 422707, Kissimmee 34742
(407) 390-9400

# Horseback Riding

There are a few places to go horseback riding in the Orlando area. Most stables offer leisurely trail rides of about an hour or so. Lessons are also available at these stables.

## Devonwood Stables

2518 Rouse Road, Orlando 32817
(407) 273-0822

| | |
|---|---|
| *Cost:* | $25 for one hour, $40 for two hours |
| *Hours:* | Tuesday to Sunday 9:00 a.m. to sunset |
| *Location:* | Half way between East Colonial Drive and University Boulevard in eastern Orlando |

## Grand Cypress Equestrian Center

1 Equestrian Drive, Orlando 32836
(407) 239-1938

| | |
|---|---|
| *Cost:* | $30 to $45, plus tax |
| *Hours:* | Daily 8:00 a.m. to 5:00 p.m. |
| *Location:* | On SR 535, about 4 miles from I-4 Exit 27 |

## Horse World

3705 South Poinciana Boulevard, Kissimmee 34758
(407) 847-4343

| | |
|---|---|
| *Cost:* | $30 to $40, plus tax |
| *Hours:* | Daily 9:00 a.m. to 5:00 p.m. |
| *Location:* | About 12 miles south of Highway 192 |

# Miniature Golf

Just as the amusement park was revolutionized by Walt and his followers, miniature golf, once a homey mom-and-pop sort of attraction, has become a multi-level "themed" extravaganza with entrepreneurs competing with each other to create the most unusual, most atmospheric, most elaborate course yet. And the Orlando area boasts some of the finest examples of the genre. For most visitors, there's nothing quite like this back home, and I think a visit to at least one miniature golf attraction should be included in every Orlando vacation.

Most of the courses are concentrated in the International Drive area of Orlando and along US 192 in Kissimmee. During the warmer months, it's best to avoid the torrid heat of the day and play at night. Don't worry, they all stay open late. Discount coupons to most (if not all) of these courses can be found in brochure racks and throwaway magazines.

# Bonanza

7761 West Irlo Bronson Highway, Kissimmee 34746
(407) 396-7536

Behind that towering rock formation over the Magic Mining Company restaurant ("Steaks & Seafood") lies a cleverly laid out miniature golf course with a Gold Rush theme. There are two complete 18-hole courses, The Prospector (the easier of the two) and The Gold Nugget. Putt your way over this three-story mountain past cascading waterfalls, old mining sluices, trestle bridges, mountain pools, and cool grottoes. The course is compact, well maintained, and a lot of fun. The entrance to Splendid China is just across the way.

*Prices:* $6 for adults, $5 for children under 9. The second 18 holes are half price.

# Congo River Golf

6312 International Drive, Orlando 32819
(407) 352-0042
4777 West Irlo Bronson Highway, Kissimmee 34746
(407) 396-6900
531 West SR 436, Altamonte Springs 32714
(407) 682-4077

Here you can putt your way up, through, around, and over Livingston Falls in a setting that evokes a storybook Africa and the memory of Stanley and Livingston. There are two complete 18-hole courses, with the "Stanley" course being the easier of the two. If you find yourself having difficulties making par, it's "Livingston," I presume. The holes on both courses are lined with small rocks and large boulders, making for erratic and unpredictable bounces. The International Drive location offers views onto Wet 'n Wild's lake, where you will see screaming riders in inner tubes being towed by jet skis.

*Prices:* $9.95 for 36 holes, $6.95 for 18, $3.95 for replays.

# Million Dollar Mulligan

2850 Florida Plaza Boulevard, Kissimmee 34746
(407) 396-8180

Before there was Astroturf, there was turf, and Million Dollar Mulligan, located right next to Old Town, is unique in offering a miniature golf experience on honest to goodness Bermuda grass. The course is impeccably maintained with each hole looking just like a grown-up golf hole, complete with sand traps. You can choose between two 9-hole courses — Emerald Isles, a putting course, and Links Par-3, a pitch-and-putt course.

*Prices:* The putting course is $7.50 or $5.75 for juniors (12 and under) and seniors (60+). The pitch-and-putt course is $11, or $7.25 for juniors and seniors.

## Pirates Cove

8601 International Drive, Orlando 32819
(407) 352-7378
Crossroads Center, Lake Buena Vista 32836
(407) 827-1242
2845 Florida Plaza Boulevard, Kissimmee 34746
(407) 396-7484

Adventure on the high seas is the theme here with two 18-hole courses named after Blackbeard and Capt. Kidd. Blackbeard's Adventure is the more challenging of the two. The design and execution of these courses is on a par with that seen at Congo River. I give Pirates Cove a slight edge, however, with the Lake Buena Vista location my personal favorite. It boasts extra height and higher waterfalls, not to mention its location next to Pebbles restaurant (a personal favorite for its tasty cuisine). At all locations, the courses are punctuated with signs offering the real-life history of their namesake pirates. (Will this edutainment never stop!) Prices are somewhat higher than at other area courses, but dollars-off coupons are fairly easy to come by.

*Prices:* Blackbeard's Adventure ranges from $6 to $7 for adults and from $4.50 to $6 for kids 12 and under; Capt. Kidd's Adventure ranges from $5.50 to $6.50 for adults and from $4 to $5.50 for kids. Prices vary by location with Kissimmee charging the least.

## Pirates Island Adventure Golf

4330 West Irlo Bronson Highway, Kissimmee 34746
(407) 396-4660

Once again the theme is piracy and once again the two 18-hole courses are named for Blackbeard and Capt. Kidd. This is one of the handsomest courses in the Orlando area, with a spectacular central waterfall cascading down in stages to a series of lagoons complete with artificial mist. The course is beautifully maintained, with smooth brick borders on each hole. There's edutainment here, too, with signs providing capsule biographies of well-known (and not so well-known) pirates.

*Prices:* Blackbeard's Challenge is $6.50 for adults, $5 for children;

Capt. Kidd's Adventure is $5.50 and $4. Play both and the second course costs $3 for adults and kids, and you can play until closing time.

## River Adventure Golf

4535 West Irlo Bronson Highway, Kissimmee 34746
(407) 396-4666

The spinning waterwheel that serves as this course's billboard says it all. A river bubbles up at the top of an artificial hill and tumbles down through a number of rocky streams to a placid lagoon below. There's just one 18-hole course with plenty of greenery. Hedges and ivy-covered rock outcroppings abound. This is yet another impeccably maintained course, with signs that announce not just the hole number and par but the distance to the hole as well. There's a "19th hole" where you can putt for a free game.

*Prices:* Adults $6, children (4 to 10) $5, children under 4 **free**. The second game is $3.

# Skydiving

## World Skydiving Center

440 Airport Road, Lake Wales (Lake Wales Airport )33853
(941) 678-1003

Ever feel like throwing yourself out of a plane? Then this is the place to come and test your resolve. Actually, it's remarkably easy, since someone else throws you out of the plane.

Allow me to explain: Would-be skydivers can experience the joys of freefall on a "tandem jump." That means you are strapped securely to a certified instructor, who knows the ropes and controls the jump. After a flight to 13,500 feet, the fun begins, with a full minute of freefall and about five minutes under a parachute to landing. No experience is necessary, but jumpers must be at least 18 years of age and weigh no more than 230 pounds.

The cost, including tax, is $125 on weekdays and $145 on weekends. If you want your dive immortalized on video, add another $75. If you can talk two or more of your friends into jumping with you, you'll all receive a discount — $10 per person. For groups of seven or more people, the discount goes to $20 a head. Licensed skydivers with their own gear can jump for just $16.50.

The first jump is scheduled for about 8:00 a.m. and the last usually goes at sunset. But since the entire experience takes about four to six hours, including a very thorough pre-jump briefing, plan on arriving early. The best idea is to reserve your jump a few days in advance. The Skydiving Center is open daily from November to April and from Thursday to Sunday the rest of the year.

# Jet Ski Rentals

Jet skis, those noisy motorcycles of the seas, are becoming increasingly popular (much to the dismay of those who prefer their lakes quiet and peaceful). If you'd like to take one out for a spin, there are a number of places that will accommodate you. No experience is necessary and driving a jet ski is the soul of simplicity. Rentals start at about $20 for as many minutes and go up from there based on your time on the water. The places listed here also offer water skiing.

## Buena Vista Watersports

13245 Lake Bryan Drive, Orlando 32830
(407) 239-6939

## Kissimmee Water Sports

4914 West Irlo Bronson Highway, Kissimmee 34746
(407) 396-1888

# PART II: SPECTATOR SPORTS

The more sedentary among us will find enough spectator sports in and around Orlando to keep them busy for quite some time. With the possible exception of the Magic, tickets are easy to come by and reasonably priced.

# Arena Football

Arena football is a scaled-down, indoor version of pro football. Two eight-man teams square off on a field about a half the size of the outdoor version. Adding interest to the game, six players on each team play both offense and defense. Otherwise, the rules are much the same as those for pro football. There are 16 professional arena football teams in the United States.

## Orlando Predators

20 North Orange Avenue, Orlando 32801
(407) 648-4444

*Season:* April to August
*Where:* Orlando Arena
*Ticket Prices:* $10 to $33 (group rates available), through TicketMaster or the Arena box office

# Auto Racing

These two racing venues, within hailing distance of each other on the far eastern fringes of the Orlando metropolitan area, are where amateurs race for the love of it. Orange County Raceway has several different tracks, all of them dirt or clay, which means their schedule is subject to the vagaries of the Florida weather. This is where you want to be for BMX bicycles, motocross, stock cars, and four-wheel-drive Mud Boggs (modified trucks). Speed World has a straight paved track with bleachers, including a platform for wheelchairs; this track is strictly for dragsters. There's usually something going on at one or both tracks on the weekends, with additional events on some weeknights, but it's a good idea to call for current information.

## Orange County Raceway

19442 East Colonial Drive, Orlando 32833
(407) 568-2271

*Season:* Year-round, call for schedule
*Ticket Prices*: $8

## Speed World Dragway

19164 East Colonial Drive, Orlando 32833
(407) 568-5522

*Season:* Year-round, call for schedule
*Ticket Prices:* $10 to $12

# Baseball, Major League

With the arrival in 1998 of the Tampa Bay Devil Rays, a new expansion team in the American League, Central Florida now can boast its own professional baseball team. Despite the name, the team plays in St. Petersburg, not Tampa.

## Tampa Bay Devil Rays

1 Tropicana Drive, St. Petersburg 33705
(813) 825-3137

| | |
|---|---|
| *Season:* | April to September |
| *Where:* | 1 Tropicana Drive, St. Petersburg |
| *Ticket Prices:* | $7 to $20 for general admission |

# Baseball, Major League Spring Training

Many major league baseball teams find Florida's spring weather ideal for their pre-season warm-ups. The training regimen includes a number of exhibition games in March that allow the teams a chance to limber up and practice under realistic conditions. They also give fans a chance to look over their favorite team's form and check out new players before the official season begins.

I have listed here the teams that have spring training camps within striking distance of Orlando, bearing in mind that a true fan's definition of "striking distance" could mean 100 miles.

## Cincinnati Reds

Plant City Stadium
1900 South Park Road, Plant City 33566
(813) 752-7337

| | |
|---|---|
| *Location:* | South of I-4 Exit 14 about 2.5 miles |
| *Ticket Prices*: | $4 to $7 |

## Cleveland Indians

Chain O' Lakes Park
Cypress Gardens Boulevard, Winter Haven 33880
(954) 523-3309

| | |
|---|---|
| *Location:* | Intersection of US 17 and Cypress Gardens Boulevard (about 5 miles from Cypress Gardens) |
| *Ticket Prices:* | $5 to $8 |

## Detroit Tigers

Joker Marchant Stadium
2301 Lakeland Hills Boulevard, Lakeland 33805
(941) 686-8075

| | |
|---|---|
| *Location:* | South of I-4 Exit 19 about 3 miles |
| *Ticket Prices*: | $5 to $8 |

# Florida Marlins
Space Coast Stadium
5800 Stadium Parkway, Melbourne 32940
(407) 633-9200
>    *Location:*     I-95 Exit 74, then 3 miles south on Fiske
>                    Boulevard
>    *Ticket Prices:* $5 to $12

# Houston Astros
Osceola County Stadium
1000 Bill Beck Boulevard, Kissimmee 34744
(407) 933-2520
>    *Location:*     Off US 192, just east of Kissimmee
>    *Ticket Prices:* $6 to $10

# Kansas City Royals
Baseball City Stadium
300 Stadium Way, Haines City 33837
(813) 424-2500
>    *Location:*     South of I-4 Exit 23, about 1 mile
>    *Ticket Prices:* $5 to $9

# Los Angeles Dodgers
Dodgertown
4001 26th Street, Vero Beach 32961
(407) 569-6858
>    *Location:*     Take SR 60 East from I-95, turn left on
>                    43rd Avenue, then right on 26th Street
>    *Ticket Prices:* $5 to $8

# New York Yankees
Legends Fields
3820 West Martin Luther King Boulevard, Tampa 33805
(813) 879-2244
>    *Location:*     I-4 to I-275, Dale Mabry (North) exit
>    *Ticket Prices:* $6 to $10

# Philadelphia Phillies
Jack Russell Memorial Stadium
800 Phillies Drive, Clearwater 34615
(813) 442-8496

*Location:* SR 60 West to Highland Avenue, then north to Palmetto Street, turn left

*Ticket Prices:* $7 to $8

## Pittsburgh Pirates

McKechnie Field
17th Avenue West & 9th Street West, Bradenton 34205
(941) 748-4610

*Location:* I-75 Exit 42, then west on SR 64, left on 9th Street West

*Ticket Prices:* $5.50 to $8.50

## St. Louis Cardinals

Al Lang Stadium
180 Second Avenue, St. Petersburg 33701
(813) 894-4773

*Location:* I-175 to end, left on First Street South to stadium

*Ticket Prices:* $7 to $8

## Toronto Blue Jays

Dunedin Stadium
311 Douglas Avenue, Dunedin 34698
(813) 733-0429

*Location:* From US 19, west on Sunset Point Road, right on Douglas Avenue

*Ticket Prices:* $7 to $9

# Baseball, Minor League

The Orlando area's two farm teams give you a chance to see some rising (and a few falling) stars in action. The Cobras (Class A) are affiliated with the Houston Astros, while the Rays (Class AA) are owned by the Tampa Bay Devil Rays but affiliated (at least for now) with the Seattle Mariners.

## Kissimmee Cobras

1000 Bill Beck Boulevard, Kissimmee 34744
(888) 592-7047; (407) 933-5400

*Season:* April to September

*Where:* Osceola County Stadium, on US 192-

441, east of Kissimmee
*Ticket Prices:* $3.50 to $5 at the stadium

## Orlando Rays
287 South Tampa Avenue, Orlando 32805
(407) 649-7297

*Season:*     April to September
*Where:*      Tinker Field, next to the Citrus Bowl, west of I-4 Exit 38
*Ticket Prices:*  $3 to $7, through TicketMaster or at the stadium

# Basketball

The Magic are definitely the hottest sports ticket in town. Don't be surprised if you find them sold out well in advance, especially if they are playing the Lakers or the Bulls. Still, tickets are sometimes available. You can always try your luck outside the Arena on the day of a game; someone just might have an "extra" ticket. Florida law prohibits the sale of a sports ticket for more than $1 over its face value, but scalpers have commanded from $225 to $1,000 for tickets to Magic playoff games.

## Orlando Magic
1 Magic Place, Orlando 32801
(800) 338-0005; (407) 896-2442

*Season:*     November to April
*Where:*      Orlando Arena
*Ticket Prices:*  $37 to $120, at the Arena box office or through TicketMaster

# Dog Racing

Orlando has two greyhound tracks, a short distance apart, which avoid competing with each other by having precisely different seasons. Seminole Greyhound Track operates from May through October, while the Sanford-Orlando Kennel Club is open from November through April. Both are just across the Seminole County line, north of Orlando. Admission is cheap, starting at $1 for grandstand seats, and both tracks allow you to bet on dog and horse races elsewhere that are beamed in by satellite. Of the two, the Seminole Greyhound Track has a slightly nicer setting, with a backdrop of trees and open skies.

## Sanford-Orlando Kennel Club
301 Dog Track Road, Longwood 32750
(407) 831-1600

## Seminole Greyhound Park
2000 Seminola Boulevard, Casselberry 32707
(407) 699-4510

# Ice Hockey
The Orlando Solar Bears are part of the International Hockey League. The team was launched in 1995 and got off to a good start, making it to the playoffs their first season.

## Orlando Solar Bears
8701 Maitland-Summit Boulevard, Orlando 32810
(407) 872-7825

    *Season:*        October to April
    *Where:*        Orlando Arena
    *Ticket Prices:*  $6 to $28, at the Arena box office only

# Jai-Alai
Jai-Alai is played on a sort of elongated racquetball court but, instead of a racquet, the players use a long curved wicker basket, called a cesta, strapped to their right hand, to catch and return the pelota (or "ball") at blinding speeds. To facilitate betting, the game is played in round-robin fashion by eight single players or two-man doubles teams. The first to reach seven points wins, with second and third place determined by point totals. Playoffs settle ties.

Reflecting the Basque origins of the game, most of the players have Basque or Spanish surnames. The action is fast and often surprisingly graceful. Points are determined much as they are in racquetball or squash. As one player (or team) loses a point, the next player takes his place. Although the program gives stats on the players, betting seems more like picking the numbers for a lottery game.

If you tire of the action unfolding in front of you, you can repair downstairs and bet on jai-alai matches in Miami or horse racing at New Jersey's Meadowlands, all of them shown on large video screens.

# Orlando Jai-Alai
Highway 17-92 & SR 436, Fern Park 32730

(407) 331-9191

*Season:*        Year-round

*Prices:*        $1 to $5, at the door

*Game Times:*    Wednesday to Saturday at 7:30 p.m.;
                 matinees Thursday and Saturday at 12:00
                 noon; Sunday at 1:00 p.m.

# Rodeo

A rodeo might seem a little too "Wild West" for Orlando, until we remember that Osceola County was the heart of Florida cattle country before Mickey arrived. Once a week, Central Florida cowhands and other rodeo enthusiasts get to show off their riding and roping skills for the general public. There's plenty of bareback riding, bull riding, bronco busting, and calf roping, along with a "calf scramble," in which kids from the audience get to chase after a mini-herd of skittish dogies.

Your host on horseback dispenses insight into the rules of rodeo along with cornpone humor ("How do you make a good impression on a lawyer?" "How?" "Steel-belted radials."). A large concession stand dispenses hamburgers, hot dogs, hot chocolate, and soft drinks, while a souvenir stand offers cowboy regalia, including straw cowboy hats for less than $10.

## Kissimmee Rodeo
958 South Hoagland Boulevard, Kissimmee 34741

(407) 933-0020

*Season:*    Year-round

*Prices:*    Adults $10, children (under 12) $5, children 3 and under **free**

*Times:*     8:00 p.m. Fridays, except closed the third week of February and Fourth of July weekend

# CHAPTER TWENTY:

# Shop 'Til You Drop

Seen all the attractions? Got some money left? No problem! Orlando makes it easy to go home flat broke and maybe with a few genuine bargains to help convince the folks back home that you're not simply an unregenerate spendthrift. Of course, for many people, shopping is an attraction in itself, bargain or no. Whatever category fits you best, you're sure to find plenty of opportunities to shop 'til you drop.

## Outlet Shopping

Once upon a time, "factory outlets" were just that — small shops located in or near the factory where seconds, rejects, overruns, and discontinued lines could be sold, at a discount, directly to the public. Factory outlets existed outside the standard retail channels and were a classic win/win proposition: The public got a bargain and the factory recouped at least some of its costs.

Today, factory outlets have become very much a part of the retail scene, located far from the factory in glossy malls and often featuring merchandise specifically designed for and marketed to the bargain-hunting segment of the market. And the words "Factory Outlet" have become a marketing buzzword used to suggest deep, deep discounts, whether they are there or not. Some factory outlets are run directly by the companies whose merchandise they sell. Others are run by entrepreneurs who contract with big name companies and then set their own prices. Still others are run by merchants who buy cheap merchandise from a variety of off-cost producers or from brokers who specialize in overstocked and "distressed" goods. All of which is to say that, when it comes to factory outlet shopping, the warning "caveat emptor" (let the buyer beware) is in full force. On the other hand, I do not mean to suggest that the outlet malls in the Orlando area are filled with shady operators out to fleece the unwary tourist. Far from it. Most of these outlets offer excellent deals on first-rate goods and any factory seconds or irregulars are clearly marked. Still, a wise shopper will arrive with a clear idea of what he or she is looking for and what the "going rate" for those items is back home.

What follows is a survey of the major factory outlet shopping venues in the Orlando area. Conveniently enough, most of them are located along International Drive in Orlando. I have listed them in the order you would encounter them when traveling from north to south along this well-traveled tourist corridor and then south to Kissimmee. The list is not meant to be all-inclusive. You may find other bona-fide outlets. On the other hand, there are many shops that use the words "factory outlet" rather loosely.

Finally, a note on sales tax. Orange County (Orlando) levies a six percent tax on all retail sales. In nearby Osceola County (Kissimmee) the sales tax is seven percent.

# Belz Outlet Mall

*Location:* At the north end of International Drive, north of the intersection of Oak Ridge Road

*Information:* (407) 354-0126

*Hours:* Monday to Saturday 10:00 a.m. to 9:00 p.m.; Sunday 10:00 a.m. to 6:00 p.m.

Belz is the 900-pound gorilla of the outlet scene with two malls and four "annexes" housing some 160 merchants who offer, according to Belz's management, up to 75% off every day. Like any self-respecting mall, this one features food courts and snack kiosks to refuel the flagging shopper. There are also games and rides for the kiddies.

# International Designer Outlets

*Location:* At the north end of International Drive, south of the intersection with Oak Ridge Road

*Information:* (407) 325-3632

*Hours:* Monday to Saturday 10:00 a.m. to 9:00 p.m.; Sunday 11:00 a.m. to 7:00 p.m.

This recent entrant to the outlet scene has an interesting marketing strategy — to bring together upscale brand name merchants offering goods at 30% to 60% off.

## Quality Outlet Center

| | |
|---|---|
| *Location:* | On International Drive, just east of Kirkman Road |
| *Information:* | (407) 423-5885 |
| *Hours:* | Monday to Saturday 9:30 a.m. to 9:00 p.m.; Sunday 11:00 a.m. to 6:00 p.m. |

There is a smaller selection of merchants at this strip mall, but they offer some excellent buys. Just across the street is the excellent Passage To India restaurant.

## Dansk Outlet

| | |
|---|---|
| *Location:* | 7024 International Drive |
| *Information:* | (407) 351-2425 |
| *Hours:* | Monday to Thursday 10:00 a.m. to 9:00 p.m.; Friday and Saturday to 10:00 p.m.; Sunday 11:00 a.m. to 6:00 p.m. |

Dansk, one of the pioneers of outlet shopping in Orlando, features an extensive selection of its Scandinavian design glassware and cooking utensils. Set well back from I-Drive, it is easy to overlook.

## Lake Buena Vista Factory Stores

| | |
|---|---|
| *Location:* | On SR 535, 2 miles south of I-4 Exit 27 |
| *Information:* | (407) 672-5644 |
| *Hours:* | Monday to Saturday 10:00 a.m. to 9:00 p.m.; Sunday 12:00 noon to 6:00 p.m. |

The newest entry in the factory outlet sweepstakes is located on the well-traveled state road that links I-4 to US 192. There's a small food court if you get hungry and a playground for the kids.

## Kissimmee Manufacturers Outlet Mall

| | |
|---|---|
| *Location:* | One mile east of the intersection of SR 535, on US Highway 192 (Irlo Bronson Highway) |
| *Information*: | (407) 396-8900 |
| *Hours:* | Monday to Saturday 10:00 a.m. to 9:00 p.m.; Sunday 11:00 a.m. to 5:00 p.m. |

Not to be left out, Kissimmee has its own outlet mall, featuring 30-

some merchants. A separate discount shoe outlet is next door and an electronics store catering to an international clientele is across the highway.

# Flea Markets

The flea market is an Old World concept. Originally the term was applied to impromptu markets, the yard sales of their day, where enterprising individuals at the frayed edge of the merchant class displayed a grab bag of merchandise, some of dubious provenance — hence the alternate term: "thieves' market." Like the term "factory outlet," the term "flea market" has evolved over the years. Today, as practiced in Central Florida, a flea market is a sort of alternate shopping mall. The market owner provides, at a modest rental, simple booths in covered arcades. The merchants are, for the most part, full-time professionals with long-term leases on their booths who differ from their counterparts in the glitzy malls only in the matter of scale.

Whereas the old flea markets of Europe held out the lure of uncovering some priceless antique at an unbelievably low price, the modern Florida flea market more often offers inexpensive merchandise, purchased from a wholesaler and offered at a price that might not be any better than you could get at Kmart. Still, savvy shoppers can find bargains here if they know what they're looking for (and at). The best bets, in my opinion, are the second-hand dealers, the craftspeople, the fresh produce vendors, and the purveyors of the sort of wacky and offbeat stuff you don't usually see elsewhere.

Whatever the drawbacks of flea market shopping, there's no denying that the atmosphere of these bazaars is a lot of fun. There's plenty of greasy and fattening food to keep your energy up and the very challenge of navigating the seemingly endless rows of wares tends to keep you going. For those who have never experienced this particular slice of Americana, I recommend it highly. For those of you who simply love the flea market experience (and you know who you are), the following flea markets should keep you busy. If you must have more, just look in the Yellow Pages in your motel room under "Flea Markets."

## Flea World

| | |
|---|---|
| *Location:* | Highway 17-92 in Sanford; I-4 Exit 50 |
| *Information:* | (407) 330-1792 |
| *Hours:* | Friday, Saturday, and Sunday 9:00 a.m. to 6:00 p.m. |

Flea World bills itself as "America's largest flea market" with 1,700 dealer booths, most of which are occupied on any given weekend. There's bingo here and an amusement park next door to keep the kids occupied. (See *Chapter Thirteen: Another Roadside Attraction.*)

## 192 Flea Market

*Location:*      4301 West Vine Street (Highway 192) in
                     Kissimmee
*Information:*  (407) 396-4555
*Hours:*         Daily 9:00 a.m. to 6:00 p.m.

Perhaps reflecting the fact that it is in the heart of tourist country, Kissimmee's flea market is open seven days a week. There are over 400 booths here with plenty of Disney souvenirs and Florida t-shirts for the budget souvenir hound.

## Osceola Flea & Farmers Market

*Location:*      2801 East Irlo Bronson Highway (Highway
                     192) between Kissimmee and St. Cloud
*Information:*  (407) 238-1296
*Hours:*         Friday, Saturday, and Sunday 8:00 a.m. to
                     5:00 p.m.

A little farther off the tourist track, this flea market offers more fresh produce than the others.

# Index to Rides & Attractions

# Other Books from The Intrepid Traveler

The Intrepid Traveler publishes money-saving, horizon expanding travel how-to and guidebooks dedicated to helping its readers make world travel an integral part of their everyday life. They include:

*Air Courier Bargains:*
*How To Travel World-Wide For Next To Nothing*

*Consolidators: Air Travel's Bargain Basement*

and

*Home-Based Travel Agent:*
*How To Cash In On The Exciting*
*New World Of Travel Marketing*

In addition, we offer hard-to-find specialty books from other publishers. For a complete catalog, write to us at:

**The Intrepid Traveler**
**P.O. Box 438**
**New York, NY 10034**

Or visit our web site, where you will find a complete catalog, frequent updates to this and other of our books, travel articles from around the world, internet travel resources, and more:

**http://www.intrepidtraveler.com**